אור השם
Light of the Lord (Or Hashem)

Roslyn Weiss is the Clara H. Stewardson Professor of Philosophy at Lehigh University in Bethlehem, PA. She holds a doctorate in philosophy from Columbia University and an MA in Jewish Studies from the Baltimore Hebrew University. She has published four books on Plato and 50 scholarly articles on mainly Greek and Jewish philosophy.

אור השם

חסדאי קרשקש

Light of the Lord (Or Hashem)

Ḥasdai Crescas

TRANSLATED WITH INTRODUCTION AND NOTES BY
Roslyn Weiss

OXFORD
UNIVERSITY PRESS

OXFORD
UNIVERSITY PRESS

Great Clarendon Street, Oxford, OX2 6DP,
United Kingdom

Oxford University Press is a department of the University of Oxford.
It furthers the University's objective of excellence in research, scholarship,
and education by publishing worldwide. Oxford is a registered trade mark of
Oxford University Press in the UK and in certain other countries

© Roslyn Weiss 2018

The moral rights of the author have been asserted

First published 2018
First published in paperback 2020

All rights reserved. No part of this publication may be reproduced, stored in
a retrieval system, or transmitted, in any form or by any means, without the
prior permission in writing of Oxford University Press, or as expressly permitted
by law, by licence or under terms agreed with the appropriate reprographics
rights organization. Enquiries concerning reproduction outside the scope of the
above should be sent to the Rights Department, Oxford University Press, at the
address above

You must not circulate this work in any other form
and you must impose this same condition on any acquirer

Published in the United States of America by Oxford University Press
198 Madison Avenue, New York, NY 10016, United States of America

British Library Cataloguing in Publication Data
Data available

Library of Congress Cataloging in Publication Data
Data available

ISBN 978-0-19-872489-6 (Hbk.)
ISBN 978-0-19-289405-2 (Pbk.)

Links to third party websites are provided by Oxford in good faith and
for information only. Oxford disclaims any responsibility for the materials
contained in any third party website referenced in this work.

Table of Contents

Acknowledgments — vii

Translator's Introduction — 1
    Crescas's Life and Works — 4
    Structure of *Light of the Lord* — 6
    Physics — 7
    Providence and Choice — 10
    About the Translation — 14

Introduction — 16
Preface — 26
Book I — 30
    Part I — 31
    Part II — 70
    Part III — 97
Book II — 120
    Part I — 120
    Part II — 142
    Part III — 166
    Part IV — 169
    Part V — 188
    Part VI — 205
Book III: Division A — 242
    Part I — 243
    Part II — 278
    Part III — 282
    Part IV — 293
    Part V — 305
    Part VI — 309
    Part VII — 313
    Part VIII — 315
Book III: Division B — 321
    Part I — 321
    Part II — 325
    Part III — 330

Book IV	331
Issue I	331
Issue II	334
Issue III	337
Issue IV	340
Issue V	342
Issue VI	345
Issue VII	347
Issue VIII	347
Issue IX	347
Issue X	349
Issue XI	352
Issue XII	352
Issue XIII	354
Bibliography	355
Citations Index	361
Subjects and Names Index	369

Acknowledgments

A full year of concerted and undistracted effort was required to complete the first draft of this translation. For affording me a year-long sabbatical, I am indebted to my home institution, Lehigh University. I thank the National Endowment for the Humanities for its financial support, without which this project could never have been completed. Several colleagues and scholars have been most helpful to me. First and foremost—and in a category by himself—is Dr Leonard Levin, who conscientiously and skillfully reviewed the entire manuscript several times, flagging errors, offering suggestions for improvement, challenging me on substantive issues which we then thrashed out together, and finding creative ways to make my task of translation proceed more efficiently. I am indebted as well to Éric Smilevitch's masterful translation of *Light of the Lord* into French. Among those who read sections of the manuscript and offered useful suggestions are Dr Warren Zev Harvey, Dr Charles Manekin, and Dr Ari Ackerman. Dr Daniel Lasker is the scholar to whom I turned when I needed help with the most recalcitrant passages. I am grateful to Ms Leslie Rubin for her skilled preparation of the index, and to Sylvie Jaffrey for her expert copyediting. I wish to acknowledge the encouragement and support of my colleagues in the Lehigh University Philosophy Department, who worked through several sections of *Light of the Lord* with me at our weekly faculty seminar in Spring 2017. Two close friends provided valued criticisms and suggestions: Dr Alan Udoff and Janette Rapp. Finally, I wish to express my appreciation to the many other colleagues and scholars who generously offered their time and assistance, and to my family, for whom I am always grateful.

Translator's Introduction

The beginning of wisdom is fear of the Lord. (Ps. 111: 10)

Ḥasdai Crescas (c.1340–c.1410) was a man of simple piety—but by no means a simple man. Suffused with an ardent and unwavering love for God and for the Jewish people, Crescas produced, out of the depths of his love, the philosophic masterpiece, *Light of the Lord* (אור השם; *Or Hashem*), a work of undisputed sophistication, monumental in scope and ambitious in conception and execution. Those acquainted with this work agree that it rivals the crown jewel of medieval Jewish thought, Maimonides' *Guide of the Perplexed*—"rivals" it, indeed, in two senses: not only does it measure up to the *Guide* in range, brilliance, profundity, thoroughness, erudition, and certainly in originality and economy of expression, but it also combats the *Guide*'s pervasive Aristotelianism. Because in his view Aristotelian physics and metaphysics deform and distort Judaism, Crescas dares to question the adequacy of the *Guide*'s arguments and to challenge its unflinching determination to place God beyond human conception and understanding and to remove from Him all anthropomorphism and anthropopathism. If there is a single driving aim of *Light of the Lord*, it is to restore to Jewish thought its Jewish soul. Without sacrificing intellectual honesty or rigor, it champions and defends traditional religious belief and worship. Crescas approaches the thorniest issues in the philosophy of religion—the origin of the universe, the nature of God, the relationship between God and the world, the proper approach to Scripture and its commandments, human choice, divine providence, prophecy, the soul, and immortality—not only with a keen and crisp intellect but with a unique religious sensibility, duly recognizing the indispensability of the passional virtues of piety, reverence, and love to the perfected human life.

Crescas is one of the great systematic philosophers: all lines of thought in *Light of the Lord* are interconnected, converging on the single unifying theme of love. Love is at the heart of every issue: creation, infinity of space and time, providence, free will, prophecy, the end of the Torah and of human existence, and the soul's immortality. Anything that cannot be subsumed under love, anything that lies outside or obstructs this central theme, is rejected. Of the three components of Torah—deeds, beliefs, and love and fear of God—it is the last, Crescas asserts, which, though smallest in quantity, is greatest in importance (*Light of the Lord*, II. vi. 1).

It is perhaps because of the centrality of love to *Light of the Lord* that the biblical figure most prominent in it is not Moses, the man of intellect who at first resists God's call, but Abraham, the man of absolute devotion who faithfully follows God wherever He leads, the only man who is called in the Bible "the one who loves Me" (Isa. 41: 18). Abraham is superior even to Adam, for Adam, despite his disposition to perfection, nevertheless succumbed to sin, whereas Abraham, despite having been raised among idol worshipers, was steadfast in his righteousness. It was therefore Abraham—and not Adam—who was deemed worthy to be the "father of a multitude of nations" (Gen. 17: 4), the "rock from which we were hewn" (Isa. 51: 1). The biblical incident recalled most frequently in *Light of the Lord* is the Binding of Isaac: its effect on Abraham was not a diminishment but rather a deepening of his love for God (II. i. 1).

The love that is central to Crescas's understanding of God, man, and their relationship displaces intellect as the essential link between the human and the divine. Not only, Crescas believes, is intellect unable to sustain a religious connection between human being and God; it cannot even adequately support the triad of root-principles (שרשים; *shorashim*) critical to monotheistic faith—God's existence, unity, and incorporeality. Philosophical speculation relies necessarily on uncertain and undemonstrated premises, so that philosophical arguments, in Crescas's view, inevitably frequently beg the question. Only the Torah, the supreme gift of God's love and the premier expression of His will to benefaction, can establish the foundations of faith. The Torah is not to be explained away—as a foil for deeper philosophical understanding (as it may well be in Maimonides' *Guide*); it is, on the contrary, the very font of understanding.

From Crescas's perspective, perhaps the most egregious sin committed by Greek philosophy is its positing of a God who has no care for human beings, who is at best an object for human intellectual apprehension. Crescas replaces the self-intellecting intellect which is Aristotle's God with a God who is engaged in infinite creation out of boundless goodness and love. Only the divine *essence*, according to Crescas, is beyond all natural human apprehension; God's attributes, however, may be to some degree accessible. They accompany the divine essence as rays of light do their source: neither essence nor attributes are conceivable apart from the other. What binds essence and attributes together is the unifying principle of God's goodness. Moreover, since the divine attributes share with the corresponding human attributes a common definition—albeit differing from them in their infinitude—one may speak of a two-way relationship between God and His human creation. Indeed, *Light of the Lord* affirms God's bond with the world He created and with all the creatures in it as an expression of His nature as a being of infinite passionate love (חשק; *hesheq*) and benefaction. Moreover, in Crescas's view, although there is no individual human being to whom God is blind or indifferent, God has a special connection with the Jewish people to whom He gave His Torah.

For Crescas, unlike for Maimonides, intellect is neither necessary nor sufficient for attachment to God: not necessary, since one becomes attached to God through observance of the commandments rather than through contemplation; and not sufficient, since philosophers need not—and generally do not—love God at all. For Crescas, the providence, prophecy, and immortality that for Maimonides are consequent upon the intellect do not require intellectual perfection; it suffices that one love and revere God. In Crescas's view the commandments make it possible for anyone—both those who are more perfect and those who are less so—to love God (IIIB. i. 1);

for Maimonides, since love of God and closeness to Him require a cultivated intellect, few people qualify.

In building his system, Crescas has many fascinating—indeed, groundbreaking— things to say about physics and metaphysics, the matters that occupied, and preoccupied, his predecessors. It is certainly legitimate, then, to mine *Light of the Lord* for the positions Crescas takes regarding nature and beyond. Yet, arguably, in offering an alternative to Aristotelian philosophy, Crescas's concern is not in the first instance to revolutionize these fields—even if his thought is nothing short of revolutionary—but rather to weaken Aristotle's iron hold on the thinking person.[1] Recognizing Maimonides as a tragic victim of the seductiveness of Aristotelian thought, Crescas was alarmed by the already devastating influence Maimonides had on Jewish intellectuals who abandoned their Judaism with the *Guide* as their warrant. Even if Maimonides himself was able to remain steadfast in his faith, refusing (at least openly) to side with Aristotle against the Torah when the two were in conflict, what assurance was there that others, including his closest disciples, would do so? Although Crescas accused Maimonides' students of distorting their teacher's claims, it is at least possible that they reached their heterodox views not by perverting but by following to their logical conclusion the "astonishing things" (דברים מתמיהין; *devarim matmihin*) (as Crescas calls them in the Introduction to *Light of the Lord*) their master had said.

For Crescas, one thing is certain: God is the author of nature; all existence and all existents owe their being to Him, and everything that exists is thus utterly dependent on Him. The precise way in which God creates or emanates is ultimately of only secondary importance to Crescas. Even an anteriorly eternal world can be accommodated, so long as it is understood that God spent all of anteriorly eternal time bringing existents into being out of nothingness. Indeed, an anteriorly eternal world is compatible for Crescas, unlike for Maimonides, with Torah and miracles. For Crescas, since even an eternal universe would necessarily be a product of divine

---

[1] Harvey (1998c: 3–5) takes issue with Wolfson (1929: 114) concerning the extent to which Crescas took himself to be advancing new views in physics as opposed to merely dismantling the Aristotelian edifice to which Maimonides was, in Crescas's view, unduly attracted. Wolfson contends that Crescas "did not mean to be anything but negative and destructive in his treatment of the physical problems of Aristotle. All he wished to accomplish was to undermine the principles upon which were based the Aristotelian proofs for the existence of God.... Still, within this destructive criticism and within these arguments which are only *ad hominem*, we may discern certain positive tendencies in the direction of the early Greek philosophers the revival of whose views is the common characteristic of all those who long after Crescas struggled to emancipate themselves from the thralldom of Aristotle." What is in dispute is clearly not whether in fact Crescas made any constructive contribution to physics—Wolfson no doubt agrees with Harvey (1998c: 3) that "Crecas' discussions of physics and metaphysics are more than only destructive" and that "he proposes new and original concepts in place of those he rejects." Rather, the disagreement concerns Crescas's conception of his project. Harvey's defense of the claim that Crescas "saw himself" (p. 5) as venturing beyond the destructive into the constructive relies in part on Crescas's remark at the start of his critique in I. ii. 1 of Aristotle's arguments for the nonexistence of empty space: "we have deemed it fit to reply and to exposit the falsity of those arguments, for there is in this no small benefit for this science" (pp. 4–5). Note, however, that what Crescas touts here as a valuable contribution to physics is precisely his discrediting of Aristotelian views.

goodness, such wondrous manifestations of God's creative love as these are surely to be expected to occur in it.[2]

The enterprise of ascertaining Crescas's position on a whole host of issues—notoriously, the free will question, but others as well, including what can be known of God—is extremely fraught, as there are many twists and turns along the way. Perhaps the virtue most needed for studying Crescas is patience: it can often seem that he has pronounced definitively on a question, when, in fact, the second shoe has yet to drop. Sometimes that shoe never drops. Yet even when we cannot be sure where Crescas stands, we need never be at a loss as to what he stands for.

Crescas's Life and Works

Hasdai Crescas was born in or around 1340, in Barcelona, Spain. He is descended from a long line of Torah scholars and was a student of the great Talmudist, R. Nissim ben Reuben Gerondi (Ran). He counted among his friends the renowned R. Isaac ben Sheshet (Ribash) and R. Simeon ben Tzemaḥ Duran (Rashbatz), and among his students the esteemed R. Joseph Albo. Crescas relied upon his students as colleagues and acknowledges in *Light of the Lord* their help in composing it.

In the first period of his life, Crescas lived relatively peacefully in Barcelona. He was a student at the local yeshiva, which was headed by R. Nissim, where, in addition to the standard curriculum of Bible and Talmud, Crescas also studied Kabbalah, science, and philosophy. In his twenties, Crescas was a merchant and communal leader and, following the death of R. Nissim, Crescas and his friend Ribash became the most prominent authorities on matters of Jewish law and practice, not only in Aragon, but possibly in of all Spain.

In 1367, Crescas was falsely accused and imprisoned (along with Ribash and Ran and other prominent members of the Jewish community)—though they were soon released. In 1387, Pedro IV of Aragon died, and his son became king. The new king, Joan I of Aragon, was, along with his French queen, Violant de Bar, a patron of the sciences and arts; and their palace in Saragossa, the capital of the Crown of Aragon, became a cultural and scientific center. In 1389 Crescas left Barcelona for Saragossa, and a year later was appointed by the royal couple chief judge of the Jews of Aragon. In 1391, while Crescas resided in Saragossa, the Jews of Barcelona fell victim to horrific pogroms. The massacres began in Castilla, but spilled over into Aragon. The king and queen tried to save the Jews and to prevent the pogrom, but they were successful only in Saragossa. Thousands of Jews were killed and, within a short time, about one hundred fifty thousand Jews—almost half the Jews of Spain—were Christian. The major Jewish communities in Barcelona, Valencia, and Gerona vanished, and with them the yeshiva in Barcelona.

Following the slaughter, Crescas was faced with a Spanish Jewish community in serious danger of disintegration. With the help of the royal palace, he worked to revive the Jewish communities of Barcelona and Valencia. Until his death late in 1410

---

[2] Crescas entertains the possibility of an infinite succession of worlds (see IIIA. i. 5 and IV. i), and suggests at more than one point that each successive world improves upon the preceding one.

or in 1411 (or possibly even in 1412), Crescas remained the spiritual head of Spanish Jewry, although it is likely that his public activity diminished during the last decade of his life. He continued to teach Torah, Talmud, science, and philosophy, and to write—it was during his last years that he wrote *Light of the Lord*—and he strove to inspire new leaders to care for the Jewish people after his death.

The terrible turn of events of 1391 undoubtedly influenced the path of Crescas's literary career. Besides *Light of the Lord*, which was Crescas's last work, he wrote several others. His first known work was an epistle to the Jewish community of Avignon chronicling the slaughter of 1391. (This work appears as an appendix in M. Wieners's 1855 edition of ibn Verga's *Shevet Yehudah* [*Tribe of Judah*].) In this letter Crescas records the course of the destruction, as it passed from one Jewish community to another. In each community, as he recounts, nearly all either perished—occasionally he provides the number of dead—whether at the hands of the marauders or at their own hands (as many killed themselves and some killed their families as well), or felt constrained to convert to Christianity, leaving in some cases no Jews at all and in others very few. He singles out among the dead the great Torah scholars of that generation as well as his son, an "unblemished lamb," yet another sacrificial Isaac demanded by God. For Crescas, the devastating loss he suffered reprised the trial of Abraham, and, just as Abraham's faith was reinvigorated as a result of his most excruciatingly painful trial, so, too, was Crescas's as a result of his.

Thus unshaken in his faith, Crescas continued to write. In 1397–8 he composed a treatise, *Refutation of the Principles of the Christians* (*Bittul Iqqarei ha-Notzerim*), spurred no doubt by the Christians' smug assertion of their faith's superiority to Judaism and by the Church's unrelenting efforts to convert the recalcitrant Jew. In this work Crescas sought to discredit, by way of reasoned argument, ten principles of Christianity—original sin, redemption, the Trinity, incarnation, the virgin birth, transubstantiation, baptism, the messiahship of Jesus, the New Testament, and demons—and thereby to challenge the Christian claim to superiority. (This text has survived only in R. Joseph ibn Shem Tov's Hebrew translation from what was probably the original Catalan.) Another work, *Sermon on the Passover* (*Derashat ha-Pesaḥ* or *Maamar Or le-Arbaʿah ʿAsar*), is likely Crescas's as well. It contends that will is irrelevant to belief and impotent in the face of miracles. *Light of the Lord*, which amplified and modified some of the ideas set forth in the *Sermon*, was surely motivated by Crescas's felt need to shore up a decimated Jewish community. His intention was to produce a work that would provide a creditable alternative to the two Maimonidean works he regarded as deeply problematic, the *Mishneh Torah* and the *Guide of the Perplexed*. Unfortunately, the second volume (to be called *Lamp of the Commandment*) of the two-volume work he hoped to write in an effort to set the record straight on both Jewish law and Jewish belief, was never written (the two-volume work was to be called *Lamp of the Lord*). Crescas was able to produce no more than the single volume, *Light of the Lord*, his challenge to the *Guide*.

Crescas's bold philosophy had fewer adherents than it should have. Later thinkers tended either to toe the Aristotelian line or to return to a less philosophically inflected Jewish traditionalism. In addition, history was not kind to Crescas: Spanish Jewry was shattered by the 1391 pogrom and by further persecutions at the start of the next century. Nevertheless, *Light of the Lord* continues to be known and studied.

Moreover, Crescas's philosophical views—particularly those on the infinite and on free will—influenced two major later thinkers, Giovanni Pico della Mirandola, who quotes Crescas extensively, and Spinoza, whose views on freedom, necessity, and love, as well as on extension and infinity, bear the Crescasian stamp. Spinoza refers to R. Ḥasdai explicitly in his Epistle 12 to Ludwig Meyer (April 20, 1663), where he paraphrases Crescas's version of the cosmological argument for God's existence.

Structure of *Light of the Lord*

The aims of *Light of the Lord* are reflected in its structure. Following, first, the Introduction, in which Crescas explains why he set out to write this work and why he thought it necessary to challenge Maimonides ("the Rabbi") despite his reluctance to do so, and, next, the Preface in which he argues—against Maimonides—that belief in God's existence is not a commandment but is rather the foundation of all commandments, he proceeds to disabuse the reader of the idea that Aristotle and his Jewish followers are the place to turn for a demonstration of the root-principles of monotheism: God's existence, unity, and incorporeality. The first order of business, then, is to challenge the Aristotelian underpinnings of Maimonidean thought by thoroughly explaining the relevant Aristotelian propositions and the Maimonidean arguments based on them, and then proceeding to undercut them by exposing the extent to which they are flawed or inadequate. Book I of *Light of the Lord* is dedicated to these two projects, plus a third: to set the record straight on the foundations of Jewish monotheism, that is, on God's existence, unity, and incorporeality, both as the Torah and Jewish tradition teach and as proper reasoning tends to confirm. Only once Aristotle is stripped of his absolute authority—and only once physics (and the metaphysics to which it gives rise) is not seen as the best (and certainly not as the only) grounds for knowledge about God and the origin of the universe[3]—can Crescas move on to the central doctrines of Judaism.

In presenting Judaism's essential beliefs, Crescas distinguishes between, on the one hand, cornerstones (פנות; *pinnot*), to which he devotes Book II, and, on the other, beliefs the denial of which amounts to heresy, to which he devotes Book III. Crescas's innovative way of distinguishing between the two is in terms of whether or not the belief is a necessary condition for the existence of the Torah—only if it is does it qualify as a cornerstone—rather than in terms of levels of importance. By drawing the distinction as he does, Crescas constructs a logical hierarchy. Just as he begins with an explication of the root-principles of all monotheism—indeed, these principles apply even to the belief in an Aristotelian unmoved mover or first cause—recognizing that they are a necessary preparation for the beliefs that ground the specifically Jewish theism which understands God as a being who loves, so he proceeds to list the beliefs without which there could be no Torah—that is, beliefs that make Torah possible—before turning to beliefs found in the Torah.

---

[3] See Book IV Issue X: "But none of this [viz. the account of creation and the account of the Chariot] can be apprehended through metaphysics, for most of what is established there is extremely weak, as was established earlier."

The six cornerstones are: God's knowledge of all existents, His providence, and His power; prophecy, choice, and end—that is, the final end of the Torah. The eight obligatory true beliefs discussed in IIIA are: creation, immortality of the soul, reward and punishment, resurrection, the superiority of Moses' prophecy, the eternality of the Torah, the reliability of the *Urim* and *Tummim* when consulted by the high priest, and the coming of the Messiah. Book IIIB presents three obligatory beliefs derived from specific commandments. They are: (1) that God is responsive to prayer and blesses the people via the priestly blessing; (2) that God welcomes the penitent; and (3) that God seeks to perfect people through the service He requires, particularly during specific seasons of the year: Rosh Hashanah and Yom Kippur and the three pilgrimage festivals. It is striking that, whereas providence and choice (i.e. freedom to choose) are counted among the cornerstones, reward and punishment are placed in the category of obligatory beliefs. In other words, in Crescas's view, the Torah could not exist without providence and choice—but it could without reward and punishment. The significance of this difference will be addressed in the section "Providence and Choice."

Light of the Lord concludes with Book IV, in which Crescas considers thirteen issues whose true resolution is not definitively established in the Torah. He presents the arguments for and against each side and contends that reason or the rabbinic tradition tilts the balance to one side rather than the other. These are: (1) whether the universe is posteriorly eternal; (2) whether another universe or many other universes might exist; (3) whether the spheres are living and rational; (4) whether the movements of the celestial bodies affect and direct the course of human affairs; (5) whether amulets and incantations affect the acts of people; (6) whether there are demons; (7) whether a human soul transmigrates, which is what one sect of Sages calls *gilgul* (גלגול); (8) whether the soul of a child who has not yet begun his education is immortal; (9) Paradise[4] and Gehenna; (10) whether "the account of creation" (מעשה בראשית; *maʿaseh bereishit*) refers to physics and "the account of the Chariot" (מעשה מרכבה; *maʿaseh merkavah*) to metaphysics, as some of the sages of our nation have held; (11) whether or not the intellect, the intellecter, and the intellected are one thing; (12) whether there is a separate prime mover; (13) whether it is impossible to apprehend the truth of God's essence.

Physics

In challenging widely accepted Aristotelian views of physics, Crescas offers alternatives to them. These Crescasian ideas, ideas that have influenced later philosophers and have indeed laid the foundations for science's modern turn, have come down to us as his settled views. It is likely, however, that Crescas proposed these views in the spirit of a defense attorney's attempt to plant reasonable doubt by offering an alternate theory of the crime—in Crescas's case, a more plausible one.

Since for Crescas the only way to know that God exists, that God is one, and that God is incorporeal is to look to the Torah and the rabbinic tradition—philosophic

---

[4] Or, Garden of Eden.

proof can do no more than incline one in a particular direction—his allegiance or commitment to any particular set of beliefs about time, space, motion, and infinity as foundations for these root-principles can be only half-hearted. Indeed, from his perspective, no grounding in physics can reliably produce the truth concerning the fundaments of theology. Whereas philosophical argument can support or confirm what the Torah has taught, and whereas proper reasoning will never conflict with the tradition's instruction, these cannot ultimately and definitively establish any of the root-principles.[5] In other words, whereas Crescas does not discredit philosophical inquiry, what he doubts is its ability to achieve the truth on its own. As Crescas says (at the close of I. ii): "And what this condition of confusion teaches is that that which provides the truth with respect to these theses has not to this day been fully grasped by recourse to the philosophers. Indeed, the only thing that illuminates all of these deep difficulties is the Torah"; and (in his introductory description in Book I to what will be its Part III): "There is no way to grasp these root-principles perfectly other than via prophecy"; see also (in I. iii. 6): "Only the Torah and the tradition furnish complete truth"; and the parable with which Book I concludes: although Abraham is inclined by way of speculation to the truth, only the light of God is ultimately decisive for him.

[5] Harvey (1988c: 84–92) contends that there is only one proof—the proof Crescas discusses at I. iii. 2 and that Harvey calls the metaphysical proof of God—which Crescas regards as successful with respect to establishing the existence of God. (See, too, Urbach (1961 116, 140, 147)). Yet Crescas seems to insist that no philosophic proof can establish on its own any of the root-principles. And indeed, despite Crescas's hyperbolic pronouncement in connection with this argument that God's existence "has thus been proved beyond a doubt," and his unequivocal assertion at the argument's conclusion that "it [namely, the determiner of existence over nonexistence] is God," there remain several grounds for doubting the argument's unique sufficiency in Crescas's estimation. First, there is its hypothetical nature. To be sure, *if* all existents are effects, then all existents have (in respect of themselves) possible existence—in which case they require a cause to determine their existence over their nonexistence. But how would it be established that all existents (or even existence as a whole) are effects? The argument's soundness is not assured; it is valid at best. Second, until it is proved that there is but a single cause that is not an effect, it certainly may not be assumed that we have arrived at God as the determiner—and Crescas concedes that we have not as yet proved that there is one God. Moreover, if there is more than one God, there would be something else besides [the first] God that is not an effect, in which case the very foundation of the argument is undermined. Third, Crescas uses expressions such as "beyond doubt" quite liberally, even when presenting a view with which he disagrees. Fourth, Harvey's claim that for Crescas it is the "totality" of effects that requires a cause seems to play no part in the argument: Crescas states that what is needed is a determiner to determine "their"—that is, the many effects'—existence over their nonexistence. (We may note that Spinoza in his paraphrase of this argument in Epistle 12 to Ludwig Meyer (20 April 1663), makes no mention of "totality." And Crescas uses the expression "totality of existents" elsewhere—see e.g. II. i. 4, where he addresses the third general difficulty—meaning by it nothing more than all existents.) Fifth, Crescas's saying, "even if we concede (כשנודה; *keshenodeh*) the existence of a first cause for the effects that follow," suggests that the conclusion is less than firmly established. Finally, there is no attention drawn by Crescas to this proof's being somehow special, different from the other proofs by which he confirms by reason what the Torah has taught. Crescas's more favorable assessment of this version of the argument may be attributed to the specific advantage he thinks it has over others: it does not require, as, for example, Maimonides' argument does, a finite number of causes. Herein lies the superiority of this argument—though not its adequacy. For Crescas, this argument, like all philosophical arguments, can do no more than supplement and confirm what is known with certainty only via the Torah and the rabbinic tradition, namely, that the one God is the cause of everything, and everything is dependent on Him.

We can expect, then—and we in fact get—a certain degree of circumspection on Crescas's part with respect to his innovations in physics. That said, Crescas must be credited with introducing a series of new perspectives that altered the character of physical theory once and for all. Crescas frees place and time from their connection to corporeal substances: place for him is an infinite, empty, three-dimensional expanse, and infinite time a (mostly) psychological phenomenon requiring not actual motion but only its conception: insofar as time applies to both motion and rest, and insofar as rest is the privation of motion, time as it applies to rest may well require the notion of motion—but that and nothing more. Furthermore, Crescas can see no grounds for withholding actual infinitude from place and time. Whereas Aristotle's universe is a sphere, with the earth at the center surrounded by a series of concentric circles or spheres the final one of which marks the world's limit, Crescas can entertain the idea of an expansive universe with no boundaries, no end or limit, an infinite magnitude. Moreover, even if, as is likely, the world we inhabit is in fact finite and closed, nevertheless, for Crescas, the empty space in which it resides is infinite. This emptiness is not pure absence, but is rather an expansiveness whose dimensionality enables it to contain the world and its fullness. Furthermore, in Crescas's view there is no reason to exclude the possibility that this endless expanse harbors many, perhaps an infinite number of, worlds. For Crescas, to limit God's creation is to limit God.

Crescas also returns to the world its unity, its undisturbed continuity: as the product of the one God, the world, too, is a continuous and homogenous unit. In viewing the world this way Crescas departs from Aristotle—and from Maimonides in lockstep with him—who sees the world as hierarchical, distinguishing within it ranks and levels and positing in particular a sharp distinction between the inferior earthly realm beneath the sphere of the moon and the superior celestial realm above. According to Aristotle, the celestial spheres differ from the earthly elements in both their motion and their matter. For him, the motion of the spheres is circular, continuous, and unceasing—in contrast to that of the elements, which is rectilinear, discontinuous, and intermittent; moreover, the celestial spheres are intelligent and yearn for and are drawn to divine perfection as the object of their thought and desire. Celestial matter is more refined and purer than earthly matter and is not, like earthly matter, subject to coming-to-be, change, or destruction.

Crescas rejects the Aristotelian privileging of heaven over earth. All motion—whether rectilinear or circular, whether of the earthly elements or of the celestial spheres—is natural and of the same kind. So, too, is their matter the same: both earthly matter and celestial matter are not raw potentiality but are actual three-dimensionality. As a result of this reorientation—that is, with earth and heaven being seen as of the same rank—human dignity is restored: the human being is no longer deficient in comparison with the celestial spheres. Whereas for Maimonides, the human being, despite being capable of intellectual activity and thus verging on the divine, pales in comparison with the eternal, unchanging, and indestructible heavens whose perfect motion reflects the perfection of God who is the object of their thought and desire, for Crescas, despite the inevitable immeasurable inferiority of the human being to his Maker, God's ultimate purpose in creating the universe was to have human beings achieve happiness through their attachment to Him.

Providence and Choice

Of Crescas's six cornerstones, two in particular stand out. Although all six are prerequisites for Torah, providence and choice are arguably the most critical. Dividing the six cornerstones into two sets of three, the first set—knowledge, providence, and power—in which the focus is on God, and the second—prophecy, choice, and end—in which the focus shifts to man, the central cornerstone of the first set is providence and that of the second, choice. Providence is the concretization of God's love for man; choice, that of man's love for God.

It is, moreover, only in the case of providence and choice that the standard formula with which Crescas closes the major sections of his text is enhanced. In place of the usual conclusion, "Praise is to God alone, who is exalted above all blessing and praise," the sections on providence and choice end as follows: "*Adulation* (שבח; *shevaḥ*) *and* praise are to God alone, who is exalted above all blessing and praise." Divine providence and human choice elicit an intensification of Crescas's ardor.

In Crescas's view, there are many ways in which God extends His providence to our world, but foremost among them is His gift of the Torah. The Torah is the means by which God accomplishes His supreme end, namely, the binding of people to Him. Yet God cannot accomplish His end unless there is causal necessity. If it seems puzzling that Crescas, whose views are, in the final analysis, fairly traditional, would embrace causal necessity to the extent that he does, the explanation surely lies in his view that everything God does is purposeful. The only way God's issuing of the Torah can be purposeful is if its commandments are effective in establishing the divine–human bond; and the only way the commandments can be effective in establishing the divine–human bond is if there is fully operative causal necessity. If the Torah is to constitute a divine benefaction its commandments must have the power to produce their intended end. Therefore Crescas asserts: "And when the grace on high determined to perfect us through the giving of the Torah ... the admonitions it contained sufficed for man to be drawn to perfection, to suppress his desires, to subdue his inclinations" (II. ii. 6). Whereas for Abraham, as Crescas tells us, one commandment, that of circumcision, sufficed to effect the connection between him and God, for everyone else many more commandments are needed. God, out of His love, consequently issues a multitude of commandments.

Yet if the world is governed by strict causation, is not the individual's freedom to choose necessarily curtailed? Is it not the case that there is in Crescas's view no choice after all? On the one hand, it seems indeed that there is not. People act in response to the causes operating on them, the Torah's commandments being one such cause. On the other hand, however, since choice counts for Crescas as a cornerstone—that is, as something without which there can be no Torah—it cannot be right simply to conclude, as many scholars have, that Crescas is a determinist.

Crescas seeks to carve out a space for choice in his discussion of the category of the possible. To that end he distinguishes between necessity in respect of itself and necessity in respect of causes: two alternatives may both be possible—in themselves—for someone, but once causes are factored in, only one alternative will, of necessity, be the one chosen. For Crescas this latter necessity is not the same as the necessity of a thing necessitated in itself, for necessitation in itself contains the element of no-matter-whatness. If one is *causally* necessitated to choose a particular alternative, it is the causes that bring about the effect. But if something is necessitated in itself, causes are irrelevant. Just as there is no cause that will change the sum of 2 + 2—something which is necessary in respect of itself and not in respect of its causes—so, too, there is no cause that will make a person poor if it is necessary in itself that he be wealthy. Put another way, to be necessitated in respect of causes is to be responsive to causes; to be necessitated in respect of itself is to be impervious to them. Phenomenologically as well, the two forms of necessitation may be distinguished. When one is causally necessitated one experiences oneself as free; when one experiences oneself as unfree, when there is a sense of helplessness, a sense of no-matter-whatness, the necessity is experienced as coercive.

Scholars have tended to see the distinction between necessity in itself and causal necessity as a distinction without a difference: if, given the causes, a person will—must—choose one and only one of the possible alternatives, then what difference could it make that the choice was not necessary in itself? Consider, for example, the words of Abarbanel (b. 1437, Lisbon; d. 1508, Venice) in his commentary on Gen. 18: 20:

And I was alarmed at seeing this pious Rabbi [viz. Crescas] escape being burnt by the fire of the commentators' heresy only to have him succumb to it in the end. For what possibility remains for the thing that is necessary in respect of its causes when it is after all necessitated and constrained? (221)

and in his book *Naḥalat Avot (Ancestral Inheritance)*:

Insofar as a thing is compelled and necessitated by its causes, what possibility remains for it in respect of itself on account of which a person should be called free (בחיריי; *behiriyi*) in truth?...And if the things are necessary in respect of their causes, how can they be subject to prescription and proscription? For the possibility they have in respect of themselves is not anything (אינו כלל; *eino khelal*)—since in respect of their causes they are necessitated. (158)

Yet if for Crescas there really is no substantive difference between causal necessity and constraint, and if he believes, as he clearly does, that people are causally necessitated, how are we to take him at his word when he affirms choice as a precondition for the very existence of Torah? What does it mean to him to insist that unless there is choice there can be no Torah?

Crescas's inclusion of choice among his cornerstones suggests that Torah cannot exist—that is, cannot exist as the gift to mankind that it was intended to be, cannot fulfill its raison d'être—without human choice. As Crescas observes, the reason the Torah is not fully efficacious, the reason it cannot guarantee that those who receive it are perfected in their attachment to God, is that people often dislike what is commanded; they consequently obey—if they obey—unwillingly and unhappily. As Crescas puts it,

And if everything painful were removed—for example, if the pursuit of all their appetites were permitted to them, and so, too, the seeking of honor in vanquishing enemies, and the amassing of wealth—and if all that were required by way of service of God were the reciting of the first verse of the *Shemaʽ* once a week, there is no doubt that there would not remain a single person who would not serve God with love. (II. vi. 2)

The Torah, then, cannot effect its end alone. Without a human agent's effort, will, or pleasure and joy, and especially if the agent is actively resistant, opposed, or displeased and sad, the commandments cannot accomplish their end. Their causal power is aided or thwarted by the person's free choice—that is, by the two things Crescas highlights as marks of human freedom: effort and attitude.

Crescas's biblical exegesis may shed some further light on his thinking in this matter. Genesis 32 describes an agitated Jacob fearful in the face of his imminent encounter with Esau. The question Crescas considers in II. iv. 2 is why Jacob is afraid; after all, God has promised to protect him. Crescas's explanation is that Jacob knew that everything that occurs is the result of a causal sequence, but he did not know in his own case which cause would produce the promised effect. He therefore saw to it that all possible causes were put in place: he prayed, prepared for war, and assembled gifts. Jacob thus regarded his being protected by God as something possible in respect of itself though necessitated in respect of its causes. It is not that Jacob thought there was a chance that God's promise would not come to pass. Rather, the fact that it would come to pass but only as a result of causes gave Jacob the opportunity to participate. What causation does is open a space for personal engagement. Jacob took the opportunity to facilitate the very effect that he had been told—and therefore knew—would occur. We see here how Crescas thinks the distinction between "in respect of itself" and "in respect to causes" operates. Were God's protection of Jacob necessary in respect of itself, such that it would occur no matter what, Jacob would have had no reason to act. Freedom is located not in escaping causal necessity but in trying to—or refusing to—participate in it.

Whereas Crescas's discussion of Gen. 32 focuses on the difficulty that arises for choice from the perspective of causation, it does not address the additional putative obstacle to choice, namely, divine foreknowledge. Here, too, turning to Crescas's analysis of a biblical text may be of use. In Ps. 139, a text pivotal to the argument of *Light of the Lord* and discussed at length in II. i. 1 (and also in I. iii. 3 and II. iv. 3), David turns to God—as the one who knows his innermost thoughts and desires—seeking to excuse his bad behavior. "O God," he says, "if only You would slay the wicked, then murderous men would depart from me." But God does not slay, and David's associations continue. Crescas derives three lessons from David's words in this Psalm. First, that God knows particulars—He knows David's thoughts and desires. (For Crescas, there is no less forgivable error than the one committed by virtually all the great philosophers, namely, imputing ignorance, "the greatest of all defects" [II. i. 3, 5], to God. To withhold from God knowledge of particulars is, for Crescas, far worse than failing to protect Him from multiplicity and change, which the philosophers were determined to do no matter the cost); second, that God knows the future—He knows that David will sin; and third, that God's knowledge does not make the possible necessary—despite God's knowledge of David's future sin, David's sinning was nevertheless not necessitated: somehow God knows what will occur without making the possible necessary. (Crescas entertains briefly in II. v. 3—and nowhere dismisses—the notion that God's knowledge is outside time, and that His eternal apprehension encompasses what does not yet exist as if it were existent. Crescas recognizes, however, that such a view presumes to know how God knows. Moreover, it appears to imply that God's knowledge "derives from existents," that is, that God knows by observing rather than by conferring existence and essence. Crescas does, however, entertain the notion that one apprehends in accordance with one's nature rather than in accordance with the nature of that which is apprehended. If this is so, it would not then be impossible to say that the eternal God apprehends, with an eternal apprehension, that which does not yet exist as if it were existent.) If it were the case that God's foreknowledge makes the possible necessary, David would need no excuse; he would not be responsible for his sin. But the reason David believes he has an excuse is that he has good intentions, intentions of which God is without doubt aware. In other words, David appeals to God's recognition of his unwillingness to sin, of his regret and displeasure with respect to his sin. David can be forgiven because God knows he is not obstinate but weak.

For Crescas, then, what will be will surely be, though, in cases in which the necessitation is causal and not in-itself, what will be is dependent on causes. Although Crescas's distinction between these two kinds of necessitation is critical to his view, it is not, we see, the whole of it. In the two biblical sources considered, Jacob and David exhibit some measure of freedom even though they cannot change what will be. Jacob exerts effort, and David adopts an attitude of disapproval toward his inevitable sin. Even though both causal necessity and divine foreknowledge entail that what will be will be, how people relate to what will be is up to them.

Thus far we have considered choice in the realm of human action. The matter of belief, however, brings with it a further complication. For in the case of belief, resolution in terms of the distinction between the two kinds of necessitation is precluded. Belief, according to Crescas, unlike action, is always and necessarily involuntary—that is, will plays no part in it: the self-evidence or incontrovertible proof of a proposition has *coercive* power. Nevertheless, here, too, a person's effort or lack thereof and his joy or displeasure are deciding factors in his closeness to or remoteness from God. Let us look then to another instance of Crescas's biblical exegesis, as he draws together at II. v. 6 two seemingly unrelated biblical texts.

The first is Exod. 19: 17, which describes the scene as the Israelites prepare for the revelation at Sinai. The verse reads: "And they stood at the bottom (בתחתית; *betaḥtit*) of the mountain"—which can also be rendered: "And they stood beneath the mountain." According to the Rabbis, this verse, when interpreted in this second way, implies that the people were constrained to accept the Torah under threat of death; will played no part in their acceptance of it. The second text is Esther 9: 27: "The Jews affirmed, and took upon themselves." As the Rabbis understand this verse, the Jews in the time of Ahasuerus affirmed, after the fact, through the joy they experienced as they witnessed the miracles and deliverance that were enacted for them then, what they had already taken upon themselves at Sinai. Crescas explains that what the Jewish people accepted at first under constraint, they later willingly embraced. Even with regard to involuntary belief, then, it is possible to be free—free to embrace the belief with enthusiasm, or to resist it, even as one cannot deny it.

One exercises freedom, then, according to Crescas, either in exerting effort or in feeling pleasure and joy with respect to acting or believing. Indeed Crescas recognizes explicitly "the exertion of effort in investigating the belief's truth" (II. v. 5). It is for how actively one is engaged in the process of causation or investigation, or for how one feels about one's acts and beliefs—how happy or unhappy one is with one's decisions and convictions—that one is rewarded or punished.

It was observed earlier that reward and punishment is not included among the cornerstones without which there could be no Torah. Instead, it is counted as one of the beliefs whose denial constitutes heresy. To be sure, Crescas has illuminating things to say about reward and punishment: that it is natural—one who touches fire is burned, one who violates God's commandments is distanced from God; that true reward and punishment are psychic or spiritual in nature—the former consists in closeness to God, the latter in remoteness from Him; that reward and punishment should not be the motivation for obeying God; that, as the Rabbis say, the reward for fulfilling a commandment is a commandment—whether an additional one or the very one performed; and that divine reward and punishment are not only not vindictive, they are also not political—that is, they are not a matter of political justice, in which desert is paramount; they are rather only for the sake of benefit, "as a father chastens his son" (Deut. 8: 5). Yet by excluding reward and punishment from the list of cornerstones, Crescas indicates that reward and punishment are not prerequisites for the Torah as God's great benefaction; it is the commandments themselves that exhibit God's grace. Whereas for other thinkers freedom to choose justifies reward and punishment (II. v. i), for Crescas what freedom to choose justifies is the commandments, as he says: "But all alternatives must be open to [a person's] simple will. Only then will an *imperative* (צואה; *tzavaah*) be appropriate and relevant" (introduction to II. v). The Torah confers benefit directly by way of its commandments—it is one's joyful and effortful embrace of commandments that ensures one's closeness to God— not by way of any further rewards and punishments that accompany their observance or violation. What causes attachment to God is not desire for good things and fear of bad but devoted service. Through issuing commandments God chooses man; through loving acceptance of the commandments man chooses God.

About the Translation

Only one complete translation of *Light of the Lord* exists in any occidental language, and that is the French translation by Éric Smilevitch, which appeared in 2010 under the title *Lumière de l'Éternel*. Although some selections of *Light of the Lord* have appeared in English, the bulk of the work has remained untranslated into English.

Partial English translations are listed in the bibliography. Notable among them are the extensive translations in Warren Harvey's Ph.D. dissertation, 'Hasdai Crescas's Critique of the Theory of the Acquired Intellect' (1973), and in his *Physics and Metaphysics in Hasdai Crescas* (1998c); and Harry Austryn Wolfson's translation of most of Parts I and II of Book I, in his *Crescas' Critique of Aristotle: Problems of Aristotle's Physics in Jewish and Arabic Philosophy* (1929). There are in addition short selections translated by Seymour Feldman in J. David Bleich's *With Perfect Faith* (1983); by Menachem Kellner in his *Dogma in Medieval Jewish Thought: From Maimonides to Abravanel* (1986); and by Charles Manekin in *Medieval Jewish Philosophical Writings*, ed. Charles Manekin (2008).

In 1990 Rabbi Shlomo Fisher rendered *Light of the Lord* into vocalized modern Hebrew print. This edition serves as the primary basis for the current translation, though I have checked it for accuracy against the original printed edition (Ferrara 1555) and a partial printed edition (Vilna 1905), as well as against the Florence and the Vienna manuscripts. I have indicated variants in the notes.

The Hebrew of *Light of the Lord* is idiosyncratic and its style compressed and notoriously difficult; moreover, the work contains discrepancies, most likely because it was written over a long span of time. It is clear from the Florence manuscript that additions were made to the original work that sought to reconcile some of the more glaringly inconsistent passages and to moderate some of the more radical opinions expressed, such as that concerning choice. I have tried in this translation to present the work as it is, preserving Crescas's voice and style and adding few embellishments in the body of the text. To the extent possible I have translated critical Hebrew terms consistently throughout. For the sake of clarity I have occasionally modified or supplemented the text, sometimes by bracketing added words or phrases and sometimes by merely inserting them. Many of Crescas's sentences are extraordinarily long and complex. Often a single sentence will contain a string of several clauses beginning with "since," and will reach its conclusion only after recording several qualifications and asides. Prudence has made it necessary in these cases to deviate from the text's original form. Long sentences have been broken into shorter ones, and often the serial "since" has been eliminated, with premises being treated as self-standing assertions, and their conclusion being signaled by the "therefore" in its independent sentence. Notes indicate biblical and rabbinic sources, and, where appropriate, explain and clarify the text. The reader will find, however, that there are stretches of text to which virtually no explanatory notes are appended, for there are passages in which Crescas's arguments, though difficult, are self-explanatory: notes would do little more than repeat the text. I have not for the most part sought to indicate Crescas's likely philosophic sources for the arguments he advances. Wolfson (1929) may be consulted for extensive discussion of Crescas's philosophic sources—among whom, as we know, are the major figures in Jewish and Islamic thought, as well as the apostate Abner of Burgos whom Crescas never mentions by name. At the start of Book I Crescas credits Maimonides with not simply reproducing the ideas and proofs advanced by others but rather distilling their essence, thereby rendering unnecessary a return to those earlier views. Crescas himself has no doubt done the same. As he says at the close of I. i. 1:

> These are the proofs that have come to us concerning this issue in the books of Aristotle and of other authors and of commentators on his books. But they came to us confused and likely to bewilder the reader, for this is a topic susceptible to error. We therefore formulated them in their [proper] form and with splendid brevity. And we reinforced them with some things that they did not mention.

It is perhaps sufficient, then, to present Crescas's arguments as he formulated them.

I have aimed in this translation to render *Light of the Lord* accessible to many readers—scholars, students, and the interested public. I have not simplified the text or offered a comprehensive commentary on it. *Light of the Lord*, even in English, remains exceedingly demanding. What I have provided is a text to be wrestled with. It is my hope that it will spark renewed engagement with a thinker who merits far more attention and study than he has hitherto received.

Introduction

A lamp unto my foot is Your word, and a light unto my path.[1]

Shine Your face upon Your servant; save me with Your kindness.[2]

For a commandment is a lamp and Torah is light; and the reproofs of instruction are the path of life.[3]

Teach me, O Lord, Your way; I will walk in Your truth; unite my heart in awe of Your name.[4]

You will make known to me the path of life; in Your presence is the plenitude of joys, and pleasures at Your right hand forever.[5]

May God's name be blessed[6] and exalted above all blessing and praise,[7] for He has been wondrously kind[8] toward His creatures, in bringing them into existence and in creating them following absolute nothingness,[9] through a kind of wisdom of whose mystery hearts cannot fathom even one part in a thousand of thousands of thousands, through the might of His greatness and His wonders and awesome deeds which outstrip the limits of a tongue to speak of things great and marvelous.[10] When the Lord God made the earth and the heavens,[11] and the heaven of heavens and all their hosts,[12] and when higher still were *erelim* and *ḥashmalim*, *serafim* and *qedoshim*[13]—thousands upon thousands, and myriads upon myriads—then He, dwelling on high,[14] sitting supremely[15] on a throne, exalted and elevated,[16] made for them a seal of perfection.[17] The Lord God fashioned the human being in the image and likeness of all His creatures—and the Lord himself at their head—as God said: "Let us make the human being in our image, according to our likeness."[18] God was joined in this effort by the totality of existent beings, in order that the human being bear the imprint of all parts of existence; and, just as all parts of

---

This Introduction is to the entire two-volume work, *Lamp of the Lord*, the second volume of which, *Lamp of the Commandment*, was never written. See n. 75. The opening of this work is composed of biblical verses interwoven with the author's words to form a continuous narrative.

[1] Ps. 119: 105.   [2] Ps. 31: 17.   [3] Prov. 6: 23.
[4] Ps. 86: 11.   [5] Ps. 16: 11.   [6] Ps. 113: 2; Job 1: 21.
[7] Neh. 9: 5. The phrase, "exalted above all blessing and praise," closes the major divisions of this work.
[8] Ps. 31: 22.
[9] "Following absolute nothingness" translates the expression, אחר האפס המוחלט (*aḥar huefes hamuḥlat*).
[10] Ps. 12: 4.   [11] Gen. 2: 4.   [12] Neh. 9: 6.
[13] These are names of various celestial beings.   [14] Isa. 32: 16.   [15] Ps. 113: 5.
[16] Isa. 6: 1.   [17] Ezek. 28: 12.   [18] Gen. 1: 26.

existence are under the governance of the Lord, so is the human being[19] under the governance of his intellect. It is for this reason that our predecessors, peace be upon them, called him a "microcosm"[20]—because God made him a miniature imprint and seal onto which all His creatures are engraved. Furthermore, in the magnitude of His kindness and the abundance of His goodness, God was provident over all from the realm of His abode,[21] and chose the house of Jacob in whose midst to rest His glory,[22] that they [viz. the Israelites] might love and be in awe of Him, serve Him, and cleave unto Him.[23] For to live thus is the pinnacle of human happiness, in pursuit of which many have become perplexed and have walked in darkness[24]—among them men wise in their own eyes and intelligent in their own estimation.[25]

With the light of His Torah God lit up for us the two great lights:[26] the lamp of God[27] and the light of the Lord,[28] which are the commandments and the beliefs,[29] respectively, in order to prepare the way for us, the way of life,[30] a way that would be so very distant without them—who could find it?[31]—unless there shone upon it the true light that is called "the radiance of the Divine Presence."[32]

The rock[33] from which we were hewn,[34] the test stone,[35] the foundation stone upon which the world was founded,[36] was the singular Abraham our father, peace be upon him, who, at the age of three,[37] from the time he attained to reason, recognized his creator and attracted others to God's service—without the Torah's having preceded him. Blessings and praises upon His great name on account of all the benefits He bestowed upon us—an abundance of goodness upon the house of Israel.[38] Indeed, because of Abraham's superlative eminence a covenant was enacted with him by way

---

[19] Whether read ויהיו, "he" (as in the Ferrara and Vilna, eds.), or (with Fisher) ויהיון, "they," the intent is that, as all parts of existence are under the governance of the Lord, so too the human being—or the imprints of all the parts of existence engraved onto the human being—are under the governance of the human intellect.

[20] עולם קטן ('olam qatan); *Tanḥuma Pekudei* 3.   [21] Ps. 33: 14.

[22] Ps. 85: 10.   [23] Deut. 11: 22, 30: 20; Josh. 22: 5.   [24] Ps. 82: 5.

[25] Isa. 5: 21.   [26] Gen. 1: 16.   [27] 1 Sam. 3: 3; cf. Prov. 20: 27: "the lamp of the Lord."

[28] Isa. 2: 5.

[29] Although the Fisher, Ferrara, and Vilna editions all have האמונות והמצוות, nevertheless, the reverse order, as found in the Florence and Vienna manuscripts, המצוות והאמונות, "the commandments and the beliefs," is followed here. Crescas associates נר (ner), lamp, with commandments, and planned to name his work on the commandments נר מצוה (*Ner Mitzvah, Lamp of the Commandment*). See Warren Harvey (1973), 235 (Heb.), 245 (Eng. trans.).

[30] Jer. 21: 8.   [31] Eccles. 7: 24.

[32] "Divine Presence" translates the Hebrew term שכינה (*shekhinah*) throughout.

[33] Reading הצור (with the Ferrara and Vilna editions and with the Florence and Vienna manuscripts) rather than כצור (with Fisher).

[34] Isa. 51: 1.   [35] Isa. 28: 16.   [36] Num. Rabbah 12: 4.

[37] Crescas's notion that Abraham was three years old when he acknowledged God is based on a midrash in BT *Nedarim* 32a concerning the verse Gen. 26: 5. This verse contains the phrase, "because Abraham hearkened to my voice." The Hebrew term for "because" is עקב ('*eqev*), whose *gematria* is 172. Since Abraham lived for 175 years (Gen. 25: 7), he must have been three years old when he first "hearkened." See, too, Gen. Rabbah 30: 8. (In *gematria*, each of the letters of the Hebrew alphabet is assigned a numerical value so that each word or phrase is the sum of the values of its individual letters. *Alef* is one, *beit* is two, and so on until *yod*, which is ten; the next letter of the alphabet, *kaf*, is twenty, *lamed* is thirty, and so on until *tsadi*, which is 90. The following letter, *kof* is 100, *reish* is 200. The final letter of the alphabet, *tav* is 400. This is the highest value a single letter can represent.)

[38] Isa. 63: 7.

of just one commandment, that of circumcision; and that alone sufficed, because of his elevated status. Indeed, for one who is worthy, all that is needed is but a few acts; there is no need for many—as in the case of the diurnal sphere as compared with the other spheres. For the diurnal sphere one motion suffices for it to achieve its perfection, the emanation of its goodness; but for the other spheres, since they are lower than it in eminence, many motions are required. It was therefore necessary, when the kindness of the blessed and exalted One determined to perfect us, the congregation of the community of Israel, that He increase our acts,[39] as is confirmed by the dictum of R. Ḥanania son of ʿAqashia: "The Holy One Blessed Be He wished to make Israel meritorious; He therefore increased for their sake Torah and commandments."[40]

Since it is the performance of the commandments that leads to this perfection, but there can be no performance of them without an understanding of them, the following dictum in the Mishnah is to be understood in its literal sense: "and the study of Torah is the equivalent of all."[41] And for this reason the Rabbis concluded that study is the greater, for it leads to performance.[42]

Since knowledge of the Torah's commandments is the straight path leading to this perfection, so that it would be appropriate that the Torah be such that knowledge of it can be attained in as perfect a manner as possible, the perfection of the knowledge of things and the comprehensiveness with which they are known turn on three things: precision with respect to them; the ease with which they are grasped; and their preservation and being remembered. Divine wisdom therefore determined that the Torah be such that these three criteria can be most perfectly met. Thus, it indeed set forth all the commandments and beliefs in written form, as well as in the oral form that was preserved through the true tradition, along with rules and signs—namely, the thirteen exegetical techniques employed in interpreting the Torah.[43] It is because the foundation of the commandments as a whole is in written form, and because they were not transmitted orally, that precision with respect to them is assured. The Torah thus insisted, in accordance with what was received through the true tradition, that: "It is not permitted to state orally things that appear in writing."[44] The Torah's intention was that these things not be entrusted to hearts alone, lest they occasion dispute on account of common forgetfulness. This is especially so considering how

---

[39] In Ptolemaic astronomy the rotation of the diurnal sphere—the supreme outermost sphere encompassing within it the spheres of the sun, moon, planets, and fixed stars—is simple: it rotates once every twenty-four hours. By contrast, the motion of the planets is complex, needing to be explained by a theory of numerous cycles and epicycles. In Crescas's analogy, Abraham, who can achieve perfection through but one commandment, is compared to the diurnal sphere, while the Israelite community, whose perfection requires many commandments, is compared to the planets.

[40] *Makkot* 3: 16; *Avot* 6: 11.   [41] *Peah* 1: 1.

[42] BT *Kiddushin* 40b. This rabbinic dictum may be understood as maintaining, paradoxically, that study is greater than performance because study leads to performance—which is greater. Alternatively, and less paradoxically, what the Rabbis may have meant is that study is greater because it leads to performance, whereas performance need not lead to study. For Crescas, however, it would seem that the reason study is greater is that there can be no performance—or, perhaps, no genuine performance—without it, for performance devoid of understanding is without merit.

[43] The thirteen interpretive techniques, known as the שלש־עשרה מדות, are found in the Introduction to *Sifra*. See n. 58.

[44] BT *Gittin* 60b; BT *Temurah* 14b.

painstaking the Torah is with respect to the form of its script and its letters—the spare form being used on some occasions, and on others the full[45]—for all this care diminishes the chance that error and dispute will befall it.

Indeed, all the commandments and their divisions and subdivisions, along with their exponential expansion—to which the necessity of perfecting us led, as was discussed above—are contained, with splendid conciseness, in the written Torah along with its orally transmitted signs and exegetical techniques. Two consequences thus follow. First, the commandments can be grasped with the greatest of ease, thanks to their utmost conciseness; and, second, they can be remembered and preserved—and this, thanks, on the one hand, to their being concise and, on the other, to the exegetical techniques that were set forth in the form of signs which are the foundations and principles of the Oral Torah. For making signs for things—lest they be forgotten—is one of the devices for facilitating memory, which is especially critical considering that the Torah mandates its own constant study.[46] All this is an important root and foundation for the commandments' preservation and for their being remembered. The Torah has indeed been most insistent in this regard, as is attested in the true tradition in which the [Rabbis] say: "It is not permitted to state in writing things that are oral."[47] This proscription stems from a concern that the oral things might depart from a person's heart so that he will come to rely on the written text and, as the subjects proliferate, this will lead to his forgetting. This is just like the Torah's insistence with regard to the written things that one may not state them orally. This proscription too derives from the Torah's fear that if someone permits himself to state the written things orally he will come to regard his having stated them orally as a reason to trust what he recalls—and this will lead to diminished precision.[48] Indeed, in order to create both love and a fierce passion to keep vigil at its gates always,[49] the Torah went so far as to organize the totality of the commandments, and to plant in them the seed of truth—which is derived from its stories about the forefathers and the heightened providence extended to them and the bounty of God's kindnesses and wonders. As a result of one's diligence and devotion, the following three ends should be attained at once: grasping the commandments easily; attaining precision with respect to them; and remembering and preserving them. Indeed, this is a path that was hardly foreign to the sages of the nations, as is suggested by what is found in their compilations. One of them, in defaming another who committed his words to writing, said to him: "You distrust your pristine ideas,

---

[45] In Hebrew certain vocalizations can be indicated—but need not be—by the inclusion of the letter *vav* or *yod*. The spare (חסר) form omits the letter; the full (Crescas's term is יתר) includes it. The technical terms for the full and spare forms are, respectively, *scriptio plena* and *scriptio defectiva*.

[46] Josh. 1: 8; Ps. 1: 2; cf. Deut. 6:7.

[47] BT *Gittin* 60b; BT *Temurah* 14b. Fisher has אי אפשר, "it is impossible," as do the Ferrara and Vilna editions. In the Florence and Vienna manuscripts, as well as in the Talmud, the expression is אי אתה רשאי, "one is not permitted."

[48] Writing down what was transmitted orally will cause excessive reliance on the written text and will diminish the capacity to remember the copious and ever-expanding body of oral material. Similarly, making oral what was written will lead to excessive reliance on possibly faulty memory and thus to error.

[49] The expression, "to keep vigil at its gates always," is based on a similar expression in Prov. 8: 34.

and instead place your trust in the hides of dead animals!"⁵⁰ Our forebears adhered to this approach from the days of Moses our Teacher to the days of the Men of the Great Assembly.⁵¹ Throughout that period no dispute or error arose concerning anything in the Torah.

When, however, the Greeks rose to ascendancy and troubles rained down on Israel following the period of the Men of the Great Assembly, the number of disciples who were insufficiently diligent in their studies increased, disputes proliferated,⁵² and several of these men allowed themselves to write down what was transmitted to them [orally]. They called these writings a "scroll of secrets."⁵³ This situation persisted until the end of the generations of the Tannaim,⁵⁴ when our holy Rabbi, peace be upon him,⁵⁵ arose and saw that hearts were contracting. Out of fear lest the Torah be forgotten in Israel, he compiled the six orders of the Mishnah, which very concisely comprise the Oral Torah. Following him came R. Ḥiyya and R. Oshaʿiya, who added the *Baraita*⁵⁶ to those very orders, declaring: "It is time to act on the Lord's behalf; they have violated Your Torah."⁵⁷ After them the *Sifra*⁵⁸ and *Sifrei*⁵⁹ were composed. All the generations of the Amoraim⁶⁰ studied these texts, along with the Jerusalem Talmud that was subsequently composed by R. Joḥanan. The period of authoritative teaching reached its culmination when Ravina and Rav Ashi arose and composed the Babylonian Talmud with the consent of the Sages⁶¹ of that generation. According to tradition, the editing of these works continued into the period of the Rabbis known as the Savoraim.⁶² They were all following the intention of the Torah to make room for the tradition in some way.

After that the Geonim⁶³—for example, R. Simeon Kayyara, the venerable R. Jehudai, R. Saadia of Fayyum, R. Samuel son of Ḥofni, and R. Hai—allowed themselves to compose works. Some, such as R. Ḥananel and Rabbeinu Nissim and, culminating with the last of the commentators of the period, Rabbeinu Solomon of France,⁶⁴ composed commentaries on the Talmud. After him, Rabbeinu Samson,

---

⁵⁰ Warren Harvey (1973a), 351 n. 1, points out that Crescas is quoting Hunayn ibn Isḥaq, *Ethics of the Philosophers* I. 1. The speaker is presumably Socrates.

⁵¹ The Men of the Great Assembly, אנשי כנסת הגדולה, were a group of scribes and Sages who served as authorities for the Jewish community in the period from the end of the biblical prophets to the early Hellenistic period.

⁵² See BT *Sanhedrin* 88b.

⁵³ מגלת סתרים; BT *Shabbat* 6b, 96b; BT *Baba metzia* 92a.

⁵⁴ The Tannaim are the Rabbis cited in the Mishnah. They flourished in the years 10–220 CE.

⁵⁵ The reference is to Judah Hanasi.

⁵⁶ החיצונה; the reference is to the Tosefta, comprising additional rabbinic oral traditions not included in the Mishnah.

⁵⁷ Ps. 119: 126. The Rabbis relied on this verse for permission to commit the Oral Torah to writing in disregard of the longstanding prohibition on doing so.

⁵⁸ *Sifra* is a *midrash halakhah*, a legal commentary, on the book of Leviticus.

⁵⁹ *Sifrei* comprises two *midrashei halakhah*, one on Numbers from ch. 5 on, and one on Deuteronomy.

⁶⁰ These are the Rabbis of the *Gemara* who flourished in the years 219–500 CE.

⁶¹ "Sage," when in lower case refers to more recent thinkers. When in upper case, it refers to the Sages of the Mishnah and Talmud. In both cases it renders חכם (*ḥakham*).

⁶² These Rabbis flourished in the first half of the 6th century CE.

⁶³ The title *gaon* was given to the heads of the Babylonian academies of Sura and Pumbedita from the end of the sixth to the end of the twelfth century.

⁶⁴ The reference is to Rashi.

the disciple of the renowned Tosafist R. Isaac, composed books and produced original arguments and dialectics on the entire Talmud. And also the great Rabbi, R. Abraham son of David,[65] composed commentaries on the whole of the Talmud. Although some [of these Rabbis] composed [legal] works drawing upon certain sections of the Talmud, there were no comprehensive compositions other than the legal composition of Rabbeinu Isaac Alfasi, which comprises three orders, and the great work composed by our master and Rabbi, Rabbi Judah Hanasi the Barcelonian, one that is of considerable length and includes the disputes of the Geonim and their responsa. There followed the comprehensive composition of the Rabbi, our teacher Moses son of Maimon,[66] which he called *Mishneh Torah*,[67] which proceeds without recording rabbinic disputes except in a few places, and without citing a Tanna, an Amora, a Rabbi, or a Gaon. He included in it that which appears in the Talmud, the *Tosefta*, *Sifra*, and *Sifrei* concerning the commandments. In addition, in order to teach the Jewish people the roots of the [proper] beliefs and views, and to illuminate the dark recesses of doubt, he composed a book which he called *Guide of the Perplexed*.

But despite what this Rabbi and author wondrously achieved in his lucid books, nevertheless, because in his composition on the commandments he omitted the disputes of the Geonim as well as their names, and also failed to cite the textual sources that are the roots of the issues, we were unable on those occasions when the books of other great authors were found to contain rulings and views opposed to his, to escape confusion and doubt. Aside from this, he did not fully cite the reasons for things or their general principles, except to allude to details found in the discourses of our predecessors. Since the great part of the commandments are in the category of the possible,[68] a category broader than the sea, and since knowledge cannot encompass their details which are infinite in number, it appears that, were a single detail of those mentioned there [i.e. in the *Mishneh Torah*] to change, we could not reach a sure determination. Indeed, just as there is no comparison between a finite number and an infinite, so, too, there is no comparison between what is grasped of the finite details that are recorded there, and what is not grasped of the infinite details that are not recorded there. It is clear, therefore, that knowledge will not be perfected through that work in even one of the three requisite ways mentioned above.[69] Precision in the

---

[65] This is R. Abraham son of David of Posquières, popularly known as Raavad.

[66] This is Maimonides.

[67] This title has been variously translated. Its sense is probably, at least in part, "recapitulation of the Torah."

[68] "The possible," האפשר (*haefshar*), is to be understood as the modality of possibility, and to refer to that which is neither necessary nor impossible. Whereas the term "contingency" might have been used (especially to avoid the error of taking, for example, "there is no possibility" to mean "it is impossible"), nevertheless, there is reason to prefer "possible" as the translation of אפשרי. For although it may be the case that things that are possible are possible because they are contingent, i.e. dependent on something else, the term "possible" does not in itself carry the implication of dependence. Crescas devotes considerable attention to whether the category of the possible is itself possible—in light of the causal nexus on the one hand, and of divine foreknowledge on the other. See I. i. 30 and II. v.

[69] My translation follows Harvey's 1973 text. An alternate version, found in the Ferrara and Vilna editions as well as in Fisher, and which is reflected in Smilevitch's translation, proceeds to list the "three requisite ways" as follows: precision in matters considered, grasping them easily (והשגתם על נקלה), and

matters considered and preservation from error [will not be secured]—for two reasons: first, because he failed to note the disputes and the texts that are the sources for the roots of the issues which would have made matters crystal clear; and, second, because he neglected to mention the reasons and general principles relevant to the issues. It is thus evident that perfect knowledge of matters will be had only when we know them in their reasons in accordance with their context. So long as our knowledge of matters is incomplete, we will not be safe from mistake and error. This is also a cause of our not inscribing them in our minds and not preserving them—which is the third problem. Even more so, we will not grasp them easily—and this is the second problem—since we will grasp only a small part, as was mentioned earlier, and even with respect to that part, our comprehension will be sorely lacking. What is most surprising and a great wonder is how it could enter Maimonides' mind and how he could imagine that, aside from his book [which would endure], books of earlier writers would be set aside, and that the whole of the Oral Torah could be contained in his work, to the point that he called it *Mishneh Torah*.[70]

In these generations, however, when strange and mighty troubles rain down on us, it is surely good to prepare a path with great precision and with much care, through which complete knowledge of the commandments of the Torah, and complete knowledge of the Talmud, will be easily attained. This, however, requires that a work be composed that contains the commandments of the Torah along with their reasons, arranged topically, and along with a conception of their definitions and general principles. In addition it should be one that clarifies them with a precise explanation, and cites their Talmudic sources, and provides a record of the disputes of the Geonim and the Rabbis, and the consensus of the Aharonim[71]—and all this with splendid conciseness.

Therefore I, Ḥasdai the son of R. Judah the son of R. Ḥasdai the son of R. Judah,[72] may they rest in peace, have taken upon myself to walk this path—with the approval of scholars and with their help,[73] and if God favors me with life. In those places, however, where I innovate and depart from what was said earlier, I will be a bit more expansive. My intention is that, in a matter in which there is disagreement, it be easy for anyone who looks into it to find the roots of the issues where they originate in the texts. Thus it would be best that one who studies this book attain in advance a familiarity with the Talmud and be engaged in Talmud study, for then he will grasp [1] easily, and [2] with precision, the matters relating to the commandments and their general principles and reasons, so that by the mere mention of definitions and general principles, once he has command of them, he will master the totality of the commandments of the Torah, which in turn will be an evident cause of his

---

preservation from error. These, however, are not the three requisite ways enumerated earlier. "Precision in matters considered" and "preservation from error" together constitute just one of the earlier three ways, and the third way mentioned earlier, "preserving and remembering," is missing entirely.

[70] See n. 67.   [71] These are later authorities.

[72] Some later manuscripts, as well as the Ferrara edition and Fisher, erroneously have "Ḥasdai the son of R. Abraham." I thank Professor Zev Harvey for alerting me to this error.

[73] This aside may be taken quite literally, as manuscripts of *Light of the Lord* contain corrections and additions that are the handiwork of Crescas's students or collaborators. See n. 95.

[3] remembering and preserving—the three things toward which the whole of our intention is directed. Because in this book things will be made crystal clear and will be purified, and because they will shine forth from the dark recesses of doubt that arise from this great part of the commandments,[74] it is appropriate to call it *Lamp of the Commandment*.[75]

This is yet another[76]—for indeed it is great[77]—namely, the cornerstones of faith and the foundations of the Torah and the principles of its roots, about which, until the sealing of the Talmud, no dispute arose. Rather, these were known and agreed upon by the Sages of our nation—except for the secrets of the Torah, among them the account of creation and the account of the Chariot[78] which were in the hands of a select few modest men who transmitted them to their disciples at special times and under special conditions. But when the generations weakened, so that those who were repositories of the received Oral Torah and of the recesses of its secrets and mysteries lost their vigor, the wisdom of our wise men dissipated, and the understanding of our intelligent ones went into hiding.[79] Then many of our people aggrandized themselves to put forth a vision[80]—though words of prophecy had been closed up and sealed[81]—in dreams and vanities[82] and foreign ideas,[83] to the point that some of our great sages were drawn to their words and decorated themselves with their discourses and adorned themselves[84] with their proofs. Chief among them was the great teacher our Rabbi Moses son of Maimon, who, despite the greatness of his intellect, the prodigious comprehensiveness of his Talmudic knowledge, and the expansiveness of his mind, was nevertheless vulnerable when he delved into the books of the philosophers and their discourses: they seduced him and he was seduced.[85] Upon their weak principles he erected pillars and foundations to support the secrets of the Torah in the book that he called *Guide of the Perplexed*. Even though the intention of the Rabbi[86] was proper, there now arose rebellious slaves[87] who turned the words of the living God into heresy, blemishing the sacred offerings and introducing defilement[88] instead of beauty[89] into the words of the Rabbi. As he

---

[74] The manuscripts have "the great part of the commandments," בחלק הגדול הזה מהמצוות, referring back, no doubt, to "this great part of the commandments" that is in the category of the possible, with regard to which Crescas faults Maimonides for not dealing with it properly. Harvey (1973) reproduces the manuscript version. Fisher and Smilevitch follow the Ferrara edition in which the word "great" is absent.

[75] Prov. 6: 23. This work was, unfortunately, never written. It may be assumed that it was to be comparable in scope to Maimonides' *Mishneh Torah* but free of those perceived deficiencies to which Crescas calls attention in this Introduction.

[76] Hag. 2: 6. "This" refers to matters of belief, which are discussed in *Light of the Lord*, the only part of the projected two-part work that was written.

[77] Esther 1: 20.

[78] The account of creation is found in Gen. 1–2. The account of the Chariot refers to Ezekiel's vision in Ezek. 1: 4–26.

[79] Based on Isa. 29: 14.   [80] Based on Dan. 11: 14.   [81] Dan. 12: 9.

[82] Based on Eccles. 5: 6.   [83] Based on Isa. 2: 6; lit., "children of strangers."

[84] The term נתיפו (*nityapu*) may well be alluding to Yefet (Japheth): see the following note.

[85] A similar expression, but used with respect to God and with a different sense, is found at Jer. 20: 7, פתיתני ה' ואפת ("O Lord, You have persuaded me and I was persuaded"); also, 20: 10, אולי יפתה ונוכלה לו ("Perhaps he will be persuaded and we shall prevail against him"). It is likely that there is an allusion, too, to יפת אלהים ליפת ("God will enlarge Japheth"—Gen. 9: 27), and thus to the allure of Greek wisdom.

[86] "The Rabbi" refers to Maimonides.   [87] 1 Sam. 25: 10.

[88] A similar expression is found in Isa. 50: 20.   [89] Isa. 3: 24.

solemnly swore them not to reveal the matters he concealed and the mysteries of his thoughts, these others indeed did not reduce his word to naught and did not violate that to which he swore them;[90] instead, they turned his words to heresy, subverting his intention. The remaining others who trembled at the word of the Lord,[91] when they saw these people rendering clean the unclean swarming thing[92]—as if in accordance with the Torah—and offering seemingly plausible proofs,[93] were not freed from confusion, and bewilderment assailed them. At the heart of the matter is that up until now there was no one to take issue with the proofs of the Greek,[94] who darkened the eyes of Israel in our times.

For this reason I, whose eyes have been somewhat opened with respect to this enterprise, have seen fit to present in writing the root-principles and cornerstones upon which the Torah in its totality rests, and the axes on which it turns, without favoring anything but truth. I will indeed accomplish this by investing, together with the most important scholars,[95] much study and great diligence. I will at the same time explain that, with respect to these principles of belief the Rabbi did not, God forbid, dissent. Nevertheless, if his book in fact turns out to contain astonishing things, it is unthinkable that we should say nothing about them. For although the words of the Rabbi our teacher, including even his remarks on secular matters, are dear to us and are loved by us, the truth is yet more beloved.[96] And it is particularly necessary [not to remain silent] when it is possible for desecration of the holy name to result from these points. For our maxim is: "Wherever there is desecration of the holy name one ought not accord deference to the Rabbi."[97] And since the source of error and confusion is reliance on the words of the Greek and the proofs he produced, it struck me as appropriate to highlight the fallaciousness of his proofs and the sophistry of his arguments—even those the Rabbi borrowed from him to bolster his own positions—in order, on this day, to show all the nations that that which removes confusion in matters of faith, and which lights up all the darkness, is the Torah alone, as he [viz. Solomon] says: "For a commandment is a lamp and Torah is light."[98] In saying this he did something extraordinary: he compared the relationship between the Torah, which in its roots and grounds is wisdom (and which is that to which this part [of my intended two-part book] is devoted), on the one hand, and the commandment, that is, the totality of the commandments (which we deal with in the

---

[90] Crescas's point is that Maimonides' students, because they lacked the necessary subtlety and discernment, did not—because they could not—reveal their master's secrets.

[91] Isa. 66: 5.

[92] The expression וטהר את השרץ, "and he purified the swarming thing," is found at BT ʿEruvin 13b and BT Sanhedrin 17a.

[93] The expression ומראה לו פנים is used in this sense at BT ʿEruvin 13b, with respect to R. Meir's uncanny ability to defend his positions, even when they seemed indefensible, with plausible arguments.

[94] The reference is to Aristotle.

[95] It is likely that these scholars, or "associates," חברים (ḥaverim), are Crescas's students, who may have prepared the collections of material and the abstracts of literature he used in this work. Talmudic Sages graciously referred to their students as "associates." See Wolfson (1929), 23. Also see n. 73.

[96] Something similar was uttered by Aristotle (EN I. vi. 1096ᵃ) with respect to "those who introduced the Forms," intending no doubt Plato's followers (cf. Metaph. III. ii. 987ᵃ⁻ᵇ). It was Plato's Socrates who first made this remark—with respect to Homer (Rep. X. 595b–c; cf. X. 607c–d).

[97] BT Berakhot 19b; BT ʿEruvin 6a.   [98] Prov. 6: 23.

other part),[99] on the other, to the relationship between light and lamp. We have therefore called this part *Light of the Lord*. Since this part is the foundation and pillar of the other part, it is appropriate that it precede it in sequence. Indeed, the name of this book, which comprises both of these parts—should God will its completion—is *Lamp of the Lord*.[100] For it is from the Lord[101] to light a path with His Torah and His commandments. From Him I request help and guidance, for there is no helper but He, and no one to rely upon but Him. Now I begin, in the name of the Lord. Amen.

---

[99] This part was never written. See n. 75.

[100] See Harvey (1973), 367, who contends that although all manuscripts and printed editions have "*Lamp of God*" (נר אלהים; *ner elohim*), nevertheless "*Lamp of the Lord*" is intended. The text's next sentence supports Harvey's view, since "Lord" is the divine name contained in the verse it cites. It is likely that the reason the manuscripts and printed editions all have "*Lamp of God*" is that their editors assumed that the verse Crescas has in mind is Prov. 20: 27—"The soul of man is the lamp of the Lord"—in which traditionally, for some reason, the Tetragrammaton was pronounced *elohim*. It seems clear, however—and it is indeed quite explicit—that the verse Crescas has in mind is the one cited in the following sentence, viz. Ps. 18: 23, in which "Lord" is the name used: "For it is from the Lord..." Moreover, it is evident that Prov. 20: 27 is the verse Crescas has in mind earlier in the Introduction, when he speaks of two lights, the lamp of God, which concerns the commandments, and the light of the Lord, which concerns beliefs. It is surely in this earlier passage that the traditional *elohim*-pronunciation of the Tetragrammaton in Prov. 20: 27 comes into play. Inasmuch, however, as "lamp of God" is reserved there for the commandments-part of the larger work, it could hardly be the name of the whole.

[101] Ps. 118: 23.

Preface

O house of Jacob arise and let us walk in the light of the Lord.[1]

The foundation of beliefs and the root of first principles[2] which will lead directly to the knowledge of truth concerning the fundamental cornerstones of the divine Torah is the belief in the existence of God. And since the intention of this part[3] is to prove the cornerstones and views of the Torah of God, it is appropriate that we investigate this root-principle and the way in which we arrived at our knowledge of it.[4]

Since the root of the first principles of the divine Torah is the belief in the existence of God, this root-principle is self-evident—since the Torah is arranged and commanded by an arranger and commander, and its being divine has meaning only if the arranger and commander is God. Anyone who included belief in the existence of God among the positive commandments therefore committed an infamous error—since commandments are relational and no commandment can be conceived without a certain commander. Thus, if we regard the belief in the existence of God as a commandment, we in effect make the belief in the existence of God precede—in the order of our knowing—the belief in the existence of God! Moreover, if we regard the preceding belief in the existence of God as itself a commandment, this, too, will necessitate a prior belief in the existence of God. And so on to infinity. It would then follow that the commandment to believe in the existence of God would go on to infinity—but this is the height of absurdity. It is clear, therefore, that it is inappropriate to count the belief in the existence of God among the positive commandments.[5]

This Preface introduces only *Light of the Lord*, the first volume of the intended two-volume work, *Lamp of the Lord*, the second volume of which, *Lamp of the Commandment*, was never written.

[1] Isa. 2: 5.

[2] Crescas echoes here the opening of Maimonides' *Mishneh Torah*. He does so, however, only to go on to disagree with Maimonides on the matter of whether there is among the commandments a commandment to believe that God exists.

[3] The reference is to this first part of Crescas's projected two-part work, the part called *Light of the Lord*. See Introduction n. 75.

[4] In addressing "the way in which we arrived at our knowledge of it," Crescas considers the extent to which speculative arguments support the view favored by Torah and tradition.

[5] These are the first two of five arguments directed against the notion that belief in God is commanded: (1) If belief in God is a commandment, it would have been commanded by God, and so it would have to presuppose belief in God *ab initio*; and (2) the presupposed belief in God entailed by taking belief in God to be a commandment (as per argument (1)) would itself be a commandment that presupposed belief in God—and so on to infinity. The first argument locates the flaw in the view that belief in God is commanded in its begging the question. In the second, the view is faulted for generating an infinite regress.

This may be seen in another way, in that it is indeed clear from the meaning of the term "commandment" and its definition that it can only find its place among things to which will and choice apply.[6] If indeed, however, the belief in the existence of God is among the things to which will and choice do not apply, it follows that the meaning of the term "commandment" will not extend to it.[7] This is something we shall investigate later on, God willing.[8] Be that as it may, because it is evident that this belief is a root and first principle of all the commandments, if we count it itself as a commandment, it would follow that it is its own premise. Yet this is the height of absurdity.

That indeed which led him [who counted belief in the existence of God as a commandment] to do so—that is, to count this root-principle as a commandment—is a statement at the end of *Gemara Makkot*, where the Rabbis say:

> 613 commandments were spoken to Moses at Sinai. What is the scriptural support for this? "Moses commanded the Torah to us."[9] Yet they objected, "But Torah in *gematria* is only 611." And they responded: "I am the Lord" and "You shall not have"—these we heard from the mouth of the Almighty.[10]

Those [who count belief in the existence of God as a commandment] came to think because of this that "I am" and "You shall not have" are two commandments, and they therefore regarded the belief in the existence of God as a commandment. But it is evident that this conclusion is unwarranted. For what is intended there [viz. in the Rabbis' response to the question they raised] is that the God who is referred to in this way [viz. as the Lord your God] is the very deity and leader *who took us out of the land of Egypt*. Therefore the Rabbi our teacher Moses, of blessed memory, did well,[11] according to this way of thinking, when, in his *Book of the Commandments* (*Sefer Hamitzvot*), he counted the first commandment concerning belief in the divine as the command "to believe that there is a cause and determinant that is the agent responsible for all existents—which is why He said: 'I am the Lord your God.'"[12] The Rabbi thus interpreted the divine name as signifying God's being the agent responsible for all existents. And for the same reason God says, "who took you out of the land of Egypt"; this, too, is a kind of proof for that belief, since it is on the basis of this event that we grasp the power of God, such that all existents stand in relation to Him "as clay in the hand of the potter."[13] Therefore, indeed, this commandment will apply to the belief that God is the one who took us out of Egypt. Nevertheless, it is

---

[6] Crescas will argue that belief is not voluntary—and certainly not once the truth of the proposition in question has been demonstrated.

[7] This is the third argument: commandment implies choice and will; belief precludes them; hence, belief in God cannot be a commandment. The fourth follows: Since belief in God is the root of all commandments, if it were itself a commandment, it would be its own root.

[8] See II. v. 5.

[9] Deut. 33: 4. The idea is that the number of commandments derives from the *gematria* of "Torah." One would therefore expect the *gematria* of Torah to be 613. On *gematria*, see Introduction n. 37.

[10] BT *Makkot* 23b–24a.

[11] Crescas's approval of Maimonides in this matter is confined to just this one view that he attributes to him, namely, that God is the cause of all existents and that this God is the very same God who took the Israelites out of the land of Egypt. Crescas disagrees both with Maimonides' interpretation of the rabbinic dictum in tractate *Makkot* and with Maimonides' view that belief in God is commanded.

[12] Exod. 20: 2.   [13] Jer. 18: 6.

clear that even this way of thinking is absurd in itself. For from the Rabbis' having said: "'I am' and 'You shall not have,'" it would indeed appear that the entire extended utterance[14] through "to those who love Me and observe My commandments" is to be included. For, note: these two utterances take the grammatical form of the first person singular—"I am the Lord"; "who has taken [first-person sing.] you"; "before Me"; "because I am the Lord your God"; "to those who love Me and keep My commandments." Since the remaining utterances proceed in the grammar of the third person—as it is said: "For the Lord will not acquit"; "for in six days the Lord made"; "He rested and was refreshed"—they agreed that "I am" and "You shall not have" issued from the mouth of the Almighty. Because all those writers who were enumerators of the commandments[15] thought it appropriate to count "You shall not make a graven image" and "You shall not bow down to them" as two commandments—and this is indeed the very truth—were "I am" to be counted as a commandment, there would be three that we heard from the mouth of the Almighty, so that there would be 614 commandments. Furthermore, if we take "You shall not have any other gods" as a commandment not to believe in any divinity other than Him, as the Rabbi wrote, their number would rise to 615.

It is therefore appropriate that we deny that the Rabbis, in saying that "'I am' and 'You shall not have'—these we heard from the mouth of the Almighty," intended each to count as a commandment. Rather, since both alike were framed in the language of the first person singular, as we noted earlier, *that* is what they meant when they said that we heard them from the mouth of the Almighty. It follows that the two commandments in the utterance "You shall not have," which are "You shall not make for yourself a graven image or any representation," and "You shall not bow down to them," which we heard from the mouth of the Almighty, will complete the [count of] 613 when added to the 611 that were heard from Moses' mouth.

What remains to be explained is why the Rabbis did not count "You shall not have any other gods before Me" as a commandment, in which case there would be *three* commandments in this one utterance. This is easily accounted for: for if beliefs are something to which will and choice do not apply,[16] the term[17] "commandment" would not apply to them. And if nevertheless the term "commandment" does apply [to "You shall not have"], then the meaning of "You shall not have" will be that we may not *acknowledge* anything else as a god.[18] It was in fact made clear in *Sanhedrin* that one who does so merits the death penalty.[19] The Rabbis did not see fit to count "You shall not have" and "You shall not bow down" as two, because these share a single common root-principle, namely, the acknowledgment of [other gods']

---

[14] I translate דבור, "utterance," when referring to any of the Ten Utterances, popularly known as the Ten Commandments.

[15] The term אזהרות (*azharot*) normally refers to the negative commandments, the proscriptions, in the Torah. In the expression, מוני האזהרות, "enumerators of the *azharot*," however, the term refers to commandments, whether negative or positive.

[16] See nn. 6 and 7.

[17] Reading *shem* ("term") rather than *sham* ("there") (contra Fisher's vocalization of שם).

[18] Acknowledgment is understood as active and hence not as a matter of belief alone.

[19] *Sanhedrin* 7: 6. Here the acknowledgment, קבלה (*qabbalah*), consists in proclaiming to the unauthorized god, "You are my God": והאומר לו אלי אתה.

divinity. But "You shall not make for yourself a graven image" stands—even if one does not worship or acknowledge it—and therefore they counted them [viz. "You shall not bow down" and "You shall not make"] as two. But it never occurred to the Rabbis to count "I am the Lord" as a commandment,[20] since it is the root and first principle of the totality of the commandments, as we explained previously.[21]

Now that it has become clear that this belief is a root and first principle of the totality of the Torah's beliefs and of the commandments, it is indeed appropriate that we examine this belief as well as how we arrived at our knowledge of this root-principle. Of the beliefs contained in the Torah, however, some are cornerstones and foundations of the totality of the commandments and others are not. Nevertheless, they too are true views. Indeed, all are alike in that they are all beliefs such that one who believes in the divine Torah must believe them and one who denies them denies the entire Torah. But there are some [beliefs] that are opinions that recommend themselves to reason; those who deny these are not considered heretics. The intention of this part[22] is to prove the cornerstones and views of the divine Torah. Because of these considerations, we have seen fit to divide this part into four Books: the first will deal with the first root-principle, which is the first principle for all the Torah's beliefs; the second, with those beliefs that are cornerstones and foundations for the totality of the commandments; the third, with the true views that we who believe in the divine Torah ought to believe; and the fourth, with those opinions that recommend themselves to reason.

Our discussion of these things will proceed along two paths: one, the clarification of their sense as the Torah determines it; and two, the way in which we arrived at our knowledge of them. May His name be praised.

---

[20] Not every utterance counted among the "ten *utterances*" need be regarded as a commandment.

[21] This completes the fifth argument, which is a refutation of Maimonides. The argument, in brief, runs as follows. Since the verse Deut. 33: 4 states, "Moses commanded the Torah to us," and since the word "Torah" in *gematria* is 611, there have to be two commandments that issued directly from the mouth of God (since, according to the tradition—for which this verse may well be the source—there are 613 commandments). Crescas contends that the two divine commandments are: "You shall not bow down" (which may comprise "You shall not have") and "You shall not make"—these are distinct from one another because one can make a graven image yet not worship it or worship it yet not make it. Crescas argues that if, as Maimonides would have it, "I am the Lord" is one commandment, "You shall not have" is another, "You shall not make" is a third, and "You shall not bow down" is a fourth, the total number of commandments would rise to 615. From Crescas's perspective, as we have seen (see n. 7), belief cannot be commanded, so "I am the Lord" cannot be a commandment nor can "You shall not have"—so long as this is viewed as a matter of belief rather than of action. As Crescas interprets the Rabbis, when they say that "I am" and "You shall not have" proceeded directly from God, all they intend is that the early part of the Decalogue was uttered by God in the first person; all commandments contained in this early part of the Decalogue spoken by God in the first person, however, forbid actions; they do not require beliefs.

[22] Of Crescas's projected two-part work.

Book I

CONCERNING the first root-principle, which is the first principle for all the beliefs of the Torah: the belief in the existence of God.

The meaning of a proposition is clarified in two ways: the first, by explaining the terms that it contains, and the second, by explaining the relation between the one term and the other—for instance, is the predicate to be affirmed or denied of the subject? It is evident, too, in the case of this proposition, namely, our assertion that God exists, that its subject-term is "God," who is absolutely inscrutable, as will be discussed, God willing, later on. Therefore, the point of this proposition is solely that the cause and first principle of all existents exists. For this reason it would seem that the study of this root-principle can be conducted in the second way alone, that is, by the way in which we arrived at knowledge of its truth.[1] It is therefore appropriate that we investigate whether we came to know the true meaning of this root-principle on the basis of tradition alone, that is, on the authority of the divine Torah, or whether we came to know it also by way of speculation and investigation.

First among those who discussed this root-principle at length from the point of view of investigation were: Aristotle in his works the *Physics* and the *Metaphysics*; the commentators on Aristotle's works, such as Themistius and Alexander; the later commentators, such as Alfarabi[2] and Averroes[3]; as well as the authors who followed him, such as Avicenna,[4] al-Ghazali,[5] and R. Abraham ibn Daud. Indeed, since the Rabbi and author who in his book called *Guide of the Perplexed* also made use of many of their propositions, stating them concisely in order to clarify this root-principle in a variety of ways, and seeing fit to join to it two precious root-principles, namely, that God is one and that He is neither a body nor a force in a body,[6] we decided to investigate Maimonides' proofs, with respect to whether they establish

---

[1] This is the second of the two ways, set forth at the end of the Preface, in which the truth of beliefs may be established. The first is via the Torah and the rabbinic tradition. The second is via speculative reasoning.

[2] Alfarabi is also known as abu Nazzr.

[3] Averroes is the Latinized form of ibn Rushd.

[4] Avicenna is the Latinized form of ibn Sina.

[5] Al-Ghazali is also known as abu Ḥamed.

[6] By "force" Crescas means to include whatever cannot exist except in something else. It includes, therefore, accidents, forms, the lower faculties of the rational soul, the internal principle of motion, and universals.

comprehensively the truth concerning these three root-principles or not. Since Maimonides' proofs derive from a synoptic grasp of the discourses of the first philosophers, one need not attend in addition to anything else that appears in their discourses.

Inasmuch as Maimonides' proofs are based on the twenty-six propositions that he posits at the beginning of the second part of his book,[7] the order of investigation herein will proceed by considering the following two questions: first, whether the propositions Maimonides uses to prove these root-principles are truly established demonstratively—for if the propositions required for the proof of the root-principles are not themselves proved demonstratively, neither will the root-principles be proved demonstratively; and second, if we do assume these propositions to be true—and to be proved demonstratively—whether the root-principles are also proved demonstratively from them. In this study, we shall proceed by addressing the author's own claims. Accordingly, it is appropriate that we divide this Book into three Parts:

Part I. An exposition of these propositions in accordance with how they were proved in the discourses of the philosophers, and an exposition of the proofs of the Rabbi. For inasmuch as we shall be examining them, it is appropriate that they be understood by us clearly and straightforwardly and free of any uncertainty—as the Rabbi intended.

Part II. An inquiry into some of the propositions and into the proofs of the Rabbi, to determine whether they have been proved demonstratively.

Part III. An account of the root-principles in accordance with what the Torah prescribes and in accordance with the way in which we arrived at our knowledge of them. In this Part the intention of Book I will be made manifest, to wit, to show that there is no way to grasp these root-principles perfectly other than via prophecy, as the Torah attests and the tradition confirms. This fact notwithstanding, it will also become evident that reason concurs.

Part I

PROOF of the propositions as they were proved in the discourses of the philosophers and in the proofs of the Rabbi as derived from the discourses of the philosophers. We have consequently divided this part into thirty-two chapters: twenty-six to explain the twenty-six propositions [of the philosophers], and an additional six to clarify the six proofs of the Rabbi.

Chapter I

PROOF of the first proposition, which states that the existence of anything whose measure is infinite is absurd.

An investigation of this proposition was conducted by Aristotle in various places in his works the *Physics*, *On the Heavens*, and the *Metaphysics*,[8] and he produced proofs

---

[7] The reference is to *The Guide of the Perplexed*.
[8] *Physics* III. iv–viii; *On the Heavens* I. v–vii; *Metaph.* XI. x.

for it: a proof of the impossibility of the existence of an infinite incorporeal magnitude; a proof of the impossibility of the existence of an infinite corporeal magnitude; a proof of the impossibility of the existence of an infinite moving thing—whether its motion is circular or rectilinear; a general proof of the impossibility of the existence of a body whose infinity is actual. Consequently, we divide this chapter into four sections, corresponding to the number of these classes of proofs.

CLASS I. PROOF OF THE IMPOSSIBILITY OF THE EXISTENCE OF AN INFINITE INCORPOREAL MAGNITUDE.

This proof proceeds as follows. He[9] asserted that the following disjunction is inescapable: an incorporeal magnitude is either subject to division or not. If it is not subject to division it surely cannot be described as infinite except in the sense in which it is said of a point that it is infinite or of a color that it is inaudible.[10] The remaining alternative is that it *is* subject to division. But if so, it is inevitable that it be either an incorporeal quantity or one of the incorporeal substances such as the soul or the intellect. Yet it is absurd that it be an incorporeal substance, since any incorporeal thing, insofar as it is incorporeal, is *not* subject to division; yet we have been proceeding on the assumption that it *is* subject to division.[11]

In addition, it is unavoidable that we say that it [viz. the incorporeal substance] is either divisible or not divisible. If, on the one hand, it is divisible, then, since that which is incorporeal is simple and homogeneous, it would follow that the definition of the part and of the whole is the same. And because it is assumed that the whole is infinite, it would be necessary that the part, too, be infinite. But it is the height of absurdity that the whole and the part be the same. If, on the other hand, it is not

---

[9] In this Part as well as in Part II Crescas frequently uses the third-person singular pronoun without specifying its referent. This translation for the most part follows suit. Nevertheless, since it is Maimonides who formulates in the Introduction to Part II of his *Guide of the Perplexed* the twenty-six propositions that Crescas presents and discusses here, the third-person pronoun usually refers to him, even when the proofs presented are not originally his. Of course, there are also discussions in which Aristotle is either explicitly (as in I. i. 1) or implicitly (as in I. ii. 1) Crescas's target. Moreover, Crescas is well aware that the proofs that undergird Maimonides' twenty-six propositions often derive not directly from Aristotle but more generally from "the discourses of the philosophers," that is, from the writings of the medieval Aristotelian commentators, especially Averroes. Crescas occasionally refers by name to a specific philosopher or commentator. He clearly relies as well on al-Tabrizi's *Commentary on Maimonides' Twenty-Five Propositions*, a digest that sets forth the medieval interpretation of the Aristotelian position. For extensive consideration of Crescas's likely sources, see Wolfson 1929.

[10] To say of a point that it is infinite or of a color that it is inaudible is to commit a category mistake: neither "finite" nor "infinite" applies to a point; a color can be neither audible nor inaudible. Whereas it is true of a point that it is infinite in the sense that it is not finite, and true of a color that it is inaudible in the sense that it is not audible, these assertions are true not because a point might have been finite or a color audible though as it happens they are not, but rather because they are not subject to this sort of characterization. The point here is that finitude and infinitude apply only to things that are subject to division.

[11] In this paragraph the argument maintains that no *in*divisible incorporeal magnitude is infinite. It proceeds to consider whether a divisible incorporeal magnitude might be infinite. The incorporeal magnitude in question might be either a quantity or a substance. Yet surely it cannot be a divisible incorporeal substance, since nothing incorporeal is divisible.

divisible, as is indeed a necessity for any incorporeal thing, we would have to be saying that it is infinite in the way that a point is said to be infinite.[12]

The sole remaining possibility [once it has been shown that the incorporeal magnitude cannot be an incorporeal substance] is, therefore, that it is a quantity, in which case it is inevitable that it be either a quantity that inheres in a substratum[13] or a quantity that is incorporeal. But it cannot be an incorporeal quantity, since number and measure, which are now being posited as infinite, are not separable from sensible things. But if it were a quantity that inheres in a substratum, then, since accidents[14] are not separate from their substratum, and since the finite and the infinite are accidents of quantity, it follows necessarily that they are not incorporeal, since quantity is not incorporeal.[15]

Since this proof is based on a premise that requires the impossibility of measure separate from sensible things, this proof would be question-begging from the perspective of one who endorses the notion of incorporeal extension, which allows for the existence of such a quantity.[16] It would seem, therefore, that he must be relying on his belief in the impossibility of empty space.[17] For were we to admit the existence of empty space, then the existence of a quantity separate from sensible things would not be impossible, but, on the contrary, its existence might actually be necessitated, for in fact, it would be capable of measurement, and we would be justified in saying of it that it is large or small or in applying to it any of the other concepts of quantity. So it is only because he denied the existence of empty space that he could base this proof on the aforementioned premise [viz. that number and measure are not separable from sensible things]. We therefore see fit to cite his proofs [for the impossibility of empty space] briefly within this class of proofs [viz. those dealing with the impossibility of an infinite incorporeal magnitude], so that we may investigate them further in the second part [viz. in Book I Part II], God willing, to see whether they establish comprehensively the truth of his view.

---

[12] This paragraph offers a further explanation of why it is that an infinite incorporeal substance cannot be divisible: since an incorporeal substance lacks internal differentiation, each part in it will be identical to the whole. Yet if this is the case then the parts would have to be infinite just as the whole is; but it is absurd that what is true of the whole, namely, that it is infinite, be true of the parts. The paragraph concludes with the application to incorporeal substances of what was said earlier regarding incorporeal magnitudes generally: that if they are indivisible they cannot be described as infinite except in the way that a point is—that is, illegitimately, by way of a category mistake.

[13] "Substratum" renders נושא (nosei), which in turn translates the Greek hupokeimenon: that which underlies and is thus the bearer of the various properties.

[14] "Accident" renders מקרה (miqreh), which in turn translates the Greek sumbebekos: a property that a thing happens to have but which is not essential to or definitive of it. "Accident" is also used more broadly to mean anything that cannot exist other than in something else. For this notion Maimonides—and Crescas as well—generally employs the term "force" כח (koah).

[15] This argument seeks to show that "incorporeal quantity" is an oxymoron: if something is incorporeal, and hence separate from sensible things, it cannot be a quantity, since quantity is not separable from sensible things; but if it is a quantity that is in a substratum it cannot be incorporeal, because quantity—whether finite or infinite—is an accident of sensible things.

[16] Whereas incorporeal quantity may be an oxymoron when quantity is regarded as a property solely of corporeal things, incorporeal quantity might be admissible if quantity may be regarded as a property of "incorporeal extension," that is, of empty space.

[17] By "empty space" what is meant is vacuum; empty space is empty of everything, including air.

Since those who maintain the existence of empty space imagine that without its existence locomotion would be impossible, he first took it upon himself to prove the falsity of this idea. In addition, he formulated four proofs for the absurdity of the existence of empty space.

The proof of the falsity of the idea [that locomotion is impossible without empty space] is as follows. If empty space were a cause of motion, it would have to be either an efficient or a final cause.[18] But it is neither efficient nor final, leading to the result that the antecedent is contradicted. The necessity of the connection between the consequent and the antecedent is evident: since it was shown that the number of causes of things is four, namely, material, formal, efficient, and final, and since it is also evident that empty space cannot be either the material cause or the formal cause of motion, the only remaining possibility is that it is an efficient or a final cause. That the consequent is necessarily contradicted is proved as follows. Since we see a variety of bodies in locomotion, some moving to the up and others to the down, it appears that the cause of this difference is either the nature of the locomoting body itself, which is the moving and efficient cause, or the nature of the that-to-which toward which the motion proceeds, which is the final cause. Since, however, empty space is homogeneous with respect to its parts and so cannot have variation in its parts—with some part of it possessing the nature of a that-from-which and some other part possessing the nature of a that-to-which—the following disjunction is inevitable: it has either the nature of a that-from-which, or the nature of a that-to-which, or the nature neither of a that-from-which nor of a that-to-which. If we posit for it the nature of a that-from-which, then any body placed within the empty space would have to be at rest forever. But if we assume for it the nature of a that-to-which, it would have to move in all directions simultaneously or else be at rest forever—since there is no more reason that it move in one direction than in another. And if we assume that it has the nature neither of a that-from-which nor of a that-to-which—and indeed it must be so since empty space is nothing but extension detached from natural things—it will again turn out necessarily that any thing placed in it would be forever at rest. It is evident, therefore, that empty space is neither an efficient nor a final cause. This is what he intended to prove with this argument.[19]

In addition he offered four proofs for the impossibility of the existence of empty space.

The first proof proceeds as follows. Were empty space to exist, there would be no motion. But there is motion. Hence, there is no empty space. In this case, that the

---

[18] Aristotle posits four causes that account for the coming-to-be of all things, whether natural or produced by art. The efficient cause is the producer; the formal cause is the form of the thing produced, that which determines the kind of thing it is; the material cause is that out of which it is composed; the final cause is its purpose or end. It is clear that empty space has neither matter nor form, hence it can be neither the material nor the formal cause of motion. Aristotle contends that in empty space there are neither starting-points nor destinations since empty space is homogeneous. In the absence of both starting-point ("that-from-which") and destination ("that-to-which") there would be only rest.

[19] This argument challenges the idea that empty space is required for locomotion. It contends that, since empty space is not any of the four causes to which the motion of bodies might be attributed, it cannot be a necessary condition for their locomotion. In the four proofs for the impossibility of the existence of empty space, immediately following, the point will be not simply that empty space is not a cause of motion, but that the existence of empty space actually precludes motion.

consequent is contradicted is evident by way of sense-perception. And the necessity of the connection between the consequent and the antecedent may be proved as follows. Motion is either natural or forcible.[20] Natural motion varies in accordance with the nature of the that-from-which and of the that-to-which, but empty space contains no variation and therefore contains no natural motion. And because forcible motion is related to natural motion, and natural motion precedes it in nature inasmuch as what is moved by force is moved by force only in that it departs from the place toward which it moves by nature, it follows that if there can be no natural motion there can likewise be no forcible motion. Furthermore, if there were forcible motion in empty space, the thing that is moved would have to rest when the mover departs from it. In the case in which an arrow departs from the string that is its mover, and then the string rests, the only reason it can propel the arrow until it arrives at its natural place is that the air in its lightness has the capacity to receive the motion. Since it is evident in the case of empty space that it has no capacity to receive the motion, the thing that is moved will of necessity come to rest as soon as it departs from the mover. Yet this is contrary to what is perceived by sense.

The second and third proofs are based on two premises. One is that the cause of swiftness and slowness in moving things is either variation in the mover, variation in the receptacle, or both. To explain: if the mover is stronger, the motion will be swifter; and so, too, if the receptacle, which is the medium in which the motion takes place, is stronger, the reception will be stronger. For instance, in the case of air, which has greater receptive strength than water, the motion in it will be swifter than in water. The second is that the ratio of one motion to another is as the ratio of the strength of one mover to another when the medium is the same; or as the ratio of the strength of one [medium's] reception to another when the mover is the same; or as the combined ratio of moving strength to moving strength and of receptive strength to receptive strength, when the movers and media vary. (How to calculate a combined ratio has indeed been explained in Euclid's *Elements*.) With the assumption that these premises are self-evident, he formulated one proof from the perspective of the receptacle and another from the perspective of the mover.

The one from the perspective of the receptacle proceeds as follows. If there were empty space, anything that moved in it would necessarily move not over time.[21] But motion not over time is impossible. Hence the antecedent is necessarily contradicted. The connection between the consequent and the antecedent is proved if we posit a single thing moved a given distance by a single mover in air and in empty space. According to the first premise, the swiftness and slowness would be a function of the variation in the receptacle, and, according to the second, the ratio of swiftness to slowness would be as the ratio of air to empty space. It is evident that in the case of these two receptacles, their ratio is as that of the finite to the infinite. It follows therefore that motion in empty space would take place not over time. But this is impossible, since motion over a given distance is inconceivable without time—since

---

[20] Natural motion is motion from within; forcible motion is motion from without.
[21] The expression, בזולת זמן (*bezulat zeman*), which I render, "not over time," means having no duration, that is, taking place instantaneously. The contrasting expression, בזמן (*bizman*), which I translate "over time," means having duration, that is, taking place over a stretch of time.

distance is divisible, and it is necessary that time be divided in tandem with the motion in it.

Averroes has maintained that the force of this proof is like that of the proof that derives from it, namely, that if there is an infinite hylic[22] moving force, that which is moved by it will move not over time.[23]

The proof from the perspective of the mover proceeds as follows. If there were empty space, the first premise would necessarily be false, despite its being self-evident. This is because if we were to assume two things moved in empty space by two movers that differed by a certain magnitude, it would follow from the first premise that one would be swifter than the other. But since it is evident with respect to any moving thing in empty space, in accordance with what was said earlier, that it would move in an instant, it would follow necessarily that, despite the variation in mover, there would be no variation in motion. This is impossible according to the first premise. And this impossibility is entailed by our asserting that there is empty space.

The fourth proof proceeds as follows. If there were empty space, it would have to be possible for one body to enter another. But the entry of one body into another is impossible, for if it were not impossible, the world could enter a grain of mustard. It follows that empty space does not exist. The necessity of the connection between consequent and antecedent may be proved as follows. Since the existence of empty space is not anything more than the existence of three incorporeal dimensions separate from body, it follows that, since they are also not bodies, and are not accidents borne by a thing, it is impossible for them to be displaced when a body enters them the way water in a trough is displaced when a stone is thrown into it. If so, the dimensions of the body could indeed enter the dimensions of the empty space. But if this were possible, it would be possible for a body to enter a body. After all, the impossibility of one body's entering another does not derive from the body's being a substance, nor from its being possessed of color or quality, but from its being three-dimensional. Thus, if the entry of a body into dimensions is possible,[24] then the entry of a body into a body is possible. But this is an outright impossibility. Therefore, empty space exists neither in the world nor outside it.

He drew further support for this view from a body's requiring a place insofar as it has three dimensions in which it resides. But if this is so, these dimensions [viz. the dimensions of the place] would in turn require dimensions, and this would go on to infinity.[25] In addition, dimensions are the limits of bodies, and a limit, inasmuch as it

---

[22] The Greek *hylē*, wood, is one of several terms generally used in philosophic contexts to designate matter. I translate Crescas's term חומרי (*homri*) as "material," reserving "hylic" for Crescas's היולני (*hiyulani*). "Corporeal" translates גשמי (*gashmi*) throughout. "Bodily" translates גופי (*gufi*).

[23] The idea here is that when any of the variables is infinite there can be no motion over time. For there can then be no ratio that would determine relative swiftness and slowness. Averroes is noting that the problem that arises when the receptive strength of the receptacle is infinite is the same as when the moving force is infinite.

[24] Following the manuscripts: אם הכנס גשם ברחקים אפשרי. Fisher, following the Ferrara edition has: אם הכנס ברחקי הגשם רחק אפשרי, "if it is possible for a dimension to enter the dimensions of a body."

[25] The thrust of this argument is that if a three-dimensional body, insofar as it is housed within three dimensions, requires a further place in which to reside, the three dimensions of this further place would in turn require a three-dimensional place in which to reside, and so on to infinity. If an infinite regress is to be

is not divisible, cannot possibly be separated from that of which it is a limit. It follows therefore that the existence of an incorporeal extension is impossible. This is the foundation upon which Aristotle relied in proving the impossibility of the existence of an infinite magnitude, and this is what he intended in this class of proof. This is the first class.

Al-Tabrizi formulated another proof to establish the impossibility of the existence of an infinite magnitude—the proof from attachment[26]—which runs as follows. If we were to posit a line infinite on only one end, and were to attach to it another infinite line beginning from the point at the finite end of the first line, then one infinite line would turn out to be longer than another infinite line. But this is impossible, for it is well known that one infinity cannot be greater than another.

CLASS II. PROOF OF THE IMPOSSIBILITY OF THE EXISTENCE OF AN INFINITE CORPOREAL MAGNITUDE.

He began first with a proof of the general rule that the existence of an actual infinite magnitude—whether corporeal or mathematical—is impossible. The proof proceeds as follows. Every body is encompassed by a single surface or by multiple surfaces; and anything that is encompassed by a surface or by surfaces is finite; therefore, every body is of necessity finite. Once it was clear to him that every body is finite, he concluded that every surface and every line is finite, inasmuch as they are inseparable from bodies. It was similarly clear to him with respect to actual number that it is finite of necessity, since every actual number is actually counted, and every number that is actually counted is either even or odd, so that every number is finite.

In addition he advanced four physical proofs to establish the impossibility of the existence of an infinite corporeal magnitude.

The first proof proceeds as follows. If there were an infinite tangible body, it would of necessity be either simple or composite. In either case, one of its elements would of necessity be infinite in magnitude, since it was proved in Book I of the *Physics* that the existence of an infinite number of elements is impossible.[27] But if one of the elements were infinite in magnitude, then, because it is also tangible and has qualities, it would, given enough time, change the other elements and cause them to pass away—since elements are elements by virtue of their qualities—and so coming-to-be would not persist. Yet this is in direct opposition to the evidence of the senses.[28] Furthermore, if one element were infinite it would be infinite in all its dimensions, since its dimensions, insofar as they are dimensions of a simple body, are all alike, such that no room would be left for the rest.

The second proof proceeds as follows. Every tangible body has either lightness or heaviness. But if it has heaviness it is located in the lower region and is separated

---

avoided, a body must be contained within its own dimensions without any need for a further place in which to reside.

[26] The Hebrew is מופת הדבקות (*mofet hadevequt*).

[27] Since there are two ways in which a tangible body might be infinite—(1) by containing an infinite number of elements, or (2) by having one infinite element—if the former is excluded, only the latter remains viable. If a body had only a finite number of finite elements, it would not be infinite.

[28] The senses attest to continuing generation.

from the upper; and if it has lightness it is located in the upper region and is separated from the lower.[29] Yet all of this is absurd with respect to a thing that is infinite.

The third proof proceeds as follows. If each sensible body is located in a place, and if places are finite in kind and measure, it follows necessarily that the body is finite, since it was proved that place is the limit that encompasses a body. But, that places are finite in kind is evident, since their differentiae are limited—they are: up and down, in front of and behind, right and left. And that they are finite in measure is necessary, since were they not finite there would be no absolute—but only relative—up and down. But we see that natural things are limited.[30]

The fourth proof proceeds as follows. If every sensible body is in a place, and if place is an encompassing limit, it follows that a body that is located in a place is finite. The necessity of the connection of the consequent [to the antecedent] is self-evident, for anything that is encompassed must of necessity be finite. But how can it be proved that place is that which encompasses? To this end, he formulated five self-evident propositions: (1) that place encompasses the thing for which it serves as place; (2) that place is separate from the thing and not a part of it; (3) that the primary place, the particular place [in which the thing resides], is equal to the place's occupant; (4) that place is either up or down; and (5) that bodies rest in their place and make their way toward it. These are the propositions that help us understand the essence of place. He also devised a disjunctive hypothetical syllogism, which proceeds as follows. Of necessity, place is seen as one of four things: either form, or matter, or the encompassing limit, or the interval between the limits of the encompasser, which is called empty space.[31] But if it is not one of the three—namely, form, matter, and empty space—it will of necessity be the encompassing limit. It is indeed not one of these three; therefore, it must be the encompassing limit.

Yet how can it be proved that it is not one of the three? With regard to its not being form or matter, this is evident, for these belong to the essence of a thing and are not separable from it. Thus, if it were either of these the second premise would not be satisfied. And even if we assume that form is a limit, it would be an encompassed limit and not an encompassing one. The truth is, however, that form is not a limit, and it is said to be a limit only in that it limits that which is hylic and sets its boundary.

What remains to be proved is that place is not empty space. Aristotle says in this regard that the assertion that there are dimensions that stand on their own leads to two absurdities: first, that a single thing by itself would have simultaneously many places—to infinity. And second, that the places would themselves be subject to motion, such that a place could be in another place.

---

[29] Aristotle held that objects are naturally light or heavy, and that each has a natural place; the absolute up for the light, the absolute down for the heavy. Furthermore, things seek out and move toward their natural place unless hindered.

[30] See Wolfson (1929: 354 n. 72), who takes "natural things," הדברים הטבעיים (hadevarim hativiyim), to refer to the "natural or proper places of the elements." The argument is designed to show that the body is finite because it occupies places that are necessarily finite—in kind, because there are only so many ways they might differ in kind; and in measure, because the up and down in which they are located are absolute.

[31] The term רחק (raḥaq) may be rendered "dimension" or "interval." I use "interval" when it appears with "between."

How this follows necessarily will be seen in what I explain. If place is the interval between the limits of a body, it is necessary that the parts of the body be essentially in that same place. This is because, just as the body as a whole is in a place insofar as its dimension is equal to it, so is each of its parts in a place insofar as its dimension is equal to it. And since we assumed that a vessel filled with water can move from place to place, it seems that just as the water moves in the vessel along with a dimension equal to that which transports it yet occupies a different dimension when the vessel as a whole has been transported from its place, so, too, the parts of the water: they, too, will be transported with the dimensions particular to them to other dimensions that will be their places. And just as we can continually divide those parts into further parts, the following two absurdities will of necessity arise: on the one hand, they will inhabit an infinity of places, and, on the other, the places will move and one place will be in another.[32]

What follows from this is that a place is a surface that encompasses something equal and separate. And with this being proved, it is confirmed without any doubt that a body that is located in a place is finite. That is what he intended in this class of proofs.

CLASS III. PROOF OF THE IMPOSSIBILITY OF THE EXISTENCE OF AN INFINITE MOVING THING—WHETHER ITS MOTION IS RECTILINEAR OR CIRCULAR.

With respect to the impossibility of rectilinear motion in an infinite moving thing he formulated three proofs.

For the first proof he introduced two self-evident propositions: first, that every sensible body has a location that is specific to it, and a place toward which it moves and in which it rests; second, that the place of the part and the place of the whole are one—for example, the place of a single clod of earth is the place of the earth as a whole. Once these two propositions were firmly established for him, the proof proceeded as follows. If there were an infinite body, its parts would have to be either similar or dissimilar. If the parts were similar, then, since the place of the whole and of the part would be one, as was explained in the second proposition, the body would not move at all. This is so since the body's place must be equal to the body. Therefore, when a part of the body is in a part of the place of the whole, it too indeed will be in its place. And a thing will not move when it is in its place.[33]

---

[32] Crescas presents as a single argument what might perhaps be better presented as two distinct arguments. One has to do with infinity of parts, the other with their transportability. The first of the two absurdities arises because if place is the (empty) interval—the bare dimensions—between the extremities of a body, each of the parts of the body will also have a place that is the interval between *its* extremities. If the body can be divided infinitely, the body's parts will be infinite and each of those parts will have a place. The body, then, would have an infinite number of places: not only its own place, but all the intervals containing all its infinite parts. The second absurdity arises because if the parts move along with the whole and take their intervals or dimensions with them, each of these intervals (= places) will be within new intervals (= places) because the new intervals are now their places too, with the result that places are nested within places, and so on.

[33] In an infinite body whose parts are alike, the parts, like the whole, are in their proper place, and motion for them, as for the whole, is therefore impossible.

Furthermore, if the parts were dissimilar, the parts would have to be either finite or infinite in number. If they were finite in number, it would be necessary that one of them be infinite in magnitude, and so of necessity it would not, just as in the earlier case, move in rectilinear fashion. But if they were infinite in number, it would be necessary that the kinds of location be infinite in number, as was established by the first proposition. The kinds of location, however, are necessarily limited, because natural location derives either from rectilinear motion or from circular motion, and rectilinear motion is either away from the center or toward the center, and circular motion is around the center. But if the body's parts add up between them to an infinite magnitude, there is no center.[34] It may not be said that the place of each one is one above the other to infinity, for if the matter were so, there would be no absolute up and down. [As we shall see, the four elements move, some to the absolute up and some to the absolute down, and some to the relative up and down. And we shall see that the absolute down is limited, and that its opposite, the absolute up is limited, since opposites are at a maximal distance from one another.[35]] It has thus been shown that, either way, the existence of an infinite body would preclude rectilinear motion. But rectilinear motion is something of which we have sense-perception. Therefore, an infinite body does not exist.

The second proof proceeds as follows. If an infinite body did exist, either infinite heaviness or infinite lightness would of necessity exist. But both infinite heaviness and infinite lightness are impossible. Therefore, an infinite body is impossible. The connection between the consequent and the antecedent in this syllogism may be explained as follows.[36] We assert that if an infinite body existed, there would necessarily exist infinite heaviness, for if there were no infinite heaviness, it [viz. the body's heaviness] would be finite. Let us then suppose that a finite body is separated off from it [i.e. from the infinite body]. It is evident that its heaviness would be less than that of the infinite body. Let us then multiply this [finite] body until its heaviness is as great as that of the infinite [body], since its heaviness [viz. the heaviness of the infinite body] is [assumed] finite and it is evident that it is possible to multiply the finite body to the point that it [viz. its heaviness] is greater than the [assumed] first finite heaviness [of the infinite body], since the infinite body had heaviness. But all of this is the height of absurdity—that the heaviness of a finite part of a body should be as great as the heaviness of an infinite body and even greater than it. The connection, then, between the consequent and the antecedent in this syllogism

---

[34] Since a body's parts each have to have a place, it follows that if a body's parts are infinite in number there would have to be infinite places. There cannot be infinite places, however, because there is motion, and motion requires set places that are the natural destination of the things that move. Indeed, there cannot be motion without a center toward which, away from which, and around which bodies move. A body whose parts jointly compose an infinite magnitude has no center. Since, however, the existence of motion is undeniable, there must be a center, and so an infinite body consisting of an infinite number of parts is precluded.

[35] In the manuscripts (see following note), this bracketed passage appears a bit later but Wolfson (1929) inserts it here because it does not seem to belong where it is found. Fisher includes the passage at this point as well.

[36] It is here that the passage that Wolfson (1929) transferred (see previous note) appears initially.

is proved by the consideration that if there existed an infinite body, an infinite heaviness would have to exist.[37]

Regarding the proposition that contradicts the consequent, namely, the assertion that it is impossible for there to be infinite heaviness or infinite lightness, this can be proved once we posit three propositions. The first is that a moving thing whose heaviness is greater will, in accordance with its natural motion, traverse a given distance in a shorter time than it takes a less heavy moving thing to traverse that same distance. The second is that the ratio between the two amounts of time is the ratio between one heaviness and the other. And the third is that every motion is over time. With these propositions established, let us consider the case in which the heaviness of an infinite thing and the heaviness of a finite thing traverse the same distance. Of necessity the ratio of one time to the other will be the ratio of one heaviness to the other. But because no ratio obtains between the infinite and the finite other than that of a point to a line and of an instant to time, it follows necessarily that [the infinitely heavy thing] will move in an instant, which is impossible. It also follows necessarily that it would traverse a great and small distance in equal time—that is, in a single instant. Were we to allot some small amount of time to the infinite [in which it would move], it is possible that some heaviness could be found such that the ratio between it and the [original] small heaviness would be the ratio between this [small amount of] time and the other time [viz. the longer time it takes the smaller heaviness to traverse the same distance]. But then this finite heaviness would move in a time equivalent to that of the infinite, and when we increase it, this finite heaviness would take less time to move than the infinite heaviness.[38] All this is the height of absurdity. These absurdities are compelled by our assumption that infinite heaviness exists. Once it is shown that infinite heaviness is impossible, the impossibility of the existence of an infinite body among simple bodies is confirmed as well.

With respect to things that are composite, the impossibility of the existence of an infinite body is demonstrable by disjunction, as follows. The existence of an infinite composite body would not be impossible if the body could be composed of things infinite either in measure, in number, or in form. But it is impossible that they be infinite in measure, for it was indeed demonstrated that simple bodies cannot be infinite in measure. Similarly, it is impossible for them to be infinite in number, for from the aspect of their contiguity they would together constitute an infinite measure, which was shown to be impossible as they are one in form. And it is impossible that

---

[37] This argument aims at discrediting the notion of an infinite body. It proceeds as follows. Let us assume that the infinite body has only finite heaviness. If so, then a finite part of the infinite body could be cut off and its heaviness multiplied until it equals or exceeds that of the infinite body. Yet how can the heaviness of a finite part equal or exceed that of the infinite whole of which it is a part? It cannot; and so it is necessary that an infinite body have infinite heaviness. Yet since infinite heaviness is impossible, an infinite body is also impossible. The argument's next step is to establish the impossibility of infinite heaviness.

[38] This argument contends in effect that once any amount of time is allotted to an infinite heaviness to traverse a given distance, a finite heaviness could be found that would do so in the very same amount of time. Moreover, this finite heaviness could in principle be made increasingly heavier so that it could conceivably move even faster—that is, it could require even less time to traverse the given distance—than the infinite heaviness.

they be infinite in form, for there would then have to be infinite places.[39] Moreover, we see that motions are finite.[40] Therefore it is proved that there cannot be an infinite body, whether simple or composite. And this addresses the issue from the aspect of motion.

The third proof proceeds as follows. If an infinite body did exist, it would be impossible for it to act or to be acted upon. But every sensible body either acts or is acted upon. The contradiction of the antecedent, namely, that an infinite body does not exist, thus follows. By being acted upon we mean being acted upon over time.

Indeed, every sensible body acts or is acted upon. This is proved by induction, since every sensible body either only acts, as do the celestial bodies, or both acts and is acted upon, as is the case with the elements and composite bodies. That it is impossible, however, for an infinite body either to act or to be acted upon will be proved by our positing three self-evident propositions. The first is that two equal receivers will be acted upon by a single agent in an equal amount of time, and a smaller acted-upon thing will be acted upon by the agent in a shorter amount of time. The second is that when two unequal agents act upon two acted-upon things, the ratio of one acted-upon thing to the other is as that of one agent to the other. The third is that an agent acts in a finite time. Once these propositions are established, it is evident that the infinite can neither act nor be acted upon, since something finite[41] cannot act upon something infinite, nor something infinite upon something finite, nor something infinite upon something infinite.

That a finite thing cannot act upon an infinite thing is evident. For if it could, let us suppose that there is one [finite thing] acting [upon an infinite thing] in a particular designated time, and another finite thing acting upon a finite thing in a different amount of time. The second time would of necessity be shorter than the first. Let us then increase the finite acted-upon thing so that it is acted upon during a time equal to the first designated time, which should be possible, as was established by the second proposition. The result would inevitably be that the infinite thing would be acted upon by the finite thing in a time equal to that in which the finite is acted upon by the finite, which is absurd. And if we increase it [viz. the acted-upon thing] even more, it will turn out, of necessity, that the infinite is acted upon by the finite in a shorter amount of time than that in which the finite is acted upon by the finite, which is most absurd.

It will also have to be the case that the infinite cannot act upon the finite. For if it could act upon it, let us suppose that an infinite thing acts upon a finite thing in a

---

[39] It was already established that there cannot be an infinity of places. Places are up and down, in front of and behind, right and left.

[40] It is unclear whether this sentence constitutes an independent argument for the impossibility that the components of an infinite composite body are infinite in form, or whether it is related to the previous sentence and so to the matter of places. As a stand-alone argument its sense would be the following. Since motions (of simple bodies) are finite, forms (of simple bodies) are finite—inasmuch as form determines a body's natural motion. Hence the components of a compound body are not infinite in form. As connected to the previous argument, its sense would be as follows. Form determines a body's natural motion; an infinity of motions requires an infinity of places; the number of places is in fact finite; therefore the number of motions is finite; and therefore the (simple) components of the infinite body are not infinite in form.

[41] Fisher, undoubtedly by mistake, has "since something infinite," שהבב״ת, instead of "since something finite," שהב״ת.

particular designated time, and that a finite thing acts upon a finite thing in a different amount of time, an amount greater than the first one. Let us then increase the finite agent until it acts in a time equal to that time, which is possible, as was established by the second proposition. The inevitable result would be that the finite will act upon the finite in a time equal to that in which the infinite acts upon the finite—the very reverse of what was assumed. And if we further increase the finite, the inevitable result will be that it will act in a shorter time than the infinite, which is most absurd.

It will also have to be the case that the infinite cannot act upon the infinite. For if it could act upon it, supposing that the infinite acts upon the infinite in a particular designated time, and supposing that a part of [the infinite] which is acted upon is acted upon by the infinite in a certain time, the latter will of necessity be shorter. Let us then increase the part that is acted upon until the amount of time in which it is acted upon is equivalent to the designated time, which is possible by reason of the second proposition. The inevitable result will be that the infinite and the finite will be acted upon by a single agent in the same amount of time, which is the reverse of what was assumed. And if we further increase the thing that is acted upon, the inevitable result will be that the infinite will be acted upon in a shorter time than that in which the finite is acted upon, and this is most absurd.

Once it has been proved that an infinite can neither act nor be acted upon, it must be concluded that no infinite exists. This was indeed proved from the point of view of the impossibility of motion—because change is a kind of motion. And indeed change is associated with rectilinear motion, since both of these go from one opposite to another. We have therefore presented this proof among those posited from the perspective of the impossibility of rectilinear motion.

From the perspective of circular motion, he formulated six proofs to prove that it, too, is impossible for an infinite body.

The first argument proceeds as follows. If an infinite spherical body moving circularly existed, it would follow that when one of its radii, which is moving circularly, reaches another of its radii, which is at rest, the former will coincide with the latter. But this is impossible. Hence, an infinite circular body cannot move circularly. Indeed the connection between the consequent and the antecedent is self-evident, since the lines that extend from the center to the circumference throughout the sphere are equal. But the contradiction of the consequent is indeed necessary, since it is obvious that the distance between any two lines extending from the center to the circumference increases with the increase in the length of the lines. Because the lines are infinite, the distance between them is infinite as well. Since it is evident that it is impossible for a moving thing to traverse an infinite distance, it is evident that it is impossible for it to coincide with the radius that is at rest. Yet we have assumed that it does coincide [with it]. It is evident that this absurdity is attributable to our assumption that the infinite moves [circularly].

One of the later thinkers[42] strengthened this proof by saying the following. How could it [viz. the revolving radius] coincide with the radius [at rest]? If we were to

---

[42] According to Wolfson (1929: 381 n. 133), the reference is to al-Tabrizi.

imagine two lines extending from the center forming an angle whose chord forms an equilateral triangle, then, if the lines are infinite, the distance between them will be infinite. And if so, the one moving line will not be able to coincide with the other line, since it would have to traverse an infinite distance. In addition it is impossible per se for an infinite to be bounded by two lines on its two ends, for the assertion that it is both infinite and bounded is a self-contradiction. This is necessary in the case of every pair of lines that extend from the center when the lines are infinite. For there is no doubt that as the lines increase, so, too, does the distance between them at the place where they form the chord; and since the lines are infinite, the distance between them is necessarily infinite. This is an evident absurdity.

The second argument proceeds as follows. If an infinite circular body moving circularly existed, it would have to move an infinite distance in a finite time, which is impossible; hence, an infinite circular moving body does not exist. The contradiction of the consequent is self-evident. Its connection to the antecedent will be established once we propose an infinite line extending from its center and posit in addition a chord in it. It is evident that it [viz. the chord] will be infinite, since the body is infinite. Let us suppose that it is at rest. When the line extending from the center moves circularly, there will be a time at which it will meet the chord and will intersect with it and a time at which it will not meet it. But since the circular body which is moving circularly moves in a finite time, the line extending from the center will necessarily traverse an infinite distance—namely, the chord that is at rest—in a finite time. But this is a manifest absurdity, since motion that takes place in a finite time must take place within a distance that is finite.

The third argument proceeds as follows. If an infinite body moving circularly existed, it would have to be possible to posit two parallel lines, one moving toward the other as it moves in a circle, and the other [at rest],[43] with which it will intersect and which it will meet, without first meeting the line's extremity. But this [consequent] is impossible; so the antecedent is likewise impossible. The reason the consequent is necessarily impossible is that it is self-evident that when two lines are assumed to be as described, the moving line will have to meet the first point at the other line's extremity before it meets its middle. The connection [of the consequent] to the antecedent is also evident, since an infinite line has no end and no beginning and no point without another point before it.[44]

The fourth argument proceeds as follows. If an infinite body were to move in a circular motion, it would have an infinite spherical form. But that is impossible. It follows that an infinite body does not move circularly. Indeed, the connection of the consequent to the antecedent is self-evident. This is seen from the definition of shape:

---

[43] Neither the manuscripts nor the editions contain the term, נח (*nah*), "at rest," though it is surely understood. I have translated the sentence so that it can be read with or without it.

[44] The argument seems to run as follows: one would expect a rotating line to intersect with a stationary line parallel to it in the middle of that line, and not to have to intersect with its end first. If the rotating line is infinite, however, it could not reach the middle of the other line without first intersecting with the endpoint of that line. Yet since the stationary line is also infinite, the moving line cannot first intersect with it at its end, for it has no end: before any given point there is always another point. Thus, the following paradoxical conclusion would result: the two lines would both intersect in the middle (*ex hypothesi*) and also not do so.

the geometer defines shape as that which a boundary or boundaries encompass. And it is evident that whatever a boundary encompasses is finite. And generally, finitude is attributable in all things to form, and the absence of finitude is attributable to matter. And since shape is form, it is impossible for it to be infinite.

The fifth argument proceeds as follows. If there were an infinite body moving circularly, it would seem to be possible that a line that we would extend from the center could move circularly to traverse a line infinite at both ends—for example, if it were an infinite line perpendicular to the diameter. But this is impossible, for the perpendicular is infinite, and it is impossible to traverse an infinite line in a finite time. Hence, it is impossible for an infinite body to move circularly.

The sixth argument proceeds as follows. Let us assume that a body moving circularly—for example, the celestial body—is infinite. It would then have to traverse an infinite distance in a finite amount of time, which is absurd. Hence, there is no infinite circularly moving body. Indeed the proposition that contradicts the consequent is self-evident. Its necessity with respect to the antecedent is established by perception, for we see that regardless of which point we mark [on the revolving body], that point will return to its place in a finite time.

It is evident from all these arguments that there cannot be circular motion in an infinite body. And it has already been shown that rectilinear motion in it [i.e. in an infinite body] is also precluded. But both rectilinear and circular motion are perceived by the senses. It follows, therefore, that an infinite body cannot exist. This was what he intended in this third class.

CLASS IV: A GENERAL PROOF OF THE IMPOSSIBILITY OF THE EXISTENCE
OF AN ACTUAL INFINITE BODY, RELYING ON THE PREVIOUS ARGUMENTS.
HE FORMULATED TWO ARGUMENTS IN THIS REGARD.

The first proceeds as follows. If an infinite body existed, it would move either circularly or rectilinearly. If circularly, it would have to have a center, because what is circular is that which circles around a center. But if it has a center, it also has extremities. But an infinite thing has no extremities. Hence it cannot move circularly. The remaining possibility is that it moves rectilinearly, but if so, it requires necessarily two places, each of them infinite. One would be for natural motion and it would be a that-to-which, and the second would be for forcible motion and it would be a that-from-which. But if the places are two, they will necessarily be finite, since what is infinite cannot be two in number. Yet they were assumed to be infinite. Thus it [viz. an infinite body] cannot move rectilinearly. Moreover, the place cannot be infinite since it is bounded, for it was shown with respect to it that it is an encompassing limit.

The second proof proceeds as follows. If there were an infinite body, it would be moved either by itself or by something else. If by itself, it would be a live sensing thing, and every sensing thing has sensible things outside and surrounding it. But anything of this description is finite. If it is moved by something else outside it, it [viz. the mover] would necessarily be infinite, so that both of them would be infinite. But this is absurd, since the sum of the two would be greater than either one alone, and that which has no limit will be greater than that which has no limit. Moreover, it would follow from this that movers and moved things would be infinite in number, each one infinite in magnitude.

He further fortified this [set of proofs] by reliance on those arguments he mentioned earlier.

These are the proofs that have come to us concerning this issue in the books of Aristotle and of other authors and of commentators on his books. But they came to us confused and likely to bewilder the reader, for this is a topic susceptible to error. We therefore formulated them in their [proper] form and with utmost conciseness. And we reinforced them with some things that they did not mention. The intention behind our doing so is that all will be ready and poised to tell truth from error and avoid the pitfalls of fallacy, favoring nothing but truth. This was our intention in this chapter.

Chapter II

PROOF of the second proposition, which states that the existence of an infinite number of magnitudes is absurd—that is, if they exist together.

Having established in the first proposition that the existence of magnitudes infinite in measure is impossible, he establishes in this second proposition that it is impossible for there to exist magnitudes infinite in number.

Confirmation of this proposition will be attained by the proofs for the first proposition, namely, that every magnitude has some measure, and if we add to it another magnitude, the sum of their measure is greater still. If magnitudes infinite in number are added together, their measure will be infinite, the impossibility of which was established previously.

Chapter III

PROOF of the third proposition, which states that the existence of an infinite number of causes and effects is absurd—even if they are not magnitudes.

If, for example, it is assumed that a particular intellect is caused by a second intellect, and the cause of the second is a third, and so on to infinity, this, too, is proved to be absurd.

Now that the impossibility of the existence of infinity with respect to things that are ordered in position, as magnitudes are,[45] was established in the second proposition, he proves the impossibility of its existence with respect to things that have a natural order, such as causes and effects. Since the cause is that by virtue of whose existence the effect exists, if the nonexistence of the cause were conceived, the existence of the effect could not be conceived. Therefore, an infinite chain of cause and effect is impossible.

This is because, on its own, an effect has possible existence and thus requires a determiner that will determine its existence over its nonexistence, and this determiner is its cause. Therefore, in an infinite chain of causes and effects it is inevitable that in their totality they be either all effects or not. If they are all effects, they indeed all have possible existence; and because they would then need a determiner to determine[46] their existence over their nonexistence, they must necessarily have a cause that is not caused. And if they are not all effects, then one of them is a cause that

---

[45] "Ordered in position" means related to one another spatially.
[46] Reading מכריע/יכריע rather than (as in Fisher and several manuscripts) מכריח/יכריח.

is not caused, which would be the end of the chain. But the chain has been assumed not to have an end; which now is an outright absurdity. This absurdity is the inevitable result of our having posited an infinite number of causes and effects.

We ought to be aware that he has not established the impossibility of infinity except with respect to things that are ordered in position, as magnitudes are, or that have a natural order, as causes and effects do. But with respect to things that have no order in position or in nature, such as intellects or souls, infinite existence was not precluded. This, at any rate, is the view of Avicenna and al-Ghazali. According to Averroes, however, the impossibility obtains even with respect to things that have no order. For he asserted that actual number is necessarily finite, because every actual number is actually counted; and anything that is actually counted is either even or odd; and whatever is even or odd is necessarily finite.

The way the matter appears to us is that this division of number is true and inescapable. But infinite number, insofar as it is not bounded, cannot be described in terms of evenness and oddness, and therefore infinity is not eliminated for it. Therefore, the Rabbi took great care in his discussion of the impossibility of infinite number, to limit himself to things that are ordered either in position, as magnitudes are, or naturally, as are causes and effects, where one is the cause of the second, the second of the third, and so on to infinity.

Chapter IV

PROOF of the fourth proposition, which states that change exists in four categories— in the category of substance, where it is coming-to-be and passing-away; in the category of quantity, where it is growth and diminution; in the category of quality, where it is alteration; and it exists, too, in the category of location, where it is locomotion. It is change in location that is called motion proper.

Since some change is over time and some not over time, when the term "change" is taken in a nonspecific and unqualified sense, this proposition is confirmed. Indeed it is virtually self-evident, inasmuch as change in quantity and in quality and in location takes place over time, but change in substance does not take place over time, as was established in *On Generation and Corruption*.[47]

What we need to be aware of, however, is why he specified these four categories, when it is evident that change exists also in other categories, such as position, and acting and being acted upon. But this is because each change has two aspects. One is from the perspective of the subject, and it is the transition of the changing thing from one condition to another. In this aspect change exists in the other categories and is not over time. The other is from the perspective of the matter undergoing the change, such as quantity, quality, and location. In this aspect change is in the category in which there is a change in the matter; and it is this aspect to which he turns his

---

[47] This paragraph is absent in Fisher. It is reproduced in Wolfson (1929), 228. הנה למה שהשינוי ממנו בזמן וממנו בזולת זמן, כשילקח השינוי סתמי בשלוח, תתאמת זאת ההקדמה. והיא כמבוארת בעצמה, כי השינוי אשר בכמה ובאיך ובאנה הוא בזמן, והשינוי אשר בעצם הוא זולת זמן, כמו שהתבאר בספר ההויה וההפסד. The idea here is that change in substance, that is, coming-to-be and passing-away, is instantaneous. See Aristotle, *On Generation and Corruption* I. iv. 319^{b}31ff.

attention when considering this issue. And since change that is in [the category of] substance depends on the motion of these [three] categories, the Rabbi specified these four categories. In this he followed in Aristotle's footsteps in the *Metaphysics*. And this appears to be the right thing to say on this issue.[48]

What remains for us to explain is why he specified in particular change in location, which is locomotion, as motion proper, when, after all, motion in quantity is also a change in location, since it involves some locomotion. Al-Tabrizi was indeed aware of this problem, and he said that since locomotion is something that is sensed, he reserved the term "motion" for it, and he did not apply it to growth, for locomotion in growth is not sensed. According to what is perceived in growth there is no locomotion, since it is known that growth in a plant is in all directions, so that there remains no determinate part of it through which locomotion from one location to another can be confirmed. Therefore the Rabbi reserved "motion" for locomotion.

Chapter V

PROOF of the fifth proposition, which states that every motion is a change and a passing from potentiality to actuality.

His assertion that every motion is a change is established by what was said earlier. But the converse is not true, for it is not the case that every change is a motion: some change is not over time, such as coming-to-be and passing-away and the transition of a subject from one condition to another, which, from this perspective [viz. being not over time], enters the category of acting and being acted upon. But some change concerns the matter involved in the change, and in this case alone is the term "motion" warranted. Know this, for the bulk of philosophizers were not mindful of this difference.[49]

---

[48] See Aristotle, *Metaph.* VIII. i. 1042^{b}3–5. Crescas's point seems to be that when the matter itself changes, only these four categories are relevant. Only changes in these categories are, so to speak, internal. When, however, something changes position, for example (position being one of the other six), the matter undergoes no internal change. Similarly in the case of acting or being acted upon, relation, possession, and time (the remaining five of the six). In all these cases, although the subject, that is, the individual thing, changes, its changes may be said to be in relation to other things, or, to put it another way, external.

[49] As Crescas explained in Proposition IV, not all change is the same, and there are four kinds of change that Aristotle, and Maimonides following him, single out, insofar as only they involve change in the matter of the thing that is changing. Despite appearances, it is unlikely that Crescas in Proposition V is asserting that it is change over time that is properly called motion, with change not over time not being properly so called. What he is in fact contrasting is the common view that only change over time can be motion—a view that he rejects—with the less widely endorsed view that only change in matter is properly called motion. The proposition that motion is change is still not convertible, because there is change that is not motion, namely, change that is not in matter—and what is relevant to the determination of whether change qualifies as motion is not whether or not it is over time but whether or not it is in matter. Change not over time includes coming-to-be and passing-away, and thus, surprisingly, motion does strictly apply even to some change that is not over time. Where the majority of philosophizers have gone wrong, Crescas thinks, is in identifying taking place over time as that distinctive character of change that qualifies it as motion. Preferring the variant אבל השינוי אשר בבחינת חמר השינוי בו יצדק שם התנועה לבד, Smilevitch (2010: 300) interprets Crescas as excluding coming-to-be and passing-away from motion. Smilevitch's text has no ממנו...ממנו contrast at all. Wolfson (1929: 522–3 n. 4), recognizing that the distinction between over time and not over time is certainly prominent enough among earlier thinkers, defers to the Ferrara edition: אבל השינוי ממנו אשר ממנו השינוי אשר הוא בבחינת חמר השינוי אשר בו יצדק שם התנועה (cf. Fisher, בבחינת חמר התנועה אשר בו יצדק שם התנועה לבד), and suggests that Crescas is arguing that the proposition is convertible after all, if one limits oneself to the forms of change cited in Proposition IV. Wolfson's view is problematic, however, in that it regards all four

Concerning his assertion that motion is a passing from potentiality to actuality, he is conforming to how motion has been defined, which is as the actualization of what is in potentiality from the perspective of its being in potentiality. There is warrant for regarding motion as actualization, since motion occurs between a that-from-which and a that-to-which. And when it is at the that-from-which it is complete potentiality [and is at rest]; when it is at the that-to-which it is complete actualization and is at rest; and when it is somewhere in between the at-rests, it is only partially actualized— with this mitigation attributable to its aspect of being still in potentiality[50]—and therefore falls short of complete actualization. It is thus confirmed that motion is a passing from potentiality to actuality.

It would appear, however, that this definition is not true of motion. For one of the marks of a definition is that its definiens is reciprocally related to the definiendum, as was established in the *Posterior Analytics*. Yet since this definiens is warranted also in the case of causing motion, it would then follow necessarily that causing motion would also qualify as motion and that for causing motion a mover would therefore be required, and this causing motion will also be motion, and so on to infinity.[51]

Therefore, the true definition, as it seems to us, is the other definition he mentioned, namely, the actualization of the moved thing insofar as it is a *moved* thing. His expression, "the actualization of the moved thing," indicates that its motion is not fully potential but[52] has some degree of actuality and actualization; and his expression, "insofar as it is moved," indicates that it falls short of complete actuality and actualization.[53]

Regardless of the definition, the *proposition* remains true, namely, that every motion is a change and is a passing from potentiality to actuality.

Chapter VI

PROOF of the sixth proposition, which states of motions that some are essential, some accidental, some forcible, and some as a part. Essential motion is as in the case of a body that locomotes from place to place. Accidental is as in the case of blackness in a body that locomotes from place to place. Forcible is as in the case in which the motion of a stone is upward because a force is forcing it in that direction. As a part is

---

forms of change in Proposition IV as "temporal," whereas change in the category of substance, that is, coming-to-be and passing-away, is explicitly said in Proposition IV to be not over time.

[50] Fisher records a variant: "when it is somewhat between, its actualization is only partial from the perspective of its being still in potentiality."

[51] See Aristotle, *Posterior Analytics* II. iv. 91ª16. Crescas's concern seems to be that, if definitions are convertible, then not only will all motion be a transition from potentiality to actuality, but anything that involves a transition from potentiality to actuality will be motion. Since that which causes motion also transitions from potentiality to actuality, it would, on this definition, qualify as in motion. And since all motion requires a mover, every cause of motion—now itself in "motion"—will require a mover. And this will go on to infinity.

[52] These words, found in the manuscripts and reproduced in Wolfson (1929), are not found in Fisher: שאינו בכח גמור, אבל.

[53] Crescas's solution (see n. 51 for Crescas's concern) is to define motion as the actualization of that which is moved insofar as it is moved, thereby preventing motion from applying to the mover as the cause of motion (even though it, too, passes from potentiality to actuality).

as in the case of the motion of a nail in a boat, for when the boat moves we say that the nail also moves. This is the case with any composite thing: when it moves as a whole, it may be said of its part that it moves as well.

What is intended by this proposition is that motion is of various kinds. It might be essential—whether natural or forcible; voluntary motion is included here as well—as the translation of a body from place to place; or accidental, when we attribute motion to something that does not move on its own other than accidentally, as, for example, when the blackness in a body moves with the body's motion; or forcible—whether essentially or accidentally—as in the case of a stone's upward motion; or by being a part, forcibly or naturally.

The distinction between [motion that is] accidental and [motion] as a part is that it is "accidental" when we attribute the accidental motion to something that in its ordinary course does not move; and it is "as a part" when we attribute the motion as a part to something that in its ordinary course does move.

What we must attend to, however, is his assertion in offering an example of essential motion: "as when a body locomotes from place to place." For since with respect to the motion of the sphere it is not the case that the body of the sphere translates from one place to another—since it as a whole does not change its place but its parts alone translate—it would follow that the whole does not have essential motion and only the parts do. But this is contrary to how it appears to us. For it is the sphere that has motion—whether voluntary and out of desire, as Aristotle held, or natural, as it appears to us. For since we generally regard motion in bodies as natural, and since the simple elemental bodies beneath the sphere—which have heaviness and lightness—move rectilinearly, it follows that the motion that is natural to the body of the sphere as a whole, which is not characterized in terms of heaviness and lightness, is circular. Therefore, the circular motion of the sphere is essential, despite its not translating as a whole from place to place—contrary to what the words of the Rabbi suggest.

Similarly, concerning his assertion in offering as an example of accidental motion: "as blackness in a body"—[this implies that accidental motion is] in something that has a certain magnitude, and which is transferable from one magnitude to another.[54] In fact, however, it may be said that accidental motion can occur even at the point at a body's extremity, and thus even when it is not in a magnitude but only at the extremity.

And concerning his assertion in offering as an example of forcible motion: "as the upward motion of a stone"—in this matter he was following the famous view of the Greek that the elements have opposing natural motions, as the downward motion of a stone and the upward motion of fire. And it was thought, therefore, that there are four elements: one of them, earth, which has absolute heaviness; fire, absolute lightness; and air and water, relative heaviness and lightness. This view apparently was not proved and will not be proved—for the following reason. One might say [instead] that each of the elements has a certain heaviness, but they differ in that

---

[54] Maimonides' use of the example of blackness in a body is not explicitly associated with magnitudes. See *Guide*, Intro. to Part II (236 in Pines 1963).

some possess less and others more. Fire indeed has an upward motion, thanks to the heaviness of the air that propels it upward, as happens when a stone that is inside a furnace in which there is molten gold or lead or mercury moves upward as a result of being propelled by the heaviness of the metals. Something comparable occurs in the case of air and water. This is also seen in our digging in the ground: air enters the area that has been dug out and that is then filled with it. Even though it is possible for someone to object that this occurs because there can be no emptiness within the sphere, nevertheless it is not impossible that this occurs because of the heaviness of the element. Regardless of how the upward motion of the stone occurs, it is in any event attributable to a force, as in this example. This observation should suffice for this chapter.[55]

Chapter VII

PROOF of the seventh proposition, which states that everything that is subject to change is subject to division, and, therefore, everything that moves can be divided and is of necessity a body. Moreover, anything that cannot be divided cannot move and cannot be a body at all.

This proposition contains five propositions. The first, that everything that is subject to change can be divided. The second, that everything that moves [i.e. is subject to motion][56] can be divided. The third, that everything that moves is of necessity a body. The fourth, that anything that cannot be divided cannot move. And the fifth, that anything that cannot be divided cannot be a body.

The fourth and the fifth are indeed self-evident. Concerning the fourth, it is proved insofar as it is the contrapositive of the second. For since it was proved that everything that moves can be divided, which is the second proposition, it follows by contraposition, that that which cannot be divided does not move, which is the fourth. Concerning the fifth, it is proved by the definition of a body and its being a continuous quantity. The first ones,[57] nevertheless, require proof.

[Aristotle's] commentators have struggled over the first. For Aristotle set forth the following proof for it in Book VI of the *Physics*.[58] Since that which is subject to change must of necessity be partly in the that-from-which and partly in the that-to-which—for when it is in the that-from-which it is at rest and not yet changing, and when it is in the that-to-which it is at rest having already changed—and since it is impossible for it to be wholly in the that-from-which and wholly in the that-to-which at the same time, it follows that it is partly in the that-from-which and partly in that-to-which; and anything in this condition is necessarily subject to division.

Because this proof applies only to things that change over time but not to things that change not over time, such as the endpoints of changes and motions, it will be

---

[55] Crescas's view is that the elements do not have proper places. Instead, all the elements have heaviness, and so, all the elements naturally tend downwards. It is only upward motion that requires an account.
[56] "Moves" here translates מתנועע (*mitno'ei'a*). The context makes clear when "moves" means "causes motion"—that is, when it translates מניע (*meini'a*).
[57] Crescas discusses the first three.   [58] *Physics* VI. iv. 234^{b}10ff.

only partial. Alexander therefore believed that everything that is subject to change changes over time, and anything that is subject to change not over time only appears so to the senses but is actually over time, though the time is not perceptible because of its shortness. This view is, however, false and clearly absurd.

Themistius, by contrast, accepted the existence of things that change not over time. Since, however, something that changes not over time is consequent upon that which changes over time, he regards the proof as generally applicable.

Avempace,[59] although he also accepted the existence of things that change not over time—specifically, things that change from nonexistence to existence, such as when form enters into matter—he nevertheless restricts "that which is subject to change" to qualitative change, as, for example, hot being cooled and cold being heated, a change which is necessarily over time.

Averroes made an even finer point. Since the endpoints of changes are not really changes, for by then they are at rest, then, insofar as Aristotle's proof extends only to that which truly changes, "that which is subject to change" will include all the kinds of change.

It is not clear to me what Avempace gained by restricting "that which is subject to change" to qualitative change, for it is evident that changes in quality have change-endpoints that are not over time. For in the case of black that becomes white, at its motion's endpoint it is white not over time.[60]

In any event, it appears that the Rabbi took it as Averroes did. Therefore, he inferred from his assertion that everything that changes can be divided that everything that moves can be divided, since that which is subject to change now includes all the kinds of change that he established in the fourth proposition. Hence the first two propositions are confirmed.

The third, his assertion that everything that moves is a body, is quite evident. For if we take motion proper as locomotion, as the Rabbi did, then, since change of location specifies a place, and since place is specific to body, it is clear that a moving thing must be a body. And if we take motion to include all kinds of change, such that they all require a corporeal subject, it is clear in these cases that that which changes must be a body.

These three first propositions have now been confirmed. But a caveat must be attached to his assertion "everything that moves," so that it refers only to things that move essentially. This is because we will find that some things that move accidentally cannot be divided. For the point that is the extremity of a line moves when the line of which it is the extremity moves, and the line moves when the surface or the body moves, yet the point cannot be divided and is not a body. What is intended is something that moves essentially.

And so the seventh proposition, which contains these five propositions, has been proved.

---

[59] Avempace is ibn Bajja. Crescas calls him Abu-Bakr Tsayigh.
[60] At the endpoint of the change from black to white, the change has no temporal duration.

Chapter VIII

PROOF of the eighth proposition, which states that anything that moves accidentally necessarily comes to rest, for its motion is not of its essence. Therefore, accidental motion cannot be perpetual.

The foundation of this proposition, it seems, is that which Aristotle posited in Book VIII of the *Physics*,[61] namely, that anything accidental has within itself the possibility of existing and of not existing. And it is inconceivable for something possible not to come to actuality given infinite time. Therefore, it indeed follows that anything that moves accidentally necessarily comes to rest.

Chapter IX

PROOF of the ninth proposition, which states that any body that moves another body will move it only if it itself moves as it moves the other.

This proposition is self-evident. But a qualification must be applied to it, namely, that the mover be an efficient [cause]. But if the mover functions the way a final [cause] does—for example, the way fire moves air to rise so that it rises to fire's surface because of the suitability of that place to air—it can indeed move another without itself moving.[62] Therefore, by his assertion, "body moves body," he intends the moving of the other by pushing or pulling.[63] An objection has been raised to this on the grounds of the way a certain thing appears to the senses, namely, that the Magnesian stone moves iron by pulling it toward itself without moving. Two sorts of response have been offered to this: the first is that one might say that the iron is moved by itself by virtue indeed of a disposition it acquires from the stone; and the second, that even if we grant that the magnet pulls it, it is still possible that when some bodies become detached from the magnet, they come into contact with that which is pulled [viz. the iron], and pull it, either by way of pulling or by way of pushing.[64]

Chapter X

PROOF of the tenth proposition, which states that all things of which it may be said that they are in a body are divided into two classes: those that exist through the body, such as accidents, and those through which the body exists, such as natural form. Both are a force in a body.

Among the ancients there were indeed those who held that a body has no composition in any way, but it is one in its essence and in its definition; and so, if we nevertheless detect composition in bodies, it is with respect to their nonessential

---

[61] *Physics* VIII. v. 256^{b}9–10.
[62] When a mover is an efficient cause, it cannot move something else—cause motion—without itself moving: a cue stick, for example, cannot cause a billiard ball to move without itself moving. But motion can be caused not only by efficient causes. It can be caused also by final causes. Ends cause motion by attraction, without themselves moving. The end of providing shelter, for example, may spur an architect to build a house, that is, it may cause the motion of the architect, without itself moving.
[63] Presumably, as efficient cause.
[64] It was held by some that bodies emit "effluences," small particles of matter.

accidents or properties.⁶⁵ Aristotle and the commentators on his books, however, dealt this view a decisive blow by saying that every body inevitably contains two essential things, matter and form. That is, we observe that all the bodies that are here are subject to coming-to-be and passing-away; and since the thing that passes away cannot receive that which is coming to be, it is necessary to posit a substratum to receive both, and this is the matter that is called *hylē*. It is evident that matter is essential to that which comes to be, because it is its substratum. Because the receiver must be distinct from the received, it follows that there must be two things in it [i.e. in the body]. And since it is said of that which is received that through it a thing comes to be, is bounded, and has its essence, it is evident that that which is received is also essential to that which comes to be. Because the substratum cannot be actual by itself—for if it were actual there would be in it not coming-to-be but alteration—it is evident that the being and existence of a thing are in that which is received, that is, in the thing's natural form.⁶⁶

With regard to accidents, which no body can escape, it is evident that they exist in the body, which comprises matter and corporeal form. For if they had being and existence in themselves, they would be substances.

Since each of these two, namely, form and accident, lacks independent existence, and both require a substratum, as was established, he seized on the term "force," and said that both are a "force in a body."

It is important to take note of his assertion that the existence of the body is through its natural form, and that he regards the body, which comprises matter and corporeal form, in its relation to its particular [or particularizing]⁶⁷ natural form, as analogous to the relation between matter and form generally, form being that through which matter has its being and existence.

Chapter XI

PROOF of the eleventh proposition, which states that some of the things that exist in a body can be divided with the body's division, and are thus divided accidentally, such as colors and other forces that are distributed throughout the body; but some of the

---

⁶⁵ I translate here in accordance with Wolfson's text, במקרים ומשיגים בלתי עצמיים, as does Smilevitch. Fisher's text, however, contains the term עצמיים modifying מקרים, as does the printed Ferrara edition. One can appreciate the oddity of speaking of "essential accidents" (see n. 14). But see I. 1. 22, where Crescas enumerates three accidents—quantity, shape, and position—which are unique among accidents in that they cannot be separated from their subjects and that bodies have them by necessity, וישיגוהו מקרים בהכרח. It is possible then that by מקרים עצמיים, "essential accidents," Crescas refers to the inseparable accidents, and by משיגים בלתי עצמיים, "nonessential properties/accidents," to the separable.

⁶⁶ According to Crescas, the Aristotelian reasoning behind the tenth proposition is as follows. All the bodies in our world come to be and pass away. If they pass away, however, what is left to receive that which comes to be? Since something that has passed away cannot receive that which comes to be, there needs to be a substratum—matter—which can be that in which both coming-to-be and passing-away take place. This substratum is essential to that which comes to be but is distinct from it. The substratum on its own is not actualized in any way; otherwise, coming-to-be would not differ from alteration, that is, the change from one actualized state (or element) to another. When a thing comes to be, the substratum receives a form. It is the form that determines the thing's nature and so it too is essential. (It also therefore has the status of "substance" in some sense.) Hence the nature of all existents is composite.

⁶⁷ Depending on whether we read, with Wolfson (1929), מיוחדת, or with Fisher and Smilevitch, מיחדת.

things through which the body exists cannot in any way be divided, such as soul and intellect.

The division of things that exist in a body and of those through which the body exists is self-evident—since some of the accidents that exist in a body are divided accidentally with the body's division, such as color and measure, and some are not divided, such as a point or a line with respect to width, and a surface with respect to depth. Similarly, some of the things through which a body exists are divided with the bodies' division, such as the *hylē* which is the thing that receives the division[68]—since corporeal *form*, which is the continuousness of dimensions, is not subject to division, inasmuch as it is not the way of an opposite to admit its opposite.[69]

What needs to be explained is his assertion, "such as soul and intellect." For although he regards them as a force in a body, nevertheless, since they are not distributed throughout the entire body, they cannot be divided with the division of the body. It will later be made evident by us, God willing,[70] that Aristotle held an opposing view, namely, that since the acquired intellect[71] is attached to the body by a connection of existence and not by a connection of mixture, it will not move accidentally with the body's motion. And so it seems too that a separate intellect moves the sphere but the intellect does not move accidentally. Since the sphere's mover is its soul,[72] he said of the sphere that it moves by virtue of its soul. The Rabbi, however, held that the intellect of the sphere is a force in a body and so does move accidentally with the motion of the sphere. He therefore devised a proof specifically to establish that this intellect is not its mover, for anything that moves accidentally necessarily comes to rest, as he explained in the eighth proposition. He also devised an argument specifically to show that a force that is distributed is not a mover, for then it would be finite[73] and its action would be finite, since it would be divided with its [viz. the sphere's] division. He therefore said that its mover is a separate intellect as is seen in what he wrote in Chapter 1 of Part II of his book, the *Guide*.[74]

Chapter XII

PROOF of the twelfth proposition, which states that every force distributed in a body is finite since body is finite.

---

[68] Reading, with Wolfson and the manuscripts, אשר הוא הדבר, "which is *the* thing..." rather than אשר הוא דבר, "which is something..."

[69] The opposites in question are continuousness and division.

[70] Wolfson and Smilevitch put a period here. Smilevitch (323 n. 1) refers the reader to II. vi. 1.

[71] The acquired intellect is the highest human faculty; it grasps the intelligible forms that exist separate from matter and is thought to be itself separate or separable from matter. It is this intellect that is immortal.

[72] Following the manuscripts which have ולהיותו מניעו הוא נפשו, "and since its mover is its soul." The editions and Fisher have ולהיותו הוא מניעו ונפשו, "and since this is its mover and its soul."

[73] Wolfson includes in brackets the beginning of this sentence up to this point. Fisher and Smilevitch insert it without brackets. It is not found, however, in the Ferrara or Vilna editions or in the Florence or Vienna manuscripts.

[74] The disagreement between Aristotle and Maimonides concerns the relationship between the sphere and the separate intellect that moves it. For Aristotle, even though this intellect is "separate," it is related to the sphere as its soul. For Maimonides, however, the separate intellect is not analogous to a soul, because the soul is for him a force in a body and thus subject to all the limitations of such a force.

Aristotle indeed proved this proposition in Book VIII of the *Physics*. He formulated the proof as follows. Every body is either finite or infinite. But the existence of an infinite body is impossible, as was proved earlier. The only remaining possibility, therefore, is that the body is finite.[75] Indeed, the impossibility of the existence of an infinite force in it will be seen once we posit a single self-evident proposition, namely, that forces that are distributed in bodies are divided with the bodies, and that the larger the body, the greater its motive force—as is seen, for instance, in that a larger chunk of the earth has greater motive force than one that is smaller than it. Once this was established, he formulated the following syllogism. If there were an infinite force in a finite body, one of two things would necessarily result: either it would move a certain movable thing in an instant,[76] or the infinite force would be equal to a finite force causing motion. Both, however, are eminently absurd.

The necessity of this will be shown in light of what I now say. Let us assume that the body in which an infinite force resides moves a movable thing in a certain amount of time. There surely could be a finite mover that could similarly move that movable thing, since we may assign to it [viz. the movable thing] a size that a finite mover could move. There can be no doubt that it [viz. the finite mover] would require a longer time to do the moving than would the infinite mover. It is inescapable that the infinite mover will do its moving of it either in an instant or over time. But if it does its moving of it over time, this time will of necessity be a certain fraction of the longer time.[77] It is well known that we could take a part of the body containing the infinite [force] such that the ratio between it and the original [body containing the] finite force[78] would be the ratio of the shorter time to the longer time. It would then turn out that a part of the infinite, which is necessarily finite, is equal in motive force to the infinite force.[79]

---

[75] Fisher's is the only available text to have הגשם, "the body," rather than הכח בגשם, "the force in the body." Yet it is Fisher's text that presents the clearly intended disjunctive syllogism: a∨b; ~b; ∴ a.

[76] Aristotle's reasoning, as Crescas presents it, is that if the greater the motive force in a body, the faster the motion, then an infinite motive force ought to move a body in an instant.

[77] Some sources have "the shorter," היותר קטן (Vilna, Fisher), rather than "the longer," היותר גדול (Ferrara edition, Wolfson (1929), Smilevitch (2010), and the Vienna and Florence manuscripts). The point of the text, either way, is clear and the same. If we take "the shorter" to be correct, then the text—יהיה ואם יניעהו בזמן, בהכרח חלק ידוע מהזמן היותר קטן—may be rendered thus: "But if it does its moving over time, it will have to be a certain portion *of time* that is shorter."

[78] Some sources have יחסו אל הבעל תכלית הראשון (Vilna, Fisher); Wolfson and the Vienna manuscript have יחסו אל הבעל תכלית האחד; and the Florence manuscript and the Ferrara edition have אל הבעל תכלית האחד. Smilevitch (327 n. 5) needlessly "corrects" Wolfson, whose text (268 l. 15) does not in fact read יחסו אל הבלתי בעל תכלית.

[79] This *reductio ad absurdum* argument works as follows. If we assume that a finite body can house an infinite force, one of two results will follow. The one result is that an infinite body will move another body in an instant—and this is absurd (see n. 76). The other is that an infinite body will move another body over time. If we assume the latter, and we suppose that there is a body that can be moved by both an infinite and a finite force, we can also assume that the finite force will take longer than the infinite force to move that body. In other words, the infinite force does its moving of the body in a fraction of the time that it takes the finite force to do its moving. We can then slice off from the [putatively finite] body that houses the infinite force a finite size that will stand to the size of the body that houses the finite force as the shorter time it takes the infinite force to move the body does to the longer time it takes the finite force. But since a part of the infinite is necessarily finite, this finite slice will contain a force whose power to move the body is equal to that of the infinite. And this is absurd.

The necessity of the connection between the consequent and the antecedent is thus established. For if there were an infinite force in a finite body, one of two things would necessarily result: either the infinite mover would move a certain movable thing in an instant or the infinite force and the finite force would be equal in causing motion.

Chapter XIII

PROOF of the thirteenth proposition, which states that it is impossible for any sort of species change to be continuous. Only locomotion can be continuous—and, within locomotion, only the circular.

The intent of this proposition is to establish that there cannot be continuous motion in the species of change—that is, between two opposite species. This is so because, as has already been shown, change is found in four categories that are different genera. Between two of them [i.e. between two *genera*], it is evident that there can be no single continuous motion, as, for example, between changing from whiteness to blackness, on the one hand, and moving from location to location, on the other. But even within a single genus, such as quality—as when there is a change from whiteness to blackness and [then] from blackness to whiteness—there also is no continuous change. This is why, he said, "any sort of species change [with species in the plural]." For it is not correct for one to say that continuous motion is impossible even within an individual species of change. Change, after all, is either over time or not over time; and change over time is necessarily continuous since time is continuous; if it were not, it would be composed of instants. But his intention was with respect to two opposite species of change.[80] Or else, what he intended by "continuous" was continuous in the sense of perpetual and eternal.

Aristotle indeed proved this proposition by arguing that since motion is called by the name of its that-to-which—as we say, for instance, of something that moves from blackness to whiteness that it is whitening—and since in motion, a certain part of the that-to-which is absolute, it is necessary that motion be at rest at the that-to-which. Otherwise, its final actualization would be in potentiality, the that-to-which would not be absolute, all opposite motions would be one, and a thing would at the same time be both becoming black and becoming white. But the situation here is the same as that of coming-to-be, namely, that motion in [the category of] substance, when it has come to be, rests, and afterwards it moves toward passing-away. Yet between the coming-to-be and the passing-away there is a midpoint, which cannot be conceived as both coming-to-be and passing-away at once.

As far as locomotion is concerned the matter is also clear, since locomotion is either rectilinear or circular or a combination of both. And it is clear in the case of rectilinear motion that between any two opposite motions there is rest, for otherwise there would be something that could be moving upward and downward at once; furthermore, the midpoint of any magnitude exists in two senses, potential and actual. This is just like what happens when a moving thing moves continuously: no

---

[80] Change within a single species can be continuous, for when change proceeds in one direction it involves no stop or pause or rest. Transitioning from one property to its opposite and back, however, is an example of discontinuous change between species. According to Aristotle, this sort of change requires a pause—if only for an instant. Rectilinear motion that reverses direction is, in Aristotle's view, similarly discontinuous: there is a pause between, for example, going up and coming back down.

actual point or line can be marked on it—because a line is not composed of points, nor a surface of lines—and only when it stops can an actual point or line be marked on it. For were it possible to mark an actual point or line on it while it was moving continuously, there would have had to be a time at which it would stop in the middle. And this is so because it is clear that its motion toward the middle and its motion away from the middle are in two opposite directions. Yet if the point or line were actual, there would have to be two actual ends to these directions, and time would have to be composed of instants. Just as this was proved with respect to [motion in] a straight line, so too must it be the case with respect to a line that combines the straight and the circular, namely, the spiral. For were we to assume that this motion [viz. the motion of the spiral] is continuous, it [viz. the spiral] would move actually upward and downward continuously, and all the previous absurdities would follow.

It is thus evident that continuousness is not possible except in locomotion—and then only in its circular manifestation—where the that-from-which and the that-to-which are one. From this perspective continuousness and eternality[81] are possible for it.

Chapter XIV

PROOF of the fourteenth proposition, which states that locomotion is prior to the other motions and first among them by nature. For alteration precedes coming-to-be and passing-away, and alteration is in turn preceded by the drawing-near [i.e. the locomotion] of that which alters to that which is to be altered. And there can be neither growth nor diminution unless preceded by coming-to-be and passing-away.[82]

Aristotle proved this proposition by induction. He intended locomotion's precedence both in nature and in time. He added a proof to the effect that circular motion precedes the other motions since it is not motion from opposite to opposite and is not subject to change. What moves in this way has no potentiality for change but has a character that resembles absolute actuality.

Chapter XV

PROOF of the fifteenth proposition, which states that, since time is an accident consequent upon motion and attached to it, neither of the two can exist without the other: motion cannot exist but in time, and time cannot be conceived apart from motion, and anything in which there is no motion is not subsumed under time.

This proposition contains four propositions: one, that time is an accident; two, that it is attached to motion in such a way that one cannot exist without the other; three, that time cannot be conceived apart from motion; and four, that anything in which there is no motion is not subsumed under time. All these will be proved as the definition of time is clarified.

---

[81] See n. 101.

[82] Proposition IV had enumerated four kinds of change, which are here placed in order of precedence: (1) locomotion, (2) alteration [i.e. change of quality], (3) coming-to-be and passing-away [i.e. change in substance], and (4) growth and diminution [i.e. change in quantity].

Aristotle defined time as the numbering of that which is earlier and that which is later in motion. (Even though the ancients differed considerably from him [in their views of time] they do not merit mention since they were expositors of nonsense.) There is no doubt that time requires a substratum, since it does not persist at all; it certainly does not persist in itself as do things that do not require a substratum. This is so because time is divided into past and future, for the present is an instant and does not exist and is not time. But the past is already gone and the future is not yet here, so that it is self-evident that time requires a substratum. This is the first proposition of these four.

Since we measure swift and slow motion by time—for motion is swift when a moving thing moves a certain measure in a shorter period of time than [it would take it to move] if the motion were slow—it is evident that time is not motion, for time cannot be captured by a definition in terms of itself. And since swiftness and slowness in motion are accidents connected to it and not separable from it, and we measure them in time, it is confirmed that time must be an accident connected to motion. This is the second proposition.

Since it is the case that time is always the measure of motion—regardless of how it is viewed, whether from the perspective of swiftness and slowness or from that of earlier and later—our saying that its definition, namely, that it is the numbering of that which is earlier and that which is later in motion, is warranted. Since motion is contained in the definition [of time], the third proposition is proved, which is that time cannot be conceived apart from motion.

The fourth proposition, namely, our assertion that anything in which there is no motion is not subsumed under time, will be self-evident, when the notion of being subsumed under time is clarified as that which is bounded by time and exceeded by it on both ends. For this reason eternal things are not essentially subsumed under time, because they are not bounded and exceeded by time. If on occasion they are subsumed under time, it is only accidentally, and only with respect to those of them that move. For since motion is indeed bounded by time, what happens when we take a fraction of it is that these moving things are accidentally subsumed under time from the perspective of their motion. But incorporeal things, insofar as they do not move, are not subsumed under time either essentially or accidentally.

Chapter XVI

PROOF of the sixteenth proposition, which states that anything that is not a body cannot be conceived in terms of number unless it is a force in a body, for these individual forces can be numbered along with the numbering of their matter or their subjects. For this reason, incorporeal entities, which are neither a body nor a force in a body, cannot be conceived at all in terms of number, except insofar as they are causes and effects.

Since the quiddity[83] of a species that contains different individuals is one in species though many in number,[84] it is evident that it cannot be conceived in terms of

---

[83] "Quiddity" throughout renders מהות (*mahut*), whatness. "Essence" is reserved for עצמות (*'atzmut*).
[84] The Florence manuscript omits, "though many in number."

number except by way of difference in place, in time, or in some accident that is present in it.[85] Since, as was shown earlier, that which is neither a body nor a force in a body is incorporeal, is not subsumed under time, is not bounded in a place, and none of the accidents applies to it, it is evident that incorporeal things cannot be conceived in terms of number, except by a difference that does exist in them, namely, their being causes and effects.

Chapter XVII

PROOF of the seventeenth proposition, which states that everything that moves must have a mover, whether something outside it, as in the case of a stone that is moved by a hand, or an internal mover, as in the case of an animate body, which is composed of mover and moved, so that, when it dies, the mover, which is the soul, is gone, but the moved, which is the body, remains in place as it was, no longer able to move in the same way. Since the mover which was present in the moved is hidden and not perceivable by sense, it is thought that animate entities move without a mover. Everything that moves because its mover is present in it is called something that moves on its own. In other words, insofar as that which moves is moved by a moving force essentially, it is present in the entity as a whole.

The point of this proposition is to prove that everything that moves has a mover, and this is so regardless of how it moves—whether naturally, as a stone moves downward; or by force, as a stone moves upward; or by choice, as a living being moves. It is evident that in the case of a thing that moves either by force or by choice, the mover is distinct from the moved. That this is so with respect to a thing that moves naturally will be clear from the following. Since things that move naturally differ in their direction, such as the downward motion of the stone and the upward motion of fire, their motion is necessarily not a matter of their being a body *tout court*. For if that were the case, they would not move in opposite directions. Rather, each of them has its own unique motion insofar as it is this particular body. Since inasmuch as they are all equally participants in corporeality, it can only be the unique form of each that imparts to them their particular motion via a force that is implanted in each and which is called nature. For this reason it is the nature of each that is its mover.

Chapter XVIII

PROOF of the eighteenth proposition, which states that when anything passes from potentiality to actuality, that which effects the transition is distinct from it and necessarily outside it. For if it were in it and there were nothing to prevent the transition, it would not for even a single instant have been in potentiality but would have always been in actuality. Moreover, if the effecter of the transition were in it and there were an impediment that was removed, there is no doubt that that which removed the impediment would be that which effects the transition from potentiality to actuality. He brought this proposition to a close by saying: "Understand this."[86]

---

[85] The point is that members of a species can be differentiated—and thus numbered—only by way of some distinguishing material feature.

[86] See *Guide*, Intro. to Part II.

This proposition may indeed be verified by induction, as follows. Anything of which it may be said that it is something *potentially* is either an agent or a thing acted upon. If it is a thing acted upon, then it [viz. its potentiality] is either in its substance or in its accidents. But if its potentiality is in its substance, that is, in its coming-to-be and passing-away, there is no doubt that that which effects its transition from potentiality is distinct from it, since it is clear that a thing cannot effect its own coming-to-be or passing-away. And if it is in its accidents, that is, in a change of quantity, of quality, or of the other categories, there is no doubt that, insofar as they require a substratum, it is the potentiality in the substratum that acts on them and effects their transition from potentiality to actuality. Yet from the perspective of the agent, that is, when we say of something that it is the agent of something that is in potentiality, there is no doubt that the potentiality is either in it or outside it. If it is outside it, then that which effects the transition [from potentiality] is distinct from it. And if it is in it, then, since the potentiality to act is within it, if there were no impediment and no unfulfilled condition, it would be always in actuality. Therefore, if it is not always in actuality, it is because there *is* an impediment, in which case that which removes the impediment is that which effects the transition.

It is necessary to attend to the following point. When we say of something that it has a certain potentiality, it follows necessarily that there is a change in the thing acted upon. But in the case of the agent, if it has within it the potentiality to act, but the receiver presents an impediment to the action, then, even if that which removes the impediment is that which effects the transition from potentiality to actuality, there need be no change in the agent. It is for this reason that he remarked here, and brought this proposition to a close by saying: "Understand this."

Chapter XIX

PROOF of the nineteenth proposition, which states that everything whose existence has a cause has possible existence from the perspective of its essence.[87] For if its causes exist it will exist, but if they do not exist or they cease to exist or if there is a change in their relation to it—a relation that would otherwise have guaranteed its existence—it will not exist.

This is self-evident. For, anything whose existence has a cause is either necessary from the perspective of its essence, or impossible, or possible, since this is what the nature of the division into alternatives requires. But it cannot be necessary in terms of its essence, for in the case of anything that is necessary in terms of its essence, its nonexistence as a consequence of the nonexistence of something else is inconceivable. In the case of anything whose existence has a cause, however, its nonexistence is necessitated by the nonexistence of its cause. It also cannot be impossible in its essence, because in the case of something that is impossible, there could not be a cause of its existence. It follows, therefore, that from the perspective of its essence it is possible—that is to say, its existence, whether eternal or noneternal, could be conceived to be nonexistent if its cause were nonexistent.

---

[87] The notion that something is necessary or possible by virtue of its essence (or in respect of itself) as opposed to by virtue of its cause will figure centrally in Crescas's consideration of free will in II. v.

Chapter XX

PROOF of the twentieth proposition, which states that there is no cause in any way or in any manner for the existence of anything whose existence is necessary from the perspective of its essence.

The truth of this proposition may be derived from the previous one by contraposition. If that whose existence has a cause does not exist necessarily, it follows necessarily that the existence of that which does exist necessarily has no cause. What is surprising is that he did not combine this proposition with the nineteenth. [This surprising phenomenon was noted by al-Tabrizi. But the Rabbi and teacher was vindicated by the explanation offered by this worthy commentator.][88]

Chapter XXI

PROOF of the twenty-first proposition, which states that in anything composed of two components, it is the composition that is necessarily the cause of its existence as it is, and its existence is not necessary by its essence, for its existence is in the existence of its parts and their combination.

Since the parts of a thing are distinct from the whole of a thing and the thing as a whole is composite, there must be a cause for the existence of the composition. We have already seen that anything whose existence has a cause does not exist necessarily. Therefore, a composite's existence is not necessary.

Chapter XXII

PROOF of the twenty-second proposition, which states that every body is necessarily composed of two elements and is necessarily subject to accidents. The two elements that constitute it are its matter and its form. And the accidents to which it is subject are quantity, shape, and position.

If the existence of a substratum is to be a necessity for coming-to-be and passing-away, it is necessary that matter exist. Since matter in itself is devoid of any form—for were it to have form, coming-to-be would be alteration and would not be coming-to-be—it follows that what individuates it is what defines its boundary and makes it exist in the actuality designated for it. It is thus proved that a body's constitutive components are matter and form.

Accidents require a substratum. Some of them are separable from their substratum and some are not. Those that are not separable are quantity, without which body is inconceivable; shape, which is in the category of quality and cannot be separated from the body since the outline of a body's shape is the line or lines that define its boundary; and position, which is the relation of the parts of a body one to the other and to other bodies outside it. These are indeed distinguished in that they are not separable from the body. And this is what he intended by saying that the body "is necessarily subject to accidents." As he then explained, these are quantity, shape, and position.

---

[88] This addition is found in the Vienna manuscript and reproduced in the Vilna edition. Wolfson (1929: 685) helpfully records al-Tabrizi's explanation for Maimonides' having devoted a separate chapter to the twentieth proposition: since this proposition is a useful one, there is value in its being established and known on its own rather than needing to be derived from the nineteenth proposition.

Chapter XXIII

PROOF of the twenty-third proposition, which states that for anything that is in potentiality, and has in its essence a certain possibility, it is indeed possible that at a certain time it will not exist in actuality.

Many commentators, such as al-Tabrizi and Narboni, have been puzzled by this proposition and it eluded them. Taking its language at face value, it appears to be inescapably tautological. For, anything that is potentially something has in its essence a certain possibility with respect to that thing. Therefore his saying, "has in its essence a certain possibility," is tautological and superfluous. For his saying, "it is indeed possible that at some time it will not exist in actuality," has no point, since [saying of] anything that [it] has a certain possibility means no more than our saying that it may or may not pass into actuality. This sentence, then, is like the sentence in which we say: "Man is man."

If his intention in saying "has in its essence a certain possibility" is that the subject of the potentiality has the possibility of existing or not existing, this does not appear to accord with his saying, "a *certain* possibility." For if his intention were the matter of its existence, his saying "a certain" would be untenable. But let us assume that this *is* what he intended. If so, the subject would already have passed into actuality. And if so, his saying, "it is indeed possible that at some time it will not exist in actuality," would be wholly inapplicable.

What appears to us to be the correct interpretation of this proposition is as follows. What is meant by "anything that is in potentiality, and has in its essence a certain possibility" is that when the possibility is a potentiality for something, sometimes the possibility is in the thing's essence, such as the way it is possible for black in its essence to change and to become white. But sometimes the possibility depends on something external to it, such as the way it is possible for the sun to blacken a thing, so long as the receiver is a moist body. He therefore asserted that [even] when the possibility is in a thing's essence, it is indeed possible for it at a certain time not to be in actuality—that is to say, for it to be in a state of privation. For when the possibility is in its essence, and nothing external is needed [to effect the actualization of the potentiality], the possibility must be present in the matter that can undergo change. Therefore, it can be in a state of privation at a particular time, since the changeable matter is the cause of privation in a substance.[89] This interpretation is consonant

---

[89] To summarize this chapter. The question is: can something have at a certain moment unactualized potential? Al-Tabrizi and Narboni are puzzled: is not this precisely what being in potentiality means, namely, that the potentiality may or may not be actualized? Crescas does not think it likely that what Maimonides has in mind is potential for *existence*, for it would be odd in that case for him to speak of "a *certain* possibility." But if potentiality for existence is indeed what Maimonides intended, then the very fact that he speaks of the potentiality that *something* has, in effect already commits him to that thing's potentiality for existence having been actualized. Crescas now suggests what Maimonides must mean. According to Crescas, Maimonides is distinguishing between two kinds of potentiality. One is the potentiality that inheres in a thing's essence, and one is potentiality that is activated by an external cause. Maimonides offers an example of each: of the first, blackness that turns white on its own, and, of the second, whiteness that is turned black by an external agent. Whereas there is nothing surprising about an unactualized potentiality when an external cause is the actualizer, an unactualized *essential* potentiality is surprising. Proposition XXIII maintains that even if something has *in its essence* a certain potentiality,

with how the Rabbi used it in [presenting] this proposition in Chapter 1 of Part II of the *Guide*.

Chapter XXIV

PROOF of the twenty-fourth proposition, which states that anything that is potentially a certain thing is necessarily material, since possibility is always in matter.

This proposition is self-evident in conjunction with what was said previously, namely, that anything that is potentially a certain thing will necessarily be a substratum for that potentiality and will remain with that thing.[90] Otherwise, that thing would not be a single thing.[91] That which behaves in this way is matter. For form does not have the potentiality to become something else. And thus it is confirmed that possibility is always in matter.

Yet it is necessary for us to be aware that possibility can be attributed either to an existing substratum, as, for example, when the matter that is bronze can become verdigris, or to a nonexistent substratum, as, for example, when verdigris might possibly come to be present in matter that is bronze.[92] Here, however, what is intended is possibility that is in the existing thing.

Chapter XXV

PROOF of the twenty-fifth proposition, which states that the first principles of an individual composite substance are matter and form. An agent—that is, a mover—is indispensable for bringing the substratum to the point that it can receive a form. This is the proximate mover, which prepares the matter of a particular individual. What is required, then, is an inquiry into motion, the mover, and the moved. What needs to be proved, however, has already been proved. As Aristotle put it, matter cannot move itself. And this is the critical proposition that leads to the investigation of the prime mover.

This proposition is self-evident. Since matter and form cannot exist each on its own by itself, and since we see that a thing that comes to be comes to be from something but not from an arbitrary something, it is evident that there must be a substratum that persists always and divests itself of one form and takes on another. Therefore the

---

that potentiality need not be realized, because one of the features of matter is that it can be, at a certain time, in a state of privation. Only something that has no taint of materiality is necessarily fully actualized.

[90] Reading with the Ferrara and Vilna editions, and with the manuscripts, וישאר עם האחד, rather than with Fisher and Wolfson, וישאר עם זה אחד, "and will remain one with this." The sense of the sentence is virtually the same either way.

[91] In this sentence, ואם לא, לא היה הוא דבר אחר, Wolfson (1929: 313) reads the last word as אחד rather than as אחר, and translates it thus: "For were it not so, it would not be the same thing." So, too, Smilevitch (2010: 352): "*Sinon il ne serait pas cette chose.*" In other words, these scholars take Crescas's point to be that the matter—the potentiality—once actualized remains with the thing, preserving it as the same thing, that is, as the same continuous thing. In my view what Crescas intends is that the matter's remaining enables the thing to be one *particular* thing, that is, a single and singular combination of matter and form. This interpretation coheres well with the manuscript version of this sentence, which is: ואם לא, היה הוא דבר אחר. In this version, the final word can only be אחר. The sense of the sentence is: "For were it not so, it would be something else."

[92] Bronze becoming verdigris is possible both in fact for an actually existent piece of bronze and theoretically for bronze that does not at the present time exist.

essential first principles of the individual substance are matter and form. Although the prior privation is also one of the principles, it is so accidentally. But since what it needs necessarily is a mover that prepares the matter to receive a particular form, it is evident that an agent is indispensable. Nevertheless, since an agent is not essential to the thing, it is not counted among the first principles. Yet since it [viz. the agent] is something inescapable—since matter does not move its own essence, but rather the mover by its essence moves the moved via motion—it is evident that inquiry into the mover leads to inquiry into motion and the moved.

Chapter XXVI

PROOF of the twenty-sixth proposition, which the Rabbi proffered by way of hypothesis. Its claim is that time and motion are eternal, constant, and exist in actuality.

The ancients held a variety of views regarding this proposition. Epicurus and his school held that time and motion are eternal without a prior cause. But there is no point in engaging with them since the absurdity of this view is easily shown by force of the previously mentioned propositions. As Aristotle saw, time and motion are eternal, caused, and necessary, as effect is necessitated by cause. But even with regard to this view later [thinkers] disagreed, as we shall see, God willing. For now, we shall simply take it as assumed. We have not seen fit to mention Aristotle's argument here, since it is being set forth solely as an assumption; [it will remain so] until the truth of the matter becomes clear in Book III, God willing.

Chapter XXVII

EXPOSITION of the first proof that the Rabbi offered for these propositions, which proceeds as follows.

It is necessary for matter that comes into being and passes away to have a mover, as was shown in the twenty-fifth proposition. When it is asked about this mover what it is that moved it and which species of motion pertains to it—the fourth proposition having shown that there are four categories of motion—this process cannot go on ad infinitum, as per the third proposition. There is then no doubt that it will terminate in locomotion, which has priority among the motions, as was shown in the fourteenth proposition[93]—for its cause is the motion of the sphere, in which all motions terminate. If we seek its mover, it is inevitable that the mover be either in it or not. If it is in it, it is unavoidable that it be either a force distributed throughout it and divisible with its division, as in the case of the heat in fire, or else one that is not divisible with its division, as in the case of the soul or intellect. This disjunction is necessary.[94] If the mover is not in it, it is inevitable that it be either a body or incorporeal. This disjunction is necessary as well. If it is impossible that the mover be one of the first three, it will necessarily be the fourth, which is, that it is incorporeal. How this is proved will become clear in what follows.

---

[93] Although the Ferrara edition has "the fifteenth proposition" (as does Fisher), the reference is clearly to the fourteenth, as in the Vilna edition and the Florence and Vienna manuscripts.
[94] "Necessary" is used here in the sense of "exhaustive": there is no third option.

It is untenable that the mover be a force in it [i.e. in the sphere]. It cannot be a force in it that is divisible with its division, for the sphere is a body and it is finite, as was proved in the twelfth proposition.[95] It would therefore be impossible for its motion to be eternal and infinite, contrary to what was proved in the twenty-sixth proposition. It is evident also that the mover is not a force divisible with its division. It is similarly evident that the mover is not a force in it that is indivisible, like soul or intellect. For if it were, the mover would move accidentally. Yet it was proved in the eighth proposition that something that moves accidentally must necessarily come to be at rest. So the mover would necessarily come to be at rest and, with its resting, that which is moved by it would necessarily come to be at rest. It would then be impossible for the motion of the sphere to be eternal, contrary to what was posited in the twenty-sixth proposition.

It is thus evident that the mover is not a force in the sphere—neither a divisible nor an indivisible one. It remains, therefore, for it to be either a body or incorporeal. But it is absurd that it be a body. For if it were a body, it would have to move when it imparts motion, as was proved in the ninth proposition. And it would require a body to move it—since it has been proved that the mover is not in it—and so that body would require another body, ad infinitum. There would then exist an infinite number of bodies, contrary to what was proved in the second proposition. It is thus established by proof that the mover is separate from body and is not a force in a body. Thus the mover is not subject to motion—not essentially and not accidentally—and division and change are impossible with respect to it, as was proved in the seventh proposition. Moreover, since it is incorporeal, it is necessarily one and not more, for it is absurd that incorporeal things be countable, except in the sense that one is cause and another effect, as was proved in the sixteenth proposition.

The existence of God, may He be blessed, is thus proved, and that He is neither a body nor a force in a body, and that He is one, and not subject to change, division, or plurality.

Chapter XXVIII

EXPOSITION of the second proof that the Rabbi formulated, his having accepted the proposition which states that when there is something composed of two things and one of the things exists by itself the other will necessarily exist by itself as well—since if their existence were such that it was necessary that they exist only as a unit, as do natural form and matter, the one could never exist without the other at all.

Once he established this proposition, he formulated its proof as follows. We find things composed of mover and moved, that is, of things that move other things and things moved by other things. There exist also moved things that do not move other things. It follows necessarily, therefore, that there exists a mover that is not moved by something else. And because it contains no motion, it is indivisible and is not a body, as was proved in the seventh proposition.

---

[95] My translation and that of Smilevitch accord with Fisher's text. Ferrara reasonably has: כמו שהתבאר בהקדמה הי"א וכח אם כן ב"ת כמו שהתבאר בהקדמה הי"ב, "as was proved in the eleventh proposition, and its force is therefore finite, as was established in the twelfth proposition." Where the Ferrara edition has the eleventh, Harvey (1998c: 66) has the first, as do the Florence and Vienna manuscripts. So, too, the Vilna edition.

Chapter XXIX

EXPOSITION of the third proof that the Rabbi formulated—borrowed from the words of Aristotle—whose point is as follows.

With regard to sensible existents, the following disjunction is inescapable, namely, that either all of them are subject to coming-to-be and passing-away, or none are subject to coming-to-be and passing-away, or some are subject to coming-to-be and passing-away and some are not. But it is absurd for all of them to be subject to coming-to-be and passing-away, for if that were the case, it would be possible for each of them to pass away. When something is possible for a species, it is necessarily impossible for it not to come to be. It must be the case, then, that all these existents will necessarily pass away. Yet once they all pass away, nothing will remain to bring anything into existence.[96] We see, however, that in this infinite time—as was posited in the twenty-sixth proposition—they have not passed away but rather they exist.[97] It is absurd, therefore, for them all to be subject to coming-to-be and passing-away. It is similarly absurd for none of them to be subject to coming-to-be and passing-away, for we see among the things that exist things that come to be and things that pass away. The remaining possibility, then, is that one thing exists that does not come to be and does not pass away, that has no possibility of passing away, and whose existence is necessary. Because among those things whose existence is necessary there is the sort that is necessary in respect of itself and the sort that is necessary in respect of its cause but possible in respect of itself, it [viz. the first existent] must of necessity be necessary in respect of itself.[98] For if it is assumed that this cause [viz. the cause of that which is necessary in respect of its cause and possible in respect of itself] is also necessary in respect of *its* cause, still another cause must be found; yet this cannot go on to infinity, as was established in the third proposition. It is therefore necessary that this first existent have necessary existence in itself. It is impossible for it to have plurality, as was established in the twenty-first proposition. It follows necessarily that it is neither a body nor a force in a body, as was established in the twenty-second proposition.

---

[96] Fisher: לא ישאר מי שימצא דבר. The Florence and Vienna manuscripts have: לא ישאר מי שימצא דבר. Harvey (1998c: 93) renders the clause as I do. Another possibility is לא ישאר שנמצא דבר : "nothing will remain in existence" (see the Ferrara and Vilna editions; cf. Smilevitch: *il n'en reste aucun*). A case could be made for preferring the first and second readings on the grounds that on the third this clause is redundant, making no new point. In favor of the third, however, we note that the next sentence makes no reference to bringing-into-being but only to existing. For the notion that every sensible body is finite, see the first proof in the second class of proofs in Part I Chapter I.

[97] Harvey (1998c: 93), following the Florence and Vienna manuscripts, renders שלא נפסדו והם נמצאים ואנחנו נמצאים: "the existing things have not been corrupted. Rather, they exist and we ourselves exist." Fisher, Ferrara, and Vilna all have שלא נפסדו והם נמצאים, rendered by Smilevitch: *qu'ils n'ont pas péri mais qu'ils existent*.

[98] The final clause in this sentence is missing from Fisher's text and from the Smilevitch translation. It is found in the Florence and Vienna manuscripts as well as in the Vilna and Ferrara editions. The Ferrara edition, however, inserts this clause after the previous instance of "necessary in respect of itself." Where the other versions insert this clause, the Ferrara edition adds yet another possibility, namely, "and there is one that is necessary in respect of its cause"—omitting all mention of its being possible in respect of itself. Following the addition of this third alternative, the Ferrara edition concludes with a repetition of: "it must of necessity be necessary in respect of itself."

He explained further that it is impossible for necessary existence to be found in two, for they would have in common necessary existence yet would differ by virtue of something else through which they are two. And there would thus be composition in them, insofar as there would be something in them that they share and something in them by which they differ. Yet, as was explained in the twenty-first proposition, something that has necessary existence cannot contain composition. From this perspective its incorporeality is easily established. For a body is necessarily composite, either from the point of view of its divisibility, or from the point of view of its being a bearer of accidents; and it must have an agent, as was established in the twenty-fifth proposition. And insofar as it is composite, it is impossible for it to have necessary existence.

Chapter XXX

CONCERNING the Rabbi's fourth proof, which proceeds as follows.

We always see things passing from potentiality to actuality; and this is impossible without there being something that effects the transition distinct from that which undergoes the transition, as was established in the eighteenth proposition. It is evident that that which effects the transition begins as an effecter-in-potentiality and afterwards is an effecter-in-actuality. The reason it was then in potentiality is either because of an internal impediment, or because of some other thing that was a condition of its existence but was absent, yet when it is present the transition to actuality occurs. Each of these two would require either an effecter, or a remover of the impediment, such that with the impediment removed, it [viz. the first effecter] would effect the transition to actuality. But this will apply also to the second effecter, though this cannot go on to infinity, as was established in the third proposition. It is necessary therefore that we arrive at an existent that is an effecter in actuality, and in which there is no possibility. And this is so because if there were possibility in it, it could be nonexistent, as came to light in the twenty-third proposition. And it is impossible that it be material, as was established in the twenty-fourth proposition. And it is therefore necessarily incorporeal. And it is therefore one, as was established in the sixteenth proposition.

Another way to prove the necessity of its oneness is as follows. If there were two, it would be necessary that there be something common to them, namely, that by virtue of which each is a God, and something else on account of which they differ from one another. And that on account of which they differ would exist either in each of them or in just one of them. It is inevitable, however, that the one that contains the difference would be composite, and so it could not have necessary existence, as was established in the twenty-first proposition.

Chapter XXXI

EXPOSITION of the Rabbi's fifth proof, which establishes unity.

This is founded on a widely accepted premise, namely, that the whole of existence[99] is like a single individual, with each part connected to another, and in which the forces

---

[99] The term is הנמצא (hanimtza). I render both this term and the related המציאות (hametziut) "existence." The latter may also be translated as "the universe." I translate העולם (ha'olam) as either "the universe" or "the world," as seems appropriate in context.

of the sphere are distributed throughout the matter and prepare it. If there were two divinities, the following disjunction would be inescapable: either one would be occupied with one of the parts of existence and the other with the other part; or one would be occupied with it at one time and the other at another time; or they would both be occupied with the whole always, so that none of the actions would be completed without the two together. The first is impossible, since existence is [assumed to be] all connected, one part to another. The second is also impossible, for several reasons: first, if at the time that the first was occupied, it was possible for the second to be occupied as well, what would have caused the first to be so occupied and the second not to be? And if it were impossible for the second [to be so occupied] at that time, there would necessarily have had to have been another cause that necessitated the action of the one and the inability to act of the other, since time is undifferentiated, and the substratum of the action is one, with one part connected to another. In addition, since each of the two is subject to time and is therefore moving, as was established in the fifteenth proposition, it would as such need a mover, as was established in the seventeenth proposition; yet a divinity has already been assumed, and it is a *first* mover. So, this is a contradiction. Furthermore, each of the two would have to pass from potentiality to actuality and each of them would require something to effect this transition, as was established in the eighteenth proposition. Moreover, there would be possibility in the essence of each of the two, and so necessarily each would therefore be nonexistent, as was established in the twenty-third proposition. For all these reasons it appears that it is not possible for one to be active at one time and the other at another. This is the second. The third is also impossible, for if no action could be completed by one agent alone, then neither one of them alone could be the agent and first cause of that action, but the cause would have to be a combination of the two. Furthermore, a combiner would be unavoidable. Yet if the combiner were one, he would be the One, may He be blessed. But if the combiner were required to be two, then their combination would require a combiner. Yet this cannot go on to infinity, as was established in the third proposition. Therefore it is necessary to arrive at one, which is the cause of the existence of this one existent.[100]

Chapter XXXII

EXPOSITION of the proof common both to those who believe in anterior eternity[101] and to us, the congregation of believers in creation, as the Rabbi formulated it.

It proceeds as follows. A moving thing in which all motions terminate—the sphere— is either subject to coming-to-be and passing-away or not subject to coming-to-be and passing-away. If it is subject to coming-to-be and passing-away, the only one who could bring it into existence after nonexistence is necessarily God, may He be blessed; for it is absurd that it should bring itself into existence. If it is not subject

---

[100] "This one existent" is the whole of existence which is assumed to be a single individual.
[101] I use the term "anterior eternity" to render קדמות (qadmut), that is, eternal on the front end or in the past. I use the term "posterior eternity" (or "eternality") to render נצחיות (nitzḥiyyut) or נצחות (nitzḥut), that is, eternal on the back end or in the future. These terms are used in place of the Latin "a parte ante" and "a parte post."

to coming-to-be and passing-away, and its motion is therefore eternal, it would necessarily be the case, according to the first, eleventh, and twelfth propositions,[102] that the mover is neither a body nor a force in a body. It is therefore established that the existence of God, may He be blessed, is necessary in respect of Himself; He is one; and He is neither a body nor a force in one.

This is what we have intended in this first part. Praise is to God alone, who is exalted above all blessing and praise.

Part II

WE shall investigate herein some of the propositions, and the Rabbi's proofs, to determine if they were proved demonstratively. Since the propositions whose truth is doubtful are the first, second, third, seventh, eighth, ninth, tenth, twelfth, thirteenth, fourteenth, fifteenth, sixteenth, twenty-second, twenty-third, twenty-fourth, and twenty-fifth, and since we shall investigate the twenty-sixth, God willing, in Book III, the total number of propositions that will be subject to investigation in this Part is fourteen. Since [in addition] there are six proofs by the Rabbi that will be subject to investigation, we have divided this Part into twenty chapters.

Chapter I

WE shall investigate herein the proofs that he formulated to establish the first proposition, in order to determine if they establish its truth on all counts. We shall divide this chapter into four speculations, corresponding to the classes of arguments produced there.

SPECULATION I. INVESTIGATION OF THE PROOF HE FORMULATED TO ESTABLISH THE IMPOSSIBILITY OF THE EXISTENCE OF AN INFINITE INCORPOREAL MAGNITUDE.

We submit that this proof is sophistical and begs the question. For, one who assumes an infinite incorporeal magnitude ipso facto affirms the existence of incorporeal measure. It would no more follow necessarily that the definition of the infinite would apply to its parts than it would necessarily hold in the case of a mathematical line. Nor would it follow necessarily that there would be any composition in it other than through its parts.[103]

---

[102] Harvey (1998c: 68), in accord with the Florence and Vienna manuscripts, has Premises 1, 8, and 12. The Ferrara edition appears to have 1, 1 again, and 12. Vilna has 1, 11, and 12, as does Fisher, whom I follow here.

[103] Crescas is challenging (at least) four Aristotelian assumptions, which, as he will argue, rely on the impossibility of empty space. These assumptions are: that no magnitude can be incorporeal; that that which is incorporeal cannot be divided; that that which is incorporeal cannot be measured; and that the parts of something infinite would themselves have to be infinite. According to Crescas, however, we may compare an incorporeal magnitude to a mathematical line: a mathematical line can indeed be measured (insofar as its parts can be measured) though it is infinite (at its ends); moreover, though it is divisible, that is, it is composite and has parts, its parts are not themselves infinite. In the same way, Crescas contends, an infinite incorporeal magnitude can be measured and can be divisible, and its parts need not be themselves infinite.

Yet this proof is based, it would seem, on the foundation of the impossibility of empty space, as was noted above in Part I, so that if we admit the existence of empty space, then the existence of measure apart from sensible things would not be precluded. Perhaps the existence of such measure would even be necessitated, since it is indeed possible for empty space to be measured, in which case our applying to it large or small or any of the other quantitative properties would be warranted. But since he rejects its existence, he based this proof on it [i.e. on the presumed nonexistence of empty space]. But because there is not in all his efforts a proof sufficient for the denial of the existence of empty space, we saw fit to refute his proofs and to prove the spuriousness of those proofs—since the benefit to this science of doing so is not inconsiderable.

Since, according to him, those who admit empty space suppose that empty space is the cause of motion, I declare that the proof adduced to point up the absurdity of that supposition is sophistical. For, those who admit empty space do not suppose that empty space is the cause of motion except accidentally. That is because they thought that if there were no empty space, locomotion would not be possible, lest one body enter another. They drew support also from growth and diminution, rarity and density, and other examples along these lines, all of which is found in the *Physics*. If empty space is the cause of motion accidentally in this way, empty space does not have to be an efficient or final cause.

With respect to the first proof he produced to refute the existence of empty space, that from the existence of motion, its illegitimacy is evident. This is so because, although there would be some grounds for this argument if those who uphold empty space were to require that it be an *essential* cause of motion, they in fact never imagined, as was noted above, that it could be anything but an accidental cause. It would not be impossible, therefore, for the elements, even if they were mixed into empty space, to incline toward their natural place, or for empty space to contain a natural distinction of that-from-which and that-to-which, depending on its closeness to or distance from the circumference or the center.[104] Therefore, the existence of natural or forcible motion is not rendered impossible by the existence of empty space. It is even more certainly the case that this proof does not compel the impossibility of the existence of empty space *outside* the world. For even if there were empty space devoid of the nature of the that-from-which and that-to-which, that would not render impossible the circular motion of a spherical body [in it]. This is self-evident.

The second and third proofs are based on two premises, one of which—the one that affirms that the ratio of one motion to another is that of the ratio of one receptacle to another when the receptacles differ—is false. For since motion entails time by its very essence, it follows that even when the receptacle is removed, the original time of motion remains—a specific time determined by its very nature, in accordance with the force of the mover. All that can therefore be proved true is that the ratio of the slowing of one original motion to the slowing of another is that of one

---

[104] Crescas's point is that since empty space is only an accidental cause, by which he means in this context a necessary condition, the homogeneity of empty space does not deprive the elements of their natural places and natural tendencies. Indeed, even homogeneous empty space may have natural places, either nearer to or further from the encompassing lunar sphere or the earth that is at the center.

receptacle to the other, in the sense in which one might say, for example, by way of analogy, that the ratio of the slowing of motion in a man who is tired to that in a man who is even more tired is that of one tiredness to another, such that if we were to remove the tiredness factor, the original motion would remain.[105] Averroes indeed made a concerted effort to discredit this objection, as Avempace before him had already done partially, yet he multiplied many words that increase vanity.[106]

One of the later thinkers sought to prove the impossibility of empty space by contending that a medium is a prerequisite for the existence of motion because a medium's nature is akin to a that-to-which. Yet this is something that has not been proved and will not be proved, since indeed one might say that heaviness and lightness are, by nature, features of moving things and do not require media. Alternatively, one might say that, since all of them have some weight, and differ only with respect to whether that weight is less or greater, therefore, those things that move upward are forced upward by heavier things. For example, when air is inside water, the air will rise because of the pressure of the heaviness of the water, which, in turn, on account of being heavier, will seek the down. This can be seen to be so, since, when we clear a space in the earth, even up to its center, it will surely fill up with water or air. Whether this is because of the necessary impossibility of empty space within the universe, or because of the weight of air, has not yet been proved, and will not be.

Moreover, even if we were to concede that a medium is a prerequisite for the existence of motion, it would still not be impossible for there to be empty space *outside* the universe, and for a spherical body to move circularly within it. For those proofs [for the impossibility of motion in empty space] render impossible only the rectilinear motion of a body located in empty space; yet a spherical body may surely move in it without changing its place. This is most evident.

The foundation for the fourth proof is the proposition that states that the impossibility of one body entering another is due solely to its having three dimensions. But to those who uphold empty space, this is an evident falsehood, because they do not impute this impossibility to nonmaterial dimensions but only to dimensions that are material. The impossibility is indeed not because of the matter alone—for if it had no dimensions it would not occupy a place. Nor is it because of the dimensions themselves, for if they were not material, they would not occupy a place either. There would then not be a need for an infinite number of places.[107] Even if we assume, however, that these two features cannot each justify on their own the

---

[105] One might say that the relative speeds of two bodies is affected by the receptacle or medium but only once their original time has been factored in.

[106] Eccles. 6: 11: ‏כי יש דברים הרבה מרבים הבל, מה יתר לאדם?‏. The word ‏דברים‏ (*devarim*) can mean either "things" or "words." Either way, the verse is less than perspicuous. Two possible translations are: (a) "Since there are many things/words that increase vanity, what advantage is there to man?"; and (b) "The more words, the more vanity; how is man the better?" Wolfson (like the Ferrara edition) has: ‏והרבה דברים מרבים הבל‏; Fisher has ‏והרבה הרבה דברים מרבים הבל‏, recording more faithfully the part of the verse in Ecclesiastes where ‏הרבה‏ follows ‏דברים‏. Fisher vocalizes the ‏והרבה‏ that precedes ‏דברים‏ as a verb to mean: "he [presumably Averroes] multiplied (*vehirbah*)…"

[107] The notion that there would be a need for an infinite number of places derives from the Aristotelian contention that if dimensions require a place, and that place has dimensions which in turn require a place, an infinite regress is generated.

impossibility of the entry of one body into another—that is, that neither one is by itself sufficient to establish this—nevertheless, they can justify this conclusion when combined.[108] For material dimensions occupy place, and from that point of view it is impossible for one body to enter another. It therefore is not established that non-material dimensions require a place. This is most evident.

With respect to his further supporting his view by maintaining that dimensions are the limits of bodies, the fact is that the advocate of incorporeal dimensionality would not concede the point, so that this is an instance of begging the question.

It has already been proved that in all that he has said regarding the impossibility of an incorporeal dimension there is nothing worthy of attention. It is this that we have intended to show.

It would seem, indeed, that the existence of an incorporeal dimension is required even according to the view of those who maintain the impossibility of the existence of an infinite body. For their view entails that there can be no body outside the universe. If there is no body at all, there is surely no fullness. And if there is no body that is full, what is it, if only I knew, that would prevent it [viz. that which is outside the universe] from receiving corporeal dimensions? For indeed incorporeal dimensions are just unoccupied place capable of receiving dimensions of a body. We say "unoccupied place" to indicate that the true place for a body is the unoccupied space equal to the body, which the body will occupy, as we shall explain at the appropriate place, God willing.

It has thus been proved that an incorporeal magnitude is in essence not impossible; and that perhaps it is even necessary. Indeed, how could it not be? It can be said of unoccupied space in its essence that it is large or small; and it may be measured by a part of itself. If one were to imagine a concave vessel having been emptied of air and not having had its air replaced, one could say of that unoccupied space that it is large or small, and it is thus measured by a part of itself. Since the definition of a continuous quantity is applicable to it, and since it is not a time, it is of necessity a magnitude. Therefore, since there is no body outside the universe according to the view of those who maintain the impossibility of an infinite body, there is of necessity unoccupied space. Since it has been proved that it is a magnitude, the existence of an incorporeal magnitude is proved. And it is impossible for it to have a limit, for if it did it would necessarily terminate either at a body or at unoccupied space. Yet it is impossible for it to terminate at a body, so it must then terminate at unoccupied space—and so on to infinity. It is therefore proved—even according to their view—that an incorporeal infinite magnitude exists.

In any case, the necessity of the existence of an infinite magnitude—whether as a body or as incorporeal—is proved. And it is with this that we see fit to bring the first speculation to a close.

Concerning al-Tabrizi's proof, which he called the proof from attachment, it is evident that what he held does not follow necessarily. For although the existence of one infinite greater than another is indeed impossible, this is so only from the point of view of measure. That is to say, when we suppose that one of them is relatively

---

[108] Neither sheer materiality devoid of dimensionality, nor sheer dimensionality devoid of materiality, but only material dimensionality or dimensional materiality, suffices to preclude the entry of one body into another.

greater, we intend greatness in measure, but there is no measure in the case of something infinite. Therefore, one line is not greater than another, since neither is subject to measure as a whole. And so one cannot be greater than the other, even if it is augmented at its finite end. This is self-evident.

This is indeed confirmed by sense-perception inasmuch as it is evident in the case of time. For, one who believes in time's posterior eternity[109] believes, too, that time is augmented at the end that is finite, despite its being, for one who accepts anterior eternity, infinite at the other end. It will be proved further in what follows, God willing, that even according to our true belief in creation, this will follow necessarily inasmuch as it is beyond doubt.[110]

SPECULATION II. INVESTIGATION OF THE PROOFS HE FORMULATED TO ESTABLISH THE IMPOSSIBILITY OF THE EXISTENCE OF AN INFINITE CORPOREAL MAGNITUDE.

The general proof with which he first begins is clearly groundless. For its minor premise, which states that every body is encompassed by a surface or surfaces, is disputed by the opponent who maintains the existence of an infinite body. Indeed, he has begged the question.

Even if we concede to him the impossibility of an infinite corporeal magnitude, the conclusion he envisioned with respect to incorporeal[111] magnitude does not follow necessarily, since it is indeed possible for dimensions to exist apart from body, as we explained earlier. We shall consider number in what follows, God willing.

As far as the physical arguments are concerned, the first is deficient in both substance and form. For it is composed of uninstructive premises,[112] and the connection of the consequent [to the antecedent] is not necessitated. This is because the premise that states the impossibility of the existence of infinite elements was first proved in the *Physics* on the basis of only two arguments. The first is that the infinite cannot be grasped by knowledge. Yet it is not necessary that first principles be known, inasmuch as they are first principles. This is self-evident. The second is that if the elements were infinite, there would be an infinite composite. This, however, is precisely the matter that is under investigation. Therefore, if we assume

---

[109] See n. 101.

[110] Through a commonsense appeal to our notion of time Crescas is here further supporting his case against al-Tabrizi, who contends that an actual infinity is impossible because one infinity could then be greater than another. Although time can be added beginning at any fixed point in time, nevertheless (regardless of whether or not time has a beginning), no matter which point is chosen, time as a whole remains always the same, namely, infinite—not a greater infinity nor a lesser one but just infinite; the infinite is not subject to measure.

[111] Fisher's text, which I follow, contains the term "incorporeal" (נבדל; *nivdal*), and it is present as well in Smilevitch's translation. But it is absent from the Florence and Vienna manuscripts and from the Ferrara edition. Wolfson's Hebrew text omits it as well. Without it, the sense of the clause is as follows: "the conclusion he envisioned with respect to magnitude *generally* does not follow necessarily." There is no substantive difference between the two.

[112] Wolfson, who renders the Hebrew, "inadmissible premises," and Smilevitch, who renders it "*premises inacceptables*," are translating הקדמות בלתי מודיעות, which is what is found in the Florence and Vienna manuscripts. The Ferrara edition, followed by Fisher, has מורות. Wolfson (1929: 426 n. 42), notes the difficulties with מודיעות but does not consider the מורות alternative. My translation follows Ferrara and Fisher.

an infinite composite, the impossibility of the existence of infinite elements is not proved. It is clear, then, that the syllogism is deficient in its substance.

From the point of view of its form, it does not follow from our assuming one of the elements to be infinite that all the rest are eliminated. For it is indeed possible that this element would be devoid of quality—since it is possible to suppose an infinite body devoid of quality, such that it could receive all qualities insofar as it is devoid of all of them and could serve as their foundation. Such a qualityless body is indeed to be found, according to their view, in the phenomenon of celestial bodies that have the ability and readiness to receive qualities. It is even more certainly the case that this proof has failed to establish the impossibility of the existence of an infinite spherical body *outside* the universe.

With respect to the further support he adduced for his view, namely, that if it were infinite it would be infinite in all its dimensions—this does not follow necessarily. For although there would be some basis for this inference if infinity were essential to dimensions per se, nevertheless, if infinity is but one of its properties and not essential to it, it will not follow for all dimensions that they must be infinite. This is most evident.

Concerning the second proof, which is based on heaviness and lightness: this argument is derived from a consideration of sensible bodies beneath the sphere. Yet the one who accepts an infinite body will attribute to it neither heaviness nor lightness, just as is the case in the matter of celestial bodies according to Aristotle's view.

Concerning the third and fourth, which have to do with place: even if we concede the definition of place that he posits, these proofs do not yield the truth as he saw it. For, one who accepts an infinite body will maintain that its place is the surface of its concavity, which is the surface that encompasses the center. From the point of view of its convexity it is infinite and it has no place from that perspective. And why would it not be so, when, after all, this description, according to Aristotle, fits the celestial body that encompasses everything; that is to say, it has no place that encompasses but only one that is encompassed.

The truth itself is, as it seems, that the true place of a thing is the interval[113] between the limits of the encompasser. The absurdities that Aristotle imputed to this view as its necessary consequences have no merit. For they are based on the notion that the dimensions inside a vessel filled with water move as the vessel is moved—and if that were the case those absurdities would indeed follow. But that is a fiction and not the truth, since, for those who accept unoccupied and empty space, the dimensions do not move. Therefore, these absurdities do not follow.

Indeed it is *Aristotle*'s view of place that entails absurdities. One of them is as follows. The celestial bodies will differ with respect to place; all of them will have an essential place, that is, an encompassing surface. But that which encompasses everything[114] will not have an essential place, since, because the surface of its convexity is not separate from it, it lacks an encompassing surface that is equal to and separate from it. For this reason, he was obliged to say that it has no essential place but only an accidental one.

---

[113] Reading with Wolfson, רחק, "interval," rather than רחקים, "dimensions."
[114] The reference is to the outermost all-inclusive sphere.

Another absurdity is that the definition he posited [of place], namely, as an encompassing surface that is equal and separate, is inapplicable to those moving things whose motion is rectilinear. For the specific place of the parts that move essentially with the motion of the whole is not one that is encompassing, equal, and separate, in the sense that it would have an affinity and likeness to all the parts of the place, as he strove to maintain. For example, the place of air, according to his view, is an encompassing surface of the concavity of fire, because it has an affinity and likeness to it. But the middle part of the air cannot but be either in its natural place or not in its natural place to which it has the inclination of which he spoke. But if it is in its natural place, it would follow necessarily that the natural place of the part is different from the natural place of the whole. Yet this is the height of absurdity.

Another absurdity is that if the place of the celestial body—whether essentially or accidentally—is that which encompasses the center, it would turn out not to have the inclination that things that occupy space generally have, for it is inconceivable that celestial bodies should have an inclination toward the down. This is especially so, considering that the element of fire seeks the up, such that, from this perspective, its affinity and likeness are to that which encompasses. How, then, could the celestial body have an affinity and likeness to the down?

Furthermore, what he envisioned, namely, that a moving sphere requires something at rest by virtue of which it would be possible to say of it that it is in a place, is a fictitious absurdity. For it would then follow necessarily that around the poles of the sphere there is something at rest; yet if that were the case, its parts would scatter. But the point at the center or at the poles is characterized neither by motion nor by rest essentially; and if it [viz. the point] moves accidentally, it does so only by virtue of its [viz. the point's] being the end of that which moves. Therefore, it cannot be said on its account [i.e. on account of the point] that the encompassing sphere is in a place.[115]

If we assume, however, that empty space is a place, then this would apply to all moving things, whether they move rectilinearly or circularly—as well as to all their parts—without our having to seek for them any inclination.

Another puzzle is that when we sought to establish a place for the earth, we maintained that it was the absolute down, yet the absolute down is not a surface but a point. A point cannot be characterized as a place.

Therefore, the truth, which provides its own verification and is in agreement with itself from every point of view, is that the true place is unoccupied space. Indeed it is fit that it be so, for it is fit that a place be equal to that which occupies it—both the whole and its parts.

Thus the proof that he has formulated does not provide the truth with respect to the matter in question. This is what we intended to show in the second speculation.

---

[115] It would seem, pace Wolfson, that בעבורה refers to the point, נקדה (fem.), and not to the center, מרכז (masc.). Indeed, Crescas does not, as Wolfson (1929: 199) has it, report Aristotle's assumption as, "that a rotating sphere must have a stationary *centre*," but only that it requires *something* at rest, דבר נח. Crescas's reasoning here appears to be that the point at the center and at the poles of a rotating sphere move accidentally with the motion of the rotating sphere by constituting its ends. If, then, the point is dependent on the sphere for its motion, then it—whether at the center or at the poles—cannot be the thing at rest that is the reason the sphere is located in a place.

It is because place was widely taken to be this [viz. unoccupied space] that there were many among the ancients who took the true place of a thing to be its form, inasmuch as form delimits and individuates a thing—both the whole and its parts— so that our Rabbis, peace be upon them, applied this term metaphorically to a thing's form and essence, saying, for example: "from its place it is determined";[116] "from the place from which you come"[117]—that is, from that thing itself; and "he fills his ancestors' place."[118] Note how they thus attested to the idea that place is the unoccupied space that will be filled by the place's occupant, in that they therefore said "fills." Had their intent been simply rank, they would have said: "he *was in* the place of his ancestors"—that is, of their rank.[119]

Therefore, since God is the form of the totality of existence, inasmuch as He created it, individuated it, and limited it, its name [viz. "place"] was applied metaphorically to Him, as in the Rabbis' always saying: "Blessed is the Place";[120] "We do not permit you to swear according to your own sense, but only according to our sense, and according to the sense of the Place, blessed be He";[121] "He is the Place of the world."[122] This comparison is wonderful, for just as the dimensions of empty space penetrate those of a body and fill it, so does the glory of God penetrate all parts of the world and fill it, as it is said: "Holy, holy, holy, the Lord of Hosts; His glory fills all the earth."[123] That is, even if He is holy and set apart by three sanctities— which allude to His being set apart from three worlds [angels, celestial spheres, and elements]—nevertheless, His glory fills all the earth, which is the most turbid[124] of the elements. This same point is made in the verse: "Blessed be the glory of the Lord from His place."[125] That is: the attribute of blessing and bounty is from His place and from His essence and nowhere else; the expression, "from His place," applies to His glory. If you prefer to regard God's glory as an emanation from Him, then the phrase may be taken literally, such that the term "place" applies to God. In other words, the glory of the Lord is blessed and flows from the place of God, that is, from His essence, since it emanates from Him. There would then be no need to resort to the Rabbi's interpretation, according to which "His place" means "His rank." For it is not proper to ascribe rank to God. With this we saw fit to close this second speculation.

SPECULATION III: INVESTIGATION OF THE PROOFS HE FORMULATED REGARDING THE IMPOSSIBILITY OF AN INFINITE MOVING THING—WHETHER ITS MOTION IS RECTILINEAR OR CIRCULAR.

The proofs he formulated with respect to the rectilinear motion of an infinite body, from which he derived the impossibility of the existence of an infinite body, are all

---

[116] E.g. BT *Shevuot* 7b.   [117] *Mekhilta, Ki Tissa* 1.   [118] E.g. BT *Horayot* 11b.
[119] If the sense of "place," מקום (*maqom*), were rank rather than unoccupied space, the expression would have been "he was in" rather than ממלא (*memalei*) "he fills."
[120] E.g. BT *ʿAvodah zarah* 40b.   [121] E.g. BT *Shevuot* 29a, 39a; *Nedarim* 25a.
[122] *Gen. Rabbah* 68; *Sefer Yetzirah* 2: 3.   [123] Isa. 6: 3.
[124] Reading העכור with Fisher and the Vienna manuscript. (It appears that this is the version in the Florence manuscript as well.) Wolfson (1929: 201), in accordance with the Ferrara edition, reads העיבור, in the sense of "impregnation," so: "which is an allusion to the element of impregnation, which is one of the elements of Glory."
[125] Ezek. 3: 12.

based on the sensible body, and therefore the conclusion they necessitate would apply only partially. Indeed, the existence of an infinite *non*sensible body has not been proved as yet. Yet when we investigate these proofs, we will find that on all counts they fail to yield the truth, even with respect to the sensible body.

Concerning the first proof, which is founded on location, one might object that the places of location, even if they are limited in species, that is, to the up and the down, are not individually limited—that is, the places *are* one higher than the other, ad infinitum. But even if there is no absolute up, this will not yield an absurdity, even though rectilinear motion is perceived by sense.[126]

With regard to the second proof, which is founded on heaviness and lightness, it turns out that, even if we assume that an infinite body has heaviness and lightness, the necessary consequences that he envisioned will not ensue. This is so because for each heaviness and lightness there is an original time, whether from the point of view of the medium in which it moves, or because of the requirement that motion be over time. It therefore does not follow necessarily that a finite weight moves in a shorter time than that in which an infinite weight does, but only that the weight of a finite body moves in a time equal to that of an infinite body. Yet from this no absurdity arises, since this occurs because of the necessity of the preservation of the original time, whether because of the medium or because of motion itself. Therefore, it also does not follow necessarily that the weight of an infinite thing moves in an instant, as he thought.[127]

Concerning the third proof, which is founded on acting and being acted upon, that which he supposed necessary, namely, that it is impossible for an infinite body to move something finite since there is no ratio between them, and that therefore its action could only take place not over time, is not so. This is because, since it is impossible that there be motion that is not over time, it is true of necessity that the motion will have an original time—if we assume that this is motion with respect to location. If we assume that it is motion in quality, then indeed, since the infinite acts and changes not over time, no absurdity will arise, and there will be no contradiction with what is sensed.[128]

---

[126] The argument that Crescas is contesting relies on the assumption that, were there an infinite body, one part of it would have to be higher than the other ad infinitum, in which case there would be no absolute up and down. If, furthermore, there were no absolute up and down, there would be no rectilinear motion, which is motion to the absolute up or down. Crescas counters that even if places can be one higher than the other ad infinitum, nevertheless, since the directions the motion remain finite—up and down—this need not preclude rectilinear motion. Crescas furthermore seems to think that the lack of an absolute up and down is no hindrance to rectilinear motion.

[127] The assumptions Crescas challenges here are that a heavier weight necessarily travels faster than a lighter weight, and that (therefore) an infinitely heavy weight must travel in an instant. Crescas contends that other factors determine speed or the "original time" of each heaviness and lightness, and that it is neither the case that there must be a finitely heavier body that travels faster than the infinitely heavy body, nor that an infinitely heavy body travels in an instant, though each heaviness and lightness has its speed, whether in a finite body or in an infinite.

[128] For Crescas there can indeed be a ratio between the motion of an infinite body and that of a finite one even with respect to locomotion, because each has original motion. And there is certainly no difficulty with respect to an infinite thing's effecting change in quality in a finite thing, for this sort of change does not even require time.

It is therefore evident that from all his efforts to prove the impossibility of an infinite body from the perspective of rectilinear motion there emerges nothing that is true of necessity.

From the perspective of circular motion, too, the conclusion does not follow necessarily, since the proofs are again based on the sensible body. One might object that indeed there exists an infinite body, but it does not move circularly, for the very reasons he offered. But when we investigate his proofs, we will find that they do not yield the truth even with respect to the sensible body. Such was the case with the first proof, in which what necessitated the contradiction of the consequent was that the distance between two radii along the circumference is infinite: since this distance increases with the lengthening of the radii, and since the radii may be lengthened infinitely, so, too, will the distance increase infinitely. It is open to the objector to say that the increase in distance is like increase in number, where finitude is always preserved. It will indeed then appear so, since the same knowledge is operative with respect to both contraries, and it was already proved in the book *Conic Sections*[129] that it is possible for distance to decrease infinitely, and yet for distance to persist. For it is possible to posit two lines, such that the more they are extended the closer together they draw to each other, yet it will never happen that they actually meet—not even if they are extended infinitely. For there is a distance that is preserved that will not vanish. This is true even more in the case of increase, because it is possible for there to be continual increase, yet for finitude to be preserved. This is the absolute truth: that there cannot be an infinite distance between two lines, even if they are infinite, since distance is always encompassed, as will yet be proved in what follows, God willing.[130]

But first we shall explain that, if the reasoning through which he established the contradiction of the consequent were sound, it would be necessary as well that the distance be infinite and finite at once. This would be so even if we do not assume that the infinite can move. For the proofs that he formulated are based on the impossibility of circular motion for an infinite body. But even if we grant that an infinite does not move [circularly], no absurdity will result. This is especially so now that it has been proved that outside the world there is either fullness or emptiness. For either way, there is an infinite dimension. And even if there is none, it is permissible for us to assume it, in the way that a geometer employs it in the definition of parallel lines and other principles. I shall now explain how it can be proved that, if the reasoning that supported it were true, the distance would be infinite and finite at once.

If it were necessary that the distance along the circumference between infinite radii extending from the center be infinite—since the distance increases as a radius is lengthened—this will obtain for any two radii extending from the center and for any angle that should form. If we were to imagine ourselves marking a point which is a certain measure from one of the radii along the circumference whose radii are at an infinite distance from one another, there is no doubt that it would be possible for us to extend a line from that marked point to the center. After all, it is one of the axioms

---

[129] A work by Apollonius of Perga (*c.*262–*c.*190 BCE).
[130] For Crescas distance is finite whether the lines extended infinitely are increasing or decreasing. And, so long as distance is finite, motion, both rectilinear and circular, is possible even for things that are infinite.

that it is possible to extend a straight line from any point to any point. A certain new angle would then be created and the radii along the circumference would be at a finite distance [from one another]. Yet it was assumed that when any radii extend, from whatever angle, an *infinite* distance [between them] would form along the circumference—in which case it would be finite and infinite at once. And this absurdity is compelled by our assuming his reasoning to be sound.

The absolute truth, however, is that even if a radius is infinite, it does not follow necessarily that the distance between two radii is infinite. For it is evident that we cannot mark a point on the infinite radius extending from the center without the line from the point to the center being finite. Since the distance between the radii cannot be infinite unless that point from which the line is drawn [to the center] is infinite—and there is no such point—there does not exist then an infinite distance between two radii. Generally, when we say of the radius that it is infinite, we have in effect said of it that it has no extremity or end. If there were an infinite distance, it would have to be at the end—yet it is devoid of an end. Thus, there is no infinite distance between radii. Although the body as a whole moves, and it is infinite, it is not the case that a part of it moves except on a finite line.[131] Although this is far from imaginable, intellect necessitates it.

It is worth your knowing that from the necessary conclusion that we inferred, namely, that the distance between two infinite radii extending from the center is finite, it follows necessarily that any [distance traversed by the] revolution of this moving thing [viz. the radius] is finite. This is easily made plain—since, if we were to create angles equal to and next to the finite angle at the center they would necessarily be finite in number, inasmuch as the distance at the center is finite. Since the number is finite, it follows necessarily that the distance will of necessity be finite.

Since it is so, it is now proved that the reasoning that he thought would prove the contradiction of the consequent in this proof is not sound. And thus is the sixth proof discredited.[132]

The second, third, and fifth proofs are based on the intersection of the revolving line with the infinite line, whether the latter be parallel to it or not. But although it was proved that it is impossible for there to be a first part of motion, since every moving thing was already moved, meeting does not require a first point.[133] Therefore,

---

[131] Fisher mistakenly has "infinite line."

[132] There is disagreement among the various editions as to which proof has been discredited, as well as which one Crescas will proceed to address. The Ferrara edition has the sixth as does Fisher; Wolfson has the fifth, in brackets; Smilevitch (407 n. 1), taking issue explicitly with Wolfson, has the sixth. Wolfson (1929: 466 n. 113) notes that all the manuscripts and editions have the sixth. With respect to what is next addressed, the Ferrara edition has the second, third, and fourth proofs (Wolfson (467 n. 114) points out that this is what all the texts have); Wolfson has second, third, and sixth [in brackets]; and both Fisher and Smilevitch have second, third, and fifth.

[133] Against the contention that if there were an infinite sphere, a revolving radius in it could never intersect a given point on an infinite line constructed adjacent to the sphere (because the revolving line would have first to intersect the line at an earlier point and before that at an earlier point, and so on ad infinitum; and without intersecting a first point it cannot intersect a later one), Crescas argues that just as motion has no beginning yet there is motion of the part in a finite time, so, too, the line, though infinite, has parts that are finite at which intersecting can take place. The line itself, as a whole, need not be finite for intersection to occur.

it is not unlikely that a line infinite in measure will meet a motion that is finite—and this because of the necessity that only the extremity of the beginning of motion is not over time.[134]

The fourth proof is based on the proposition that states that an infinite body that moves circularly has a spherical shape. But this is absurd, since an infinite body is devoid of extremities, and therefore has no shape. It is true that if circular motion necessitated spherical shape, there would be some grounds for objection. But indeed it is possible for any shape to move circularly. And once we divest the body of borders, we also divest it of shape. And therefore it need not be finite.

It has already been established that there is not, in all the proofs he formulated, anything that requires the denial of circular motion to an infinite body. But it was further made evident by what we said, that motion is possible for an infinite body. And indeed the necessity of its possibility is made evident by sense-perception. That is, we see that a luminous body revolves in a finite time. And if we imagine a luminous ray to be infinite, and we use this the way a geometer does, it will turn out not to be impossible for it to move in its infinite motion in a finite amount of time, even if the ray is infinitely extended. And even should it prove to be the case, according to the view of the objector, that the infinite does not exist, intellect will nevertheless dictate that, if it were possible for the ray to be infinite, it would not be impossible for it to move. This is self-evident.

Further, even if we were to imagine that the ray is not infinite, nevertheless it is inevitable that in its motion it will make contact at a point within the infinite magnitude, whether that magnitude be something full or something empty, as was proved necessary in what we said. Therefore, when we imagine in that magnitude an infinite line parallel to the posited ray, the extremity of the ray when it moves will make contact at a point on that line that is parallel to the ray. In this way the opposite of the conclusions of the proofs he formulated is easily established. This will suffice for the third speculation.

SPECULATION IV. INVESTIGATION OF THE PROOFS HE FORMULATED TO ESTABLISH A GENERAL PROOF FOR THE IMPOSSIBILITY OF THE EXISTENCE OF AN ACTUAL INFINITE BODY.

Although these proofs derive their force from the previous proofs, nevertheless, regarding the first proof it may be said that circular motion does not entail a center. This is so since, insofar as it [viz. the infinite] is devoid of extremities, it has no center. Regarding the second, [it may be said] that it is indeed possible for it to move on its own, such that it is not necessary that it have sensibles surrounding it from the outside. Regarding the rest of what was said on this matter, its refutation is evident from what was said.

It is evident from all this that in all the things he thought would confirm this proposition, there is not anything adequate. Because an error in first principles leads

---

[134] Crescas has argued that motion in its parts is finite and over time, even if it is infinite and not over time at its extremities. So, too, is the line finite in its parts though infinite at its extremities. (In the case of the sphere's radius, this is so at one extremity only.) There is, therefore, nothing to prevent a finite part of the infinite moving radius from intersecting with a finite part of the infinite line.

to an error in what follows from these first principles, this one led to the conclusion that there are no other worlds. This is what he concluded first, namely, that outside the world there is neither fullness nor emptiness, and he reasoned that if there were other worlds there, the elements would move from one world to another. And he added delusions and words that increase vanity.[135] Since the error in his first premise is evident, inasmuch as the necessity of the existence of an infinite magnitude and the necessity of either infinite emptiness or fullness outside the world were already proved above, it is evident that the existence of many worlds is possible. It is not necessary that the elements move from one world to another, for each of the elements moves within that which encompasses it to the place that is most suitable for it. Everything that was said herein to establish the impossibility [of many worlds] is vanity and a striving after wind.[136] Since this possibility is true and beyond doubt, yet there is no way available to us, and no inroad by way of investigation, by which to know the truth of what is outside this world, our Sages, peace be upon them, restricted inquiry and investigation into "what is above, and what is below, what is in front, and what is behind."[137] With this it is appropriate to bring to a close this fourth speculation of the first chapter.

Chapter II

INVESTIGATION of the second proposition, which states that the existence of an infinite number of magnitudes is absurd.

It is evident that the foundation of this proposition is the proof of the veracity of the first proposition. And once the first is proved false, the falseness of this second proposition is easily proved. It is open to an objector to say that even without proof of the first proposition, the veracity of the second can be established on the grounds of the impossibility of an infinite number, as follows: let us say that every number is either even or odd; even and odd are each limited and finite; therefore, every number is finite. Yet it was already noted by us, in Chapter III of Part I, that this was not the view of the Rabbi. And al-Ghazali and Avicenna agree with him. Averroes, however, was aware of this point in his *Commentary on the Physics*. What is pertinent to the matter is that actual number—that is, things counted by number—are limited. And anything limited is necessarily finite. But for things that are subject to number—that is, things that are in their ordinary course subject to being counted—but are not actually counted, infinity is not impossible, even if it is assumed that they are even or odd, for it is possible for even and odd to be infinite.

The absolute truth is that the division of number into even and odd applies to what is finite and limited in number. But with respect to infinite number, since it is not limited, it is not described as even or odd, as we already noted in the aforementioned chapter.

Chapter III

INVESTIGATION of the third proposition, which states that the existence of an infinite number of causes and effects is absurd.

---

[135] Eccles. 6: 11.   [136] Eccles. 1: 14.   [137] BT Ḥagigah 11b.

Let me say that the proof that al-Tabrizi formulated in this matter, which we noted in Part I Chapter III, and which is hinted at in the eighth book of the *Physics* and in the *Metaphysics*, is inadequate in the Rabbi's view. For the only things for which an infinite number is impossible are those that have order and grade either in their position or by nature. Therefore, one intelligence can be the cause of an infinite number of intelligences. Generally, if an emanation of more than one effect is possible for a single cause, there is no impossibility in the existence of infinite effects having a single cause. Since it is not impossible for effects to be infinite, even if they all have the same cause, it follows that the existence of one cause for all of them does not necessitate the impossibility of infinite effects. Therefore, if we assume causes and effects in which the first is the cause of the second and the second of the third, and so on ad infinitum, how, if only I knew, could the existence of a single cause, were we to assume it, necessitate the impossibility of infinite causes and effects? For this could not be necessitated simply by there being a first cause for all of them. For by assuming infinite effects we indeed concede a first cause for all of them, and it is evident that this does not render impossible their being infinite since infinity in number is not precluded for things that have no order in position or by nature. But even if we assume also that infinite effects are each a cause for the next one, no absurdity will result. And we will need something that will determine their existence rather than nonexistence, since all are possibly existent. We have already acknowledged a first cause, without its necessitating a limit to the effects; and it is this that will determine their existence.[138]

Indeed one commentator[139] strove to prove this proposition by putting the point in the following words: "Anything that will not be realized essentially unless it is preceded by something infinite, will not be realized and cannot come to exist."[140] If the precedence were temporal, there might be grounds for this argument—but even so, it is open to dispute. For we see that it does in fact happen that a thing that is not realized unless being preceded by something infinite is realized. One might say, by way of analogy, that this day that we are in is realized, even though it could not have been realized unless it were preceded, according to those who subscribe to the anterior eternity of the universe, by something infinite.[141] Although in this case the realization was accidental,[142] nevertheless, our conceding the possibility in the case of the accidental while maintaining its impossibility in the case of the essential requires justification.[143] But even if we concede this distinction[144] in the matter of priority in

---

[138] Crescas maintains that there is no greater absurdity in the idea that a single cause has an infinite number of effects when the effects are causally or sequentially ordered in relation to one another than it is when the effects are not so ordered. When all these (even ordered) effects have possible rather than necessary existence, a cause is required to determine their existence over their nonexistence.

[139] The reference is to Narboni.

[140] Anything that requires an infinite causal chain for its coming to be will never come to be.

[141] The counterinstance is that the current day, which, assuming anterior eternity, could not have come to be unless an infinite number of days preceded it, nevertheless has come to be.

[142] The sense of "accidental" here is that there is no causal connection between the preceding days and the current one. One day is succeeded by another but is not caused by it.

[143] Crescas's point is that once we concede the possibility in the case of accidental coming-to-be that a thing that could not come to be were it not preceded by something infinite does in fact come to be, we need to justify our withholding the same concession in the case of essential, that is, causal, coming-to-be.

[144] Between accidental and essential.

time, there are no grounds for it in the matter of causal priority, in the case in which they are contemporaneous. For since this [viz. the possibility of realization] holds for things that are contemporaneous, by what necessity is it impossible for each one to be the cause of another, while it is possible for them all to be effects [of a single cause], once we recognize the possibility that they can be infinite simultaneously?[145]

What this proposition aims at, however, and what we require from it, is the existence of a first cause that is not caused, whether the effects are infinite and each a cause of another, or they are finite.

Chapter IV

INVESTIGATION of the seventh proposition, which states that everything that is subject to change is subject to division.

We find that a rational soul is subject to change in its acquisition of intelligibles, sensibles, and imaginables—although this acquisition is not over time—as well as in its psychic motions, such as joy and fear, which must be over time.[146]

Al-Tabrizi was struck by this objection and said, in an attempt to resolve it, that what is intended here is corporeal qualities. It seems that he was following Avempace's view in his interpretation of Aristotle's words, as we noted in Part I Chapter VII. Indeed, even according to Averroes' view, we can say, in agreement with his [viz. al-Tabrizi's] interpretation, that what is intended here are corporeal qualities and motions. But if so this entire proposition is redundant and superfluous—in particular, his saying in effect that anything that moves with corporeal motions is a body. Furthermore, if this proposition is only partial, singling out corporeal qualities, he [viz. Maimonides] could not have used it later in speaking generally of what is subject to change.

The solution to the objection, as it seems, is in accordance with the caveat we noted in connection with the moving thing, which is, that we must qualify it by speaking of the thing that moves *essentially*. We can say the same thing with respect to the changing thing, namely, that we are speaking of the thing that changes essentially. Since the rational soul does not change essentially, but only with respect to what happens to it insofar as it is hylic, the truth of this proposition is not impugned.[147] The proof of whether the change that it undergoes can be essential or not will be taken up in what follows, God willing.

---

[145] Causes and effects (with respect to which there is priority "in nature") when the effects are contemporaneous are not vulnerable to the argument of the commentator. For it is admitted that a single cause can have an infinity of concurrent effects.

[146] The rational soul is a putative counterexample to the seventh proposition, inasmuch as it is subject to change but not divisible.

[147] If what the seventh proposition intends is only that essential change entails divisibility, then the rational soul, insofar as it changes only nonessentially, need not, according to the seventh proposition, be divisible, and the proposition therefore remains intact. Crescas rejects al-Tabrizi's solution, according to which the seventh proposition should be understood to say that anything *corporeal* that is subject to change is subject to division. For Crescas, the proposition thus stated is redundant.

Chapter V

INVESTIGATION of the eighth proposition, which states that anything that moves accidentally necessarily comes to rest.

This proposition, namely, that anything that exists accidentally will cease to exist, applies only when it is not necessitated by a thing whose existence is essential. For it is indeed possible for a body to move accidentally constantly, so long as it is necessitated to do so by something else that moves essentially, just as in the case of a ball of fire[148] which is moved forcibly by virtue of the constant motion of the sphere. So, too, in the case of the surfaces of the sphere and their parts which move accidentally with the essential motion of the sphere. This is the species of accidentally moving things to which the Rabbi alluded in his illustration in the sixth proposition.

This had already troubled al-Tabrizi and others, so that Narboni thought to clarify this proposition by saying that what it meant was that anything that moves accidentally, insofar as it moves accidentally, will come to rest of necessity. For by way of analogy one might say that the human soul—which causes a person to move, and, in doing so moves accidentally but does not move essentially—necessarily comes to rest insofar as in causing motion it moves [only] accidentally. The same may be said for the soul of the sphere that moves the sphere, namely, that since it moves accidentally through causing motion, it would necessarily come to rest, were it not for the adjoining of some other separate mover that does not move even accidentally.

When we put effort into investigating this matter we will find that it is not compelling. For when we attribute accidental motion to the soul of the sphere, it is only through its connection—a connection of existence or of admixture—to the sphere which moves essentially. And since it has motion in no other way than this, it is evident that incapacity in this respect [viz. in respect of perpetual motion] could not derive from it.[149] Therefore, since we are assuming that it moves the sphere with an eternal and essential motion, it follows that the accidental motion we attribute to it will be joined to the essential, and we must indeed assume that it is possible for it to move forever. And nothing absurd arises from this. [For we find that accidental things necessitated by essential things are constant with the constancy of the essential things.][150]

Chapter VI

INVESTIGATION of the ninth proposition, which states that any body that moves another body will move it only if it itself moves as it moves the other.

---

[148] The reference is to the celestial spheres (especially the sun), which are maintained in their constant motion across the sky by the all-encompassing sphere. The next sentence concerns the epicycles whose motion, according to Ptolemaic astronomy, is synchronized with the larger cycles within which they are embedded.

[149] Since the soul of the sphere, even if we say that it moves accidentally, moves insofar as it is connected to the sphere which moves essentially, it need not come to rest.

[150] Fisher brackets this sentence, calling it an alternate version. It is absent from the Ferrara edition. It appears in both the Florence and Vienna manuscripts, as well as in Wolfson. Smilevitch treats it as integral to the text.

The two reasons they mentioned, derived from what appears to be the case when the Magnesian stone attracts iron, are self-evidently deficient. For it is improbable and nearly impossible that iron would acquire a disposition just from its proximity to the magnet, when each of them has a large measure of natural power, and are manifestly by their nature highly resistant to modification. From the same perspective it is most improbable that bodies become detached from the magnet and pull the iron and move it.[151] Furthermore, it is inevitable that these [putative] motion-causing bodies that exit from the magnet act by way of either pulling or pushing. If by pushing, the bodies would have to move in two opposing motions in first pulling the iron and then bringing it toward the magnet. And if by pulling, the bodies would in this case also have to move in two opposing motions with respect to the iron, having afterwards[152] to pull it and move with it in the direction of the magnet. If only I could fathom how this might be. But all of this is the height of absurdity.

It therefore appears that the correct solution in the matter of the Magnesian stone is that iron has a natural motion toward the magnet, in a certain relation to its nature, just as it has a natural motion toward the down, whether because of its affinity to that place or because of some property it has of which we would be ignorant were it not verified by sense-perception.

Chapter VII

INVESTIGATION of the tenth proposition, which states that all things of which it may be said that they are in a body are divided into two classes: those that exist through the body, such as accidents, and those through which the body exists, such as natural form.

It is fitting that you know that Avicenna, al-Ghazali, and their followers maintained that matter and form exist in every body, including the celestial bodies. For in their view, the corporeal form is but the continuousness of the three dimensions intersecting with each other at right angles. And since continuousness is distinct from the continuous thing—for continuousness is not subject to division—a substratum is required to receive the division and the continuousness. Intellect thus mandates two essential things for each body, namely, matter and form. For Averroes, however, since the celestial body is not subject to *actual* division, it would seem that it contains no plurality or composition. For this body is [for Averroes] one in reality; it is only from the perspective of coming-to-be and passing-away that the intellect mandates that a body be composed of a bearer and a borne, since what has passed away cannot receive any coming-to-be, as we explained earlier in Part I Chapter X. Thus, with respect to the eternal body [viz. the celestial sphere], which is not governed by coming-to-be and passing-away, the intellect does not mandate composition containing matter at all.[153]

---

[151] See n. 64. Crescas thinks it unreasonable to suppose that a magnet emits effluences that move toward the iron and pull it toward the magnet.

[152] That is, after moving toward the iron.

[153] Some manuscripts have: "does not mandate composition of matter *and form.*" So, too, Wolfson (1929: 261). Neither the Florence nor the Vienna manuscript contains "and form." Nor does the Ferrara edition. In any event, the critical point for Averroes is that the celestial body contains no matter.

With respect to Averroes's view, what, if only I knew, could necessitate that we not say this very thing in the case of bodies that come to be and pass away, namely, that the matter they contain is their corporeality, and their form the form that is specific to each one and serves each one as the perfection of its corporeality? Corporeality, which he calls "corporeal form," would then function as matter with respect to its specific form. If so, the matter, even without its specific form, would be in need of a place and would exist in actuality. Behold, my witness is in heaven,[154] since the celestial body, which is a body without matter, is one that exists in actuality. In this way, many difficult and perplexing questions regarding hylic nature as it is generally understood will be resolved.

It is open, therefore, to an objector to say that it is not a specific form through which a body exists, but that the corporeal form, which is the substratum in actuality, is that which sustains the specific form. It would still not be appropriate to say of the specific forms that they are accidents, since they have singular features that distinguish them from accidents, such as that they have specific places and are not subject to increase and decrease, etc. What must be said of them is that they are substantive things. But that the sustaining of the body in its existence is through it [viz. the specific form]—no. For the corporeal form, which is the substratum, is always in actuality, and is that which sustains the existence of the form that perfects it.[155]

Chapter VIII

INVESTIGATION of the twelfth proposition, which states that every force distributed in a body is finite since body is finite.

I say that the reason he gave for this proposition has already been discredited in what was said above, namely, that the impossibility of an infinite body has not been proved. Let us assume it nevertheless. I will then still say that it is invalid, because we do not concede the necessity of the connection of the consequent to the antecedent in this syllogism. For motion not over time does not follow necessarily, since every motion inevitably has an original time. Equality between the time of an infinite force and that of a finite is also not necessary, because the ratio of force to force enters into the time added to the particular natural original time. For the infinite could move within no other time than the original time, but the finite would require some additional time. And even if a finite mover is assumed to move *something* in the original time alone, no absurdity will result, since there might indeed be a difference between them [i.e. between the finite and infinite mover] in the case of moving a large object, in which case a finite mover would require time to move it in addition to the original time, but the infinite would move it in the original time alone. In this way the proof is discredited.

It is necessary to be aware, however, that, even if we grant this proof, it is to be understood that what is meant by infinite is infinite in strength. For it is evident that

---

[154] Job 16: 19.
[155] Crescas contends in this chapter that, not only is it possible for matter, in the sense of corporeality, that is, of being three-dimensional, to exist in actuality without specific form, but that it is this corporeality that sustains the specific forms that are the bodies' perfections, rather than that the forms sustain the bodies.

the infinite can be spoken of in two senses, either that of strength or that of time. For even if we grant the proof with respect to the infinite in strength, it will not follow that it applies to the infinite in time. For it is indeed possible for a force in a finite body to produce motion with finite strength but over infinite time, so long as there is no cause of fatigue and weakness, as, for example, in circular motion that involves neither pulling nor pushing, and, a fortiori, in the case of the celestial body, about which there is agreement among them [viz. the philosophers] that it has no qualities and suffers no infirmity or old age, as appears in the book *On the Heavens*.[156] Furthermore, it is possible for it to be said with respect to circular motion that it is natural for the celestial body just as rectilinear motion is natural for the elements. This is evident.

Chapter IX

INVESTIGATION of the thirteenth proposition, which states that it is impossible for any sort of species change to be continuous. Only locomotion can be continuous—and, within locomotion, only the circular.

If Aristotle's arguments in this regard are closely inspected, they will be seen to be nothing but imaginings and delusions. For when black moves to white, even if it does not come to rest at the white but instead proceeds to blacken, it will still not be necessary that it whiten and blacken simultaneously, but rather that it do so from two perspectives, thus: insofar as it first whitened it is appropriate to say of it that it whitens; and insofar as it subsequently moves to the black it is appropriate to say that it blackens. No absurdity arises from this.

This is all the more the case in rectilinear motion, which does not require rest between the two [opposing] motions, but rather it is possible that it be continuous—though this matter is not resolvable by sense-perception, as Aristotle said. But it is necessarily the case that, if we imagine a light thing of maximal lightness moving in the upward direction, and a mountain of maximal size falling on it, there can be no doubt that it [viz. the heavy thing] will move it [viz. the light thing] in the downward direction. If there were rest between these two opposing motions, it would be necessary that the mountain stand still, despite the extremity of its size.

The necessity that he imagined, namely, that it follows from the fact that motions are opposite that there is an actual instant [between them], is mistaken. It is evident in the case of an instant that is the end of passing-away and the beginning of coming-to-be, or the end of a previous coming-to-be and the beginning of a later coming-to-be, that it is necessary that there *not* be an actual instant. And how not? For the motion of coming-to-be is consequent upon the motion of quality, and the instant between two qualities does not exist actually, even though the first quality is the end of the previous coming-to-be and the second the beginning of a subsequent one.[157] This is most evident.

---

[156] See Aristotle, *On the Heavens* I. iii. 270^{b}1–4.

[157] Wolfson (1929: 226–7) offers the example of a cold thing becoming a hot thing. There is no moment of rest between the cold thing's passing away and the hot thing's coming to be, because there is no moment of rest in the transition from cold to hot. But Crescas seems to be considering instead the moment when a process reverses course. His point is not that there is no pause when a cold thing becomes hot, but that there

Chapter X

INVESTIGATION of the fourteenth proposition, which states that locomotion is prior to the other motions and first among them by nature. For alteration precedes coming-to-be and passing-away, and alteration is in turn preceded by the drawing-near of that which alters to that which is to be altered. And there can be neither growth nor diminution unless preceded by coming-to-be and passing-away.

With respect to ongoing coming-to-be this proposition is confirmed, but with respect to the beginning of coming-to-be, if it is ex nihilo, as will be explained, it will be proved that coming-to-be precedes the other motions, and that the motions of quantity and quality precede locomotion, since things are subject to quality and quantity before they move, and absolute quantity[158] precedes quality.[159]

Chapter XI

INVESTIGATION of the fifteenth proposition, which states that, since time is an accident consequent upon motion and attached to it, neither of the two can exist without the other: motion cannot exist but in time, and time cannot be conceived apart from motion, and anything in which there is no motion is not subsumed under time.

I contend that if we attend closely to the definition of time, we shall find that the four propositions, which, as we saw previously in Part I, are contained in this proposition, are false. For since it is self-evident that rest is said to be great when something rests for a long time, and small when it rests for a short time, it is evident that time is measured with respect to rest without there being actual motion. Even if we measure rest by conceiving the measure of something moving in it, it is still confirmed that there is no need for there to be actual motion in that time. Even more is this the case considering that rest, even without our conceiving of motion in it, is differentiated in actuality in terms of much and little. Since this is so, why, if only I knew, may time not be measured in it [i.e. in rest] without our conceiving of motion. For the correct definition of time, as it seems, is: the measure of the continuousness of motion *or rest* between two instants. Indeed it is clear that the genus most appropriate to time is measure.[160] Since time belongs to continuous quantity, but number to discrete, were we to posit it as number, that would be assigning it to a genus that is neither essential nor primary. Yet it is measure in both motion and rest, since our conception of the measure of their continuousness is time. Therefore, it appears that the existence of time is in the soul.

---

is no pause between the cold thing's becoming hot and its then beginning to cool. (See n. 80.) In this same way, generally, a passing-away leads into a coming-to-be without halting, and so, too, one coming-to-be into another.

[158] In speaking of "absolute quantity" Crescas intends the condition of being subject to number or measure (as opposed to having a specific number or measure).

[159] In considering the order in which the categories would come to apply to a world created after nonexistence, Crescas inverts the order in which the categories apply to an uncreated world. In an uncreated world the order is: locomotion, alteration, coming-to-be and passing-away. In a created world the order is: coming-to-be, alteration (in the sense of possessing quantity and quality), locomotion.

[160] Measure—as opposed to number.

Since this is so, the first proposition, which states that time is an accident, is true if what we intend by it is that time is not a substance. But if we intend by its being an accident that it exists outside the soul, it is false, since it depends on rest as on motion, and rest is the privation of motion, and privation has no existence. Therefore, it is necessary that time depend on our conceiving of a measure of continuousness, whether in motion or in rest, since in each we say great or small.

With respect to the second, which states that time is connected to motion, such that one cannot exist without the other, this is also false. For indeed time is found without motion, and is measured in rest, or in a mere conception of motion even when it is not actual.

With respect to the third, which states that time cannot be conceived other than with motion, this, too, is false for this same reason. But what we may say is that, since rest is the privation of motion, when we measure the time of rest, we conceive of motion. But, that time cannot be conceived of except as being with motion—that is not so.

With respect to the fourth, which states that whatever contains no motion is not subsumed under time, [it may be said that] the separate intellects,[161] although they do not move, are nevertheless subsumed under time, since it is confirmed that they came to be with time preceding them—since time does not require the existence of motion in actuality, but only the conception of the measure of motion or rest. The statement of R. Judah son of R. Simon, "This teaches that the order of time was prior to this,"[162] is therefore established in accordance with its literal meaning. And it is not necessary to go as far as the Rabbi's interpretation of the first verse of the Torah which says: "*bereishit* (בראשית) God created," according to which it means "by being the first principle." This would be a superfluous redundancy, for if He created it, He was the first principle and cause of it. And to say that the description of creation was for the sake solely of establishing that there was an initiator and cause—far be it from the Rabbi to hold this view, for he indeed spoke at length and expansively in refutation of Aristotle's proofs for anterior eternity, and innovated sufficient proofs to support belief in creation, as will be shown, God willing.

Chapter XII

INVESTIGATION of the sixteenth proposition, which states that anything that is not a body cannot be conceived in terms of number unless it is a force in a body, for those individual forces can be numbered along with the numbering of their matter or their subjects. For this reason, incorporeal entities, which are neither a body nor a force in a body, cannot be conceived at all in terms of number, except insofar as they are causes and effects.

It will indeed be seen that this proposition is also false. For souls that continue on after death must be conceived numerically, since the following disjunction is inescapable: either that which continues on after death is the substance of the intellectual soul, or it is the intellect acquired by the human being through his senses and powers. But if it is the substance of a soul, each of the souls will be individuated in accordance

---

[161] The separate intellects are the movers of the spheres.   [162] Gen. Rabbah 3: 7.

with what it grasps of the intelligibles or in accordance with its attachment to God, blessed be He; and what one soul grasps is indeed different from what another does. They will therefore be countable, just as individual substances are countable, since each of them has accidents by which it is individuated, even though their essence is one. Even if that which continues on [after death] is the acquired intellect, it is evident that the intelligibles acquired by one soul are indeed different from those acquired by another. Therefore, they are indeed countable without being causes and effects. To say that that which continues on [after death] is a predisposition that will become attached to the active intellect[163] and will become one with it and that therefore being counted is impossible for them [viz. incorporeal entities]—this view will be shown later to be an untenable view. Far be it from the Rabbi to hold this view. Rather, it will be seen that what the Rabbi intended in speaking of incorporeal entities is things that were always incorporeal and were at no time in the past forces in a body.

Chapter XIII

INVESTIGATION of the twenty-second proposition, which states that every body is necessarily composed of two elements and they are the two elements that constitute it and are its matter and its form.

This proposition was investigated in Chapter VII of this Part. According to Averroes this proposition is not a necessary one, for indeed there can be a body that is not composed of matter and form, namely, the celestial body. We have already said enough there with respect to this proposition.

Chapter XIV

INVESTIGATION of the twenty-third proposition, which states that for anything that is in potentiality, and has in its essence a certain possibility, it is indeed possible that at a certain time it will not exist in actuality.

Here, too, in accordance with what was said earlier in Chapter VII, a body may exist in actuality without having a specific form if it has in itself the possibility of receiving a form. And it is untenable that in itself[164] it not exist in actuality, for corporeality remains in it always. This observation is indeed relevant to the twenty-fourth and twenty-fifth propositions. With respect to the twenty-sixth, we shall investigate it in Book III, God willing, and we will show there that there is no doubt as to its being false.

Chapter XV

INVESTIGATION of the first proof that the Rabbi formulated to establish God's existence and unity, and His being neither a body nor a force in a body.

---

[163] The term "active intellect" (or "agent intellect") is notoriously difficult to define. For some, it is a transcendent entity, the last of the ten intellects to emanate from God. Others see it as something with which human intellect can become conjoined. It is the latter to which Crescas appears to be alluding here.

[164] Wolfson, like the Vienna manuscript, has בענינה; Fisher has בעינו; the Ferrara edition and the Florence manuscript have בעינה.

We shall investigate this from two perspectives, the first, the perspective of discrediting the premises needed to substantiate this proof; the second, granting the truth of the premises, asking whether this proof is decisive, as the Rabbi said.

With respect to the first, it will be proved easily, once we inspect the proofs one by one. When we inspect the first, we shall find that it requires propositions whose falseness has been shown to be possible. For it requires the first proposition; otherwise, it would be possible for the body that imparts motion to be infinite and to have infinite force. [It requires the second; otherwise, it would be possible for one body to be moved by another—ad infinitum. It requires the third; otherwise it would be possible for the movers to be infinite.[165]] It requires the eighth;[166] otherwise it would be possible for the mover to be an indivisible force in a body, like the soul and intellect. It would also require the twelfth; otherwise, it would be possible for the force of the body that causes motion to be infinite. It requires the sixteenth; otherwise it would be possible for number[167] to apply to incorporeal entities. It requires the twenty-sixth;[168] otherwise it would be possible for the mover to be a force distributed in a body, in which case its force would be finite, or possible that it have a force that is not distributed and its force finite. But, as the veracity of these propositions was discredited earlier, this proof is likewise discredited. The number of its refutations is the number of propositions the proof of whose veracity has been discredited. This is the first perspective.

Regarding the second, in which it is granted that the premises are true, I respond that this proof is still discredited on two grounds. One is that it is indeed possible that a mover be a force distributed in a body. For even if we concede the twelfth proposition, which states that any force that is distributed in a body is finite since the body is finite, nevertheless, the finiteness must be understood as finite in *strength*. For indeed it is possible for a finite force in a body to move a moving thing with a motion that is finite in strength though infinite in time—when the moving thing has no cause of fatigue and weakness, as was proved with respect to the celestial bodies. Moreover, it is indeed possible that their circular motion is natural to them, just as rectilinear motion is natural to the elements. Should one object that the natural motion of the elements applies only when they are out of their place but that rest is natural to them in their place, it is open to the responder to say that there is a difference between the elements and the celestial bodies in that, whereas rest is natural to the elements in their place, motion is natural to the celestial bodies in their place. And this is the first way in which the proof is discredited, namely, by showing that it is not proved of God that He is incorporeal.

---

[165] Fisher brackets these two sentences, found in both the Florence and Vienna manuscripts. They are indeed absent in the Ferrara edition.

[166] Fisher has the eleventh rather than the eighth. But the Ferrara edition, as well as the Florence and Vienna manuscripts, have the eighth. Similarly, Harvey (1998c: 69). (For further discussion, see Smilevitch, 448 n. 3.)

[167] Reading המנין with the Florence and Vienna manuscripts, rather than הממני with Fisher, since Proposition XVI concerns number. The Ferrara manuscript replaces the final letter with an apostrophe.

[168] Following the Florence manuscript and the Ferrara edition; Fisher has the twenty-seventh. The number is missing in the Vienna manuscript.

The second is that, even if we grant that it [viz. the mover] is incorporeal, I maintain that it is not proved of it that it is one, for if we grant the sixteenth proposition, that things that are not a body cannot be conceived as numbered unless they are causes and effects, it is evident that even if they had different relations, for example, if one thing were a cause of one effect, and another the cause of another effect, there is no doubt that, from the point of view of their different relations, number would be conceivable with respect to them. Thus it has not been established by this proof that one thing cannot be the cause of one sphere and another the cause of another sphere. And even more is this so considering that the possibility of other worlds was proved by us earlier, so that one could be the cause of one world and another the cause of another. And this is the second perspective from which the proof has been discredited. For it did not prove that God is one.

Chapter XVI

INVESTIGATION of the second proof that the Rabbi formulated concerning these three theses. We shall investigate this one as well from two perspectives.

From the first perspective, the second proof is one for which he uses the proposition that states that when we find something composed of two things, and one of them exists in isolation, the second one will of necessity exist in isolation. He in fact argued for this proposition by saying that if their existence requires that they be found together, as is the case with natural matter and form, it could not happen under any circumstances that the one would be found without the other. Let me say first that it is a sophism to regard this implication as necessary. For the [impossibility of the] existence of the one in isolation does not necessitate that their existence must be such that they can be found only together.[169] What it does compel is what must be the case solely with respect to one of them, that is, that *its* existence is not possible apart from the other. Moreover, even if the implication were true, the existence of the one would not compel the necessity of the existence of the other but only the possibility of its existence. But the implication is not true nor is the proposition true. For, once something completes the process of perfecting another thing, the fact is that the perfecter cannot exist without the existence of that which it perfects, but the perfected thing can exist without its perfecter. The case of the animal and the vegetative, for example, illustrates this point: anything animal is also vegetative,[170] but the vegetative might exist in isolation, even though the animal cannot be found by itself. Therefore it is evident that the proposition itself is false, and for this reason the proof too is discredited.[171]

---

[169] The manuscripts and editions differ on the precise formulation of this sentence. Fisher reasonably inserts המנעות (himane'ut; "the impossibility of") so: שלא יחיב [המנעות] מציאות האחד לבדו, and I follow him. For further discussion, see Smilevitch 452 n. 2.

[170] The vegetative includes the life-functions of nutrition and growth, but not the higher functions of sense-perception and emotion, or the still higher ones of morality and rationality.

[171] Crescas contends that although it is true that there can be a composite of A and B such that A cannot exist apart from B, it does not follow that B cannot exist apart from A. Although it is true that when B completes A's process of becoming perfected, B cannot exist without A, but A can exist—indeed A has existed—without B. Thus matter can exist without the particular form that completes it before the process of completion has run its course. The example Crescas offers is that of animal as the completion of something vegetative. Although anything animal is composite, containing both the animal and the

From the second perspective, even if we grant that this proposition is true, it does not compel the existence of a mover that does not move even accidentally. For there can be a mover that is also moved, as well as a thing that is moved which is also a mover but only accidentally. For the last moved thing causes both the motive force and the corporeal accidents that are attached to it to move accidentally. Therefore there necessarily exists a mover that is moved only accidentally. Hence it is possible for there to be a force in a body that is a mover essentially but is moved accidentally. And therefore this proof does not establish the mover's incorporeality.[172]

Chapter XVII

INVESTIGATION of the third proof that the Rabbi formulated concerning these theses. We shall investigate this one as well from two perspectives.

From the first perspective, when we inspect this proof carefully we find that the Rabbi used the third proposition in it, for otherwise it would be possible to seek for each cause its cause, ad infinitum. Now we have already shown the possibility of such a thing. At the same time he also requires the twenty-sixth proposition, for otherwise it would be possible for there to be a future passing-away.[173] The falsity of this [proposition] will be indeed proved below, God willing. This is the first perspective.

From the second perspective, even if we grant that this proposition is true, I maintain that the proof does not yield the truth of the theses. For the necessity that he attributed to the disjunction is not true, since even if all existents were subject to coming-to-be and passing-away, and it were possible for each of them to pass away, it would still not be necessary that they all pass away together, but rather it could happen that as one comes another would go. If the attributed necessity were true, it would necessarily be the case that *we* do not exist. In the species human being in general, passing-away is possible for each human being, and it would thus be necessary that all pass away. Therefore, it is indeed possible that all existents are subject to coming-to-be and passing-away. The proof is discredited from this perspective, even if we grant that the propositions that he used, namely, the third and twenty-sixth, are true.

This [viz. that the proof is discredited even if we grant the truth of the propositions on which it relies] can be seen indeed from another perspective as well. For even if we grant that there is one existent that neither comes to be nor passes away, it still

---

vegetative, which the animal perfects, and although the animal therefore cannot exist without the vegetative, nevertheless the vegetative can exist in isolation; it need not be united with the animal.

[172] Crescas argues that even if matter, which is at the lowest level of the chain of motion, is moved but does not cause motion, it does not follow that there must be something that causes motion but is not moved (and so is incorporeal). Because, just as matter is moved essentially but causes motion (in its motive force and in its accidents) accidentally, there can be something that causes motion essentially but is moved accidentally. Such a thing could be a force in a body and hence not incorporeal.

[173] Fisher and the Ferrara edition have: שאם לא, היה אפשרי המציאות בעתיד. The Florence and Vienna manuscripts have, more plausibly, שאם לא, היה אפשרי הפסד המציאות בעתיד. I follow the manuscripts here. Maimonides' twenty-sixth proposition takes the universe's eternity to be necessary, thus precluding its passing away. Without this proposition, on Fisher's reading, the world's posterior eternity is a possible—though not a necessary—thing. On the manuscript reading, it is the world's passing-away which is said to be possible.

does not follow necessarily that it has necessary existence in itself, for if it derives necessary existence from its cause, it will also be absolutely impossible for it to pass away,[174] since its cause has necessary existence in itself. Therefore, even if we grant that a composite does not exist necessarily in respect of itself, since composition is its cause—why, if only I knew, if this composite is a necessary existent, such that passing-away is impossible for it, and if it is the case that this composite does not cease and will never cease, and that nonexistence is therefore precluded for it, could it not be a prime mover? From this perspective it is indeed not proved that the mover must be incorporeal, although a body is necessarily composite, as he understood.[175]

Chapter XVIII

INVESTIGATION of the fourth proof that the Rabbi formulated concerning these theses. We shall investigate this one as well from two perspectives.

From the first perspective, if we inspect this proof carefully we find that the Rabbi used his third proposition in it, for otherwise the actualizing agent would have potentiality to be actualized, and so on ad infinitum. And he requires the sixteenth proposition, for without it, there is no necessity that the agent be one. And similarly he requires the twenty-third proposition, for without it the proof would be compelled to arrive [in some other way] at an existent who is an actualizer in actuality and contains no possibility.[176] The twenty-fourth proposition would be needed as well, for otherwise it would be possible for the actualizer in actuality to be a body. The possibility that these are false has already been shown previously. This is the first perspective.

From the second perspective, if we grant that the proposition is true, it still will not be evident that the agent is one. For they will differ from one another, for one will be a cause for one thing, and another a cause for another. The implication that he posited, that if there were two the one would necessarily be composite, was not shown to be impossible, once passing-away was eliminated and it was seen that this composite neither ceases to be nor will ever cease to be so, having no prior cause.[177]

---

[174] It seems that critical words are missing in Fisher's text. Fisher has: הנה לא יתחיב שיהיה מחויב בשום פנים ; the manuscripts have: הנה לא יתחיב שיהיה מחויב המציאות בבחינת עצמו, זה שכאשר הוא מחויב המציאות בבחינת סבתו הנה א"א בו ההפסד בשום פנים.

[175] Crescas sees no reason why a body—that is, something composite—could not have necessary existence, if not in respect of itself (since composition is its cause), then in respect of its cause. And any being that has necessary existence, one for which nonexistence is impossible, seems a good candidate for a prime mover. And so, there is not sufficient proof that God, qua prime mover, could not be corporeal.

[176] The text reads: "for without it he will necessarily arrive at an existent that actualizes in actuality and contains no potentiality." As this cannot be Crescas's intent, I take him to be saying that the Rabbi would have to find *some other way* to arrive at the fully actualized actualizer. The alternative is to insert a "not," as Smilevitch does, so: "*sinon ce process [n']aboutit [pas] nécessairement à un être qui soit un agent [toujours] en acte...*" (458).

[177] The reasoning here might appear to be problematic, inasmuch as it seems as if Crescas in the previous chapter allowed that a prior cause is needed to effect composition. In admitting, however, that a composite is caused, Crescas concedes no more than that it is caused by composition (לפי שסבתו ההרכבה); he does not concede that a distinct prior cause is required. As is evident in the next chapter, Chapter XIX, Crescas believes—and is satisfied that he has already shown—that a composite does not require a "combiner."

Chapter XIX

INVESTIGATION of the fifth proof that the Rabbi formulated concerning these theses. We shall investigate this one as well from two perspectives.

From the first perspective, if we inspect it carefully we find that the Rabbi used the third proposition in it; otherwise, it would be possible for there to be a combiner for the combiner, ad infinitum. He thus also requires the fifteenth proposition, for without it, even if something is subject to time, it would not necessarily have to cease to exist. Similarly, he needs to use the twenty-sixth proposition, even though it was not mentioned there, because, according to the [competing] belief in creation, the cause, prior to creation, was not causing motion, and with this view, the absurdities he mentioned would not occur. Therefore, this proof is evidently disqualified. This is the first perspective.

From the second perspective, even if we grant that these propositions are true, this proof does not yield truth, for several reasons. First, even if we grant that this existent [viz. the universe] is one individual, and that it is impossible that there be one [divinity] involved with one part and another with another—even if this impossibility has not been shown, for it is indeed possible for each to know what is needed by the other[178]—even if we grant this, it is still not impossible that the one would be involved in one world, for it is as one individual in its totality, and another with another world. Moreover, the nature of the disjunction he posited is such that it is not necessitated. For it remains possible that the one will act but the other will not act at all. And so it was easily proved previously that a composite does not require a combiner, for it is possible for a composite to have necessary existence such that it does not cease and will never cease.

Chapter XX

INVESTIGATION of the sixth proof, common both to those who believe in anterior eternity and to us, the congregation of believers in creation, that the Rabbi formulated concerning these theses. We shall investigate this one as well from two perspectives.

For this proof the Rabbi used the first proposition; otherwise it would be possible for a mover that is a body to produce infinite motion. He similarly requires the eighth proposition; for otherwise it would be possible for it to be a force in a body that need not cease to exist. He also needs the twelfth; otherwise, it would indeed be possible, even for a finite body that causes motion, to produce motion that is infinite. Yet the truth of these was nullified. This is the first perspective.

From the second perspective, even if we grant that these propositions are true, the only thing that follows necessarily from the fact that a body is finite is that it cannot produce motion infinite in strength, as was explained previously. It is indeed possible, however, for it to produce motion finite in strength but infinite in time, so long as the body is not subject to fatigue and weakness. All the more will this be the case if circular motion is natural to it, as we mentioned. Moreover, it does not follow

---

[178] In other words, coordination among causes is possible.

necessarily from the disjunction[179] that, if the mover is subject to coming-to-be and passing-away, it will come to be after having not existed such that it would require a bringer-into-existence. For it is indeed possible that there be continuous coming-to-be and passing-away, as is the case with individuals in a species. Therefore what he presented as following necessarily does not in fact follow necessarily.

This is the totality of what we saw fit to say in our concise manner by way of response to the Rabbi's proofs. It is evident that the number of responses from the first perspective parallels the number of propositions that we mentioned that the Rabbi used. These are in addition to the responses from the second perspective in which we granted the truth of those propositions. What this condition[180] of confusion teaches is that that which provides the truth with respect to these theses has not to this day been fully grasped by recourse to the philosophers. Indeed, the only thing that illuminates all of these deep difficulties is the Torah. This is what we intended to show in this second part. Praise is to God alone, who is exalted above all blessing and praise.

Part III

AN exposition of these root-principles in accordance with what the Torah has affirmed, and of the way in which we arrived at our knowledge of them. And since there are three root-principles, and there are two investigations into each in what follows, we have divided this Part into six chapters.

Chapter I

EXPOSITION of the first root-principle, which is the existence of God, may He be blessed.

Although we have already dealt briefly with the clarification of this proposition and with the way in which we arrived at it, it is nevertheless unthinkable that we not expand somewhat our discussion of it. For there is benefit in it, as is obvious, inasmuch as disputes have arisen among scholars with respect to it.

Let me say that the content of this assertion will become clear as its terms are clarified, and as the relationship of one term to the other is clarified. Yet since it is certain that the relationship in this assertion is one of affirmation, for in our stating, "God exists," we are in effect affirming existence with respect to Him, all that remains in clarifying this assertion is the clarification of the terms alone. The term that is the *subject* of this assertion, namely God, is something on which all scholars and the writings of the Torah agree: He is concealed to the highest degree of concealment, such that it is impossible for another to grasp His quiddity in itself. Indeed the

---

[179] The disjunction referred to is: the sphere either is or is not subject to coming-to-be and passing-away. Maimonides assumes that if it is, it would have to be brought into existence after nonexistence—by God.

[180] Ferrara has מצמ where Fisher has מצב. The translation of the Ferrara version would be: "This is what is indicated from the perspective of the confusion..." Both the Florence and Vienna manuscripts have שהממסיר instead of מצב or מצמ. The translation would then read: "This is something that teaches that what removes the confusion and provides the truth with respect to these theses has not to this day been fully grasped by recourse to the philosophers."

investigators have striven to establish a proof for this, as the Rabbi noted in Part I of the *Guide*, in the chapter in which he explained that the intellect and the intellected are one thing. And in this connection he said that God denied to Moses this apprehension when Moses asked of Him: "Show me, please, Your glory,"[181] by which he meant that God should make known to him the reality of His essence and its true nature. What must be explained, however, is how it is that what was clear to each of the philosophizers regarding this impossibility was not clear to the master of the prophets, who, according to the Torah's testimony reached the highest level, exceeding that of all other prophets. How could he require a large measure of basic instruction in a divine science concerning that which is obvious, and about which the Rabbi could expound at length in his book? What the Rabbi therefore had to say by way of resolution is that these requests by Moses were in visions of prophecy, and it is not implausible that something that had become evident to a prophet earlier by way of proof is subsequently made known to him in a vision of prophecy, in a dialogue, or in a question-and-answer format. Yet it is inescapable according to this that Moses used some sort of riddle [in making his request]. This, however, is the opposite of the commentators' consensus, and of what seems to be the case from the verses in Scripture: "Mouth to mouth I spoke with him";[182] "And the Lord spoke to Moses face to face, as a man speaks to his companion";[183] and many others of this sort. We have an explanation, which you will hear in what is to come, God willing. Moses never asked to apprehend the divine quiddity. And what is written [in the Torah] does not attribute or assign to the master of the prophets, God forbid, the folly of making a request in allegories or riddles, since the impossibility of apprehending the divine essence is obvious to and recognized by even philosophical novices. It is apparently for this reason that the Men of the Great Assembly instituted a formula for benedictions in language that is at once in the second person and in the third.[184] For His existence is evident and known, but His essence is concealed to the highest degree of concealment. Now, since this is quite evident with respect to the subject-term of this proposition, namely, God, we shall not express anything at this point other than what is signified by our saying "the cause of the totality of existents." This is sufficient for the clarification of this term.

With respect to the predicate-term in this proposition, which is our saying God *exists*: since a dispute arose in connection with this among the commentators on Aristotle's works, we must address it at length, inasmuch as it is a most important root-principle, the pillar and essential first principle of all. Indeed, Avicenna and al-Ghazali, as well as the Rabbi, who followed them, held that existence is distinct from quiddity, and that it is an accident that occurs in it. Averroes and some of the later thinkers held that existence is not something distinct from quiddity. Therefore, we must explain each of the views of these commentators, so as to determine what needs to be understood by this term in this proposition.

---

[181] Exod. 33: 18. [182] Num. 12: 8. [183] Exod. 33: 11.
[184] The terms נמצא (*nimtza*) and נסתר (*nistar*) indicate, respectively, the second and third person. The standard benediction-formula is: "Blessed are You [in the second person], O Lord, who [in the third person]..."

According to the view of Averroes, there is no doubt that since God's existence and His quiddity are one, and since His quiddity is different from any other quiddity to the highest degree of difference, it follows that His existence is also different from any other existence to the highest degree of difference. Therefore it is necessary that the term "exists" be applied to God, may He be blessed, and to things other than God, only with absolute equivocation, and without any sort of analogy.[185] This is so because the various kinds of analogy allow some relation, with the difference [between the analogous terms] being a matter of priority and posteriority.[186] But since the quiddity of God has no relation whatsoever to any other quiddity, it follows necessarily that the term "exists" as it applies to Him and to anything else is absolutely equivocal. This is all the more certainly the view of the Rabbi, for whom, since all existents have accidental existence, it is necessary that the term "exists" apply to God, may He be blessed, [and to anything else] absolutely equivocally and without any sort of analogy. For since it is evident that no accidents apply to God, may He be blessed, it is necessary that His existence be no different from His quiddity. Therefore, it is necessary that His existence differ to the utmost, just as His quiddity and reality do, from that of anything else. It is evident therefore, that, according to the view of all, the term "exists" is predicated absolutely equivocally of God and all other existents. This is what the Rabbi wrote explicitly, for even though the commentators differed regarding the term "exists" as it applies to other existents, they surely agree with respect to "exists" as predicated of God, may He be blessed, that existence is not something extrinsic [to His quiddity].

Now, if only I could fathom what this term signifies when it is applied to God, may He be blessed. For when we say, "God exists," such that the term "exists" is applied to something whose existence is not extrinsic, it is as if we had said, "God is God." This difficulty will indeed befall all existents according to the view of Averroes and his followers, for whom existence is nothing but quiddity: when we say, "the man exists" or "the whiteness exists," then, according to his statements, it is as if we had said, "the man is man" or "the whiteness is whiteness." Even if one should say in this regard that this is but a partial definition, the redundancy remains. For when we say "man," what is immediately understood by this term is: animal, rational, existent. Therefore our saying "man" is tantamount to our saying "the rational existent animal."[187]

By the same token, a not inconsiderable difficulty will befall the view of one who says that the existence of the other existents is distinct from their quiddity and is but an accident that occurs in it. For if existence is merely an accident, then it is necessary that it be found in a substratum, in which case the existence will have existence. If this second existence is also an accident, it too will be found in a substratum, and it too will require a substratum, and it will have yet a further existence. And so on, ad infinitum. Furthermore, existence would take the guise of form to matter, inasmuch as the substratum, according to their statements, will be nonexistent without this

---

[185] The term ספוק (*sippuq*) suggests less than full-fledged synonymy, but also less than full-fledged homonymy.

[186] For an attribute to apply to two entities by priority and posteriority is for it to belong fully and absolutely to the superior entity, but to belong, too, albeit in an inferior and derivative way, to the lesser one.

[187] If existence were quiddity, then it would be tautologous to say "God exists."

accident. If this accident confers existence and persistence on the substance, then it would necessarily be prior to the substratum in the determination of the substance, since form takes precedence over matter in the determination of a substance, as was explained in Book I of the *Physics*. Yet it was already conceded that, with respect to accidents, this reversal [in which an accident takes precedence in determining a substance] is untenable. Since it follows necessarily from this that existence is not an accident of the existent, and since the previous difficulty necessitated that it not be the quiddity itself, what then is existence?[188] If only I knew.

That it is absurd for existence to be an accident of quiddity may now be seen to be both true and necessary. It is therefore necessary that existence be either the essence of the quiddity, or essential to it. Since it has been proved that it is not the essence of the quiddity, as is evident from the first of the previous difficulties, the only remaining possibility is that it is essential to the quiddity. For among the conditions of quiddity is that it be outside the mind; as it might be said, by way of example, that the quiddity of man is his animality and rationality, and that it is among the conditions of quiddity that these exist outside the mind. Therefore, there is a single sense of existence common to all other existents [i.e. all existents other than God], especially when the accidents are not hierarchically related to one another.[189] Of the existence of substance and accidents, however, one may speak only by way of analogy. Since existence is outside the mind, it may be applied with priority to substance but only by posteriority to accidents. But the all-inclusive signification [of "exists"] is that anything to which it applies is not nonexistent. It is in this sense that existence is said primarily of God and secondarily of other existents. It is therefore evident that "exists" cannot be predicated of Him and of the other existents with absolute equivocation but rather by a kind of analogy.[190] Thus have this term and this proposition been clarified in accordance with what we said earlier in our concise manner.

Chapter II

THE way in which we arrived at our knowledge of this root-principle.

According to what was said in the third proposition, and in Part II Chapter III of this Book, regardless of whether causes and effects are finite or infinite, there is no escaping that there is a cause for their totality. For if they were all effects, they would have only possible existence in respect of themselves and would require a determiner to determine their existence over their nonexistence. It is God, may He be blessed, who is the cause of all of them, the cause that determines their existence. His existence has thus been proved beyond any doubt. Although according to the intent

---

[188] With quiddity disqualified as what is meant by "exists," Crescas looks to the possibility that "exists" is an accident of the substance. But, says Crescas, accidents are not that which determines a substance, yet would we not expect "exists" to be determinative?

[189] When things are on the same ontological level, "exists" applies to them in the same way. A horse, a chair, a flower, for example: all of these exist in the same sense.

[190] "Exists" applies to all existent things in the negative sense of "is not nonexistent." And so there cannot be absolute equivocation in using the term with respect both to God and to other things. Nevertheless, it applies more fully and more perfectly to God than to other things. It is most accurate, therefore, to say that "exists" applies to God and to other things by priority and posteriority.

of this proposition, a cause of the totality of existents itself exists, nevertheless, even if we concede the existence of a first cause for the effects that follow, how can we arrive at His being the single cause for all existents? This is what we shall clarify in the second root-principle. What we intended in this chapter has now been established.[191]

Chapter III

EXPOSITION of the second root-principle, namely, that God is one.

Because the relation of predicate to subject in this proposition is also a relation of affirmation, and the subject of all three propositions is the same, namely, God, may He be blessed, and since we have already spoken of this previously, what remains for us to clarify in this root-principle is the term that is the predicate—that is, our saying "one." About this the commentators have been divided: Avicenna and al-Ghazali, as well as the Rabbi, who followed them, held that unity in the substance of a thing is distinct from its quiddity,[192] and is something added to it and an accident that occurs in it. Averroes held that unity is not distinct from quiddity and is subject to the same rule as existence. It appears to us that unity is neither the essence of quiddity nor something added to it, but is an essential aspect of anything that exists in actuality, and is a rational inference from the absence of multiplicity in it. For if unity were the essence of quiddity, our saying it with respect to a certain substance, for example, "the man is one," would be tantamount to our saying "the man is man." As for its being a part of its definition, we have already dealt with this with respect to existence, and it adds nothing to our understanding of the matter. Indeed the sense of "one" is universally known: it signifies the absence of multiplicity. Were we to say that unity, insofar as it signifies the absence of multiplicity, is the quiddity in a substance described as one, it would follow necessarily for all substances described as one that their quiddity is one. It is therefore evident that unity is not the essence of quiddity. It is also evident that it is not an accident in it. Since form is more truly determinative of a substance, conferring existence on the existent and delimitation and differentiation in actuality, it follows that unity and existence and delimitedness are not distinct from it. It is therefore evident that unity is not an accident, and not something added to a substance, but something essential in every actual and delimited existent, and a rational inference from the absence of multiplicity in it.

Now that this has been established, since unity is essential to every actual existent, it is evident that the existent whose existence precedes all other existents, and who is forever in actuality, is more truly and more primordially designated one than is anything else. Insofar as unity defines and distinguishes an existent, it is evident that the existent who is at the highest degree of difference from all existents, even if He is not subject to limit, is more truly called one than is anything else, since "one" is applied to an existent to distinguish it from another, and not insofar as the existent is limited to a place. And when it is proved as well that the Blessed One is at the highest degree of simplicity and of absence of multiplicity, it will be seen from this

---

[191] For further discussion, see Translator's Introduction n. 5.
[192] According to this view, whether a thing is one in number is different from what the thing is.

aspect as well that He is, as compared to anything else, more truly and more preeminently called one.

The Rabbi of the *Guide* indeed kept positive attributes away from God, may He be blessed, to a very great extent and, in particular, those attributes that might apply from any of four perspectives: those that describe Him by definition; or by partial definition; or by something extrinsic [to His essence], for all this is impossible with respect to Him; or by relation to something else. Since the species of relation is not the essence of the thing, and is not in the essence of the thing as quality is, it would seem at first glance that these would be permitted with respect to the Creator, may He be blessed; but this is not the Rabbi's view. [That there is no relation] is evident with respect to some things: for example, it is evident that there is no relation between Him and place; and no relation between Him and time, since time is an accident consequent upon motion, and motion applies to corporeal things, and God is not a body.[193] There is also no correlation between Him and the existents, for it is a peculiarity of correlated things that they have reciprocal relations, yet since God has necessary existence and everything else only possible existence, there can be no correlation—no relation at all—between them. And there is no relation except between two things of the same species, and certainly not between things that belong to two distinct genera and do not even share a genus, as, for example, wisdom and sweetness do, insofar as both belong to the genus of quality. How, then, could there be any relation between God and anything else, if the difference between them is one of very existence? Therefore, no affirmative attribute is permitted with respect to Him, for it would lead to one of the four [unacceptable] things: to corporeality; to being acted upon and to change; to privation, as when something in Him is not in actuality but will come to be in actuality; or to some likeness to something in His creatures, for likeness is a kind of relation, and where there is no relation there can be no likeness. As it is said: "And to whom will you liken Me that I will be his equal?";[194] "And to whom will you liken God?";[195] "there is none like You."[196]

He went even further, for existence and unity cannot be predicated of God [and of other things] other than equivocally, as we previously explained. And so, too, anterior eternity. In the end, no attribution is permitted with respect to Him other than an attribute of something in action, and not even an attribute of the action in the essence of the agent. And multiplicity is only in the actions that He performed, for if one performs this and does that, this would not necessitate change or multiplicity in the essence of the agent, but the multiplicity would be confined to the acts alone. Therefore, the only essential attributes permitted with respect to God are negative ones, since they render unique that which is described. Anyone who increases negative attributes increases specificity,[197] and in this way the ranks of the perfect ones are differentiated. Superiority among the apprehenders rests indeed on this: that the negation of a thing with respect to God is evident to some but not evident to others—not that some [but not others] apprehend something positive in God.

---

[193] Crescas is here presenting Maimonides' view of time—not his own view. The latter is found in l. ii. 11.
[194] Isa. 40: 25.   [195] Isa. 40: 18.   [196] Jer. 10: 6.
[197] In the case of negative attributes, with each additional instance of saying, "God is not this," God becomes increasingly differentiated from all other things and more particularized.

For if we were to affirm of God any perfection among the perfections that apply to something other than Him, there would then be a relation between Him and something else. In any event, if we affirm something of Him, He will have that which we have affirmed of Him, and He would be subject to composition, which is impossible with respect to the necessary existent, as was explained in the twenty-first proposition, which states that anything composed of two things is not a necessary existent.

[According to Maimonides,] once this became well known, it became established among the Sages that the apprehension of God is impossible for anyone, and that no one would know what He is but He himself. And therefore silence in praising Him became necessary, as the Psalmist says: "To You is silence praise."[198] And as he furthermore says: "Speak in your heart upon your bed, and be silent. *Selah*."[199] And the Rabbi was supported in this by one passage in *Berakhot*. They said: "Someone who came into the presence of R. Ḥanina said [in his prayer]: 'God the great, the valiant, the terrible, the mighty, the strong, the tremendous, the powerful.' R. Ḥanina said to him: 'Have you finished all the praises of your Master? Now, even the three [praises] that we say we could not have said had not Moses our Teacher said them and had not the Men of the Great Assembly instituted them in the liturgy, yet you come and say [all these]! To what may this be compared? To a flesh-and-blood king who has thousands of gold dinars and is praised for having silver ones; is this not an insult to him?'"[200] Now since R. Ḥanina silenced this man, preventing him from multiplying attributes, the Rabbi explained that the three [attributes] that we are permitted to say are permitted on two grounds: the first, that Moses said them; and the second, that the prophets instituted them in the liturgy; otherwise, we would not be permitted to say them except in reading the Torah. He further explained, by way of a parable, that the praises we say are not of the species of praises that apply to Him. For he [viz. R. Ḥanina] did not say: "And they praised him for having one hundred gold [dinars]."[201] And so he [viz. R. Ḥanina] concluded by saying, "Is this not an insult to him?" From all this it is evident and apparent [according to Maimonides] that affirmative attributes are forbidden, and are precluded with respect to God. Indeed they are offensive and shameful on the part of anyone who utters them even if he does so unawares. This is the gist of what emerges from the words of the Rabbi of the *Guide*, although he spoke about it at length and extensively.

It is impossible for us to refrain from commenting on doubts raised by what he said. We shall then explain that the things he regarded as following necessarily are not necessary.

First, once the attributes that describe God in relation to other things and which imply privation are precluded with respect to Him—for example, that there is in Him something that is not currently in actuality but then comes to be in actuality—how

---

[198] Ps. 65: 2. [199] Ps. 4: 4. [200] BT *Berakhot* 33b.
[201] In *Guide* I. 54 Maimonides applauds R. Ḥanina's parable for recognizing that the insult lies in praising the king for having silver when he had gold (a qualitative difference), rather than in praising the king for having 100 gold dinars when he had thousands (a mere quantitative difference). The difference between God and everything else is certainly not merely one of quantity. For Maimonides, to think God literally does or has anything that others do is to commit a category mistake.

could Maimonides permit the kind of attribute that describes a thing in action, saying, for example, that He acted, made, or created, insofar as these imply privation, for prior to the acting or the making or the creating He was in potentiality and only afterwards came to be in actuality?

Second, if the inference Maimonides drew were true, namely, that affirmative attributes are precluded with respect to Him inasmuch as they entail composition which is impossible with respect to something that is necessarily existent, there would be no superiority in the apprehension of the perfect ones over that of philosophical novices. His notion that this difficulty could be eliminated by [the difference in their abilities to] increase negations is inadequate. For it is evident upon minimal reflection that apprehension of the divine essence is impossible. Also, its having been established that His existence is necessary, [it is easily seen that] it is necessary that He not be described by any affirmative attributes inasmuch as these entail composition which is precluded with respect to Him. It follows then that anyone who apprehends that every attribute, no matter of what kind, is impossible with respect to God insofar as He is a necessary existent, and that He has nothing but His essence which is at the height of inconceivability, indeed apprehends all that the master of the prophets has apprehended. Knowing the details of the attributes that are impossible with respect to Him will not improve upon the general knowledge that the philosophical novice has, for his knowledge is demonstrative knowledge, and the proof regarding all the attributes is essentially the same. Therefore, the essence of everyone's apprehension [of God] is the same in kind: what one cannot apprehend of God is His essence alone, and this essence is what the master of the prophets and the other prophets could not apprehend.

Third, if this proof determines the impossibility of essential attributes with respect to God, it is highly improbable that Moses, in saying, "Show me, please..." would have been requesting, whether in a vision or in a waking state, to have that essence made known to him, as we hinted in Chapter I of this Part.

Fourth,[202] it is known and agreed on by all those whose words have reached us, that the great and explicit name of God, namely, the Tetragrammaton, which was pronounced in the Temple the way it is written, and in outside environs using a substitute appellation, is His proper name, and that all His other names derive from His actions. And so the Rabbi wrote explicitly that the reason the Tetragrammaton is called "the explicit name" is that it indicates God clearly and without equivocation, and it instructs specifically that there is no association between Him and anything else. Yet once knowledge of His essence is excluded, it is impossible for this name to signify His essence. It is likewise impossible that it signify an essential attribute, for it has been proved that it is impossible for Him to have essential attributes. Therefore, there is nothing for this name to signify. It appears that he was indeed vexed by this problem, for this is what he said, verbatim: "It is possible that the name signified, in a language of which we have but little that remains today, and in accordance with how it should be read, the necessity of His existence."[203] Why, if only I knew, would the Rabbis

---

[202] The Florence and Vienna manuscripts designate this a fourth ground rather than a continuation of the third. The Ferrara edition and Fisher treat it as a continuation of the third.

[203] See *Guide* I. 61.

oppose teaching this meaning more frequently than once in seven years,[204] when it is indeed fitting that this be known even to the masses, since the matter of the necessity of His existence is not something about which the people should be ignorant? Even understanding the proof for this is not beyond their reach, such that it is not necessary to conceal this secret, but rather it is fitting that it be publicized throughout the congregation of Israel. Even more astonishing is his having said that the name consisting of twelve letters is lesser in sanctity than the name consisting of four letters, and that it [viz. the twelve-letter name] indicates something more particular to God than the name of *alef-dalet*,[205] and that they used to use that name the way we use the name *alef-dalet*. In this way he in effect affirmed an essential attribute, for if what this [twelve-letter name] involved was simply a multiplicity of negations, it would not have required concealment. Furthermore, his saying that they used to pronounce [the twelve-letter name in the Temple] does not seem correct. For we maintain this principle: "In the Temple, as it was written."[206] But since the twelve-letter name consists of the Tetragrammaton repeated three times with different vocalizations, as is relayed in the book *Bahir*,[207] then, because of the requirement to conceal the explicit name with its unique vocalization, the priests would obscure it via their brothers' singing of the twelve-letter name, in order to pronounce it as it is written but without its explicit vocalization.[208] They drowned it out in order to conceal its vocalization from the masses, so that they not use it in their speech in their frivolous quotidian conversation. And this is because of the importance of the name. However this might be, there is nothing in the signification of the name that is a negative signification. And therefore, as it seems, the affirmative attributes are not excluded.

One must also wonder how Maimonides concluded that there is no correlation between God and any of His creatures on the grounds that correlatives are reciprocally related. It is inescapable that God is a cause and first principle, yet a cause is a cause of an effect, and a first principle is a first principle to that to which it is a first principle. Therefore it is evident that from this perspective there indeed is a relation between Him and His creatures. He further maintained that there is no relation between Him and time, since time is an accident of motion, and motion is among the accidents that apply only to bodies. Yet even if we grant this, then, if time is eternal, there is a relation and similarity between Him and time in their shared eternality. And even more is this the case in light of what became evident from what we said in the second Part, namely, that the proposition that maintains that time is an accident consequent upon motion is false. And so, from all these perspectives it

---

[204] BT *Kiddushin* 71a; *Hilkhot Tefilah* 14: 10; *Guide* I. 62.

[205] A shortened version of this substitute for the Tetragrammaton: *alef-dalet-nun-yod*.

[206] *Sotah* 7: 6. In *Guide* I. 62 Maimonides quotes BT *Yoma* 39b (also BT *Menaḥot* 109b), which says that there came a time after the death of Simeon the Just, when the Tetragrammaton was no longer pronounced in the Temple; Maimonides asserts that the priests pronounced the twelve-letter name in its place.

[207] Fr. 107. *Sefer Habahir*, or *Book of Brightness*, is an anonymous mystical work (traditionally, though incorrectly) attributed to a 1st-century rabbinic Sage Neḥunya ben Hakkanah, because it begins, "R. Neḥunya ben Hakkanah said." It is also known as the *Midrash of Rabbi Neḥunya ben Hakkanah*.

[208] Rather than replacing the Tetragrammaton with a substitute name consisting of different letters, the four letters of the Tetragrammaton as written would be variously vocalized.

appears that attributes by which God is described in relation to something else are not precluded with respect to Him.

What remains for us to explain is how it can be that the conclusion he derived from the arguments on which he relied is not necessitated—whether from the impossibility of any likeness, as the biblical verses attest; or if we draw support from the statement of R. Ḥanina; or because of the impossibility of composition in a necessary existent, which serves for him as the decisive proof of the impossibility of attributes.

We say that there is no doubt concerning the necessity of dismissing all likeness between Him, may He be blessed, and His creatures. For even if the perfections [in God and His creatures], as, for example, knowledge or power, belong to one genus, nevertheless, since there is an enormous difference between God and His creatures, whether that between necessary existence and possible, or that between finitude and infinity, the distance between them is great enough to preclude any likeness between them. And even if a broader use of language allows the term "likeness" to apply to them, still, insofar as they are at the greatest distance from one another from these two perspectives, it is fitting that likeness be excluded. And so it is written: "To whom will you liken Me, that I will be his equal?"[209] This indicates that even if the perfections belong to the same genus, nevertheless, the impossibility of equality between them and its preclusion is established, for from no conceivable perspective is there anything equal to Him to which He can be likened. As it is said: "To whom then will you liken God, and what likeness will you measure to Him?"[210] It is thus clear that the likeness that is excluded with respect to Him is a likeness that has some measure, and since the likeness between Him and His creatures has no measure, inasmuch as there is no relation and measure between the infinite and the finite, it is impossible to measure a likeness to Him. But it would seem that a likeness that has no measure is not impossible.

When we look more closely into the statement by R. Ḥanina we will see that it indicates just what we have said. The Rabbi based his view on: "Have you finished all the praises of your Master?" Yet it is most evident that the reason R. Ḥanina silenced the prayer-leader was the excessiveness of his multiplication of praises. Because he could not recount them all, it was not fitting that he multiply praises. For their multiplication and the descent into their details indicated that his intent was to praise God with them. Therefore it would appear to those who heard that had he known further praises he would not have refrained from uttering them. Therefore one could infer insult from this praise, inasmuch as it indicates that there are no other praises that apply to Him. For this reason we would not permit ourselves to say them [viz. the three standardized praises] in prayer—insofar as the number of attributes [that we say] is three, which is the first number of plurality[211]—had the Men of the Great Assembly not instituted them in the liturgy and had Moses not uttered them. For according to our principle that, "One ought always first arrange his praise of the Holy

---

[209] Isa. 40: 25.   [210] Isa. 40: 18.
[211] By simply entering the realm of plurality we appear to indicate that there is a certain finite number of praises that apply to God.

One Blessed Be He and then supplicate,"[212] it is indeed fitting that the strictures with respect to the multiplying of praises apply when the arrangement [of praises] is mandatory, for there would be in that case, as is obvious, the danger of its appearing that one is arranging [before supplication] all the praises. Therefore he said: "The Men of the Great Assembly came and instituted it in the liturgy." For it is certain that once Moses uttered them he in effect permitted them, but the entire danger lies in arranging praises when they are mandatory, for in this case the multiplication of praises suggests that one is recounting all or most of them.[213] There is no danger, however, in the praises themselves, for it suffices for us that the master of the prophets uttered them. It indeed seems too that the many praises uttered by the person who came into the presence of R. Ḥanina also appear in various places in Scripture. But the danger lies in multiplying them in one place, and even more so in a place where arranging praise is mandated. Therefore he [viz. R. Ḥanina] added the matter of the permission by the Men of the Great Assembly. And indeed he said: "and they praise him for having silver ones," for insofar as the praise is such that it appears that he is praising him [viz. the king] for how much money he has, that is an insult to him. It is true that he said, "silver ones" rather than "one hundred gold ones," but that is because of the two differences that we noted between praises of God and praises of anyone else. First, there is the difference between one who has necessary existence and one who has possible existence, and in this sense they are not really from the same species. And, second, because all His praises are infinite in excellence and the praises of others finite. Therefore there were these two differences in the parable. For, once it appeared that he was limiting something that is infinite in number, it was appropriate to suspect him of limiting something that is infinite in power of existence. And, in general, the problem is that he did not distinguish between an attribute of God and an attribute of someone else. This is what R. Ḥanina saw, and not that attributes are precluded with respect to Him—so long as there is no succumbing to the danger of appearing to be recounting all the praises.

For this reason we were permitted, in prolonging our supplications, to describe God with the thirteen divine attributes, since we have a clear indication that the purpose of their recitation is to ask for forgiveness and not to formulate and magnify praises.[214] And so too, therefore, those attributes and praises found in the Psalms of the Psalmist whose utterance is permitted both to the Psalmist himself and to others, as it is said: "*My* mouth shall speak the praise of the Lord, and let *all flesh* bless His holy name forever and ever."[215] And he says as well, with regard to the extensive multiplying of praises: "How precious are Your thoughts [lit. friends, רֵעֶיךָ (re ʿekha); see directly below] to me, O God; how mighty are the chief among them. If I count them, they will exceed the sand; when I awake, I am still with You."[216] Indeed, after he

---

[212] BT *Berakhot* 32a.
[213] Since praise of God is rabbinically mandated in prayer—it is to precede prayer's supplicatory element—any plurality of praises might suggest to the congregation that they are meant to be exhaustive.
[214] The thirteen divine attributes are proclaimed by God to Moses at Exod. 34: 6-7. They attest in the main to God's mercy and kindness and are included in the liturgy as a prelude to requests for divine forgiveness.
[215] Ps. 145: 21.
[216] Ps. 139: 17-18. Although the term רֵעַ (re ʿa) most often means friend, in this verse the sense of this term is "thoughts." See Ps. 139: 2, where the word רֵעַ clearly means "thought." Just below Crescas plays on

extensively recounted the praise of God and His knowledge of particulars, he closed his utterance by saying: "but to Him, He is one through them [בהם; *bahem*],"²¹⁷ that is: from the perspective of God himself, He is one in all the things He knows. For there is no multiplicity in His essence on account of their multiplicity; there is multiplicity only from the perspective of the Psalmist. And so, too, in his saying, "How precious are Your friends to me, O God," he intended the essential virtues that are not separate from Him, as if they were His friends. He indicated the essence of each by itself, its necessary existence and its being infinite in power of existence, by saying: "How precious"; "how mighty are the chief among them." And so, too, their vast numbers, in saying: "If I count them, they will exceed the sand." Here he compared the number of infinite [divine virtues] to the vastness of sand which they exceed. Indeed since their number is so vast, he treated being occupied with recounting them as akin to sinking deep, as he said: "When I wake, I am still with You." By this he meant that when he is roused and awakens from having sunk deeply into that recounting he finds himself still with God. In other words, by recounting so extensively he does not abandon God's essence, for the [divine attributes] are essences that do not separate [from Him], and God is one with them to the highest degree of simplicity. Even if they [viz. the attributes] are not absolutely equivocal they are related by a priority and posteriority that preserves the difference between the finite and the infinite.²¹⁸

Once this is resolved, the request of the master of the prophets, in his saying, "Show me, please, Your glory," is seen to be proper for him. For his first request, his saying, "Make known to me, please, Your way," was a request to know the ways of God's acts and governance, as the Rabbi of the *Guide* said. And in God's making these known to him, Moses would find favor in His eyes. But the second request, his saying, "Show me, please, Your glory," was a request to know the essential attributes that are not separate from Him. And he compared this apprehension to seeing, for seeing with the senses is possible only in the presence of the thing seen, for it [viz. what is seen with the sense of sight] is something not separate from it. The essence of a thing, however, is not apprehended by sense. And so, too, in the case of that apprehension [viz. Moses' apprehension]: although the apprehension of God's essence is impossible, the apprehension of His essential attributes was possible for Moses.²¹⁹

---

the "friends" sense to refer to the essential attributes as inseparable from the divine essence. The term ראשיהם (*rasheihem*) which I have rendered, "the chief among them," is frequently translated, "the sum of them."

²¹⁷ Ps. 139: 16. The clause, ולו אחד בהם, has been variously translated. Its most likely meaning, retaining the reading form, ולו, rather than the written form, ולא, is: "but to Him they [the days] are as one." Crescas takes the clause to mean that to God, His absolute uncompromised unity persists—is one—*through* them, that is, through the plurality of details He knows. Crescas later interprets both versions—in nonstandard ways. See II. i. 1 n. 13.

²¹⁸ Each of the divine attributes is infinite and exists in God essentially. Human beings who have attributes of the same name have them finitely, and so the gap between human attributes and divine ones of the same name remains, even if they are not completely homonymous.

²¹⁹ Crescas is taking note of an important difference in Moses' two requests. In the one—the request concerning God's ways and governance ("Your way")—Moses uses the term הודיעני (*hodi'eni*), "make known to me." But in the other—the request concerning God's essential attributes ("Your glory")—he uses the term הראיני (*hareini*), lit. "make seen to me." The essential attributes, Crescas contends, are like the

And so the response to him came in this matter: "You cannot see My face."[220] God called this apprehension [of the attributes] seeing the face, since what is seen is the face of things. But He designated for Moses the seeing of His back,[221] by which He meant that even if Moses fails to apprehend the essential attributes entirely, he will apprehend them somewhat; and He compared the relation between this and the apprehension that he requested to the relation between back and face. But according to the Rabbi's view, what God designated for him in this matter was the apprehension of what follows from Him, namely, His entire creation, as he said in discussing the equivocal nature of "back."[222] But if this is so, then "You will see My back" is redundant and superfluous, since God had already promised him this in response to his first request, in saying: "I will pass all My goodness before you."[223] This [viz. "You will see My back"], however, is God's response to the second request, that answer being that Moses will apprehend [the divine attributes] partially, which is in addition to what He promised him in response to the first.[224]

With this matter resolved, to say that the explicit name indicates a nonseparate essential attribute, whose secret the Sages transmitted to their students under the conditions mentioned above, is not implausible. And so, too, the twelve-letter name. They therefore did not transmit it to any but those in the priesthood who were modest, as is required insofar as in the benediction that was recited uniquely by them in the Temple, [the divine name was pronounced] as written. We shall elaborate on this explanation, God willing, in Book IV.

It remains for us to explain how, once we grant the proposition which states that anything composed of two things cannot be a necessary existent, the negation of essential attributes is not necessitated. This is not in fact difficult, for two reasons. First, although from our perspective attributes are separate, they are one from God's. And the infinite goodness that is His essentially includes them all and renders them one on all counts. Second, that proposition is true from a certain perspective, namely, when that which is conjoined and composed requires a conjoiner and composer so that each [of the things conjoined and composed] may be a part of the essence. In this case we say that the composition is a product of the composer, which, in turn, is the cause of the composition. But God has no parts in His essence, since His essence is one, simple to the highest degree of simplicity; and all-encompassing goodness is a

---

visible characteristics of things, which are not only seen but are seen as not separate from things. Since essences are not seen at all, Moses, according to Crescas, never asks to see—or know—God's essence. Moses knows, as even a theological novice does, that God's essence is beyond human capacity. What he asks to understand are God's acts in the world and what he asks to "see" are God's essential attributes. Translations frequently obscure this critical difference. See e.g. how Pines (1963: 123) renders both terms identically in his translation of Maimonides' *Guide* I. 54. Friedländer (1904, 75) does the same. But cf. Munk (1856: I. 217) who renders the one "*Fais-moi donc connaître*" and the other "*Fais-moi donc voir*."

[220] Exod. 33: 20.
[221] Exod. 33: 23. Crescas contends that Moses' apprehension of the divine attributes will not be complete—which would be seeing God's face—but will be partial: Moses will see God's back.
[222] See *Guide* I. 38.
[223] Exod. 33: 19. If when God said He would pass all His goodness before Moses what He intended—even according to Maimonides—was His creation, His creation could not be what God intended by "His back."
[224] The response to Moses' first request, namely, to have God make known to him His way, was "yes."

necessity for Him—indeed, an essential necessity. What, then, could preclude the necessity of His existence to His essence? If we infer necessarily from His essence the good in general, or infinite knowledge and power in particular, or the other virtues, would it not be like inferring light necessarily from a light source? If this were to be set forth as an analogy, could light, were it to emanate essentially from a certain light source necessarily existent in itself, be denied the necessity of existence of that light source? No. For the light is not an essence separate from the essence of the light source such that a conjoiner or composer would be required, but is something essential by which the light source is properly described. Such is the case in the matter of attributes in God, may He be blessed; and, a fortiori, in the matter of His anterior eternity, for it is a matter of rational inference that He did not come into being. And such is the case, too, with respect to His existence, which indicates that He is not subject to nonexistence. And so, too, in the case of His unity, which signifies that He is free of multiplicity in His essence and has no duality in any respect. This is what ought to be understood according to the truth in itself, and according to what the Torah posits.

And now that it has been established that what the Rabbi believed to be necessitated is not necessary, it is fitting to investigate further to determine if it is actually impossible. Since, however, this investigation is very important, especially insofar as it obviously entails great danger, we may not be lax with respect to it but must assert our own views if they appear to us to sanctify the name of God. Concerning such things it was said: "Wherever there is desecration of the holy name one ought not accord deference to the Rabbi."[225] And it has already become evident beyond doubt that what he regarded as necessary is actually impossible. And this for several reasons.

One of these, which was already established above, is that "exists" and "one," when predicated of God, are essential attributes. Therefore, there is no avoiding affirming essential attributes of God.

Another, which was also already seen, is that when we attribute to God knowledge and power, if what the term "knowledge" indicates is the absence of its negation, namely, ignorance, and the term "power," the absence of impotence, it is evident that each of these terms that is applied to Him necessarily indicates something affirmative. For what absence of ignorance signifies is a certain knowledge and apprehension. Even though His knowledge is different from our knowledge, as His essence is different from our essence, nevertheless there is no avoiding the fact that the absence of ignorance indicates the presence of something affirmative that we understand. For there is only one thing that is indicative of the negation of ignorance, namely, apprehension. I say, therefore, that if what the term "knowledge" indicates and what is meant by it is not something affirmative that is essential to God, it can then only be His very essence. For it is impossible that it be an accidental attribute, for there is no possibility of accidents in relation to God. But if it *is* His essence, one of the following absurdities would follow: either God's essence would be apprehended by us, as if there is nothing in His essence beyond what we understand by the term "knowledge"; or there is something in His essence beyond what we understand by the

---

[225] BT *Berakhot* 19b; BT *ʿEruvin* 6a.

term "knowledge," in which case His essence would necessarily be composed of two things, namely, that which we understand of the term "knowledge," and that of which we are ignorant. But each of these is the height of absurdity. For that it is impossible that God be apprehended by us is evident to every philosophical novice. And that His essence is also composed is impossible, for that would entail that He has merely possible existence. Therefore what is necessary is that the term "knowledge" and the term "power" are essential affirmative attributes of God, while His essence is one and necessarily existent. Anyone who attributes to Him the term "knowledge" *as* His essence, is, without realizing it, necessitating compositeness in Him. It has thus been established that what the Rabbi thought necessary is in fact impossible.

Another reason, as was explained, is that the meaning of the terms "knowledge" and "power," when we apply them to God, are affirmative things that we understand, since we understand something of both the absence of ignorance and the absence of impotence, that is, of the negation of ignorance and the negation of impotence. Indeed it is evident that what is understood of the negation of ignorance is not the same as what is understood of the negation of impotence. Therefore the meaning of the one is necessarily different from the meaning of the other. It therefore follows necessarily that the meaning of each one cannot be His essence; for if it were, His essence would be composed of different things.

Another reason is that if the entailments that he derived from the denial of essential attributes were true, namely, the impossibility of composition and the impossibility of any relation or likeness between Him and anything else, then, insofar as the terms "knowledge" and "power," for example, apply to anything else, it would be impossible for us to invest them with any positive meaning [when applied to God]. For what is impossible is not simply our knowing His essential attributes but His having any essential attributes. And if so, both apprehension and power will necessarily remain devoid of any meaning for us, and they will be applied to Him neither as His essence nor as an essential attribute. Since it is evident that He is devoid of all ignorance and impotence, He will be devoid, too, at the same time, of both contraries or opposites—that is, devoid of both knowledge and ignorance, and of both power and impotence. All of this is the height of absurdity and nonsense. In general, when we say of God that He is not nonknowing, we have in effect affirmed of Him that He is knowing. The meaning of this is apprehended by us. And if knowledge were His essence or part of His essence, it would similarly be necessary that His essence or a part of His essence be apprehended by us. And this is the height of absurdity.[226]

Indeed, what would be necessitated is something so absurd that nothing is beneath it in terms of nonsense and absurdity. For what is necessary with respect to knowing is also necessary with respect to being powerful and to having will, and so, too, for the other attributes. Once their meanings are apprehended by us, then knowledge is not power and will, but the three are distinct matters. Since His essence is one, then the two, if they are His essence or a part of His essence, would be one on all counts. It would be as if one were to say: "He is one but He is three, and three are one." It is even

---

[226] It follows, then, that such things as knowledge and power must be God's essential affirmative attributes.

more impossible for us, the congregation that believes in creation, to escape the necessity, once He acted, that He necessarily knew to act, was able to act, and wanted to act. What follows necessarily from His having acted is understood by us. It is evident that what is understood by us with regard to knowledge, power, and will, is that they differ from one another. If they were His essence, two absurdities would necessarily follow: first, that His essence would be understood by us; and second, that His essence would, God forbid, contain multiplicity.

What follows necessarily, then, is something about which there is no doubt, namely, that these are essential attributes—since His essence, that is, the essence of God the necessary existent, is one. Therefore the Psalmist waxed eloquent in recounting expansively the plurality of essential attributes, and said: "but to Him, He is one through them," indicating that His essence is one even as the essential attributes, at whose plurality he hinted with the word "through them (בהם (*bahem*))," which is an expression that indicates plurality, are many. He further explained them by saying, "And to me how precious are Your friends, O God, etc.," as we discussed earlier.

Since the truth is witness to itself, and is in agreement from all sides, it appears that the author of the *Sefer Yetzirah* (*Book of Creation*) would agree with this. He said, "as a flame is connected to a live coal."[227] This attests to an unbreakable unity. This is the truth about His essence, for as the essence of a substance cannot be conceived apart from its existence, nor its existence apart from its essence, so, too, the existence of an attribute cannot be conceived apart from that which it describes, nor that which it describes apart from the attribute. This includes the absolute good which contains all the species of perfections. This is what we wished to establish.

I will say furthermore that what this investigation has led to and confirmed regarding what is indubitably true of attributes agrees necessarily with the view of the greatest philosophers, such as Avicenna, Alfarabi, Averroes, and R. Moses Halevi,[228] but only after our having posited two propositions as self-evident. The first is that the apprehension of God's quiddity by someone other than God is impossible. This will be confirmed for us in what the philosophers have agreed on, namely, that intellect, the intellecter, and the intellected are one. And therefore, if God's quiddity were intellected by the intellect of another, His quiddity would become one with and would constitute that intellect, insofar as intellect is constituted by[229] what it intellects.[230] The second is that the intellection of a part of His quiddity is impossible. This is because if a part of His essence were intellected, absurdities would necessarily follow. First, there would be multiplicity in the essence of God, and there would be composition in His essence, since there would be in Him a part that is apprehended and a part that is not apprehended. Second, since the intellect is

---

[227] *Sefer Yetzirah* 1: 6.
[228] The reference is to R. Moshe ben Yosef Halevi of Seville, who lived in the 13th century and whose major work is *Maamar Elohi* (*Divine Word*).
[229] I translate the term מתעצם (*mit'atzem*), which literally means "is made a substance," simply as "is constituted."
[230] Since an intellect is constituted by what it intellects, were another intellect, a human intellect, to intellect God's quiddity, God's quiddity would unite with and constitute that intellect. "Intellect," as a verb, translates להשכיל (*lehaskil*). It is said then of the intellect that it intellects.

constituted by what it intellects, it would be constituted by what it apprehends of a part of His essence. This is the height of absurdity.[231]

Now that these propositions have been established, let me say that, when the views of the philosophers concerning the causal chain of existents deriving from the first cause is studied, it will be seen that the philosophers were puzzled by how a composite could derive from something simple. They agreed that the first effect was composed of various intellected things—of what it apprehended of the essence of the first cause, of what it apprehended of its own essence, and of what it apprehended concerning that the quiddity of the essence of God is its cause and it is the effect of that cause. They thought it fitting that the most worthy object of intellection be what it [viz. the first effect] intellects of the essence of the first cause. From this object of intellection the second effect necessarily derives. The second most worthy object of intellection to follow is what it apprehends of its own essence, and from this the form of the sphere derives. From what it apprehends concerning *that* God is its cause the matter of the sphere derives. Since it was proved from the propositions that the apprehending of God's essence or of a part of His essence is absolutely impossible, it follows necessarily that we should understand that what they [viz. the philosophers] meant when they declared the apprehension of a part of God's essence more worthy is: what is intellected of His essence by way of essential attributes. For the apprehension of negation is essentially the apprehension *that* He is its cause—for the first effect, in knowing that God, may He be blessed, was its cause, knows of itself that it was the effect of His essence. Indeed, they made this the least worthy object of intellection. Therefore the most important object of intellection must be that which is intellected of God's essence by way of essential attributes.

This is the language that R. Moses Halevi used in a treatise that he composed concerning the first mover. He said, and I quote:

It is necessary that there be a causal chain in this way. The mover of all, since it intellects what it intellects of the necessary existent, and intellects its own essence, and knows that it is the effect of the necessary existent, and since each one of these is known to it by its rank of existence and perfection, in accordance with whatever He decreed would flow from His existence to another, it is necessitated that the mover of all necessitate three existents. It is most fitting, in the natural course of things, that the more important among the effects be necessitated by the more important among the causes. Therefore, what was necessitated by the mover of all, insofar as it has knowledge of God's essence, may He be blessed, is the existence of the form of the sphere of the fixed stars;[232] and insofar as it intellected its own essence it necessitated the form of the sphere that was moved by it; and since it intellected that of which it is the effect, it necessitated the existence of the matter of the sphere.

---

[231] The absurdity lies in that the human intellect, in apprehending a part of God's essence, would be constituted by the part of the divine essence that it apprehends and would thus itself become, absurdly, divine.

[232] Fisher includes a parenthetical note found in the Ferrara edition that indicates that this phrase requires a correction in line with the correction required in the language of R. Moses Halevi. The correction would presumably replace "form of the sphere of the fixed stars" with "mover of the sphere of the fixed stars."

Averroes as well, who disagrees with Avicenna and Alfarabi regarding the first cause, agrees with this, in making the intellected thing that is first in importance that which the effect apprehends of God's essence, may He be blessed. And there is no path to this other than through essential attributes. We therefore need to say that, if some sages banish affirmative attributes and increase the use of negation, they need to be understood as intending attributes that indicate essence. It is for these that affirmation is indeed impossible, but not for the others. Know this.

Chapter IV

THE way in which we arrived at our knowledge of this root-principle.

This root-principle contains two matters: the first, that God, may He be blessed, is one in himself to the highest degree of simplicity; and the second, the impossibility of duality. For even once God's simplicity and oneness in himself are posited, whether there might be more than one divinity is still subject to doubt.

The first is proved easily based on what was said previously. For it was proved that the totality of existence is like a single individual with all its parts connected one to another, and that the forces of the sphere are distributed in this matter and prepare it.[233] It is inescapable that the sphere has a mover, [and so on,] until we ascend to the necessarily existent mover. The necessarily existent mover cannot be composite, as was proved in proposition twenty-one. It is evident that the necessary existent is simple with no composition at all, and this is the first species of unity.

With respect to the second species, which is [that there is no] duality:[234] If we assume that God, may He be blessed, is simple, but that there is more than one, it is inescapable that one would either be occupied with the governance of existence or of a part of it, or not. It is absurd that He be occupied with a part of it, for existence as a whole is connected end-to-end and is like a single individual, such that it is fitting that it be governed by a single agent. But even if He were not occupied with the governance of this existence, it would be open to an objector to say that there is a God who governs a different world, which is possible, as will be proved in what follows—that is, the possibility of many worlds will be proved. Yet when it is proved in Books II and III that God's power is infinite in strength, it will be evident that one God is sufficient for all. As for the possibility that one governs and another not, the doors to the investigation of this possibility are locked.[235] In order to remove this confusion and this doubt, and to abolish all skepticism with respect to this great root-principle, the Torah opened our eyes, the eyes of us, the community of believers, by saying: "Hear O Israel, the Lord our God, the Lord is one."[236] It emphasized this by repeating the great name in order to indicate that there are two species of unity. The Torah juxtaposed the first instance of the name to "our God," to indicate the first species, for the God who is our God and governor is one in His essence, that is, He is simple. For

---

[233] The forces prepare the matter to receive forms.

[234] By duality, שניּות (sheniyyut), Crescas means there being not one but two deities.

[235] This sentence and the previous one appear in the margin of the Florence manuscript, though they are found in the Vienna manuscript and in the Ferrara edition. Perhaps they should be excised: is there any point in entertaining the possibility of a God who governs nothing, who is wholly inactive?

[236] Deut. 6: 4.

from the perspective of His divinity over us and His governance of us, He is one. But God, even apart from our recognition of His governance of us, is one, and there is no second—neither one who governs other worlds, if they exist, nor one who does not govern elsewhere. This God is one and there is no second. This is the second species of unity. Indeed our Rabbis, peace be upon them, have agreed to this root-principle, that is, to God's governance of other worlds, to the point of hyperbolically setting their number, in many midrashic texts, at 18,000. This is what we intended in this chapter.

Chapter V

EXPOSITION of the third root-principle that was posited, namely, that God is neither a body nor a force in a body.

It is evident, whether by way of speculation or by way of the Torah, that the quiddity of God is at the highest degree of concealment, such that apprehension of His essential attributes was impossible even for the master of the prophets, as we discussed earlier.[237] And what he said shows this. When he made his request, saying: "And should they say to me, 'What is His name?' what shall I say to them?"[238] his desire, as it appears, was to teach God's essence, for this was the very start of his prophecy. The answer was that this instruction is impossible for them, as He said: "I shall be what I shall be"[239]—that is: they may have no commerce with My quiddity, for I shall be what I shall be. This hints at the concealment of the essence, but shows that existence is quite openly revealed, for Moses returned and said: "'I shall be' sent me to you."[240] In other words, with respect to My essence it is not possible to indicate anything; it is possible to do so only with respect to My existence. Indeed God indicated the necessity of His existence is saying, "I shall be what I shall be." The word אשר (*asher*) [here translated "what"] takes the place of a cause, for He requires no cause, as if to say, "I shall be because I shall be." This applies only to a necessary existent. For anything that in itself has possible existence exists because its cause exists. Therefore, in indicating its existence, it is untenable to say, "I shall be because I shall be," but only, "I shall be because of something other than myself that will be," namely, its cause. And it is not improbable that the impossibility of knowing God's essence is indicated in this verse, even as His existence is dealt with in these words.

Since it is evident and well known that attributes, even if they are negative, confer specificity and some knowledge of a thing, as the Rabbi of the *Guide* wrote, there is very great danger in this inquiry. Even more is this so if we permit to ourselves the assigning of anything affirmative to the thing that was specified by negative attributes. This would be like our affirming something in God's quiddity of something other than Him, which would engender scorn, abuse, insult, and the assigning of divinity to things other than God. So too, in specifying by negations, if we negate something that it is not fitting for us to negate with respect to Him, that, too, engenders scorn and rebelliousness and the removal of divinity from Him, God forbid. Therefore it is fitting that we be perfectly certain concerning what we negate

---

[237] What Crescas in fact had said earlier (I. iii. 3) is that apprehension of God's essential attributes was not fully—but only partially—possible for Moses.
[238] Exod. 3: 13.   [239] Exod. 3: 14.   [240] Exod. 3: 14.

with respect to God. If doubt infects this investigation, we should abandon it, and not expend efforts toward that end, other than what the true tradition dictates. And so, if the Sages forbade looking into four things, "what is above, and what is below, what is in front, and what is behind,"[241] as the Mishnah says explicitly, how much more would they withhold permission when it comes to looking into and investigating that which is the cause of all, may He be blessed. It is therefore fitting for us in this investigation that we be perfectly certain regarding what to affirm and what to negate. Once this is resolved, I will assert that, since the second root-principle was established for us, namely, the necessity of the unity of God, may He be blessed, on all counts—both from the perspective of speculation and from the perspective of the Torah—it is incumbent on us to negate anything with respect to God that contradicts this root-principle. Since it is evident with respect to sensible bodies, and with respect to those that contain forces, that they are composite, it is evident that it is necessary to negate this of Him. The extent of this investigation is sufficient. It is at the highest degree of confirmation and certainty.

Because every passion,[242] insofar as passions are corporeal, must necessarily be denied with respect to God, it is fitting that we inquire into one such matter that we have found attributed to Him both in prophecy and in the dicta of our Rabbis, of blessed memory, and that is, joy. It is found in the Writings,[243] where the Psalmist says: "Let the Lord rejoice in His works";[244] and in the words of our Rabbis of blessed memory, as they instituted the formula of the benediction: "in whose habitation there is joy."[245] This idea appears frequently in the Writings and in midrashic texts. Moreover, since contraries are known by a single knowledge, then, if sadness is attributed to Him, as, for example: "He was saddened in His heart";[246] "They saddened His holy spirit";[247] "I will be with him in his travails";[248] it is fitting that we attribute joy to Him. According to the early thinkers [here, the Sages], however, although it is impossible that sadness be attributed to Him in any way[249]—such that what Scripture sought to indicate, by way of metaphorical and figurative speech, was only that someone has acted in a way opposed to the purpose God intended for him—it remains appropriate, in any event, to attribute joy to God.

The foundation of Aristotle's argument, and that of his followers, in this matter, is as I shall explain. Apprehension is pleasurable for those who apprehend; and to the extent that pleasure and joy increase as the apprehension of things is more noble, and since God apprehends all things in the most noble way possible, it follows necessarily that the pleasure and joy He experiences is of the highest degree possible. Accordingly, the interpretation of their [viz. the Sages'] expression, "in whose habitation (במעונו—*bime'ono*) there is joy" would be: at His rank. For, "habitation" and "place"

---

[241] *Ḥagigah* 2: 1.
[242] "Passion," הפעלות (*hipo'alut*), which often indicates being acted upon, is here to be understood as emotion.
[243] The Hebrew Bible contains three divisions: the Pentateuch, the Prophets, and the Writings. It is often unclear whether by כתובים (*ketuvim*) Crescas intends Scripture as a whole or specifically the Writings.
[244] Ps. 104: 31.
[245] *Ketubot* 8: 1. This expression is inserted into the Grace after Meals at a wedding celebration.
[246] Gen. 6: 6.   [247] Isa. 63: 10.   [248] Ps. 91: 15.   [249] BT *Ḥagigah* 5b.

as used in this matter are the same, the term "habitation" being equivocal in the same way that "place" is, and used here in its sense of rank.[250]

Yet this argument is evidently mistaken, as it seems, for two reasons. First, it is known that joy and sadness are contraries and belong to the same genus of passion. And this is the truth itself. For joy is nothing but pleasure in the will, whereas sadness is conflict in the will. These are both passions of the soul. Therefore, if we are happy when we apprehend, that is because we have souls that have will. But for the one who is fully an intellect, which intellects, and which is the object of intellection, as the philosophers have agreed, and who has no soul, it is unimaginable that He experiences joy and pleasure, except loosely speaking, for these have no place in the intellect. Second, if we concede that pleasure can be attributed to Him, it could not be for the reason they supposed. For it is inappropriate to compare our apprehension to His at all. For the pleasure we take in apprehending something accompanies our transition from potentiality to actuality. Therefore, when we attain new knowledge of which we had previously been ignorant, we experience joy, for we have made a sudden transition from ignorance to knowledge. Indeed an indication of this is that the joy is more intense when the apprehension is fresh, but the pleasure fades following the apprehension. Yet another indication of this is that when the object of intellection is quite recondite the pleasure is greater. For in this case we have to use more elusive premises, and the transition from ignorance to knowledge is greater. It is even the case that when the object of intellection is not recondite, even if it is higher in rank, we do not experience pleasure as great as with a recondite object of intellection, even if the latter is lower in rank. And what is inescapable proof of the veracity of this is that we do not attain pleasure from first intelligibles.[251] Therefore it is not fitting that we compare the pleasure of our apprehension, which is due to the transition from ignorance to knowledge and the newness of apprehension, to [that of] the one whose objects of intellection are always first intelligibles, and who never transitions [from ignorance to knowledge] and for whom apprehension is never new. It is therefore evident that pleasure cannot be attributed to Him in the way they supposed.

It has been proved, beyond any doubt as to its truth, that God is, by intention and will, the true agent of all existents, and that He sustains their existence by the constant overflowing of His goodness. It is for this reason that the Rabbis instituted [the prayer],"who renews each day in His goodness the work of creation," as will be explained in Book III, God willing. It follows, then, that insofar as He, by will and intention, causes His goodness and perfection to overflow, He necessarily loves bestowing goodness and having it overflow. This is love—for there is no love without pleasure in the will—and this alone is true joy. As it is said: "Let the Lord rejoice in His works,"[252] which means that the joy is in His works, and it derives from the overflow of His goodness to them in keeping them in constant existence in the most perfect way. From this perspective our Rabbis of blessed memory have said in several

---

[250] The final two sentences of this paragraph appear in brackets in Fisher and are absent from the Ferrara edition. They appear, however, in both the Florence and the Vienna manuscripts.
[251] First intelligibles are truths which are in us by nature, the basic truths of logic and mathematics.
[252] Ps. 104: 31.

places that the Holy One Blessed Be He "craves the prayers of the righteous."²⁵³ What they meant by this is that, since pleasure and joy derive for Him from the overflow of goodness, and since the most perfect goodness that a man can have is in adhering to God, which is the secret of prayer, as will be explained, God willing, it follows that when this goodness extends from Him, He takes pleasure in it, and, figuratively speaking, it is as if He craves it. And the opposite holds in the opposite case, for the knowledge of opposites is one. And indeed the formulation of the benediction, "in whose habitation there is joy," is to be taken literally, and there is no need to posit an equivocation on "place" to mean rank. On the contrary, since this joy is common to the Creator, may He be blessed, in His causing His goodness to overflow, and to the created, insofar as they receive the overflow, it follows that true joy is in His place, that is, in His dwelling-place, figuratively speaking—by which they meant in His kingdom, the kingdom of heaven, which they designate the dwelling-place of spiritual beings.

It is indeed possible at first thought to raise the objection that surely the recipient experiences greater pleasure than the agent—and this for two reasons. First, it is thought that the greater joy is experienced by the recipient upon the receiving of good than by the bestower in bestowing; and, second, because the one on the receiving end experiences pleasure from two sides: first, from having received goodness and existence from God; second, from apprehending God, may He be blessed, who is the greatest possible object of apprehension. This occurs when the apprehension is new, whether it be on the part of the separate intellects, whose existence is created, or on the part of souls, which are also created, insofar as they transition in these cases from ignorance to knowledge. If this is so, however, it would be conceivable that their pleasure would be greater than God's. We must therefore explain that, even though their pleasure is exceedingly great, as our Rabbis of blessed memory indicated: "The righteous sit with their crowns on their heads and they enjoy the radiance of the Divine Presence,"²⁵⁴ there is still no proportionality or comparison with God's pleasure in conferring good. For since it has been confirmed that He takes pleasure, it is necessary that it be through His essence, and therefore it must be a virtue and perfection. Since there is no proportion or relation between God's perfection and the perfection of another, it follows necessarily that there is no proportion or relation between God's pleasure and the pleasure of another. Since it was proved that pleasure is love and is pleasureful passionate-love, and, according to the conventions of language, חשק (*hesheq*) signifies ardent love, we find that with respect to the love God has for the Patriarchs, the term חשק is used, as it is said: "It was your forefathers that God passionately loved,"²⁵⁵ but with respect to the love the Patriarchs had for God, the term אהבה (*ahavah*) is used, as it is said: "Abraham who loves Me,"²⁵⁶ rather than "who loves Me passionately," in order to indicate this distinction. Because of this love it is fitting and required of us that we thank God and bless His name, and therefore a specific benediction was instituted to precede the *Shema'*, as we shall see,

---

²⁵³ BT *Ḥullin* 60b; BT *Yevamot* 64a; also *Tanḥuma Toldot* 9; *Song of Songs Rabbah* 2: 32.
²⁵⁴ *Berakhot* 17: 1.   ²⁵⁵ Deut. 10: 15.   ²⁵⁶ Isa. 41: 18.

God willing. Our intention here, however, was to establish the truth of God's pleasure and joy, though not in the way they imagined. This is what we have sought to clarify.

Chapter VI

THE way in which we arrived at our knowledge of this third root-principle.

Since it was explained in our discussion of this root-principle that it depends on the second root-principle, and since one indubitable fact was explained, namely, that only the Torah and the tradition furnish complete proof, it is evident that this root-principle too is proved by the Torah and the tradition which illuminate all that is obscure. Indeed it was stated by the Rabbis of blessed memory in many places that there are in God no corporeal manifestations. Even if the Torah permits itself to use language that contains indications of corporeality, this was by necessity, as was discussed extensively by the Rabbi of the *Guide* in many places in his book. Indeed our Rabbis of blessed memory suggested as much when they said: "The Torah speaks in accordance with the language of human beings."[257] And by this they made clear that the root-principle of prophecy, according to what the Torah attests and what was shown by the tradition to be true, is what opened our eyes to the road on which we should walk to confirm these root-principles perfectly. And it is confirmed accordingly that speculation does not conflict with it but rather agrees with it from all perspectives, which is the nature of truth—that it attests to itself and is in agreement from all perspectives. How appropriately have the Rabbis of blessed memory said in the Midrash:

This may be compared to a person who was walking on the road from one place to another and saw a palace ablaze [or illumined]. He said, "One might say that this palace has no governor." The master of the palace looked at him and said: "I am the master of the palace." So did Abraham our father say, "One might say that this world has no governor." The Holy One Blessed Be He looked at him and said, "I am the master of the world," etc.[258]

By this they meant that, even though Abraham was inclined to the truth, he was not free of all doubt until God caused His light to flow onto him. This is prophecy. This is what we wished to show in our concise manner in this first Book. Praise is to God alone, may He be blessed.

---

[257] *Berakhot* 31: 2.
[258] *Genesis Rabbah* 39: 1. Note the connection between this midrash which tells of "a person who was walking on the road" and remained in the dark until he experienced prophetic revelation, and the text immediately preceding it which asserts that the root-principle of prophecy opens our eyes to "the road on which we should walk" if we wish to confirm the truth of the root-principles.

Book II

CONCERNING the cornerstones of the Torah, that is, the foundations and pillars upon which the house of God is erected. Through their existence the existence of the Torah is conceivable as God has arranged it. Were the absence of even one of these conceivable, the entire Torah would collapse, God forbid.

When we inquired into them, we found that there were six cornerstones: (1) God's knowledge of existents; (2) His providence with respect to them; (3) His power; (4) prophecy; (5) choice; and (6) end.[1] For since the Torah was an act of will, issuing from the commander who is the agent, to the commanded who are the acted-upon, it follows necessarily that the agent is one who knows, one who wills, and one who is powerful; and that those who are acted upon exercise will and make choices and are not necessitated or compelled. Since the agent's act acts upon those who are acted upon, it is inevitable that there be some relationship between them. It is necessary, therefore, that there be a relationship and a kind of connection between them, which is prophecy. And since every act, whether natural or a product of art—and especially an act that is willed, issuing from an agent who is infinitely perfect—is aimed at a specific end, it is inescapable that this perfect act is aimed at an important end. We have thus seen fit to divide this Book into six Parts.

Part I

CONCERNING God's knowledge of existents. This will include both the establishment of this cornerstone and the way in which we arrived at our knowledge of it.

Many of the philosophers have strayed from the path of truth, and have thought to contradict this cornerstone as it is affirmed by the true tradition. Even some of the

---

[1] "End" translates *takhlit* (תכלית), which corresponds to the Greek *telos*. This end is the end of the Torah.

sages of our nation who engage in speculation were inclined to some degree in their direction, and fabricated notions that are not correct.[2] We set as our task in this Part to explain this cornerstone as the Torah directed, as well as the contradictions that they imagined it contains; to resolve difficulties; to refute what they thought; and to take note of the way in which we arrived at knowledge of this cornerstone. We therefore saw fit to divide this Part into five parts.

Chapter I: an exposition of this cornerstone in accordance with the dictates of the Torah.

Chapter II: an exposition of the difficulties that might confound one and on account of which some of our sages stumbled with respect to this cornerstone.

Chapter III: an exposition of the even more serious difficulties in what they affirmed in connection with this cornerstone.

Chapter IV: resolution of the difficulties they raised in connection with this cornerstone, in accordance with the view of the Torah.

Chapter V: an exposition of the way in which we arrived at our complete knowledge of this cornerstone.

Chapter I

EXPOSITION of this cornerstone in accordance with the dictates of the Torah.

It is evident, as we saw earlier, that the issuer and arranger of the Torah, may He be blessed, must necessarily know what He commands and arranges. Yet with regard to the way in which He knows, commentators differed widely. Three points are necessarily affirmed according to the roots of the Torah, so far as we can apprehend: first, that God's knowledge encompasses the infinite; second, that God's knowledge extends to the nonexistent;[3] and third, that God has knowledge concerning possible alternatives without their nature as possible being changed. How this necessity can be proved according to the three root-principles of the Torah is as I shall now explain.

Concerning the first: It is evident from the Torah—in its narratives, in its individual commandments, and in its predictions—that God apprehends particulars; [it is evident] as well from the perspective of the tradition, as many of the Writings attest to this. It is said: "for the Lord searches all hearts, and understands all the intentions of one's thoughts";[4] and in the Psalm [which opens with], "O Lord, You have searched me and known me,"[5] the Psalmist speaks expansively of God's detailed knowledge; indeed, the entire Psalm is based on this—that is, on God's knowing and apprehending particulars, as in its saying: "You know my sitting down and my rising up; You understand my thought[6] afar off. You have measured my going out and my lying down; and You are acquainted with all my ways."[7] The remaining verses that follow in this Psalm indicate God's apprehension of particulars in minute detail.

---

[2] 2 Kgs. 17: 9.
[3] What is intended is future existents—in other words, things not yet existent.
[4] 1 Chr. 28: 9.   [5] Ps. 139: 1.
[6] *Re'a* (רע) in Psalms often means "thought." See I. iii. 3 n. 216.   [7] Ps. 139: 2–3.

Once this is established—and since it is evident that particulars are infinite—it follows necessarily that God's knowledge encompasses the infinite. This is the first.

Concerning the second, namely, that God has knowledge of the nonexistent: This is evident from the fact that there are predictions made in the Torah and in the books of the Prophets regarding what does not yet exist. If it appears that there are in the Torah some verses that indicate new knowledge, as, for example, when God says [with regard to Sodom and Gomorrah]: "I will go down now and see whether they have done altogether according to the cry of it which has come to Me; and if not, I will know,"[8] our Rabbis of blessed memory have indeed accounted for verses such as these by asserting: "The Torah speaks in accordance with the language of human beings"[9]—especially when the thing [which God knows] is already in existence. It is hardly likely that this [existing thing] [at first] eluded God and that His knowledge of it came to be subsequently; rather, it occurred in a prophetic vision, and the language of human beings was used. Since, however, God's saying, "for now I know that you are God-fearing,"[10] occurred while Abraham was awake during the incident of the Binding, as the true tradition affirms, it seems to me that this should be taken literally. It is based on a certain proposition established in political philosophy, namely, that deeds inculcate permanent traits or qualities in the soul, especially if they are strengthening ones that have already taken root. With this proposition established, I can go on to assert something of which there can be no doubt, namely, that although Abraham was imbued with fear of God even before the incident of the Binding, this God-fearingness was strengthened in his soul and increased further after this incident. Thus it is evident that this level had not been achieved by him before the incident. Since this is so, and since the text, in saying, "God-fearing," intended: at the level known to God, its saying, "for now I know that you are God-fearing," is warranted. For before the incident, the degree to which Abraham was God-fearing was not the degree indicated by "that you are God-fearing." And so, it was not possible that what was known to God was something different from what was the case. Rather, what was known to God before this [i.e. before the Binding] is that Abraham would be "God-fearing" in the future, inasmuch as he was not yet at that level. For it is an absolute necessity that God have knowledge of what does not exist at present. This is the second point.[11]

Concerning the third, namely, that God knows alternative possibilities—that is, that He has knowledge of which of two alternatives will be realized, without the nature of the possible changing: the necessity of this according to the Torah is evident. For if God's knowledge were to compel the alternative that He knows will be realized, there could be no element of command in the prescriptions and

---

[8] Gen. 18: 21. [9] BT *Berakhot* 31b. [10] Gen. 22: 12.

[11] If "God-fearing" is understood to refer to the higher level of God-fearingness, the level not achieved by Abraham until the incident of the Binding, then what God knew before that incident is that Abraham would later become God-fearing to this greater extent. God could not and did not know before the Binding that Abraham *is* at this higher level of God-fearingness, because Abraham indeed was not at that level then, and God cannot and does not know what is not the case. (Crescas understands truth as correspondence between what is in the mind and what is outside it.) It is therefore quite accurate for God to have said at the Binding—though not before—that He now knows that Abraham *is* God-fearing. This knowledge is not, however, strictly speaking, new knowledge. God knew earlier what would later be the case.

proscriptions of the Torah. For unless it is assumed that the one who is commanded acts voluntarily and not by compulsion or necessity, there is no possibility of commanding him. This is self-evident. Indeed the [contrary] notion is self-contradictory. For if God's knowledge were to compel one alternative, then this [compelled] alternative was never a possible thing. For what it means for a thing to be possible is that it might exist and might not exist. But if one alternative is compelled, then it is not a possible thing. Yet it was assumed to be a possible thing. It therefore follows necessarily that God's knowledge that one alternative will be realized does not make the nature of the possible necessary. This is the third point.

These three points were fully verified in the Psalm we mentioned above. The first was verified at the beginning, as we saw earlier, as well as at its end, as it is said: "My frame was not hidden from You, when I was made in secret and intricately wrought in the depths of the earth. Your eyes did see my unshaped flesh; for in Your book all things are written; the days also in which they are to be fashioned; but to Him, He is one through them." Since the word that appears in the written text as "not," לא, with the letter *alef*, is to be read, according to the tradition,[12] "to Him," לו, with the letter *vav*, both versions require interpretation. According to the Masoretic tradition, the written form is interpreted in terms of what preceded it,[13] and refers back to "was not hidden." In other words, not one of all the particulars that God recalled was hidden from Him. According to the form in which it is to be read, it is to be interpreted "to Him"—that is, from His perspective—thus: despite His having many cognitions, "He is one through them." But from our perspective, what is said afterwards applies: "How precious are Your thoughts to me, O God..."[14] This Psalm clearly affirms the multiplicity of God's cognitions in minute detail. This is the first point.

God's knowledge of what is not existent is alluded to in the verse: "For no word is yet on my tongue; and lo, O Lord, You know it all."[15] In other words, the word that I will speak in the future is not yet on my tongue—that is, I have not uttered it—yet You knew it completely. This indicates God's knowledge of the future. This is the second point.

Concerning the third, which is that God's knowledge does not make the possible necessary[16]—this is self-evident. For this Psalm is apparently based on David's excusing himself for the days he spent associating with men who were murderous and desperate and fleeing their creditors. That is why he formulated praises of God with respect to His knowledge, saying that God knows the inner recesses of his heart and the hidden depths of his thoughts. He therefore began poetically as

---

[12] The reference is to the Masoretic text. The aim of the Masoretes (7th–10th century) was to preserve the authentic text and to instruct as to the proper way to read particular words in cases in which the written text was deemed flawed, though without replacing the problematic written form.

[13] Ps. 139: 15–16. The Masoretes (see previous note) determined that this final clause should be read: ולו אחד בהם, despite that in its written form the clause appears as: ולא אחד בהם. The latter would be translated roughly: "and *not* one of them [was hidden]"; the former, "but *to Him* [He is] one through them." Other possible interpretations are: "But to Him the *days* are as one"; or, referring not to God but to גלמי, "To my unshaped flesh there was [allotted] one of them [namely, the days]."

[14] Ps. 139: 17. From God's perspective, the many things He knows do not threaten His perfect unity. From our human perspective, however, what we see is simply God's knowledge of many things.

[15] Ps. 139: 4.

[16] Fisher cites an alternate version: "does not make the one alternative [viz. the one God knows will occur] necessary."

follows: "O Lord, You have searched me, and known me," as if God engaged in investigation and research to examine his condition, although God already had knowledge of him prior to this. By this he indicated that which is the very truth itself, namely, that God's knowledge is eternal and unchanging. And he elaborated expansively in detail on this notion. The purpose of all this was to excuse himself, and so he said: "O God, if only You would slay the wicked, then murderous men would depart from me." In other words, had You slain the evil men—alluding to Saul and Ahitofel—thereby implementing justice for me, I would then have said to the murderous men: "Depart from me," and I certainly would not have associated with them—and all this is evident to You. He therefore closed by saying: "Search me, O God, and know my heart..."[17] "and lead me in the everlasting path."[18] In other words, he asks that God's providence accompany him on the everlasting path that he will traverse, even though it would appear on the surface that he is unworthy. It is thus evident that if God's knowledge made what He knew necessary, David would not have needed to seek to excuse himself.[19] This Psalm has thus verified these three points. This is what was intended in this chapter.

Chapter II

EXPOSITION of the difficulties that might arise with respect to this cornerstone as it has been posited.

Some of the following difficulties are general and some specific. We shall mention the general ones first, namely, those that raise doubts concerning the three points that were posited with respect to God's knowledge of existents. They are five.

The first is: If God knew any existent other than himself, then, since it is evident that knowledge is a perfection in the knower, it would follow necessarily that the superior [viz. God] is perfected by the inferior [viz. the existent that God knows]. This, however, is the height of absurdity. And anything from which an absurdity follows is itself necessarily false.

The second is: If God knew any existent other than himself, then, since the intellect is constituted by what it knows, there would of necessity be multiplicity in God's essence, that is, [it would include] His essence plus what He knows—in addition to [the first absurdity] that the superior would be constituted by the inferior. Moreover, if there were many things known, the multiplicity [in God's essence] would correspond to the number of things known [by God]. If the latter are infinite, the multiplicity would be infinite. This is the height of absurdity and nonsense.

The third is: Since particular things are not apprehended other than by a hylic faculty,[20] such as sense or imagination, and since God has no hylic faculty, it follows necessarily that He does not apprehend particulars.

---

[17] Ps. 139: 23.   [18] Ps. 139: 24.

[19] That David sought to excuse himself shows that he held the following two beliefs: first, that God was aware of his good intentions; and, second, that God's knowledge does not compel. For were God unaware of his intentions there would have been nothing to mitigate his offense; and had God's knowledge compelled his association with unsavory men, he would have had no need for an excuse as there would have been no offense.

[20] The hylic faculty is the rational faculty that is connected to the body rather than separate from it.

The fourth is: Since particular things are in time, and since time is an accident consequent upon motion, it follows that one who cannot be described as either in motion or at rest does not apprehend particulars.

Since it is evident from the three points that were posited concerning God's knowledge that they confirm God's knowledge of particulars, it is clear from these difficulties—namely, the third and fourth—that they apply to all three points.

The fifth is: The deplorable condition of the order as it applies to the human species[21] entails that God does not apprehend such things. We shall not expand on this difficulty here, because it pertains more directly to Part II, where providence is discussed.

The following are the specific difficulties.

With respect to the first point we made, namely, that God's knowledge encompasses the infinite, there are two difficulties.

The first is: Since knowledge encompasses and includes, and since the infinite is neither encompassed nor bounded, it seems that the affirmation that there is knowledge of the infinite must be a self-contradictory statement.

The second is: If God's knowledge were to encompass the infinite, then something impossible would be possible. For it has already been shown with respect to continuous quantity, that it is perpetually divisible. Yet if God's knowledge is encompassing in relation to the infinite parts into which the continuous quantity can be divided, it would be impossible for any one of the parts to be subject to the [infinite] division to which, qua quantity, it is subject. For if it were subject to this division, God's knowledge would not be true.[22]

With respect to the second point, namely, that God's knowledge extends to what is nonexistent, there are also two difficulties.

The first is that true knowledge appears to be necessarily of something existent. For truth, with respect to existent things, is the correspondence of what is in the mind to what is outside the mind.

The second is as follows. The way knowledge works, if it is true, with respect to the nonexistent is that [it is knowledge of] that the nonexistent does not exist yet but will exist in the future. When, however, the nonexistent actually comes to exist, the knowledge of it is that it is something that exists now. It then follows inescapably that there is a change in God's knowledge. And since the intellect is constituted by what it knows, it would follow necessarily that God's essence changes. This is the height of absurdity.

With respect to the third point, namely, our having said that God has knowledge of possible alternatives without the nature of the possible being changed, there are also two difficulties.

---

[21] What is meant is the apparent absence of justice in the human realm, where it seems as if the righteous suffer and the wicked flourish.

[22] The difficulty here is as follows. Insofar as knowledge is something that encompasses that which is known, it follows that that which is known cannot be without end. Thus, if God knows a continuous quantity—that is, a quantity that has parts that are necessarily infinitely divisible—then either the parts God knows are not a continuous quantity, which, *ex hypothesi*, they are, or God does not know the parts. For to know something is to know it completely. And only something finite can be known completely.

The first is as follows. If what God knows is which one of two possible alternatives will be realized while, as appears to be the case, the contrary alternative remains possible, then, when indeed the first of these alternatives is realized, the [second alternative's] possibility is eliminated, and God's knowledge with respect to it will have undergone change. Since the intellect is constituted by what it knows, God's essence would necessarily undergo change. This is the height of absurdity.[23]

The second is as follows. It is posited that God knows which one of two possible alternatives will be realized, while the contrary alternative remains possible. Yet it is evident with respect to any possible thing that when its existence is posited, no absurdity arises. Nevertheless, when we posit its existence [i.e. the existence of the contrary alternative], two absurdities do follow: the first, a change in God's knowledge and thus in His essence—inasmuch as the intellect is constituted by what it knows; the second, that the earlier knowledge was not in fact knowledge but was an erroneous conjecture. All this is the height of absurdity and nonsense.[24]

These are the difficulties that spurred some of the early thinkers to dispute this cornerstone as it was posited, so much so that some of them divested God of all knowledge of anything but himself, whereas others eliminated knowledge of particulars that are subject to coming-to-be and passing-away while allowing it with respect to universals and eternal individuals.

Many of the sages of our nation[25] felt constrained by the Torah to accept God's knowledge of particulars; and, since particulars are infinite, it would appear that God's knowledge encompasses the infinite. Moreover, the literal sense of the prophecies indicates that God has knowledge of particulars before they come to be, to the extent that He even conveys them to His prophets, as it is stated: "For the Lord God will not do anything without revealing its secret to His servants the prophets."[26] So, too, with respect even to possible things that involve choice, as in: "For the king of Egypt will not permit you to go, if not for a mighty hand."[27] They would then indeed be obligated to believe in this cornerstone as it was posited, in this respect as well. Yet since they also felt constrained by speculation, and by what they imagined speculation necessitates in terms of discrediting these points, they sought to fulfill the vision, and failed.[28] For although they posited God's knowledge of particulars, it was not of particulars qua particulars but rather of particulars qua parts of universals.

---

[23] The difficulty Crescas envisions on behalf of the objector is as follows. God knows initially that (a) and (b) are both possible, but knows, too, that (a) is the alternative that will be realized. Once (a) is realized, however, (b) ceases to be possible. Since God always knows what is the case, then what God now knows is that (b) is not possible. His initial knowledge that (b) is possible has thus been replaced by His subsequent knowledge that (b) is not possible. Hence, His knowledge has changed and, insofar as God's essence is constituted by His knowledge, God's essence will have changed as well.

[24] Crescas presents the following scenario on behalf of the objector. God knows that two alternatives, (a) and (b), are both possible. He also knows that alternative (a) is the one that will be realized. Alternative (b), however, is still possible, in which case it ought to be possible to posit its existence without generating absurdity. Yet if (b) is the alternative that is realized, two absurdities result: first, that God's knowledge changes (since God originally knew that (a) would be realized but now must know that the realized alternative is (b)); and, second, that God's initial knowledge was mistaken and so was not knowledge after all.

[25] Crescas may well be referring to Gersonides (whom he calls R. Levi), yet he does not mention him here by name. The first explicit mention of Gersonides comes in II. i. 3.

[26] Amos 3: 7.   [27] Exod. 3: 19.   [28] Dan. 11: 14.

[They maintained that] even [God's knowledge of] these universals [is only] from the perspective of their constituting the perfection of each other—that is, from the perspective from which the parts are unified in accordance with a comprehensive order which [achieves] [1] in God's essence the height of perfection, [2] in the soul of the active intellect somewhat less perfection, and [3] in the soul of the sphere a degree of perfection well below that of both of them. They imagined that neither religion nor speculation would dispute this. With respect to whether religion would dispute this, [these sages were confident] that it would not, since they accepted that God has knowledge of particulars, and accepted too that He indeed knew the particulars before they came to be and conveyed them to the prophets; but [they thought that] His knowledge of them was not of them qua particulars but rather was of them from the perspective of the comprehensive order that exists in His essence, before the particulars even came to be. As to whether speculation would not dispute this, this will be explained in what follows.

The difficulties that seem to entail the impossibility of God's knowing any existents other than himself are not hard [for them] to resolve.

The first is based on the notion that knowledge is a perfection in the knower, so that if God were to know something other than himself, the superior would be perfected by the inferior. This is easy to resolve. For since the existence of that which is other than God is derived from God's existence, and since anything intelligible that is other than God derives from the Intelligible itself, we need not conclude that the superior is perfected by the inferior. For it has been posited that His knowledge of what is other than himself derives from the comprehensive order that is in His essence.

The second is based on the notion that the intellect is constituted by what it knows, so that if God knows something other than himself, that would entail, along with the multiplicity in what He knows, a multiplicity in His essence. The resolution of this is simple as well, based on what was said: God's knowledge, which is His essence, bequeaths existence to what is other than Him. Indeed the comprehensive order that is in His essence, even if it includes many known things, includes them from the perspective that they perfect each other, and from this perspective they are also unified. Take, for example, the human being whose definition is: nutritive, sentient, and rational. Despite his including many different things, nevertheless, since one perfects the other, he is one through them. It is therefore evident that God apprehends known things from the perspective from which they are one in Him, and therefore His essence is not subject to multiplicity.

The third is based on the notion that an individual thing is apprehended only by a hylic faculty. But it is self-evident that it does not follow necessarily from this that God cannot know the intelligible order of things.

The fourth is based on things' being subject to time. But it is evident that the intelligible order is not time-dependent.

The fifth is based on what is thought to be the deplorable condition of the order as it applies to the human species. But once it is shown that this order is at the highest degree of goodness and importance, this difficulty will be dispelled. This will be fully explained in Part II of this Book, God willing.

The first difficulty concerning the first of the three points is based on the infinity of what is known, insofar as it cannot be encompassed. It would thus appear that knowing and encompassing with respect to infinity is a self-contradiction. Yet the resolution of this difficulty is easy. It is true that there would be grounds for this difficulty were the knowing considered from the perspective of the infinity of that which is known. But the knowing, according to what was posited, is from the perspective from which it is finite—that is, from its being intelligibly ordered.

The second is the one based on continuous quantity. It is evident that [God's] knowledge of this operates not from the perspective of the quantity's being infinite but from the perspective of its being intelligibly ordered, according to which it has the potential to be perpetually divided. There is no necessity that God's knowledge of infinite parts be knowledge of them *as* infinite.

The first difficulty concerning the second of the three points is based on that true knowledge is necessarily of something existent. Yet from our saying that God knows them in accordance with the comprehensive order in His essence, it follows that what He knows is something existent, indeed something whose existence is at the height of importance.

The second is based on the change in God's knowledge when the things that are known change. This, too, is easily resolved. For whereas there would be grounds for this difficulty were the knowing applied to particulars qua particulars, the knowing here applies, as was posited, to the comprehensive order in God's essence, and it is therefore always of one unchanging thing.

The two difficulties regarding the third point concern the nature of the possible. But according to what was posited, there are no grounds for them. For as is evident, things that are possible are ordered from one perspective and not ordered from another: from the perspective of the comprehensive order they are ordered but from the perspective of human choice they are not ordered. It was indeed posited that they are subject to knowledge from the perspective of the comprehensive order, which is the perspective according to which they are ordered and limited. Thus, from the perspective from which they are not ordered and limited, they are not subject to knowledge. For if they were subject to knowledge, they would indeed be ordered and limited. But they were assumed to be neither ordered nor limited. It is therefore necessary, according to what was posited, that the knowledge of possible things be only of *that* they are possible, but not of which one of the possible alternatives will be realized.[29]

This is what emerges from their statements. This is what was intended in this chapter.

Chapter III

EXPOSITION of the even more serious difficulties incurred by what they affirmed in connection with this cornerstone.[30]

---

[29] This solution—one advanced by Gersonides—simply denies that God knows which of two possible alternatives will be realized.

[30] Now that a solution has been proposed to the objections that might be raised with respect to the cornerstone that God knows particulars, Crescas raises objections to the proposed solution, objections that he considers to be even more serious than those the solution presumably resolved.

I maintain, in accordance with what was established previously, that the root-principles of the Torah entail God's knowledge of particulars, along with the three points mentioned above. For that is indeed what the narratives and the predictions the Torah contains suggest, and what the texts indicate first and foremost and essentially. But one who wishes to be strangled and to be hanged on a tall tree[31] reveals facets of the Torah contrary to what is lawful.[32] For in no language are there arguments to compel allegorists to admit their sophistry. We therefore saw fit to expose more of the flaws in their positions, both in terms of the root-principles of the Torah and in terms of their sort of speculation.

They affirmed two points: first, that God's knowledge of particulars is not of them qua particulars but is only [of particulars] from the perspective of the comprehensive order; and second, that His knowledge of things that are possible is limited to His knowing *that* they are possible, but He does not know which of two possible alternatives will be realized. A third follows, too, for them, namely, that once one of the possible alternatives is realized, God will not have knowledge of it. This is entailed by the two earlier points. It is entailed by the first of them, insofar as, once one of two possible alternatives is realized, knowledge of it becomes knowledge of a particular qua particular, yet this sort of knowledge was already eliminated. It is entailed by the second because, according to what is posited of God, namely, that He has no knowledge of which alternative will be realized before it is realized, it follows that if He did have knowledge of it after it is realized, there would be a change in His knowledge. Yet this is something they avoided at all costs, since this is the most serious of the difficulties that led them to their view. Moreover, the claim that God's knowledge originates in something outside the mind entails that God's knowledge has its cause outside Him, such that He has an acquired intellect. This, however, is the height of absurdity and nonsense, inasmuch as its acquisition is inconceivable other than through a hylic faculty. Therefore, it is evident that this third point is necessitated for them.

Now that this has been established, we shall make evident the absurdities that arise from these points, both according to the Torah and according to speculation.

According to the Torah, this view precludes the truth of all narratives in the literal sense of the text. For since these thinkers affirm that God's knowledge is not of the particulars that are alluded to, then [according to them] God did not know the Patriarchs, did not call them by name, and did not offer them specific promises. They will say of all these things that God knew only that which is ordered in the [comprehensive] order. Yet the Torah cries out: "But You said, 'I knew you by name,'"[33] and "whom God knew face to face";[34] and it speaks of particulars, so that every believer is compelled to concede that God has particular knowledge.

Since they also affirmed that God does not know which of two possible alternatives will be realized, they were compelled to deny the [validity of] predictions concerning matters in which choice is involved. On their interpretation, these things are predicted from the perspective of the probable and reasonable, as they are presumed to conform to the workings of the celestial constellations—on condition that they not

---

[31] BT *Pesaḥim* 112a.   [32] *Avot* 3: 11.   [33] Exod. 33: 12.   [34] Deut. 34: 10.

nullify [human] choice. In the verse [in which Moses says], "For I know that after my death you will surely become corrupted,"³⁵ [they read "I know"] as "I think." But this amounts to the destruction and denial of the principles of religion. So, too, with respect to Samuel's statement to Saul, in which he predicted that Saul would encounter a certain number of men on the road, and they would say specific things to him: are these also uttered from the perspective of probability and opinion, even though the prophet calls them signs?³⁶ All this is craziness and folly.

Since they also affirmed that once one of the two possible alternatives is realized, God will not know it, the verse that says, "For now I know that you are God-fearing," is devoid of significance. For it is not really knowledge, since they affirm that God has no knowledge of anything newly existent. Nor is it something God thought, because the thought that Abraham is God-fearing could not have been newly produced after this event, so as to justify the use of the expression, "Now I know."³⁷ It is therefore evident that this view stands in opposition to the Torah and the true tradition, several of whose texts attest to God's knowledge of particulars in minute detail. It is superfluous to prolong this discussion.

Even with respect to speculation I maintain that through the approach they adopted not only were they unable to extricate themselves from difficulties but they became vulnerable to even more serious difficulties. With respect to their not having freed themselves of difficulties, it is evident that knowledge, even as they saw it, cannot escape multiplicity of the things known—and perhaps even of an infinite number of such known things. This is so for several reasons.

First, there is complete knowledge of things when their proximate and remote causes are known. Therefore, the knowledge of composite things from the perspective of their each being one thing will be complete only when the simples out of which the composites are composed are known, for these are the elements and causes of the things composed out of them. Thus, when the composite is known, a multiplicity of the things known is inescapable.

Second, that the totality of existents proceeds along the path to perfection from one existent to the next, and that it is from this perspective that they become unified, is, to be sure, verified by the genera that perfect each other and that are perfected by their species. For example, the vegetative is the perfection of the mineral, and the animal of the vegetative, and the rational of the animal. But it is not true of final species that one perfects another. For the horse does not perfect the donkey, nor the donkey the sheep. Similarly, it is not true of individuals that are primary substances that one perfects the other.³⁸ Therefore, if we suppose that God has knowledge of final species, it is inescapable that there will be a multiplicity of the things known.

Third, it is posited that God's knowledge operates from the perspective of the comprehensive order as applied to the celestial bodies and the separate intellects, which are individually eternal and differ from each other in species. From the perspective from which they differ, that is, in species, they are not unified. Therefore,

---

[35] Deut. 31: 29.   [36] 1 Sam. 10: 2; 10: 9.

[37] Since for these thinkers—for Gersonides—God has no knowledge of any new particular, it cannot be that on the occasion of the Binding God came to know—or think—that Abraham is God-fearing.

[38] Primary substances are the individual members of a species: this horse, this donkey, this person.

the knowledge of things whose essences differ in species necessitates a multiplicity of the things known.

Fourth, even if we concede that the separate intellects perfect each other—since one is the cause of the next and from that perspective they are unified—nevertheless, if God knows the immortal souls, which are not causally related to one another, it is inescapable that there is a multiplicity of things known.

Fifth, if God knows particulars from the perspective of the order of the celestial spheres, and they have a numerical order—for example, a certain number of revolutions or a number of degrees, as is known to anyone who has even a modest familiarity with the laws of astronomy—and if from this perspective a prophet is informed of a definite time, as was the case in the words Samuel spoke to Saul, it is inescapable that knowledge be of a particular number, for example, three or four. Therefore, knowledge is of particulars. If it were objected that the knowledge is not of the particular qua particular—for example, not this three or four but any three or four that should come to be—nevertheless, since it is inescapable even so that God has knowledge of some number, does He, if only I knew, know all the remaining numbers, or not? If He does know them, then, since any number is infinitely augmentable, His knowledge would be of infinite numbers. If He does not know all of them, there will necessarily be a limit beyond which He does not know. The question then remains, why would He know the numbers up to that limit, and not know them beyond that; is His knowledge subject to weakness and fatigue? The infinite multiplicity of known things is then inescapable from all perspectives.

Sixth, let us assume that God knows particulars from the perspective of the order of the celestial bodies; and that this order is in accordance with the arrangement of the planets at the moment of their inception, their zenith, and in their aspects, along with the other conditions that are not unfamiliar to the masters of this science. Let us assume, too, that if the number of positions of the planets in their orbits, from the point of view of their ascendance, their zenith, and their aspects, is infinite—inasmuch as the great circle of the celestial sphere, based upon which the ascendance is determined, is a continuous quantity and is always infinitely divisible—it would follow then that the orderings from the perspective of the celestial bodies is infinite. The infinite multiplicity of known things is thus inescapable.

And so it is evident from all perspectives that they did not extricate themselves from the difficulties stemming from the multiplicity of known things.

It will become evident as well in what follows that they became vulnerable to even more serious difficulties. In avoiding attributing to God a multiplicity of cognitions, they instead attributed to Him the defect of ignorance, the greatest of all defects. Indeed, they attributed ignorance to Him in each of three points, to the greatest possible extent.

The first is that God's knowledge is not of particulars qua particulars. Since particulars are infinite, they affirmed of Him ignorance of things that are infinite. Now, since what He knows is finite, it turns out that the ratio of what He knows to what He is ignorant of is that of the finite to the infinite.

The second is that He does not know which of two possible alternatives will be realized. Yet since the modality of the possible is wider than the ocean, and the modality of the necessary is small in measure by comparison, they indeed attribute to God ignorance of most things.

The third, which is entailed by what they hold, is that once one of the possible alternatives is realized, God has no knowledge of it. Since all events are composites, insofar as they are dependent on and mixed with human choice[39]—and indeed this is how they always are—it follows that, even though thousands of years have passed, and certain possible alternatives have always been realized following certain other alternatives, and even though this sequence has continued in the same way for all that time, God must be ignorant of all this and know nothing about any of them. For example: since Jacob's going down to Egypt belongs to the modality of the possible and depends on his choice, it would follow [according to these thinkers] that once he chose to go down—at which point God became ignorant of that choice and knew nothing of it—God also had no way of knowing all that followed from that choice, and, a fortiori, all that followed from the many choices that were made from among the possible alternatives. But this is madness on their part and heresy and confusion of heart.[40]

What is most surprising in their view is that they attribute to God ignorance of eternal things and of most existents, and perhaps to an infinite degree. For the continuing-on of immortal souls after death is a consequence of the good choices people make while they are still living their lives. Their immortality is therefore initially something that might come to be and might not come to be. But once it does come to be, God would not know of this immortality. As the number of immortal souls multiplies, it indeed becomes possible for them to outnumber greatly the eternal separate intellects and the individual celestial bodies. It is possible for their number to increase infinitely in accordance with the nature of number, so that the measure of the eternal existents of which God is ignorant will be much greater than the measure of those He knows, and this surfeit will increase infinitely. All this is the height of nonsense.

It will furthermore become evident in what follows that it is impossible for God not to have knowledge of particulars qua particulars.

Since God is the agent for all existents, whether substances or accidents, and since the particulars qua particulars are existents—either as substances or as accidents—it follows that particulars qua particulars flow from God's essence.[41] It is evident that if God is ignorant of something that flows from His essence, then His knowledge of His own essence will be a defective knowledge; may He be exalted above that.

Furthermore, it is evident from propositions that are accepted and to which the senses attest, that prophets and diviners can communicate particular things qua particular to people who are indicated to them. And of necessity they know these things through one who communicates—either God, may He be blessed, or an angel. Either way, if the communicator does not know these things, how will he communicate them to another? If only I knew.

Averroes was aware of this difficulty in his book *On* [Aristotle's] *Sense and Sensibilia*. But he did not resolve it adequately. He proposed that, just as the intellect

---

[39] The astrological order and human choice jointly determine the course of events.
[40] Deut. 28: 28.
[41] A line appears to be missing from Fisher's text (138). The text should read: והיו הפרטים במה שהם פרטים נמצאים עצמים היו או מקרים א"כ הפרטים במה שהם פרטים שופעים מעצמותו.

confers forms as universals, and matter receives them in a reception that is particular, so the intellect confers general order, and the imagination receives it in a reception that is particular. Yet these are things that can be uttered by the mouth but cannot be conceived by the mind. This resembles what R. Levi[42] of blessed memory said, namely, that whereas particular existence flows from the general order from the perspective of the nature of the matter in which the accidents inhere, and each of the existents is individuated by particulars determined by the position of its constellation, there are not in the imaginative faculty [of the communicator] individual accidents that account for the particularity of the communication. Yet how can this be if the communication[43] concerns specific accidents?

R. Levi of blessed memory made a concerted effort to resolve this difficulty by contending that the communication does not concern this individual qua individual; rather, knowledge of the order that pertains to this individual as determined by the celestial bodies arrives from the active intellect with respect to him insofar as he is an individual who happens to be born when the celestial bodies are in that specific configuration. And it so happens that this person is the one seized upon because it so happens that in the vicinity of the one who received the communication there is no other person who meets this description.

Yet it is evident that the fact that it so happens that there is not at that time in the vicinity of the one who receives the communication another person who meets this description is not sufficient to account for the prophet's communicating this specific thing. For the fact that this person [viz. the person who is in the prophet's vicinity] meets this description is not known to the prophet on his own. So it is evident that he would need someone to communicate to him that this person meets the description—if he were indeed in need of such a communication. Yet it is evident from the testimony of the senses, even with respect to the diviners of our day, that he is not in need of this communication. This is all the more the case with respect to the prophets, as it is affirmed in the true tradition, insofar as they communicate wondrous and time-specific particulars, whether concerning the past or the future, as well as possible things.[44]

---

[42] The reference is to Gersonides, R. Levi son of Gershon. This is the first explicit mention in this work of Gersonides, whose views, as we have noted (see n. 25), have already very probably been alluded to and discussed—but anonymously.

[43] Fisher records "knowledge" (ידיעה; *yediʿah*), found in the Ferrara edition, as an alternative version. Both the Vienna and Florence manuscripts have "communication" (הודעה; *hodaʿah*).

[44] According to Crescas's presentation of Gersonides' view, the specifics of the divination or prophecy apply broadly to all those who at birth share a particular astrological constellation. The way in which the divination or prophecy then applies directly to a particular individual within that group is that it is that individual who happens to be in proximity to the diviner or prophet at the time the communication is received. Crescas regards this approach as clearly insufficient, for if it is the constellation that makes the communication pertinent to the current individual, the bearer of the divination or prophecy would need to know that the particular person he was addressing was born under that constellation, and he could know this only if it were communicated to him by someone. But surely diviners (and certainly prophets) have no need for such a communication and indeed receive no such communication from anyone. And that can only be because from the start the communication they receive contains particulars relevant to a specific individual.

Most surprising concerning R. Levi is that even were we to accept his solution with respect to particular communications, there would be no escaping that, in what he maintained with respect to the kind of providence he posited, there is particular knowledge. We shall comment further on this, God willing, in Part II Chapter III.

It is evident in yet another way that God's knowledge necessarily encompasses an infinite number of known things. We shall posit in this regard two propositions, the first of which was established in the book, *On Generation and Corruption*, and the second of which is self-evident.

The first is that form comes to be in a compound through composition and blending, as oxymel comes to be through the blending of vinegar and honey. The second is that when the proportions in the blending are changed the form changes. For example, when the proportions of the ingredients in Theriac[45] change vis-à-vis one another, the form of Theriac changes, and it takes on a different form. And even more is this the case when the simple components of the compound change.

Once these propositions are established, I say that, since the magnitudes of the parts are always infinitely divisible, the variation in their blendings increases infinitely, and so, the forms of things that differ in species are infinite. It follows necessarily, therefore, that the conferrer of forms[46] must apprehend an infinity of forms. If this is confirmed for it, then it is certainly confirmed for God.

This should suffice to discredit what they imagined with respect to this cornerstone. This is what we wished to show in this chapter.

Chapter IV

RESOLUTION of the difficulties they raised in connection with this cornerstone, in accordance with the view of the Torah.

The Rabbi of the *Guide*, of blessed memory, resolved them in his own way; and with it he severely reprimanded[47] the philosophers. He saw the foundation of all their difficulties in the likening of God's knowledge to our knowledge. Since it is evident even from their claims that the term "knowledge" as predicated of God and of us is utterly equivocal, and since it is known that one cannot draw any proof from the one to the other when the two terms are applied equivocally, it follows that there are no grounds for their difficulties at all. This is because God's knowledge is His essence; and just as the level of His existence is higher than ours, so is His knowledge higher than ours. Therefore, our attempt to know how God would know which alternative from among the possible alternatives is the one that will be realized—but without necessitating it— would be like our attempting to know His essence. In this way, it is reasonable that He would know an infinite number of different particulars before they come to be, without the nature of the possible changing, and without His knowledge changing as the things known change—as is the view of the Torah according to the true tradition.

---

[45] Theriac was a pharmaceutical made from a mixture of the flesh of a serpent (which was believed to be poisonous) and several herbs and minerals to counteract the venom of the serpent. One of its uses was to thwart plague. Because it frequently contained opium, it actually was effective in easing certain symptoms.
[46] The reference is to the active intellect. See I. ii. 12 n. 163.
[47] Or, "frequently reprimanded."

Yet R. Levi of blessed memory vigorously responded to him in his book *Wars of the Lord*. He thought to topple Maimonides' edifice with two propositions. The first is that it is impossible for the equivocation between God's knowledge and our own knowledge to be absolute. The second is that, with respect to God, it is impossible for that which is confusion or error in us to be knowledge in Him.

The second of these is self-evident. The first he establishes as follows. The knowledge that is predicated of us and of God, may He be blessed, is a matter of priority and posteriority.[48] Anything that is predicated by way of priority and posteriority is not predicated with absolute equivocation.[49] It follows necessarily that the term "knowledge" is not predicated of God and of us with absolute equivocation.[50]

The major premise is self-evident. Anything that is predicated with absolute equivocation cannot be predicated by way of priority and posteriority, for the things that are designated in this way (namely, with absolute equivocation) bear no relation to one another. For example, the term ʿ*ayyin* (עין) is not predicated by way of priority and posteriority in the case of an ʿ*ayyin* of water [i.e. a spring] and an ʿ*ayyin* of vision [i.e. an eye].

The minor premise is also easily established. For it will indeed be thought that when we attribute to God or deny of Him any of the things that are found in us, what we affirm or deny is what that thing means when we have it, for we will neither affirm nor deny the bare term alone. For this reason it would appear that when we attribute knowledge, which is one of the things that we have, to God, we affirm its sense, namely, the absence of ignorance, and not the term alone devoid of its sense. Yet since this sense is not predicated synonymously of Him and of us, what it necessitates is predication by way of priority and posteriority. Thus is the first proposition established, namely, that it is impossible that the equivocation between God's knowledge and ours be absolute.

Once these propositions were established to his satisfaction, R. Levi thought to topple the wall of the edifice that the Rabbi of the *Guide* had erected around the Torah's view [in order to protect it]. For since [for R. Levi] the term "knowledge" is not predicated of God and of us by way of absolute equivocation but rather by way of priority and posteriority—which is the first proposition—it is fitting for us to liken God's knowledge to ours in terms of priority and posteriority. The difficulties that then arise out of the multiplicity of things known and out of their changing remain intact.

Since it is evident that it is impossible for something that is a confusion or error on our part to be knowledge on God's part—which is the second proposition—it is impossible, regardless of how the matter is considered, for God's knowledge concerning which of the possible alternatives will be realized not to render the possible necessary. For if it did not render that alternative necessary, the contrary alternative would remain possible. And when anything possible is posited as existing, no

---

[48] In the discussion immediately following, this statement will be referred to as the minor premise. (On priority and posteriority, see I. iii. 5 n. 186.)

[49] This statement will be referred to as the major premise.

[50] This conclusion will be referred to as the first proposition.

absurdity ensues. Therefore, the knowledge of the [first] alternative before it is realized is for us confused or erroneous. Nor can it avoid being changed after the [second] alternative is realized. But it was assumed that anything that is confused or erroneous on our part cannot be knowledge on God's part.[51]

This is the upshot of all R. Levi's arguments and objections against the Rabbi, though he babbled on at some length. For our part, even though the resolution of R. Levi's difficulties is not hard for us, as will become evident, God willing, from our remarks in what is to come, we see fit to explain first, that the way in which he sought to discredit the statements of the Rabbi are not worthy of attention. For the Rabbi's words are correct and true; they contain neither perversion nor distortion.

Let us begin by stating that, of necessity, [according to the Rabbi,] the term "knowledge" is not predicated of God and of us by way of priority and posteriority. For, any term that is predicated of things by way of priority and posteriority must of necessity designate essentially one sense. For if the senses designated by the term were different, then to speak of priority and posteriority with respect to them would be untenable. For there would be no commonality between them beyond the term alone. This is self-evident.

An example of this is the term "exists," which is predicated of substance and of other categories by way of priority and posteriority. The term "exists" has the same sense in all cases, because it intends existence and being, which is understood in one sense in all cases, and the difference is only one of priority and posteriority. For existence and being arise in the other categories through the existence and being of substance.

Once this is established, if the term "knowledge" when predicated of God means His essence, and if God's essence is at the extreme of difference and distance from the sense intended by the term "knowledge" when predicated of us, then it follows necessarily that this term does not apply to Him and to us by way of priority and posteriority.

Since a shared term that is predicated of things neither synonymously nor by way of priority and posteriority can only be predicated by way of absolute equivocation, this is what the Rabbi's words intended when he said that the term "knowledge" is predicated of God and of us by way of absolute equivocation. For even if both [viz. the term "knowledge" predicated of God and the term "knowledge" predicated of us] participate, by way of priority and posteriority, in indicating absence of ignorance, nevertheless, insofar as the term also indicates something positive, and in its positive signification it applies to things that differ absolutely in this respect, this term as applied to God and to us would necessarily be absolutely equivocal.

Indeed it is fitting that this be what is understood by the Rabbi's words. For he likened knowledge to existence in saying that, just as the degree of God's existence is

---

[51] Until one of two possible alternatives, (a) and (b), is realized, both are possible. If the one we "know" will be realized is (a), but (b) is also possible, then no absurdity should ensue if (b) is the one realized. Yet if (b) is realized, our knowledge that (a) would be realized was not knowledge but a mistake and a confusion on our part. How could that same sort of confused or mistaken cognition be knowledge on God's part? Moreover, our knowledge that (a) would be realized changes if (b) is realized, since what we now know is that (b) is realized. It must be the case, then, either that God's knowing that (a) will be realized renders (a) not possible but necessary, or that God does not know which alternative will be realized.

higher than that of our existence, so, too, is the degree of His knowledge higher than that of our knowledge. He himself explained that God's existence is God's essence, but the existence of anything else is an accident that happens to it. Therefore it is necessary that the signification of the term "existence" in its positive sense differ absolutely [when applied to God and to anything else], as God's essence differs from another's accident, even as the signification of the term "existence" in its negative sense is the same for both, namely, the indication of the negation of nonexistence. Indeed since the primary signification of the term is a positive one, he is justified in saying that the term "existence" is predicated of God and of us by way of absolute equivocation. And similarly in the case of the term "knowledge." And once this is clarified, the foundation of the edifice the Rabbi erected in his way is firm and abiding.[52]

The second proposition, which states that, concerning God, it is impossible that that which is confusion and error on our part be knowledge on God's part, is true and self-evident. But God's knowledge of which of two possible alternatives will be realized is knowledge that is true, clear, and definite; and His knowledge does not change the nature of the possible since the nature of the possible concerns only matters of choice, as will be explained in Part IV,[53] God willing. Therefore the nature of the possible does not change, and God's knowledge concerns only which alternative will be realized through choice.

R. Levi's objection that, if the nature of the possible is not changed [as a consequence of God's foreknowledge], we should be able to posit the existence of the contrary alternative—since it has indeed been established, on the basis of the definition of the possible, that when the contrary alternative is posited as existent, this positing will not engender an absurdity—may be resolved as follows. This positing will not engender an absurdity from the perspective of the nature of the possible, but rather will do so from the perspective of God's knowing which alternative the person will choose. It is evident that the absurdity does not stem from the nature of the possible, but from God's knowing the choice. But, how God knows the alternative which will be the object of choice from among things posited as possible by their nature—this could be apprehended only if God's essence were apprehended, since His knowledge and His essence are one.

This, as it appears, is the Rabbi's approach to resolving these difficulties. It is a comprehensive approach, correct and excellent and beyond doubt, regardless of how the term "knowledge" is understood—that is, whether it is thought to apply by way of absolute equivocation, as the Rabbi would have it, or whether it is predicated by way of priority and posteriority and indicates, as it seems to us, an attribute of God's essence—since knowledge is essential to Him, as we saw in Book I Part III.[54]

---

[52] BT *Baba batra* 160b, 161a. "Firm and abiding" (שריר וקים) is an expression that often appears at the end of legal documents.

[53] The manuscripts and the Ferrara edition all say Part IV, but the main discussion of free will actually takes place in Part V.

[54] Crescas is determined to commend Maimonides' solution, even as he acknowledges his disagreement with Maimonides' view that the term "knowledge" as applied to God's knowledge and to human knowledge is absolutely equivocal. Indeed, he attempts to soften Maimonides' position by suggesting that it is not with absolute equivocation that knowledge, at least in its negative sense of absence of

What remains for us to do is to address the resolution of difficulties in a special way that will be adequate, as we promised. Let us preface this by saying that there is a special distinction between God's knowledge and our knowledge, as has been established both by speculation and by the true tradition, and as will be further established in our discussion in Part III, God willing. Whereas known things acquire their existence from God's knowledge and the shaping force of His will, our knowledge emanates from and is acquired from the known things by means of the senses and the imagination, as was established in Aristotle's book *On the Soul*.[55] This is the special true foundation by which most of the difficulties will be eliminated.

The four general difficulties,[56] which concern the three points that distinguish God's knowledge,[57] will be eliminated via this foundational principle. The first derives from the notion that knowledge constitutes a perfection in the knower. In this connection it might be thought that if God were to know something other than himself, the superior would of necessity be perfected by the inferior. In fact, if God's knowledge emanated from something other than himself, there would be a basis for this difficulty. But once it has been established that God's knowledge is that which confers existence on others, it is no longer confirmed that the superior is perfected by the inferior. This is so because God's knowledge and His perfection are one, and from His knowledge that is himself, and from the shaping force of His will that is himself, the existents other than himself acquire their existence.

The second derives from a proposition that states that the intellect is constituted by what it knows. In this connection it might be thought that if God were to know something other than himself He would necessarily be constituted by something other than himself, and there would necessarily be multiplicity in His essence in

---

ignorance, that Maimonides thinks it applies to God and to human beings. It would appear that for Crescas, even if the relation between divine knowledge and human knowledge is one of priority and posteriority (as Gersonides holds, and, as Crescas here implies, he does as well), the difference between how God knows and how human beings know is so great that it remains illegitimate to draw conclusions from the latter to the former. As Crescas will go on to maintain, God's knowledge confers existence on—and is not acquired from—known things. Moreover, it is possible that Crescas agrees with Maimonides that, insofar as knowledge is not predicated univocally of God and of human beings, the precise way in which it operates remains of necessity mostly opaque to us.

Harvey (1998c: x–xi n. 2) contends that Crescas's inconsistency with respect to whether attributes when applied affirmatively to God and to human beings are utterly homonymous, as Maimonides claimed, or whether they apply by priority and posteriority, as Gersonides held, may be resolved by recognizing that the discussion in our current book, Book II, which supports Maimonides (at least until this last sentence), was written before the discussion in I. iii. 1 and I. iii. 3 which supports Gersonides.

[55] See *On the Soul* II. v–III. viii.

[56] Deviating slightly from the manuscripts, the Ferrara edition, and Fisher, all of which have: זוה, שהספקות הארבעה הכוללים העניינים השלשה אשר תיחד בהם ידיעת השם, I read: בעניינים השלשה, "which concern the three," which allows me to take הכוללים to mean "the general" rather than "which include." Without this emendation, the sentence in question would begin: "The four difficulties, which include the three points that distinguish God's knowledge." It is evident, however, that Crescas's intention is to deal first with the four general difficulties before turning to the two specific (חלקיים) ones he considers next. (It is also quite unclear what it might mean to say that these difficulties "*include* the three points that distinguish God's knowledge.")

The three points, as enumerated in II. i. 1, are that: (1) God's knowledge is infinite; (2) God's knowledge extends to the not-yet-existent; and (3) God's knowledge knows which of two possible alternatives will be chosen without changing its nature as possible.

[57] There is also a fifth general difficulty which will be taken up later.

accordance with the number of things known. Indeed, even if this generally accepted proposition [viz. that the intellect is constituted by what it knows] were justified [with respect to intellects generally], it is evident with respect to God's knowledge that it confers existence and essence on existents other than himself, and it is certainly evident that God is not constituted by something other than himself and that His knowledge of things does not necessitate multiplicity in His essence. For although if it were the case that God is constituted by the things He knows, then multiplicity in His essence would be necessitated, nevertheless, since it has been established that He confers existence on existents other than himself, it follows that He is the single, simple source and wellspring, who with His essential, eternal will confers existence on that which is other than himself, whether one or many. All the more is this difficulty groundless if this generally accepted proposition [viz. that the intellect is constituted by what it knows] is not correct, as will be shown in Book III, God willing.[58]

The third derives from the idea that individual things are apprehended only by a hylic faculty. It is evident, however, that this is true specifically of knowledge that is acquired from an existent thing, since [in such a case] the particular is not apprehended or known other than by means of sense and imagination. But in the case of knowledge that confers existence on the totality of existents, whether they be substances or accidents, species or individuals, it is not necessary that it know by means of sense and imagination. Rather, the individual is that which acquires existence from the knowledge that is in God's essence.

The fourth derives from the notion that particulars are in time, and time is an accident consequent upon motion. Yet even if this is accepted, there is no basis for this difficulty. For God's knowledge is that which confers existence on them as well as on time and on motion. That there are no grounds for doubt is even more certain in light of its having been shown in Book I that this notion is false, for time is not an accident consequent upon motion.

The fifth derives from what is thought to be the deplorable condition of the order [in the human realm]. Yet when it is shown that this order is at the height of goodness, this difficulty will vanish. This will be shown in Part II, where we shall discuss providence, God willing.

As for the specific objections. The first [specific] difficulty in relation to the first [of the three points that were posited with respect to God's knowledge of existents] is based on the idea that knowledge is something that encompasses and includes, yet things that are not finite are not encompassed or bounded. Whereas this objection would be true if [God's] knowledge were finite, no absurdity arises from His knowing an infinite number of things if instead we posit His knowledge as infinite. For the infinite does not exceed the infinite.

The second specific difficulty [related to the first point] is based on the notion of a continuous quantity. For if God were to know the relations of the parts into which a continuous quantity can be divided, He would know them as infinite, and He would know that there is no final part. Yet there is no impossibility when infinite knowledge

---

[58] The reference should probably be not to Book III, but to II. vi. 1. In IIIA. ii. 2, Crescas refers back to this earlier discussion in Book II.

correlates to infinite known things in the way that one infinite line correlates to another infinite line: in such cases the one does not exceed the other.

The first [specific] difficulty in relation to the second [of the three points that were posited with respect to God's knowledge of existents] is based on the notion that it is fitting that true knowledge concern an existent thing. Indeed this is true with respect to the cognitions we acquire from existent things. But with respect to God's knowledge, which confers existence on things, it is sophistical. For the knowledge God has of things belongs to an existent thing whose existence is the most sublime possible, that is, it is within the essence of God who is the one who confers existence on things and streams existence onto them. The fact that these things are known to Him from eternity suffices for them to be in existence.[59]

The second [specific] difficulty [in relation to the second of the three points that were posited with respect to God's knowledge of existents] is based on the idea that God's knowledge changes, for from this follows a change in God's essence, insofar as the intellect is constituted by what it knows. It is not hard to resolve this difficulty through what was said earlier. For this proposition [viz. that the intellect is constituted by what it knows] is not correct. But even if we were to accept it, nevertheless, since it was in His eternal will that a particular thing should come to be at the time that His wisdom directed, then, when the time for the coming-to-be of that thing arrives, there will be no change in the essence of His knowledge.

The first [specific] difficulty in relation to the third point is also based on a change in God's knowledge—in this case, when one of two possible alternatives is realized, insofar as the nature of the possible is eliminated. Its resolution replicates that of the previous difficulty: if we do not accept that the intellect is constituted by what it knows, then there are no grounds for this difficulty. But even if we do accept it, nevertheless, since God knows eternally that at that time the nature of the possible will change, then, when the time comes, and what occurs is just as He knew it, there is no change in His knowledge.[60]

The second [specific] difficulty [in relation to the third point] is based on the idea that, if we posit as possible the contrary alternative to the one God knows [and it is that contrary alternative that is realized], two absurdities necessarily follow: the first, a change in God's knowledge; and the second, that His previous knowledge was not knowledge but was an erroneous conjecture. It is evident that this difficulty is inescapable if we draw an analogy between our knowledge and God's—unless we posit, regarding the alternative that He knows, that from one perspective it is possible, and, from another, necessary. And then, from the perspective from which the alternative is necessary, there is no change in God's knowledge or in His essence

---

[59] Since God's eternal knowledge of things brings them into existence, they need not already exist in order for Him to know them.

[60] Crescas should not be taken to be conceding here that the *nature* of the possible changes when one of two possible alternatives is realized. He is merely countering the first specific difficulty, granting for the sake of argument that the nature of the possible could change. In other words, even if such a thing were possible, and even if God's intellect were constituted by what it knows—two propositions that Crescas vigorously denies—nevertheless, insofar as God's knowledge of the change was in place from eternity, His knowledge would not change at the time the nature of the possible (allegedly) changes.

and, from the perspective from which it is possible, the status of possible is not annulled for possible things.

This will become clear in what I shall now say. There is no doubt that if a thing is necessary from one perspective, it does not follow that the thing is necessary in itself. This will be evident in things that are possible in themselves and exist now perceived by sense. For in the case of human knowledge, once it is known that a possible thing exists, its existence is positively necessary. And its contrary is not existent from any perspective. But this necessity does not change the nature of the thing's possibility and does not compel the thing's necessity in itself.[61] Therefore, God's having knowledge with respect to things that are subject to choice does not compel their necessity in themselves and does not change at all the nature of the possible. This will indeed be clarified more expansively in Part IV, God willing.[62] There the truth with regard to this matter will be established beyond doubt. In fact, most of those who have engaged in speculation have stumbled with respect to this issue, because they could not conceive of a necessity which the Torah's divine justice can accommodate. This suffices with respect to what we intended in this chapter.

Chapter V

THE way in which we arrived at our complete knowledge of this cornerstone.

I say that this cornerstone, as we have posited it, aside from its having been verified for us by tradition, as was explained above, is also proved for us by speculation, in two ways.

The first, which is evident, is that the refutation of the arguments and the resolution of the difficulties that induced some of the investigators to deny knowledge to God, suffice to sustain this cornerstone—since it is not fitting to attribute to Him the defect of ignorance, which is the greatest of all defects. Therefore, taking into account its having been demonstratively established that nothing in all their arguments against this cornerstone invalidates it, along with what was established for us by speculation regarding the nature of the possible, it is fitting and necessary that we confirm this cornerstone as we posited it.

Second, it was already established previously that, from the point of view of speculation, it is necessarily impossible for God not to have knowledge of particulars qua particulars, as was explained in Chapter III of this Book.

What will add illumination and completion to this cornerstone is the decisive establishment of the root-principle that is the belief in creation. For then it will become clear beyond any doubt that God is the agent and the one who brings all existents into existence by His simple will. And it is inconceivable that He is their agent yet does not know them.

---

[61] Crescas here introduces a contrast between the existence of one of two possible alternatives, (a) and (b), on the one hand, and the nature of this alternative, on the other. Once alternative (a) exists, one could say that (a)'s existence is necessary (since at the moment of its existence it cannot be nonexistent), and (b)'s existence is absolutely precluded. Yet the nature of (a) as a possible thing has nevertheless not changed from possible to necessary. Crescas's way of putting this point is to say that (a) is not necessary in itself.

[62] As noted earlier (n. 53), there is some discussion of this matter in Part IV, but the fuller discussion is found in Part V.

One thing that will be established easily is that, once we concede that the creation of all things is accomplished by His will, and that among these [created] things is the nature of things, it will follow that the nature of things is also consequent upon His will, as, for example, that fire burns because He wished to give it a burning nature. Had God wished to give fire a cold nature, despite its being extremely fine, and to give earth a hot nature, despite its being extremely dense, fire and earth would have those natures. It is necessary therefore that the nature of the possible, which is among the existents, is something that God conferred by His will.[63] It is inconceivable that God, may He be blessed, wished not to know what He would know if He had not wished not to know it. For if this were possible for God, so, too, would it be possible, without any absurdity resulting, for God to endow something with a nature over which He would then have no power—even though it was the sort of thing over which power might conceivably be had. Yet this is the height of nonsense and heresy. This root-principle will indeed be established in Book III, God willing.

We have now completed what we wished to establish in this Part. Praise is to God alone, who is exalted above all blessing and praise.

Part II

CONCERNING providence.

We already stated at the beginning of this Book that God's providence with respect to existents is a cornerstone of the Torah, without which the existence of the Torah is inconceivable. Therefore it is necessary for us to investigate it, both by explaining this cornerstone and by specifying the way in which it comes to be known. This is indeed in accordance with our practice—that is, to explain this cornerstone as the Torah posited it, along with citing the difficulties that impelled some of the sages to tread the Greek path. We will resolve the difficulties; and we will restore the path that caused the sages consternation. We will take note, too, of the way in which we have arrived at our knowledge of this cornerstone, and we will investigate some issues relevant to it. We therefore saw fit to divide this Part into six chapters.[64]

Chapter I: an exposition of this cornerstone as the Torah posited it.

Chapter II: an exposition of the difficulties that can arouse confusion concerning it, on account of which some of our sages have deviated from the correct path regarding this cornerstone.

Chapter III: an exposition of the difficulties in what they affirmed in connection with this cornerstone.

Chapter IV: resolution of the difficulties they raised in connection with this cornerstone, in accordance with the view of the Torah.

Chapter V: the way in which we arrived at our complete knowledge of this cornerstone.

Chapter VI: an exposition of the issues relevant to it.

---

[63] The word translated here as "conferred" is הטביעו (*hitbi'o*), which contains the root טבע (*teva'*), nature. Crescas thus subtly reinforces a point he has already made, namely, that nature is not independent of God but is rather determined by God's will. I owe this point to Leonard Levin.

[64] Fisher erroneously has "three chapters."

Chapter I

EXPOSITION of this cornerstone as the Torah posited it.

I assert that, since it is evident from the perspective of providence, which is a cornerstone of the Torah, that God is providential with respect to human beings in order to direct them to their happiness, it is fitting that we investigate this matter in three ways: first, in respect of the providential agent; second, in respect of the providential subjects; and third, as concerns the manner of providence.

In respect of the providential agent, which is the first, the investigation must consider whether providence proceeds by means of an intermediary or in the absence of an intermediary. If providence proceeds by means of an intermediary, the investigation needs to consider what the intermediary is and if it is one or many. In respect of the providential subjects, which is the second, the investigation must consider if the providence extends only to collectives or also to individuals. If it is to individuals, then [the investigation must consider] whether providence extends equally or varies, by being lesser or greater, even to the point that it might extend to some and not to others. Concerning the manner of providence, which is the third, the investigation must consider the things that direct toward happiness, which is providence's aim.

The first is evident from the Torah and the true tradition. According to these sources, providence indeed occurs [in all three ways]: via an intermediary, or in the absence of an intermediary, or both. There are many intermediaries, and they vary in accordance with the rank of the providential subjects. It is necessary for you to know that in saying "intermediaries" we intend entities that are provident through choice and will. For there are many intermediaries through which providence operates that are in the category of instruments, such as natural forces and acts that do not operate through choice and will. Much that is recorded in the Torah and the prophets concerning acts of God which are not in accordance with the natural order are of this [second] type: "And the Lord caused the sea to go back by a strong east wind";[65] "Take your staff";[66] and many others. But what is being referred to at present is intermediaries that act through choice and will. This is easily explained in light of what is written in the Torah concerning the Patriarchs. You will find in connection with Jacob when a man struggled with him: "'Let me go, for the day breaks.' And he said: 'I will not let you go unless you bless me.' . . . And he blessed him there."[67] With respect to this, Scripture said of him: "And he strove with an angel and prevailed."[68] And he himself named the place Penuel, "for I have seen *elohim*[69] face to face and my soul was spared."[70] Furthermore when Jacob blessed his son Joseph, he said: "The *elohim* before whom my fathers Abraham and Isaac walked, the *elohim* who was my shepherd all my life until this day, the angel who redeemed me from all evil, will bless the lads."[71] It is possible, moreover, that in saying, "the *elohim* before whom my fathers walked," Jacob was hinting at the first providential agent, may he be blessed.

---

[65] Exod. 14: 21. [66] Exod. 7: 9. [67] Gen. 32: 27, 30. [68] Hosea 12: 5.
[69] *Elohim* in this context seems to indicate an angel. [70] Gen. 32: 31.
[71] Gen. 48: 15–16. Because of the parallel structure of the clauses in this blessing, since "angel" occupies the same place in the clause in which it appears, as "*elohim*" does in the clauses in which it is featured, there is reason to think that *elohim* in this context denotes not God but an angel.

Indeed it was said to Moses, "Behold, I send an angel before you, to watch over you on the way";[72] "and to Moses he said, 'Go up to the Lord,'"[73] which was interpreted homiletically in the Mishnaic tractate *Sanhedrin*.[74] There they objected: "He might have said, 'Go up to Me.' This is then Metatron whose name is like the name of his master."[75] There is indeed also an occasion on which an angel appeared to Joshua and commanded him to remove his shoe.[76]

That there can be providence without an intermediary was already attested to in the verse, "And the Lord spoke to Moses face to face as a man speaks to his companion";[77] "Mouth to mouth I spoke with him";[78] "whom the Lord knew face to face."[79] And we find a case of providence involving both an intermediary and the absence of an intermediary in the plague of the firstborn. It is said: "And I will pass through the land of Egypt, etc.";[80] "and He did not permit the destroyer to come to your house to smite."[81] In respect of the Egyptians there was an intermediary, but in respect of the sparing of Israel there was no intermediary, as the true tradition affirms in the Sages' saying: "'And I will pass through the land of Egypt'—I and not an angel."[82] Yet according to the view of our Sages, of blessed memory, it appears that, even in respect of the Egyptians, there was providence in the absence of an intermediary, as they say: "'And I will smite every firstborn'—I, and not a fiery angel."[83] According to their view, its saying "and He did not permit the destroyer," hints at an intermediary whose status is that of an instrument that operates without providence[84] and will.[85] There are, then, many intermediaries. Some are angels, like those who appeared to Jacob, Joshua, and Gideon. The angels that arrived in Sodom were also of this type, since they indeed directed Lot to escape the destruction. Some were prophets, such as the Patriarchs who directed others to the belief in God, as it is said: "And the souls they made in Haran,"[86] culminating in the master of the prophets who came and directed the whole of our nation to worship God. So, too, the prophets who followed him, generation after generation. Some were judges and Sages who remonstrated with the people, and who kept watch over the sacred through Torah and through commandment.

The first way, then, the one in respect of the providential agent, has been settled from the point of view of the intention of the Torah, as follows. God is a providential

---

[72] Exod. 23: 20. [73] Exod. 24:1.

[74] BT *Sanhedrin* 38b. The manuscripts and the Ferrara edition have *Sotah* rather than *Sanhedrin*. Fisher preserves the reference as *Sotah*; he brackets *Sanhedrin*.

[75] The Tetragrammaton, then, and not only *elohim*, may indicate an angel.

[76] Josh. 5: 15. The expression here is שר צבא ה', "the captain of the Lord's host."

[77] Exod. 33: 11.   [78] Num. 12: 8.   [79] Deut. 33: 10.   [80] Exod. 12: 12.

[81] Exod. 12: 23.   [82] In the Passover *Haggadah*.   [83] In the Passover *Haggadah*.

[84] The expected term here is בחירה (*beḥirah*), choice; yet the term that appears is השגחה (*hashgaḥah*), the term for providence. Since Crescas had said, however, that what is intended by "intermediary" is an entity "*provident* through choice and will," it follows that intermediaries that function as instruments are not provident; they indeed "operate without providence and will."

[85] Crescas first considers the possibility that an intermediary, a "destroyer," smote the Egyptian first-born, but God himself, directly, spared the Israelites. Taking into account, however, the Rabbis' view that the smiting of the first-born Egyptians was performed directly by God, Crescas concludes that the destroyer was not an angel endowed with choice and will but an instrument—and thus not a true intermediary.

[86] Gen. 12: 5.

agent who operates both through intermediaries and in the absence of an intermediary; there are many intermediaries; and intermediaries are of three species: angels, which are the separate intellects; prophets; and Sages. Whether or not there is a fourth species is something to which we have no access from this perspective—neither from the point of view of the tradition nor from the point of view of speculation. For, some of the sages—among them the Rabbi of the *Guide*—held that the spheres are alive and think. Indeed, the straightforward meaning of the Scriptures and some of the midrashic texts agree with this view. If this is the case, there would be a fourth species of intermediary that acts with choice and will, namely, the celestial bodies, which act, and conceive of what they do, in accordance with an order that is in their souls, and which is a matter of will.

That the rank of those who are subjects of providence varies is evident from what appears in the Torah and in the stories it relates about the world's Patriarchs. The providence and guidance extended to the master of the prophets took place without an intermediary, face to face. The guidance extended to other prophets was through an intermediary, as Scripture attests, for they are of lower rank than Moses. Since the community of Israel is lower in rank than the prophets, their guidance was accomplished by means of the prophets. When the generations declined, their guidance came via the judges and Sages. Since the community of our nation is the people that God chose as His inheritance, they received guidance from Him, sometimes without an intermediary and sometimes through the mediation of His prophets and Sages, such that the mediation was necessarily founded on, constrained by, and relative to the level of perfection of the providential subjects in accordance with time and place. But God's providence for the other nations was through the mediation of the celestial bodies,[87] from which necessarily follows a general guidance, not related to the rank in perfection of the providential subjects in accordance with time and place. It appears to follow that the spheres are lower in rank than the Sages, since, as it seems, the more God's guidance is related [to the perfection of the providential subject], the higher the rank [of the subject]. Some of the sages were drawn to this view. In any event, however, it is verified according to the Torah and the true tradition that the intermediaries vary with the difference in the providential subject. This should suffice now for the first.

The second, the one concerning the providential subjects, is evident from what the Torah says, namely, that providence indeed extends to the whole and to individuals; and that providence varies with respect to them by being lesser or greater, to the point that it is possible that it extend to some and not to others. For besides the general guidance provided to the nation as a whole, particular guidings and promises and blessings were extended to the Patriarchs and to the prophets, each one by name. It would appear from what was said concerning the difference among providential subjects that providence varies by being lesser or greater to the point that it is possible even that it not extend at all to some, because of how far their level falls short of perfection and the human end. With respect to people of this sort it is said: "And

---

[87] See Deut. 4: 19–20.

I will surely hide My face";[88] "I will hide My face from them."[89] This is sufficient now for the second.

With respect to the third, which concerns the manner of providence as derived from the Torah and the tradition, and as proved as well by sense, it will be easily shown that sometimes it operates at the species level and is general, and sometimes it is individual. Of providence that is general, some is general absolutely, and is ordered and defined, and is not relative to the perfection of the individuals subject to it; and some is general in one way, and particular in another, and varies from mostly general to slightly general. The mostly general is also ordered and defined, and is natural and not relative to the perfection of the providential subjects. The slightly general is ordered and defined, but is not natural and is somewhat relative to the perfection of the providential subjects. Individual providence is also not natural. Some of it is ordered and defined and is absolutely relative to the perfection of the providential subjects; some of it is ordered and defined and is only partially relative to the perfection of the providential subjects.

An example of fully general providence may be found in that all composite existent individuals are equipped with instruments and qualities and desires, and with psychic and active faculties, to preserve their existence and enable them to avoid harm. This providence, even if it varies from species to species, is equal for all individuals within a species. An example of providence that is general in one respect and particular in another is found in the human species. For since this species is more perfect than the other species it has a practical intellect which can organize many activities that preserve its existence, and a theoretical intellect which is the greatest vital force for the acquisition of human perfection. This providence is natural, and it is equal for individuals from the point of view of potential and disposition. Even if it varies from the perspective of the agent, the variation is not relative to the perfection of the individual providential subjects. For, one whose rank in human perfection is great might enjoy a smaller measure of this providence than does someone whose rank is lower, since this type of providence follows either the temperament of each individual or the order of the celestial spheres that obtained when this individual was born, as is explained by the science of astrology. But this is general providence insofar as it affects the entire species of man, and it is particular providence insofar as it affects *only* the species of man, such that it is natural and inclusive of the entire human species.

An example of providence that is slightly general is the grace that was shown to the whole of our nation, to us, the congregation of believers, in the Torah that was given by God, may He be blessed and His name praised forever, through which, essentially and first and foremost, perfection is acquired. Yet this is only slightly general inasmuch as it does not include the entire species. Moreover, it is not natural, inasmuch as it depends on the will of one who wills with respect to a particular nation and a particular time. It is not, however, relative to the [perfection of the] individual providential subjects. For even though it is the most excellent providence

---

[88] Deut. 31: 18.   [89] Deut. 32: 20.

possible, nevertheless, since it is the nation as a whole that is the preeminent providential subject, this providence is not relative to individual providential subjects, for it applies equally to all individuals in the nation. Even though there are differences among the individuals in the nation, in that for some of these individuals Scripture prescribed a greater number of commandments—for example, more commandments are obligatory for men than for women and slaves, more are obligatory for priests than for Israelites—the reason for this is the difference in status of the groups: males, for example, are of higher status than females and have greater potential for perfection, and the priests who were sanctified with the priesthood of Aaron are of higher status than the rest of Israel and have greater potential for perfection. Nevertheless, the providence with respect to individuals within each of the groups is equal. It is therefore evident that this providence is not fully relative to the perfection of the individuals subject to it. To the extent, however, that this providence varies with respect to parts of a species, it is somewhat relative to the perfection of the subjects of providence. It is also somewhat true that this providence is a means and preparation for a providence relative to individual providential subjects.[90] Yet even if it is a means and preparation for individual providence, it is nevertheless self-evident that individual providence does not follow from it.

An example of individual providence is the reward bestowed on those who serve God and the punishment visited upon the transgressor, as the Torah and tradition affirm. Its being non-natural is evident on its face, for it is not by nature that one who builds a sukkah and takes the lulav and avoids mixed kinds is the recipient of God's kindness, nor [is it by nature] that one who eats fat and blood is subject to excision. But the form of providence that is completely relative to the perfection of the providential subjects is the form of providence that is affirmed in the true tradition, namely, psychic reward and punishment.[91] It is evident that this form of providence is precisely proportional to individual providential subjects according to the rank of each of them. And it is also evident that this providence is ordered and defined by God's eternal will, in accordance with His wisdom.

An example of providence that is ordered and defined and relative to the perfection of providential subjects, but incompletely so, is the form of this providence that is explicit in the Torah, namely, corporeal reward and punishment. Since the obedient individual is rewarded and the transgressor punished, it is evident that this providence is relative to the perfection of providential subjects. Since, however, there is confusion and perplexity with respect to what is seen of this providence by the senses, as will be discussed later, God willing, it is confirmed that this providence is not precisely proportional to the perfection of the providential subjects.

The manner of providence has thus been established. This was the third way.

---

[90] Fisher brackets this sentence as it is absent from the Ferrara edition. The Florence manuscript adds the following phrase which is absent from the Vienna manuscript and from Fisher, היותה מתיחסת לשלמות המשגחים, "in that it is relative to the perfection of the providential subjects."

[91] "Psychic" is used throughout in the sense of "pertaining to the soul." Psychic reward and punishment are experienced after death.

Chapter II

EXPOSITION of the difficulties that can arouse confusion concerning this cornerstone, as it has been posited, on account of which some of our sages have deviated from the correct path regarding it.

I assert, according to what has been supposed in this cornerstone, that since individual members of the human species are subject to providence in the particulars of their deeds, it is evident that the same objections that they [viz. some of our sages] raised with respect to God's knowledge of things may well be raised here. There is no need to repeat those things, especially since they were already fully resolved. But the great difficulty, which has not been fully resolved, and whose solution we promised would be provided in this Part, is what is thought to be the deplorable condition of the order [in the human realm] insofar as it appears that many excellent men are mere doormats[92] for lesser men, and, generally, that the righteous suffer and the wicked prosper. It is this that has perplexed the prophets and the sages to this day.

Since the Rabbi has written that it is possible to resolve the issue, whether we concede the proposition—namely, that the righteous suffer and the wicked prosper—or whether we deny it, and, if we deny it, whether we do so from the perspective of the predicate or from that of the subject,[93] it is necessary to examine this response [viz. the Rabbi's response] to see if it is adequate. The way to respond [according to the Rabbi] in the case in which we concede the supposition is to attribute the good that accrues to the wicked and the bad that accrues to the righteous, not to providence but to naïveté and ignorance. For if the righteous man does not wish, in his naïveté and ignorance, to pursue appropriate causes, the fault does not lie with God. And occasionally something good will ensue from naïveté and ignorance. Such is the good that accrues to the wicked.

The response in the case in which we deny the supposition from the perspective of the subject is that the righteous person who appears righteous is not in fact righteous. Even if we see him doing good, it is still possible that, considering his potential, he fell short in doing good, and his good act was therefore regarded as an act of rebellion. So, too, the wicked person who appears wicked may not in fact be wicked, for, considering his potential and temperament, he does good by refraining from doing the bad to which he is disposed.

The response in the case in which we deny the supposition from the perspective of the predicate is to say that the bad that accrues to the righteous person is not truly bad, since its end is the good. Insofar as it is a means to the good, it is considered good. Similarly, the good that accrues to the wicked person, insofar as its end is the bad, is considered bad.

When we looked into this response, however, it appeared inadequate. For in the case in which we conceded the supposition [that the righteous suffer and the wicked prosper], the response was inadequate, since from the perspective of his deeds the righteous person, even if we see him pursuing appropriate causes lest he experience

---

[92] Deut. 2: 5. The expression is מדרך כף רגל, "that upon which the sole of a foot treads."
[93] The righteous and the wicked are the subjects; the predicates are their respective suffering and prospering.

many and terrible afflictions, does not receive the good he deserves. And the wicked person experiences great happiness.[94] The response in the case in which the proposition is denied from the perspective of the subject is also inadequate, because the very same person has bad things happen to him when his deeds are directed to the good, and good things happen to him when they are not directed to the good. And the response in the case in which the proposition is denied from the perspective of the predicate is also inadequate. For, many bad things whose end is not the good affect the righteous person, and good things whose end is not the bad affect the wicked person. The difficulty thus remains the same: it derives from the senses, from the fact that we see that the righteous experience bad and the wicked experience good.

Objections have indeed been raised with respect to this doctrine [of individual providence] both from the perspective of speculation and from the perspective of the Torah. From the perspective of speculation, it is challenged by a single proposition which was corroborated in the *Metaphysics*[95] and which states that bad ensues from God only accidentally but not essentially, and from the necessity imposed by matter. Indeed, the Sages of blessed memory accepted this proposition, when they said, "No bad thing descends from on high,"[96] along with other dicta that agree with this one. Once this proposition was established for them, they composed the following syllogism: If God were to exercise providence with respect to human beings and take note of their deeds such that good would accrue to the good and bad to the bad, it would follow that the bad would derive from God essentially; but this consequent is false; and so it follows that the antecedent is false. Therefore this doctrine is discredited from the perspective of speculation. For it is unlikely that God would exercise providence with respect to man, for man is inferior in relation to Him.

This doctrine of individual providence [may be contested] from the perspective of the Torah as well, since, as it appears, the bad it foretold in accordance with the great rebellion took the form of abandonment and concealment of the Face, as God said: "And I will conceal My face from them";[97] "And I will surely conceal My face";[98] and in the tradition [here "the tradition" refers to the Prophets]: "I will not take note of your daughters when they are promiscuous."[99] All of this indicates that a punishment consisting of something bad involves concealment of the Face and abandonment to the accidents of time.

Some of our sages,[100] feeling pressed by the Torah and by speculation, accepted this cornerstone in the sense that individual providence extends to some people and not to others. For as it is proved in the book, *Parts of Animals*,[101] the more eminent the animal, the better equipped it is with organs to preserve its life. Since man is

---

[94] Even if we accept that the righteous suffer and the wicked prosper, we can say, with Maimonides, that they acted out of ignorance and naïveté: in the case of the righteous, they failed to pursue appropriate causes; in the case of the wicked, it was by happenstance that their fecklessness led to good results. Crescas objects, however, that the righteous and the wicked who act not out of ignorance and naïveté still respectively suffer and prosper.

[95] Aristotle, *Metaph.* IX. ix. 1051^{a}15ff.   [96] *Gen. Rabbah* 51: 3.

[97] Deut. 32: 20.   [98] Deut. 31: 18.   [99] Hosea 4: 14.

[100] The reference is (at least) to Gersonides. Certain aspects of the view Crescas challenges may be found in Maimonides as well.

[101] See Aristotle, *Parts of Animals* X.

immeasurably the most eminent, to the point that there are those who believe it to be possible for him to become conjoined with and to become one with the active intellect, it follows necessarily that anyone who is closer to the active intellect in rank, will, because of his importance, be more subject to providence, and anything[102] that is farther in rank will, because of its deficiency, be unworthy of having providence attach to it. It is fitting that it be so. For it is evident that, for God, all the intelligibles are actual, and man is in potentiality with respect to many of them. And it is evident with respect to that which is actual that it perfects and actualizes that which is in potentiality; and when there is transition from potentiality to actuality in the intelligibles, the agent and the acted-upon are one in some way. Therefore, from this perspective, it is fitting that the perfect man who intellects in actuality and who is conjoined to God and is one with Him, should have providence extend to him; and it is fitting that he who, despite having the potential and disposition, does not intellect in actuality since he has not acquired this union and attachment, be abandoned on account of his deficiency and defectiveness. It is thus confirmed that this providence, which depends on one's attachment to and union with God, and thus, in turn, on the acquisition of the intelligibles in actuality, is a matter of individual nature. Therefore, it is fitting that providence be in accordance with the degree of this attachment and union.

Because the purpose of this providence is in general to produce appropriate causes for attaining the good, it would appear that this providence extends to human individuals by communicating to them the good things and the bad things that are poised to accrue to them, so that they will avoid the bad things and direct themselves to the good. This communication would reach the perfect ones perfectly via prophecy—within which there are also degrees—and would reach others through a weaker means of communication, as, for example, by introducing into them psychic desires to turn toward the good and to flee the bad, without their having to calculate. Occasionally, something painful will lead to a good end, as it is said: "I will thank You, O Lord, for You were angry with me,"[103] as our Sages, of blessed memory, explained. Just as this providence is for those who are good, in that such communication reaches them, so too is it for the bad, in that this communication does not reach them, they are abandoned to the accidents of time, and they are not protected from the bad things that are poised to come upon them in accordance with the constellation.

It is evident that this type of providence does not guarantee that the good things that are poised to befall the wicked in accordance with the constellation will not reach them. Thus, what appears to the senses, namely, that the wicked man experiences good, is not contradicted by this hypothesis of ours, for that good befalls him on account of the constellation and not on account of providence—just as it does not contradict what appears to the senses in the case of the righteous experiencing bad. For that bad is possible for the righteous person for various reasons. One such reason is, for example, that the children of fathers whose punishment was exile were not sufficiently meritorious to be redeemed from that exile by way of a miracle or

---

[102] Fisher reasonably has "and anyone" (ומי), but the Ferrara edition and the manuscripts all say, "and anything" (ומה).

[103] Isa. 12: 1.

wonder. Another is so that the bad might result in a good end, whether to protect people from the bad thing that was poised to come upon them, or to protect them from yielding to their own deficiencies. Another is because of their undoing of their bond and attachment to God, for since their providence is in virtue of this union, once a person is separated from God, it is fitting that he be abandoned and surrendered to the influence of the constellation, and that he not be protected from the bad things that are poised to come upon him.

With regard to the ordering of the constellation itself, even if what results from it is occasionally good for the wicked and bad for the righteous, it is not fitting that this be attributed to any wrong or weakness, since it is obvious from its character that, in relation to the preservation of existents in the world and to the flourishing of species, it is at the height of perfection. And even if it is possible that there are some individuals whom good things befall, despite their being evil, it is not fitting to discount the general good for that reason. This is especially so in light of its being evident that true reward and punishment is a matter of the soul's happiness and the absence of its happiness, and not a matter of merely illusory goods.[104] This is their view with regard to this cornerstone. The matter of the deplorable condition of the order as it appears to the senses was thus resolved for them. And [they recognized] that bad does not ensue from God essentially, for the bad that befalls a wicked man when he is abandoned befalls him on account of his having happened to be born under a certain configuration of the celestial bodies.

They made a concerted effort to resolve two difficulties in this supposition. The first is that if providence extends to the perfect person by means of communication, it is likely that some of this communication would reach the wicked who are intellectually perfect, on account of the union they have with God through the perfection of their intellect; this, however, is not right in respect of divine justice. The second is that we find bad things promised in the Torah, and what is intended seems to be these things themselves and not the abandonment and concealment of the Face.

They resolved the first by saying that, although true reward is nothing but psychic happiness, so that there should be nothing to prevent the possibility of this communication's reaching the wicked, in point of fact, this is not correct. For, a person who is perfect with respect to intelligibles nevertheless loses his attachment when he inclines toward lusts and shameful deeds; for his being drawn to matter prevents him from using the intelligibles he has already apprehended and will certainly prevent him from further apprehension. Therefore, it is not possible that communication will reach him in the way it reaches the perfect person. This is the whole of what they said in resolving the first difficulty.

With respect to the second they said that the promises of punishment to the transgressor are a matter of providence. To those who are novices in evil, they are issued in order that they turn away from it. And for those who are steeped in evil, they are for the good of the nation as a collective. For if some individuals adopt

---

[104] The idea here is that bad things and good things are illusory, מדמות (*medumot*), when they are material—as opposed to psychic. No material bad is a genuine harm and no material good is a genuine benefit. Examples of faux harms would be such things as poverty and illness; faux benefits would include wealth and bodily vigor, victory over enemies and glory.

shameful deeds, God will attempt to punish them as an admonition to the nation as a whole, lest it sink to [the commission of] such deeds. This is the sum total of what emerges from their words regarding this cornerstone.

Chapter III

EXPOSITION of the difficulties in what they affirmed concerning this cornerstone.

It is fitting that we note first the places along the path on which these thinkers became bewildered, where they deviated from what our Sages of blessed memory set down as root-principles and from what is written in the Torah. There are two such places of deviation: the first is with respect to what they affirmed concerning the reward of the righteous; the second is with respect to the punishment of the wicked.

The reason they deviated with respect to reward for the righteous person is that they held that providence involves the communication to him of the good things poised to befall him [in accordance with the constellation]. Yet it is evident from what is written in the Torah and from the stories that have come by way of prophecy regarding the promises to the Patriarchs and to others, that providence with respect to them lies in the flowing of good things to them that exceeds the measure and custom of nature, and which could hardly be ordained by the celestial bodies: for example, that ten will chase one hundred and one hundred chase one thousand,[105] that the produce of the sixth year will suffice for three years,[106] that "there shall be no poor among you,"[107] for it is not possible that the stars could be responsible for this ordering every sixth year. And there are many standing miracles for which providence is responsible, such as the administering of the water to the woman suspected of adultery,[108] the assurance that no one will covet our land when we go up [to Jerusalem] for the pilgrimage festival,[109] and the other miracles accepted by tradition that occurred in the Temple by way of individual providence.

It appears that the reason they fled from reward of this kind is that it entails God's having knowledge of particulars. For they imagined that the communication to the person who is perfect is made possible by some sort of union with the active intellect, and that it was on account of this union that he received the communication—without God's knowing the particular individual. But, in the miraculous production of particular goods for a particular individual, it is unavoidable that the producer of the particular good know that particular individual. Because they banished such knowledge, however, they fled from this kind of providence. It is nevertheless evident that this is a deviation and departure from the roots of truth.

With respect to the punishment of the wicked person, this is even more evident. For it was supposed that his essential punishment would be that he would be abandoned to the accidents of time—rather than that illusory bad things not ordained by the cosmic order would be produced for him. When the predictions in the Torah are cited in objection to them, inasmuch as it certainly appears that these punishments are directed [to specific wicked individuals], they say that it is not they

---

[105] Lev. 26: 8. In this verse it is said that five—not ten—chase one hundred. Fisher's text does, however, concur with the manuscripts.
[106] Lev. 25: 20–2.   [107] Deut. 15: 4.   [108] Num. 5: 11–21.   [109] Exod. 34: 24.

that are so directed, but that they remain a matter of providence: [they serve as a warning] to those who are novices in evil to turn away from it; and, in the case of those who are steeped in evil, [they serve as a warning] to the nation which, as a collective, is good.

Even if it were as it was supposed, however, there would still be no avoiding God's knowledge of particulars. For even if the bad thing that befalls the wicked person is intended to reach him on account of providence for good men, that bad thing could not reach him without an agent to confer the bad thing on that person. After all, there is no way for it to reach him by way of union with and closeness to the conferrer, for he is very far removed from Him and abandoned. Therefore, it is impossible to conceive of this sort of providence without an agent who knows the righteous and the wicked individuals, for it is evident that nature cannot become a prophet knowing good and evil. Therefore, it is impossible for the one who produces the causes that will afflict a particular wicked person not to know him. It is therefore evident that, even in accordance with what they posited, God's knowledge of particulars is necessitated—yet this is the very thing from which they fled.

That which they supposed contradicts the plain meaning of Scripture. For in the punishment of the generation of the flood which was general, it indeed appears that had Noah not found favor in God's eyes, the entire human species would have been obliterated. Yet according to their hypothesis, if Noah had not found favor in God's eyes, the entire generation would have been free of punishment.[110] Yet this is the height of nonsense. And there is no way to avoid this, other than to say that the flood was ordained by the constellation, and that the providence was for Noah, to save him in order that the species survive. As much as their view is opposed to the plain meaning of the scriptural texts, which posit punishment for the wicked, it is also impossible. For what would have had to happen is that from the order attributable to the celestial bodies, which is providential with respect to preserving this inferior existence, something essentially bad would have derived for the entirety of this chosen species within it.[111] Yet this, too, is contrary to their supposition. And there is no doubt that it was intended as a punishment for that generation; and were Noah of their ilk, he too would have been afflicted along with them.

In addition to this, thirty-six excisions are mentioned in the Torah for certain transgressions. Does the Torah contain any mention of a connection [between the transgressors and other people] or stipulate as a condition that the transgressors must be known to others? Yet according to their supposition, one who eats fat[112] or blood[113] is not excised by way of punishment unless it is known to others who are righteous—because his punishment is a matter of providence for the righteous alone.[114] Our Rabbis of blessed memory have already made explicit, in various places,

---

[110] The reasoning here is that if, as "their" view would have it, the punishment of the wicked is only for the purpose of warning the righteous, then, in the absence of anyone righteous, there would be *no* punishment.
[111] The reference is to the human species.   [112] Lev. 7: 23–5.   [113] Lev. 7: 26–7.
[114] If the purpose of punishment for those who transgress is to deter the righteous from sin, the punishment is pointless if the righteous are unaware of it, in cases where they have no connection to the sinners or do not know them.

that excision entails the death of the body. Further, it is inescapable that this excision be either of the body or of the soul. But if it is of the body, it is necessary that the transgressor in private not be punished. And if it is of the soul, and if its purpose is providence for the *souls* of the righteous—which would [presumably] be cognizant of that soul's demise—would it keep them from sinking further into [wicked] deeds? If only I knew.[115] All of this is but a destruction of the foundations of the Torah and a complete betrayal of the true tradition.

Moreover, according to this supposition of theirs, punishment of the wicked is for the sake of providence for the righteous. Yet true punishment of the wicked is by way of the soul's demise, a punishment that cannot be directed toward the providence of the righteous for it must be natural and not judicial. According to their view, such a punishment would indeed be natural for an individual who does not activate the intelligibles. But for one who does activate the intelligibles and acquires them, punishment for deeds is precluded. In several places in the Talmud,[116] however, informers, those who strike terror in the land of the living, and others of their sort are told of the extraordinary punishment to which their souls will be subjected. Someone might say that this, too, is for the sake of providence for the righteous man, who will know that the wicked man is irrevocably destined for the demise of his soul, and who will therefore be deterred from those deeds. Yet this is vanity and chasing after the wind.[117] For the righteous man does not know unless he believes, and if he believes, there is no need for that form of providence or for that bad thing [viz. the soul's demise] to occur miraculously after death to the very soul whose immortality was guaranteed by dint of its having acquired the intelligibles.[118]

From all this it appears that everything they have supposed, whether with respect to the reward of the righteous or with respect to the punishment of the wicked, contradicts the principles of the Torah and its roots.

Now that we have noted the places where they have deviated and departed from the religion, we shall explain the difficulties in what they affirmed in connection with this cornerstone.

We assert that the first difficulty that spurred them to their supposition regarding this cornerstone remains intact.[119] For it is self-evident, as well as accepted by them,

---

[115] The absurdity here seems to be that if it is the *soul* of the wicked that is punished, how would the righteous know about it so as to be deterred by it from sinning unless they were already dead and witnessed it—in which case it would hardly be of value?

[116] *Tosefta, Sanhedrin* 13: 4–5; BT *Rosh Hashanah* 17a.   [117] Eccles. 1: 14.

[118] Crescas recognizes that punishment by the demise of the soul for the sake of the righteous is not consonant with the philosophers' allegiance to strictly natural punishment. Natural punishment in the form of the soul's demise, even if it accrues to the wicked, is not related to their wicked deeds but only to their souls' having failed to become conjoined with the active intellect. Souls, even wicked ones, that, while still associated with living human beings, successfully acquire the intelligibles and engage actively with them are necessarily immortal and cannot perish. How, then, would the righteous be able to deduce from the demise of a soul that wicked deeds are to be avoided? It is the Talmud that links such extraordinary punishment to wickedness. Yet the righteous have no verification of the dire consequences of evildoing of which the Talmud speaks: if they take it on faith they require no further proof; they surely do not require the actual demise of the souls of the wicked in order to be deterred from transgression. Does their continued righteousness depend upon their witnessing a miracle—that of the perishing of souls which, because of their acquisition of intelligibles, cannot perish?

[119] The first difficulty was that the wicked prosper and the righteous suffer.

that true reward and punishment are psychic reward and punishment. Therefore it is necessary, according to their hypothesis, that one who acquires the intelligibles in large measure, yet inclines to evil deeds, be punished with a psychic punishment. This should especially be the case if he is a member of one of the groups that, as is accepted according to the root-principles of the Torah, have no portion in the world-to-come. Therefore it is inescapable that this punishment, namely, the bad and the destruction that befalls this soul, derives from God essentially. For the statement that this punishment arrives after death to admonish another person is an absurd one.[120]

There is indeed another difficulty associated with their position, one no less serious than this one[121] according to their approach. For according to them, this soul, which has acquired the intelligibles, and which is by its nature an eternal substance at the time it is annihilated by divine decree as punishment for its deeds, will then pass either into something or into nothing. This is a necessary disjunction. It is impossible that it pass into nothing, on their approach, because those who hold this view believe that coming-to-be from nothing or passing-away into nothing is an impossibility whose nature is stable.[122] It is necessary, therefore, that it pass into something. If only I knew into what thing. For disjunction dictates that it be either a substance or an accident. It cannot be an accident, because an accident can be predicated only of a subject, and its existence is inconceivable without it. It is therefore necessary that it be a substance. But a substance is either incorporeal or not incorporeal. It cannot, however, fail to be incorporeal, for a soul after it departs is an incorporeal substance. And for an incorporeal substance not to be incorporeal is a contradiction in terms. It is necessary therefore that the substance be incorporeal. Yet if it is an incorporeal substance, no causes can effect its passing-away, and it will remain necessarily immortal, and it will have a portion in the world-to-come. It was assumed, however, that it has no portion in the world-to-come.[123] It is proved, then, that the difficulty that spurred them to this view remains intact; indeed, it is even stronger.[124]

Indeed their other difficulty, the one that supposed that it is unlikely that God's providence would extend to human beings because of man's inferiority in relation to God,[125] remains intact as well. For what they proposed in resolving it was inadequate, namely, that the union that is reached as a result of God's having all the intelligibles in actuality and of man's being in potentiality with respect to many of them necessitates providence. For as was proved in what we said in Part I of this Book, knowledge and intellect are not predicated of God and of us univocally. And

---

[120] With the discrediting of the idea that punishment as destruction of the soul is for the benefit of the righteous and hence actually a good thing, there is no avoiding the conclusion these thinkers were desperate to avoid at all costs, namely, that something bad—punishment whose end is not something good—derives from God essentially. For, those whose intellects are developed—no matter how wicked—could not suffer destruction of the soul by purely natural means.

[121] The manuscripts have איננו למטה מזה; the Ferrara edition has איננו למטה. Fisher suggests איננו מעטי.

[122] This impossibility has a "stable nature," קים טבע (*teva' qayyam*), in the sense that it is firm and fixed.

[123] This sentence does not appear in the Ferrara edition but it is found in the Florence and Vienna manuscripts: וכבר הונח שאין לו חלק לעולם הבא.

[124] The reference is to the second difficulty, which is that God cannot be essentially the source of bad.

[125] This was the third difficulty, namely, that God's providence would not extend to those who are inferior to Him.

things that are not predicated univocally do not unite in such a way that God's providence with respect to man is necessitated. This is especially true according to the view of the Rabbi, who holds that they are predicated equivocally. So, the difficulty stands: that man, despite his intellecting, is at the height of inferiority in relation to God, to the point that the ratio between them is infinite. And therefore it is improbable that God's providence extends to him.

It has thus been proved that the difficulties that led them to this view remain intact,[126] in addition to the difficulties in the matter of God's knowledge, which we discussed previously in the relevant Part, and which we noted in this chapter.

Chapter IV

RESOLUTION of the difficulties they raised in connection with this cornerstone, in accordance with the view of the Torah.

It is not difficult to resolve the objection that was raised from the perspective of the deplorable condition of the order [in the human realm], in accordance with what was supposed, namely, that true punishment and reward is psychic—and this is the very truth. For the foundation of this objection is the bad that the righteous experience and the good that the wicked experience. Indeed the bad that the righteous experience, aside from the bad that they suffer on account of their fathers, as was noted earlier, can occur for various reasons, as was also noted earlier. It may occur either because of the occasional dissolution of the bond and attachment between the righteous person and God insofar as the righteous person is a corporeal being; or it could be the kind of bad whose end is good, whether corporeal or psychic, as, for example, something distressing that leads to a corporeal good, or to the person's not inclining toward the lusts to which he was disposed, or to making him perfect or acquiring for him a firm hold on psychic virtues. This to me is the matter of trials mentioned in the Torah to which the nation as a totality is subjected, when considered from the perspective of those tested. Yet this is in line with the verified proposition that states that deeds help one acquire stable character traits and virtues in the soul, and, a fortiori, strengthen those already acquired. It thus proves true that one who is tested by a certain deed or deeds, will, if he passes the test, acquire a further perfection beyond his [current] perfection. It will be confirmed in this way that something became known to God that He did not know prior to the test, since it did not yet exist.[127] Therefore, when Scripture says with respect to the nation: "for the Lord your God tests you, to know whether you love the Lord your God,"[128] it does not say, "whether you *will* love," for this is something God already knows. For since

---

[126] The problems that spurred the untenable and now discredited solutions persist. They are: the problem of theodicy; that of bad deriving from God essentially; and that of God's concerning himself with inferior beings.

[127] The point is that God knows before the test that after the test—and as a result of the test—the person tested will be perfected beyond his current perfection. What God comes to know only after the test is that the person *is now* in this state of enhanced perfection. As Crescas explains, God could not know *this* at the earlier time because it was not then true.

[128] Deut. 13: 4. God knows in advance that the people *will* love Him in the future, but He does not know that they love him at the present time because they do not.

the commandments were issued to the nation as a totality to make us perfect in the love of God, as will be explained, God willing, it follows that we will acquire perfection by means of the commandments, and God therefore knows that we will then be lovers of Him. But before the trial He did not know that we were [then] lovers of Him, since in truth we were not lovers of Him until after the trial. This is precisely what happened in the trial of the Binding of Isaac—"For now I know that you are God-fearing"[129]—as we noted in Chapter I of Part I of this Book. The Rabbi of the *Guide* interpreted this differently, taking "to know" in the sense of "to make known" to all the nations that you are lovers of Him—but there is no need to interpret it this way. In any event, a bad thing that arises in this way, even if its end is not a corporeal good, is nevertheless a perfect good, since it has been supposed that true reward is the good of the soul. This to me is the "afflictions of love" mentioned in the dicta of our Sages of blessed memory.[130] These are not afflictions whose end is a corporeal good, as R. Levi thought. There are, then, no grounds for this objection from the point of view of the bad that befalls the righteous person.

Since it is the same knowledge that knows both opposites, it is confirmed that there is similarly no difficulty with respect to the wicked person's experience of good. For the good that the wicked person experiences, aside from the good that he experiences on account of the fathers, may befall him for various reasons. At times it may be that he does something good and, on account of that good, he is not punished at that time by being deprived of the good that was set to befall him via the celestial bodies.[131] Or the good may be of the type whose end is something bad, whether corporeal or psychic. That is to say, a good may befall him that leads to a corporeal bad end or a good may befall him via the celestial bodies but he turns away from that good to wallow in lusts and vices. In this case there is no fault with respect to God[132] or with respect to divine justice in depriving him of that good.

The bad that befalls the righteous and the good that befalls the wicked might arrive as well in a different way, other than those already mentioned. This would be in accordance with the root-principle in our true tradition that "the world is judged according to the majority."[133] This is unique, however, to corporeal promises. For with respect to psychic true reward and punishment, each individual person has a certain rank, as is stated in tractate *Shabbat*, where the Rabbis say: "This teaches that each person makes for himself a dwelling-place in accordance with his eminence."[134] But from the perspective of corporeal recompense, good befalls the wicked person and bad the righteous one when the person is not at so high a rank that the [influence of the celestial] order is changed on his account. In this there is no fault with respect to divine justice. For since corporeal reward and punishment are general, they are

---

[129] Gen. 22: 12. God knew before the trial that the level of God-fearingness Abraham would reach at the trial would be higher than that reached by him prior to the trial. It is not until the trial that God knows that Abraham *is* at this higher level.

[130] *Berakhot* 5: 1.

[131] Rather than visit bad upon the wicked, God may permit a wicked person who has done something good to receive, on account of that good, the good to which he was destined in accordance with the constellations.

[132] The Florence manuscript has: "with respect to providence," בחק ההשגחה.

[133] BT *Kiddushin* 40b.   [134] BT *Shabbat* 152a.

ordered by the celestial bodies in accordance with the majority. The planets that bestow illusory good fortune generally also bestow for the most part good character traits, and the harmful ones that bestow bad things generally bestow for the most part bad character traits.[135] It is indeed compatible with divine justice that one is judged according to the majority, since true reward and punishment are psychic reward and punishment. As far as explaining why the Torah does not mention the true reward, here is my strongest reason: the promises that the Torah mentions concern the nation as a whole, who are judged according to the majority. Whereas the reward that is designated for individuals may be only hinted at in some places in the Torah, it is explicit in the true tradition. In any event, no difficulty remains from the perspective of what might be inferred from the deplorable condition of the order [in the human realm].

The second difficulty is the one founded on the proposition that states that bad does not come from God essentially. For if God were to punish the wicked, bad would come from Him essentially. This difficulty is not hard to resolve. For the bad that befalls a wicked person for the purpose of providence for the righteous person begins as a good. The bad that befalls the wicked person as a punishment, since it is an effect whose end is an act of right and justice, is also good, since divine justice is good in itself. It is thus proved that the bad that befalls the wicked, in whichever way, whether for the sake of providence for the righteous, or for the sake of doing right and justice, is actually good. That is why our Sages of blessed memory have interpreted the verse, "And God saw all that He had made and behold it was very good,"[136] to mean that "death is good."[137]

Since the goodness that pervades reality is permanent, and the bad in it is little, as the Rabbi of the *Guide* has argued at length, and since the small amount of bad is for a good end, the Psalmist therefore said: "For His anger endures for a moment, but life is what He wills."[138] Here he compared the proportional relation between anger—which alludes to sensed bad—and good, to that between a moment and time. In this he spoke emphatically, saying that in that short moment of anger, "life is what He wills," that is, what is desired and yearned for in it is life and good. This is what we intended here, and through it the second difficulty is resolved.

The third has its foundation in the inferior rank of man in relation to God, because of which, it seems, man is too distant from God for God's providence to extend to him. The resolution of this difficulty is not hard, once it has been established that God constantly brings forth and creates existents through His will. God's willing something is nothing but His loving the thing willed. It is not unlikely that the thing loved by God would be subject to His providence, regardless of whether its relation to Him is far or near—even, indeed, at the very farthest distance. It follows from

---

[135] The same celestial fate that shapes character also then distributes accordingly the "illusory" goods and bad things.

[136] Gen. 1: 31.

[137] *Gen. Rabbah* 9: 5. Both the natural order and God's providential order are good, and each of these contains death. There is a play on words here between מאד ("very") and מות ("death").

[138] Ps. 30: 6.

this that the more beloved of God something is, the more it is the subject of His providence. Since that which is more important is worthy of being more beloved by God, and since the most important of the inferior existents is man, it is fitting that man be most subject to God's providence. It is therefore evident that this difficulty, whose foundation is the great distance between God and man, is not something that would entail that man not be subject to God's providence. Since this providence is a matter of the love God has for His creatures, and not a matter of intellect at all, as will be established in Part V of this Book, God willing, it is evident that the problem they invented concerning the wicked person who acquires some of the intelligibles, to wit, that, even if the punishment he receives is a psychic one, bad would still be coming from God essentially, is not difficult. For even without relying on the fact that this difficulty was already resolved in what preceded, inasmuch as that bad [was seen to be] a manifestation of divine justice and rectitude, which is the perfect good, it is indeed resolved in accordance with the truth itself. For it is on account of one's wickedness that one is spurned and distanced, for the cause of love is not intellect; and therefore the punishment was natural and essential to that soul; and it has nothing in its nature and essence in virtue of which God would change it for the better. Whether or not the soul receives a particular punishment inflicted by God volitionally will be investigated in Part III, God willing.

Chapter V

THE way in which we arrived at our complete knowledge of this cornerstone.

I say that this cornerstone, aside from what was verified for us from the perspective of the tradition as we posited it, is also upheld for us through speculation. For it is evident that refuting the objections and resolving the difficulties with which the commentators sought to invalidate particular providence, suffice to uphold this cornerstone. It is not fitting to attribute to the perfect governor, the one who knows, any failure to govern what He knows. It was proved in Part I that He knows particulars qua particulars. Moreover, it was proved as well, to the greatest extent possible, that there was nothing in all they said by way of objecting to this cornerstone that would invalidate it. It is therefore not fitting to attribute to God a failure to govern them. On the contrary, it is fitting that the more perfect providence be extended to the more perfect being, and therefore it is fitting that there be a more perfect providence extended to the human species than to other species. Since the community of our nation is the most perfect within the human species, it is fitting that the providence extended to it be still more perfect. What will add clarity and completeness with respect to this cornerstone is the full exposition of the root-principle that is belief in creation. For in that connection it will be proved, in a way that is beyond doubt, that God is the agent and the one who brings forth all the existents with His simple will. It is inconceivable that He would make them by His will without loving what He makes. It is improbable—nay, nearly impossible—that He would know something and love it yet withhold His providence from it. This root-principle will be proved in Book III, God willing.

Chapter VI

AN investigation of three issues relevant to this cornerstone.

Since it was posited that the most perfect providence extended to the human species is the providence over the community of our nation, the first issue is whether there is something special, aside from this Torah, that is characteristic of the nation in general, such that it would receive an extra measure of providence, or whether there is nothing special. The second is whether there is one [geographical] place that receives an extra measure of providence and another not. For it indeed appears from some scriptural texts and some dicta of our Rabbis of blessed memory that there is a difference between places in this respect. The third issue is whether one time is subject to an extra measure of providence and another not. For it indeed appears, too, from some scriptural texts and some dicta of our Rabbis of blessed memory that there is a difference between times in this respect. Yet it seems very surprising that there would be a difference in providence corresponding to a difference in places and times.

With respect to the first issue, it indeed appears according to the tradition that the commandment of circumcision that was given to Abraham our forefather, which is something unique to the community of the nation, is something on which providence depends in part. This is seen in the formulation of the blessing that our Rabbis of blessed memory instituted. They said: "who sanctified this beloved one from the womb.... As a reward for this, the Living God, our portion, our Rock, did order deliverance from destruction of the beloved holy seed, our flesh, for the sake of the covenant that He set in our flesh."[139] It is evident that the deliverance from annihilation and from descending into destruction consists in everlasting immortality, which is a large part of providence. Therefore, what it is necessary to explain is how this commandment relates to this providence, as is seen in the formulation of this blessing. And even if it does relate, why did they deem it necessary to include in it deliverance from destruction, which reminds us of punishment, and did not include in it a mention of immortality, which is reward?

To explain both these matters it is necessary that we present briefly that which our Rabbis of blessed memory stated in one of their dicta: "From the time the serpent accosted Eve it polluted her. When Israel stood at Mt. Sinai, this pollution ceased."[140] The explanation of this, as it seems, is that the sin of Adam and Eve was a serious rebellion against the first root, and against the rock from which the human species as a whole was hewn,[141] and indeed introduced pollution into the human species by deeply impressing into it an attraction to materiality. On account of this the species as a whole was disposed to annihilation and destruction. When the grace on high determined to perfect us through the giving of the Torah, this pollution ended, for the

---

[139] BT *Shabbat* 137b. This is a blessing recited at circumcisions.   [140] BT *Shabbat* 146a.

[141] "The rock from which the human species as a whole was hewn" refers, in the Introduction, to Abraham, in accordance with Isa. 51: 1, but may refer here to God who is called "our Rock" in the previous paragraph in the quote from BT *Shabbat* 137b. Note, however, that in this quote, God is "*our* Rock," that is, the Rock of the Jewish people, and so, too, later on in this chapter. What Crescas explains here is that because of Adam and Eve's rebellion against God, the distinction of being the root of humanity was transferred from them to Abraham—see directly below in the text: "he [viz. Abraham] was worthy to be the root and beginning of this chosen species." The same idea appears again in the next paragraph, where Abraham is the father of "a multitude of nations."

admonitions it contained sufficed for man to be drawn to perfection, to suppress his desires, to subdue his inclinations, as will all become clear in this Part of this Book, God willing. Abraham was diametrically opposite to Adam, who, despite being the handiwork of God and disposed to perfection to the greatest extent, nevertheless rebelled and indulged in sin. But this one [viz. Abraham] who was born among idol-worshipers nevertheless indulged in love, which is the height of human perfection, as will be discussed below, God willing. Thus, when the sun of Abraham rose, he was worthy of being the root and beginning of this chosen species and of having God bring him into a new covenant which would put an end to the pollution of his children and the members of his household. They are for this reason distinguished with the sign of the holy covenant in the very organ through which the survival of the species and its perpetuity is realized. This mark was to be in the community as if a sacrifice of their blood and flesh, of their reproductive organ, to God, along with its being a mark of a distancing from materiality and of a dispelling of desires, since the desire borne by that organ is the strongest of the desires. It is therefore proved that this commandment in particular is for the sake of delivering the beloved of our flesh from the destruction[142] to which we were disposed on account of the first sin. They therefore explained and instituted it as a reminder of our having been saved from punishment, implying thereby that, were it not for this commandment, we would be vulnerable to it.

It will be seen that the whole of the Binding of Isaac was directed to the special divine governance of this nation. For it is surprising that there could be room for such a command following the favorable promise that was made to Abraham which contained an explicit reference specifically to Isaac, as it is said: "For in Isaac will your seed be called."[143] One would have thought it appropriate that the command to bind Isaac precede this promise, and that this promise be made to Isaac because of the merit he earned through the Binding. But upon investigation of the matter it appears that the incident of the Binding is attributable to this promise, and that it is fitting on all counts that this promise should have preceded the Binding. For God chose Abraham to be the father of a multitude of nations,[144] and especially to be a root and beginning of a nation chosen to be God's portion and the lot of His inheritance.[145] They were governed by God especially, for which reason they were called a "people preferred over all the nations":[146] God apportioned the celestial constellations and their motions to the nations as judges, but God drew all the Israelites near to His worship, and removed them from general governance through a sacrifice[147]—the incident of the Binding—that encompassed the nation as a whole, and this, through Abraham's sacrifice to God of his son Isaac, the son who was the subject of the promise. It was therefore as if he had already sacrificed to God both Isaac and all Isaac's progeny, who in this deed were removed from being under the governance of another and were singled out for God's governance. It was indeed proved in the

---

[142] BT *Shabbat* 137b.
[143] Gen. 21: 12. The puzzle is: How can God command the sacrifice of Isaac when, if Isaac were to die, God's prior promise to Abraham that his legacy will be perpetuated through Isaac would be nullified?
[144] Gen. 17: 4. See n. 141.   [145] Deut. 32: 9. See n. 141.   [146] Exod. 19: 5.
[147] Crescas plays on the root קרב, which signifies both sacrifice and drawing near. I owe this point to Leonard Levin.

science of astrology that it is possible for the act of an agent to bring about an emanation of the influence of a celestial sphere, even if this was not ordained by the individual's nature, as explained in Ptolemy's *Book of Fruit* (הפרי; *Haperi*).[148] Therefore, when divine wisdom decreed the singling out of this nation, it examined it and also prepared it by means of this event to receive God's governance and to be removed from that of the other, even if its nature did not destine it thus. Therefore, you will find that when Abraham sacrificed the ram in place of his son, designating it a ransom and exchange for his son, he said: "The Lord will see."[149] What he intended by this was that with this act he became worthy to have God himself be his supervisor and providential agent. Therefore God's name was written as the Tetragrammaton, which is God's special name. For before this event, when Abraham said: "God will see for himself the lamb for the offering, my son,"[150] he referred to God with the term *elohim*, for he was not yet quite ready for this special providence. It indeed appears that the barrenness of the matriarchs was also directed toward this end. For in this way it came about that it was specifically God who was the origin and root of this nation that issued from them.[151] The people were thus more disposed to this special providence, which is in accord with the goal of the Binding.

It indeed appears fitting that this deed, which was a kindness to our entire nation, the descendants of Isaac, should leave its impress on them, even as it serves as a great aid to the preservation of their unique governance. Therefore, it appears that the intention of the two daily offerings, the morning offering and the evening offering, which take place at the times of change (from night to day and from day to night), is to indicate that this is an atonement for all Israel, so as to remove them from the governance of the servants [i.e. the constellations] and to distinguish them as governed by God. It is as if these daily offerings are in exchange for all Israel and, in offering them, the entirety of the people are drawn nearer to the worship of God.[152] Therefore the daily offerings were lambs, which come from the ram, just as the nation as a whole is a descendant of Isaac. They were therefore purchased with the finances of the Temple treasury, which were public funds, as is recorded in tractate *Shekalim*.[153]

It would appear that the reason behind blowing the shofar made from a ram's horn on Rosh Hashanah, which is the day of judgment according to the tradition, is this one as well: to establish as our ruler the rule of Him who rides the heavens,[154] and to single us out for His governance. As our Sages of blessed memory said: "Declare three things before Me: kingship, remembrance, and shofar. Kingship—so that you will elect Me your king; remembrance—so that I will remember you for good; by what means?—by means of a shofar."[155] This accords very well with what we have said, namely, that the shofar, which is an instrument customarily sounded on the day of the coronation of a king, as it is said: "And they sounded a shofar and the entire

---

[148] The book's Latinized name is *Liber Fructus*. For the identity of this book, see Harvey (1991), who identifies *Sefer Haperi* as Pseudo-Ptolemy's *Centiloquy*, of which there is an 1822 English translation by J. M. Ashmand, as well as more recent English translations. There are also two medieval Hebrew translations, one by Kalonymus ben Kalonymus and one by Jacob ben Elijah.

[149] Gen. 22: 14. [150] Gen. 22:8. [151] See n. 141.
[152] See n. 147. A similar play on the root קרב occurs here. [153] *Shekalim* 4: 1.
[154] Deut. 33: 26. [155] BT *Rosh Hashanah* 16a.

people proclaimed, 'May the king live,'"[156] is worthy of being present on the day when the kingship of Heaven is affirmed in its uniqueness, in memory of the ram of Isaac that was caught in the thicket by its horns.[157] It is in the nature of truth that it attests to itself and agrees with itself from all perspectives.

It is thus established here that the community of our nation, in addition to their uniqueness on account of the Torah, have other things unique to them, such as the commandment of circumcision and some other commandments that will yet be explained in Part VI, God willing, and the singularity of the Binding, which is impressed upon the daily offerings. On account of these they enjoy an extra measure of providence and unique governance. This is what we wished to establish; it is the first issue.

The second issue is whether there is greater providence in one place than in another. The Torah and the Writings indicate that there is a great difference among places. Jacob our father said, referring to the place where he rested on the way: "How filled with awe this place is; it is none other than the house of God."[158] And of the place of the sphere facing it: "And this is the gate of heaven."[159] And it is said in the Torah: "And there I will meet with you, and I will speak with you from above the covering, from between the two cherubs";[160] "And let them make Me a sanctuary that I may dwell among them."[161] And it is said as well: "The eyes of the Lord your God are always upon it, from the beginning of the year to the end of the year";[162] "And My eyes and My heart shall be there forever."[163] And the Psalmist said: "The Lord loves the gates of Zion more than all the dwellings of Jacob";[164] "How beloved are Your dwelling-places, O Lord of Hosts! My soul longs...";[165] and many others. This was so firmly established for our Rabbis of blessed memory that they expanded on it extensively in their discussions and said: "Whoever lives outside the Land [of Israel] is like one who worships idols"[166]—to the point that they forbade leaving the land of Israel for the Diaspora. According to the tradition, a slave sold to the Diaspora acquires his freedom, as the Rabbis said in tractate *Gittin*.[167] They were also punctilious with regard to facing Jerusalem in time of prayer, as was indicated in the Book of Daniel: "And he had windows open in his chamber toward Jerusalem."[168] One who is standing [during prayer] in Jerusalem faces toward the Temple and the Holy of Holies, as is indicated in the prayer of Solomon, who said: "And they pray to You towards their land... and [to] the house that I have built for Your name,"[169] as is explained in tractate *Berakhot*.[170]

What needs to be clarified is the reason for this difference in providence, considering that all places bear the same relation to Him. This is not, however, difficult to explain. For despite the fact that the providential agent stands in the same relation to the various places, nevertheless, if the providential subject does not stand in the same relation to them, that will entail a difference in providence. Indeed, it is evident that the subject does not stand in the same relation to them. For as the places differ, so, too, do the necessary dispositions for the worship of God, such as seclusion and

---

[156] 1 Kgs. 1: 39. [157] Gen. 22: 13. [158] Gen. 28: 17. [159] Gen. 28: 17.
[160] Exod. 25: 22. [161] Exod. 25: 8. [162] Deut. 11: 12. [163] 1 Kgs. 9: 3.
[164] Ps. 87: 2. [165] Ps. 84: 2. [166] BT *Ketubot* 110a. [167] *Gittin* 4: 6.
[168] Dan. 6: 11. [169] 1 Kgs. 8: 48. [170] BT *Berakhot* 30a.

solitude; and this is indeed due to both celestial and earthly causes. Therefore the Rabbis of blessed memory have indicated that, with respect to places, the land of Israel is special to them in this way, inasmuch as the tradition teaches that prophecy is not found anywhere but in the land of Israel, as it is said in tractate *Mo'ed katan*.[171] Since that place was chosen over others, the wisdom of God dictated that that should be the place of the fashioning of man, as was transmitted to them. They said: "Man was created from the place of his atonement."[172] Therefore that place was chosen for the sacrificial rite, especially because the continuity of the rite in that place greatly influences the reception of emanation and perfection, since deeds profoundly influence the emanating of the divine overflow, as was explained previously. Now the second issue has been explained.

The third issue is whether there is greater providence at one time than at another. According to tradition, this is also evident. They said: "The world is judged at four seasons..."[173] And they explained there: "When does 'Seek the Lord when He is present'[174] apply? During the ten days of repentance between Rosh Hashanah and Yom Kippur."[175] They said further: "Three books are opened on Rosh Hashanah."[176] And many others besides. Considering what was said previously, however, it is not difficult to provide the reason for this difference among times. Even though they all stand in the same relation to the providential agent, they are different from the perspective of the providential subject, in the sense that as the times differ so do the necessary dispositions for the worship of God differ—either on account of the time itself or on account of the special acts performed at those times. For example, there are four seasons that were singled out for special rites relevant to those times, as will be explained in Part VI, God willing. Among these there is the "month of the strong,"[177] which was decked out in special commandments and rites—for example, the acceptance of the sovereignty of Heaven, and the acceptance of the exclusive governance of God, which arouses joy. Therefore Ezra said: "For this day is sanctified to our Lord; do not be sad."[178] For on this day there is the bestowing of God's special sovereignty and the removal of the rulership of another—through the worship ritual of that day and the sounding of the shofar. There is also the awakening of repentance on those days of awe, until the arrival of the special day of fasting [viz. Yom Kippur], which involves the general sacrifice on behalf of the individual members of the nation, along with seclusion and the subjugation of desires, as is obvious. For indeed it is fitting that it be so. For this period has two aspects: exclusive sovereignty and rulership, and service. It is therefore fitting that the governed be obligated to be happy and joyous by virtue of exiting the rulership of another and entering into being sheltered by His shade,[179] as it is said: "Eat sumptuously, and drink sweet beverages..."[180] The reason for this is: "For this day is sanctified to our Lord," which indicates the sanctity

---

[171] Although the Ferrara edition and the manuscripts all specify tractate *Yoma*, the idea expressed here is actually found in BT *Mo'ed katan* 25a.
[172] *Gen. Rabbah* 14: 8.   [173] BT *Rosh Hashanah* 16a.   [174] Isa. 55: 6.
[175] BT *Rosh Hashanah* 18a.   [176] BT *Rosh Hashanah* 16b.
[177] The month of Tishri is intended. See 1 Kgs. 8: 2.   [178] Neh. 8: 10.
[179] See Ps. 36: 8.   [180] Neh. 8: 10.

of Lordship. And so, too, by virtue of service, that is, by radical seclusion and self-sacrifice—rather than the sacrifice of another, as with other sacrifices. So we have found in the case of some of our Sages, who used to say on the day of fasting: "Master of the universe, it is revealed and known before the throne of Your glory... may it be Your will that my fat and my blood that have been diminished be as if laid on the altar, so that You receive me with favor."[181] Since joy arises when that which opposes it departs, it is fitting that it be at the [year's] beginning—which is the time when that which opposes leaves—that is, with the entry into God's governance and the taking leave of the governance of the other. [It is fitting] to embark [at that time] on a path of separation [from sin] and of repentance, until one is perfected to the greatest possible extent. This is the special fast.

There are several reasons for all this being at this time. One is because of the nature of the time, for it is suited to seclusion, since it is the start of the cold and dry season. Another is that at this season of the year there is a strong influence [by the celestial spheres] on the life of those born then, and therefore it is necessary—especially within the chosen nation—to transfer that influence from that which is other than God and to give it to God. Another is that it was in that period of time that God was appeased by Moses in the second round of forty days.[182] In addition, since this time was designated for the judgment of water, which is the lifeline of this world, the commandment concerning the four species was issued.[183] These are the choice species, whether in height, taste, aroma, or other qualities, but they have in common that they endure for the entire year and grow near any body of water. This is indeed to bring the people close to God, and to demonstrate in this way that this providence and this judgment comes from God. It is therefore fitting that we offer to God the choicest among the species, and those that grow near all bodies of water. Since the willow is the most affected by the influence of water, the custom of the prophets in the Temple was to rejoice with it particularly on the seventh day, on which the festival is completed. This festival was also distinguished by the [ceremony of the] pouring of the water, as is found in the *Gemara*: "Pour the water before Me on the festival [viz. Sukkot] in order that the rains of the entire year be blessed for you."[184] In accordance with what was already said, namely, that by means of deeds the influence of the emanation may be either secured or removed, it is not surprising that by means of deeds at certain times the governance of the planets and of princes [i.e. the celestial bodies] may be removed, and governance will be the province exclusively of God. Thus is the third issue clarified, and this should suffice for this Part. Adulation and praise are to God alone, who is exalted above all blessing and praise.

---

[181] BT *Berakhot* 17a.
[182] The reference is to the second forty-day period during which, following the sin of the Golden Calf, Moses ascended once again to the mountain and received a second set of tablets.
[183] Based on Lev. 23: 40, the Rabbis determined the four species to be the citron (*etrog*), date palm (*lulav*), myrtle (*hadas*), and willow (*'aravah*).
[184] BT *Rosh Hashanah* 16a.

Part III

CONCERNING God's power.

It is evident that this cornerstone is a foundation and pillar of the Torah, without which its existence is inconceivable. For since the Torah is an act that proceeds from the Commander to the one commanded, God must have the power to perform it. This is even more the case, insofar as the axes upon which the Torah turns are the signs and wonders and promises that it contains and whose existence would be inconceivable without it. Therefore, our discussion of this cornerstone will consider both its establishment in accordance with the dictates of the Torah and the way in which we arrived at knowledge of it.

Chapter I

EXPOSITION of this cornerstone in accordance with the dictates of the Torah.

I assert that, since it is evident that weakness would be a defect with respect to God, it is necessary that His power be infinite on all counts, with regard to everything whose existence can be conceived by the intellect—even if it is impossible by nature. Indeed the necessity of God's infinite power is evident. For if He were finite and limited, then, beyond that limit, where His power is imagined not to operate, He would, God forbid, be necessarily weak. Indeed our saying "infinite in every respect" is driven by the fact that "infinite" has two aspects: one, infinite in time; the other, infinite in strength. If He were finite in either of these two aspects, He would indeed be, God forbid, weak in that aspect in which His power was limited.

We set a condition, however, and said: "with regard to anything whose existence can be conceived by the intellect," since it is evident that power is inapplicable from every perspective with respect to anything whose existence is inconceivable by the intellect—for example, the negation and affirmation of the same thing with respect to the same thing.[185] For with respect to anything the possibility of whose existence is not conceivable by the intellect, the term "power" does not apply. Therefore, the absence of power with respect to that thing does not represent any weakness at all.[186] Therefore, it does not apply to the power to annul first intelligibles, since their annulment would involve simultaneous affirmation and negation. And generally, things that do not result from the act of an agent, such as apodictic demonstrations, are in the same category. For their presence and absence distinguish the true from the false, and their annulment entails simultaneous affirmation and negation. Therefore you will find among our Rabbis of blessed memory those who say: "He who enters a city and hears the sound of screams and says: 'May it be Your will that this not be coming from my house,' is uttering a prayer in vain."[187] And the reason they say this is that, if the scream is coming from his house, it has already entered into reality; and for something

---

[185] "Negation and affirmation of the same thing with respect to the same thing from the same perspective" is what we would call a contradiction or a self-contradiction.
[186] It implies no deficiency in God if He is unable to do things that involve logical impossibility. If a thing cannot be done, an agent's inability to do it should not be construed as a weakness or a limitation on his part.
[187] BT *Berakhot* 54a.

that has already occurred not to have occurred is simultaneous affirmation and negation. It is superfluous to go on at length in this vein.

Our saying "even if it is impossible by nature," includes everything whose existence is not inconceivable by the intellect.[188] Since it is evident that creating something in the absence of matter that precedes it is not among the things the impossibility of whose existence is conceived by the intellect, it is evident that power in this case may be attributed to God. For it is evident that a thing whose existence is impossible for the intellect to conceive is simultaneous affirmation and negation from the same perspective. Therefore, if our saying "something comes to be from nothing" were comparable to our saying "the ring comes to be from gold," one could object that in so saying we have in effect negated and affirmed simultaneously;[189] but since our saying "something comes to be from nothing," says only that there is something with nothing preceding it, there is no simultaneous negation and affirmation. This will be explained further in Book III, God willing.

Chapter II

EXPOSITION of the way in which we arrived at our knowledge of this cornerstone.

I assert that Aristotle, for whom the eternity of motion and of the celestial spheres is necessary, and for whom it was established that a finite body cannot contain an infinite force, inferred the necessity of a first principle that is intelligent, a mover, and incorporeal. Yet even if we concede this necessity to him, the only thing necessitated [to move the universe] is a force infinite in time. A force infinite in strength, however, is not necessitated, either in actuality or in potentiality—that is to say, one that can increase infinitely in number and measure. For an objector might say that the force that moves the diurnal sphere is limited in that it moves it within twenty-four hours, without being able to move it in a shorter amount of time. It is therefore evident that what opened our eyes to this cornerstone is the belief in creation, as the Torah and the tradition posit it. For in Book III something indubitable will be proved, namely, that existence as a whole was created by God, via absolute will, even though nothing preceded it. It is therefore evident that the agent operates in this case without any relation to the receiver of the action, since His act depends on will alone. Since this is so, it is evident that He does not have limited power. For a limit to power can be caused only by a determinate relation between the agent and the receiver of the action. Since God acts without any determinate relation, He is not limited. Therefore, it is the belief in creation, as it has been accepted by the nation and in accordance with the truth itself, that fully opened our eyes to this cornerstone.[190]

---

[188] Although God's infinite power does not enable Him to do that which is logically impossible, it does enable Him to do that which is merely physically impossible. Such physically impossible things would include the biblical miracles—for example, the sun's standing still. Crescas's example of something physically impossible that God can do is creation in the absence of matter.

[189] In saying "something comes to be from nothing" on analogy with "the ring comes to be from gold," one implies that, after all, "nothing" is something—just as gold is. It is this contradiction that the intellect cannot accommodate.

[190] The eternity of motion can establish at most the necessity of a mover infinite in time but not one infinite in strength. Only creation can establish a mover infinite in strength.

It follows necessarily from what was said that what has been proved here regarding infinity in strength and time is not a matter of mere potential, that is to say, of perpetual infinite increase in actuality. Rather, what follows is the existence of a power having infinite strength in actuality. For it has already been established with regard to this power that it does not have a determinate relation, and the power that fits this description is without limit, since its foundation is will alone. Infinity is nothing other than this, namely, other than the impossibility of limit.

This [cornerstone] will indeed be established from another perspective, in accordance with what is contained in the Torah and the tradition concerning the miracles of the creation of substances and their destruction, as, for example, the staff's turning into a serpent or the plague of the firstborn. For it is indeed established with respect to natural things, that their coming-to-be and passing-away are inescapably the result of motion. Indeed, in the miracle of the staff, although the plain meaning of the text indicates that this took place not over time, one might object that some time elapsed in the coming-to-be of the serpent. Nevertheless, in the plague of the firstborn, according to tradition, its saying "at midnight"[191] marks that it was precisely then. This is indeed indicated by the change in language, for when it was told to the Egyptians it said, "around midnight."[192] And so, too, in *Gemara Berakhot*.[193] Since the true midnight is an instant, it is necessary that the destruction took place not over time. As we already said, if passing-away requires motion, it follows that either there is motion not over time or that there is passing-away without a prior motion. All this shows that God acts without a determinate relation. This entails a power infinite in strength. It appears that our Rabbis of blessed memory indeed agreed with respect to this plague that it took place without an intermediary, for this plague in particular indicates unlimited power.[194]

The necessity of an unlimited power derives from what is said in the Torah and the tradition regarding the opening of the mouth of the donkey.[195] For the creation of the order of intelligent speech in the mouth of the donkey appears more improbable than the creation of speech without a subject. Since the creation of speech is a great wonder, its creation is all the more wondrous in a subject that is antithetical to it. It will therefore be seen that this is something that indicates an unlimited power, whose foundation is will alone. Some of the sages of our nation stumbled with respect to this miracle and proposed the fiction that the speech of the donkey was actually a prophetic vision. They thus interpreted the Torah incorrectly and in opposition to the tradition. This happened to them because they did not understand the purpose of this miracle and its reason, which we will discuss in Part IV, God willing. Let this now suffice for this Part. Praise is to God alone, who is exalted above all blessing and praise.

---

[191] Exod. 12: 29.
[192] Exod. 11: 4. The contrast is between בחצי הלילה at Exod. 12: 29 and כחצת הלילה here. That the plague took place precisely at midnight indicates that it was instantaneous. Since all natural events require time, the durationless nature of this miraculous event is an indication that God's power is unlimited.
[193] BT *Berakhot* 3b–4a.
[194] We saw in II. ii. 1 (also see above n. 85) that the Rabbis insist that God himself, unassisted by any volitional aide, performed this plague.
[195] Num. 22: 28. The reference is to Balaam's donkey.

Part IV

CONCERNING prophecy.

As we have already seen, the existence of a divine Torah, which is a commandment or commandments, from a commander, who is God, to the commanded, who are the nation as a whole, is inconceivable without some relation and connection between them, which is prophecy. It is fitting that we explain the subject-matter of prophecy in this Part, as per our usual procedure. We have divided it into four chapters.

Chapter I: an exposition of the term "prophecy" and its subject-matter, in accordance with the dictates of the Torah.
Chapter II: an exposition of the essential properties of prophecy.
Chapter III: resolution of some of the difficulties concerning prophecy, some of which were noted by earlier thinkers, and some of which were not.
Chapter IV: herein we shall provide guidance to the path by which the rank of prophecy is achieved, in accordance with the dictates of the Torah, with which speculation concurs.

Chapter I

EXPOSITION of the term "prophecy" and its subject-matter, in accordance with the dictates of the Torah, with which speculation concurs.

Prophecy, according to what is known of it, is an overflowing, which overflows to a person's intellect, is spiritual and epistemic,[196] from God, either through an intermediary or without an intermediary, which informs him—even without the premises that entail them—of some matter or matters of which he is ignorant, and does so with respect to all modalities, for the sake of guiding him or of guiding others.

Indeed by our saying in this definition an "overflowing, which overflows," we specify prophecy as belonging to the genus of all the overflowings that flow from that which overflows to that which receives the overflow. Our saying, "to a person's intellect," is to distinguish this overflow from the overflows that reach other species such as animals and plants. Since we designated "intellect" as the receiver of the overflow, dreams and magic are excluded, for the faculty that receives these is the imagination, as Aristotle explained in the book, *Sense and Sensibilia*. Our saying, "spiritual," is to distinguish it from material, corporeal overflowings. Our saying, "epistemic," is to distinguish it from spiritual overflowings that are in potentiality—that is, the overflow that overflows onto a person and renders him one who intellects potentially. Our saying, "from God, either through an intermediary or without an intermediary," also eliminates dreams and magic, and hints that the prophecy of Moses took place without an intermediary and that of the rest of the prophets occurred through an intermediary. Our saying, "informs him of some matter or matters—even without the premises that entail them," distinguishes this from the overflow that overflows to a person and renders him one who intellects in actuality but cannot intellect the truth of what he intellects without the

---

[196] "Epistemic" renders מדעי (*mada'i*). As Crescas will soon explain, this kind of overflowing imparts actual—not potential—knowledge.

premises that entail it—whether what he intellects be an intelligible, a sensible, or a commonly known traditional truth, as was explained in its place. Indeed, our saying, "of which he is ignorant," distinguishes these matters from first intelligibles, for of these this man is not ignorant, since he is assumed to be a man of intellect. Our saying, "and does so with respect to all modalities," indicates that prophecy can occur with respect to the modality of the possible as well as with respect to the other modalities. This is seen in most of the prophecies and promises, as we have noted in Part I of this Book. Some of the sages of our nation stumbled in this matter, because they thought that God's knowledge applies only to the modality of necessity. Yet not only does this constitute an utter heresy with respect to the Torah, it is also self-evidently unsustainable, as we explained earlier and as we shall discuss further in Part V, God willing. Our saying, "for the sake of guiding him or of guiding others," indicates the category of ends. For ends are contained in definitions, since the final cause is the strongest of the four causes, as was explained in its place. Indeed, according to what appears in the Torah and the Writings, there are some prophecies that were for the guidance of the prophet, such as most of the prophecies that our Patriarchs received; and some that were for the guidance of others, such as the prophecy of the master of the prophets, which was for the guidance of our nation as a whole, as well as the prophecies of the prophets who were sent to Israel and to other nations. This is what appears fitting with respect to explaining the term "prophecy," according to what is known of it.

It appears that this [characterization of prophecy] encompasses all ranks of prophecy. For according to the tradition, the term "prophecy" applies essentially to the prophets who are sent, and this [viz. the description of prophecy just given] is generally characteristic of the prophetic books. Metaphorically, however, the term is applied as well to those who speak through [any form of] divine inspiration,[197] and this is generally characteristic of the Writings. Within each of these there are ranks as well. For in prophecy, there are differences between the prophecy of Moses our master, may he rest in peace, and that of the other prophets, as the Torah makes explicit. There are differences, too, among these other prophets. For some receive their prophecy through the medium of a dream, some through the medium of a vision, some in parables and riddles, and some in speech. Among those who speak when divinely inspired there are also differences. For some, the inspiration comes in the form of spoken words that predict the future—indeed, without a dream or vision. It is thus said: "The spirit of the Lord spoke within me; His word was on my tongue."[198] This is the rank of David in his Psalms, Solomon in the scroll Song of Songs, and Jeremiah in the scroll Lamentations, for although Jeremiah was a prophet, it was not antithetical to him to speak through divine inspiration—even though this is of a lower rank than prophecy—at times when he was not actively prophesying. This is self-evident. This is also the rank of Daniel, according to the tradition. Some of these individuals did not receive, through their inspiration, predictions of the future, but rather accounts of past events. What is meant is that, because they were

---

[197] Not all instances of divine inspiration, רוח הקדש (ruaḥ haqodesh), rise to the level of prophecy.
[198] 2 Sam. 23: 2.

divinely inspired, they were precise in their language, just as the Scribes were in preserving the written and oral forms, the full and spare forms, the large and small letters, and the closed and open sections.[199] Persons of various ranks are all included in the Writings, just as prophets of various ranks are all included in the Prophets, even though there were manifest differences among ranks. This variation is attested in Chapter 2 of Ḥagigah, where the Rabbis said: "Whatever it was that Ezekiel saw, Isaiah saw more." There are thus three general ranks: the rank of the master of the prophets, which appears in the Torah; the rank of the other prophets, which appears in the Prophets; and the rank of those who speak through divine inspiration, which appears in the Writings. This is what our Sages of blessed memory expressed in Chapter 1 of *Baba batra*:[200] Torah, Prophets, and Writings.

Although there is a vast difference between the prophecy of Moses our Teacher, may he rest in peace, and the prophecy of the other prophets, it did not seem fitting to count this [difference] as a cornerstone among the cornerstones of the Torah, just as we did not count [as a cornerstone] the difference between the miracles of Moses our Teacher and those of others, about which the Torah is explicit—since the Torah's existence is conceivable without our conceiving a difference between the different prophecies and miracles. This is self-evident. But since this is the view of our Torah, and since one who rejects this view is like one who rejects the Torah's narratives, it seems fitting to us that we establish it, God willing, in Book III, which contains the true views of the Torah. We shall expand there on its explanation. For the Rabbi raised issues in his discussion which, as it appears, do not accord with our tradition.

Chapter II

EXPOSITION of the essential properties of prophecy.

According to what we know of prophecy, it appears that it has three essential properties. One of them is the same and equal for all prophets, involving no disparity among them; the other two vary with the difference in rank among the prophets. The first is the veracity of the prophets' predictions—this is the same and equal for all ranks. The second is the signs and wonders that have a certain end and are created through the intermediation of the prophet: the ranks of the prophets differ in this regard. The third is the fierce passion and the courage to summon others to the worship of God. In this respect, too, the prophets differ.

Concerning the first, which is the veracity of the prophet's predictions, the Torah says explicitly: "When a prophet speaks in the name of the Lord, if the thing follow not, nor come to pass, that is the thing which the Lord has not spoken."[201] It is said regarding Samuel: "And the Lord was with him, and did let none of his words fall to the ground; and all Israel from Dan even to Beer-sheba knew that Samuel was established to be a prophet of the Lord."[202] This is most evident. What it is necessary

---

[199] Occasionally, the way a word is written in the Torah is not the preferred way of reading it, but the written form is nevertheless not "corrected." Spellings of words have full and spare forms that are not used consistently (see Intro. n. 45). Some letters in the Torah are oversized and some unusually small. Also, sections are either open—that is, they begin at the start of a new line; or closed—that is, they do not begin at the start of a new line.

[200] BT *Baba batra* 13b.   [201] Deut. 18: 22.   [202] 1 Sam. 3: 19–20.

to be aware of, however, is what occurs in the prophecy of Jonah, who proclaimed the prophecy to the people of Nineveh: "Yet forty days, and Nineveh shall be overthrown."[203] When the people came to believe in God, however, and declared a fast and repented of their wicked ways and of the violence in which they were engaged, "God repented of the bad, which He said He would do unto them; and He did it not."[204] It is explicit, too, in the Book of Jeremiah: "At one instant I may speak concerning a nation, and concerning a kingdom, to pluck up and to break down and to destroy it; but if that nation turn from their evil... And at one instant I may speak concerning a nation, and concerning a kingdom, to build and to plant it; but if it do evil in My sight... then I repent of the good, wherewith I said I would benefit it."[205]

By way of resolving this difficulty[206] the commentators have said that a prediction of good may not be rescinded, but one of bad may be rescinded. The prophet is testable therefore only with respect to predictions of good. For it is possible that the predictions of bad will not come to pass, because God is gracious and merciful and repents of the bad when people return to Him with all their hearts, as happened in Nineveh. According to this, what is intended when the Book of Jeremiah says: "at one instant I may speak," is that, "at one instant I may speak to My heart"—but God will not speak through prophecy, for then He would not be able to rescind the prediction.[207]

When an objection was raised with respect to Jacob's fear and dread of his brother Esau, in light of Jacob's already having been promised in a prophecy: "And, behold, I am with you, and will keep you wherever you go, and will bring you back into this land; for I will not leave you..."[208] they offered two solutions. The first was that the prediction of good may not be rescinded when it is delivered through the mediation of a prophet who is sent expressly to convey it to another—though even under these conditions a prediction of bad may be rescinded, as was the case in Jonah's prediction to Nineveh and in Isaiah's prediction to Hezekiah. Since the prediction to Jacob occurred in the absence of a prophet sent expressly to convey it to another, he became afraid lest his sin cause him [to forfeit the prediction].[209] This is the approach the Rabbi of blessed memory took. According to this, "at one instant I may speak" can be to a prophet, provided that he is not sent to the nation. For whereas its saying: "at one instant I may speak to pluck up and to break down," can accommodate a prophet's being sent to a nation and a kingdom, because a prediction of bad can be rescinded, its saying: "And at one instant I may speak concerning a nation, and concerning a kingdom, to build and to plant it," cannot accommodate this interpretation because a prediction of good cannot be rescinded when the prophet is sent to a nation.

The second solution was the approach taken by R. Levi. He maintained that, because the bad that the prophet foretells is for the purpose of preventing it, and

---

[203] Jonah 3: 4.   [204] Jonah 3: 10.   [205] Jer. 18: 7–10.

[206] The difficulty is that the Torah suggests both that what a prophet predicts will always come to pass and that God can revoke His promise. A further difficulty arises if God can revoke His promise: how can one assess the legitimacy of a prophet?

[207] God may change His mind even with respect to a promise of good, but not once the initial intent is announced to someone by a prophet.

[208] Gen. 28: 15.   [209] BT *Berakhot* 4a.

that it is for this end that the communication was received by the prophet, it stands to reason that the prophecy will not come to fruition, when the end for the sake of which the communication was issued is fulfilled, that is to say, when a person or a people, as a consequence of having received a prediction of something bad, improves his/its ways. But when a good thing is ordained to happen to a person, it is improbable that it will not occur, for man is endowed with choice in order that he correct what is defective in the order ordained by the celestial bodies—and not in order that he pervert it.[210] From this perspective the test of the prophet is complete when the good that he predicted does not come to pass. This needs to be understood from the perspective of the celestial order.[211] But with respect to a prediction of good that derives from individual providence, and which is attributed to the providence of God without the mediation of the celestial order: in this case even if no explicit condition is stipulated, it must be understood to be tied to the condition of serving God and being attached to Him.[212] Therefore Jacob feared lest his sin cause him to forfeit [the prediction of good he received], for that good was ordained as a matter of individual providence. This became clear to him because it is unreasonable that he would be perfectly protected by the order of the celestial bodies wherever he went. Thus, with respect to what our Rabbis of blessed memory have said, namely, that "Every promise of good that is issued by God, even if conditional, is not rescinded [when the condition is not fulfilled],"[213] it is fitting that this be understood to hold when the condition is nonessential. As they explained in the matter of Moses, when God said to him: "Now therefore let Me alone, that My wrath may wax hot against them, and that I may consume them...,"[214] it is not fitting to say that the promised good [to Moses] is a reward for [his] withholding prayer.[215] This is what this sage [R. Levi] said.

From our point of view this is far from plausible. For, first, if we posit this we shall have to reject the text that says: "When a prophet speaks in the name of the Lord, if

---

[210] The point is that, if one learns of a prediction of good deriving from the celestial order, one is unlikely deliberately to sabotage that good.

[211] From the perspective of the celestial order, if the predicted good does not come to pass, then, according to Gersonides, the prophet who predicted it can be known to be a false one.

[212] According to Gersonides, if a prophet predicts good as a matter of direct individual providence, the good can fail to materialize even if the prophet is legitimate. This could occur if the subject of the prophecy fails to uphold the condition attached to all such predictions, whether the condition is made explicit or not, namely, that he not violate God's commandments. This condition is constant and may be presumed to attach to all direct individual predictions of good.

[213] BT *Berakhot* 7a.   [214] Exod. 32: 10.

[215] According to Gersonides, as Crescas reports, the Rabbis hold that divine conditional favorable promises are not rescindable even if the condition is not fulfilled, so long as the condition is nonessential. When the condition is essential, that is, when the fulfillment of the promise hinges on one's not violating the commandments (even when this condition is not made explicit but is merely understood), then the promise is rescindable when the condition is not fulfilled. In the case of Moses, the promise of good that God conveyed to him at the end of the verse Exod. 32: 10, namely, that He will make a great nation of him and his descendants, if only he would leave God alone and not pray for the people, is a conditional promise whose condition is nonessential, so that the promise cannot be revoked even if the condition is not fulfilled. In other words, once God told Moses He would make a great nation of him, nothing Moses would do or not do could cause God to renege. Moses did not have to refrain from praying for the people in order to be made a great nation.

the thing follow not, nor come to pass, that is the thing that the Lord has not spoken."[216] For [according to R. Levi] when a prophet promises something good by way of individual providence, it is possible that that thing will not materialize and will not come to pass. For although, according to the Rabbi's approach, when God promises something good it will happen absolutely so long as there is a messenger, according to this sage [viz. R. Levi], it would have to apply only to the case of a good that comes by way of the order of the celestial bodies. This is highly implausible. Furthermore, when the [good] thing [predicted] does not materialize and does not come to pass, if only I knew how the prophet would be tested! For indeed, the prophet could excuse himself by saying that the promise of good came by way of individual providence, which, as was supposed, might well not materialize.[217] Moreover, if we assume that the promised good was one that comes from the celestial bodies, it follows that, even if we concede that it is improbable that it will not occur, it is still not impossible—for the person *might* make a bad choice. And since it is possible that it will not occur—even if the possibility is small—it remains in the category of the possible, which does not yield an absurdity when it is assumed to occur. I cannot fathom, then, how a prophet can be tested by it.[218] But all of this is a fiction, and an edifice without a foundation—even with regard to what he explained in Jacob's case, namely, that it was clear to him that the promise was indeed a matter of individual providence because it is unlikely that the order of the celestial bodies could protect him completely wherever he goes. Yet even if this were the truth [viz. that the promise to Jacob was a matter of individual providence], nevertheless, the reason R. Levi gave [viz. that the celestial bodies could not completely protect him] is worthless. For whereas it would be possible to say this if the promise concerned both him and his descendants, for in such a long stretch of time it would indeed be impossible for the protection [by the celestial order] to be comprehensive, it is not impossible for one person to be protected and secure [in this way] for an entire lifetime. All the more is this so considering that the promise was made to him after the greater part of his life had passed. Yet according to R. Levi's approach it would be possible for us to conclude, from the fact that Jacob was afraid, that the promise came from individual providence and that this is why he was not certain that his sin would not cause [the promise to be rescinded]. Yet even from this very perspective, as we have said, the prophet cannot be tested when the promised good does not materialize

---

[216] Deut. 18: 22.

[217] According to Gersonides, only when good is predicted from the perspective of the celestial order is it nonrescindable. Therefore it is only when a prophet predicts such a good and it does not come to pass that he has been tested and exposed as a fraud. Yet since the prophet can always say that the prediction of good was individually providential and not celestially so, in which case, according to Gersonides, the prediction is rescindable, we could never know in the case of a prediction of good that did not materialize that the prophet is illegitimate.

[218] According to Gersonides, the coming-to-pass of a predicted good from the celestial perspective is only probable. For however unlikely it is that the subject of a promise of good would sabotage the favorable prediction, it is not impossible. How can we tell, then, from the mere fact that the prophecy is not fulfilled, that the prophet is a false one?

and does not come to pass, for [according to R. Levi] it is possible for this to happen in cases of individual providence.[219] This approach indeed has nothing to support it.

We have already noted that even on the Rabbi's approach the saying in Jeremiah poses a difficulty, where God says: "At one instant I may speak." For as we hinted, in this utterance the promise of good and the promise of bad are equal. Further, according to the Rabbi's approach, when it is said, "When a prophet speaks in the name of the Lord," this must refer to a promise of good alone—yet this is opposed to the straightforward meaning of the text. What must have brought them to this view,[220] however, as it appears, is something Jeremiah said to Ḥananiah son of Azur: "As for the prophet who prophesies of peace, when the word of the prophet shall come to pass, then shall it be known of the prophet that the Lord has truly sent him."[221] It followed for them from this that there can be a test of a prophet [only] with respect to the prediction of good. We accordingly would have to say that the intention of this text was to make precisely the point that if the word of the prophet is not realized, it is known that in truth God did not send him. If what the text says is true, it may be assumed that its intention was precisely to derive the negation of the consequent from the negation of the antecedent, even though this does not follow necessarily.[222] But according to them,[223] what the text actually says is *not* true. For the test is not [for them] in effect "when the word of the prophet shall come to pass ... that the Lord has truly sent him," but rather when it occurs repeatedly,[224] for it is possible even for something that comes by magic or in a dream to materialize. And so it is said with respect to Samuel: "... and [the Lord] did let none of his words fall to the ground; and all Israel from Dan even to Beer-sheba knew that Samuel was established to be a prophet of the Lord."[225] The words, "when the word of the prophet shall come to pass," however, apply equally whether he prophesies of peace or of war. But according to them, there is no test unless what fails to materialize is the word of the prophet who prophesies of peace. In addition, according to their approach, what Samuel said in the previous verse, namely, "The prophets who have been before me and before you of old prophesied against many countries, and against great

---

[219] Even if we could be sure that the promise to Jacob of good was a matter of individual providence, it still would not provide grounds for testing the prophet who predicted it when it failed to materialize. This is because even for Gersonides, individual providential promises of good can be rescinded—when the subject of the promise sins.

[220] "Them" refers to Maimonides and Gersonides. [221] Jer. 28: 9.

[222] According to the text, if the prophecy comes true, then it is known that the prophet is sent by God. Crescas recognizes that, if the text is to support Maimonides and Gersonides, the text must be taken to be making the further point—a point that is not, however, logically entailed, since a proposition does not entail its inverse—that if the prophecy does not come true, then it can be known that the prophet is not sent by God.

[223] Maimonides and Gersonides do not accept that a prediction of good that comes to pass proves that the prophet is legitimate, but only that a prediction of good that does not come to pass proves that a prophet is illegitimate.

[224] Fisher has בהשנות הרב; the Florence and Vienna manuscripts have בהשנות רב, which I follow. The Ferrara edition has בהשנות הרע. Maimonides and Gersonides do not accept Jer. 28: 9 as it stands because they hold that a prediction may come true even when its source is other than genuine prophecy. A prophet of good could only be known to be legitimate if his predictions consistently came to pass.

[225] 1 Sam. 3: 19–20.

kingdoms, of war, and of evil, and of pestilence,"[226] is superfluous and of no import; and it is lacking its predicate.[227]

In my view, however, in these texts it is as if Jeremiah is mocking Ḥananiah and responding to him, saying that when the prophet's [i.e. Ḥananiah's] words come to pass[228] it will be known that God has truly sent him. The truth is indeed that which he claimed,[229] for he used a true premise in this proof. What he intended by it is that if the prophets who preceded them, that is, recognized prophets, prophesied that bad things would happen to the lands, but another prophet subsequently prophesied that there would be peace, thereby disputing them, it would be known, when the latter's prophecy comes to pass, that God has truly sent him. For since they were recognized prophets, and they prophesied of bad things, it would indeed be seen, when the word of the one who prophesied of peace[230] materialized, that their overflow came from the order of the celestial bodies. It therefore says: "that the Lord has *truly* sent him," for even if the others were also sent by God, they were not sent "truly" and without an intermediary. And so it should be, for it is fitting for the bad to be attributed to the celestial order, and the good to individual providence. This is why Jeremiah took this as his example. For Jeremiah was himself a recognized prophet, and he forecast bad things; but when the word of Ḥananiah, who promised good things, would come to fruition, that would indicate that God sent Ḥananiah "truly," that is, with no intermediary, and that Jeremiah, too, was sent, but through an intermediary, namely, the [celestial] order. He took this approach as if to say: "now we will see if God sent you truly." We therefore have no proof from this that there is a test only when a prediction of good does not materialize.[231]

Yet what it is possible to say with respect to this, as it appears, is that there is no difference between a prediction of good and of something other than good, as the straightforward sense of the text indicates. For it is said: "when the prophet speaks in the name of the Lord...,"[232] and the text does not differentiate among the things of which the prophet speaks. Nevertheless, the concern here is with when the prophet speaks to make it known that he is a prophet. This will be known either through the

---

[226] Jer. 28: 8.

[227] According to Crescas, both Maimonides and Gersonides ignore the verse Jer. 28: 8, treating the following verse, 28: 9, as if it stands on its own. Yet, Crescas argues, the "predicate" with which 28: 9 ends, "then shall it be known of the prophet that the Lord has truly sent him," must apply to 28: 8's prophets of war, for otherwise they are left hanging with no predicate. Crescas contends that the closing "predicate" of 28: 9 applies equally to the prophets of good of 28: 9 and to the prophets of bad of 28: 8.

[228] That is, *if* they come to pass, which they in fact do not.

[229] Vocalizing מה שאמרו as *mah sheamaro*, "that which he claimed," rather than, with Fisher, as *mah sheameru*, "that which they claimed."

[230] The Vienna manuscript has "of bad," הלרע, where the other manuscripts, the Ferrara edition, and Fisher have "of peace," לשלום. Crescas's point is that the legitimacy of those recognized prophets who prophesy of coming bad, even if the bad does not materialize, cannot be automatically impugned. It may simply be the case that the prophecy of peace comes directly from God rather than via the celestial intermediary and supersedes the legitimate prophecy that came by way of an intermediary.

[231] Crescas contends that, according to Jeremiah, there may be proof of the legitimacy of a prophet of good when the predicted good does materialize—and not only a discrediting of such a prophet when the good he foretold does not materialize—in the case in which the prophet's favorable prophecy contradicts that of established prophets who had prophesied of forthcoming bad.

[232] Deut. 18: 22.

creation of a sign, in which case, if there is no suspicion concerning that sign, just one time will suffice as verification; or through prediction of future occurrences, in which case repetition will be required. When the prophet speaks for this purpose, then, if God has sent him, it is not possible for what occurs to be other than what was predicted, whether the prediction is of good or of bad. This is what the text indicates in the preceding verse, where it is said: "And if you say in your heart: 'How shall we know the word that the Lord has not spoken?'"[233] For it is clear from this that the intention is for us to have a way of knowing if he is a prophet who is sent by God, and it is precisely for this purpose that he makes himself known. This is confirmed by the true tradition which maintains that, when the speech of the prophet is for this purpose, that is, to make it known that he is a prophet sent by God, it cannot happen[234] that "the thing follow not, nor come to pass." As it is said: "If I be a man of God, let fire come down from heaven."[235] The master of the prophets preceded him by saying: "If these men die the common death of all men, and be visited after the visitation of all men, then the Lord has not sent me."[236] Were it possible that the prediction of bad made for this purpose could be rescinded, it would be possible for these men to die like all men yet it be true that God sent Moses.[237] How could it not? Besides, what obstacle would cause the prophet himself not to know if his prediction would be rescinded or not? But those who deny [to God] knowledge of the possible indeed reject this as well.[238] May God protect us from the sword of their tongue![239]

At times, however, the prophet's speech is not of this kind, that is, its purpose is not to validate his prophecy but to predict bad or good, as is widely acknowledged with respect to those occasions when a prediction of good and bad is a matter of reward and punishment which are necessitated by individual providence. Indeed, the Torah specified the double condition: "If you walk in My statutes, and keep My commandments, and do them";[240] "and if you shall reject My statutes, and if your soul abhor My ordinances."[241] Should the prophet, in issuing these predictions, omit the condition and fail to mention it, it is nevertheless as if it had been stated explicitly. Should the good or the bad that was promised not materialize, the words of the prophet are not contradicted, for it is well known that what he says in these matters has to do with reward and punishment, for which the double condition appears in the Torah. It follows from this, too, that when the prophet speaks without a promise of

---

[233] Deut. 18: 21.

[234] The words אי אפשר, found in the manuscripts, are missing from Fisher and from the Ferrara edition.

[235] 2 Kgs. 1: 10.   [236] Num. 16: 29.

[237] As we have seen, both Maimonides and Gersonides are of the opinion that a prediction of bad can be reversed, and the purpose of the prediction would presumably make no difference from their point of view. For them, then, despite Moses' status as a true prophet, if what he predicts is bad, its coming-to-pass cannot be assured. Thus, if Moses predicts the unnatural death of these men—a bad thing—as proof that God has sent him, and has further stipulated that if they die a natural death that is proof that God has not sent him, it would remain possible from Maimonides' and Gersonides' point of view for the prediction not to materialize yet for Moses to have been sent. From Crescas's point of view, when a prediction is made for the express purpose of proving the legitimacy of the prophet, it is not possible, even in the case of a prediction of bad, for the prediction not to come to pass yet for the prophet to be legitimate.

[238] If the prophet receives his knowledge from God, it stands to reason that he should know if God has decided not to fulfill the promise. But if God knows only the necessary, this question is moot.

[239] Ps. 64: 4.   [240] Lev. 26: 3.   [241] Lev. 26: 15.

good and bad, but rather speaks about things that will happen or have happened, such as in the case of what Samuel said to Saul regarding the donkeys,[242] these things must be fulfilled; if they are not, these words were not God's. When Scripture speaks generally and is not specific in its predictions, they may be taken in a straightforward sense. For when the prophet issues promises of good things or bad things, it is as if he explicitly states the condition, for it is accepted by us and is set in our mouths by the written Torah. Therefore, when our Rabbis of blessed memory said: "Every promise of good that is issued by God, even if conditional, is not rescinded," they intended this to pertain to when the condition is not essential, as was said earlier.

If we have no choice but to concede that this dictum is to be taken in its straightforward sense, then there is a difference between a promise of good [which cannot be rescinded] and a promise of bad [which can]; and [it must also be the case that] when it is said in Jeremiah, "At one instant I may speak," this concerns when God does not communicate with the prophet—without our distinguishing between a prophet who is sent and one who is not. If we hew to the straightforward sense of Scripture and the dictum of our Sages of blessed memory, then the best we can say is that, in respect of the prophet, that is, when he gives a sign that he is a prophet, God will not assent to the invalidation of that sign, whether the prophecy is for good or for bad, once He has authorized him to give that sign. Thus the words of Scripture can be taken literally, "When a prophet speaks in the name of the Lord, if the thing follow not, nor come to pass, that is the thing which the Lord has not spoken."

What remains, then, to be explained is Jacob's fear and dread and his efforts to escape from his brother Esau,[243] even though he received a promise of good—if we do not distinguish between a prophet who is sent to deliver a prophecy and one who is a prophet whose prophecy pertains to himself. This is in accordance with the dictum of our Sages of blessed memory, which says: "Every promise of good that is issued by God," and which does not distinguish between a prophet who is sent and one whose prophecy pertains to himself. Even more is this so, since they proved this from that which is said: "Let Me be ... and I will make of you a great nation," since here the prophecy was conveyed only to the person himself. It would appear, therefore, that the distinction drawn by the Rabbi does not conform to this rabbinic dictum—even though it is always possible to say that a prophecy, once it is written, becomes like that of a prophet who is sent.

The solution to the matter of Jacob's fears and efforts is not difficult. For the prediction of a prophet with regard to possible things must occur because of God's knowledge of them and from the causal chain that leads to them. And because the prophet does not know the chain, it follows that even if the arrival of something is predicted, it is fitting that he prepare the causes that might reasonably bring it about. Since Jacob our forefather, despite the fact that protection was promised to him by God, did not know the causal chain by means of which the protection would come to be, he prepared himself with all the possible means through which, as he thought, the protection might come about. This is in accordance with what our Rabbis of blessed

---

[242] 1 Sam. 10: 2.
[243] The manuscripts contain the word להנצל, "to escape," which has dropped out of the Ferrara edition.

memory have said: "For a gift, for prayer, and for war."[244] And since it is possible that the prediction by God to him was predicated on God's knowing that Jacob would pray fervently to be saved from his brother Esau whom he feared, or that the protection would come through a gift or through war, it was fitting that Jacob not stint on any one of these, as if he were not sure [of God's protection]. For it is possible that the promise was made with God's knowledge of the way in which Jacob would prepare himself through these causes. This is evident to those who study Parts I and V of this Book. So when it says, "Then Jacob was greatly afraid and was distressed,"[245] this signifies that he prepared himself for prayer with great concentration, since he assessed, while in this great danger, that through this the promise of protection would materialize. This is what we wished to clarify with regard to the first property of prophecy, namely, the validation of the words of the prophet.

The second is that, with respect to the signs and wonders created through the prophet, the prophets differ in rank. Although the signs and wonders are essential properties of prophecy, nevertheless, when we investigated and researched what is available to us about them, we did not discover in Scripture any wonders that did not take place through the intermediation of a prophet—and this, whether they were for his own direction or for the direction of another, and whether they were predicted before they happened or were known only along with his performance of them. It was even discovered that a wonder could originate after the death of the prophet, as occurred in the case of Elisha.[246] For there can be no doubt that the astounding miracle of resurrecting the dead was created in his merit, just as good flows from one person's individual providence to another, as is seen in the Torah: "Then I will forgive all the place for their sake";[247] "I have forgiven according to your word."[248] Good can also continue on after one's death. Since a wonder is consequent upon the attachment of the prophet to God and upon his perfection, it is manifestly appropriate that the higher the rank of the prophet, the greater the signs and wonders created through him. Therefore the signs and wonders that were created through Moses our Teacher were greater than those created through any other—in terms of their number, wide dissemination, and duration, as will be discussed in Book III, God willing. For despite the tradition's report of Joshua's staying of the sun, that is, the delay of all the celestial motions in a fixed relation, Moses' wonders were superior in the three ways mentioned—and all the more so insofar as our Rabbis of blessed memory received through the tradition that this wonder [viz. the staying of the sun] was also performed by Moses. This should suffice for this matter as well.

The third is the fierce passion to summon others to the worship of God, and in this respect, too, the prophets differ. What is found constantly in the words of the prophets should suffice, namely, that they never withheld their admonishment of the people, even though the people insulted and harangued them. Isaiah, for example, said: "I gave my back to the smiters, and my cheeks to them that plucked off the hair";[249] and Jeremiah as well: "And if I say: 'I will not make mention of Him, nor speak any more in His name,' then there is in my heart as it were a burning fire shut

---

[244] *Tanḥuma Vayishlach* (Buber ed.) 6.   [245] Gen. 32: 7.   [246] 2 Kgs. 20.
[247] Gen. 18: 26.   [248] Num. 14: 20.   [249] Isa. 50: 6.

up in my bones, and I weary myself to hold it in, but cannot."[250] Also in what is found in the tradition from our ancestors. But since this requires the perfection of the prophet and the strength of his love in serving God, it follows that the greater his perfection, and the stronger his love, the greater the desire and passion to summon others to the worship of the beloved. It is evident therefore that the prophets differ in rank in this matter. This is what I wished to establish with respect to the third feature.

It is fitting that we explain that the second and third features are relevant to perfected persons even when they are not prophets, as appears in various places in the Talmud. But they are essential to the prophet, insofar as they derive from the perfection of the prophets' attachment to God and their love of Him, which are an essential cause of prophecy, as will be discussed in Chapter IV.

Chapter III

RESOLUTION of some of the difficulties concerning prophecy. We shall comment now upon those which were posited in previous chapters.

Regarding the first. What was said previously by way of defining prophecy is that it is an overflow overflowing from God; we distinguished it in this way from dreams and from magic. It is evident that the prophet is not at all doubtful about his prophecy, and because of this we were commanded to listen to him and to follow him. The prophet who transgresses against his own words merits death, according to what is found in the tradition,[251] and as will be explained in connection with the incident of the Binding [of Isaac]. We may add to this the self-evident proposition that, for those prophets who did not prophesy regularly, activities of the imagination, such as dreams and magic, were possible—at times when they were not prophesying—just as activities of the rest of the senses were not impossible for them. A not insignificant difficulty follows from this, however, namely, that when a prophet prophesies via a dream, as it is said explicitly: "If there should be a prophet among you ... I will speak to him in a dream,"[252] how will the prophet know that he is prophesying? In the case in which there is a sign attesting to the prophet's prophesying, how, if only I knew, would the sign be prevented from occurring in a dream? Is there something that cannot be apprehended in a dream, such that only that thing might be supposed to be a sign that the prophet is prophesying?

The second. It was posited earlier that there is an enormous difference between the prophecy of Moses our Teacher, of blessed memory, and that of other prophets, as well as between their wonders, as is attested by Scripture's saying: "And there has not arisen since a prophet in Israel like unto Moses."[253] This is quite puzzling, if indeed prophecy is something natural, as was widely accepted among the speculative thinkers, and as is indicated by Balaam's prophecy—for if prophecy were not a natural phenomenon but was instead a miraculous one, it is highly improbable that so great a miracle would have been performed for the wicked Balaam. Therefore, insofar as Moses' prophecy is attainable by the human species, there are grounds for

---

[250] Jer. 20: 9. [251] BT *Sanhedrin* 89a. [252] Num. 12: 6. [253] Deut. 34: 10.

great surprise as to why this good would be withheld from human beings, and no other like him would arise.²⁵⁴

The third. In connection with what was posited earlier regarding this difference [between Moses and the other prophets], it would seem that it is in contradiction to the midrash that our Sages of blessed memory proposed: "In Israel no such one arose but among the gentiles one such did arise, namely, Balaam."²⁵⁵ It is a source of great puzzlement that prophecy should devolve upon such a wicked one. It is indeed agreed—and speculation concurs—that the attainment of prophecy requires preparation and perfection.

These are the difficulties which we deemed fitting to note with regard to what was posited in Chapter I.

In Chapter II, the first essential property posited was the verification of the predictions of the prophet, which is equal and in agreement for all prophets. One may indeed wonder, in the case of predictions of good that were established by way of covenant and oath, why the covenant and oath were needed, when, after all, "God is not a man, that He should lie; neither a human being, that He should regret"²⁵⁶— certainly in the case of predictions of good, as was said.²⁵⁷ If the prediction of good may be reversed if it is not uttered along with a sign, the difficulty is not hard to resolve; for we shall then say that it is the prediction that is accompanied by an oath that is irreversible. But if we say that a prediction of good is not rescinded, what is the purpose of the oath? If only I knew!²⁵⁸

It was also posited there that in the case of the second property, namely, the miracles and wonders that were created to serve a definite purpose through the intermediation of the prophet, the ranks of the prophets differ. This is subject to two difficulties. The first is that we find no good purpose in the miracle that occurred when the mouth of the donkey was opened, even if we assume that Balaam was a prophet. The second is that if the ranks of the prophets differ in these cases, why did the Torah neglect to inform us of the great miracle that is found in the tradition of the sun's standing still for Moses?²⁵⁹ For indeed it seems that this miracle that was enacted for Joshua, to the extent that its subject [viz. the sun] is more prestigious, was a greater miracle than all the miracles that were performed by Moses' hand. It is even fitting to add to this a further difficulty, namely, what is the purpose of the moon's standing still in the valley of Ayalon, when the revenge taken against the enemy had already been accomplished before sunset?

---

²⁵⁴ If prophecy is natural, why would it be impossible for others to attain Moses' level of prophecy? Yet how can it be miraculous if so wicked a man as Balaam prophesied? He would hardly be worthy to have a miracle wrought on his behalf.

²⁵⁵ *Sifrei* on *Parashat Berakhah* 16.   ²⁵⁶ Num. 23: 19.

²⁵⁷ One may wonder why predictions of good, which are generally irrevocable, would require confirmation by way of a sign or oath.

²⁵⁸ If we were to suppose that a promise of good unaccompanied by a sign is in fact revocable, we could easily resolve this difficulty by saying that it is when the promise is accompanied by an oath that it is irrevocable. But if our position is that a promise of good is generally not reversible, why would an oath— why would anything confirmatory—be needed?

²⁵⁹ BT *Ta'anit* 20a; BT *'Avodah zarah* 25a.

Similarly with respect to the third property that was also posited there, namely, the fierce passion and the courage to summon others to the worship of God. This property is true and indubitable. Yet if so, why did not the first prophets strive to summon the other nations to worship God and to take shelter under the wings of His Torah? Indeed, according to the tradition, in the time of Solomon proselytes were not accepted; and there are dicta by our Rabbis of blessed memory that indicate their discouragement of this practice. Indeed this is also a source of puzzlement. These are the difficulties that we deemed it fitting to take note of here.

By way of resolving them I say the following. With respect to the first, which concerns the sign that enables the prophet to know that he is prophesying when he is spoken to in a dream, it is self-evident that anything the prophet imagines in a prophetic dream is something which it is possible by nature for him to imagine in a dream that is not prophetic. But by God! if there is nothing by which a dream is known to be a prophetic one issuing from God, nothing that cannot be imagined in a non-prophetic dream, the prophet himself would have to know [whether or not his dream contains a prophecy] on his own; yet this is highly unlikely. The only remaining possibility is for the [distinguishing] sign to be the force of the feeling in this imagining. For just as the feeling in sense-perception is stronger than that of imagination such that the one having the feeling knows that he is awake and is not having the feeling in his imagination alone, that is, in a dream, so, too, the feeling of prophetic imagining, even if in a dream, is stronger than that of an imagining that is not prophetic. This is the true sign by which a prophet knows he is prophesying, even if he is dreaming. Perhaps this is what is alluded to in the verse: "I shall behold Your face in righteousness; I shall be satiated, when I awake, by Your likeness."[260] That is, when I see Your face truly, when it is a veridical instance of my seeing Your face, for example, in a dream, then, when I awaken, I will be satiated by Your likeness. This is the precise opposite of what is said with respect to a simple dream: "And it shall be as when a hungry man dreams, and, behold, he eats, but he awakes, and his soul is empty."[261] Since the imagination varies in being stronger and weaker, and since it is possible for the imagination in a dream to be accompanied by strong feeling—indeed by a feeling nearly as strong as the feeling in sense-perception—the prophet requires great precision in evaluating that feeling and relying on his own assessment. I think Ḥananiah son of Azur who was thought to be a prophet, as the straightforward sense of Scripture attests, erred with regard to the measure of the force of his imagination, and imagined that what he dreamed concerning the king of Assyria was a prophetic dream. For it is hardly in accord with human nature for one to lie with respect to something that will inevitably be put to the test, and, a fortiori, it is not in accord with a prophet's nature. Scripture called him simply a "prophet." There can be no doubt, therefore, that it was his error regarding the strength of his imagination that led to this. Indeed, a mistake in such things [on the part of a prophet] amounts to a deliberate wrong.[262] He was therefore punished. This also shows that he was not

---

[260] Ps. 17: 15.   [261] Isa. 29: 8.
[262] A prophet is held responsible for an error just as a layperson is held responsible for a deliberate wrongful act. This is an application of the broader principle that professionals are held responsible for errors they make in the practice of their profession.

one of the prophets of Baal. For if he were, he would have received the far greater punishment one receives for being a prophet of idolatry, which is far worse than simply prophesying something that was unauthorized, as it is said: "the Lord has not sent you."[263] The Rabbis concur in the chapter on hangings[264] that he was a true prophet, and they attributed his error to a fortiori reasoning.[265] Perhaps this a fortiori reasoning brought him to err with regard to his imagination. This should suffice for the first difficulty.

The second concerns the superiority of Moses' prophecy to that of all the other prophets. For suppose we concede that Moses' prophecy did not depart from the natural course of things; and also that there is [by nature] no limit that limits human perfection, but rather, the more one increases one's worship of God, the more one's perfection increases.[266] This [latter] is the opposite of what some of our sages imagined, since they supposed that perfection depends on intellect alone, and they accepted that human intellect is limited, which entails that human perfection is limited. But the very truth is that perfection has no limit; it can keep increasing continually, as will be shown in Book III, God willing. Unlimited [human] perfection, however, will not exist in actuality. Since God's knowledge of the possible does not make it necessary, as was shown in Part I of this Book, it is not unlikely—indeed, it is necessary—that God knows what the greatest perfection is that will be actualized in the human species. This perfection was Moses'—though God's knowledge of this fact does not make it impossible for someone else to attain this perfection; it remains possible for someone else to do so. But God simply knows that no other human being will actually attain that limit of perfection, as was established. This will further be shown in Part V of this Book, God willing.

It would appear, however, that the view of our Rabbis of blessed memory is that, even though prophecy is generally something that does not depart from the natural course of things, still, the prophecy of Moses our master did depart from the natural course of things and was miraculous in the way other miracles are. This is in order to establish in our souls the perfection and eternality of the Torah, such that it would not be fitting to pay heed to another prophet who would seek to abrogate it. They therefore offered the following midrash: "In Israel no such one arose [like Moses], but among the gentiles one did arise; and who is this? Balaam."[267] They thus taught that Balaam's prophecy did not occur by way of the natural course of things.

---

[263] Jer. 28: 15.   [264] BT *Sanhedrin* 89a.

[265] Jeremiah stood in the upper market place, and said, "Thus says the Lord of Hosts, 'Behold, I will break the bow of Elam'" (Jer. 49: 35). Ḥananiah the son of Azur then drew a conclusion from this proclamation by way of a fortiori reasoning: if God said to Jeremiah that He will break the bow of Elam, when Elam came only to assist Babylon, then God would certainly break the Babylonians themselves. So Ḥananiah went to the lower market place and proclaimed, "Thus speaks the Lord of hosts, the God of Israel, saying, 'I have broken the yoke of the kingdom of Babylon.'" It was inappropriate for him to draw this conclusion.

[266] The problem is this: If Moses' prophecy is natural, yet he is superior to all other prophets, it would seem that, contrary to what is to be expected with respect to natural perfection, there would have to be a limit to human perfection, a limit that he alone has reached. If, however, there is, as we would expect, no such limit, on what grounds can we be assured that no one else will attain prophecy of a rank that equals that of Moses?

[267] *Sifrei* on *Parashat Berakhah* 16.

For prophecy requires proper dispositions and perfections, and these were absent from that wicked man. Therefore, Scripture calls him a magician. When he appeared before Balak, he prophesied by way of miracle and wonder. This is because of the providence that Israel enjoyed that prevented him from cursing them. Deeds and speech do have an effect on others, as the author of the *Kuzari* argued at length and as will be shown in Part IV, God willing. And they also have the effect of showing Israel's [distinguished] rank, and of weakening the resolve [of Israel's enemies], so that Israelites few in number were able to triumph with amazing alacrity over a numerous opponent. Yet since this wicked man is far removed in his nature from the acquisition of his prophecy—indeed by a distance greater than that which separates Moses our master in his nature from the prophecy he acquired—the Rabbis explained that in Israel no one arose who reached Moses' level, for whom a miracle was performed like for no other, but among the gentiles such a one arose, for whom perhaps an even greater miracle was performed.[268] This is what needs to be said by way of resolving the second and third difficulties, according to the view of our Rabbis of blessed memory. But the idea that Moses' prophecy was miraculous is something that originated with R. Nissim, of blessed memory, as a way of resolving the second difficulty. We have in this way resolved the difficulties noted in Chapter I.

Regarding the difficulty associated with the verification of the promises of the prophet, the oath that was mentioned in promises of good might have either of two reasons: the one, to indicate the eternality of the prediction, as in the covenant with Noah and with the Patriarchs—for even if a promise of good is not rescinded, it is possible that, without the oath, the eternality of the promise would not be necessitated in every way; the other, because the promise involves something bad that will happen to someone else, as, for example, in the matter of the promise to Abraham regarding the inheritance of the land. Although this is a good thing for Abraham, it is bad for others; though if the others repent, God might forgive them. Therefore we find that Abraham believed immediately in the promise to his descendants, as it is said: "And he believed in the Lord; and He counted it to him for righteousness,"[269] but he also said, "O Lord God, whereby shall I know that I shall inherit it?,"[270] and what followed was the covenant between the pieces.[271] So, too, the oath with respect to the obliteration of any vestige of Amalek—since this was something bad for Amalek. And so, too, the general covenant at Horeb and in the plains of Moab, inasmuch as it encompassed the prescriptions of the Torah and its proscriptions and thus contained promises of both good and bad. So, too, the covenant of circumcision through which Israel entered into a covenant with God, as will be explained in Part VI of this Book, God willing.

---

[268] According to the Rabbis, the gap between the prophet's nature and his ability to prophesy was so much greater in the case of Balaam than in Moses' case, that a greater miracle was needed (and did in fact occur) to close the gap for Balaam than was needed for Moses.

[269] Gen. 15: 6. This is a promise of good with no attendant bad for someone else. Hence, there is in this case no need for an oath.

[270] Gen. 15: 8.

[271] Here an oath is required because the promise of inheritance of the land contains a promise of something bad for others.

Regarding the first difficulty associated with the second property, which concerns the purpose of the miracle that occurred in causing the donkey to speak, I think that it was in order to grant us a true view, and to expose that wicked man, lest he become arrogant and fancy himself a perfected prophet. For this reason it was indicated to him that his attainment was miraculous and wondrous and not in accordance with his nature, just as it is not in accordance with the nature of a donkey to speak and to be credited for it. That this aim of the speech of the donkey was known to our Rabbis of blessed memory is seen in their Scriptural interpretation according to which the donkey recognized Balaam's deficiency and bad character in saying: "Am not I your ass, upon which you have ridden all your life long unto this day?"[272] as explained in the *Gemara*.[273] And because some of our sages were ignorant of this, they interpreted the Torah improperly, in a way that does not accord with the tradition of our predecessors of blessed memory, of whose waters we drink.[274]

Regarding the second difficulty, which concerns the superiority of Moses' miracles, we already indicated in Chapter II that the superiority consisted in their number, their wide dissemination, and their duration. To be sure, the sun's standing still is reckoned a great merit due to the eminence of its subject [viz. the sun]; but if we do not accept that the heavens are living and rational, there are no longer grounds for this difficulty. For this miracle involved no more than the cessation of its motion or its delay, which is an accident of moving bodies, whereas the miracles of Moses were of substance, as some of the plagues involved the coming-to-be of substances. Even if, however, we do accept that the heavens are living and rational, as the literal sense of Scripture indicates,[275] and as most of the philosophers believed—even if there is no proof of this—nevertheless, what is found in the tradition suffices for the resolution of the difficulty.

The puzzle, however, concerns why the Torah neglected to mention this miracle [among Moses' miracles]. The answer is that the miracle was hardly widely known. For as it appears, the time of revenge was close to the setting of the sun, as is attested by its saying: "and hastened not to go down as on a whole day"[276]—that is, it did not set rapidly, just as the sun's motion seems slow to sense-perception when the sun is in its zenith because the day is in its fullness and perfection. Since it is possible that revenge came swiftly, and that the sun did not delay more than half an hour, it is quite likely that the people did not sense its delay. After all, with the exception of those who were not engaged in the war, the rest were engaged in war, the time was short, and they were not informed of it in advance. It is likely, then, that only those few who were trained in this science would have sensed it. The aim of a miracle consists either in the utility that arises from it in the form of a bodily good or in promoting faith; the purpose of its being recorded in a book is solely to promote faith. Therefore, since this miracle was hardly well known, the Torah neglected to mention

---

[272] Num. 22: 30.
[273] BT *Sanhedrin* 105b. According to the Rabbis, this verse shows that Balaam did not even know his own mind—let alone the mind of God. Balaam's donkey had to point out to him that *it* was his constant companion and that he never rode a horse.
[274] *Avot* 3: 11.
[275] Crescas is referring to Ps. 19: 2: "The heavens declare the glory of God." See his discussion of Issue III in Book IV.
[276] Josh. 10: 13.

it with respect to Moses. Indeed some of our sages have stumbled with respect to this point,[277] and denied this miracle, saying that the swiftness with which the copious revenge was accomplished made it only seem as if the setting of the sun was delayed. Yet, what mandates that the miracle be taken literally is the moon's standing still in the valley of Ayalon. For since the revenge had been accomplished during the day, there was no point in mentioning this, other than to indicate that the matter is to be taken literally. This also informs us of a delay in the other planets as well, in equal measure, lest the fixed order of the celestial bodies, as decreed by divine wisdom, be disrupted. And since the luminaries are the great presiders, insofar as their motion is sensed more, it was sufficient to mention the sun and moon. In Book III, God willing, we shall further clarify the resolution of this difficulty. Thus have these difficulties with respect to wonders been resolved.

Regarding the difficulty associated with the third property, which concerns the reason for the prophets' neglecting to summon the other nations to the worship of God, the solution is simple once we accept one noble dictum of our Rabbis of blessed memory. They said: "Proselytes are as hard for Israel as a sore."[278] This means that, as was proved elsewhere, the celestial bodies direct this inferior world, and the happiness as well as the troubles of those who are born are attributable to their fathers, as is explained in *Book of Fruit (Haperi)*, by Ptolemy the king.[279] Insofar as nature falls short of perfecting man, there is something that derives from God's wisdom in directing the nation to its task, namely, the Torah, whose whole aim is man's attainment of human perfection, which depends on sustained faith and worship. Thus the proselytes who come from other nations are hard for Israel, for they are not disposed to this perfection.

And how could they not be hard? After all, they harbor in their souls their fathers' attraction to idolatry. The situation is even worse when the Israelites are mixed with peoples in such a way that no trace is left of the [Israelite] nation. Since it is thanks to divine kindness that this nation had the merit of receiving the Torah, as per the dictum of Rabbi Ḥanania son of ʿAqashia at the end of tractate *Makkot*,[280] divine wisdom contrived not to summon any other people but us. This holds until such time as he [viz. the Messiah][281] comes and teaches righteousness, for by means of our exile and our dispersion among the nations, the name of God will become known among the nations, and the miracles of the prophets and God's wonders will be recalled. When the truth is revealed, all will come to worship Him in unison. The name of idolatry will be erased from the world, as it is said: "For then will I turn a pure language to the peoples."[282] This is what appears to be the resolution of these difficulties. This is what we wished to say in this chapter.

---

[277] One such sage is Gersonides.　　[278] BT *Yevamot* 47b.

[279] Crescas appears to have confused Ptolemy the astronomer (2nd century CE) with Ptolemy the king (3rd century BCE). For further information on this book, see n. 148.

[280] BT *Makkot* 23b. "The Holy One, Blessed Be He, wished to make Israel worthy, therefore He increased for them Torah and commandments; as it is said: 'The Lord was pleased, for His righteousness's sake, to make the law great and glorious.'"

[281] The manuscripts, but not the Ferrara edition, contain the words "the Messiah."

[282] Zeph. 9: 3. The verse continues: "that they may all call upon the name of the Lord, to serve Him with one consent."

It did not seem fitting to mention here the difficulty that some of the sages raised. They said that there is no escaping the following: if God creates wonders or even a single separate intellect, then either He has a new piece of knowledge and a change of will along with the creation of these wonders, or it was all ordered and determined from before, in which case the nature of the possible is eliminated. But as was already explained, God's knowledge of the future does not nullify the nature of the possible. This will be explained more completely in Part V of this Book, God willing.

Chapter IV

EXPOSITION of the path by which the rank of prophecy is achieved, in accordance with the dictates of the Torah, with which speculation concurs.

I assert that, since it was established in the definition of prophecy that it is an overflow overflowing from God onto man, it is clear that the one who is disposed to this perfection is he who is attached to God and who continually secludes himself to worship Him. Therefore, if it is shown that by means of the Torah and the commandments a connection and attachment to God, which is the height of perfection for the human species, is secured, it is evident that the correct path by which this rank is achieved is the attainment of the end: true worship and love. It will indeed be conclusively established in Part VI that this attachment and connection, which is the highest of all ends, is one that can be attained [only] by means of the Torah. It is therefore evident that the more this connection and love is reinforced, the more one will be disposed to this attainment. If one persists in this connection, and abounds in loving seclusion, there can be no doubt that the divine overflow will overflow onto him, so long as he is not subjected to some affliction. Indeed our Rabbis of blessed memory set conditions and said: "Prophecy does not devolve on anyone who is not wise, brave, and wealthy."[283] Wisdom is an essential condition for a prophet, for the Torah's wisdom is that which leads essentially to this end, and without it this end would not be attained, as our Sages of blessed memory hinted when they said: "One who is ignorant is not pious."[284] Moreover, since the prophet is particularly disposed to guide others, and for this task he fortifies his soul, they set the condition, as was explained in Chapter II, that he be brave, so that he have the strength of heart to reprove others. They required, too, that he be wealthy, that he lack nothing on account of which he would have to toil to supply the needs of survival, and he would be content with his lot, as the Mishnah established.[285] For the thoughts of one who chases money[286] are stupefied by this disturbance, and this will loosen his connection [to God] and weaken his attachment. Therefore, when a wise man secludes himself in love for God, and all conditions are met and all dispositions perfected, and no external affliction oppresses him, there is no doubt that the prophetic spirit will overflow onto him. In addition, according to what is found in the tradition, among the conditions for this overflow is one's locale, as will be explained in Part VI, God willing.

---

[283] BT *Shabbat* 92a.   [284] *Avot* 2: 5.
[285] *Avot* 4: 1: "Who is wealthy? He who is content with his lot."   [286] Prov. 28: 22.

The view of the philosophers in this matter, as found in their discourses, is that a person who has achieved excellence in his intellect and his moral virtues will undoubtedly prophesy when his imaginative faculty is fully developed, and when he readies himself with the requisite preparations. Thus the man who is disposed to prophecy cannot but prophesy. The Rabbi supported this view, but added that one who is disposed to prophecy can be prevented from prophesying by the will of God; and this for him has the stamp of the miraculous. For if one accepts the view of the philosophers, it remains surprising that, during all the time in which events have been transmitted to us, not a single person who reached this level emerged from any nation but the chosen one, in the period following the giving of the Torah. Because the wisdom of the Greeks and the Chaldeans is very well known, the Rabbi was forced to attribute their failure to attain prophecy to a miracle. Yet we must still wonder how this miracle could have affected all of them, that is, all the wise of the nations. Once we posit the true doctrine as we posited it, however, there is no longer room for this surprise. For the true worship and love through which this rank is attained is perfected essentially through the Torah and the commandments. It is also very unreasonable for us to maintain that there might be someone who is ripe for prophecy and ready for it, but God would create a miracle in order to deprive a rightful owner of the good due him.[287] What is said to Baruch son of Neriah: "And do you seek great things for yourself? Do not seek them,"[288] is not relevant to this matter, contrary to what the Rabbi maintains.[289] For in the case of Baruch son of Neriah prophecy indeed constitutes "great things."[290] Yet in the case of one who is disposed to prophecy and suffers no external affliction it is impossible that he not prophesy, so long as he does not become entangled in the cares of time and of things external to him, on account of which prophecy has ceased in this exile, as our Rabbis of blessed memory have said: "Prophecy devolves on someone not out of laziness or sadness, but out of joy, as it is said: 'And it came to pass, when the minstrel played, that the hand of the Lord came upon him.'"[291] This is what we wished to clarify in this chapter.

With this we conclude Part IV of this Book. Praise is to God alone, who is exalted above all blessing and praise.

Part V

CONCERNING choice.

We have already noted that one of the foundations of religion is choice, such that each person is given freedom to choose. For the term "commandment" does not apply to one who is constrained and compelled to do a definite thing, but all

---

[287] Prov. 3: 27. [288] Jer. 45: 5.
[289] For Maimonides in *Guide* II. 32, Baruch son of Neriah serves as an example of one who is miraculously prevented from prophesying despite his presumed fitness for prophecy.
[290] Crescas regards Baruch as unfit for prophecy and therefore as not validating the notion that God may withhold prophecy from someone who is worthy. Maimonides takes note of the possibility that Baruch is unfit and at least appears to dismiss it. See *Guide* II. 32.
[291] 2 Kgs. 3: 15. BT *Shabbat* 30b. The prophet Elisha was able to prophesy when his spirit was soothed by the music of the minstrel.

alternatives must be open to his simple will. Only then will an imperative be appropriate and relevant.

The foundation of choice is the existence of the nature of the possible. Early thinkers struggled with this matter, and we have found various views within those writings of theirs that have reached us. We must investigate them in accordance with the Torah and in accordance with speculation. Since the views we found among them align with two contradictory sides, we have divided this Part into three chapters. The first two deal with these two views and the arguments for them contained in the force of their words; in the third we report on what the Torah and speculation necessitate, as it appears to us.

It is fitting that we not be overcome by indolence in this investigation, for this cornerstone is a great foundation and pillar concerning God's knowledge of existents, as we hinted in Part I, such that an error in this matter leads to great and enormous errors concerning God's knowledge and providence with respect to existents.

We have therefore added three more chapters, as will be seen in our discussion in this Part, God willing.

Chapter I

EXPOSITION of the view of one who accepts the existence of the nature of the possible. This will be established both from the point of view of speculation and from that of the Torah.

From the point of view of speculation, this [viz. that the nature of the possible exists] is plausible from several perspectives. One of them [the first] is as follows. It is evident that things—whether natural or a product of art—do not come to be unless preceded by four causes, which are: the efficient, material, formal, and final, as was explained in the *Physics*.[292] We see that for some things some of these causes exist and some do not exist, but it is possible for all to exist or for all not to exist. Since the causes of things are possible, it follows necessarily that the things themselves are possible.

Another [the second] is as follows. We see many things that depend on will. It is evident that a person can will or not will. If, however, one of these were necessary there would be not will but compulsion or necessity. It is therefore evident that the nature of the possible exists.[293]

Another [the third]. It was already explained in the *Physics*[294] that some things come to be by chance or by luck or by themselves. Yet if all things were necessary, as would necessarily be the case were the nature of the possible nonexistent, each of the existent things would exist by necessity. Yet what exists by necessity cannot rightly be said to exist by chance, for it is not right to say that the sun will rise tomorrow by chance. It is therefore evident that not all things are necessary, and that the nature of the possible exists.

---

[292] *Physics* II. iii.
[293] This entire passage is missing from Fisher's text. It reads as follows: ומהם שאנחנו נראה הרבה הדברים מהדברים ניתלים ברצון. ולפי שהוא מבואר, שהאדם לו שירצה ושלא ירצה למה שאם היה האחד מחויב, לא היה רצון, אבל הכרח וחיוב. הנה אם כן הוא מבואר שטבע האפשר נמצא. It is found in the Ferrara edition and the manuscripts.
[294] *Physics* II. iv-vi.

Another [the fourth]. If the nature of the possible did not exist, and man's acts were necessitated, then effort and industriousness would be futile. Futile, too, would be study and training, as well as preparation and initiation, and so also zeal in accumulating goods and useful things and in avoiding harmful things. This is the opposite of what is well known and sensed.

Another [the fifth]. Since the human will is consequent upon the rational soul, which is separate from matter, it is not fitting that it be acted upon by material things, as the bodies of the celestial spheres act upon the lower [terrestrial] bodies. For it is evident that the incorporeal is designated to act, and matter is designated to be acted upon, as was explained in the *Metaphysics*.[295] It is therefore not fitting that it be thought that the spheres, which have bodies, act upon and compel the human soul. Rather, the will is unconstrained and is free of all necessity.

From all these perspectives it would appear that from the point of view of speculation the nature of the possible exists. But from the point of view of the Torah this is also evident from several perspectives.

One of these [the first] is as follows. If all things were necessary, and man were constrained in his deeds, then the prescriptions of the Torah and its proscriptions would be futile, since they would be of no use if man's deeds are compelled and he has no power or will over them.

Also [the second], that if man were constrained in his deeds, reward and punishment for them would constitute an injustice on God's part, God forbid. For it is self-evident that reward and punishment for deeds do not apply other than to voluntary human deeds, but with respect to deeds in which he is constrained and compelled, reward and punishment are untenable. Since reward and punishment is one of the root-principles of the Torah, it is necessary that man be in possession of will, unconstrained in his deeds, and free of all compulsion and constraint.

On this basis it is established that the nature of the possible exists. This is the intention of this chapter.

Chapter II

EXPOSITION of the view of one who holds that the nature of the possible does not exist.

This will be explained as well, both from the point of view of speculation and from the point of view of the Torah.

From the point of view of speculation this is plausible from several perspectives. One of them [the first] is as follows. It has been explained in physics that the existence of all things subject to coming-to-be and passing-away is necessarily preceded by four causes. When the causes are present, the effects necessarily ensue and, therefore, the existence of the effects is necessary and not possible. When we investigated, too, the existence of the causes, we found that it is necessary that these causes be preceded by the existence of other causes, whose existence necessitates those causes. Of necessity their existence is necessary and not possible. When we seek further causes for these causes, the same rule will apply, until the series culminates in

---

[295] *Metaph.* IX. v–ix.

the first existent whose existence is necessary: God. It is thus established that the nature of the possible does not exist.

Another [the second]. It is self-evident and agreed-upon that a possible thing that can exist or not exist requires a cause to determine its existence over its nonexistence; otherwise, its nonexistence would persist. Therefore, when something possible exists, it is necessarily the case that it was preceded by a cause that necessitated and determined its existence over its nonexistence, so that the existent that was assumed possible turns out to be necessary. And if we investigate the earlier cause, if it, too, was assumed to be possible, and we posit it as existent, then the necessity that turned out to apply in the case of the first possible that was posited as existent will apply to it as well. This will continue until the series culminates in the first cause and first existent, whose existence is necessary: God.

Another [the third] is that it is self-evident and agreed-upon that anything that passes from potentiality to actuality requires something external to effect the transition. It is therefore necessary that when the volition[296] to do something newly arises in a man, this volition, which was in potentiality and passed into actuality, was necessarily actualized by something external to it that moved the appetitive faculty[297] to join and concur with the imaginative faculty. This conjunction, as was explained in *On the Soul*,[298] is the cause of the volition. When this conjunction, which is the cause of the volition, exists, the volition indeed will exist of necessity; and the conjunction is also necessary when its mover exists.

Were it to be objected that the mover of this volition is the volition alone, so that this is actually the opposite of necessity, one of two absurdities would follow. The first is that a thing would be its own mover and would be able to effect its own transition from potentiality to actuality. Yet this stands in opposition to an agreed-upon proposition.[299] The second is that this volition will have a prior volition that will move it and effect its transition from potentiality to actuality. But then the prior volition will have one prior to it, so that one volition will require an infinite number of volitions. Yet this is the height of absurdity—on top of which, each one will be necessitated by the previous one, and so will not be something possible.

Another [the fourth]. It is self-evident, as was said, that everything that comes into being requires an originator to bring it into being, for nothing can bring itself into being. Therefore, if we imagine two people in the same condition, with the same temperament, the same traits, and standing in the same relation to a particular thing, with no distinction between them at all, it cannot happen that one will choose the existence of a particular thing and the other its nonexistence. Rather, it is necessary that the one will choose and desire just what the other chooses and desires. For were they to differ in choice and desire, so that a new distinction between them would arise, there would have to be something to create this distinction. Yet what could be

---

[296] רצון (*ratzon*) is rendered "volition" when it denotes a particular instance of wanting. As a faculty, it is rendered "will."
[297] The term is הכח המתעורר (*hakoaḥ hamit'orer*).
[298] Aristotle, *On the Soul* III. x.
[299] The proposition referred to is that it is not possible for something to move itself from potentiality to actuality; something actual is needed.

the cause of this distinction's coming-to-be when the two are alike in temperament and birth and traits in every respect?—if only I knew! Although the existence of two such people is impossible, the necessity [of the argument's conclusion that they will choose and desire identically] derives not from the perspective of its impossibility [i.e. that it is impossible in fact for there to be two such identical people], but from the perspective of its possibility [i.e. that it is theoretically possible for there to be two such identical people]. Since it is necessary that they have the same volition, their choice is necessary and constrained—not possible.

Another [the fifth]. It was already established in Part I of this Book that God's knowledge encompasses all particulars qua particulars, even if they are nonexistent and have not come into existence. It is therefore necessary that when God knows which one of two possible alternatives will come into existence, that is the one that will necessarily come into existence. For otherwise what He has is not knowledge, but conjecture or error. Therefore, inescapably, what was presumed to be something possible is actually something necessary.

Another [the sixth]. If the nature of the possible were to exist, we would necessarily have to concede that the existence of a volition for one of two alternatives, without a necessitating cause, is possible. It would then necessarily be the case that God's knowledge of it does not derive from His essence as does His knowledge of existents insofar as He is their cause; rather, His knowledge would be acquired and would emanate from *their* existence. Yet it is the height of absurdity that His knowledge should originate outside Him.

Another [the seventh]. It is evident that providence with respect to particulars, inasmuch as it does not operate from the perspective of the general order, is impossible—other than by a hylic faculty. But this is impossible with respect to God. Yet if an alternative comes to exist without a necessitating cause, it cannot be apprehended by means of the general order.[300] On the basis of all these considerations it appears that, from the point of view of speculation, the nature of the possible does not exist.

From the Torah's point of view, it was established in what we have already discussed—beyond all doubt as to its truth—that God's knowledge encompasses all particulars, even if they are [as yet] nonexistent. In the case of the prophets as well, we find that they related many particulars prior to their coming-to-be, even if they were not in themselves necessary—that is, even if they were dependent on choice, as in the case of Pharaoh.

All of this is patent proof that the nature of the possible does not exist. This is the intent of this chapter.

---

[300] The thrust of this argument is as follows. God can know particulars only through the general order which is necessitated. Any other knowledge would be of particulars that are possible and not necessary, and knowledge of this kind requires a hylic faculty, that is, a material faculty capable of sense-perception, which God does not have. Since, however, things that come to exist outside a strict causal order, viz. "possibles," cannot be part of the necessary general order and cannot, therefore, be known by God, it is not possible for possibles to exist.

Chapter III

EXPOSITION of the true view according to what the Torah and speculation necessitate.

We assert that, since there are arguments that entail the existence of the nature of the possible, and arguments that entail its nonexistence, the only remaining option is for the nature of the possible to exist in one respect, and not to exist in another. What are these respects? If only I knew!

I say that, when we investigate the arguments that entail the existence of the possible, what emerges is that the only way in which they entail its existence is in respect of itself.[301]

Regarding the first argument, which contends that there are some things for which all the causes either do exist or do not exist, this begs the question. For the possibility of the causes is also in question. Therefore, this does not resolve the matter regarding this question.[302]

The second argument is based on will, that is, on that it is evident that a person can either will something or not will it. Yet this, too, is question-begging. For one who maintains that the nature of the possible does not exist will say that the will has a mover that moves it and, since the mover necessitates that the will be directed toward that thing or to its alternative, the mover is the cause of the will. Therefore, that mover will necessitate the direction of the will, even as the will remains a will and is not a matter of necessitation or constraint. For in itself, it might will each of the alternatives equally, were it not for the mover that necessitates that it will the one. The person, however, senses no constraint or compulsion. Since it is possible for the person in himself to will both alternatives equally, it is called will rather than necessity.[303]

The third derives from what has been explained in physics, namely, that some things occur by chance. This possibility is not necessary, however, except in respect of itself: from this perspective it is true that the things occurred by chance. But the possibility of their having causes that necessitate their occurrence has not been eliminated.

With respect to the fourth, which is based on industriousness and effort, it is evident that these do not require anything but the possibility of things in [respect of] themselves. For example, if a person were constrained in himself to become wealthy, then efforts on his part to accumulate goods would be futile. But if we assume possibility in himself but necessity in respect of his causes—which in this case just *are* his industriousness and effort—his industriousness and effort would not be

---

[301] What is meant by "in respect of itself" is: without looking beyond it to its causes. Thus, what is voluntary or a matter of chance in itself may not be so from the perspective of its causes.

[302] Crescas is contending that, if we say some things are possible because their causes are possible—that is, these causes may or may not exist—we will have prejudged precisely that which is at issue, namely, whether the causes themselves are possible or necessary.

[303] When two alternatives are equally open to the person who is to choose, it remains possible that his or her choice of one alternative over another is actually determined by a cause. If this is so, then, from the point of view of the cause the choice is necessary, even if in itself—that is, if one looks no farther than the chooser—the choice is up to the chooser. Even if one's will is necessitated by a cause, one need not feel coerced or constrained.

futile but rather would be the essential cause of his accumulating goods, and the accumulation of goods would be their effect. There is no way to say that the coming-to-be of the cause is futile with respect to the effect, unless the effect is necessary in itself, necessitated by its essence, regardless of whether the cause exists or not. It would then, however, not be an effect.[304]

The fifth argument proffers nothing true in any respect. For the rational soul is not incorporeal but hylic, and it is acted upon by the temperament of the soul's possessor. Therefore, it is possible that the corporeal celestial spheres, and certainly their movers, will also act upon the temperament of the soul's possessor, and will move his appetitive faculty. When this faculty concurs with the imaginative faculty, the will is created, as was explained in the book *On the Soul*. Thus, this argument will not resolve the matter of whether the moving is necessary or whether its being possible is still a viable option.

It is evident, then, that in all the arguments from the point of view of speculation, what is entailed is the existence of the nature of the possible in the things that are—in respect of themselves but not in respect of their causes.

The arguments from the point of view of the Torah also fail to entail the existence of the nature of the possible except in respect of the thing in itself.

It is evident that the argument derived from the prescriptions of the Torah and its proscriptions, to the effect that if things were necessary, the prescriptions and proscriptions would be futile, necessitates only the possibility of things in respect of themselves. For although it is true that, if the things were necessary in respect of themselves the prescriptions and proscriptions would be futile, nevertheless, if the things are possible in respect of themselves and necessary in respect of their causes, the prescriptions and proscriptions would not be futile but would rather have an important purpose. For they would be the causes that move things that are possible in themselves, just as do other causes that are causes of their effects, such as industriousness and diligence in the accumulation of goods and in the acquisition of beneficial things and the avoidance of harmful things. It is therefore the case that this argument offers nothing that would necessitate the existence of possibility in respect of the cause.

The second argument derives from reward and punishment. If a man were necessitated in his deeds, reward and punishment for them would constitute an injustice on God's part. This appears to be a strong argument for the nullification of all necessity. Yet if we delve into it, its resolution is not difficult. For if reward and punishment follow necessarily upon good works and transgressions [respectively] in the way that effects follow necessarily upon causes, they would not be said to be injustices, just as there is no injustice when someone who approaches fire gets

---

[304] Crescas is suggesting that, even in a world of causal necessity, there is no reason to think that industriousness and effort play no role in a man's becoming wealthy. On the contrary, it is only if the man *must* be wealthy, that is, if his being wealthy is necessary in itself, that effort is in vain, for only in such a case is there no cause that could have any effect. So long, however, as a man's becoming wealthy is not something that will occur no matter what, industriousness and effort make all the difference: they are the very causes of his material success. These causes, however, may well be themselves necessitated by causes, and so, from the point of view of causes, the man's becoming wealthy may be necessary.

burned, even if he approaches the fire involuntarily. This will be explained in Book III, God willing.

It is therefore evident that none of the arguments, whether from the point of view of speculation or from the point of view of the Torah, offers anything that would entail the existence of the nature of the possible in respect of causes. I will also say that, when we examine the arguments for the necessity of the nonexistence of the possible, these will be found to entail it only in respect of its causes.

It is evident that the first, second, and third arguments, which derive from the causes of things and from the movers that effect the transition from potentiality to actuality—and so, too, the fourth necessity argument—support necessity only in respect of causes, while in respect of themselves, the things remain possible. Just as it might be said with respect to prime matter that, although in respect of itself it is capable of receiving all forms in succession, this is not so when it is considered in respect of its movers. For example, although it is necessary in respect of causes that bronze become verdigris, bronze in respect of itself does not lose its possibility [either to become or not to become verdigris], so that becoming verdigris remains for it in itself only a possible outcome. Therefore, when verdigris appears, the bronze is subject to a temporary necessity in respect of its cause but it retains a permanent possibility in respect of itself, which it never forfeits.

So, too, it is evident that the arguments deriving from God's knowledge of the future, and from the prophets' prediction of future events—especially regarding those things dependent on choice—fail to disqualify possibility in respect of the thing itself. Indeed, things are possible in respect of themselves and necessary in respect of their causes; and it is from their aspect as necessary that knowledge precedes their existence.[305]

It is evident therefore that in none of these arguments, whether from the point of view of speculation or from the point of view of the Torah, is there anything to compel the necessity of things in respect of themselves. Therefore, the complete truth is, in accordance with what the Torah and speculation require, that the nature of the possible exists in things in respect of themselves, but not in respect of their causes. Nevertheless, to publicize this thesis is harmful to the multitude, for they will regard it as an excuse for wrongdoers, and they will not sense that punishment is consequent upon transgressions as an effect is consequent upon a cause.

Therefore, the divine science saw fit to set the prescriptions and the proscriptions as means to move people, and as powerful causes to direct them to human happiness. And this is indeed a manifestation of God's simple goodness and kindness. This is the righteousness of God alluded to in Scripture's saying: "As a man chastens his son, so the Lord your God chastens you."[306] It is known that a father does not chasten his son with the intent of taking revenge, and not even for the sake of doing justice, but only to benefit his son. When, therefore, God chastens man, His intent is not to take revenge on him, and not even to achieve political justice—which is fitting only if the

---

[305] The manuscripts have היותם (heyotam) instead of חיובם (hiyyuvam), "their existence" instead of "their necessitation." Knowledge precedes existence not only when existence is necessary but also when there is knowledge of the causal chain that will produce the effect.

[306] Deut. 8: 5.

person is acting fully voluntarily without any constraint or compulsion. Rather, the intent of chastening is for the good of the nation generally; this is its intended aim. It is therefore fitting as well even when the person is necessitated in respect of his cause, for his cause is the good for man.

It is necessary to be aware, however, that this necessity obtains when the agent does not feel compulsion and constraint. This is the secret of choice and will. When, however, acts are constrained and compelled, that is, when a man acts under constraint and compulsion, and does not act by his will, then, since he does not act by the concurrence of his appetitive faculty with his imaginative one, what he does is not an act of his soul, and it is not fitting that punishment should follow. This is so because compelled deeds are unaffected by prescriptions and proscriptions which are able to move people to do or to avoid them. For inasmuch as these have no effect on a person, there is no point in issuing prescriptions and proscriptions to him. Punishment for transgression would not stem then from divine justice, for no good is consequent upon it.

If, however, we have no alternative but to say that the nature of will in fact entails that one wills or does not will without an external mover—and this view is the correct one according to the Torah[307]—it is then possible that a distinction along the lines of that drawn in Part I of this Book applies. According to this distinction, things are possible both in respect of themselves and in respect of their causes, but are necessary in respect of the cause that is God's knowledge—just as the possible, when it is posited as existent and known, is possible in respect of itself but necessary in respect of its existing at the time and in respect of its having become known. If God's knowledge of things precedes their coming to be, then, since a thing that is possible is not necessary before it comes to be, it follows that things are possible, not in respect of God's knowledge, but in respect of themselves. And since God's knowledge is not subject to time, His knowledge of the future is like our knowledge of things that exist: it does not entail constraint and necessity in the essence of things.[308] If, however, we were to object, saying: "Does God's knowledge derive from existents?" as per the last two difficulties,[309] we would respond: "We do not know how God knows, since His knowledge is His essence." This is the Rabbi's approach, in our view.

Yet another possible reply is as follows. It is evident that things that are apprehended are apprehended, not in accordance with the things apprehended, but in accordance with the nature of the apprehender, as is seen in the matter of sense-perception. For the sense of touch will apprehend the object of its apprehension when it draws near to it and touches it, and will apprehend heat or coldness, hardness or

---

[307] Harvey (1980b) points out that several passages that appear in the Florence manuscript as marginal notes and found their way into the editions of *Light of the Lord* reflect Crescas's (or, more likely, one of his students') concern that his determinism stands in some tension with the Torah's view.

[308] When human beings have knowledge of a current state of affairs that was previously possible, that state of affairs becomes necessary—not in respect of itself or its nature—but because it cannot but be the case now that it exists in fact and is known. One would not say, however, that this human knowledge caused the state of affairs to be necessary in itself. Similarly, when God knows that a future state of affairs that is now possible will come to be, the existence of that state of affairs is necessary insofar as God knows it, but its nature in respect of itself remains possible.

[309] The reference is to the sixth and seventh doubts in Chapter II, just above.

softness, at the point of contact alone; but the sense of sight apprehends its object's colors at a distance; and so, too, the other senses. Therefore, since this apprehender is eternal and not subject to time, it is fitting that He apprehend the object of His apprehension in accordance with His rank and not be subject to time, for His apprehension is a feature of His essence. He therefore apprehends what does not [yet] exist, with an eternal apprehension—as if it were existent.[310]

The principle that emerges from these considerations is that it is inescapable that that which is possible is necessary in respect of its cause and possible in respect of itself—so long as choice is not involved. And with regard to things in which choice is involved, if we say that the nature of will necessitates that it can will something or not will it with no external mover—and this is the correct approach according to the Torah—these things will be possible in respect both of their causes and of themselves, but necessary in respect of God's knowledge. And since they are possible in respect of themselves, industriousness is fitting with respect to them, as are the prescriptions and proscriptions, and as are their being subject to reward and punishment. For if the person were to choose the alternative, God's knowledge would be of the alternative. The only remaining question is: how does God know things that are possible? But we have already answered this, both in accordance with the view of the Rabbi and in accordance with our own view. Generally, since God confers existence on all other existents, His knowledge of them is fitting and necessary.[311] Either way, the root of the entire matter is possibility in one respect, necessity in another. This is inescapable.

Indeed, the perfect one who entered in peace and left in peace[312] attested to all these profound matters in one short statement. He said: "All is foreseen [or, seen—צפוי (tzafui)], but freedom [to choose] is granted. The world is judged by goodness. And all is according to the preponderance of deeds."[313] By saying, "All is foreseen," he indicated that all things are ordered and known. Although this is a critical root-principle whose truth is indubitable, some of our sages have stumbled with respect to it. What has induced us to reveal this secret is that many of our nation defy it even today. By saying, "but freedom is granted," he attested to the secret of choice and will, namely, that the freedom of each person is granted to him in respect of himself, for commands do not apply to one who is constrained and compelled. By saying, "The world is judged by goodness," he attested to the divine justice in judgment, that is, in reward and punishment. For their purpose is not revenge, and their intent is not to

---

[310] Some manuscripts contain the term "eternal," נצחי: "as if it were eternally existent." Fisher's text omits it. Smilevitch includes it. It is found in the Vienna and Florence manuscripts as well as in the Ferrara edition. The view Crescas presents here as a possible solution to the difficulty of divine foreknowledge—namely, that apprehension is determined by the nature of the apprehender, and that God's superior apprehension, unlike inferior forms of apprehension, is not subject to time—is reminiscent of a view propounded most vigorously by Boethius, who, in his *The Consolation of Philosophy* (written in prison c.523–524), contends that God's apprehension is outside time, that He sees all time in a single instant and so may be said merely to observe the present and not, strictly speaking, to have *fore*knowledge.

[311] The current paragraph up until this point appears to be another mitigating gloss inserted into the text by Crescas or his students. See n. 307. Fisher designates it an alternative version. It is found as well in the Ferrara edition and in the Vienna manuscript.

[312] The reference is to R. Akiva, who was, according to legend, the only one of four Sages to emerge whole after having entered Paradise. See *Tosefta, Ḥagigah* 2: 2.

[313] *Avot* 3: 15.

secure popular political justice—though it is a necessity from a causal perspective—but for benefit, as we said earlier.[314] And by saying, "And all is according to the preponderance of deeds," it is possible that he attested to the necessity of causes, both proximate and remote, that affect the world, as it is said: "for one higher than the high watches."[315] It is also possible that he is hinting at the well-known root-principle of the tradition, namely, that the world is judged according to the deeds of the majority.[316] Yet another possibility is that he is hinting at an important root-principle that will be explained in Part VI, God willing.

Chapter IV

However this view concerning necessity is understood, whether as necessity in respect of causes or as necessity in respect of God's knowledge, it is alluded to in places in the Writings, particularly in Ecclesiastes, and in certain places in the dicta of our Rabbis of blessed memory. They say: "A person does not bruise his finger below, without its having been decreed above."[317] They interpret Scripture's saying, "if the faller fall from there,"[318] as follows: "At the six days of creation it was ordained that this individual fall, for even before he fell, Scripture called him 'the faller.' For merit is brought about at the hand of the meritorious, and blame at the hand of the blameworthy."[319] Thus, even though what occurred was an instance of the possible, nevertheless, from the six days of creation, it was ordained that this man would fall. The proximate cause was the absence of a parapet. But even though the fall is attributed to chance, and even though knowledge of it eludes human beings—since human knowledge cannot encompass all particulars inasmuch as they are infinite—nevertheless, the fall was necessary from the perspective of one who is infinite and whose knowledge is infinite.

A further dictum of theirs attests to this. They say: "It was not like David to commit that [sinful] deed, nor was it like Israel to commit that [sinful] deed. Rather, it was meant to show that if an individual sins he should be told: 'Turn to that individual'; and if the community sins, it should be told, 'Turn to that community.'"[320] Nevertheless, they were punished. The only way this can be made sense of is in the way we have specified.[321]

---

[314] The Florence manuscript and the Ferrara edition insert a "not," לא (*lo*), into the qualifying phrase, as follows: "though it is not a necessity from a causal perspective" See n. 307.

[315] Eccles. 5: 7. On this reading of *Avot* 3: 15, the "deeds" whose preponderance is decisive are the natural causes at work in the universe.

[316] BT *Kiddushin* 40b.   [317] BT *Ḥullin* 7b.

[318] Deut. 22: 8. One is required to build a parapet on one's roof lest someone fall from it. One who fails to build a parapet is held liable when someone falls. The Torah calls the person who falls "the faller" (הנופל; *hanofel*).

[319] BT *Shabbat* 32a.

[320] BT *ʿAvodah zarah* 4b–5a. The allusion is to David's sin with Bathsheba and the Israelites' sin of the Golden Calf.

[321] These sins were meant to teach the possibility and importance of repentance, at both the individual and communal levels. The reason David and the Israelites committed their respective sins was to encourage repentance in others who sin. Nevertheless, punishment follows upon sin.

Another dictum that also points to necessity is their saying: "When the Holy One Blessed Be He said to the Israelites: 'Who might grant that they have such a heart [to fear Me always and follow My commandments]?'[322] they ought to have said: 'You be the one to grant.' Yet Moses did not even hint at this to the Israelites until forty years had passed.... From this it may be derived that a person does not plumb the depths of his teacher's thought until forty years pass."[323]

There are many such dicta apart from those mentioned that appear to increase doubt and confusion, yet, when taken in this way, in accordance with their literal sense, make good sense.

As far as something that teaches the compatibility of effort with necessity, there is their dictum: "If I am not for myself, who will be for me? And if I am for myself alone, what am I? And if not now, when?"[324] There are in addition many others like this, although there is no need to mention them. For example, they say in *Gemara Sukkah*: "The sun is eclipsed on account of six things."[325] And in tractate *Makkot*: "If the high priest dies before a certain person's trial was concluded, and another high priest is appointed and the trial is brought to a conclusion in his lifetime, the accused returns only after the death of the second one." The *Gemara* then says: "What should this one have done? He ought to have petitioned God for mercy so that the trial culminate in an acquittal, yet he failed to do so."[326] None of these statements can be sustained unless the matter is understood as has been established, namely, as that all things, whether natural or volitional, are ordered and known by God. This should suffice for what we have intended. In Part VI we shall introduce points that agree with and are

---

[322] Deut. 5: 26.

[323] BT *'Avodah zarah* 5a. Forty years after the revelation at Sinai, Moses chastises the people for not having asked God, when they had the chance, to grant them a heart that would fear God and observe His commandments. In other words, since the rightly disposed heart is the cause of God-fearingness and observance of the commandments, the people should have asked God (the remote cause) to bestow this heart (the proximate cause) upon them.

[324] Avot 1: 14. As Crescas interprets this dictum it encourages our efforts despite causal necessitation.

[325] BT *Sukkah* 29a. The *Gemara* with which we are acquainted lists just four: on account of an *av beit din* (i.e. head of the rabbinical court) who died and was not mourned fittingly; on account of a betrothed maiden who cried out aloud in the city and there was none to save her; on account of sodomy; and on account of two brothers whose blood was shed at the same time. This rabbinic dictum implies that, despite the seeming imperviousness of the natural course of the motions of heavens to the deeds of men, the heavens are in fact affected by human deeds and events. Fisher emends the text, substituting "four" for "six." The manuscripts and the Ferrara edition say "six."

[326] BT *Makkot* 11b. This passage in the Talmud concerns one who has slain another. If it is found that the slaying was unintentional, the perpetrator is exiled until the death of the high priest (Num. 35: 28). If, however, the trial does not conclude until a second high priest is in office, the unintentional killer must await this second high priest's death before he may return from the city to which he had been banished. The Rabbis explain that, although this second high priest was not in office when the killing occurred, he might have prayed to God for a merciful outcome—but he failed to do so. Since he did not pray when he might have, he is in some way implicated in the crime for which his death is a partial atonement. According to Crescas, it is evident from this that the Rabbis must have believed that, despite the necessitated verdict, human effort should have been expended. Even though the outcome of the trial would be what it would be, the high priest still should have prayed (for perhaps his prayer was to have been the cause of a merciful outcome).

congenial to this view, for the nature of truth attests to itself and is in agreement from all perspectives.

The great difficulty which, in Part I of this Book, we promised to resolve, a difficulty with respect to which many of our earlier scholars have stumbled, has thus been resolved. They were in error in not having recognized that necessity accords with the divine justice of the Torah, even if it cannot accommodate popular political justice, [and, a fortiori, since the Torah's view, which is the correct one, accords with popular political justice. Know this.][327] Praise is to God alone, who is exalted above all blessing and praise.

Chapter V

An additional exposition of this view [or, of the two views[328]] in order to resolve the serious difficulty with respect to which the ancient thinkers never ceased from their perplexity, namely, how divine justice in the meting out of reward and punishment can be reconciled with necessity. And if they are reconciled, what is the difference between necessity in respect of causes in which there is no feeling of compulsion or constraint and necessity in which there is a feeling of compulsion and constraint?

It might be thought that, if deeds done in observance of the commandments and deeds done in violation of them are causes, if reward and punishment are their effects, and, in addition, the deeds are themselves necessary, it would not be fitting to distinguish necessity unaccompanied by a feeling of constraint from necessity accompanied by a feeling of constraint and to take reward and punishment to be effects of the one but not effects of the other. For necessity is utterly inescapable in either case. Even if we were to concede such a distinction—namely, that when there is a feeling of compulsion and constraint there is no room for reward and punishment, for in such a case, the deed was not at all volitional, yet when no constraint is felt, then, even if the deed was constrained, it is called volitional—how could there be reward and punishment for *beliefs* held concerning the Torah's cornerstones? If only I knew! Moreover, it is explicit according to the tradition that punishment for them is severe. It is said, for example: "But for the apostates and the heretics and those who deny the Torah and the resurrection of the dead..."[329] And in the Mishnah it is said: "These are the ones who have no portion in the world-to-come..."[330] Yet it would seem that will and choice have no role in beliefs, for several reasons.

First, if will were required for belief, then the degree of belief would not be determined by the force of the truth [but by the will]. That is, since will has the

---

[327] See n. 307. Fisher presents the bracketed text as an alternate reading. The Vienna manuscript does not include it at all. It appears in the Ferrara edition. The bracketed text contradicts what precedes it. The preceding text implies that the divine justice of the Torah is at odds with popular political justice; in the bracketed text, the two are in accord and both are endorsed.

[328] Fisher presents the bracketed text as an alternate reading. This bracketed text is not found in either of the manuscripts. In fact, they do not have even the words "of this view." The Ferrara edition has only "of this view."

[329] BT *Rosh Hashanah* 17a. A severe punishment follows: descent into Gehenna for all eternity.

[330] BT *Sanhedrin* 90a. The beliefs held by these people are: that resurrection of the dead has no source in the Torah, and that the Torah does not have a divine origin.

discretion to want or not to want, one could presumably believe two contradictory things one after another, continually, so long as one wished to do so. Yet this is the height of absurdity.

Second, if will were required for belief, then the truth of that which motivates and creates the particular belief would have to be in doubt. For if the truth of that which propels the belief were not at all doubtful, there would be no need for will. Yet if the truth of that which creates the belief is in doubt, then the truth of the belief is in doubt.[331]

Third, it appears from this perspective that will has no role in the matter of belief. For belief is nothing but the affirmation that something outside the mind is as it is within the mind. Whatever is outside the mind is independent of the will to believe of it that it is so. Therefore, belief is independent of will.

Now that this has been clarified, I assert that it is impossible for one who holds a certain belief, particularly if it is a belief that is demonstrated, not to feel utterly necessitated and constrained to hold that belief. For when a proof is decisive, as it is in the case of a belief presumed to be demonstrated, necessitation by the mover [viz. the proof] is strong and inescapable. Therefore, necessitation and constraint are evident, obvious, and felt by the one who holds the belief, such that it is impossible for him to believe the contradiction of that belief. Therefore, if reward and punishment are not fitting for this sort of necessity, that is, for necessity that is felt, as was posited, I cannot fathom how reward and punishment could be tenable for beliefs.

What is fitting to be said by way of resolving these difficulties is as follows. First, since divine justice is always directed toward the good and toward perfection, and since the good and perfection serve as motivating causes for deeds of goodness, it follows with respect to divine justice that commandments would be issued subject to reward and punishment, so that they serve as motivating causes for deeds of goodness. Indeed they are motivating causes, for reward and punishment are consequent upon them as effects are consequent upon causes. Therefore will and choice propel one toward that to which it is fitting to draw near and away from that from which it is fitting to keep one's distance. It therefore stands to reason that divine justice as exhibited in reward and punishment accords with necessity.

The distinction between necessity unaccompanied by a feeling of compulsion and constraint and necessity accompanied by a feeling of compulsion and constraint is a necessary one, as I shall explain. This matter will be clarified below, God willing, in Part VI, both from the perspective of speculation and from that of Scripture, and in a way that is in accord with the dicta of our Rabbis of blessed memory which are found in various places. These state that the end yearned for in worship and deeds of goodness is the love and joy one takes in them, which is none other than the pleasure of the will in doing good. For since God is the height of love and pleasure in bestowing and doing good, connection and attachment to Him are a matter of walking in His ways to the greatest extent possible. Therefore, when this desire and pleasure is in the soul, there follows an act of the soul through which attachment to

---

[331] In other words, if a reason is not strong enough to compel a belief so that a space opens up for will to step in, will cannot close the gap: it cannot remove the uncertainty of the belief's truth. By the same token, when a reason is strong enough to compel the belief, will is superfluous.

or detachment from God occurs. It is therefore fitting that reward and punishment derive from this act as effect derives from cause. When the soul is devoid of this desire, as when a person feels compulsion and constraint in his deeds, his soul will not perform his deed, and attachment and detachment will not be necessitated by it. Since the act will have been disengaged from the soul's will, reward and punishment would not be fitting at all. The distinction has now been legitimated.

Now that the legitimacy of this distinction has been established, [the question arises:] how can reward and punishment for beliefs be justified? For promises of reward and punishment for them are not capable of drawing will and choice toward particular beliefs, nor are they causes that move them, since it has been posited that one adopts beliefs involuntarily, such that will has no role in them.

Some of our sages, as would appear from the force of their words, have indeed been seduced by the idea that reward for beliefs does not fall within the jurisdiction of justice and injustice because reward is natural and necessarily derives from the intelligibles. In other words, when the truths of beliefs are established in the human soul, and when they become intelligibles within the person as they are outside his mind, these beliefs indeed constitute his soul as an immortal substance, which is the ultimate reward for a human being.

It is evident that the way of the Torah excludes such a position, as will be explained further in what follows, God willing. For if this position were correct, the few views that are found in the Torah would have sufficed to guide us, and we would not have required the expansive multiplication of commandments and their offshoots and the offshoots of their offshoots—by God!—unless this profusion [of commandments] were philosophical conclusions. Surely, however, the number of commandments of this type [viz. philosophical commandments] is fairly small.

If it were the case that souls are constituted by intelligible truths, then one would expect that, since the book *Elements*[332] and the book *Conic Sections*[333] contain many intelligibles, the geometer's soul would be composed of many more truths than would a soul engaged in Torah. But it is evident that this view is false according to the Torah; and it will be further clarified, God willing, that indeed the position that holds that the [highest] reward consists in the continuing-on [beyond death] of intelligibles is far-fetched in itself.

If only I knew with respect to a soul that intellects one of the intelligibles established in the book *Elements*—for example, that the angles of a triangle are equal to two right angles—and intellects nothing else, if this intelligible alone would constitute it so that it would achieve immortality. And if this soul does achieve immortality, would it resemble the soul that was constituted by another intelligible that was also established in that book, namely, that the square of the diagonal of a square is equal to the sum of the squares of the two adjacent sides, or some other? If the one differs from the other, in what does it differ? This, however, is all foolishness and false imaginings. But the Philosopher [viz. Aristotle], since his eyes were never illumined by the light of the Torah, and since he was also pressured by strong indications pointing in the direction of the immortality of the human soul, invented

---

[332] The reference is to Euclid's *Elements*.   [333] The reference is to Apollonius's *Conics*.

things and thought up things to bolster those indications, even though these inventions are extremely remote from intelligence, and a fortiori, from the Torah. So, let us abandon this approach.

Let us say that, once it is established that there is no place for will in beliefs, and that it is inescapably true that the believer feels the necessity of believing, it is evident that we must attribute choice and will to something that is attached and joined to beliefs, something that borders on them, namely, the pleasure and joy we experience when God graciously endows us with belief in Him, and the exertion we exercise in apprehending its truth. This is something that is without doubt a matter of will and choice. Indeed, a true belief can be conceived without the believer's being aware of any stirring of joy associated with his being the holder of that belief. It is therefore evident that it is the stirring of joy and the exertion of effort in investigating the belief's truth, things which are consequent upon will and choice, to which it stands to reason that reward and punishment would apply, as will be further clarified in what follows, God willing.

I will say further that, if we look into deeds, we will find that the reward is not first and foremost for the deeds themselves but for the person's choice of the deed in performing it. For when a person does something, he actualizes one of the contrary alternatives that were equally open to his power of choice. Since it is evident that something that is actualized, from the perspective of its being actual, is not in potentiality or possible for him, but is a matter of necessity and constraint for him, it follows that reward and punishment that have to do with choice and will, apply not to the deed itself when he performs it but to his choice of the deed when he performs it.

How appropriate with respect to this question is the dictum of our Rabbis of blessed memory: "Thoughts of transgression are worse than transgression."[334] The reason for this is that transgression is composed of two things: the deed itself and the choice and willing of it. The punishment that results is only on account of the will and the choice, which in this dictum is called thought. It is evident that, of the two, will is the worse—and this is the thought.

This will be verified as well when we conceive of them as separate, that is, of the deed without the thought and will—in other words, a compelled deed; or of the will without the execution of the deed. The punishment will devolve on the thought and will, as the true tradition asserts in the Sages' saying: "A burnt-offering atones for the thought in the heart."[335] One is not punished for a deed alone, as per one of our root-principles: "In the case of coercion, God exempts him."[336] The reason it says "worse," is because there is no doubt that the punishment for will when it is joined by the actual deed is greater than the punishment for the will alone when no actual deed ensues. This is what is indicated: that the punishment applies from the perspective of the deed as well, yet the more severe one applies from the perspective of the will—and particularly when will is joined to deed. This is true without any doubt.

Thus is the great difficulty resolved. It was established that reward and punishment with respect to beliefs applies to the pleasure and joy we take in them, and to the

---

[334] BT *Yoma* 29a. [335] *Lev. Rabbah* 7: 40. [336] BT *Nedarim* 27a.

industriousness with which we exert effort to understand them. This is what we wished to explain.

Chapter VI

To show that what was established regarding this issue from the perspective of speculation accords with the view of our Rabbis of blessed memory.

Two things have been established regarding this issue: first, that belief with respect to views that one holds is acquired without will; second, that reward and punishment pertain to will—reward for the passionate love and effort and joy at belonging to this sect of believers, and punishment for the opposite. Both of these matters were hinted at in a single dictum in the "Rabbi Akiva" chapter.[337] There the Rabbis said: "'And they stood at the bottom of the mountain.'[338] This teaches that God overturned the mountain onto them like a casket, and said: 'If you accept the Torah, fine; if not, here is your grave.' Rava said: This provides a powerful claim against the Torah. To which someone responded: Yet even so, they accepted it [willingly] in the days of Ahasuerus, for it is written: 'The Jews affirmed, and took upon themselves.'[339] They affirmed what they had already taken upon themselves."

The sense of the dictum according to this is as follows. Since it was established that will can have no part in belief acquired by means of rational propositions, and all the more so when acquired by means of the prophecy heard at that eminent assembly,[340] it follows that they had to believe, whether they wished to or not. Thus, they were constrained to believe. This constraint was likened to the overturning of a mountain upon them like a casket, so that they would accept the Torah by constraint, and, if not, would die on the spot, which is blatant compulsion and constraint. So, too, [if they were constrained to believe by] the many magnificent miracles. At the conclusion of their assembly, they believed in the Torah by constraint, believing that if they would depart from it, they would be straying from the correct path, the path of life,[341] a straying that is called death and burial. Therefore that Sage [viz. Rava] said: "This provides a powerful claim against the Torah." For even though the Torah is true without a doubt, nevertheless, insofar as the belief in it was constrained, will played no part in it, and perhaps the people did not accept it of their own free will, which is what would bind us to follow it. For it is evident that, although the belief is true without a doubt, nevertheless, if we failed to accept it, the path to severe punishment would be closed, as would not be the case if we accepted it of our own volition. Therefore the Rabbis responded: "Yet even so, they accepted it [willingly] in the days of Ahasuerus, for it is written: 'The Jews affirmed, and took upon themselves'—that is, they affirmed what they had already taken upon themselves." The sense of this is that, since, through the joy they experienced as they rejoiced over the miracles and deliverance that were enacted for them in those days, they affirmed that which they had already taken upon themselves, their claim [against the Torah] was nullified on

---

[337] BT *Shabbat* 88a.
[338] Exod. 19: 17. The verse can be rendered hyperliterally to mean: "And they stood under [בתחתית] the mountain."
[339] Esther 9: 27.
[340] The reference is to the assembly at Mt. Sinai.   [341] Jer. 21: 8; Prov. 6: 23.

its own. For pleasure and joy, on which reward for beliefs depends, reached completion in the days of Ahasuerus. This in its entirety provides a lesson for what was established in our discussion: both that belief with respect to views is not volitional, and that reward is for the will and joy of the one who holds the belief.

Since this joy is a delight and pleasure to the believer, and since our root-principle is, "It is forbidden to a person to derive pleasure from this world without reciting a blessing," the Sages formulated a blessing for this: "Blessed is He who did not create me a gentile, a slave, or a woman." We shall explain this further in Part VI, God willing. What we have said should suffice for now in accordance with our intention. Adulation and praise are to God alone, who is exalted above all blessing and praise.

Part VI

CONCERNING the end.

Although the Rabbi of the *Guide* regards it as pointless to seek the final end of the whole of existence, even according to the creation view, nevertheless it is obligatory to seek the end of this Torah. For the final cause in the case even of natural things is quite evident, as was established in its place, and the Rabbi conceded this concerning some things at the level of first end.[342] This is so all the more in the case of products of art that are a result of rational action.[343] Thus, the result of the act of the First Intellect, who is the true originator of all the other intellects that bear no comparison or resemblance to Him, cannot but be for the sake of some important end. Therefore, it is necessary that this Torah have an important end; otherwise, its existence at God's initiative would be inconceivable.

Since the final cause is the most important of the causes of things, it is fitting that we not succumb to laziness in this inquiry—especially because it has great utility. For when we have come to understand the true end of this Torah, then the reasons for some of its commandments, those that never ceased to puzzle our predecessors, will readily become manifest to us. We shall therefore conduct the investigation in this Part in our customary way. We have divided it into five chapters.

Chapter I. Here we shall explain the true end of this Torah.
Chapter II. Here we shall explain how it is established that this end is necessitated by this Torah.
Chapter III. Here we shall explain that the end of this Torah is the end of existence as a whole.
Chapter IV. We shall establish this necessity from the perspective of speculation and on the basis of the dicta of our Rabbis of blessed memory.
Chapter V. We shall explain that the search for a final end for the totality of existence is fitting and necessary, while reconciling it with the view of the Rabbi.

---

[342] In a natural thing, according to Aristotle, the efficient, formal, and final causes converge. This final cause, a thing's first finality as distinguished from its ultimate end, is its being fully the kind of thing it is. If it has an ultimate end, that end lies outside itself.

[343] A product of art (מלאכותי; *melakhuti*) is something manufactured.

Chapter I

EXPOSITION of the true end of this Torah.

We say regarding the end of things, that there is a first, a final, and an intermediate end. It is the final end that is the true end, for all the earlier ends exist for its sake and it is their cause. Therefore it is necessary that we investigate the final end of this Torah. Since the intended end for things is the good and a certain perfection, in respect of which the cause is final, the approach to the investigation into this matter will be inductive. Thus, we shall investigate whether the good and the perfection that result from the Torah are one or many. If they are one, they are without doubt the final end. And if they are many, then, since the ultimate good of things is just one—a simple unity in all things, as was explained in the *Metaphysics*[344]—and that is the perfection that is reached via the Torah, it is necessary that we investigate which one of them is suited to be the final end. For it is not impossible that the first or intermediate end be many, but it is imperative on all counts that they point to one thing which is the final end for the sake of which they all exist.

When we investigated the Torah as well as what is found in the tradition, we discovered that the Torah directs us to the perfection of virtues and views, and to bodily and psychic happiness. Therefore, what remains for us to investigate is whether the final end is one of these or something else. If it is something else, and these are first or intermediate ends, then [we must investigate] how it will be verified that they all point to the final end, as is necessitated by their being ends—now that it has become clear that the final end can only be a single one.

That the Torah guides us to these four perfections will be established by what I will now say. Let us consider the first, which is the perfection of the virtues. The perfection of the virtues and their deficiency involves how a person conducts himself with respect to himself, with respect to the members of his household, and with respect to fellow-citizens. When we attend to the ways of the Torah, we find that in the case of each one of these, the Torah directs the person to the end of perfection.

In the matter of a person's conduct toward himself, the Torah does this through the restraint and abstinence it enjoins with respect to forbidden sexual relations and with respect to forbidden foods that promote bad character traits in a person's soul, both by their nature and by their properties, some of which are well known. They [viz. the forbidden things] extinguish the light of the intellect through whose perfection the soul is perfected. The holiness that arises from the prohibition of impure things impresses cleanness and purity upon the human soul, as will be explained later in this very Part, God willing.

In the matter of a person's conduct toward the members of his household, which includes his conduct toward his wife, his children, and his servants, this will be seen as well. According to the tradition, the Torah is painstaking in providing properly for a wife's every need in terms of food, clothing, and sexual relations. The rulings the Rabbis issued oblige the husband to provide food, adornments, medical care, ransom, and burial, and to continue to provide for his wife and her daughters when she is

---

[344] Aristotle, *Metaph.* XII. vii.

widowed, and to set down in writing what her sons will inherit. She, too, is obligated to serve her husband, so that her handiwork and what comes her way and the fruits of her property are his; and if she dies, her husband is her heir. It seems that she was released from time-bound commandments on account of her obligation to serve him.[345] It would not have been right, however, for her to be released from commandments that are not time-bound, since, in the case of those that are not time-bound, if it does not work out for them to be fulfilled at one time they can be fulfilled at another. And there is certainly no release from obligatory prohibitions, for in order to fulfill them one need do nothing. The intention of all these is to foster a peaceful home, about which the Rabbis of blessed memory were most insistent, and for the sake of which they were very lenient in various places, as when they said: "If there is a choice between the light of Chanukah and the light of the home, the light of the home is to be preferred—for the sake of the peace of his home"[346]—and many other things of this kind, to the point that they required that the husband honor his wife more than himself.[347]

In the matter of children, the Torah takes pains to ensure that the union of the parents takes place in a holy way, by restricting licentiousness and evicting lust. Its intention is that there be perfection in the formation of children, that they take after the rock from which they were hewn.[348] For the thoughts of the agents at that moment [of conception] influence the nature [of the child conceived]. So, too, the Torah obligates the father with respect to certain commandments that render the child's soul and body fit, as, for example, the commandments to circumcise him, to teach him a craft, and to provide his sustenance for a certain amount of time, in accordance with the ruling at Usha.[349] So, too, are the children obligated to revere and honor their parents, which is a foundation and great pillar of the tradition. And so, too, in requiring the death of a stubborn and rebellious son, the Torah seeks to improve conduct.

In the matter of slaves, the Torah warns not to work Hebrew slaves with rigor,[350] and not in such a way as to cause them humiliation. And it requires of masters that they nourish them as they do themselves, as this dictum of the Rabbis of blessed memory attests: "He who buys a Hebrew slave buys himself a master"; "Let it not be the case that you eat fine bread and he coarse bread.[351] It commands them to provide for them generously when they depart. It protects the honor of Israelite daughters more than that of males: if she presents signs [of puberty], she is set free, lest they degrade her as she matures; and [she is protected] even in her childhood, for the Torah commands that the father or the son see to her betrothal, because someone might have second thoughts about marrying her once she has been enslaved. As the tradition records: the commandment to betroth takes precedence over the commandment to redeem.

---

[345] Some of the commandments in the Torah must be performed at specific times. The Rabbis released women from the obligation to perform positive commandments that are time-bound in this way.
[346] BT *Shabbat* 23b.   [347] BT *Sanhedrin* 76b.
[348] The reference is surely to Abraham. See n. 141.
[349] BT *Ketubot* 49b.   [350] Lev. 25: 46.   [351] BT *Kiddushin* 20a, 22a.

If the servants are Canaanites, the Torah looks out for them by commanding that they be brought under the wings of the Divine Presence, as the tradition mandates. It also obligates them with respect to the very commandments that women are obligated to observe, for the reason we mentioned, that is, insofar as they have a duty to work and serve. Therefore, once they are freed they are like Israelites in every respect. It furthermore commands that they go free if their limbs are damaged.[352] Moreover, in its graciousness to them, the Torah frees a slave who escaped from outside the land of Israel to the land of Israel, as is explicit in the tradition's interpretation of the verse:[353] "You shall not deliver unto his master [a servant who has escaped]."[354]

In the matter of one's conduct toward the people of one's city, the Torah provides guidance with respect to virtues such as justice and equity through its individual commandments and its stories about the Patriarchs. In addition, it also says: "You shall keep yourselves far from a false matter; and slay not the innocent and righteous,"[355] which our Rabbis of blessed memory interpreted to mean that we are to distance ourselves from various sorts of subtleties that are the opposite of equity.[356] They also interpreted the verse: "Justice, justice, you shall pursue, that you may live," to mean: "Seek a proper court of law,"[357] as well as that one should avoid bribery even when it is offered for acquitting the innocent.[358]

The Torah also teaches courage, as it is said: "You shall not be afraid of the face of any man; for judgment is God's";[359] and it commands, with respect to the war against the Seven Nations and the effacing of all traces of Amalek, not to be afraid, as it is said: "Fear not, nor be affrighted at them."[360] Abraham our father, peace be upon him, indeed conducted himself in accordance with this virtue when he fought the five kings with great zeal, and with a very small entourage by comparison with theirs.

The Torah also seeks to inculcate generosity, by way of the requirement to give charity and gifts to the poor, and to treat one's colleagues better than is required by the strict demands of the law, as per the tradition and as the prophet [Abraham], peace be on him, conducted himself in his dealings with the kings. Within the same category the Torah contains laws about the sabbatical years and the jubilees,[361] and it prohibits usury—for all of this is the path and direction toward ameliorating human affairs and steering clear of destruction and corruption in the human condition. It also enjoins humility, which characterized the master of the prophets [viz. Moses], peace be on him. The Torah guides us wondrously in this respect by forbidding arrogance in kings, to the extent that, despite the wide gap between the king and his people in terms of sovereignty and rank, it issues an explicit directive "that his heart be not lifted up above his brethren."[362] In accord with this is what our Rabbis of blessed memory have said: "Be very, very humble of spirit."[363] It also seeks to curtail

---

[352] Exod. 21: 26-7. See BT *Kiddushin* 24b-25a. [353] BT *Gittin* 45a. [354] Deut. 23: 16.
[355] Exod. 23: 7. [356] BT *Shevuot* 30b, 31a. [357] BT *Sanhedrin* 32b.
[358] *Sifrei* on Deut. 16: 19-20. [359] Deut. 1: 17. [360] Deut. 31: 6.
[361] Every seventh year the fields are to lie fallow (Lev. 25: 1-7) and debts are to be cancelled (Deut. 15: 1-11). Every fiftieth year there is to be no agricultural work done, all landed property is to revert to its original owner, and slaves are to be set free (Lev. 25: 8-17).
[362] Deut. 17: 20. [363] *Avot* 4: 4.

flattery, as we see in connection with the matter of reprimanding, for it is said: "You shall surely rebuke your neighbor."[364]

The Torah also prohibits hatred, revenge, and bearing a grudge, as it is said: "You shall not hate your brother in your heart.... You shall not take vengeance, nor bear any grudge against the members of your people."[365] Beyond all this, the Torah guides us with a commandment that encompasses all affairs between persons, namely, to love, as it is said: "You shall love your neighbor as yourself."[366] Hillel the Elder indeed replied in this way to the person who came to him seeking to convert—provided Hillel would teach him the entire Torah while he stood on one foot. Hillel said to him: "'You shall love your neighbor as yourself': what is hateful to you do not do to your fellow; the rest is commentary; go forth and gain understanding."[367] Thus does the Torah guide us with wondrous guidance with respect to the moral virtues.

As far as the perfection of views is concerned, it is most evident [that the Torah provides guidance in this regard]. For it guides us with respect to God's existence, which is the root of the pillar of the Torah and the fruit of all the sciences; with respect to His unity; with respect to His being neither a body nor a force in a body; with respect to His knowledge, His providence, and the enormity of His power, both in His creation of the universe as a whole, and in the miracles and wonders that occurred in it, which are commemorated by established festivals; with respect to the root-principle of prophecy; and, generally, with respect to all the cornerstones and views of the Torah that are included in this book—and more—as will be explained below, God willing. As to the happiness of the body, the promises to the Patriarchs and the promises attendant upon the fulfillment of the commandments should suffice.

As to the happiness of the soul, this too has been made explicit in general promises. Thus Scripture says at the eminent assembly, "Now therefore, if you will hearken unto My voice indeed... then you shall be My own treasure... and you shall be unto Me a kingdom of priests, and a holy nation."[368] And it is said: "And the Lord has affirmed you this day... and to make you high above all nations that He has made..."[369] And: "Happy are you, O Israel; who is like you? A people saved by the Lord, the shield of your help..."[370] Although it is possible to interpret these verses as promising illusory happiness, such as victory over enemies and glory, the true tradition has set us straight concerning their actually referring to eternal happiness, which the Sages conceive of as the world-to-come. This is the immortality of the soul that basks in the radiance of the Divine Presence. When this is examined with precision, it will be seen that the written Torah, too, contains hints and indications of this, as will yet be discussed, God willing.

Once it has been established that the Torah provides the utmost guidance toward these perfections, what remains for us to consider is whether the final end is one of these or if it is something else. If it is indeed one of them, it is necessarily the most important among them. For once it is established that they are ends, in whatever way they are ends, it is necessary that they point to the final end. If we append to this the

---

[364] Lev. 19: 17. [365] Lev. 19: 17–18. [366] Lev. 19: 18. [367] BT *Shabbat* 31a.
[368] Exod. 19: 5–6. [369] Deut. 26: 18–19. [370] Deut. 39: 29.

self-evident principle that it could hardly be the case that the deficient and lesser is the end of the perfect and superior, it follows necessarily that the superior one is the final end. Since there is no comparison between eternal happiness and temporary happiness even when they are of the same species, and, even more so, if eternal happiness is of an infinitely superior species, it is then evident that if the final end is one of these, it lies in eternal psychic happiness. For all other forms of happiness are temporary, and they are incomparable to it in importance, for it is impossible to conceive of a good of greater importance than that of attachment to the radiance of the Divine Presence.[371]

The truth of our assertion that the other forms of happiness, whether the happiness of the body or that of the perfection of the virtues, are temporary is evident. With respect to the perfection of views, note that, insofar as the human intellect is joined to a body, it is not always in actuality. Even once it separates from the body, the eternality of the [intellected] intelligible is not yet proved, as will be shown below.

Since it is evident that one's eternal human happiness[372] [viz. the happiness of the soul] is, in terms of its importance, the final end, and since this final end indeed must be the same as the final end in the Torah, it is indeed fitting that the final end of this Torah be considered the final end.[373] Since it is inescapable that the other perfections will be oriented toward this if indeed this is the final end, it is fitting that we ascertain whether they are indeed oriented toward it.

We shall say that what is evident with respect to the other perfections is that they are oriented toward this perfection—if indeed it is the final end. For it is obvious with respect to the happiness of the body, that, insofar as the soul of a person acts through corporeal organs, their being in good and optimal condition is a prelude and preparation for the body's actions in observing the Torah. And with respect to the perfection of the virtues, there is no doubt that they are an essential cause of the purification of the soul and its light, and of the removal of its dross, and of its becoming purified of impurities, of lusts, of jealousies, and of contentiousness, which are the proximate causes of the extinction of its light, all of which is a prelude to and preparation for the development of the intelligibles in it.

With respect to the perfection of views, this is indeed thought to be more essential to this end. There is no alternative to expanding on this point, since, as it seems to us, some of the sages of our nation have stumbled with respect to it. At the same time we will set ourselves aright in grasping the true end of this Torah.

I say that they all agree that the intellect is constituted by what it apprehends of the intelligibles, out of which is created an acquired intellect unmixed with the hylic intellect.[374] Since the acquired intellect is separate from the hylic, even though it comes to be and is created, it remains eternal, since there are no causes for

---

[371] The final clause of this sentence is missing from the Ferrara edition: למה שהדבקות בזיו השכינה אי אפשר שיציר טוב גדול כמוהו בחשיבו.

[372] The Florence manuscript has: בהצלחה הזאת הנצחית, "this eternal happiness."

[373] Reading this final clause with the manuscripts: והתכלית האחרון בזאת התורה ראוי להיות כן כבר יחשב בה שהיא התכלית האחרון.

[374] The hylic intellect or the intellect in potentiality is the rational human faculty that is connected to the body.

its passing-away, as was explained in the *Metaphysics*,[375] for matter is the cause of passing-away and evil, and therefore eternal happiness resides in the acquired intelligibles. The more concepts we apprehend the greater will our happiness be—and especially when the concepts are in themselves more precious.

It is also agreed by them that each of the apprehenders will rejoice and delight after death in what he has apprehended. And they supposed that, as much as we acquire pleasure in our lifetimes when we apprehend intelligibles, we will take that much more pleasure after death when we apprehend them all together and continually. It is therefore necessarily the case that there is no comparison between the pleasure that derives from the lesser intelligibles and that from the superior intelligibles, for the pleasure that we take in the intelligibles in our lifetimes differs considerably [from that taken in the intelligibles after death].

This is the entirety of what they hold in common and agree upon. There are, however, ways in which they differ. One holds that this happiness would be greater the greater the number of apprehensions of existents, whether they be of material things or of incorporeal things.[376] And this is because, since the order of all the existents is in the soul of the active intellect, the rank of whoever draws closer to the active intellect in his apprehension of intelligibles is higher. Another holds that what lasts is that which is apprehended correctly by the intellect of a man [but only] with respect to the existence of God and his angels.[377] Whoever apprehends more [of these incorporeal things] has the higher rank. What this means, as it seems, is that the intellect is constituted by the apprehension of incorporeal things alone, and it is this that remains eternal. The more one apprehends of them, the greater one's happiness. These two views, even as they destroy the Torah and uproot the tradition, are also evidently false from the point of view of speculation.

That they destroy the principles of the Torah and the tradition may be seen in several ways. One is that, according to the Torah and the tradition, a person secures for himself eternal life by performing commandments, as it is said explicitly in the Mishnah: "He who performs one commandment is treated well."[378] The interpretation found in the *Gemara* is that this good treatment is that which is reserved for the righteous.[379] According to these [other] views, however, the practical commandments are but a prelude to the intelligibles, and since the intellect is not constituted by them, there is no advantage in performing them.

Another way is that, according to the Torah and the tradition, the practical prescriptions and proscriptions involve certain notions of reward and punishment that are untenable on those views. There is reward, for example, for those who sacrifice their lives in sanctification of the Name, as the Rabbis said: "No creature can stand in the area [in heaven] reserved for the martyrs of Lydda [or Lud]."[380] There is no assumption here that these martyrs were constituted by intelligibles; moreover, if they were, what advantage would there have been in the death of their

---

[375] Aristotle, *Metaph.* VII. xv. 1039^{b}23ff.; VIII. v; and IX. ix. 1051^{a}15ff.
[376] Gersonides holds this view.   [377] Maimonides holds this view.
[378] *Kiddushin* 1: 10. In context this dictum concerns the one commandment that shifts the balance of good deeds and transgressions, causing the former to outweigh the latter.
[379] BT *Kiddushin* 39b.   [380] BT *Baba batra* 10b; BT *Pesaḥim* 50a.

bodies? There is also punishment for informers, for traitors, and for the person who shames his fellow in public: according to the tradition, these "have no portion in the world-to-come."[381] Yet if their intellect had been constituted by intelligibles, it would not have been possible for it not to continue on eternally. The only way it could fail to continue on is if God were to create a miracle for them and punish that acquired intellect, so that it would pass away despite its natural course of immortality. Moreover, included in this category are the heretics, those who deny even just one root-principle of the root-principles of the Torah, as, for example, he who maintains that the resurrection of the dead is not affirmed in the Torah. Yet if his intellect is constituted by other intelligibles, then, even if the intelligible on whose account he is called a heretic does not continue on, why would the other intelligibles fail to continue on? Nevertheless, according to the true tradition, he has no portion in the world-to-come.

Another way is that it is indeed well known and accepted in the nation that the preponderance of delight or suffering of the soul is determined by the preponderance of a person's merits or transgressions—as there is much in the tradition and in the midrashic homilies devoted to the matter of Paradise[382] and Gehenna. But according to these [other] views, reward and punishment are, respectively, immortality for the acquired intellect and its passing away—and nothing else. Yet the statement that the intellect delights in the intelligibles after death is evidently false, as we shall see below, God willing. Even if we concede, however, that this is a possibility in the case of delight, there is no way to make sense in this way of the notion of suffering, even if one should be willing to be most inventive.[383]

Another is that, according to our Rabbis of blessed memory, the end is in fact the performance part [of the study–performance pair], as we find some of them having said that "the greater thing is the performance [i.e. it is greater than study]," yet, in the end, they voted and concluded that "study is greater, for study leads to performance."[384] Thus, they posited the active part [viz. the performance] as the final cause of the intellecting part [viz. study]. From all these perspectives it is evident that these views are opposed to the roots and principles of the Torah.

That they are false in themselves from the point of view of speculation will also be seen from several perspectives. One is that, according to these views, the end of the Torah for man turns out to be for a species other than man. For according to these views, the immortal acquired intellect is incorporeal, unmixed with man. It is thus neither a man's form nor an accident that attaches to him, once it is supposed that it is incorporeal and that it is something that is constituted by intelligibles. Furthermore, the passing-away of a man is conceivable without the acquired intellect's passing-away, as is supposed by its continuing on after death. Anything whose passing-away is possible without the passing-away of something else—insofar as it is not mixed with it—is necessarily individually different from that other thing. And that which is individually different from something, and is not connected with it, cannot be its form. In addition, the passing-away of the incorporeal in man is indeed

---

[381] BT *Rosh Hashanah* 17a; *Avot* 3: 15. [382] Or, Garden of Eden.
[383] Straddling the more common אם ירצה לברא בריאה and Fisher's אם ירצה לבדא בדיאה.
[384] BT *Kiddushin* 40b. See Introduction, n. 42.

conceivable without his passing away, just as the possibility was supposed of a man's passing-away without the incorporeal in him passing away. Once it is established that the acquired intellect is not a man's form, it follows that the end of the Torah, which is [assumed to be] the immortality of this intellect in man, pertains to something other than man. Indeed, that it pertains to something other than the species man is easily seen, from a consideration of the nature of each. For man by his nature is headed toward passing-away, and it is impossible for an individual man to be immortal. Yet the acquired intellect, it is supposed, is individually immortal, so that passing-away is essentially impossible for it. Anything for which this is the natural course differs in species [from man].

Another way is that it is inconsistent with divine justice for there to be true reward and punishment for anything other than serving God or rebelling against Him.

And another is that the proposition that the intellect is constituted by the objects of its apprehension and is created, and that it is separate from the hylic intellect, is evidently false, for the following reasons:

One is that, since it is supposed to be non-hylic, it has no material substratum to serve as its bearer and as that from which it could come to be. Since it is supposed to be created, it is necessary that it come to be from nothing. Yet this is an evidently false proposition. For coming-to-be from nothing is among the impossibilities whose nature as impossible is stable,[385] unless it occurs by way of a miracle by God.

Another is that this proposition is self-contradictory. For if it is supposed that the intellect is constituted by the objects of its apprehension, then what is intended cannot be the hylic intellect. For the intellect that is thus constituted has already been supposed to be separate from the hylic intellect. But if we intend by it the acquired intellect, then, when we say that *it* is constituted by the objects of its apprehension, we necessarily suppose it existed before it came to be. By God! We might as well say that the thing brought itself into existence. This is evident nonsense and absurdity.[386]

Another is that it is evidently absurd for the intellect to be constituted by the objects of its apprehension. For the following disjunction is inescapable. Either intellection, which is the act of apprehending an intelligible, is itself an intelligible, as the philosophers agree—for them, the intellect, the intellecter, and the intellected are one and the same—or not. If intellection itself is an intellected intelligible, one of two absurdities will follow. One is that the one intelligible is the same as the other, and all the intelligibles are also one and the same intelligible, such that the same unvarying intellection would pertain to all the intelligibles. Yet this is evidently absurd. For if this were the case, then one who apprehends many intelligibles would be no better than, and would not be superior to, one who apprehends but one intelligible. The other is that one intelligible is distinct from another, and the act of intellection with respect to one intelligible differs from the act of intellection with respect to another intelligible. It would follow in this case that if the intellect is constituted by one intelligible, and subsequently apprehends another intelligible, it

---

[385] See n. 122.
[386] If we say that the acquired intellect is constituted by the intelligibles that it apprehends, what is doing the apprehending? If the acquired intellect does the apprehending but is constituted by what it apprehends, it must constitute itself, that is, it must bring itself into existence.

will have been made as many substances as the number of intelligibles it apprehends, or the one will be changed and will be constituted by another, and will thus become another substance different in species from the previous one. This is the height of absurdity. Further, since the essential form of man is continually created anew according to this, it would follow that the person in question would be changing from one substance to another and would be different each time. This is the height of absurdity and nonsense.

Another is that this acquired intellect which was constituted by intelligibles is, inevitably, either alive, dead, or not the sort of thing to which "alive" and "dead" apply. Yet it is not the case that it cannot be described by these terms, for in order to be that sort of thing, a thing must be an inanimate body or one of the accidents. It is also not the case that it is dead, for then it would not be better or superior on account of its eternality. Hence, it is necessarily alive. Since it is self-evident that life is other than intellection, it is necessary that this intellect be composed of life and intellection. It therefore must have a substratum. But it was already assumed to be incorporeal. This is a contradiction.

From all these perspectives the manifest probability of the illegitimacy of these views is apparent. The first view is more nonsensical from one point of view, and the second from another.

What follows from the first is that immortality resides in the apprehension of the intelligibles of philosophy, so that the principles of the Torah would be a derivative of philosophy. And it would follow that one who intellects one intelligible among the intelligibles of geometry, since they exist in the soul of the active intellect, will continue on to eternity. Yet these are wild imaginings without any basis.

With respect to the second, intellection of the essence of incorporeal substances is not affirmative but negative, as the Rabbi expounded at length. Therefore, there cannot be complete apprehension, and, a fortiori, what is in the intellect cannot correspond to what is outside the mind. How, then, can this deficient intelligible, which does not exist outside the mind in this way, constitute a substance? If only I knew.

These views were inventions of the philosophers, as if the nature of truth compelled them to believe in the immortality of the soul. They therefore thought their thoughts and multiplied many words that increase vanity.[387] Some of the sages of our nation were seduced and followed them, and they did not sense, nor did it occur to them, that in this way they were destroying the wall[388] of the edifice that is the Torah and breaching its enclosures,[389] even though the position is itself groundless.

Since it has been shown with respect to the perfection of views that it does not necessitate this end in the way they supposed, and since it was shown as well with respect to the other perfections that they are but a prelude to the intelligibles, it follows that that [final] end is necessitated, primarily and essentially, neither by views nor by deeds. Since this end is necessary to the Torah, as the tradition avers, it must be necessitated, primarily and essentially, by a part of the Torah that concerns neither views nor deeds absolutely. When we investigated the Torah and its parts, we found

---

[387] Eccles. 6: 11. [388] This expression is based on Jer. 30: 15 and Ezek. 26: 12.
[389] This expression is based on Ps. 80: 13 and 83: 41.

in it one part, small in quantity but large in quality, that concerns neither views nor deeds absolutely. This part is the love of God and the true fear of Him. I say that this is what guarantees this end in every respect, both according to the Torah and the tradition, and according to speculation.

With respect to the Torah, we have the verse: "And now, Israel, what does the Lord your God require of you, but to fear the Lord your God, to walk in all His ways, and to love Him, and to serve the Lord your God with all your heart and with all your soul?"[390] And: "in that I command you this day to love the Lord your God, to walk in His ways."[391] And: "to love the Lord your God, to hearken to His voice, and to cleave unto Him."[392] In connection with the acceptance of the yoke of the kingdom of heaven [we have]: "And you shall love the Lord your God with all your heart and all your soul"[393]—as if the root-principle of unity[394] was put to use to serve as a cause of this love with all one's heart and with all one's soul, as will be discussed below, God willing. It is said as well: "And it shall come to pass, if you shall hearken diligently unto My commandments which I command you this day, to love the Lord your God, and to serve Him with all your heart and with all your soul..."[395] It thus appears that the end sought by the Torah is to hearken unto God with extraordinary zeal to fulfill His prescriptions, and to exercise great caution lest one transgress His proscriptions, [and to do both] with joy and with a happy heart, which is the secret of true worship, and love, and fear,[396] as many scriptural passages and[397] rabbinic dicta attest. Since this [viz. fulfilling the commandments with zeal] is the end sought in the Torah, and since it is evident from the Torah[398] that this [end] guarantees happiness and eternal life, it is evident, too, that this end guarantees happiness and eternal life according to the Torah and the tradition.

With respect to speculation itself, this [conclusion] is indeed established once three propositions that are beyond doubt are posited. The first is that the soul of man, which is his form, is a substance that is spiritual, that is disposed to intellection, yet that does not intellect in actuality in itself. Second, one who is perfect in his essence loves the good and perfection and desires it; and love and pleasure in desire is proportional to one's perfection. The third is that love and pleasure in desire are distinct from intellection. We may add to these a fourth, which is self-evident, namely, that it is fitting that perfection of the soul and its attachment to God guarantee this end.[399] The way in which these propositions will be proved is as follows.

To begin. Regarding the first one, our saying of the soul of man that it is "his form"—this is self-evident. For when the form separates from the body, the man passes away in such a way that his definition no longer properly applies to him. Our

---

[390] Deut. 10: 12. [391] Deut. 30: 16. [392] Deut. 30: 20. [393] Deut. 6: 5.
[394] Crescas maintained in I. iii. 4 that the preceding verse, Deut. 6: 4, "Hear, O Israel, the Lord your God, the Lord is one," is the prooftext for the unity of God.
[395] Deut. 11: 13.
[396] והיראה ("and fear") is missing from the Ferrara edition.
[397] ו־ כתובים ("scriptural passages and") is missing from the Ferrara edition.
[398] The word ממנה ("from it") is found in the manuscripts but is missing from Fisher and the Ferrara edition.
[399] Reading with the manuscripts and the Ferrara edition ראוי שיחיב, as opposed to, Fisher's ראוי שיהיה. Fisher includes the former in brackets as an alternate reading.

saying of it that it is "a substance"—this too is self-evident. For it was proved in Book I of the *Physics* that with respect to the term "substance" form takes precedence over matter. Our saying of it that it is "spiritual"—this is evident, since within it are faculties that the will employs without any of the senses, such as the faculties of imagination and memory and intellect. Our saying of it that it is "disposed to intellection" is evident, inasmuch as it is proved that it is the substratum of the intellecting faculty, since this faculty is predicated of the body through the intermediation of the soul. For it is inescapable that the substratum of this disposition[400] is either intellect or soul or body, for there is no fourth possibility. It cannot be intellect, as some of the commentators on Aristotle's books have thought, for several reasons. First, because if the substratum of this disposition were[401] intellect, it would be mixed with intellective form, and it would be impossible for it to intellect all forms. For [generally] a thing can receive all things only if it is devoid of all of them. So, if we were to posit the intellect as the substratum of this disposition, then, in receiving the intelligibles, it would be constituted by them by way of a reception into which this [intellective form] is mixed. Yet this is impossible, since it is not then devoid of all forms.[402] If, however, we were to posit the soul as the substratum of this disposition, then, whereas we would indeed make it a condition of the disposition's existence, it would not be affected by the reception of the intelligibles. For, the substrata of the disposition to receive things vary greatly with respect to reception. In some cases, the substratum is affected in some way by the specific species that it apprehends, as in the matter of the sense of touch; in some, the substratum receives them in such a way that the substratum is not affected by the specific species it apprehends, as in the matter of the reception of colors by the sense of sight; for it does not receive the hue from the perceived color—yet it is affected by it somewhat. Therefore, it will not sense a weak sensation that follows a strong one. The common sense will be affected even less by the things it apprehends, for its apprehension is spiritual. Furthermore,[403] since the imagination is more spiritual, it follows its will. And furthermore, the intellective disposition receives things without its substratum being affected by them; therefore, when the substratum is taken to be the soul, it is able to receive all forms. But when the substratum is taken to be the intellect, this cannot be said of it. For if we assume that the reception by which the disposition receives the intelligibles is one in which the substratum is not mixed, the following disjunction is unavoidable. We must take the substratum either to be or not to be something that intellects. Yet it is impossible for the intellect not to be something that intellects. It must, therefore, of

---

[400] The text from here through "because if the substratum of this disposition were" in the next paragraph is absent from Fisher. The missing text, found in the manuscripts, reads as follows. (The words in brackets are absent from the Florence manuscript.) אם שכל או נפש או גשם לפי שאין בכאן מציאות רביעי, והנה אי אפשר שיהיה [קצת הנושא] שכל כמו שחשבו המפרשים לספרי אריסטו, וזה אמנם מפנים. ראשונה שאם היה הנושא לזאת ההכנה...

[401] The Fisher text resumes here.

[402] The question is: could the intellect be that which anchors the disposition to intellection, that is, to the reception of intelligibles? Crescas's argument is that it could not, because such a substratum would have an intellective form. And once the substratum has a form, it cannot be receptive to all forms, since only something devoid of form can be receptive to all forms.

[403] Missing from the Ferrara edition is the following text, which is included here: יהיה הדמיון יותר רוחני ולזה יהיה הדמיון נמשך אחרי רצונו. עוד אחר כך...

necessity be something that intellects. But then, were we to posit one intelligible from among the intelligibles that the disposition might receive, it would have to be in it both potentially and actually.[404] This is absurd—unless, by God, one conjures fantastical imaginings such that there can be an intelligible that bears no relation to the intelligibles the disposition might receive.[405] Yet this is the height of absurdity and nonsense. It is therefore evident that the substratum of this disposition is not intellect.

Second, if the substratum of this disposition were intellect, it would inevitably either come to be or not come to be. If it were to come to be, it is unavoidable that this substratum would emerge either from another substratum or out of nothing. If from another substratum, the first substratum would necessarily have to change so that this substratum might emerge from it. Yet it has already been established that anything that changes is a body, so it would in this case have to be a body. Yet since it is self-evident that it is impossible for something incorporeal to come to be from something corporeal, it follows necessarily that this substratum also be a body. Yet it was already assumed to be intellect. This contradiction is what follows from the assumption that the substratum comes to be.

It is necessary, then, that it not come to be. In that case, it is inevitable that it be either incorporeal or not. If it is not incorporeal, it is necessary that the intellect of the individual alluded to[406] be hidden and concealed in matter before the individual comes to be. Since the intellect of the individual from whom this matter will come to be is already manifest[407] in him, it is necessary that there be in him another intellect, and the same will apply to the matter from which that matter came to be, and so on, ad infinitum.[408] It will be necessary that all the matters that come to be and pass away possess intellects to infinity—unless, by God! the intellect transfers from the outside with the coming-to-be of the matter and hides in it until such time as its actions are perceived. Yet this is the height of absurdity and nonsense.

If, however, we assume that it is incorporeal, then, either the intellects of Reuben and Simeon are different from one another such that their forms differ—or not. If we assume their forms are different, then they are necessarily different in species, for agreement at the species level and difference at the level of the individual are inconceivable with respect to incorporeal things, as was explained in its place. Yet it is false that they differ in species, for if that were so, individual members of the

---

[404] Insofar as the intellect is necessarily something that intellects, it must intellect in actuality at least one intelligible which its disposition intellects potentially.

[405] In order to avoid the absurdity of an intelligible's being in the disposition both potentially and actually, one would have to say that there is no relation between the intelligible actually intellected by the intellect and the intelligibles the disposition is disposed potentially to receive. This is, Crescas maintains, absurd.

[406] "Of the individual," האיש, is missing from the Ferrara edition.

[407] Reading נגלה with the Florence manuscript rather than הנגלה, as found in Fisher as well as in the editions and other manuscripts.

[408] If a new individual possessing intellect is to come to be, but this intellect does not itself come to be and is also not incorporeal, it would have to be hiding in the matter of its progenitor. Thus the progenitor who gives rise to the matter of this new individual will contain not only the hidden intellect of his issue but his own manifest intellect. But the progenitor's manifest intellect would in turn have had to reside concealed within the matter of his progenitor, and so on, ad infinitum.

same species would differ in species. If Simeon's intellect does not differ from Reuben's either at the level of species or at the individual level, then the forms of individual members of a species would be one in number, and one individual in a species would be the same as another, and the other the same as the one—each the same as the other. Furthermore, this one intellect would be in potentiality and in actuality at once. For the intelligibles that Reuben has in potentiality, Simeon has in actuality. Moreover, the individual members of the species would not require a sense for the acquisition of intelligibles, so long as one individual among them used his senses in the acquisition of those intelligibles.

It is evident, then, that from our positing intellect as the substratum of this disposition, many absurdities follow. It is therefore necessary that the substratum be either body or soul. Yet it is evident that if body were posited as the substratum, it would not receive the intelligibles without an intermediary. For it is inconceivable that those forms that it is the nature of body to acquire without an intermediary would be devoid of body. Therefore it is necessary that, if body were to receive this disposition without an intermediary, all bodies would possess intellect. It is also evident that, if we posit the soul as the substratum, it could not be the substratum of the disposition on its own [i.e. without the intermediation of matter]. For it is not in the nature of forms to be substrata of one another, except through the intermediation of matter. And since this is how things stand, it is evident that the substratum of this disposition is the soul, through the intermediation of the body. Therefore, our saying with respect to the soul of man that it is "a substance" disposed to intellection is established.

We said "disposed," since the potentiality of this disposition is in it. And we said "which does not intellect in actuality in itself," for whereas our saying "disposed" indicates that the intellection is not in actuality, our saying "which does not intellect in actuality in itself," indicates that the substance of the substratum is not constituted by intellection. Many of the ancients stumbled with respect to this. For since the substratum of this disposition is [for them] a substance outside the soul,[409] if it were to be constituted by intellection, it would change from one substance to another.[410] The proposition that the acquired intelligibles become substances separate from the substratum, and that from this a separate intellect comes to be, is groundless, as was established earlier in our discussion.

This should suffice, in our concise manner, to verify the first proposition.

The second proposition will be established as follows. Since it is known that God is the source and origin of all the perfections, and that He in His perfection, which is His essence, loves the good, as is seen from His deeds in bringing existence as a whole into existence and preserving it and continually creating it anew—and all this indeed by His simple will—it follows necessarily that love of the good is an essential property of His perfection. It follows necessarily from this that the greater one's perfection, the greater the love for and the pleasure one takes in the object of desire. This accords

---

[409] That is, the intellect is not, for the ancients, in the soul but is a distinct incorporeal entity constituted by intelligibles.

[410] The change in substance would reflect the variation in the intellected intelligibles that constitute the intellect.

strongly with what is found in the Torah. For when the Torah mentions the love of the Patriarchs for God, it uses the term *ahavah* (אהבה), love,[411] but when it mentions God's love for the Patriarchs, it uses the term *ḥesheq* (חשק), passionate love, which indicates the love's intensity. It is said: "Yet the Lord did passionately-love your fathers, to love them,"[412] which indeed will be seen to support what we have said. For it will be seen that the degree of love is proportional to the grade of the good that is loved, such that the greater the good, the greater the love. Thus, when the good is infinitely large, it is fitting that the love be infinite. Therefore, although it would seem that the love of man for God should be greater to the point of infinity, so that the term "passionate love" should apply to the love of the Patriarchs for God and the term "love" for God's love for them, in fact, since love is an essential property of perfection, and since the perfection of God is infinitely great, it is fitting that God's love for the good be greater, even if the good that is loved is very low in degree. This should suffice for the second proposition.

The third is self-evident from the definitions of its terms. For the will is nothing but the coming-together of and relation between the appetitive and imaginative faculties—that is, their agreement regarding the things that are wanted. And pleasure in the will is in accordance with that relation. Intellection is conception and verification, both of which are performed by the intellective faculty, as was established in the book *On the Soul*.[413] Since the intellective faculty operates without the appetitive faculty and the imaginative faculty, it is shown that love and pleasure in desire are not matters of intellection. This is the third proposition.

Now that these propositions have been established, I shall say that it was established in the first proposition that the soul of man is a spiritual substance, such that immortality following its separation from the body is possible, since it is not subject to the causes of passing-away, insofar as it is then immaterial. So, too, is separation from the body possible for it, insofar as it is an intellective substance, and we have seen that this substance exercises its intellection more powerfully at times when the corporeal organs are weak, which is one of the indicators that it can exist on its own and that it does not pass away as do the other forms when the things of which they are forms pass away. Since existence on its own is possible for it when it separates from the thing of which it is the form, its eternality is necessary for it by virtue of its nature, insofar as it is devoid of materiality which is the cause of passing-away—when the acted-upon powers do not yield to the acting powers, as has been established in its place.[414]

Since it was explained in connection with the second proposition that love of the good and pleasure in it are proportional to one's perfection, it is evident that the degree of perfection is proportional to the degree of the loved good.[415] Therefore, it is

---

[411] Abraham is referred to as "the one who loves Me" (אוהבי; *ohavi*) (Isa. 41: 8).
[412] Deut. 10: 15.   [413] Aristotle, *On the Soul*, III. vii–viii.
[414] Passing-away occurs in the body, that is, in the material aspect of the human being, when, as Aristotle states in *Meteorology* IV. i, the passive elements, namely, the dry and the moist, no longer yield to the active elements, namely, the hot and cold. Since the soul by its nature has no materiality, it has no cause of passing-away.
[415] Reading with the manuscripts, הטוב האהוב, rather than with the Ferrara edition, האהוב הטוב.

established that the love of God who is infinitely good is required for the greatest conceivable perfection of the soul.

Since it was explained in connection with the third proposition that love and the pleasure in it are distinct from intellection, it follows that that which is essential to the perfection of the soul is something distinct from intellection, namely, love. It is evident with respect to love that it engenders attachment to God, inasmuch as it is evident in the case of natural things as well that love and mutual attraction are the cause of their perfection and unity, so much so that one of the ancients maintained that the first principle of coming-to-be is love and coming-together, and the first principle of passing-away is strife and breaking-apart.[416] All the more is it the case with spiritual things, that the love and the mutual attraction between them engenders attachment and unity. Since it was established previously and will be further established below in Book III, God willing, that God's love for the good is great, it is evident that the greater the love between God and man, the more intense and greater the attachment.

It was established in connection with the fourth proposition that it is fitting that the perfection of the soul and its attachment to God entail this end. Therefore, it is established beyond all doubt that speculation agrees with what was established by the Torah and by the tradition, namely, that genuine love is what guarantees this end of eternal continuing-on. This is an idea accepted in the nation and one on which we were raised. The Torah illumined it for us, even as this notion is in agreement with speculation and does not contradict it.

Since the truth bears witness to itself and is in agreement from all perspectives, what has been transmitted to our Rabbis of blessed memory concerning the features of the world-to-come relates very well to this true view, and is far removed from the views of the ancients. For in the Rabbis' dicta there are three points that are congenial to this view and very remote from those views. First, there is what is found in their dicta regarding the reward of the righteous—namely, that their souls delight in the radiance of the Divine Presence, each one in accordance with its rank—and regarding the punishments of the wicked, which also vary, as many of their dicta report. Second, there is further what is found in their dicta with respect to the reward of the righteous: they designated circumscribed places for reward and punishment—as many midrashic homilies speak of the matter of Paradise[417] and Gehenna. The third is how expansively they spoke in their dicta of the reward of schoolchildren, as, for example, their saying: "There is no comparison between breath that contains no sin and breath that contains sin."[418] In *Tanḥuma* we find: "They said in the name of R. Meir: When do children become deserving of life in the world-to-come? When they know how to answer amen, as it is written: 'Open the gates, that the righteous nation that keeps faithfulness may enter in.'[419] Read not 'that keeps faithfulness' but 'those that say amen,' that is, those who know how to answer amen."[420] This agrees

---

[416] The reference is to Empedocles.   [417] Or, the Garden of Eden.

[418] BT *Shabbat* 119b. The editions of the Talmud in our possession reverse the order of the parts of this dictum as they appear in Crescas. The sense, however, is the same.

[419] Isa. 26: 2.

[420] BT *Sanhedrin* 110b. The Rabbis change the vocalization of the word אמנים to produce this play on words. Our current editions of *Tanḥuma* do not contain this midrashic homily.

with what they said in tractate *Shabbat*: "And the spirit returns unto God who gave it; give it to Him as He gave it to you."[421]

With respect to the first, namely, the reward the righteous receive in the form of the delight and enjoyment their souls experience in the radiance of the Divine Presence, it is most appropriate that, in return for their service with love and fierce devotion, and for the attachment of their desire and will to God, they attain enjoyment and intense pleasure in the attachment for which they yearned while they were yet joined to matter. This enjoyment and pleasure is possible since the pleasure is not intellective, as was explained earlier: because the essence of the soul is something other than intellection, it is subject to will and passionate love and pleasure, as we explained. But I say that, in the views of the ancients, this pleasure and enjoyment is impossible. Even though they sought to support their view with arguments which they devised—as if the nature of truth compelled their view—nevertheless they committed an infamous error in light of their view. There is no alternative but to mention their arguments and the places where their arguments went awry.

To begin, I say that, according to their view, pleasure is impossible, since it was established that pleasure is not a matter of intellect. Therefore, if for them the acquired intellect is at once intellect, intellecter, and intellected, and if pleasure is not a matter of intellect, then it is also not a matter of the intellecter and intellected. Since the intellect is something simple and not composite, it is impossible that it contain pleasure, for it would then be composed of pleasure and intellection, which were established as distinct. Since pleasure in things makes an impression in the substratum of the faculties through which pleasure is experienced, as, for example, the pleasure of tastes takes place in its substratum [viz. the tongue], so the pleasure of intellection takes place in its substratum, which is that which has the potential for intellection, namely, the soul as a whole. But if we posit intellection as separate from the soul, as they imagined, then it would be impossible for pleasure to take place in the substratum, inasmuch as it has no substratum on their view. For intellection and the intellecter are but one thing, in their view.

What they imagined would support their view that this pleasure exists is that there is pleasure in our lives in the apprehension of intelligibles: how much more so, then, after death, when we will intellect them all together and continually. Another indication for them is the wondrous pleasure that attends the apprehension of the superior intelligibles, for there is no comparison between that pleasure and the pleasure of apprehending [inferior] others. But this is a blatant sophistry. For the pleasure that exists in our life arises from the attainment of something for which we yearn. The person is in potentiality with respect to the apprehension of intelligibles, and he yearns for them. This yearning is nothing other than the excitement of the will—which has already been shown to be other than intellection—in anticipation of attaining the thing for which it yearns. It follows that when the yearned-for apprehension, which was formerly in potentiality, is in actuality, great pleasure is experienced, for the nature of being something yearned for so dictates. It is therefore

---

[421] BT *Shabbat* 152b.

necessary that when the thing that is yearned for is very valuable and precious, the yearning is more intense, and the pleasure in the attainment is greater.

Related to this is what happens when the apprehensions are precious. Insofar as they are profound and subtle, the potentiality for them is more remote than that for the inferior intelligibles, so that when one who has them in potentiality makes the transition to having them in actuality, the pleasure experienced will be greater inasmuch as he began farther away and transitioned from one extreme to the other. This resembles what occurs in musical melodies, where the melody in the ratio of the all and in the ratio of the double[422] is more pleasant—insofar as the distance between the tones is in that ratio, and insofar as it involves a transition from one extreme to another. Therefore, after death, when intellection is constantly in actuality, and there is no transition and no distance between potentiality and actuality, and no yearning—for the intellect has no will, as we explained earlier—it is not likely, and it is certainly not necessary, that there will be pleasure then.

Another thing that will indicate the correctness of what we said is what is true of our apprehensions of first intelligibles: in this case we feel no pleasure at all. This is indeed so because the transition from potentiality to actuality is not felt, and because there was no yearning for their apprehension prior to the apprehension of them. It is therefore evident that what they imagined would support their view is a sophistry and not a proof.

According to our view, which is that the soul is a substance that has an intellective faculty, the pleasure it takes even in the intelligible is both possible and necessary from the point of view of the excitement of attachment to God that we experience in our apprehension. It is this that is the essential cause of pleasure. It has thus been established that the Rabbis' dicta concerning the delight experienced by the souls of the righteous are in accord and in agreement with the true view, and not at all in agreement with their [viz. the ancients'] views. This is all the more the case with regard to the punishment of the wicked, which has no place in their [viz. the ancients'] view, since, according to their view, what happens to them is only that neither immortality nor the intelligible is available to them.

It is fitting that we be aware that what the Rabbis maintain regarding this first matter, namely, that rewards and punishments are assigned in different degrees, accords very well with our view. For it is fitting that the pleasure of reward be proportional to the level of attachment, and it is likewise fitting that the pain borne in the soul's essence in punishment[423] be proportional to the level of punishment. Thus the first matter is very much in agreement with the true view from every perspective.

With respect to the second, namely, that the Rabbis designated circumscribed places for reward and punishment, in Paradise and Gehenna, respectively, we see this in their dicta which, as Ramban[424] of blessed memory explained at length in his

---

[422] It may be that both the "whole" and the "double" refer to the octave, where the harmony produced is from tones that stand in a 2:1 ratio and are farthest from one another—farther, that is, than the tones in the fourth or the fifth are from one another.

[423] Reading, with the manuscripts, בעונש, rather than בעצם, as in the Ferrara edition.

[424] This is R. Moshe ben Naḥman, commonly known as Naḥmanides.

book, *At the Gate of Reward*,[425] are not susceptible of metaphorical or figurative interpretation. Ramban agrees with this view,[426] and does not agree with those [philosophic] views. For according to our view concerning the substance of immortal souls, it is not far-fetched that they would be situated, after their separation [from their bodies], in a circumscribed place, just as they are situated in relation to the bodies of people while they are still attached to the body. But if we were to assume that what continues on after death is the acquired intellect, which is an incorporeal substance that bears no relation to place, their being situated in a place designated for souls would be impossible in itself.

Regarding the third, namely, that the rabbinic dicta imply that the soul is disposed to immortality in itself, without the acquisition of intelligibles, this too accords with the true view and does not agree with—indeed disputes—those [philosophic views]. The Rabbis said explicitly: "Give it to Him as He gave it to you."[427] Indeed, insofar as the mysteries of wisdom in the prophetic-rabbinic science were revealed to them, it is not far-fetched that they, who fixed the moment [at which one merits the world-to-come] as "when they know how to answer amen," were recipients of the tradition according to which it is at that moment that the soul of man is perfected. Perhaps that is the very moment at which some of the first intelligibles are attained. This could be explained by the notion that the soul of a human being is perfected when he attains its faculties. Since some of those faculties precede others in time—that is, the nutritive precedes the vegetative, and the vegetative, the sensitive; and last of all in time is the intellective faculty, all of which was established in the book *On the Soul*[428]—it is likely that this intellective faculty is not perfected so long as it remains impossible for it to transition to actuality. Therefore, if it is the case that this faculty is perfected at this moment [in the child's development], since it is at this time that it has the possibility of becoming actualized to the point that it apprehends some of the first intelligibles, it is not far-fetched that the soul's perfection by nature should occur then, and that it would acquire its immortality all by itself, independent of any prior reward due to the possessor of that soul, as will be explained further in Book IV, God willing.

Yet, according to the views of the ancients, who hold that the immortality of the soul applies to the acquired intellect in accordance with its acquisition of acquired intelligibles, there is no way to account for the immortality of children, unless, by God, they believe that immortality attaches even to the acquisition of first intelligibles. If only I knew how it could be that the souls of two children, one of whom apprehends that the whole is greater than the part, and the other of whom apprehends that things equal to the same thing are equal to each other, would be separate substances, each through its own intelligible, and would not resemble one another. But this is surely something for which a lengthy explanation is superfluous. The

---

[425] בשער הגמול; *Besha'ar Hagemul*, par. 123. See IIIA. iv, n. 181.
[426] Reading, with the manuscripts, לדעת הזה ("with this view"), rather than לדעת השני ("with the second view" or "with the other view"), as in the Ferrara edition.
[427] BT *Shabbat* 152b.
[428] See Aristotle, *On the Soul* II. iii. 414^{b}27ff.; III. xii–xiii.

Rabbis indeed issued many statements that indicate the truth of this view [viz. our view]; there is no need to mention them.

Now that this has been established, I assert that it is easily established according to both the Torah and speculation that this love is necessarily at the highest possible level of intensity. The Torah says explicitly: "And you shall love the Lord your God with all your heart and with all your soul,"[429] which the Rabbis interpreted to mean: "even if He takes your soul,"[430] as if the whole intention is that the thoughts of man will be directed to this end out of this love, as they said: "And all your deeds should be for the sake of Heaven."[431] One is to reach the point at which one loves nothing unless it is for the sake of this love and this service, as another sage has discussed at length.[432] For this reason there are proscriptions forbidding the worship of anyone but God, as it is said: "I am the Lord your God ... a jealous God."[433] The Torah attributes the trait of jealousy to God, for it is the way of the jealous to view harshly their lovers' loving someone else. For, according to the Torah, it is not fitting that a greater love than this one [viz. the love for God] be conceivable. According to speculation, the degree of strength or weakness of the love of the good should correspond to the degree of good in that which is loved. And the degree of good in the one loved who is God is infinite. This is true all the more when the one who loves is loved by the beloved with a great love, as we explained earlier and will explain further, God willing. Thus, even by speculation alone it is fitting that this love be such that no stronger love is conceivable.

Now that this has been established regarding this love [of God], I assert that it is necessary that it have no other end outside itself. For if it had another end, that end would be more loved, and therefore this love, which was posited as being the strongest one conceivable, would not be strong in the way described.

This is confirmed by something found in the Mishnah: "Be like servants who serve the master not for the sake of receiving a reward."[434] Since this is so, it is necessary that this be understood to encompass eternal reward as well. That is to say: it is not fitting that this love be for the sake of the world-to-come. For, so long as it is for the sake of some end, that end will necessarily be more loved, and the service of love weaker than the level required of it. Once this is established of this love, we will have discovered the final end of the Torah, which is true love and service. This is how the greatest of the wise men concluded his book: "The end of the matter, all having been heard: fear God, and keep His commandments; for this is the whole man."[435]

Since eternal life and eternal attachment to the radiance of the Divine Presence is the good such that no other can be conceived to be as good, the final end is also this. It seems to follow from this that there is more than one final end.[436] Yet from the

---

[429] Deut. 6: 5.   [430] Berakhot 9: 5.   [431] Avot 2: 17.

[432] The reference is most likely to Maimonides—specifically to ch. 5 of his *Introduction to Tractate Avot*, also known as *Eight Chapters* (שמונה פרקים).

[433] Exod. 20: 3–5; Deut. 5: 7–9.   [434] Avot 1: 3.

[435] Eccles. 12: 13. This wisest of men is Solomon who, according to tradition, is the author of Ecclesiastes.

[436] The two apparent final ends are: eternal attachment to God after death; and love of and service to Him (in life).

perspective of speculation the opposite of this has been established, as was confirmed in its place.

The existence of two ends is necessary, as was explained earlier, but from different points of view. In respect of the one who is commanded, the final end is love and true service;[437] but in respect of the one issuing the command, the final end is the acquisition of the good and the eternal attachment to the radiance of the Divine Presence. These are alluded to and explicit in the Mishnah, where the Rabbis say: "A single hour of repentance and good deeds in this world is better than all of life in the world-to-come."[438] By this they intended that for the one who serves God and loves Him truly, the end of his passionate love is service, and that is the whole of his purpose; he considers nothing else. This was the intent of the master of the prophets when he said: "Let me go over,"[439] as our Rabbis of blessed memory interpreted this plea: "Many commandments can be fulfilled [only] in the land of Israel."[440] For even though he was assured of eternal life and of delighting in the radiance of the Divine Presence, it was fitting that he should yearn to serve, despite the advantage that would accrue to him through having his soul separate [from his body]. Moreover, the more he would serve, the more his attachment to God would increase and grow.

Be that as it may, one who serves yearns only to serve, and it is this that is, for the one commanded, the final end. For this reason, it appears, the Rabbis voted and reached the conclusion in Gemara 'Eruvin: "It would have been better for the human being not to have been born."[441] Their intent in this dictum was that for the person who serves it is fitting that he choose nonbeing over being. For the true servant does not consider his advantage but only service; and therefore all his good[442] counts for nothing; the only thing that matters is that he not for even a single hour do something wicked before God, or slacken in his service, which for him would be tantamount to great rebellion. Since there is no excuse in this matter, as it is said: "For there is no man who is righteous in the earth,"[443] they arrived at the proposition that for the man who is perfect it is better—taking the term *noaḥ lo* (נוח לו), "it is better for him," in the sense of *munaḥ lirtzono* (מונח לרצונו), "it is in accordance with his will"—not to have been born.[444] In this way the Rabbis made it abundantly clear what the final end is for the one who is commanded. The final end of the one who commands, however, is that with which the (earlier) *mishnah* concludes, when they say: "A single hour of bliss in the world-to-come is better than all the life of this world."[445] Thus the final end of the Torah has been established, both from the perspective of the one commanded and from that of the one issuing the command.[446] It is evident that all perfections are directed toward God, as was established implicitly in our discussion, and as will be further established in what follows, God willing. This was the intention of this chapter.

---

[437] The words והעבודה האמתית ("and true service") do not appear in the Ferrara edition.
[438] *Avot* 4: 22. [439] Deut. 3: 25. [440] BT *Sotah* 14a. [441] BT *'Eruvin* 13b.
[442] Reading כל טובו כאין, rather than, with Fisher, הכל כאין.
[443] Eccles. 7: 20. [444] That is, lest he fail in his service to God.
[445] *Avot* 1: 3. The first part of this *mishnah* was quoted earlier.
[446] From the human perspective, the final end is love of God and service to Him in this life. From God's perspective, the final end is our attachment to Him after death.

Chapter II

EXPOSITION of how it is established that this end is necessitated by this Torah.

I assert that it is evident that the final end in respect of the commander is necessitated by the final end in respect of the one commanded, namely, service and true love. For, once it is explained how it is that this genuine[447] love derives from this Torah, it will become clear how the final end is necessitated in respect of both the one commanded and the commander. Since love requires will and resolute desire, we must explain, with respect to this Torah, how it arouses and awakens this love via the desire and resolute will without coercion by the commander. This will be easily explained on the basis of what was already said.

It was already established in the previous chapter that one who is perfect in his essence loves the good and perfection. It follows from this that the more praiseworthy the loved good, the greater the love. It was established there as well that the Torah perfects us in two perfections—namely, in virtues and in views, which are the foundation of human happiness. Insofar as God is the good that is infinitely praiseworthy, it is necessary that the love of the perfect for Him is the strongest one conceivable. Yet since this love is guaranteed only for the perfect one, I assert further, that the Torah undoubtedly endows the hearts of all those who follow it—both of those who are perfect and of those who are imperfect—with love. For it has already been established in another place that everyone yearns for the good. There is therefore no doubt that the absolute good that is God is in every religious person, and all love Him passionately and yearn for Him. If everything painful were removed—for example, if the pursuit of all their appetites were permitted to them, and so, too, the seeking of honor in vanquishing enemies, and the amassing of wealth—and if all that were required by way of service of God was the reciting of the first verse of the *Shemaʿ* once a week, there is no doubt that there would not remain a single person who would not serve God with love. And if a person were made aware that he is the recipient of God's generosity, his love would grow even more. It is thus the burden of the prescriptions and proscriptions, along with the pressure exerted by the appetites, and also the forbidding of jealousy and arrogance, that prevent most people from serving God with the love for which they yearn. This is so because the human being, though an intellecter in potentiality, is a material being, and, as such, is constantly tempted and is always both one who acts and one who is acted upon in actuality. Since the nature of service requires steadfastness in attachment to God, and a connection that is not severed, the Torah was therefore clever with a wondrous cleverness, in the proliferation of its commandments, in setting forth the root-principles of faith, and in establishing the seven notions that are the principles of its branches, its shoots, its flowers, and its fruits.[448]

The first [of these seven notions] that the Torah shows is the magnitude of God's transcendence and power. The second, His many kindnesses to us. Third, His

---

[447] האמתית, found in the manuscripts, is absent from the Ferrara edition.
[448] Reading, with the manuscripts, אשר הם עקרים לענפיה שריגיה פרחיה ופרותיה, rather than with the Ferrara edition (and Fisher): אשר הם עקריה וענפיה שריגיה ופארותיה, "that are its principles, its branches, its shoots, and its boughs."

bequeathing to us true views and the apprehension of as much as can be apprehended of God and His creations. Fourth, the punctiliousness of His providence and guidance with respect to us. Fifth, two kinds of promises. Sixth, His giving us wonderful reminders and wake-up calls to awaken the heart of those constantly asleep in their foolishness. Seventh, His giving us the love and attachment to Him that is our end. To these are directed the narratives in the Torah and its prescriptions and proscriptions. It is not possible for us to fail to take note of them in brief in this place. We shall assign to them seven sections corresponding to the number of notions.

Concerning the first: that the Torah shows the magnitude of God's transcendence and power. It is sufficient in this regard to cite what may be derived from the narratives in the Torah concerning the act of creation, the exodus from Egypt, the unique and eminent assembly [at Mount Sinai], and the other miracles and wonders that are explicit or traditionally accepted, through which[449] we were singled out for extraordinary renown, acknowledged in so many words by our adversaries who were themselves renowned both for wisdom and for the long duration [of their miracles]— the two considerations that tend to dispel all kinds of suspicion. Indeed, in addition to what is necessitated by the promises that attest to the good will of the one who promises, the observance of the commandments requires to some degree God's enacting a miracle or sign. Thus was it promised with respect to the commandment of the pilgrim festivals that we need not fear the enemy. Thus the Torah says explicitly: "neither shall any man covet your land, when you go up to appear before the Lord your God three times in the year."[450] Similarly, in the matter of administering the drink to the woman suspected of adultery, there would inescapably be a sign—either way: "if you have gone astray" and "if you have not gone astray."[451] This is in addition to what has been transmitted through the tradition concerning the constant miracles that took place in the Temple. In this way the magnitude of God's transcendence and power is easily established, as discussed previously in Part V of this Book, and as will be further discussed in Book III, God willing.

The second is the many kindnesses God bestows upon us. Considering that the details in the Torah and the tradition are too numerous to count, we may note generally God's creating us among the existents as a whole as a simple act of kindness; His taking us out of Egypt with a mighty hand and with signs and terrors; His bringing us to His service, to be His kingdom of priests and a holy nation;[452] and His giving us His Torah, in which the punctiliousness of His providence with respect to us is made clear, along with the magnitude of His transcendence as contrasted with our extreme inferiority. The end intended by all this is attachment to God despite our being at the greatest distance from Him in terms of existence. This should suffice to establish this notion in the Torah.

Some of the Torah's commandments call attention to the first two notions. Those that call attention to the first include the reading of *Hallel*;[453] the special songs sung in

---

[449] Reading בם with the Fisher and the Ferrara edition, rather than רובם, "most of them," with the manuscripts.
[450] Exod. 34: 24.   [451] Num. 5: 19–20.   [452] Exod. 19: 5.
[453] A prayer recited on festivals, which contains Psalms of praise to God.

the Temple; the various tributes that we were commanded to offer in the house of God and through the use of its vessels, out of reverence and awe; the sanctity of those who serve God and are members of the tribe [of Levi] who were selected for this service; the honor and reverence accorded those who love God, who are Sages of the Torah; the honor and reverence accorded to the king and to judges; and the severe punishments visited on those who disobey them, on those who disturb the order in the Chosen House.[454] All this represents the magnificence and transcendence of Him who has chosen this House as a dwelling-place for His Name.

Those that call attention to the second notion include the blessings and prayers of thanks—most of those recited each day contain the details of some [of God's kindnesses]; in general the blessings accompanying the reciting of the *Shemaʿ*—the first of which speaks of creation and the fixing of the celestial lights that rule in the day and the night and are more important than all the sensible existents that serve human needs, the second of which speaks of the kindness and love that God bountifully showed us in giving us His Torah. All this is suited to awakening people as much as is possible to love with a true love this One who loves. For this reason they were placed near the prayer in which the yoke of divine sovereignty is accepted, whose end is this love, as it is said: "And you shall love the Lord your God."[455] The third blessing concerns the redemption [from slavery] in Egypt, which is the kindness felt in our very being to this day, as our Sages said: "And if the Holy One, blessed be He, had not taken our ancestors out of Egypt... then we and our children and our grandchildren would be enslaved to Pharaoh in Egypt."[456] All of this awakens a person's heart to be grateful to God and to praise Him, and to arrange the praises of God to precede prayer, as our Rabbis of blessed memory said: "One ought always to arrange one's praise of God first and pray [only] afterwards";[457] and for this reason they cautioned us to place the [blessing of] redemption close to prayer.[458] Yet another thing indicates this, namely, the statutes incumbent upon us regarding the chosen tribe [of Levi], including the gifts to priests and Levites. So, too, the gifts to the poor, such as tithes, gleanings, forgotten sheaves, and the uncut corner of the field, the sabbatical year, the release of one's slaves, charity, deeds of kindness, love of truth—since truth is beloved of the One who loves—and, a fortiori, distancing oneself from injuring and oppressing others. All this seeks to fix in our souls the idea that we are the recipients of God's kindnesses, inasmuch as He loves doing good absolutely.

The third notion concerns His bequeathing unto us true views and the apprehension of as much as can be apprehended of God and His creations. It is sufficient to point here to the Torah's cornerstones and to the true views that have been transmitted, via the tradition, to those whom God has graced with knowledge, as well as to the allusions that are contained in the Temple and its vessels, in the modes of purification, in the number of days and their sprinklings, and others. To those

---

[454] בית הבחירה (*beit habeḥirah*), another name for the Temple.
[455] Deut. 6: 5.
[456] This rabbinic dictum is found in the Passover *haggadah*.
[457] BT *Berakhot* 32a.
[458] The blessing that culminates in "who redeems Israel" directly precedes the central prayer known as the ʿAmidah.

adept at Kabbalah,[459] other indications are the account of creation and the account of the Chariot.[460]

Some of the commandments act as a wall or barrier for this [viz. to safeguard the true views], as, for example, the injunction to obey the high court [i.e. the Sanhedrin], the admonition not to deviate from what they say, and the severe punishment that awaits one who repudiates their ruling with his own singular teaching. So, too, to obey one's parents, as it is said: "Ask your father, and he will declare unto you, your elders, and they will tell you."[461] All of this is protection and an ingenious barrier lest one be left to one's own sinfulness, believing whatever one imagines at first thought. It ensures that one follow instead what was established by the Sages of the nation and was received from the prophets and the Patriarchs. The Torah dealt expansively with this issue, so that the tradition commented on the biblical verse, "you shall not turn aside from that which they shall declare unto you, to the right or to the left,"[462] as follows: "even if he tells you of the left that it is right and of the right that it is left."[463] All of this is to distance people from even entertaining the thought that the high court might have erred. This shows great wisdom and [erects] a great protective barrier to ensure that they will be obeyed. And it is indeed seen in what the Torah decreed with respect to conspiring witnesses: "then you shall do unto him as he had purposed to do unto his brother,"[464] and does not say "as he had done to his brother." According to the tradition,[465] this is lest it be publicized that the high court erred in its ruling and unlawfully put a soul to death, which would cause doubt to enter the hearts of men with respect to the court's rulings, and cause the wall which is most necessary for the Torah's protection to be breached.

The fourth notion concerns God's punctiliousness in His providence and guidance with respect to us. The narratives in the Torah and in the Prophets and their rebukes are replete with [instances of] this, and especially with respect to the chosen nation, as is hinted at in the Torah's saying: "For the portion of the Lord is His people, Jacob the lot of His inheritance."[466] Our master David spoke expansively about this in his Psalms, and particularly in the Psalm that begins: "O Lord, You have searched me, and known me,"[467] which is wholly devoted to the extraordinary punctiliousness with which God knows and is provident with respect to the details of man, despite the magnitude of His transcendence. This Psalm, it seems, is based on David's excusing himself for consorting with all sorts of desperate men fleeing their creditors, and therefore he said: "If You would but slay the wicked, O God,"[468] referring to those who were in pursuit of him, such as Doeg the Edomite, and Saul, who was, in David's judgment, wicked. Also: "Depart from me, therefore, you men of blood,"[469] that is to say that he would imminently be parting ways with such men, for they were murderers. He therefore said: "Search me, O God, and know my heart,"[470] for God knows the hidden thoughts of the heart, as he said in another place: "for the Lord

---

[459] Crescas's term is יודעי חן. To those initiated into the esoteric traditions, Gen. 1 and Ezek. 1 reveal secrets of which the uninitiated are unaware.
[460] This refers to the famous vision of the prophet Ezekiel, found in Ezek. 1: 4–26.
[461] Deut. 32: 7.   [462] Deut. 17: 11.   [463] *Sifrei* on Deut. 17 11.
[464] Deut. 19: 19.   [465] BT *Makkot* 5b.   [466] Deut. 32: 9.   [467] Ps. 139.
[468] Ps. 139: 19.   [469] Ps. 139: 19.   [470] Ps. 139: 23.

searches all hearts, and understands all the intentions of one's thoughts."[471] Indeed, our Rabbis of blessed memory expanded on this theme, too, in Chapter I of tractate Ḥullin, where they said: "A person is not injured in his finger below without its having been decreed from above, as it is said: 'It is of the Lord that a man's goings are established.'"[472] This is the whole truth, as was discussed in Part V regarding matters beyond doubt.

Some of the commandments indicate this, such as the daily worship in prayer; fasting in times of trouble,[473] as it is said: "then you shall sound an alarm with the trumpets";[474] and reciting the precise blessings in all their details, as specified in *Gemara Berakhot*. Among these commandments is included the sacrificial service as well. For since beliefs are fixed in the soul by the constant performance of deeds, it was an act of divine providence to set in our souls the belief in providence by providing much guidance to us by way of the sacrificial service, through which, in effect, we acknowledge that all benefactions in matters of sustenance and the needs of our senses are supervised and influenced by God, and therefore it is fitting that we set aside the choicest of the species, either offering all of it to God, as in the burnt-offerings, or offering some of it to those designated to serve Him, such as sin-offerings and guilt-offerings. Those offered wholly to the One on high include the burnt-offering. Those designated for both the One on high and the owners include the paschal sacrifice. Those designated for both the One on high and those who serve Him include the sin-offering, the guilt-offering, and the meal-offering. Those designated for the One on high, for those who serve Him, and for the community of Israel include the peace-offering. Those designated solely for those who serve Him include the showbread. It is fitting that the kind of thing designated solely for the One on high be of the finest species, namely, animals; and that that which is designated for the priests be of a less choice category, such as produce. It is fitting that there be a candelabrum, to teach that the bounteous light comes from God. It has seven branches to teach that there are seven servants that overflow from Him.[475] For this reason the candelabrum is lit from the altar of God.[476] Also relevant in this category are the many stories in the Torah—such as the Binding of Isaac and the barrenness of the Matriarchs—and the commandment to circumcise the male organ. So, too, the blowing of the shofar, the joy on New Year and on the special Day of Atonement, the four species of the palm branch, and the service on Sukkot, as we explained in Part II of this Book. The ritual of the two goats of expiation[477]—the one designated for God, the other for ʿAzazel—appears not to be outside this intention. For this makes a strong impression in terms of removing us from the guidance of others—that is why

---

[471] 1 Chr. 28: 9.   [472] Ps. 37: 23. BT Ḥullin 7b.
[473] The manuscripts have תפלות, that is "prayers in times of trouble." The Ferrara edition has תענית, "fasting."
[474] Num. 10: 9. This verse begins: "And when you go to war in your land against the adversary that oppresses you..."
[475] The reference is to what were, in ancient astronomy, the seven known planets: the sun, the moon, Mercury, Venus, Mars, Jupiter, and Saturn.
[476] See *Tamid* 6: 1. If the western lamp was no longer burning, the candelabrum would be lit from the ashes on the altar.
[477] See Lev. 16.

one of the goats is sent to the wilderness—and consigning our guidance solely to God: for this reason, one is a sin-offering to God. In addition, this teaches the obvious connection between the inferior and the transcendent. In this category are included, too, the sabbatical year and the jubilee year, the laws concerning the fruit of immature plants[478] and of first-fruits. For since it is fitting that there be something for God separated from the first-fruits, and since the fruit of the first three years is not choice, God saw fit to forbid the fruit until the fourth year, at which time its redemption is permitted. In this category, too, is the demarking of the first-fruits for the festival of ʿAtzeret [i.e. Shavuot],[479] for they were not brought earlier, in accordance with the tradition that on the festival of ʿAtzeret one is judged with respect to the fruit of trees. Similarly, in accordance with the tradition that on Passover one is judged with respect to grain, the offering of the ʿomer was of grain.[480] All of this constitutes an acknowledgment that all benefactions flow from God, and therefore it is fitting that we sacrifice the first of things. Since the cultivation of grain is very important and necessary, it is fitting that we sacrifice too from the first of our dough.

The offering of two loaves on ʿAtzeret is, it seems, to indicate the connection between Passover and ʿAtzeret. For it is evident that the whole intention and the desired end of the exodus from Egypt, which is commemorated by the Passover festival, is the giving of the Torah, which is commemorated on ʿAtzeret. Therefore, the Torah commanded that the counting run from the day of the ʿomer, which is an offering on Passover, until ʿAtzeret. In this way it suggests that we are to yearn for the arrival of that time, and our thoughts should always be directed toward this end. When we reach it, we will have attained the true bread, as it is said: "Come, eat of My bread,"[481] and "Not a famine of bread, nor a thirst for water, but of hearing the words of the Lord."[482] These two [festivals] are importantly related, for the offering of the ʿomer, which concerns bodily happiness, in accordance with the law of the festival, involves the grain without any alteration of it by way of work; but the offering that concerns the perfection of happiness, which is acquired through the intermediation of the Torah, includes two kinds of happiness, bodily and psychic, as the Rabbis said: "If there is Torah then there is flour."[483] This refers to the two loaves, which are precisely crafted to the greatest possible degree. In addition, the communal peace-offerings express the unity of the laborer with the One for whom he labors, as will be discussed later, God willing.

In this category are [also] the prescriptions and proscriptions in the Torah that include the foods and types of sexual intercourse that are forbidden. This is indeed to guide us to the health of the soul and the body, as it is widely known with respect to some of them that they lead to disturbance and unclarity in the intellect, and with respect to some others, to bad psychic traits, such as cruelty and indifference and

---

[478] These are: ערלה and כרם רבעי.
[479] The festival of Shavuot is called ʿAtzeret by the Rabbis to signal that it is the completion of the festival season that begins with Passover.
[480] See Lev. 23: 9–14.   [481] Prov. 9: 5. The bread refers to wisdom—or, for Crescas, to Torah.
[482] Amos 8: 11.   [483] Avot 3: 21.

being mired in lusts, all of which are things that are most harmful to soul and body. All of this shows the punctiliousness of God's guidance and providence with respect to us. The Torah indeed was most severe with regard to illicit sexual unions, for in these the very organ singled out for the service of God, in which the sign of the covenant resides, as was said earlier, is one engaged in defying God's word. Therefore it is fitting that sexual offense be regarded as a serious defiance. In this category are also the laws of purity and impurity, and the admonitions to the priests and the Nazarites with regard to certain impurities, since these are uniquely positioned to cause intellectual and moral impairment. Some use such things to engage in some form of idolatry and its sacrifices, as is known—for example, the impurity of the dead. Sacrifices and incense from repugnant things are used also in the various kinds of magic, which are a manifestation of idolatry. All of this attests to God's providence in distancing us as far as is possible from anything that approaches or contributes in some way to idolatry, and especially from using [for idolatry] cultic rituals designated for the worship of God. In addition, there are indications of things necessary to the end of the Torah, as will yet be explained, God willing. It is not far-fetched but is rather the truth itself, that in the matter of the commandments there are purposes, indications, and hints of various things, all of which are designed to direct the person to his ultimate perfection.

The fifth concerns the two kinds of promise. The promises regarding bodily happiness are explicit in the Torah in various places and, although the promises of psychic happiness are not quite as explicit in the Torah, they are nevertheless verified in the tradition and hinted at in Scripture, as will be explained in Book III, God willing. Because it is evident that a human being contains a material aspect and an intellectual one, it is also evident that these two types of promise will lead him to the perfection of service. The material promises will address him insofar as he is materially engaged, and the psychic ones will do so when he favors his intellect and is not engaged in or vanquished by his material aspect. This is self-evident.

The sixth concerns the wake-up calls to awaken the heart of those constantly asleep in their foolishness. The temporal commandments are in this category: for example, the festivals, which awaken hearts to remember God's wonders and kindnesses that He wondrously conferred on us in those days and at that time. Since the root of all these wonders to which the Torah alludes is our ceasing from activity on the Sabbath day, the Torah was most exacting with respect to it. But the Torah joined to this reason for observing the Sabbath a second reason, namely, our redemption [from slavery] in Egypt, to teach that we are beholden to God over this as well. For this reason divine wisdom decreed that the occasions that indicate that we are beholden to God, such as, for example, the sabbatical years and the jubilee years, are based on sevens. Even though the jubilee year is the fiftieth year, it is the completion of the sabbatical years and represents complete emancipation, suggesting the perfect emancipation that we achieved on the day of the giving of the Torah, which took place on the fiftieth day of the exodus from Egypt.

So, too, the commandment regarding the mezuzah, which, even though it is not temporal, is in this category. For when a person sees the biblical passages housed within the mezuzah, namely, the portion of the *Shema'* which concerns the acceptance of the yoke of the sovereignty of Heaven, and that of "And it shall come to pass, if you shall hearken diligently..."[484] which contains the bodily promises, then, either way, whether one's intellect or one's material aspect prevails, the person will be aroused to return to God—either because of his love for the truth itself or because of his hope for the fulfillment of the promises. Thus was the Torah prescient in enjoining the presence of the mezuzah in all entryways, whether in homes, yards, or villages, as it is said in Chapter I in *Yoma*: its intent is to arouse a person wherever he is.[485] And since this arouser is located outside the person, the Torah devised, too, the commandment of fringes, which constitutes a sign and reminder of all the commandments. For since this commandment is not relevant to the accepted purpose of the making of clothing—whether because the garment must have four corners and does not cover the entire body, or because fringes are not customary—it will be, at any rate, a reminder that one is commanded. This is all the more the case if, in addition, one considers the hint or hints that are found in the homiletic *midrashim*. Either way, this arouser is very close to the person, closer than the mezuzah. Yet since this arouser is general, applying to all the commandments, the Torah saw fit, in addition, to provide another, more specific one, which is the phylacteries, which contain four biblical passages. We therefore have the tradition with respect to phylacteries of the hand, that there is to be no obstruction between them and the person's flesh, and so, too with the phylacteries of the head, although there are those who were doubtful about this.[486] The actual truth, according to the principles of the Talmud, is that there is no distinction between those of the hand and those of the head. This is what the discussions in tractates *Zevahim* and *Menahot* demonstrate. Furthermore, it is evident there that the phylacteries of the head are analogous to the phylacteries of the hand; and we have a root-principle that does not permit a partial analogy. For this reason, this arouser must be attached to the person. Yet since even this one is outside the person himself, the Torah determined to give us yet another—one which is attached to the person himself at all times. This is circumcision, through which one sacrifices to God one's blood and one's flesh, to indicate that it alone is fit to be the arouser. It is therefore said in tractate *Menahot*: "When David entered to bathe he glanced at his circumcision and sang [God's] praises. Therefore it is written: 'For the Leader; on the eighth'[487]—that is, on circumcision, which is performed on the eighth [day]."[488]

In this category is also the matter of sacrifices, for they arouse submissiveness in service to God. That the burnt-offering is entirely consumed, and atones for bad intentions, as the tradition tells us, suggests that, by the measure of justice, a person deserves to be destroyed even for bad intentions alone, but it is by virtue of God's kindness that the burnt-offering serves as an atonement and replacement. In this [expiation] anyone who designates a part [of the animal] to God participates. And the various kinds of purifications and immersions and sprinklings arouse the person, since transgressions leave an impression on him like a garment that requires washing. By means of the act of immersion in water in which one's body is completely

---

[484] Deut. 11: 13.   [485] BT *Yoma* 11a.
[486] There was disagreement concerning whether it is forbidden that there be an obstruction between the head and its phylacteries.
[487] Ps. 12: 1.   [488] BT *Menahot* 43b.

submerged, it is impressed anew on the soul that one must remove from oneself the filth of those transgressions. The Torah wisely determined that with respect to serious impurities, namely, the impurity of the dead and that of the skin disease *tzaraʿat*, what is required is sprinkling. Just as a dirty garment cannot be cleaned by washing in water alone, but requires detergent, which is composed of water and ash, so, by analogy with this more powerful way of cleaning, purification is accomplished by the sprinkling of water and ash. Divine wisdom decreed that the ash should be taken from the larger animals that are sacrificed, in accord with what is well known, namely, that the most potent ash is the ash derived from an animal [as opposed to from a plant source], once the artisans remove the sulfur from it. The details [of the purification rite] contain allusions [to various secrets], some of which were discovered by R. Eleazar Hakalir. The sprinkling is done by means of plants—specifically, the cedar tree and hyssop—to indicate submissiveness, as it is stated, and with minimal employment of materials. These were chosen because they do not produce edible fruit. In addition, this imitates the cleaning that is customary for things that require cleaning by way of laundering, which is called in the language of Scripture, purgation, as it is said: "Purge me with hyssop, and I shall be clean."[489] For this reason they were called, "waters of purgation."[490]

There are as well many commandments in addition to these that are connected to this notion, commandments wonderfully aimed at arousing people, such as the number of festival days and the number of sacrifices, of which others have spoken at length. For example, there is the commandment concerning the *sukkah*, which signifies both commemoration and gratitude, as it is said: "so that your generations may know that I had the children of Israel live in booths."[491] Its precise details, according to the tradition, contain hints and arousers, as the Rabbis say: "only that which grows from the ground and cannot contract impurity may be used as covering for the *sukkah*,"[492] yet the Rabbis were not similarly insistent on the requirements with respect to the walls. There is no doubt that protection from the rain is accomplished by the roof of the *sukkah*, yet this requires something to support it, namely, walls. Matter is the support for the soul, which is the true form of a human being that protects him. To indicate that submission to the soul is necessary, it is fitting that the roof of the *sukkah*, which indicates submissiveness, be made from something that grows from the ground, which is the lowliest of the elements. To show that it is fitting to distance oneself from the impurity of matter and its passing-away, it is fitting that the roof of the *sukkah* not be made from anything that is subject to impurity. All of this is a hint and wake-up call for man. So, too, are the prohibitions concerning mixed species in this category. They are intended to arouse the person to direct his deeds to one end, namely, true service. In addition, some of them put us in mind of a certain kind of idolatry and distance us from it, as the Rabbi mentioned.

The seventh concerns the notion that love and attachment are the end. A number of commandments lead to this, besides those that are explicit, such as: "You shall love

---

[489] Ps. 51: 7.   [490] The Hebrew is: מי חטאת.   [491] Lev. 23: 43.   [492] *Sukkah* 1: 4.

the Lord your God,"[493] and "and Him you shall serve, and unto Him you shall cleave."[494] Indeed, the commandments in general participate in this end and are oriented toward it, as was said previously. Those that are specific to this end are in the category of service through sacrifices, since they make an extraordinary impression, and serve as a model, insofar as they are an expiation for our souls. It is as if through them we sacrifice our essence to worship God. We appear in our eyes as nothing, and as naught in our souls. So, too, our possessions—especially as compared with God's glory. That is why it is through sacrifices that those who perform the service attain the emanation of His overflow and attachment to the light of the Divine Presence, whether it is sensed or not sensed—sometimes even feeling as if fire is descending from the heavens. The priests had a path to, and a part in, this unification with and attachment to God by way of sacrifices. As our Rabbis of blessed memory said with respect to the priests: "When the priests receive their portion, they receive it from the table of the Most High."[495] Since this unification was extended to the nation as a whole, the owners of the sacrificial animals partook of some of the sacrifices, namely, the peace-offerings, so long as they were private peace-offerings. For the sacrifices of the communal peace-offering could not be distributed to all of Israel. Therefore, the priests served as representatives of all Israel in this matter.

Among the commandments specifically signifying attachment to God is that of the *Urim* and *Tummim*, upon which were inscribed the tribes of Israel with majesty and glory, along with the explicit name of God, as the tradition affirms. Since Aaron was the high priest of his generation and the representative of Israel, if a king or a prophet who were leaders of the community were with him when the *Urim* and *Tummim* were set upon his heart, and if their thoughts then turned to unification with God and attachment to Him, it would be fitting and necessary that they attain the emanation of the divine overflow. Even more is this the case in the Temple, which was the house of God, as it is said: "And let them make Me a sanctuary, that I may dwell among them."[496] Praised be the One who drew us near to His service, and sanctified us with His Torah, in order that we draw near to Him and that He cause His glory to dwell in our land.

These are the seven notions that the Torah intended, to which we alluded briefly. No person should be deceived and imagine that this suffices for understanding the reasons for the Torah and its commandments. For the intentions of the Torah and its details are too numerous to count. But I assert that the things we have discussed are among the Torah's purposes and intentions. In this way that which we wished to establish is verified, namely, that the Torah engenders love in the heart of both the perfect and the imperfect who are drawn to follow it. As our Rabbis of blessed memory said: "If someone repulsive assails you, lead him to the house of study: if he is of stone, he will dissolve; if of iron, he will shiver into fragments, for it is said: 'Is not my word like a fire? says the Lord.'"[497] This was the intention of this chapter.

---

[493] Deut. 6: 5.   [494] Deut 13: 4.   [495] BT *Beitzah* 21a.   [496] Exod. 25: 8.
[497] Jer. 23: 29. The verse continues: "and like a hammer that breaks the rock in pieces?" BT *Kiddushin* 30b.

Chapter III

EXPOSITION of the proposition that this Torah's end is the end of existence as a whole.

I assert that since it was established in the *Metaphysics*[498] that existence is good, and since this Torah's end is the acquisition of the good, as was established earlier in this Book, it follows that the end of all existents and of the Torah are of the same genus, namely, the good. But I assert as well that their end—that is, the end of existence as a whole and of this Torah—are of the same species. Moreover, the end of the existence of the lower realm as a whole and of this Torah are one and the same individual thing.

That the end of the whole of existence in its entirety and of this Torah are one in species will be established as follows. Existence as a whole has three parts: the higher, which is the realm of the angels; the intermediate, which is the realm of the celestial spheres; and the lower, which is the realm of the elements. The following disjunction is inescapable: either they are all eternal, that is, they are not subject to passing-away, even if it is established that they are created; or they are all subject to passing-away; or some are eternal and some pass away. There are no causes for the angels to pass away, for matter is the source of passing-away and evil, as was established in its place. That leaves but two alternatives: either they are all eternal,[499] or some are subject to passing-away—but either way, they are of one species. For if they are all eternal, then their end is of the same species,[500] for it is the good that is found in eternal life. But if some of them are subject to passing-away, then the cause of their passing-away is that they are only the precondition for the existence of something else, which is their eternal aspect. For example, the realm of the elements is the precondition for the existence of the human species, that is, for human souls. Or the realm of the spheres: even were it to turn out that they are in the category of things that pass away, nevertheless, insofar as they are the precondition for the eternal aspect, it is indeed established for existents as a whole that their end is eternal life. It is thus established that the end of existence in general as a whole and of this Torah is of one species.

That the end of the whole of inferior existence and of this Torah is one and the same individual thing is easily established, since it was established in another place that the end of the inferior world[501] is the species man. And it was established that the end of human perfection is in this Torah, whose end is eternal life and attachment to God. Thus, their end is one in number. This is what we wished to show.

Chapter IV

VERIFICATION of this necessity from the perspective of speculation and from the dicta of our Rabbis of blessed memory.

---

[498] See *Metaph.* I. iii. 983ᵃ32.

[499] Missing from the Fisher and the Ferrara edition is the following text found in the manuscripts: או שיהיו קצתם נפסדים. ואיך שיהיה התכלית בהם אחד במין. וזה שאם כולם היו נצחיים. The Ferrara edition resumes at: "then their end is of the same species."

[500] Missing from the Fisher and the Ferrara edition is the following text found in the manuscripts: והוא הטוב הנמצא בחיים הנצחיים. The Ferrara edition resumes at: "But if some of them..."

[501] עולם השפל. The manuscripts have: "the world of composition," עולם ההרכבה.

I assert that the ancient thinkers established that this existence is as a whole like one individual thing, connected one part to another, and the Rabbi of the *Guide* expanded upon this idea.[502] And it is fitting that it be so, inasmuch as the source of its existence is one simple producer. It is thus fitting that its end be, as a whole, one, insofar as it is one individual. The final end of its parts is the final end of the whole, which is one. For since it is one individual connected one part to the other, one part is a precondition for the other. If the final end of one part were other than the final end of the whole, then existence as a whole would not be a single individual thing, for the end is consequent upon the form, as was explained in its place. Therefore, when the form is one, the end is necessarily one. Since the ancients were confused about this, we have no alternative but to discuss the matter at length, especially insofar as this discussion will establish what we mentioned with respect to this necessity, namely, the necessity that there be one end.

I assert that there is something well known and agreed-upon, namely, that from a simple one there can emerge only a simple one. Since it has been established with respect to God's essence that He is a simple one at the height of simplicity, and we appear to be substances composed of matter and form that emanate from Him, this proposition would seem to provide grounds for a major objection—especially if substances composed of matter and form come to be through the intermediation of other intellects,[503] that is, from the tenth intellect. Since the first effect emanates from the first simple without an intermediary, that effect would have to be simple. So, too, for the second effect, for insofar as it is an effect of the first effect which is a simple one,[504] it would necessarily have to be a simple one. And so, too, for the last effect. Therefore, I am utterly amazed at how bodies come to be from intellects that are simple.

What the ancient thinkers said by way of resolving this difficulty is that, although the proposition that states that, from a simple one nothing but a simple one can come to be, is true in respect of its quiddity, nevertheless, in respect of the necessity of its existence a certain composition must be created. For although the effect is a simple one in respect of its quiddity, as is necessitated by its emanation from a simple one, it is impossible that there not be created in it a certain composition in respect of the necessity of its existence. For from the perspective of its cause, the effect's existence is necessary, but in respect of itself, its existence is possible.[505] Thus, the second effect, insofar as its cause is composite, also takes on composition. All the effects that are links in that chain will also take on composition, until we arrive at the tenth intellect, which, because of the increase in its composition, will give rise to a body composed of form and matter. This is what they said by way of resolving this difficulty, or this is what derives from the force of their statements. Yet the flaw in this position is

---

[502] *Guide* I. 72.
[503] Fisher follows the Ferrara edition, which has: "other incorporeal intellects," שכלים נפרדים אחרים; the manuscripts have: "other intellects," שכלים אחרים, omitting נפרדים, "incorporeal." I follow the manuscripts.
[504] Fisher, following the Ferrara edition, has: מהאחד הראשון שהוא פשוט; the Florence manuscript has, more intelligibly: מהראשון שהוא אחד פשוט. My translation follows this manuscript.
[505] The first effect is both necessary and possible with respect to its existence—necessary in respect of its cause, but possible in itself—and is therefore, in one sense, composite.

patently obvious. The composition that exists in the intellects that are effected derives from the possibility and the necessity of their existence; but in respect of their quiddity they are simple, with no composition. This proposition entails only that from a one that is simple only a one that is simple *in its quiddity* can come to be. This proposition does not, however, mandate simplicity with respect to the necessity and possibility of existence. Indeed, how could this be mandated when the first effect is necessarily composite in respect of its existence? Therefore, even if the effects increase in composition, so long as they are simple in respect of their quiddity, how could new things that are composite in quiddity[506] emerge from them? If only I knew.[507]

What is fitting to be said by way of resolution of this difficulty is what I shall now say. If the effect were to follow from its cause with absolute necessity, this objection would have a basis. But since the effect follows from its cause via a willed apprehension, the resolution of this difficulty is not hard. For even if intellect requires that a simple one also have a single simple will, this unity of the will is manifest in the phenomenon of benefaction, that is, in the overflow of as much good as is possible, or in the good that God's wisdom decrees. Since the whole of existence is good, as was established in its place, it is fitting that divine benefaction, which is, as it should be, the greatest conceivable benefaction, would not stint in producing as much good as it is possible to produce. Therefore, even if in producing the good some bad thing results, nevertheless, insofar as it is still the good in its essence, even the bad is a kind of good, for it would not be fitting for the perfect divine will to stint in this regard. It is therefore not impossible that bodies that are composite in their quiddity would derive from a simple one with no intermediation, since they are necessitated by way of the single simple will, which is the will to produce every possible good, or the good that God's will decrees. This is one way in which the production of all existence by God as an act of will is established, as we will see in Book III Part I, God willing. But it became necessary to speak of this [here] in order to indicate that the end of God's will is one simple thing, which is the production of good, both for the whole of existence and for things that are its parts. Since the most perfect possible good is the attachment to God, it is fitting that that good overflow from Him to all those who are capable of receiving it. This is now established from the perspective of speculation.[508]

Our Rabbis of blessed memory explained this—that is, that the end of the whole world and of the Torah is one and the same—in various places. They said that the Torah preceded the universe by two thousand years.[509] This shows that the Torah precedes the universe as its anterior cause, since the end is the first of the causes, inasmuch as the end of something precedes it chronologically in thought. In order to establish that the Torah is the end of the universe, they exaggerated the time and said

---

[506] במהותם ("in their quiddity") is missing from the Ferrara edition.

[507] Crescas objects to this view insofar as it allows a body that is not simple in its quiddity to derive from an original one that is simple in its quiddity.

[508] Crescas solves the problem of composite nature's deriving from simple nature by understanding this simple nature as goodness and benefaction which can produce composition as a manifestation of that single generous nature. Everything produced is one insofar as goodness is one.

[509] *Gen. Rabbah* 8: 2.

"two thousand years," as Solomon did in saying, by way of exaggeration, "though he live a thousand years twice told."[510] Indeed, in speaking of the Torah, they intended the end of the Torah, which is the eternal attachment to God. This is the absolute truth. And this was their explicit intent in saying: "Were it not for the Torah, the heavens and the earth would not endure."[511] But since the end of existence as a whole and in its parts is goodness, they interpreted the verse in the following way in order to make that point explicit. "'And God saw every thing that He had made, and, behold, it was very good'[512]—goodness is death."[513] For the end of the universe is eternal life. It is affirmed at the beginning of the great Hallel prayer that good is a genus encompassing all varieties of goodness: "Give thanks to the Lord, for He is good. His kindness endures forever."[514] What is intended here is that God is the absolute good. Since it is fitting that the absolute good be eternal, it is said: "His kindness endures forever." After noting the inclusive genus, the Psalmist takes note of various kinds of goods in the remaining verses that follow, concluding with: "O give thanks unto the God of heaven"[515]—hinting at God's being the lord and ruler of the heavens, as the marvels that he mentions indicate. Along these same lines, our Rabbis of blessed memory formulated the grace after meals: "Who nourishes with His goodness, His graciousness, His kindness, and His mercy." Note that they mention first the good that is the inclusive genus for all the various kinds of kindness, and then enumerate the three species, as will be discussed further, God willing. Indeed there are many rabbinic dicta concerning this matter that establish its truth. There is no need to mention them.

Chapter V

WE shall explain that the search for a final end for the totality of existence is fitting and necessary, while reconciling it with the view of the Rabbi.

The search for the final end of the totality of existence is fitting and necessary. This may be seen in that, according to the true view, the view of our Torah, which illumines our eyes with the belief in creation, it is evident that the totality of existence is a work produced with intention by one who intends, and with will by one who wills, and by a being whose intellect has no peer and nothing comparable among the other intellects. To suggest that the act of such an intellect is in vain and without an end is patently false and nonsensical. Therefore, there is no escaping that there must be an end. I affirm that there needs to be a final end. For it is true of any end that is posited that, insofar as it also originates in the intention of one who intends it, it either has a further end or not. If creation has a further end, then the further end is subject to the same disjunction as the first one. If creation has no further end, then either it is an end in itself or it is not an end in itself. But it is impossible for it not to be an end in itself, for if it were not an end in itself the act would be in vain, since it has been assumed not to have a further end. It is evident that if it had another end, it would be necessary for us to inquire about the end of that end. Since this cannot go on ad infinitum, it is necessary that the matter come to a stop with the final end

---

[510] Eccles. 6: 6. [511] BT *Pesaḥim* 68b. [512] Gen. 1: 31.
[513] *Gen. Rabbah* 9: 5. See n. 137. [514] Ps. 136: 1. [515] Ps. 136: 26.

which is an end in itself. It is evident, therefore, according to our view, the view of the congregation of believers in the creation of the world, that it is necessary that there be a final end to the totality of existence.

I affirm that this is necessary as well for the group of believers in anterior eternity. For they indeed acknowledge an intelligent divine first principle for all existents. And natural science seeks the end of every natural existent. It is indeed found with respect to natural existents that they are so wisely constituted that it is impossible for them not to be oriented toward an end. This is why Aristotle said that nature does nothing in vain. Since this is so, and since, insofar as the natural world derives from an intelligent principle, it is impossible to escape the conclusion that there is an end,[516] then, either it is an end in itself or it is oriented toward another end, in which case that would be the final end. For if not, that first end would be a work in vain, which is, however, excluded by the law of nature, since it derives from an intelligent principle. It is indeed thus established that, even for those who believe in anterior eternity, a final end for the totality of existence is necessitated. All the more is this the case for us, the congregation of believers in the Torah of Moses.

It might indeed be thought that what we say with respect to this end could not be more remote from what the Rabbi says. For he made a concerted effort to establish, in Part III of his book, that searching for the end of the totality of existence is futile according to every opinion.[517] Nevertheless, he conceded, verbatim, as follows: "Whenever an agent acts with intentionality, it is impossible for the thing he has done not to have an end for the sake of which it was done. This is evident according to philosophical speculation and does not require a demonstration."[518] Moreover, he accepted that, even according to the view of anterior eternity, it is impossible for any natural existent not to have an end, for nature does nothing in vain.

It is most evident from these propositions which the Rabbi acknowledged, that there is no avoiding a final end on either of the two views. Since this did not escape his profound understanding, it would appear that the Rabbi's view would indeed favor the search for the end. Of course, even if we assume that this end exists, nevertheless, the search for it is difficult and nearly impossible, as the Rabbi hinted when he said: "Indeed, everyone who discoursed on nature recognized the impossibility of forgoing a final end. But knowledge of this entity is very difficult, especially as it is the end of the totality of existence."[519] To be sure, the Rabbi worked at the question of knowing the final end in accordance with the statements of Aristotle. But he sought to establish the difficulty of its existence even according to the creation view. For he saw that the question would not come to a stop regardless of what the end turned out to be, as the Rabbi suggested when he said: "Even if all is for the sake of man, and the final end of man is, as has been said, to serve God, the question

---

[516] Following the manuscripts: אי אפשר המלט מתכלית אחד. Fisher has: אי אפשר המלט התכלית ההוא מתכלית אחר, which would mean something like: "it is impossible that this end do without another end."

[517] That is, according to the opinion both of those who believe the universe was created and of those who believe in its anterior eternity.

[518] *Guide* III. 13. The translations of Maimonides' *Guide* in this section are my translations of Crescas's quotations. They are not direct translations from the Arabic.

[519] *Guide* III. 13.

remains, what end is there in his serving, when God's perfection will not increase if he serves Him. And if we say: it is not for God's perfection but for ours—for it, namely, our perfection, is the good for us—the following question would necessarily arise: and what is the end of our existing with this perfection? It is necessarily not possible for the matter not to culminate in our specifying as the end: this is what God wanted, or this is what His wisdom decreed."[520] This is what appears explicitly in the Rabbi's discussion.

The Rabbi drew support for his statements from the formulation of a particular prayer, and concluded, saying: "They established that there is no end [for the totality of existence] other than will."[521] We will have to interpret this somewhat loosely, as saying that there is no end *known to us* aside from will. This is what appears to us in explaining his words. It was already established previously, however, that benefaction and the conferring of kindness is something essential to the perfect one and to the absolute good [viz. God]. Since everyone desires the good, it is evident that when an agent acts for the sake of a good end, the question is resolved at that end, insofar as it is good: it is an end in itself. Therefore, when the absolute good, in whom benefaction is an essential property, does something, its end is benefaction. The question is resolved there.

Do you not see in the discourse of the Rabbi his saying:[522] "What end is there in his serving, when God's perfection will not increase?" It may be seen from this that if God's perfection were to increase, the question would be resolved, since that end would be good for Him.[523] Thus, once it is established that benefaction is a good essential to Him, something indubitable is established, namely, that this is the true final end.

The formulation of the prayer in which they say: "Yet who shall say unto You, What is it You are doing?; and if he is righteous, what does this give You?" is intended to indicate that there is no one who can increase the perfection of what God has produced, such that he might say: "What is it You are doing?" For "if he is righteous," that will not increase its perfection. But they did not intend that there is no end other than God's will alone, as the Rabbi apparently would have it. God forbid that one attribute to God something that would be a grave defect in any intelligent being.

This is what we intended in this chapter. With this, Part VI of Book II is completed. Praise is to God alone, who is exalted above all blessing and praise.

---

[520] *Guide* III. 13.

[521] *Guide* III. 13. The prayer to which Maimonides refers is one recited on the Day of Atonement in the Neʿilah service: "You have set man apart from the beginning and acknowledged him that he should stand before You; yet, who shall say unto You, What is it You are doing?; and if he is righteous, what does this give You?"

[522] Fisher and the Ferrara edition have: "And this was established in the discourse of the Rabbi, who said." We follow the manuscripts which have: והלא תראה בדברי הרב אומרו.

[523] Reading לעצמו, with the Florence manuscript, rather than בעצמו, with the Ferrara edition and Fisher.

Book III: Division A
CONCERNING the true beliefs that we who believe in the divine Torah believe, the denier of any one of which is called a heretic.

When we investigated these beliefs, which are in addition to the six cornerstones discussed in Book II, we found that they fall into two categories. One category contains beliefs not tied to specific commandments. The other contains beliefs tied to specific commandments.[1]

The first category contains eight beliefs: (1) creation of the universe; (2) immortality of the soul; (3) reward and punishment; (4) resurrection of the dead; (5) eternality of the Torah; (6) the difference between Moses' prophecy and that of other prophets; (7) that the high priest receives his answers via the *Urim* and *Tummim*; and (8) the coming of the Messiah. We have therefore divided this Division [of Book III] into eight Parts.

It did not strike us as appropriate to include these beliefs among the cornerstones. For even though belief in them is obligatory, and their denial constitutes so egregious a rebellion that one who denies them is regarded as belonging to the class of heretics, nevertheless, the Torah's existence is conceivable without them. Therefore, we did not posit them as the Torah's foundation or roots.

It is puzzling that the Rabbi of the *Guide* introduced, in his commentary to the chapter called Ḥeleq,[2] thirteen principles that he posited as foundations of the religion. For if by "principles" he intended true beliefs whose denial qualifies as heresy, then there are more than fifteen.[3] But if by "principles" he intended the

---

[1] These are beliefs that may be inferred from the commandments with which they are associated. The beliefs are: (1) that God is responsive to prayer and blesses the Israelites through the priestly blessing; (2) that God welcomes the penitent; and (3) that God seeks to perfect people in service and attachment to Him.

[2] The reference is to Maimonides' *Commentary on Mishnah Sanhedrin*, ch. 10.

[3] Crescas does not say how he counts required beliefs so that they add up to "more than fifteen." It is likely that the fifteen are his own six cornerstones, plus these eight true beliefs (which are not connected to specific commandments)—beliefs whose denial constitutes heresy though the Torah is conceivable without them—plus the belief in God's existence. In saying "more than fifteen" Crescas may be alluding to the three additional beliefs that are tied to specific commandments to be discussed in Division B of this Book. (This is Kellner's view (1986: 124).) Another possibility might be the addition—to his six cornerstones plus these eight true beliefs—of his root-principles of divine unity and incorporeality, which, if included, would bring the count either to sixteen (if one were included) or to seventeen (if both were). A third possibility—in my opinion, the most likely one—is that the possible sixteenth required belief is belief in the divinity of the Torah. Since the two possible additional beliefs that Crescas adds to his cornerstones at the end of this

cornerstones and foundations of the religion without which the Torah[4] is inconceivable, then there are no more than seven, if we include among them the existence of God, or eight, if we also include among these cornerstones the Torah's being a divine Torah from Heaven.[5]

The following objection might be raised against us, on the basis of what was agreed upon and was widespread among some of the ancients, namely, that the belief in creation is an axis upon which the Torah turns. For this belief entails that God is powerful and that all existents are to Him as clay in the hand of the potter.[6] Without this belief, the Torah's essential existence would not be conceivable at all, and, more specifically, neither would the signs and wonders recorded in it, which are its foundations and its sustaining pillar. Indeed for the believers in eternity, who regard the existence of the universe as a necessity deriving from God, the Torah's existence is inconceivable in every respect. And since this is so, it is appropriate to count belief in creation as a great pillar and cornerstone alongside the other cornerstones mentioned in Book II.

It is not difficult, however, to resolve this objection, once the necessity of God's power is established even for the believers in eternity.[7] It is this that eluded the ancients. Just how this is to be established will be discussed in what follows, God willing. Since, however, the necessity of believing in creation is established in accordance with the Torah and the tradition, it is necessary that we investigate, as is our custom, what one ought to believe, and the way in which we arrived at our knowledge of it. We have placed it [viz. the belief in creation] in Part I of this Book.

Part I

CONCERNING the belief in creation.

The commentators on Aristotle's books wrote profusely and argued extensively in support of the belief in anterior eternity. The Rabbi of the *Guide* responded to these arguments, introducing arguments in opposition to eternity and in support of creation; and R. Levi exerted further efforts in establishing proofs and arguments in support of creation, while rejecting the approach of the Rabbi. We must therefore

---

paragraph to bring their number to seven or eight are belief in the existence of God and belief in the divinity of the Torah, it stands to reason that if the first of these is what brings his count of required beliefs to fifteen, the second of these is what would bring his count to more than fifteen.

[4] The text contains only a feminine form of "which is inconceivable," אשר לא תצויר, and might well refer to the immediately preceding term, "the religion," דת. But Crescas appears to be concerned to categorize beliefs in terms of whether or not they are so fundamental as to render the Torah inconceivable without them.

[5] Crescas is adding to his own six cornerstones either just one or at most two further beliefs. The first is the belief in God's existence, which is one of Crescas's own root-principles. The second is the belief in the divine origin of the Torah, which is one of Maimonides' thirteen principles but is not explicitly among either Crescas's root-principles or his required beliefs not tied to specific commandments or his required beliefs tied to specific commandments.

[6] An expression found in the High Holiday liturgy, quoting Jer. 18: 6. Maimonides in the *Guide* uses this simile of "clay in the potter's hand" in III. 13, where he presents and discredits the view of "the philosophers," Plato among them, that God created the world from pre-existent matter, which, though dependent on God, is nevertheless co-eternal with Him.

[7] Once the believers in anterior eternity concede God's power, belief in the Torah becomes conceivable even for them. Therefore, creation is not a belief without which the existence of the Torah is inconceivable.

cite their discussions as concisely as possible, and distinguish in our concise manner between that in their approaches which is justified and that which is not. We therefore saw fit to divide this Part into five chapters.

Chapter I, in which we review the arguments of the commentators in support of anterior eternity.

Chapter II, in which we review the responses of the Rabbi of the *Guide* to them, as well as his arguments to establish absolute creation.

Chapter III, in which we review the proofs, arguments, and responses of R. Levi in support of creation in accordance with his conception of it.

Chapter IV, in which we distinguish as best we can that which is correct from that which is incorrect [in their positions].

Chapter V, in which we establish that the view concerning creation is true without any doubt, and its denial tantamount to the destruction of the roots of the Torah. Nevertheless, this is not a foundation or cornerstone without which the existence of the Torah would be inconceivable.

Chapter I

WE shall review the arguments offered by the believers in anterior eternity, such as those we encountered in the books *Physics* and *Metaphysics*, which reinforce their belief in this view—in respect of time, in respect of motion, in respect of the celestial body, in respect of prime matter, and in respect of the agent.

In respect of time, they offered three arguments. The first proceeds as follows. If time is eternal, there must necessarily be something that moves eternally; time is indeed eternal; hence, there must necessarily be something that moves eternally. In this case the consequent is self-evident, insofar as time is an accident consequent upon motion, and motion without something moving is inconceivable. And the antecedent is established as follows. If time came to be, it would necessarily have come to be before its coming-to-be. This, however, is absurd. How is this absurdity established? In the way I shall now explain. If time came to be, there would have been no time before it existed. Our saying "before," however, involves one of the divisions of time, so that time would have to exist and not exist at once. It is proved, too, that time cannot pass away—in precisely this same way. If time neither comes to be nor passes away, it is necessarily eternal. The Philosopher strengthened this argument by saying that it is an accepted proposition that anything that comes to be, comes to be in time.[8]

The second is as follows. If time came to be, there would have to be an instant that is not preceded by time. But this is absurd. This absurdity is proved by the fact that the instant divides the before from the after; the before and the after are divisions of time. How is it necessitated of the instant that it divide the before from the after? Because it may indeed be imagined that the condition of the instant is like that of the point that divides a line. There is a point that exists in actuality, such as that at the end of a line, and one that exists only in potentiality,[9] which is the one that divides

---

[8] The implication is that time itself could not come to be if all coming-to-be takes place in time.

[9] "In potentiality" here may be close in meaning to "theoretically."

the line. The point that is in the latter condition is both a beginning and an end at once. The instant never exists in actuality: since time itself never exists in actuality, so, a fortiori, the instant. Furthermore, if it existed in actuality it would have to exist over time and be divisible. Therefore, it is evident that it exists only in potentiality. It is therefore necessary that the first instant divide the before from the after. But it was supposed that it was first. This yields a contradiction.

The third proceeds as follows. If the universe came to be, it would be necessary that its existence be in potentiality prior—chronologically—to its existence in actuality, for potentiality and actuality contradict one another, and it is impossible for them to exist at the same time from the same perspective. But if time existed before, there would have been eternal motion and an eternally moving thing. For if it were created, the existence of its potential would have to have preceded it chronologically, and so on, ad infinitum. Therefore, in respect of time, the moving thing must be eternal.[10]

In respect of motion, they offered two arguments. The first proceeds as follows. Since it is established in physics that locomotion precedes the other forms of motion and that it is necessary that motion terminate[11] in a first moving thing that is self-moved, it follows that, if the universe is posited as coming to be, it would require that there be something that locomotes to which the universe's coming-to-be may be traced back. This would be true with respect to that moving thing if it, too, came to be. Because it is impossible that this process go on ad infinitum, it is necessary that it terminate in a first moving thing that does not come to be.

The second proceeds as follows. If it is impossible that motion is created absolutely, it is necessary that there be an eternal moving thing; it is impossible that motion be created absolutely; hence, there must be an eternal moving thing. The necessity of the consequent is self-evident. The way the antecedent is established is as follows. If we suppose a first motion that is created absolutely, it is inevitable that that which moves with that motion either come to be or not come to be. If it comes to be, then the motion that was posited as first is not first, because it would have had to be preceded by the motion of coming-to-be. And if we posit the motion of coming-to-be as first, it too would necessarily not be first. This is so whether in respect of the agent or in respect of that which is acted upon.

In respect of the agent, this is because it is indeed thought that when the agent acts at a moment following its having been inactive, there is necessarily a change created in it on account of which it was spurred to act. If we suppose that this change is first, it is necessary for there to have been another change before it. This would go on ad infinitum. This necessity in respect of the agent is therefore equivalent to that which was posited with respect to the first moving thing, that is, that it either comes to be or does not come to be.

---

[10] If the universe comes to be, it must be in potentiality before it comes to be. "Before it comes to be" is the *time* in which it exists in potentiality. But time entails motion, which in turn entails a moving body—in actuality. This moving body in actuality in turn requires a prior time in which it exists in potentiality. But this time, too, entails motion, which in turn entails an actually moving body—and so on, ad infinitum.

[11] The self-moved mover is the starting point of motion but is its *endpoint* when motion is traced backward.

In respect of that which is acted upon, this is because it is indeed thought that anything that comes to be is necessarily preceded by a change, and therefore the motion of coming-to-be that was posited as first cannot be first. If we posit that change as first, it must be preceded by the possibility of the creation of a change. For the potential precedes the actual in all created things, and the possibility of the creation of a change is also a change that follows a change. This goes on ad infinitum. It is evident from this, too, that the necessity in respect of that which is acted upon is equivalent to that which was posited with respect to the first moving thing, that is, that it either comes to be or does not come to be. They thus established in respect of motion that there must be an eternal moving thing.

In respect of the celestial body, they offered two arguments. The first proceeds as follows. Anything that comes to be, comes to be from its opposite and passes away into its opposite. It is accordingly necessary that anything that has no opposite not come to be and not pass away. Since it was established in physics that the celestial body has no opposite,[12] it follows necessarily that it neither comes to be nor passes away.

The second proceeds as follows. Everything that comes to be passes away. It is necessary, then, that the celestial body, which cannot pass away, therefore not come to be. Indeed, that it is impossible for the celestial body to pass away was already established in the book *On the Heavens*,[13] since there are no causes for its passing-away. With respect to the previous proposition, namely, that everything that comes to be passes away, Aristotle offered many arguments and wrote extensively on this matter.

Aristotle said[14] that if a thing that is in itself one contains the potentiality for two opposing things, then these potentialities would have to be limited, and the time in which they are actualized would have to be limited. It is thus impossible that there be in a thing, which is in itself one, opposing potentialities that are unlimited, that is, a potentiality for existence that is infinite and so, too, a potentiality for nonexistence that is infinite. For if this were possible, one of three things would follow necessarily. Either we would not posit the actualization at any time of either one of the two potentialities—yet this is absurd with respect to existence and nonexistence, for in their case there is no intermediate; or we would posit the actualization of both potentialities existing concurrently all the time—yet this too is absurd; or we would posit the actualization of one of the two potentialities being always present, and the actualization of the other being always absent, inasmuch as the potentialities are assumed to be unlimited. This [third] alternative would appear to be possible, but in fact it is not. For if we suppose that the celestial body contains a constant potential to exist and to not-exist, and, furthermore, that the actualization of its potentiality for existence is always present and the actualization of its potentiality for nonexistence not present at any time, the following is inescapable with respect to the potentiality

---

[12] The celestial sphere has no opposite because its motion is circular.

[13] Aristotle, *On the Heavens* I. xii.

[14] This compressed argument is designed to show that anything that comes to be passes away, doing so by demonstrating that anything with infinite potentiality to exist—that is, anything that is anteriorly eternal—must continue to actualize its infinite potentiality to exist.

for nonexistence: its transitioning to actuality is either possible, or necessary, or impossible. It is absurd that it be either necessary or impossible, because each of these negates the possibility it presumably contains. We must therefore assume that its existing and transitioning to actuality are possible. If we assume that this possibility does not transition to actuality, its status as possible is belied.[15] But if we assume that it is actualized, an absurdity will necessarily ensue, namely, that two opposite actualizations will coexist, that is, that a thing that is in itself one will be always in existence and always in nonexistence. And so,[16] that which is always in existence has no potentiality at all for nonexistence. Therefore, it will necessarily turn out on their view that it is impossible for something always in existence in the past to pass away in the future.[17] And in this way in itself it will be proved of anything that comes to be that it cannot continue on eternally.[18]

Furthermore, since the time during which the universe exists is infinite, and similarly the time during which it was nonexistent is infinite, it would be necessary on their view that it be existent and nonexistent simultaneously. For if we assume that the past time in which it was nonexistent is infinite, and the future time in which it will exist is infinite, one infinity will be part of another, yet this is impossible. It would therefore be necessary according to Aristotle that each of these times be finite and limited.[19]

In addition, it might be thought that the intermediate that lies between always-existent and always-nonexistent could well be viewed as the negation of both extremes, that is, as neither existent always nor nonexistent always. But anything

---

[15] We cannot assume that this possibility is not actualized without undermining its nature as possible.

[16] That is, the same reasoning applies: If something has infinite existence—that is, its infinite potentiality for existence is actualized—how could it have infinite potentiality for nonexistence? For if that potentiality were realized, the thing would be always existent yet also always nonexistent at the same time.

[17] The argument advanced on Aristotle's behalf runs as follows. If it were possible for the existent thing to contain two infinite opposing potentialities—one for existence and one for nonexistence—yet it clearly could not be the case either that both are actualized or that neither is, then perhaps it can contain the one, namely the infinite potentiality for existence, in its actualized form, and the other, namely, the infinite potentiality for nonexistence, in its potential but unactualized form. Yet, as Crescas continues in Aristotle's name, any potentiality that is possible is one that might be actualized. If, then, the entity's infinite potentiality for nonexistence were actualized while its infinite potentiality for existence were also actualized, the entity would be, *per impossibile*, both actually existent always and actually nonexistent always.

[18] Because a proposition does not entail its inverse, the conclusion, "Whatever comes to be passes away," does not follow from the proposition, "No anteriorly eternal existent thing (i.e. no existent thing that has not come to be) can pass away. Perhaps, then, what Crescas intends by, "And in this way," is that the same reasoning that Aristotle employs with respect to an existent that has not come to be may be applied to an existent that has come to be: if potentiality is possibility, and if possibility is not merely theoretical, then, just as an existent that has not come to be cannot have the potentiality for infinite nonexistence—for if that potentiality were actualized, the existent would both exist and not exist always—so, too, an existent that has come to be cannot have the potentiality either for infinite existence or for infinite nonexistence. For if either potentiality were realized, then that which is now existent but was previously nonexistent would exist and not exist at the same time. Hence, whatever comes to be passes away.

[19] Since infinities are not larger or smaller than each other, the infinity before existence and the infinity of existence would collapse into one another. The only way coming-to-be is possible, then, is if both the time before existence and the time of existence are finite. In other words, because the time of nonexistence ends and the time of existence then begins, neither time is infinite. And if the time of existence is finite, then that which comes to be necessarily passes away.

that has this property both comes to be and passes away, inasmuch as it contradicts both extremes.

In addition, things that do not come to be and do not pass away cannot be this way accidentally but only in respect of their natures. For it is because of the difference in the natures of things that some admit coming-to-be and passing-away and some do not. Therefore, if this nature [viz. the nature of the celestial body] were such that it were subject to coming-to-be and passing-away, it could not continue on eternally unless the nature of the possible could undergo a change to the necessary.

Furthermore, it would appear through induction regarding individual existents, that everything that comes to be passes away and everything that passes away comes to be. Therefore it is necessary for Aristotle that the celestial body, which is not subject to passing-away, also not be something that comes to be.

In respect of matter, they offered two arguments. The first proceeds as follows. Prime matter neither comes to be nor passes away. For if it were to come to be, it would require a substratum from which to come to be. But since prime matter can exist only in potentiality, it itself would have to be the substratum; otherwise, it would have to exist in actuality, for it is inconceivable that there be a substratum for that which does not exist in actuality.[20] Once it is established that prime matter does not come to be, and the well-known proposition that it is impossible for prime matter to be without form is conjoined to this, it follows necessarily, on their view, that there is an anteriorly eternal universe.[21]

The second proceeds as follows. Were prime matter not anteriorly eternal, and the totality of the universe came to be absolutely, then it would have to have come to be from nothing. But this is absurd. For the coming-to-be of a body from nothing is an absurdity. According to this assumption [viz. of the absolute coming-to-be of the universe], it is also necessary that there be empty space. Similarly, the coming-to-be of a body from matter devoid of form is impossible in itself, for matter cannot be devoid of form. Therefore, they deemed it necessary that body not come to be.

In respect of the agent, they offered three arguments. The first is that they noted that when an agent in potentiality transitions to actuality, it is necessary that there be a change. This is especially so if it was in potentiality for an infinite time, which is necessitated if we assume that the universe comes to be. Yet change cannot be attributed to God.

The second is in respect of the relation of the agent [to the action], for indeed a relation to the created action would itself be created. Yet this, too, is impossible with respect to God—especially since it is a puzzle as to what might have brought God to act at this particular time rather than at another.

The third is that, since God is the law of existents, and as such is that which orders and directs them, it would not be legitimate to regard Him as independent of

---

[20] Since a substratum is that from which that which exists in actuality comes to be, and since prime matter is essentially potentiality—indeed, it is putatively the potentiality from which everything actual comes to be—it follows that prime matter cannot have a substratum, for if it did, it would be actual. And since it cannot have a substratum, prime matter cannot come to be.

[21] If prime matter cannot come to be and also cannot exist without form, then the universe, as formed matter, must have been in existence always.

existents. For an intelligible that has no substratum outside the soul is thought to be a fiction.[22] This is the case even more if God is the mover specifically of the first of the spheres, to which [if the universe came to be] He would be at one time connected and at another not. Aristotle further reinforced his view with the words of the ancients, who posited the heavens as the abode of God, by virtue of their eternity.

These are the arguments with which those who believe in anterior eternity supported their view. This is what we intended in this chapter.

Chapter II

WE shall review the responses of the Rabbi of the *Guide* to them, and then his arguments to establish absolute creation.

What follows are the Rabbi's responses to the arguments with which the believers in eternity thought to support the eternity view. He offered first a general response to the arguments they formulated in respect of time, in respect of motion, in respect of the celestial body, and in respect of matter. The foundation of these arguments is [he said] the analogy between partial coming-to-be and comprehensive coming-to-be. It is self-evident, however, that this analogy is invalid—as he sought to show by way of illustration. It is evident that these arguments [advanced by the believers in eternity] do not provide the truth with regard to this issue.

With regard to the first of the arguments in respect of the agent, he said that, even if it is true, in the case of material things, that if they act at one time and not at another they inevitably undergo change as well as transition from potentiality to actuality, there need not be change in the case of incorporeal things. He brought as proof the active intellect which acts at one time but not at another and nevertheless does not change.

With regard to the second argument he also responded by saying that creating a relation does not constitute a change in the case of incorporeal things. To the question of what brings such a thing to act at one time and not at another, he responds that the question is illegitimate when the will has no further end for the sake of which it acts. Since God's will has no end outside itself, the nature of His will necessitates that He act whenever He so wishes.

With regard to the third, here, too, the solution is simple. It is as follows. If the law [of the existents] were acquired from them, there would be grounds for this objection. But since this law is bestowed upon the existents by God, it is not implausible that their law be true in Him even before they have existence outside the soul. Even if we assume that He is the mover of the sphere, this moving is solely an act of will and has no other cause. This is the sum of the Rabbi's responses to those arguments.

In order to *support* creation, the Rabbi offered the following two arguments. The first is taken from the fact that the celestial bodies differ from one another, despite sharing the same matter. For the cause of there being a difference among elements and compounds despite their also sharing the same matter is evident to anyone who has studied physics. In the case of compounds, the difference is on account of

---

[22] The universe—the totality of existents—is viewed here as the substratum of God qua intelligible. An intelligible that has no anchor outside the mind has no reality; it would be the mind's invention.

blending and mixing; in simples, it is on account of their proximity to or remoteness from the periphery [of the sphere]. But the difference among the celestial bodies, whether in respect of their motion, or in respect of their acceleration and slowing down, or in respect of the conjunction of the various natures—of planets, on the one hand, which give light but are not transparent and are at rest, and of spheres, on the other hand, which are transparent but do not give light and do move, despite sharing the same matter—cannot possibly be attributed to anything but a will that brings them into being and creates them. And even more is this the case if we accept Ptolemaic astronomy, which posits things that are contrary to nature, such as the eccentric and the epicycle.

The second is taken from a proposition accepted by the Philosopher, namely, that from a simple one nothing can derive but a simple one. Since the intellects emanate via cause and effect, the last one would necessarily have been characterized by unity and simplicity: multiplicity in any respect could not pertain to it, except from the perspective of its existing by both necessity and possibility. Consequently, it is impossible that the sphere, which is a body composed of matter and form, emanates from the last intellect by necessity. The only remaining option is that it comes to be via the will and intention of one who intends. To claim that something is intended by an intender yet is not created is self-contradictory. It is necessary then that the universe, in its totality and in its parts, be created from absolute nothingness. Time, too, is in the class of created things. This is the way of the true tradition, which it is both fitting and required that we follow. It is our inheritance bequeathed to us by the fathers of the world, Abraham and Moses, peace be upon them.

This is what may be understood from the words of the Rabbi as found in his responses and his arguments. This is what we wished to accomplish in this chapter.

Chapter III

WE shall review the proofs, arguments, and responses of R. Levi in support of creation in accordance with his conception of it.

Because R. Levi's responses are based on his view regarding creation, we wished to begin by reviewing it. He maintains that the universe and its parts, including time, are created—though not from absolute nothingness but rather from an anteriorly eternal body stripped of all form and devoid of any stable shape. What brought him to this view of creation is that everything that is found in the universe, both in its totality and in its parts, has all the features of things that come to be insofar as they come to be. In investigating the properties of things that come to be, we discovered that there are three.

The first is that it is possible for that which comes to be to have a final cause. For according to what is thought, to say of what does not come to be that it is for the sake of a certain end is self-contradictory. For that reason, no final cause is posited in geometry, for it is not the act of an agent.

The second is that it is possible for that which comes to be to contain things that are not necessary for it essentially. But it is not possible for there to be in that which does not come to be anything that is outside its nature. For if it contained things other than through its nature, they would necessarily be accidental. But being accidental is impossible for things that do not come to be but are permanent. For the accidental is not permanent.

The third is that it is possible for that which comes to be to contain in its essence things that are for the sake of something else. But since it is not feasible for that which does not come to be to have a final end, it is certainly true that it will not have an end that is for the sake of something else.

Once all this was established for him, he arranged his proofs and reached his conclusion based on the generally acknowledged intrinsic order of the celestial bodies, in which these bodies are at the height of perfection in perfecting the [inferior] existents, such that if the order of the celestial bodies were even slightly impaired, those existents would pass away. It is evident that, for example, the distance of the celestial body from the earth, the distance between the various [celestial bodies], the size of the planets, their order and their place in their spheres, their span, the difference in their radiance, and many other such phenomena, have a final cause. It has thus become necessary for him[23] that the celestial bodies are the work of an agent.

Once it was proved for him that the celestial bodies are the work of an agent, it was necessitated that they be created absolutely, as is established by the first feature associated with coming-to-be. The number of proofs in this matter will be the number of things of which it is proved that they are for some end.

Since it was established as well that the nature of the celestial body is one, yet there are found in the celestial bodies things which, from the perspective of their nature, are not necessary for them, such as their variation in quantity—whether in motion, in brightness, or in transparency, as was previously attested in the Rabbi's proofs—it was necessitated for R. Levi, too, that they be created, as was established by the second feature associated with coming-to-be.

Since it was established as well that everything found in the celestial bodies, for example, their distances and their inclinations and the variation in the radiance of the stars, is for the sake of something else, namely, to perfect the inferior existents—this is the third feature associated with coming-to-be—it was also necessitated for him that they be created.

Since it might indeed be thought, however, that things act on something else insofar as the latter emanates from them constantly—as, for example, in the cases in which the celestial bodies' motions emanate from their apprehension of the laws of existents, and in which light emanates from luminous bodies—an objector might argue that, even if it is established of the celestial body that it is the act of an agent, it is not thereby established that it is created. For its existence could flow from the agent constantly, in which case it would be established that it is the result of the act of an agent, even if it is not created.

R. Levi made a concerted effort to resolve this objection. He said that it is not feasible to draw this sort of analogy except to accidents that do not exist in themselves, such as motion and light. But in the case of things that do exist in themselves, it is untenable in every respect. For the assumption that that which exists in itself

---

[23] Reading with the manuscripts, חיב אצלו, rather than חיב שתאמת אצלו, "it thus becomes necessary that it be confirmed for him."

constantly emanates from something else yields many absurdities. Among them is that things come to be from nothing and pass away into nothing; that time is composed of instants; that the celestial bodies do not exist in actuality; and that there is no continuous motion.

For indeed our assumption that the existence of the spheres emanates constantly from God entails that the spheres pass away immediately upon their emanation.[24] For if we were to say that God brings them about from previously existent spheres, there would be no act, for they are then always in some mode of existence.[25] Moreover, it would be necessary that they be at one instant both coming to be and passing away. For if we posit them coming to be at one instant and passing away at a contiguous instant, motion would not be continuous. And it would be necessary, too, that one instant succeed another, and that time be composed of instants. Since the existence of the spheres could not persist for more than one instant, the spheres would not exist in actuality.

These absurdities and many others besides are entailed by our assumption that the spheres emanate constantly from God. It is therefore necessary that they were created by choice and will.

After this was established for R. Levi, he proved that time, too, is among the created things. From this it became evident that the view of some of the ancients was absurd, since they believed that one universe succeeded another ad infinitum.

The way he proved that time is created is as follows. First, he posited the idea found in the *Physics* that time is a continuous quantity whose substratum is not a specific thing—that is to say, its substratum is motion. Even if time is attributed specifically to diurnal motion, this is a matter of convention and not of nature. For before and after can be measured with respect to any motion whatsoever—and this is time.

It was proved there as well that time exists between potentiality and actuality. For past time acts in accordance with the rule of actuality, and future time with that of potentiality. For whatever is in potentiality will invariably be spoken of in terms of the future.

It is established as well that it contains no essential plurality. For if it contained plurality, there would be present in it defined extremities, as is the case with individual things, and it would be impossible for the extremities to be midpoints. But extremities that exist in time can be midpoints. And therefore what is necessitated is that time be one in essence.[26]

When this too was posited, R. Levi proceeded to prove that time is finite. He proved this in several ways. One is by saying that it was already supposed that time is in the category of quantity. And quantity qua quantity is finite insofar as it measures

---

[24] If the spheres are constantly emanating, that can only be because they lack existence in themselves and so lack any sort of permanence.

[25] If the emanation proceeds from already-existing spheres, then the emerging spheres exist already in potentiality and one may no longer speak of them as the act of an agent. Therefore, the objector's attempt to cast constant emanation as an alternative to creation which would nevertheless count as the act of an agent fails.

[26] In the case of individual things, their extremities do not serve as midpoints for other things. In the case of time, however, the end of any segment can be the midpoint of a larger segment because time is, as Gersonides puts it, one in essence; it is not composed of discrete parts.

and limits that which is quantified. He concluded, in accordance with the first syllogistic figure, that time is finite.[27]

Even though the major premise is self-evident, nevertheless it is further verified by our review of the [various] species of quantity and our finding that all of them—the solid, the surface, the line, and the place[28]—are finite. Even if number can be infinitely increased, nevertheless it is infinite only in the act of increasing or in the act of division. In all other species [of quantity], however, finitude is always preserved. It is therefore evident that time is finite.

Once this was established for him, he deduced that time is created. For it is impossible to say that before this finite time there is another finite time, and so on, ad infinitum. For it was already posited that time is one and continuous and contains no plurality in its essence.

The Philosopher sought to draw a parallel between the infinity that applies to measure and number and that which applies to time. He said that what these suggest is that the existence of infinity applies to that which is in potentiality. Therefore, since the existence of time is not in actuality, it must have infinite existence.

Aristotle committed two errors here [according to Gersonides]. The first is that he used "infinite" equivocally. For in the case of number and measure, infinity is predicated of the act of increasing, which is one of the properties of quantity. But in the case of time, infinity is predicated of the quantity itself. Second, in the case of measure and number, infinity is predicated of its increasing, which is a pure potentiality. But in the case of time, it is predicated of the past, which conforms to the rule of the actual.

We therefore say that the reason body and measure are necessarily finite is not that they exist only in actuality, as he imagined. For if so, it would be possible for time, which was posited not to be completely in actuality, to be infinite. But it is because of the nature of quantity [that body and measure must be finite]. Therefore it is necessary in the case of time that it be absolutely finite and created.[29]

Another support for the finitude of time is that it is proved by induction. For body and all its properties, in all categories, are essentially finite. Since time is consequent upon motion, and motion is consequent upon the moving thing, and the moving thing is a body, it appears that by necessity time is essentially finite; it can be without end only accidentally. He expanded on this proof to establish that body and all its properties are essentially finite. We have no need, however, to deal with this matter here. For it may be established with minimal study by anyone who studies physics. We shall return to where we were in the order of his proofs to establish that time cannot be infinite.

---

[27] The first syllogistic figure is one in which the middle term is the subject of the major premise and the predicate of the minor premise. In this case: All quantity is finite; time is a quantity; therefore, time is finite. "Quantity" is the middle term.

[28] Fisher seeks to correct the text by changing "place" to "point," נקדה. A point, however, is not a quantity.

[29] Body and measure are finite because of the nature of quantity—not because they exist in actuality. If they were finite because they exist in actuality, it could not be inferred that time is finite, since time does not exist fully in actuality. Time, however, is also related to the nature of quantity; that is why it is finite.

Another of these is that it is established that celestial bodies vary in their motion in terms of swiftness and slowness, since it was shown that the diurnal sphere is faster than the sphere of the fixed stars. It is necessarily impossible that past time be infinite, when we combine this proposition with another one that is self-evident, namely, that there is no infinity greater than another infinity. For, everything, whether swift or slow, would revolve an infinite number of times, and it would then follow that there can be no fast or slow, contrary to what appears to the senses.

Another is that, if past time were infinite, it would be necessary that the moon be eclipsed for an infinite amount of time. And so, too, the sun. And since each infinity is equal to every other infinity, it follows that the luminaries would always be eclipsed.

Another is that, since it is proved with respect to time that its parts are homogeneous, it is fitting that the category of "when" pertain in the same way to any part of time whatsoever. But if it is supposed that past time is infinite, there will be one time to which the category of "when" will not apply, insofar as it is infinite. But it has been posited that the category of "when" should pertain to all parts of time in the same way.[30]

Another is that time is continuous and comes to be in tandem with the coming-to-be of motion as it is occurring. That which comes to be, insofar as it comes to be, must continually increase so long as the coming-to-be persists. Thus time increases with the coming-to-be of motion. But since we posited past time as infinite, motion could have no effect on the increase in time, for even if we were to subtract some part of the motion, the time would neither increase nor decrease.[31]

Another is that time measures motion as it is occurring. That which measures must be limited and finite.

Another is that, if past time were infinite, this infinity could not be arrived at by our positing one time, and then, after it, another time, and so on, ad infinitum. For a past infinity could not be created unless we were to posit one time, and then, *before* it, another time, and so on, ad infinitum, such that the coming-to-be of time would be a function of going back in time. Yet this is evidently absurd, for it was already supposed that the potentiality [of time] stands only in relation to what comes later and not in relation to what precedes.

Another is that, since it is the time that comes later that is fully in potentiality, it is more appropriate that *it* be infinite. Thus, when it is proved that its limit is forever fixed, this characterization will apply all the more to past time.

Another is that, if past time is infinite, then the motion moving in it is infinite. Yet it is evident that time is the number of the motion of the celestial body in respect of before and after, when conceived as a whole.[32] Since it is proved of the celestial body that it is created, it is necessary that time be created.

---

[30] If time is infinite, there will always be time that cannot be specified as a particular "when."

[31] Infinity does not grow larger or smaller.

[32] Time makes it possible to speak of a before and after in the motion of the celestial body. This argument regards time and motion as mutually dependent. If time were anteriorly infinite, the motion of the celestial body would be anteriorly infinite as well. Since the celestial body is created, however, and its motion therefore anteriorly finite, so, too, the time that numbers it—so that it has a before and after—is created and anteriorly finite.

Just as R. Levi established [creation] in respect of time, he did so as well in respect of motion, using similar proofs.

He went on to establish that it is apparent from the emergence of the earth that it is created, since it is characterized by the properties of coming-to-be that were mentioned earlier. For it indeed appears that the end for the sake of which this part of the earth [viz. the visible part] emerged was the coming-to-be of the inferior existents in it.[33] It is evident that the natures of the elements water and earth do not account for the emergence of the earth. On the contrary, their natures mandate that the earthly element be surrounded by water. The nature of the celestial bodies cannot account for it either. This is evident to anyone who has any training at all in mathematics and astronomy. It is therefore evident that the emergence of the earth is created. It is therefore necessary that the species, at the inception of their coming-to-be, are created by something outside their own species.

Once this was established for him, he garnered support as well from the fact that the sciences were only recently perfected. For since human beings are naturally drawn to the sciences, it is not credible that the human species is anteriorly eternal yet its sciences only recently created. The same is true of the divine Torah: laws were egregiously defective until God sought to make Israel meritorious [through the Torah's commandments], but it is highly implausible that an infinite amount of time would have passed during which laws were defective.

The same may be seen from the variety of languages. It is evident that they are conventional, as was explained in its place. It is necessary that those who agreed on the conventions preceded their agreement chronologically. It is not credible that an infinite amount of time would have elapsed without an agreement, inasmuch as people are naturally political and require community with others for the means of survival.

This should suffice with respect to the universe's status as created. But with regard to R. Levi's view that it is created from an anteriorly eternal body devoid of all form, he offered the following proof. It is indeed thought that the nature of disjunction dictates that creation be either something-from-something or something-from-nothing. The impossibility of the from-something alternative has already been established by the force of what we have said. For the something would have had to have some form, for matter is never devoid of form. And if it had form, then it would have been subject to natural motion and rest, and that entails an anteriorly eternal time, whose impossibility we have established. With respect to something-from-nothing, [its impossibility] is evident for several reasons.

One of these is that the coming-to-be of a body from nothing is hard to conceive. For even if the active form creates forms out of nothing, nevertheless, it must bestow form on matter that is prepared to accept it. And, generally, it would bestow a form that resembles something in its own essence. How, then, could it bestow corporeality, when there is no relation at all between them?[34]

---

[33] One of the properties of created things is their having an end outside themselves.
[34] That is, between the incorporeal active form and corporeality.

Another is that it would be necessary that there be empty space before there could be a universe. And this is because the empty spaces in which the universe resides must contain the possibility for a body to reside in them. For empty space is nothing but this.

Another is that, since the unoccupied space is prepared to receive the influence of the efficient cause in a uniform way, it is necessary that the body emanate uniformly throughout the unoccupied space. And so, the body would be infinite. For there is nothing from the perspective of the agent, and nothing from the perspective of the unoccupied space, on account of which the form would be received in just one specific place.[35]

Another is that it is inevitable that before the world existed it had to be either necessary, possible, or impossible. If it were necessary, its being could not fail to be. If it were impossible, it could not come to be. Therefore, it could only have been possible. But possibility requires a substratum.

Another is that, since the agent and the receiver of the action are correlatives, and since correlatives are found together, it follows that when the agent is in potentiality, the receiver of the action is also in potentiality. But the receiver of the action that is in potentiality is a body. It is therefore necessary that there be a body before the coming-to-be of the universe.

Once it is established that coming-to-be, whether as something-from-something or as something-from-nothing, is impossible, it becomes necessary that it be something-from-something in one respect, and something-from-nothing in another. In being something-from-something it is from a body. In being something-from-nothing it is from a body devoid of all form.

In this way all difficulties are resolved. For the difficulty that they [viz. those who oppose creation] posited with respect to something-from-something was on account of motion. But when we posit it as devoid of all form, it can have no motion. The difficulties that were related to the assumption of something-from-nothing stemmed from their failure to posit a substratum for this coming-to-be. Once we posit a substratum, all the difficulties vanish.

R. Levi therefore accepted the proposition that the creation of the world was from an anteriorly eternal body, stripped of all form and not preserving any stable shape—that is, it was devoid of a nature from which there could derive a body that preserves its shape. His conception of creation was that [God] made one part that would preserve its shape, namely, the celestial body, and created in it planets and spheres; and one part that would not preserve its shape, and this He placed among the eccentric spheres whose centers differ, in order that there be no empty space between them. In this way, this sage remained true to his view of the astronomy of the spheres. The reason it is possible for God to bestow different forms on a matter which is the same in itself is that coming-to-be is something willed.

Once this was settled for him, he took up the task of resolving the difficulties that the believers in anterior eternity raised, as we saw in Chapter I of this Book, after first

---

[35] Gersonides, like Aristotle, rejects both empty space and infinite body.

resolving some of the difficulties he raised with respect to his own hypothesis. The latter are the following.

First, it is indeed necessary, with respect to this body, either that nothing remain of it at creation or that something remain. If something remains, it would appear that this excess is superfluous. And if nothing remains, how would it happen that its size would coincide with the size of the universe? For as it appears, the size of living things is limited. So, if the body has a certain dimension, it must have the nature of an individual.[36] Furthermore, it could not fail to be spherical, or to have another shape, prior to the coming-to-be. If it is spherical, it is puzzling that its sphericity happens to coincide with that of the universe. And if it is not spherical, there would have to be empty space, for we assume that God assembled it and gave it a spherical shape.[37]

Second, the coming-to-be of the universe would have to be accidental, for it just so happened that this body was of the measure required to perfect the universe. For if it were not for this accident, God would be such that nothing could emanate from Him.[38]

Third, for there to have been something anteriorly eternal along with and other than God is utter nonsense. For it would then appear that there were, God forbid, two powers.

Fourth, it would indeed seem that this body must be either in motion or at rest. Either way, it must have a nature and a form, which is the opposite of what was supposed.

Fifth, matter cannot be devoid of form. It certainly cannot be devoid of form for an infinite amount of time.

Sixth, a thing can be deficient in its nature only for a short time, and the time during which it is in its perfect character is very long. Yet according to our hypothesis, the body would be in its deficient state for an infinitely longer time than that during which it is perfect.

Seventh, we find in every coming-to-be that it does not arise from just anything. Therefore, how is it conceivable that all the natures in the universe came to be from one matter? And who compelled this matter to receive all these forms?

Eighth, it appears that there are upper places and lower places. If so, there must already be elements and a celestial body.

Ninth, what is it that caused the agent to act at that moment? Was there some new knowledge created in Him that He did not previously have, or was there some obstacle that was removed? All of this is evidently absurd.

These are the difficulties that he raised with respect to his own hypothesis. He resolved them in the way that I will now explain.

---

[36] If the universe is generated from an original body with no remainder, and if it has a precise and fixed size, then the body that generates it must be like it in having that very precise and fixed size. But if the original body has a precise and fixed size, then it, like all living things, is an individual, and so is not devoid of form.
[37] If the first body was not spherical but had some other shape, and God subsequently formed from it the spherical universe, then empty space would have had to emerge to surround the spherical universe.
[38] God would be powerless to create the universe if the anteriorly eternal body from which it was formed did not happen to be sufficiently large to contain it.

To begin: Since this body is not the work of an agent, even if something of it were to remain after the coming-to-be of the universe, none of it would be superfluous, for it is impossible for it to have a determinate end. Thus is the first difficulty resolved.[39]

As for the second, it is not necessitated. For there is no defect in the benefactor if there is nothing to receive the benefaction. Just as there is no defect in God if He does not create the universe when there is no body at all to receive creation, so there is no defect in Him if He does not create a universe when the body receiving the creation lacks the requisite measure.

As for the third, it does not follow from the body's being anteriorly eternal that it is a divinity. For divinity does not stem from a thing's being anteriorly eternal but rather from the force of its exalted stature such that the good and the order of existence might emanate from it. The body in question was in its essence deficient to the utmost and devoid of goodness. Since the more a thing acquires goodness the more perfect it becomes—which is why the animal is more perfect than the plant, and the human being than the animal—this body, insofar as it is utterly deficient, is very far from divinity.

Regarding the fourth, according to which a body must be either at rest or in motion, this applies only to natural bodies. A body that is totally devoid of any nature cannot properly be subject to natural motion and rest—just as it is improper to apply vision or blindness to a stone.

Regarding the fifth, it appears that it is not implausible that there be a body with no specific form; indeed, it might be necessary. For although we find form with matter, as in the case of hylic forms, we find, too, form without matter, as in the case of incorporeal forms. It is thus fitting that there be matter without form—even though matter without form would not be possible for actual existents since, insofar as they are garbed in primary qualities that serve as forms even for the elements, they could not be absolutely stripped [of form].[40] Moreover, what was said of it, to the effect that it would have to have been without form for an infinite amount of time, is false. For it was already said that there was no time before the creation of the universe.

As for the sixth, it was indeed established that the notion of a longer time of perfection [as compared to deficiency] is relevant for something that has a nature, because that nature will lead it and direct it to perfection. But it was already posited of this body that it does not have a nature. And it was also established that this body did not persist in its deficiency for any length of time prior to the creation of the universe.[41]

Regarding the seventh, there can be no analogy between partial and comprehensive coming-to-be—especially when the latter is volitional. For the comprehensive coming-to-be is attributed to the will of God and He confers on things the nature to receive His will. In addition, we have already recognized the force of the subjugation of matter to the agent of incorporeal form, in how wondrously living things are created by the moving of matter, so that selected from it is precisely that which is

---

[39] To speak of something being superfluous is to presuppose purpose. If there was never any purpose associated with this body, there can be no place for concern that any left-over part of it is superfluous.

[40] Gersonides contends, according to Crescas, that, although it is true of all actual things that they have form—even the basic elements, namely, the hot, the cold, the wet, and the dry, bear qualities and so have form—there is in principle no reason to exclude the possibility of formless matter.

[41] Since there was no time before the creation of the universe, it is senseless to speak about how much longer the universe was in a state of imperfection than in a state of perfection.

suited for the making of each organ. And so, too, in the case of voluntary motions, as when a man, in his envisaging of sounds, marvelously moves his vocal cords without consciously thinking about them.

Concerning the eighth, upper and lower are not a matter of spatial relations but a matter of where light and heavy things are located. It was already assumed of that body that it is neither heavy nor light.

Concerning the ninth, since the end of creation is benefaction and grace, the material first principle indeed necessitates that this benefaction have a temporal beginning. Therefore, the question of why God did not initiate its coming-to-be sooner is unreasonable. For no matter what the reply, the question would be asked: and why not sooner?

This is the extent of R. Levi's resolution of these difficulties. He resolved the difficulties raised by the class of believers in anterior eternity in the following way.

Concerning the first of the difficulties in respect of time, it does not follow from our saying that there was time after there was no time that there was a time before this time. For even if we use words that indicate time, time is not what we intend by them; what we intend is that time was created and it was not anteriorly eternal.

To be sure, the definition that they agreed upon is that every coming-to-be occurs in time. Yet if time came to be, it is impossible that it came to be in time. Moreover, there are cases in which something created is not created in time. For example, the change that is implicitly created in that which is changed is not itself in time. Since time is an accident consequent upon every change, and is created with its creation, it is necessary that if it comes to be it does not come to be in time.

The second is in respect of the instant. The instant that is the beginning of coming-to-be does not divide the before from the after. Even if this is beyond the reach of the imagination, it is still true. For not everything that is beyond the reach of the imagination is false. For we say that an instant has two aspects. One is that it divides the before from the after. The other is that it limits a given part of time. Indeed, the instant's being in potentiality does not require that it divide the before from the after. For the nature itself of time entails that it is impossible for the instant to be in actuality concurrent with that of which it is the beginning. For as was said earlier, time itself cannot exist in simultaneity.[42]

The resolution of the third is simple. For the precedence of potentiality to actuality obtains in the case of partial coming-to-be, for in this case potentiality resides in a substratum and time exists. But in the case of comprehensive coming-to-be this is not the case, for time is created along with its creation. Furthermore, when the potentiality is in the that-from-which, the existence of time need not pertain to its existence.[43] For there is as yet no motion.

---

[42] With respect to the future, time does not exist as an actual beginning instant, but rather as bare potentiality.

[43] Gersonides speaks of two kinds of potentiality: that in which the change occurs in the that-from-which, and that in which the change occurs between the that-from-which and the that-to-which. Comprehensive coming-to-be involves the kind of potentiality in which the change occurs in the that-from-which, in which case there is as yet no motion, and hence there is not as yet any time. See *Wars of the Lord*, VI. i. 23.

In response to the first of the difficulties concerning motion it may be said that the fact that locomotion precedes [all other forms of motion] in the case of partial motion does not necessitate that it precede comprehensive coming-to-be. Here the motion of coming-to-be is the one that precedes.

With respect to the second, in which we posited that the motion of coming-to-be is the first motion, it does not follow necessarily that motion precede it. First, [it does not follow] from the perspective of the agent, since God acts in an instant after not having acted. Even if we were to concede that His acting involves a transitioning from potentiality to actuality, it is nevertheless not necessary that there be any change in Him. For whereas the transition from potentiality to actuality in that which is acted upon in being acted upon does involve change, this is not the case with respect to the agent in acting. For otherwise, there would be two simultaneous motions: one of being moved and one of causing-to-move. Yet it was already established in the *Physics* that there is only one motion in the substratum, though it be in two respects. That is, when it is attributed to the mover it is called "causing-to-move" and when it is attributed to the moved it is called "being moved."[44]

Nor [does it follow] from the perspective of that which is acted upon. Even if it is the case, as concerns possibility as it exists in nature, that a change must precede the creation of the possibility of change, it is not necessitated, in the case of possibility from the perspective of the simple will, that it must be preceded by a change. Rather, the possibility of change is a relation that is the same at every time. Therefore it is not justified to require with respect to this possibility that change precede it.

In response to the first of the difficulties in respect of the celestial body, even if the case of partial coming-to-be is a matter of transitioning from one contrary to the other, this is not necessitated in the comprehensive coming-to-be, and, a fortiori, not in the coming-to-be that is attributable to will.

Concerning the second. When one thing has potentiality for two conflicting results, it is warranted to say that each of the two potentialities is limited by the potentiality contiguous to it[45] that is transitioning to its result. If, indeed, we were to maintain that, by necessity, the time during which this potentiality is transitioning to coming-to-be is infinite, there would be grounds for this objection. But what was posited is that the universe came to be by will, without the will's having been applied to it before it came to be.[46] It is also not impossible that the universe will continue on eternally, since there are no causes for its passing-away. Even its being nonexistent for an infinite amount of time by will does not contradict the possibility of its existence, since its existence is the product of will.

---

[44] Although we speak of the motion of the mover as well as of the motion of the moved, there is in fact only one motion. And it is only the moved that is changed.

[45] Fisher has בכח הקרוב, vocalized as: *bekhoaḥ haqeruv*. He includes in brackets the possibility that it should be vocalized: *bakoaḥ haqarov*. The Florence manuscript seems to settle the issue in favor of the bracketed reading, followed here, since it says: בכח אשר הקרוב.

[46] Crescas here expounds Gersonides' view that, since there is nothing absurd in supposing that an act of will by God brought the celestial body into existence, we need not attribute to the celestial body an infinite potential both to exist and to not exist. The problems that arise when the conflicting infinite potentialities for existence and nonexistence are thought to transition to actuality over infinite time dissipate once it is posited that an act of will brought the celestial body into existence.

What strengthened his argument is that if it is supposed that both existence and nonexistence are possible, and it is supposed as well that one of those possibilities is realized eternally, an absurdity will arise. The absurdity, however, arises only if we suppose that its realization is necessary. But if we suppose it to be merely possible, no absurdity follows.[47]

Another notion strengthened his argument. It is [supposed] necessary that the universe be both existent and nonexistent simultaneously, for if not, an infinite amount of time will be a part of another infinite amount of time. But even if we concede that the universe was nonexistent for an infinite amount of time, this conclusion is not necessitated, except in the way that it would be necessitated for the Philosopher who maintains anterior eternity. For if we assume an instant that separates the before from the after, with each segment being infinite, each will be a part of the composite whole which is similarly infinite. From the perspective of its being finite, however, this is possible.[48]

His argument was strengthened as well by the following. It is indeed thought that the intermediate between that which is eternally existent and that which is eternally nonexistent is that which comes to be and passes away. This is not so, however. The true intermediate is that which is existent sometimes and nonexistent at other times.

He drew support for his argument as well from the nature of the celestial body. For if it had a nature that receives coming-to-be and passing-away it would be impossible for it to continue on forever. But since it was assumed that this thing has no nature other than the one that God bestowed on it in the comprehensive coming-to-be, it is not necessitated that it pass away, even if it came to be. Even if it appears in the case of individual existents that that which comes to be passes away, the same cannot be said of comprehensive coming-to-be, and especially of the celestial bodies that have no causes of passing-away—either in respect of the agent or in respect of that which is acted upon.

With regard to the difficulties in respect of matter, what is impossible in the case of prime matter is that it be devoid of form after receiving a nature and being garbed in forms. But before that, it is not impossible for that body[49] to be devoid of form, as was posited.

With respect to the second, it is not necessitated that that which comes to be arise from absolutely no body but only that it arise from a body having no form.

With regard to the difficulties concerning the agent, since divine wisdom decreed this benefaction, and since the material first principle necessitates that the universe be created in time, there is no change in God in this respect. For He exists at all times

---

[47] For Gersonides, so long as the conflicting infinite potentialities for existence and nonexistence are possible and not necessary, it is possible for the universe to come to be and then to exist forever. Only if the eternal existence of the universe were necessary could there be no potentiality for nonexistence at any time.

[48] If Aristotle allows a point—an instant—that divides the before from the after (as he must), then there is a sense in which time is finite, in that it has a limit at the start of the after. Similarly, if we regard the universe as beginning, then, although time is infinite from the point of creation on, there is a sense in which it is finite in that it has a limit at its beginning point. And even if we add infinite past time on the past side of the beginning point, there still remains a sense in which time is finite and part of it is "smaller" than the whole.

[49] Reading בגשם ההוא rather than, with Fisher, בגשם ההוה, "for the body that comes to be."

with the will to confer benefit, but it was on account of a necessity in the receiver that it was created.

Even if we were to admit that there was an infinite time in which there was no law for the existents, that would only affect our position if God derived the law from them. But since God bestows the law on them, it poses no threat.

With regard to the support the Philosopher drew from the ancients' designation of the heavens as the abode of the spiritual beings, it may be said that they did so only because the heavens are eternal and attest to the power of their originator.[50]

It is therefore especially fitting and obligatory for us to support the truth as derived from the straightforward sense of the Torah's words which attest to the validity of this view as this sage saw it and as he expounded it at great length. We chose the requisite conciseness in presenting this chapter.

Chapter IV

WE shall distinguish[51] herein as best we can that which is correct from that which is incorrect [in their positions].

Here we review with precision what was said [by the Rabbi and R. Levi], both in their responses to the arguments of the adherents of the eternity view, as well as in what they laid down as foundational via their own views.

Let me address first the general responses of the Rabbi of the *Guide*, to the arguments in respect of time, motion, the celestial body, and prime matter. These responses are correct and reveal the truth, and suffice to refute the arguments [of the advocates of anterior eternity]—not to mention that these latter arguments themselves are very weak.

The responses of the Rabbi concerning the first of the arguments in respect of the agent, however, require considerable reflection. He decisively asserted that the transitioning from potentiality to actuality does not constitute a change in the case of incorporeal entities. With regard to this point arguments may be advanced and objections raised.

For it is inconceivable for a thing to transition from potentiality to actuality without a cause being created, whether it be in the thing itself or outside it. [In the case of God], the cause could not have been outside it, because there was nothing outside it. So, the creation of the cause had to be in the thing itself. Yet the creation of a cause is a change.[52]

In addition, [he argued that] an incorporeal entity, insofar as it is incorporeal, is not subject to potentiality. So, to say that it transitions from potentiality to actuality is

---

[50] Gersonides is apparently unimpressed with Aristotle's argument from consensus among the ancients.

[51] Following the Florence manuscript's נבור, "we shall distinguish," rather than נבאר, "we shall establish/clarify," found in Fisher and in other manuscripts and in the Ferrara edition. Note that in previewing the chapters to come in this Part, Crescas uses נברר.

[52] Crescas argues against Maimonides that, although God is incorporeal, His transitioning from potentiality to actuality in creating the world does constitute a change. Since transitions from potentiality to actuality require a new cause, then, even though in this case the cause was necessarily in God himself—since at creation there was nothing in existence other than God—nevertheless, there was still a new cause. This new cause constitutes a change.

a self-contradiction. Thus, when the active intellect acts at one time and not at another, this signals only that there is a deficiency in the receiver of the action; in itself it is always active: it contains no potentiality. But in a case in which there is no deficiency in the receiver, as in the case at hand, then, when the agent does not act it is inevitable that potentiality be attributed to it.[53] Yet it has already been posited that, insofar as it is incorporeal, it is always in actuality. This is a contradiction that cannot be sustained.

His response to the second argument, which poses the question: what caused God to act at one particular time and not at another? is invalid. The reason he offered is as follows. Since God's will has no end outside itself, the nature of His will necessitates that He act as He wishes. If what the Rabbi intended was that God's will has no end outside itself, he is correct. God's will is His essence; and, just as His essence has no end outside itself to compel His existence, so, too, His will has no end outside itself. Yet the question nevertheless stands, as we shall see. If what he intended is that God's particular will to act at this time has no end outside itself, he would be attributing to God an act without an end. For even if [for the Rabbi] God's acts are generally directed toward an end—that of benefaction and grace—nevertheless, His acting at a certain time would still be an act without an end. Yet this is sheer nonsense with respect to any intelligent being, and, a fortiori, with respect to God. The question then remains: what caused God to act at one particular time and not at another?

It is not possible to settle this matter by suggesting that although God's end at that time is opaque to us, God knows why His wisdom dictated that He act at that time rather than at another. For as it appears, it is impossible that there be any end other than the will itself. For it is inevitable that, if there were another end [outside the will itself], it would be either in respect of the agent, or in respect of that which is acted upon, or in respect of something outside both the agent and that which is acted upon, such as the instruments of action. But it cannot be in respect of the agent, for God's relation to all times is the same. Nor can it be in respect of that which is acted upon, for there is nothing there but absolute nonexistence, and the agent's relation to all times is also the same. It is certainly impossible that it be in respect of something outside the agent, for there is nothing outside the agent. Furthermore, the agent does not use instruments in acting. Therefore what is necessitated is that there not be any other end in the singling out of this time but the will alone. What may be said, therefore, in this regard is that, as God's wisdom dictated that the universe be brought into existence following absolute nonexistence, it is inappropriate to seek an end for a specific time. For the relation would be the same for all times.[54]

---

[53] According to Maimonides, the universe comes into being after nonexistence at the hand of God and there is no universe and hence no receiver at the moment of creation. If so, says Crescas, God's acting at this time and not at another cannot be resolved by recourse to a deficient receiver—in the way it might be in the case of the activity of the active intellect as it acts on an existing receiver. How, then, can we avoid attributing potentiality to God?

[54] Crescas is recognizing that in the end Maimonides cannot account for why God created at one moment and not at another.

This is what it appears necessary to be aware of in connection with the Rabbi's responses.

With respect to his arguments on behalf of absolute creation, let me say first that, even if we concede that they supply the truth in this matter, they do not compel the view that creation is from total nothingness; perhaps there was anteriorly eternal matter, as Plato held, and as some rabbinic dicta, which the Rabbi cites in his book, indicate. For the arguments, when they are closely examined, do not require more than the intention of one who intends and the will of one who wills. I assert, however, that it is always open to the objector to say that they do not, in any way, require creation following nonexistence.

The first argument, which derives from differences among the celestial bodies in spite of their sharing the same matter, does not, in any way, appear to necessitate creation. For it is not impossible for things that agree in definition to differ with respect to accidents, so long as this is for a definite end. That there is a final end is something our opponent concedes with respect to natural things. As it appears, the more eminent a thing is, the more eminent its end. Therefore, that argument entails the existence of an end for the celestial bodies. Nevertheless, it is not impossible for their [diverse] existence to derive from God by necessity, along with that very end. Even if this diversity is impossible without requiring a will that wills, what would prevent that will, too, from being anteriorly eternal?[55] If only I knew.

With respect, too, to the second argument, which is based on the proposition that from a simple one only a simple one can derive, an objector might say that this does not necessitate creation. For even if this proposition necessitates a will that wills, it also implies that the will is present in a simple one, for when a will is in a composite, it appears that the will, too, is composite, since the will is distributed throughout all the parts of the composite. Therefore, what this proposition necessitates with respect to it [viz. the universe] is that, despite its being composite, nevertheless, insofar as of necessity it is one in the perfection of benefaction and grace derived from God, it is reasonable—indeed, it is fitting and necessary—that it derive from God, despite God's being simple to the utmost. Since this is so, I cannot fathom what obstacle would prevent it from deriving the perfection of benefaction from this unity by way of necessity. And if this is impossible unless there be a will that wills, what prevents this will from being anteriorly eternal? This argument, therefore, does not necessitate creation. Moreover, it is certainly the case that the creation of time is not necessitated. For it is easily shown, based on what was already discussed in Book I, that time is not the act of an agent, even if we concede that the universe is created from absolute nothingness, as the tradition would have it, and as will be explained further in what follows, God willing.

We shall now return to our promise regarding a close examination of R. Levi's words—in terms of his view, his proofs, and his responses. Let us say, first, that there is nothing in his arguments—not in a single one—to establish the truth in this matter [of creation] as he posited it. But perhaps—or not perhaps—it will be easily shown

---

[55] There is no reason to assume, Crescas argues, that, if the diversity of the celestial bodies can only be a product of will, then there must be creation. That will, too, might reach back infinitely.

that what he posited in connection with his view concerning creation is a mendacious fiction. That indeed there is nothing in all his proofs that would necessitate creation in the way he supposed will be shown through what I will now say.

All the proofs R. Levi proffered, despite their profusion, are of two kinds. The first kind is based on the properties of coming-to-be; the second kind, on the infinite.

It is evident concerning the first kind that, if an opponent were to object by saying that the properties that R. Levi assigned to coming-to-be may be assigned just as well to that which emanates from an intelligent being, all the arguments of this kind would founder. Our earlier discussion confirms that this is indeed so. For it was said of that which emanates from an anteriorly eternal intelligent being, that, insofar as it is caused by an intelligent being and the latter is its cause, it fittingly and necessarily has an end. It is not unlikely that such a thing would contain things that are not essential to its essence for the sake of something else. For this would be requisite for the intelligent first principle on account of its perfection, since benefaction and grace are a perfection in a benefactor and bestower of grace. Therefore, the proposition that that which emanates from the intelligent first principle has some end—even if it is not created—is not self-contradictory, as he assumed. For in our saying "it has some end," we do not intend that it was *created* for some end. What we intend is that it emanated from this intelligence to a certain end, even though it was not created. And, a fortiori, if we say that it emanated not by necessity but by an anteriorly eternal will, the proposition that it has some end is justified without necessitating created coming-to-be.

It is therefore evident with respect to all the proofs of the first kind that they are question-begging, since R. Levi's assumption with respect to the properties of coming-to-be is precisely what is at issue.

What is utterly surprising is that such an error escaped the perception of one as wise as R. Levi, a man of penetrating astuteness. Apparently, he was troubled by something similar when he sought to preserve the impossibility that something that has independent existence might emanate constantly from something else. For this [he thought] would entail many absurdities. The first of these is that something would come to be from nothing and pass away into nothing. Also, time would be composed of instants. Furthermore, the celestial bodies would not be in actuality. And there would also be no continuous motion.

The first absurdity that he assumed, namely, that a thing might come from nothing and pass away into nothing, even if we were to concede it, does not actually result in an absurdity. For it is not impossible that something which acts by apprehension and will alone, without instruments, would, as it wishes, bring something into being and have it pass away into nothing. Indeed, this is necessary, as will be shown in what follows, God willing.

But I say that it need not pass away at all, neither into something, nor, a fortiori, into nothing. For the apprehension and will of the one who brings-into-existence and brings-into-being are tied to His essential perpetuity, and so, a fortiori, coming-into-being will be constant. What obtains here is what obtains in the case of the bestower of forms[56] which emanates forms constantly through its apprehension and the

---

[56] The bestower of forms is the active intellect.

streaming of its light onto all things that will receive them. It follows, a fortiori, that the forms that emanate from God will be, through His apprehension, constantly sustained. For since things are disposed to receive forms to the point that, owing to their disposition, they in fact receive them, and since the streaming of the light of the forms proceeding from the bestower of forms is constant, it is not possible for their existence not to be constant. This is most evident.

Since this is so, it is evident that neither are the other absurdities that R. Levi noted necessitated. For because of the continuousness of God's apprehension and will there is necessarily continuous existence, along with the continuousness of time and of motion.

The great puzzle is how R. Levi arrived at the distinction between that which exists independently and the accidents that do not exist independently, such as the motions of the celestial bodies that emanate constantly from these bodies' apprehension of the law of existents, or the light that emanates constantly from the luminous bodies. For even if the accidents are not necessarily vulnerable to the first absurdity—for since they are accidents, it is possible that their existence comes from nothing and their passing-away goes into nothing—nevertheless, if they were to pass away, as is [presumed] necessitated for something that emanates constantly, they would be vulnerable to the other absurdities, namely, that time would be composed of instants, that motion and light would not exist in actuality, and that motion would not be continuous. But then motions that emanate from apprehensions, and light that emanates from a luminary, would also last for but a single instant.[57]

The solution to all these difficulties lies in our proposal that the emanator who bestows existence, will, a fortiori, through the continuousness of His emanating, bestow continuousness on sustained existence—whether what emanates is an accident or something independently existent. This should suffice with respect to the first kind of proofs.

With respect to the second kind of proofs, that are based on the notion of infinity, let me say, too, that there is nothing in them that necessitates [creation], and indeed nothing plausible.

First, R. Levi made assumptions about time that concur with what was shown in the book, the *Physics*. We shall not respond to these now. Even though it was established by the force of our discussion in Book I, and will be established further in this Part, God willing, that some of these assumptions are unsound, nevertheless we shall assume for now that they are sound. I shall say that the first proof is unconvincing. For the major premise, which states that quantity insofar as it is quantity is finite, is dubious. For, one who maintains that time is infinite will not grant it. R. Levi's reason, namely, that time measures and limits that which is quantified, is no reason. For, one who holds that time is infinite, even if he were to define quantity as that which measures a part of it, would simply intend the part of it

---

[57] Crescas sees no validity in Gersonides' distinction between independent existents and accidents. For if the constant emanation of independent bodies gives rise to a whole host of absurdities, the constant emanation of accidents gives rise to them as well. The only exception might be that it is not absurd for accidents—as it is for independent existents—to come into being from nothing and pass away into nothing.

that it is possible to measure. And if [the argument is that] the use of the term "quantity" indicates a definite measure, nevertheless, insofar as language is a matter of agreement, this does not hold. For the speaker did not agree to posit a name for that in time which is not perceived. And so no absurdity follows. What strengthened R. Levi's proof based on the various species of quantity is that they are all finite.

The second proof as well, which is based on an argument by analogy—since the body and all its properties are finite—does not require a response, since induction does not, in any way, provide the truth. And this is especially so since it was shown that time is not one of the properties of body, as will be explained, God willing.

The third argument, whose foundation is swiftness and slowness, is sophistical. The swift completes a number of revolutions in a certain amount of time, a number that the slower completes in a greater amount of time, for number is spoken of in terms of much and little, and time in terms of great and small. These categories, however, apply only to things that are finite, in which case it is impossible that something fast and something slow move in the same amount of time. But when time or number is infinite, neither much and little nor large and small nor equal applies. For these are the limits of measure, and measure is impossible in the case of infinite things. Therefore, no absurdity results from the swift and slow completing an infinite number of revolutions. For with respect to infinite revolutions neither large and small nor equal apply. Even though this is self-evident, it finds verification in our conceiving of the duration of these motions as anteriorly eternal, and it will not prevent the possibility that the universe emanates constantly from God in this way always.

On the basis of what has been said, the fourth proof can similarly be easily shown not to compel anything of what R. Levi imagined. For even if one infinity cannot be larger than another, it is not necessitated that the celestial luminaries be eclipsed always. The error resides in taking our assertion that one infinity cannot be larger than another to mean that they are equal, when it was established that the term "equal" does not apply to infinity. What we intended by our assertion is that infinity is not the sort of thing of which it may be said that one is larger or smaller than another. Therefore, nothing that he thought to be necessitated by this proof is in fact so necessitated.

The fifth proof is sophistical as well. For even if time is infinite, the category of "when" does not apply to it as it applies to the finite. For, any stretch of time that we would limit with a "when" would, by the very fact of being limited, be finite. This is self-evident.

The sixth proof is founded on [the notion] that time increases with the increase in motion. Yet although the increase of something infinite is impossible from one perspective, it is possible from another. [On the one hand,] from the perspective of infinity as a whole it is impossible—for large and small cannot be predicated of it; and so, too, from the perspective of the direction in which it is infinite [viz. the past, which has no starting point], it is not subject to increase, for this very reason. But [on the other hand,] from the perspective of the direction in which it is finite [viz. the future, whose starting point is now], it is both possible and necessary that it be subject to increase. Therefore, time increases from the perspective of its being finite, as motion progresses forward.

The seventh proof is rhetorical. For even if time is the measure of motion forward, part for part, it is not necessitated that time as a whole be limited and finite. For not everything that is true of something when it is separate is true of it when it is within a composite whole.

The eighth proof is without substance. For although potentiality is from the perspective of what is to come, it has already been posited that the side that is past, from which perspective time is infinite, has the status of actuality. The past is not created by positing a time, and then another time before it, but rather, through the anteriority of endless time, it has already transitioned to actuality.

The ninth is merely imagined and so requires no response.[58]

The tenth, which relates to the creation of the celestial body, is manifestly untenable, for two reasons: first, since it has not yet been established that the celestial body was created; and second, because even if we concede its creation, the creation of time is not proved. For it is possible to regard time in relation to another motion [viz. a motion other than that of the celestial body], as was explained in its place. This is true all the more if it is possible to regard it in relation to a motion that is not in actuality, as we saw earlier.

It is thus established that in all of these proofs proposed by R. Levi there is nothing that confirms that time is finite. It is evident that these same refutations apply to all his proofs regarding the finitude of motion.

It is similarly evident that the proofs he formulated with regard to the creation of the emergence of the earth, which rely on the properties of coming-to-be, fail to confirm creation as he thought, for the reasons we noted with respect to the refutation of the proofs of the first kind. For it is fitting for the objector to say that this was arranged, [arising] from an intelligent cause for a good end, by an anteriorly eternal providence and will. It is therefore evident that in all the proofs R. Levi formulated, despite their profusion, there is nothing to confirm that the truth in this matter is in accordance with what he posited.

R. Levi indeed drew support from some of the arguments he borrowed concerning the creation of the sciences and religions and languages. But even if these arguments favor creation, they do not ensure that the creation of these things could not have occurred at some other time, with the repeated destruction and creation of the human species.

Now that it has been established that in all that this sage imagined there is nothing that necessitates that which he posited, it is incumbent upon us to establish that which we promised, namely, that creation as he posited it is illusion and fiction.

He posited the creation of the universe from an anteriorly eternal body devoid of all form. Let us assume for the moment the possibility of its existence. I assert that it is impossible that it be anteriorly eternal. For it would then have to have necessary existence in respect of itself, or else be possible in respect of itself and necessary in

---

[58] All versions of the text pass directly from Crescas's response to the eighth proof to his response to the tenth and eleventh. In fact, what appears as the response to the tenth constitutes Crescas's response to the ninth proof, and what appears as Crescas's response to the eleventh is actually his response to the tenth. I have changed the numbers so that response corresponds to proof.

respect of its cause. For possible existence in all respects is inconceivable in the case of an eternal body that does not cease and cannot be made to cease.

That an anteriorly eternal body devoid of all form is necessary in respect of its cause is false for three reasons. First, it is inconceivable that its existence is necessitated in respect of its cause unless its existence is constantly emanating from the cause. For since it has permanent existence, it is inconceivable that there be a certain time in which there occurs an emanation of existence, followed by an emanation of permanence. Once this is established—and since this sage accepts, as was said earlier, that there is no way that a thing might act such that something permanently existing would emanate from it—it follows that it is impossible that its existence be necessary in respect of its cause.

Even if R. Levi would not accept this, and would point to the possibility that an extended emanation might produce something permanently existent, he would, if so, nevertheless have to concede of necessity the invalidation of all his proofs of the first kind. For it would then indeed be possible for the existence of the world to be constantly emanated from a permanent anteriorly eternal will. If so, what he devised would be illusion and fiction.

The second is that, since this body is deficient in the extreme, it is impossible that its necessary existence would derive necessarily from that which is perfect to the infinite degree of perfection—and, a fortiori, that its infinite duration would derive from it.

The third is that it is inconceivable that a thing would act upon another thing when the former, that is, the agent, is the direct opposite of that which is necessitated by it. It is therefore evident that the anteriorly eternal body does not have necessary existence in respect of its cause.

That it is not necessary in respect of itself is easily shown. First, the positing of a necessarily existent body in itself requires that it not be the effect of a cause outside itself. It follows, then, that we must posit it as a first cause. But then there would be two first causes, the one at the height of perfection, the other at the extreme of deficiency. Not only does this result—namely, that the totality of existence is not the effect of a simple one—constitute heresy and destruction [of the Torah], but it is most absurd even if we admit that it is not a deity. This is something on which there is consensus, since the world as a whole is one individual, and it is therefore necessary that it be the effect of a simple one.

Second, if we posit that this body is necessarily existent in respect of itself and is not an effect of God, how could it willingly submit to being acted upon? Would this body either intellect or sense God's perfection and its own extreme deficiency? Submission of matter to form is indeed generally tenable, inasmuch as the form constitutes it and actualizes it and is connected to it. But in the case of something whose existence suffices for itself and is not connected to another, how could there be such willingness? If only I knew.

Third, once it is posited that this body exists necessarily in itself but is a nonpreserver of its shape, it follows that it is by its essence that it is a nonpreserver of its shape. Since this is so, how could it be that someone who has no connection to it could compel it to accept the preservation of a shape in contradiction to its nature?

Fourth, the statement that it is necessarily existent and is a nonpreserver of its shape and is devoid of any nature is itself self-contradictory. For in being necessarily existent in itself, it will also by its essence be a nonpreserver of its shape. But insofar as it is by its essence that it does not preserve its shape, it follows that it indeed *has* a nature by virtue of which it is necessary that it not be a preserver of its shape.

In addition, its being a nonpreserver of its shape does not free it from having secondary qualities, such as those of softness and hardness. That it is characterized by secondary qualities but not characterized by primary qualities is hardly conceivable. This also contradicts R. Levi's supposition that it is devoid of all nature.

Once it is established that this body does not exist necessarily—either in respect of itself or in respect of its cause—it turns out that this view is invalid and self-refuting.

Furthermore, however the necessity of this body's existence is construed, the anterior eternity of time is necessitated, since time is spoken of in relation to any kind of change whatsoever. And, indeed, this body could not avoid change—that is, for all of anteriorly eternal time it was characterized by the preservation of shape in actuality, and it was subsequently changed so that it did not preserve it. Thus it rested from change in shape in actuality, and subsequently moved inasmuch as its shape then changed.[59]

Furthermore, there is inevitably a change in will for no reason. This is most absurd with respect to every intelligent being, and, a fortiori, with respect to God. But how can change in will for no reason be established? Yet change in will is self-evident. For before creation God did not will the perfecting of that deficient body, and subsequently He did will it. And that there was no reason for this change will be easily shown based on what was said earlier. For if there was a reason for the change in this will, it was necessarily either from the perspective of God or from the perspective of the body, for there was nothing else in all existence. And since God's relation to all instants is the same, and the relation of that body and all that comes to be from it to all instants is also the same, it is impossible for there to have been any reason for the change in will in singling out a particular moment.

If we have no alternative but to believe that because there is a reason behind the change in will, namely, benefaction and grace, there is no harm in saying that there is no reason for the singling out of a particular instant—something that is far from conceivable with respect to God—it is open to an objector to say that [in that case] the change in will itself has no reason. For it would indeed be more fitting that the

---

[59] The difficulty of this passage is no doubt what caused Smilevitch (2010: 973) to add "[*non-*]" before his term *conservation*, and to understand the final "it" in the penultimate sentence of this paragraph ("so that it did not preserve it" (ולא שמרה; *velo shemarah*)) to refer, not to shape (which is what one would expect) but to the *attribute* of nonconservation of shape, so: "*Or ce corps ne peut éviter le changement en cela que, pendant toute la durée éternelle, il avait pour attribut la [non-]conservation de la figure en act; puis il se modifia et perdit cet attribut.*" According to Smilevitch, then, Crescas was noticing how odd it would be if for all eternity the material body had *no* actual stable shape and then at some point suddenly did. Although it is possible that Crescas meant to say "nonpreservation," let us proceed instead on the assumption that he meant what he said. Perhaps, then, what struck him as improbable was Gersonides' view that a purportedly necessarily existent body was for all anterior eternity a nonpreserver of its shape. If so, Crescas is assuming that before this body became a nonpreserver of its shape, it was a preserver of its shape. And if so, then, when it became something that does not preserve its shape, it "rested" from the change from preserver to nonpreserver until it again was changed when it took on definite shape. If this always-existing body is one that has undergone change, then time, which presumably measures change and not only motion, must be anteriorly eternal.

will to benefaction and grace be both anteriorly and posteriorly eternal than that the body remain at the height of deficiency for an infinite amount of time.

What is surprising with respect to this sage is that with this supposition he indeed rendered it necessary that God have knowledge of the particular insofar as it is particular, namely, of this individual body that does not preserve its shape, when God acts on it with His will. He was thus ensnared by the very thing from which he fled, as was discussed in Book II. Even more absurdly: according to what he posited, God's knowledge of this body is necessarily acquired from it, that is, His knowledge is acquired from something other than himself, something whose impossibility was established with respect to God. This is especially egregious for R. Levi's view, according to which the knower is constituted by what he knows. All these absurdities follow from his assumption. This is what we intended for this chapter.

Chapter V

WE establish that the view concerning creation is true without any doubt, and its denial is tantamount to the destruction of the roots of the Torah. Nevertheless, this is not a foundation or cornerstone without which the existence of the Torah would be inconceivable.

I say, first, that even if we do compare partial coming-to-be to comprehensive coming-to-be, there is nothing in the arguments of those who endorse anterior eternity that is worthy of attention. For the arguments in respect of time, motion, and the celestial body will all be discredited by our positing creation after absolute nonexistence. This is so even if we use words that indicate time, such as "before" and "after," and, a fortiori, if it is confirmed that time is not consequent upon motion, and is not the act of an agent. So, too, the first argument, the one that is in respect of matter, will completely disintegrate, because, according to this supposition of ours, there is no primordial matter.

With respect to the second argument, R. Levi added things to compel the impossibility of something from nothing, as was discussed in Chapter III. Since the foundation of the entire argument is constructed on this fiction—and this is what blinded that man, the chief believer in anterior eternity, despite the greatness of his stature in wisdom—we have no alternative but to expand on this matter in order to reveal the error of those who so believe.

I say, first, that that from which they fled cannot be escaped in any respect. For it was already established above that there is nothing that is necessarily existent in respect of itself except God. And everything other than God—however we posit it, whether as created or as anteriorly eternal—is, in respect of itself, something possible, and it emanates from Him. There is thus neither matter nor form nor corporeality that does not emanate from Him. There is no escaping that emanation must be either a matter of necessity or a matter of will. Either way, we indeed concede a corporeal existence that emanates from form, and a form that emanates something and bestows something that is unlike itself. It cannot emanate something or bestow something on the receiver, because it bestows on the receiver its very existence.[60] We do not intend

---

[60] Until existence itself is bestowed there is no receiver on whom anything can be bestowed.

in saying "something from nothing" anything but this. For even if in saying "something from nothing" we were to mean that "nothing" is a substratum, as in "the verdigris is from bronze," this would not follow from our assumption of necessary emanation, inasmuch as [even on this assumption] the possibility of the coming-to-be of something from [absolute] nothing remains in force. But our intention in saying "something from nothing" is that it comes to be after nonexistence, and there was no previously existent subject, but rather matter and form together both emanated after nonexistence, without their having a previously existent substratum. When we say, too, that they both emanated by necessity, here, too, the intent is precisely that they had no previously existent substratum and that their entire existence emanated from God. There is no doubt that there is no difference between these two statements other than with respect to the power of God. For by positing the universe as anteriorly eternal, what is implied is infinite power through time, whereas by positing it as created, what is implied is finite power through time. Furthermore, the positing of it as anteriorly eternal compels its emanation and its permanent necessitation from God, since the relation between the agent and that which is acted upon is the same with respect to all instants. As was posited, there is no special instant at which the emanation of existence occurs, and a different time for the emanation of its permanence. It is therefore necessitated by our supposition—namely, that the permanent emanation of existence is a matter of necessity—that the infinite power is necessarily always in actuality. For power would be finite if there were a fixed relation between the agent and that which is acted upon. But when there is no relation between them, the power is necessarily infinite.

I would further say that from this supposition—namely, the necessity that existence derives from God—it is necessitated that it be a matter of will. And this for two reasons. The first is that from our positing of the necessity that existence arise from an intelligent cause, it follows that it is a matter of apprehension. Insofar as it [viz. this intelligent source] bestows existence by way of an apprehension, it is necessary that the apprehension be perfect—that is to say, an apprehension of the natural order of existents and an apprehension that bestows existence on the natural order and on the existents themselves, in general and in particular. For there is nothing that does not acquire existence and quiddity from being apprehended. Since the source is an intelligent one, it must will what it apprehends. There is no content to will other than this—that it is an apprehender that wills and bestows [existence on things] by way of intellection and an apprehension of their existence.

Second, from the agreed-upon proposition that from a simple one nothing but a simple one can derive, it follows necessarily that the emanation of existence is volitional. For since it was established that the existence of matter and corporeality emanates from God and from no other originating source, there is only one way of avoiding the difficulty of how this composite, containing matter and corporeality, emanated from a simple one at the height of simplicity. What might be said is the following. Existence as a whole is a single individual, as good in the extent of its perfection as is possible for the receiver; it is the way of the good to impart goodness in the sense of grace, for in this sense there is perfection for the good to impart; and the good, as good, is a simple one. It would then follow that, even though existence as a whole is composed of parts—and from this perspective it is many—nevertheless, the good and perfection that are found in it are found in it not insofar as it is many but rather insofar as it is one.

Furthermore—and this is self-evident—when the good is active, its perfection is greater beyond measure when it involves the exercise of will than when it operates without will. Since this is so, it is evident from our supposition that existence derives necessarily from God[61] that it must be volitional. In accordance too with what has already been established, it is necessary that this volition be constant.

Since the truth attests to itself and is in agreement from all perspectives, we can draw support for this—that is, for God's acting by will—from what is generally recognized with regard to the wonders and signs of the prophets. For even if we did not apprehend them with our senses, it is indeed fitting that we rely on what has been accepted by those of our predecessors who are trustworthy. For it is inescapable that God is the agent behind these wonders and signs. And there is no way to act on individual matter—for example, a staff's turning into a snake[62]—other than through a providential agent who exercises will. This is self-evident to one who delves into this book.

Yet with respect to how it is to be established that the agent is God, I say the following. According to what is true of signs and wonders, namely, that they obviously involve benefaction and aim at a good end and that they are created, they are necessarily the acts of an agent. It is inescapable that, if their proximate agent is not God, then it is either a prophet, or someone perfect, by means of whom they are created, or the celestial bodies, or their movers. Yet it is easily established that none of these is the agent. For with respect to man it is evident that he is not the agent. If he could be, his being the agent would be a matter of his perfection and attachment to God. Now this is not entirely impossible, and there is no doubt that man has a role to play [in wonders and signs]. But that he is the agent? Indeed a certain sect of people imagined that this could be so, for because of the perfection of man's intellect and his solitary contemplation, he understands[63] the faculties of the soul. But they were mistaken. For, one who is an agent in this way is so because of his contemplation of them [viz. the soul's faculties], and his coming to be a form for them, and therefore [their] matter of necessity yields to him, particular matter yielding to particular form. Yet it is evident that it is impossible for man to have complete knowledge of the natural order of existents, in such a way that he attains the level at which he is form to its particular matter. But only from this perspective would the possibility of his being the agent be thinkable. It is therefore evident that a man is not the agent.[64]

---

[61] The text does not say explicitly that it is from God that existence derives necessarily. It is possible that Crescas intends "the good" as this source of existence. The following paragraph, however, names God explicitly as the volitional agent.

[62] "Snake" renders תנין (tannin), which may well be a crocodile.

[63] Reading מבין "*mevin*," "understands," rather than (as per Fisher's vocalization) "*mibein*," "from amid." And so, rather than: "because of the perfection of his intellect and his solitary contemplation amid the faculties of the soul," I render: "because of the perfection of his intellect and his solitary contemplation, he understands the faculties of the soul."

[64] It is possible for man to be the form of the faculties of the soul because through his understanding of them they yield their matter to him. But in order for him to be the agent of miracles he would have to know the natural order completely, for only then would it yield to his form.

It is similarly evident that the celestial bodies or their movers are not the agents. For they bestow a natural order and arrangement on the existents, but miracles, which depart from the established arrangement and order, cannot be created by the very things that impart arrangement and order.

Even if R. Levi indeed imagined that the agent behind the wonders and signs is the active intellect, and thought he could resolve this difficulty by saying that the creation of miracles is part of the order that God ordained such that it is by means of man, in accordance with the level of attachment to God that he attains, that miracles are created, nevertheless, even if this is the very truth—that is, that miracles are part and parcel of the order and arrangement—it is impossible for man to be the agent. For the agent [of a miracle] acts on particular matter, and the particular matter obeys him despite not being so disposed. For example, it is impossible for the matter of the staff to submit to accepting the form of a snake[65] despite not being disposed to accept that form, without there being particular knowledge and a particular will—things remote indeed from the nature of the active intellect. This is especially so when the thoughts of the prophet or of the perfect man are not engaged in the act, as in the case of Elisha who revived the dead man by the man's being touched by one of Elisha's skeletal bones.[66]

Therefore what is necessitated is that the agent of miracles be God exercising individual providence and individual will. This is indeed consequent upon the arrangement and natural order that His wisdom ordained out of benefaction and grace. And this is through a permanent arrangement when there is an appropriate receiver.

It has now been established that from our supposition of necessary existence the power of something coming to be from nothing—that is, after absolute nonexistence—follows necessarily, as does volitional coming-to-be. It is fitting therefore that we mention the difficulties some have raised in connection with this supposition, in order that no confusion remain with respect to it.

They said, first, that we see in the case of all things that come to be, that the forms come to be and not the corporeality. Second, since form bestows only what is like itself, how, then, could it bestow corporeality? Third, from our positing "something from nothing," empty space is necessitated, something that was established as absurd. Yet this necessitation is evidently required on their view [i.e. on the view of those who endorse volitional coming-to-be after absolute nonexistence]. For before the universe came into existence it would have to have been already possible for the dimensions in which the universe is located to house a body. Indeed this accords with the definition of empty space, namely, that it is a place empty of body in which it is possible for there to be a body.

Fourth, since there was no specific nature before the coming-to-be of the universe, there was no possibility of there being a specific place in which the universe would be located as opposed to any other unoccupied place. Since the relation of unoccupied space to the agent is the same for all places, the following question arises of necessity:

---

[65] Or crocodile. See n. 62.

[66] 2 Kgs. 13: 21. Elisha was dead and buried, when another dead man was tossed into Elisha's grave. When the latter's body came into contact with Elisha's bones, the man was revived.

how did the universe come to be located in that specific place? It would have been fitting that it be located in all unoccupied space, but if so, there would exist an infinite body, which has been established as impossible. Fifth, there is no escaping that the existence of the universe, prior to its coming-to-be, had to be either necessary, impossible, or possible. If it were necessary, its being could never fail to be. If it were impossible, it could never be. Therefore, what is necessitated is that its existence be possible. But possibility requires a substratum.

These are the difficulties raised against our positing of "something from nothing." Yet applying what was discussed earlier will make their resolution simple.

With regard to the first, it does not even qualify as problematic, for even if we do not accept that corporeality can come to be in partial coming-to-be, it is not therefore impossible that it come to be in comprehensive coming-to-be. This is self-evident. And this is especially so in accordance with what was established, namely, that, even for those who believe in anterior eternity, it is inescapable that the emanation of something corporeal from nothing can only originate with God.

With regard to the second, whose foundation is that it is not fitting that form give rise to corporeality inasmuch as corporeality does not resemble form—its resolution is not difficult. First, if coming-to-be were necessarily not volitional, there would be room for doubt, but inasmuch as coming-to-be is volitional, there is no room for doubt. Furthermore, as was discussed earlier, coming-to-be is an act of benefaction and grace, and in this sense it gives rise to something that resembles it; for it has already been established that the end of coming-to-be is that it be good, for "the Lord, moreover, gives that which is good."[67]

With regard to the third, which requires that empty space exist, its solution, too, is easy. For one might say that prior to the universe dimensions were not in existence, but God brought them into being when he brought the body into being out of nothing. And further, even if we concede the necessity of empty space, no absurdity will arise, for the necessity of empty space was already established in Book I of this work, in opposition to what they imagined.

With regard to the fourth: Even if all the places that are unoccupied stand in the same relation [to the agent], there is no necessity that an infinite body exist if its existence as such is impossible. Rather, [it may be said that the agent] gave rise to a specific, limited measure, appropriate to the universe's perfection as it is in it.

In response to the question, why did He create the universe in this empty place rather than in that one? the following may be said. Since all places are equivalent, then, no matter which place was the one into which He brought it into being, the question of why did He not bring it into being in another place would remain. In this very way did R. Levi respond to the question, why did He create at this instant, when, after all, all instants stand before Him as equivalent? Yet whereas this response is adequate in resolving the current difficulty [concerning place], it is not adequate in resolving that one [concerning instants]. For since all instants are equivalent for Him, it is necessary that His will be eternally anterior to all instants. But that all places are equivalent does not require that He [cause the universe to] fill all places—either

---

[67] Ps. 85: 13.

because an infinite body is impossible, or because the requirements of the perfection of the universe demand a determinate measure.[68]

The fifth is just rhetorical. For when we posited "something from nothing" there was no substratum to receive the disjunction of necessary, impossible, and possible from the perspective of the entity acted upon. Possibility was from the perspective of the agent alone. This is self-evident.

It is therefore indeed established that, with respect to our supposition—of absolute creation after nonexistence—there is no confusion. But it is also established that, even if we suppose that the existence of the universe proceeds by way of necessity from God, what is entailed is constant creation but not out of a thing. God's power would necessarily produce miracles as a matter of benefaction and grace, since He is constantly bestowing benefaction when its reception is not impossible from the perspective of the receiver. This is a matter of the level of intellect possessed by the agent—and this agent acts constantly, at every instant that there is a receiver so disposed. Therefore, the existence of the Torah and the miracles it contains are conceivable, even if we believe that the existence of the universe proceeds necessarily from God as a benefaction.

The absolute truth according to what is found in the tradition is that God created and brought the universe into being at a certain instant, as it is said, "In the beginning God created..." and so on through the entire passage. Yet the question indeed remains: why did He bring it forth at a certain instant, when, whether from the perspective of the agent or from the perspective of that which is acted upon, all instants are equivalent?

This difficulty, even if it is rather formidable, may be resolved in one of two ways. One is by our saying that God's wisdom ordained, for a certain reason, that the universe have a beginning of created coming-to-be. In this case the question of why God brought the universe into being at this particular instant when all instants are equivalent with respect to creation would no longer pertain. The other is by our permitting to ourselves what appears in some of the dicta of our Sages of blessed memory, dicta which are quoted by the Rabbi of the *Guide* and which no one we have encountered disputes. They said: "This teaches that He would construct worlds and destroy them."[69] And another: "This teaches that the order of times preceded this."[70] The intent of these dicta, as it appears, is to indicate that there is constant creation, but that worlds come to be at a certain instant and pass away at a certain instant, whether [simply] with the coming-to-be and passing-away of individual worlds, or

---

[68] Crescas is able to explain why God chose a particular place in which to put the universe. He points to a necessary feature of body, namely, that it requires finitude—either because such is the nature of body or because such is the nature of the perfection of body. According to Crescas since God must choose one place rather than another, the question of why *this* particular place can be adequately answered by saying that no matter which place God had chosen, the same question could be asked. What Crescas notes, however, is that this response is one that Gersonides illegitimately proposes to the question of why God chose one particular *instant* rather than another for the universe's creation. Since God's will must be eternally anterior to all instants, Crescas contends, He in fact could not choose one instant over another. Perhaps Crescas differentiates between time and place because, whereas God's not being able to create in every space would imply only a limitation in the created body, His not being able to create at every instant would imply a limitation in Him.

[69] Gen. Rabbah 3: 7.

[70] Gen. Rabbah 3: 7. That is, the order of times preceded the first day of creation.

with each world exceeding the preceding one in its level of perfection. It is possible that the world in which we exist will persist forever, and it is also possible that it will pass away and another world will follow it, exceeding this one in its degree of perfection as the animal exceeds the plant in perfection. Here the doors to speculation are locked, but the matters are ancient, [known] to the receivers of the truth.[71] Even if some sages took strong exception, on the grounds of speculation, to the passing-away of the universe, it is easily established that there is in what they said nothing that compels what they sought to prove—as will be discussed in Book IV, God willing.

In this way the difficulties from the perspective of the agent are also resolved. The conclusion that arises out of this entire discussion, one that is confirmed by speculation, is that it is absolutely the case that creation is not from a thing. This was made known to Abraham in the court of Shem and Eber. "He [viz. Melchizedek] said: 'Blessed be Abram of God Most High, Maker of heaven and earth.'"[72] And the Sweet Singer[73] said: "The heavens declare the glory of God, and the firmament shows His handiwork."[74] For the firmament indicates that which is beyond doubt, namely, that it is the work of God's hands. This is what the Rabbis instituted in the formulation of the benedictions: "He who renews each day, constantly, the work of creation"—since the creation of the totality of existence not from a thing is constant.

It appears that in order to highlight this creation,[75] which includes both form and matter, the Rabbis instituted the following formulation of the benediction: "who forms (יוצר; *yotzer*) light and creates (ובורא; *uvore*) darkness." Even if this benediction was instituted to refer literally to the luminaries, nevertheless, it is not implausible to take it to be indicating the principle of creation (בריאה; *beriah*). Since form bestows determinate quiddity, and matter on its own has no standing and has no concrete stamina, this formulation associates light with form and darkness with matter. But this formula goes further in associating formation (יצירה; *yetzirah*) with form (צורה; *tzurah*), and creation (בריאה; *beriah*) with matter—for since there is no formation without form, what it is doing is associating creation with matter, inasmuch as creation is from nonexistence. Indeed, it has already been established that creation following nonexistence is necessary from the point of view of speculation.

It was established, too, even for the believers in anterior eternity, that God has the power to bring forth a body not from a thing, though this is the opposite of what they imagined. For this reason we did not place the belief in creation among the cornerstones without which the existence of the Torah is inconceivable. The famous dictum of R. Yitzḥaq[76] confirms this. He said: "The Torah did not need to begin other than with 'This month is for you the first of the months.'"[77] R. Nissim, of blessed memory, indeed took note of this dictum in the commentary on the Torah that he began. And

---

[71] This dictum is cited by the kabbalists.   [72] Gen. 14: 19.
[73] The reference is to the composer of Psalms, traditionally taken to be David.   [74] Ps. 19: 2.
[75] "Creation" normally renders Crescas's term חדוש (*ḥiddush*). In this passage, however, Crescas uses both the term חדוש and the term בריאה (*beriah*), since he is dealing with the term for creation used in Genesis and is distinguishing its sense from that of another related term here rendered "formation," viz. יצירה (*yetzirah*).
[76] This dictum is cited by Rashi, in his commentary on the verse Gen. 1: 1.
[77] Exod. 12: 2. According to Crescas, the reason R. Yitzḥaq suggests that the Torah might just as well have started with the commandment concerning the paschal lamb as with an account of creation is that the Torah's legitimacy does not depend on the truth of creation.

the Rabbi[78] brought this view to the attention of the Khazar king, saying to him: "If one faithful to the Torah felt constrained to believe in and to accept anteriorly eternal *hylē*, as well as the existence of many worlds prior to this one, this would not constitute a flaw in his faith. For he believes that *this* universe was created at a certain time, and that in this universe mankind began with Adam and Eve."[79]

With this, what we promised in this chapter is completed. Praise is to God alone, who is exalted above all blessing and praise.

Part II

CONCERNING immortality of the soul.

This discussion concerns two matters: the quiddity of the soul, and its immortality. With respect to quiddity, this is something we discussed, sufficiently for the intent of this book, in Book II Part VI. Therefore, what remains for us to present is an account of the soul's immortality. We shall proceed as is our custom, that is: with an account of how this ought to be understood in accordance with the dictates of the Torah and of speculation, and of the way in which we arrived at our knowledge of it. We therefore assign two chapters to this Part.

Chapter 1

AN account of how immortality ought to be understood in accordance with the dictates of the Torah and of speculation.

I assert that the soul that continues on after death continues on eternally by nature, endures in itself, does not change with respect to species or as an individual—according to the dictates of the Torah with which speculation is in agreement.

We said, "that continues on after death," because not all the souls of human beings continue on, but some perish in their time, such as the souls of some of the wicked, as will be discussed, God willing, in Part III. We said, "continues on eternally by nature," because the soul contains in itself no causes of passing-away, and therefore, if not on account of punishment, as the tradition teaches and as will be discussed below, God willing, the soul continues on eternally by nature. And we said, "endures in itself," since it was established that by definition it is a substance, and not merely a disposition as Averroes imagined. We said, "does not change with respect to species," to indicate the worthlessness of the view of one who imagines that the aspect of souls that continues on unites with the active intellect, such that it *is* it, for insofar as the soul of man is different from the active intellect, were it to unite with it in such a way that it would be correct for us to say, "it is it," then, indeed, it would have changed with respect to species.[80] And we said, "or as an individual," to indicate the

---

[78] The reference is to the fictional character in R. Judah Halevi's *Kuzari*.

[79] See R. Judah Halevi, *Kuzari*, I. 67.

[80] This translation follows the version of this text found in both the Florence and the Vienna manuscripts and reproduced in Harvey 1973: כבר נשתנה באופן שיהיה הוא הוא, כי למה שנפש האדם היא מתחלפת לשכל הפועל, אם היה שתתאחד עמו באופן שיצדק עליו אמרנו הוא הוא, במין. The shorter version, found in the Ferrara edition and reprinted in Fisher, is: באופן שיצדק עליו אמרנו היא כבר תשתנה במין, which would be translated as: "in such a way that our saying that it does not change with respect to species is justified."

worthlessness of the view of those who believe that there is no multiplicity of souls after they separate [from the body] but they are one in number. This is a most worthless view, according to tradition and to speculation itself.

Chapter II

THE way in which we arrived at our knowledge of it.

I assert that the immortality of the soul as posited may be known from the Torah and the tradition, and speculation concurs.

Indeed in the Torah, even if the immortality of the soul was not explicitly stated in the form of a promise, there are nevertheless many texts that attest to it as something basic, accepted and well known by the nation. With respect to Enoch we find: "And he is not, for God took him,"[81]—that is, God took him and placed him among the ranks of His angels. The same language is found concerning Elijah: "Today the Lord will take your master from your head."[82] This notion was so widely known that Balaam yearned to be like Israel at the end, and he therefore said: "May my soul die the death of the righteous, and may my end be like his."[83] Because this was well known among the people, Abigail said: "But the soul of my lord shall be bound in the bond of life, and the souls of your enemies, them shall He sling out, as from the hollow of a sling."[84] Moreover, God said: "Behold, I have set before you this day life and good."[85] And Ezekiel also promised this same life: "Turn, and live!"[86] There is no doubt that it is not corporeal life that is intended, because life and death are common to the righteous and the wicked. Indeed the Psalmist in his prayers called the wicked "dead," as he said: "the dead do not praise the Lord."[87] He also said: "And we shall bless the Lord from now until forever."[88] And he said, in addition, again attesting to this: "But God will redeem my soul from the hand of Sheol, for He will take me. Selah."[89] Moreover, he said elsewhere: "until I arrived at the sanctuaries of God."[90] Solomon his son further said explicitly: "And the spirit will return unto God who gave it."[91] One could expand on these as another did.[92] Nevertheless, there is no explicit promise other than the corporeal promise, for the reason we shall mention in Part VI, God willing.

In the tradition, this doctrine is well known to our Sages, who mentioned the subject of the world-to-come in many places; there is no need to recall them. Therefore, the matter of immortality is most evident according to the Torah and the tradition.

That the immortal soul does not change with respect to species or as an individual, as was posited, is seen from the perspective of the Torah. For insofar as true reward and punishment for man lies in the continuing-on of souls after their separation [from the body], then, if the soul were to unite with the active intellect, or if the souls were to unite and all become one—as one of the sages of our nation imagined and on account of which he stumbled because of his attraction to the way of the Greeks[93]—this would not be a correct and appropriate reward, since

---

[81] Gen. 5: 24. [82] 2 Kgs. 2: 3. [83] Num. 23: 10. [84] 1 Sam. 25: 29.
[85] Deut. 30: 15. [86] Ezek. 18: 32. [87] Ps. 115: 17. [88] Ps. 115: 18. [89] Ps. 49: 16.
[90] Ps. 73: 17. The verse continues: "and considered their end." [91] Eccles. 12: 7.
[92] The reference is to Abraham ibn Daud, in his *Emunah Ramah* (*Exalted Faith*).
[93] The likely referent is Maimonides. See *Guide* I. 74, "Seventh Method."

there would be no advantage to the obedient one over someone who did not achieve one-thousandth of his rank.

This is most evident as well in the dicta of our Rabbis, of blessed memory. They said: "The righteous sit with their crowns on their heads, enjoying the radiance of the Divine Presence."[94] They said as well: "Moses' face is like the face of the sun; Joshua's face, like the face of the moon."[95] And further: This teaches that each is given a dwelling-place in accordance with his eminence."[96] There are many other such statements besides. Expanding on this would be superfluous.

With regard to whether speculation concurs with this, the question of immortality is something about which the commentators on Aristotle's books have been perplexed. Some have denied its existence, and some have affirmed it. They multiplied arguments and words. It is therefore fitting that we present, with splendid conciseness, that which merits attention in the support they gleaned for their view. For in this way the truth of what we seek will be established.

I assert that there are three propositions to which all agree and on which they erected their edifices. First, that the human intellect, which they called the acquired intellect, is constituted by its intelligibles. Second, that everything that comes to be passes away, and everything that passes away has come to be. And third, that if it is supposed that it is possible for the human intellect to intellect the active intellect, it is necessary that it be eternal. Their dispute, however, concerns two propositions. The first is whether the intelligibles that are in this realm come to be or do not come to be. The second is whether it is possible for the human intellect to intellect the active intellect.

The party that denies immortality of the soul holds that the intelligibles in this realm come to be, and that the human intellect cannot intellect the active intellect. They infer from this that human intellect cannot be eternal. For when it was confirmed for them that the intellect is constituted by its intelligibles, as is affirmed in the first agreed-upon proposition, and that the intelligibles in this realm come to be, it followed that they will necessarily pass away, as is affirmed by the second agreed-upon proposition. This obtains so long as the human intellect does not intellect the active intellect. Thus, once it was confirmed for them that it is impossible for the human intellect to intellect the active intellect, it followed necessarily that the human intellect cannot be eternal.[97]

One member of the party that accepts immortality[98] maintains that the intelligibles in this realm do not come to be. And once it was verified that the intellect is constituted by its intelligibles, as per the first agreed-upon proposition, it followed that the human intellect is necessarily eternal, since the intelligibles are eternal, insofar as they do not come to be—as per the second agreed-upon proposition. He infers from this the necessity of immortality. Other members maintain that it

---

[94] BT *Berakhot* 17a. [95] BT *Baba batra* 75a. [96] BT *Shabbat* 152a.
[97] The text of this sentence is not found in the Ferrara edition or in Fisher or Smilevitch. וכאשר נתאמת לו שאי אפשר בו שישכיל השכל הפועל, הוליד בהכרח שהשכל האנושי אי אפשר בו שישוב נצחי. It is found in both the Florence and Vienna manuscripts and is reproduced in Harvey 1973a.
[98] The manuscripts have מהם מי שיראה; Fisher has simply יראה. The reference, according to Gersonides (citing Averroes) in *Wars of the Lord* I. viii, is to Avicenna. According to Gersonides, the "other members" include Alexander, Themistius, and Averroes.

is possible for the human intellect to intellect the active intellect. Relying on the third agreed-upon proposition, they infer the necessity of the immortality of the human intellect when it intellects the active intellect. These are the extremes of their approach.

We assert, however, that the falsity of the first proposition, which is the foundation of the entire edifice, was established beyond doubt in Book II Part VI. So, too, the second proposition. R. Levi indeed dealt it a severe blow, but even if we were to grant its truth, it would not apply to coming-to-be which is a product of will. It has already been established in our earlier discussion that comprehensive coming-to-be is willed and is from nothing; this renders eternality all the more possible. The falsity of the third proposition will be easily established via the falsity of the first. For the human intellect's apprehension of the active intellect does not impart eternity to the human intellect unless we say that the intellect is constituted by its intelligibles. This is self-evident.

Therefore, since it was stipulated in the definition of soul that it is an intellectual substance that contains in itself no causes of passing-away, it is fitting to say with respect to the necessity of immortality that, when the soul is perfected in its bond [with God] and in its love [for Him], by means of what it apprehends of the Torah and of God's miracles, it is fitting that it persist in its perfection and in its strong bond [with God] and in the light's unceasing streaming, thanks to the removal of the barrier that darkens its way—namely, matter.

Since this is so, it is evident that speculation does not refute anything with respect to immortality. Rather, it appears that it necessitates it, for since it is evident in the case of a composite that passes away and that separates into its simple components that each component returns to its simple essence, and since man is composed of a material part and a spiritual part whose essence[99] emanates from an emanating intellectual substance—whether an angel or something else—it is fitting and necessary that the spiritual part not pass away, just as it is evident that the material part returns to its simple components and to the elements. Therefore immortality is evident and necessitated in itself according to correct speculation. It is to this that Solomon alluded when he said: "But dust shall return to the earth as it was, and the spirit shall return unto God who bestowed it."[100] There is a difference, however, between the material part and the spiritual. The simple components of the material will return to its elements and unite with them, since they are homogeneous and did not acquire through matter a stable perfection, since matter is constantly moving and changing. But it is fitting and necessary that the spiritual part, insofar as it acquired, by way of its apprehension, perfection and attachment to the Supreme Light which is stable and unchanging, remain stable in itself and in its perfection. This indeed necessitates immortality. This should suffice in accordance with the intention of this book.

That the soul does not change with respect to species or as an individual is evident from our earlier discussion. For it is evident in itself that that which changes with

---

[99] Reading, with Ferrara and Fisher, עצמותו, rather than עצמותיו, found in the Florence and Vienna manuscripts, which would mean, "an essential spiritual part."
[100] Eccles. 12: 7.

respect to species or as an individual is converted from one substance to another—whether it be a species or an individual—and the substance from which it is converted necessarily passes away. For if it did not pass away, a single thing would harbor in itself two substances—an outcome whose absurdity has been established. Since it has been established that the intellective soul has no causes of passing-away, it follows necessarily that it does not change either with respect to species or as an individual.

What led some of the commentators on Aristotle's books to this error is their acceptance of the proposition that the human intellect is constituted by its intelligibles. And when it was verified for them that the intellecter, the intellected, and intellection were one thing, and that intellection excludes multiplicity of individuals, it followed necessarily for them that souls, upon separating [from bodies] were a single thing. We have already established in our earlier discussion the nonsensicalness and falsity of this proposition. We maintain that the soul has an essence beyond its intellection, even though its quiddity remains obscure to us. Indeed, our Rabbis of blessed memory called it, in several places, light, as Scripture says: "The soul of man is the lamp of the Lord."[101] It is worthy of this name, inasmuch as it illumines the eyes of the blind and the benighted. For this very reason they attributed light to the Divine Presence, and said: "delighting in the radiance of the Divine Presence."[102] Scripture says, too: "The light dwells with Him."[103]

What is surprising about them is that, since intellection in itself is one, and it excludes plurality, nevertheless, since the intellection and the intellected are also one, the intelligibles, despite their great number, may be just one individual. This is the height of absurdity and nonsense.[104] In fact, what they have said is illusion and fiction and, in addition, utterly defies the Torah and the tradition, as was discussed earlier.

We have established here what we saw fit to establish in this Part. Praise is to God alone, who is exalted above all blessing and praise.

Part III

CONCERNING reward and punishment.

We assert, in accordance with our previous discussion, that, according to the Torah and the tradition, reward and punishment are of two kinds: corporeal, and—for the soul after its separation from the body—spiritual. It was established as well that, with respect to the spiritual kind, speculation concurs. And so their existence is established. What remains for us to establish are three matters. First, the modes of reward and punishment—in a way that speculation would not dispute them. Second, an account of the two kinds of reward and the two kinds of punishment, with respect to whether they differ, and, if they differ, with respect to the way in which they differ.

---

[101] Prov. 20: 27.   [102] BT *Berakhot* 17a.   [103] Dan. 2: 22.
[104] Fisher's text adds the words אל השכל, "for the intellect," translated in Smilevitch as "pour l'intelligence."

Third, the resolution of some difficulties that arise for both kinds [of reward and punishment]. We therefore assign three chapters to this Part.

Chapter I

CONCERNING the modes of reward and punishment—in a way that speculation would not dispute them.

I assert that corporeal reward and punishment were explicitly set forth in the Torah in several places. Because of the way in which they were posited it is evident that speculation will not dispute them. For their primary intention is benefaction and the imparting of perfection, as was discussed earlier. From the perspective of the promise of good, [these goods are achieved by] the removal of the obstacle that prevents perfection, combined with the extraordinary informing of man that there is something providential above him and a seeing eye. From the perspective of the promise of bad, even though it contains this notification [of something bad] for him or for another, its usefulness lies in that it vanquishes and rebukes the destroying angel—the angel of death which is the evil inclination. Since this benefaction and grace is the essential intent of reward and punishment, as the verse teaches in saying, "And you shall consider in your heart that, as a man chastens his son, so the Lord your God chastens you,"[105] it is evident that speculation will not dispute it—since it is established with respect to God that He is the true good, and that it is fitting that His perfection impart benefaction—once the indubitable has been established, namely, that He has the power to do so.

Since the essential end and primary intent of the promise of good is the imparting of perfection through the removal of the obstacle to it, the first promise in the Torah is the removal of bad, as it is said: "If you will diligently hearken to the voice of the Lord your God...and will give ear to His commandments...I will put none of the diseases upon you, which I have put upon the Egyptians; for I am the Lord who heals you."[106] It is as if this is to teach what we have said, namely, that the primary intent of the promise of good is the removal of the obstacle to it. And it therefore concludes: "for I am the Lord who heals you." That is to say: because it is not in the course of nature for God who is the good and the powerful and the truthful to be your healer—by "your healer" what is intended is the director of your health and the health of your soul—it is fitting that you believe in Him. And if the primary intent of reward were the bestowal of corporeal good to reward the obedient one, and the bestowal of bad to punish the transgressor, it would have been fitting for the first promise of reward to have been the bestowal of corporeal good. But the primary and essential end of reward and punishment is the removal of the obstacle and the impediment to perfection. This reflects the benefaction of the true benefactor, may He be blessed and exalted. From this perspective speculation concurs.

Now that this has been established with respect to reward and punishment, I assert that, of the modes of corporeal reward and punishment as they were expounded in

---

[105] Deut. 8: 5.
[106] Exod. 15: 26. The two omitted phrases are: "and will do that which is right in His eyes"; and "and keep all His statutes."

the Torah, some are general and some particular. By the general I mean that they apply to all the commandments; these appear in well-known places in the Torah. By the particular I mean those that apply to particular commandments, such as the promise of good in the commandment of *shemittah*: "and it shall bring forth produce for three years";[107] in the commandment of appearing: "neither shall any man covet your land";[108] in the honoring of father and mother and the sending-away of the mother bird: "that it may be well with you, and that you may prolong your days,"[109] which our Rabbis of blessed memory interpreted at the end of *Gemara Ḥullin*[110] to mean, "in a world that is all good and lengthy"; in the case of a promise of bad, such as excision for certain transgressions;[111] and in the matter of the woman suspected of adultery, in which case, according to the tradition, either an extraordinary reward or an extraordinary punishment is inevitable under certain specific conditions.[112]

All have in common three things, according to the Torah and the tradition. One is that reward and punishment are related respectively to the performance of a commandment and its transgression. In this there is considerable benefit, for as is obvious, it contains a profound lesson. It is what Jethro said, when he sensed that the death of the Egyptians, and particularly the smiting of the first-born, was a matter of "measure for measure," as it is said: "My first-born child, Israel...";[113] and in the parting of the Reed Sea and the drowning of the Egyptians in the water, where the decree affected them in their persons, as it is said: "Every son who is born you shall cast into the river and every female child you shall keep alive."[114] Thus divine wisdom and providence proceeded in such a way that the first and last plagues were accomplished through water, and in the very same place a magnificent miracle would be wrought for Israel.[115] For this reason, the final benediction in the recital of the *Shemaʿ* was instituted in commemoration of these miracles.[116] It is fitting for Jethro to have said when he sensed this: "Now I know that the Lord is greater than all gods, for in that in which they dealt arrogantly against them."[117] Since this thing [viz.

---

[107] Lev. 25: 21. The reference is to the commandment to allow the land (of Israel) to lie fallow every seventh year.

[108] Exod. 34: 24. The reference is to the commandment to appear before the Lord in the Temple in Jerusalem on the three pilgrimage festivals.

[109] Deut. 22: 7; also 5: 16.   [110] BT *Ḥullin* 142a.

[111] The manuscripts specify thirty-six as the number of sins punished by excision.

[112] A woman whose husband suspects her of adultery is subjected to an ordeal that will determine her guilt or innocence. If she is guilty, she will become infertile; if innocent, fertile.

[113] Exod. 4: 22. As the Egyptians enslaved and tormented God's first-born child, Israel, so were the Egyptians subjected to the plague of the smiting of their first-born.

[114] Exod. 1: 22. The Egyptians were drowned in the Reed Sea to repay Pharaoh, measure-for-measure, for his decree that all male Israelite newborns were to be tossed into the river.

[115] In the first plague, the waters of the Nile turned to blood; in the last plague the Egyptians drowned in the Reed Sea. It was at the Reed Sea that the Israelites experienced the great miracle of being able to cross without being drowned.

[116] The reference is to the prayer that begins עזרת אבותינו (*'ezrat avoteinu*), "The help of our forefathers."

[117] Exod. 18: 11. This verse appears to end before Jethro completes his thought. It ends: "for that in which they [viz. the Egyptians] dealt arrogantly against them [עליהם, *'aleihem*]," and one expects it to continue: "God repaid them in kind, measure for measure." It is possible, however, to render (עליהם *'aleihem*), "He was above them," and to understand the verse so: "Now I know that the Lord is greater than all gods, for in that in which they [viz. the gods of the Egyptians] dealt arrogantly—He was above them."

measure-for-measure recompense] is of the greatest benefit and goodness, with which it is fitting that the Divine Name be associated, the Psalmist said: "Unto You, O Lord, mercy belongs; for You render to every man according to his work."[118] That is to say: divine recompense resembles and is in proportion to a man's deed. The Psalmist was most emphatic in saying "for You," that is: despite the supremacy of Your exaltedness and transcendence, You punctiliously compensate individuals measure-for-measure—for their benefit. These words indicate as well God's graciousness, for He compensates individuals in accordance with their deeds, that is: the requital is in respect of the obedient or the rebellious individual, and not in respect of the issuer of the command, may His name be blessed and exalted. For from God's perspective, nothing is owed the person who is obedient, in light of the fact that He already bestowed His graces upon him, as was discussed in its place; and so he who defies God's word in even a small thing merits the most severe punishment. It is therefore evident, in respect of the person and not in respect of the issuer of the commandment, may His name be blessed, that reward and punishment are without doubt an act of grace. And this is the case all the more considering God's punctiliousness in compensating individuals measure-for-measure, as our Rabbis of blessed memory say: "In the measure in which a man measures it is meted out to him."[119] There are many instances mentioned in the Talmud that attest to the truth of this adage. This is the first point common to the various corporeal promises.

The second is that it has already been seen that these [corporeal promises] are not meant absolutely, such that nothing else might occur. This is hinted at by our Sages of blessed memory in several places. In the Torah, too, it is said: "and He repays those who hate Him to their face, to destroy them."[120] It is possible, then, that the promise of a corporeal bad thing to the transgressor may not come to pass [in the here and now]. And the same applies to a promise of corporeal good to the obedient, for knowledge with respect to opposites is the same, namely, that it is indeed possible that it will not come to pass, either for the sake of the purgation of certain transgressions, or for the purification of the obedient man's soul to perfect it. These are the afflictions of love that are mentioned in various places in the dicta of our Sages of blessed memory. And a case in point are the trials by which our Patriarchs were tested, in order to impart to them the greatest perfection possible for them in terms of what is attainable by way of deeds, as was mentioned earlier.

Indeed it is clear, from the incident of the woman suspected of adultery, that under certain conditions, as the tradition maintains, nothing other than what was promised can occur, whether for good or for bad. In this case, these conditions are met: the name of God is effaced in water mixed with the dust of the floor of the Tabernacle for the purpose of investigating the woman [and exonerating her if she is innocent], and otherwise, [in the case of her guilt,] to forbid her to her husband since she indeed acted [sinfully] in secret.[121] But as for other promises—whether general or particular—it is possible for them not to come to pass, as was discussed earlier. This is the second point.

---

[118] Ps. 62: 13.   [119] BT *Sotah* 8b.
[120] Deut. 7: 10. As Rashi explains, the wicked are compensated for their good deeds in this world in order that they may be utterly destroyed in the next.
[121] See Num. 5: 11–31.

The third is mentioned by our Rabbis of blessed memory in *Gemara Kiddushin*,[122] where they say that a person is judged according to the majority of his deeds, and the world according to the majority of its people. They used this notion to alert the person—by having him see himself, as he acts, as if his deeds, or the deeds of the world as a whole, are half transgressions and half meritorious—to his deeds' being such that he can tip the balance for himself and for the whole world to the side of merit. It is indeed clear that this law obtains for the state and for each and every city, even if it is not explicit in the Talmud. This is the third point common to the various corporeal promises.

The modes of spiritual reward and punishment, however, are not explicit in the Torah, although they are hinted at in many places in the tradition. The upshot of all of them as a whole is that after the obedient soul separates from the body it delights in the radiance of the Divine Presence—that is, it takes pleasure in its apprehension of God, an apprehension precluded while it is still in the body. This is "the light that is stored for the righteous."[123] The soul's constant attachment [to God] will be strengthened for infinite time. The ranks of individuals will differ [in their pleasure][124] in accordance with how their love and [the strength of] their bond differed while they lived their lives of body-and-soul. Similarly, the soul of the rebellious transgressor, after it separates from the body, will experience severe pain as it dwells in a darkness contrary to its nature. The Rabbis likened this to the pain of burning and called it "the fire of Gehenna,"[125] insofar as fire is the thinnest of the agents: since the spiritual soul which is affected is thin in relation to the thickness of things corporeal, they chose the thinnest pain-inducing agent among the sensible agents.[126] The ranks of the transgressors also differed in this [i.e. in their pain], as the tradition teaches, such that some experience the pain and the purgation for a limited time, as divine wisdom ordains. Many details concerning this matter appear in *Gemara Rosh Hashanah*.[127] There is no need to mention them.

What remains to be established is how speculation regarding spiritual reward and punishment concurs with what has been said. This will be easily established through what has been said. For since it is established of the soul that it is a spiritual substance, it is evident with respect to it that it will attain the ultimate joy and delight when it is attached to the spirituality for which it yearns by its nature. Through its attachment to the Divine Presence—which is the most wondrous spirituality possible—what will follow necessarily is immeasurable joy and delight. Nevertheless, souls will be of different ranks in the kind of delight they attain, in accordance with the measure of their prior love and attachment [to God] while they were in bodies. Since knowledge with respect to opposites is the same, it follows that when the soul does not attain that for which it yearns by its nature, it will experience severe pain, to the point that

---

[122] BT *Kiddushin* 40b. All the versions cite *Rosh Hashanah*, but Fisher corrects the reference in brackets.
[123] BT *Ḥagigah* 12a.   [124] בזה, "in this," is missing in the Ferrara edition and in Fisher.
[125] BT *Rosh Hashanah* 17a.
[126] The text following the colon is omitted in Fisher and Smilevitch and in the Ferrara edition. It is found in both the Florence and Vienna manuscripts and is reproduced in Harvey 1973: ולהיות הנפש רוחנית המתפעלת דקה ביחס אל עובי הגשמות, לקחו המצער היותר דק שבפועלים המוחשים.
[127] BT *Rosh Hashanah* 17a.

possibly, as a result of the pain, it may utterly pass away over a stretch of time. For, as was established above, since the soul is a substance apart from intellection, and since love and passionate love are distinct from intellection as well, it is not implausible from the point of view of speculation that this pain will bring about the passing-away of the substance of the soul over a stretch of time. This is what we intended in this chapter.

Chapter II

CONCERNING the two kinds of reward, and the two kinds of punishment, with respect to whether they differ; and, if they differ, with respect to the way in which they differ.

I assert that it indeed appears from what was said that the two kinds of reward and punishment differ in three ways and agree in three. Of the three in which they differ, the first is that the corporeal promise applies to man insofar as he is body-and-soul; therefore, it is necessarily limited. But the spiritual promise applies mainly to the soul after it separates from the body; therefore, it is unlimited. Second, it might happen that the corporeal promise will not come to pass, as we established. But it cannot happen that the spiritual promise will not come to pass. Third, the corporeal promise is determined for the world in accordance with the majority of people. But in the case of the spiritual promise, the fate of each person is determined by his own deeds.

Of the three ways in which they agree, the first is that the promise of good applies to the obedient individual, and the promise of bad to the transgressor. Second, the promise in each case operates in terms of measure-for-measure. How the corporeal promise operates was established already in the previous chapter. As for the spiritual promise, this is easily established. Since the end of obedience is attachment [to God], and the pleasure experienced by the soul after it separates from the body is also attachment to the radiance of the Divine Presence and its apprehension, it follows that the reward is fitting to the utmost. And so, too, in the case of the opposite, the punishment of the transgressor is most fitting: in his lifetime he is far from attachment [to God], and he is punished by the distancing of his soul from the apprehension of that which by its nature [it yearns to apprehend]. Third, man's fate, too, according to what appears in *Gemara Rosh Hashanah*,[128] is determined by the majority—that is, by the majority of his deeds. It is possible that it is to this that R. Akiva was alluding at the end of his statement: "All is in accordance with the majority of deeds."[129]

Chapter III

THE resolution of some difficulties that arise for both kinds of promises [of recompense].

With regard to the corporeal promise, the following difficulties might be raised. First, were it to happen that, for one of the reasons we mentioned, it does not come to pass, how can it be posited in Scripture—and particularly in the case of a promise of good, since according to our root-principle the promise of good is never rescinded? Second, we see just the opposite of what is found in Scripture in the statements of our Rabbis

---

[128] BT *Rosh Hashanah* 17a.   [129] *Avot* 3: 15.

of blessed memory. They say: "There is no reward in this world for the performance of a commandment."[130] Also: "Children, life, and sustenance do not depend on merit but depend on the constellation."[131] The straightforward sense of these dicta contradicts Scripture. Indeed, Rabbinic dicta contradict one another, for in another place they say: "Israel is unaffected by the constellation."[132] Third, the tradition transmits the following teaching: "The world's fate is determined by the majority." Yet this is surely surprising: how could it be that, when God's punitive attribute holds sway, the minority of righteous people who dwell in a city in which the majority of people are wicked, would come to grief on account of the transgression of the wicked? It is clear that this would be the opposite of the principle we laid down concerning individual providence. These are the difficulties that might be raised with respect to the corporeal promise.

With respect to the spiritual promise, here, too, it is possible for difficulties to be raised. First, it is quite astonishing—considering that this [viz. spiritual reward and punishment] is the essence of true reward and punishment, and that it could never happen that it not come to pass—that it is not explicitly set forth in the Torah, yet the corporeal, which is not the true reward and punishment, and which might not come to pass, is explicitly set forth.

Second, since we endorse the root-principle, "No bad thing descends from on high,"[133] and since this is the truth itself with which speculation concurs, how can anything that is bad for the soul ensue from God? It is not possible that it does so by way of reprimand so as to benefit someone else, for the bad thing that affects the soul is not sensed by anything other than the soul itself.

Third, how is purgation and punishment for a specific amount of time conceivable in the case of a soul? Yet the tradition posits it so. The Rabbis say: "The length of the sentence for the wicked in Gehenna is twelve months."[134]

Fourth, since it is a root-principle of the tradition that the souls of sinners are obliterated, to the point that the Rabbis said, "they will be ash beneath the soles of the righteous,"[135] how curious it is that passing-away is conceivable for an intellectual entity which contains no causes of passing-away. If it is assumed that it will pass away, into what will it pass?[136] Will it pass into ash, as the literal sense of the dictum suggests?

Fifth, the Rabbis' dictum with respect to this promise, to the effect that a man's fate is determined by the majority [of his deeds], is surprising. For it would seem that the following unavoidable disjunction applies to the minority of his deeds which are transgressions: either he repents of them, or he does not and remains defiant. If he repents of them, how can his fate be determined by the majority? For it is then as if he has not transgressed at all, as many rabbinic dicta attest.[137] And if he remains defiant, how is it tenable that despite how remote he is from obedience to God, he

---

[130] BT *Kiddushin* 39b. [131] BT *Moʿed katan* 28a. [132] BT *Shabbat* 156a.
[133] Gen. *Rabbah* 51: 3. [134] *ʿEduyot* 2: 10. [135] BT *Rosh Hashanah* 17a.
[136] This last clause, found in both the Vienna and Florence manuscripts, is absent from the Ferrara edition and from Fisher and Smilevitch. It reads: ‏אל מה יפסד?‏.
[137] In this case it is as if all the person's deeds are righteous, and the idea of being judged "by the majority" would not apply to him.

merits the pleasantness of closeness and attachment?[138] Indeed, our Rabbis of blessed memory held in this connection that one may not take a bribe, not even a bribe in the form of the observance of a commandment. Their intention in this was that even if a transgressor observes a commandment, the commandment will not atone for the transgression; he must repent of the transgression.[139]

Sixth, our positing that reward and punishment occur after death is contrary to political justice; how, then, could it plausibly accord with divine justice? For it is evident that man as he is, that is, body-and-soul, which is his mode of being when he is either obedient or the opposite, differs in species from his soul following its separation [from the body]. This is seen in that the definitions of the two are not in agreement. Indeed, according to political justice, it is not tenable for Reuben to be rewarded for a service performed by Simeon, even though they are of the same species, for they differ as individuals. It is even less thinkable to reward someone who differs in species from the performer of the service. Would it be thinkable to reward [the angel] Michael for the service performed by [the human being] Abraham?[140]

Seventh, let us suppose that this *is* acceptable according to divine justice as it pertains to the soul, insofar as the soul is the noblest of the human being's parts—even if in truth[141] this is not sufficient grounds, since a simple thing when it is in a compound is not the same substance as when it is separate, for if it were there would be two substances in the compound.[142] Let us suppose nevertheless that it is acceptable in this respect. Why, if so, did God not find a way to reward or punish the person, who as a person[143] is body-and-soul, for indeed this appears more correct and more suitable? These are the difficulties that might arise with respect to the spiritual promise.

It is fitting that we say the following by way of resolving these difficulties. Let us begin with the corporeal promise. The first difficulty concerns the following. Since recompense is posited explicitly in Scripture, and especially in the case of a promise of good, how could it happen that it not come to pass? This is particularly problematic considering that one of our root-principles is that a promise of good is not rescinded. Resolving this problem is not difficult. For if we investigate the promises, we will find that the promises of good are dependent on and are on condition of the fulfillment of all the commandments, statutes, and ordinances. And there can be no doubt that for anyone who fits this description it will not happen that he will fail to attain the corporeal promise as it appears in Scripture, since he needs no purification or purgation to overcome his evil inclination. The only exception is by way of testing him in order to increase his perfection, as was the case of Abraham our father of

---

[138] If a person remains defiant of God and does not regret his wicked deeds, why should he be rewarded in accordance with the majority of his deeds which are righteous?

[139] See Maimonides' commentary on *Avot* 4: 22.

[140] Since a body-and-soul human being, on the one hand, and this same human being's soul alone when separated from his body after death, on the other, are not of the same species, how can it be just to reward or punish the soul alone for the deeds of the body-and-soul human being?

[141] The Florence manuscript does not contain the word באמת.

[142] If the body-soul compound is a single substance—a body whose form is the soul—it follows that the separated soul which is a substance in and of itself is not the same as the soul that is a component of this compound. For if it were, a person would be composed of two distinct substances.

[143] The manuscripts contain the words והוא אדם.

blessed memory. But according to our root-principle, "Everything is in accordance with the majority of deeds," we believe—even if it does not say so explicitly—that the promise of good will be fulfilled for the one who is obedient in accordance with the majority of his deeds. Yet it might indeed happen that this promise will not come to pass, for one of the reasons we mentioned. Even if it does not come to pass, however, that does not mean that the promise of good has been rescinded on account of this. For the illusory bad that comes to pass for the righteous is in truth a benefit. For its end is the attainment of the truly high rank, which is something that one cannot attain without that bad thing or that test. It is therefore verified that, despite the failure of the corporeal good to come to pass, the promise is nevertheless not rescinded for one who is obedient in the majority of cases, and even if the promise of good[144] is not explicitly written. But with regard to a promise appearing in writing in the Torah, it cannot happen from any perspective that it will not come to pass.[145] We say, "from any perspective,"[146] for even if there were a city and boundary in which most were wicked—considering that our root-principle is that the world is judged according to the majority—the individual would escape punishment, insofar as he is subject to individual providence, as we set down earlier. This should suffice for the first difficulty.

The second and third concern reconciling the dicta of our Rabbis of blessed memory. It is not difficult to resolve them. The general propositions in the Talmud derive their force from their indeterminateness. For it is indeed an important root-principle in the Talmud that, "Inferences are not to be drawn from general rules, not even where an exception is specified."[147] Thus the intent of the adage, "Children, life, and sustenance do not depend on merit but depend on the constellation," is that they do not depend *fully* on merit, that, although they require merit, nevertheless, "they depend [also] on the constellation"[148]—somewhat. For when the constellation ordains something good or its opposite, often what the constellation has ordained is not abrogated on account of merit or its opposite. For Rabbah, despite his being a righteous man like R. Ḥisda, suffered "sixty pains,"[149] but the good reserved for him because of his merits was stored away for him in the world-to-come, which is the true good. Their saying, "Israel is unaffected by the constellation,"[150] means: not affected absolutely. In other words, it is indeed possible for someone to be of such a rank that the providence to which he is subject is the opposite of what the constellation ordained. But when people are not of the rank at which they are subject to special providence, it will be true that their fate will reflect that of the majority of the city, or the country, or the world. The bestower of reward may be trusted to compensate them for the corporeal reward they forfeited because of the wickedness of those nations[151] by bestowing on them the true good in the measure appropriate to them. But when they achieve the rank at which they are subject to individual providence, they do not come to grief on account of the transgression of others.

---

[144] הטוב is absent from the Ferrara edition.   [145] שלא יגיע is absent from the Ferrara edition.
[146] ואמרנו משום צד is absent from the Ferrara edition.   [147] BT ʿEruvin 27a.
[148] BT Moʿed katan 28a.   [149] BT Baba kamma 92b.   [150] BT Shabbat 156a.
[151] This phrase is based on Deut. 9: 4 and 5: ברשעת הגוים האלה, "because of the wickedness of these nations."

By their saying, "There is no reward in this world for the observance of a commandment,"[152] they intended that the true reward for observing the commandments is not bestowed in this world, as was discussed earlier. This adage suggests that corporeal good is not in the first instance to reward the observance of a commandment but rather to remove from the person the obstacle to his perfection. The true reward pertains to the soul. This should suffice with respect to [resolving the difficulties concerning] the corporeal promise.

Turning to the spiritual promise, the first difficulty, one that has never stopped troubling the earlier thinkers, is actually not difficult to resolve. For there is no doubt that the divine Torah, in its essence and nature, requires a spiritual promise for the souls of those who are obedient, in light of their bond and attachment to the end of spirituality. This is something that was well known to Abraham our father, to his sons, and to his students, as he himself received it from Shem and Eber, and as it was verified for him by the promise he received in the matter of the Binding. For the assurance Abraham and Isaac received by God's saying, "for through Isaac will your seed be called yours,"[153] would have been senseless if it were impossible to compensate him by replacing the illusory good with the true good. This faith [viz. that a promise of good can be fulfilled spiritually if it is not fulfilled illusorily—that is, materially] was very well known to them, and the fathers bequeathed it to their children and to all their descendants. Therefore the Israelites suffered their difficult slavery to the Egyptians without worshiping their gods. For it might be thought that if Israel would have listened to the Egyptians and would have worshiped their gods, the Egyptians would have been favorably disposed to them, accepting them as one of them. The fact that they suffered poverty and misery for not worshiping their gods attests sufficiently to their hoping for a spiritual reward for adhering to the faith of Abraham, which demanded belief in creation and the performance of circumcision, in addition to the observance of the seven commandments issued to Noah's children. Otherwise, there is no doubt that they would have chosen the bodily happiness of being released from the vicissitudes of slavery. How could it be otherwise? Indeed, the first commandment that was issued to the human species was the prohibition on meat-consumption.[154] No promise—neither one of corporeal nor one of spiritual reward—accompanied it. When meat was permitted, and the children of Noah received their seven commandments, no promise of spiritual reward was issued to them. When the commandment of circumcision was originally issued to Abraham, it was not accompanied by a spiritual reward. For spiritual reward, as far as the divine Torah is concerned, is something that goes without saying and was accepted by them. Therefore, when the perfect divine Torah was completed, spiritual promise was absolutely superfluous. For the prior directives, insofar as they too were divine,

---

[152] BT *Kiddushin* 39b.
[153] Gen. 21: 12. Unless this promise were understood by Abraham to be such that it could be fulfilled through spiritual reward, he could not take seriously the trial he is about to be subjected to, the trial in which God will command him to sacrifice Isaac: Abraham would know that his son would not actually die, for if he did, then the divine promise—if it were solely a corporeal one—would not be fulfilled.
[154] Gen. 2: 16 states: "And the Lord God *commanded* (ויצו) the man, saying, 'Of every tree of the garden you may freely eat.'" Crescas interprets this verse to imply that the eating of anything other than what was mandated—and so, the eating of meat—was forbidden.

were understood to be promising a spiritual reward, even though it was not written. The corporeal promise in the divine Torah had never been heard, however, until that time, except in the case of Abraham, and only specifically with respect to the commandment of circumcision. That the divine Torah must deliver a corporeal good is something that had to be written and publicized, for it is against nature and is something miraculous and wondrous. This should suffice for the first.

The second, third, and fourth depend on a clarification of how something bad can befall the sinning soul when our root-principle maintains: "No bad thing descends from on high." And if something can happen, how is purgation or passing-away conceivable in the case of an intellectual substance? Even though this is a major difficulty, it is fitting that we point out by way of its resolution that it was established through the definition of a soul that it is a spiritual substance which is distinct from intellection. The delight that was posited—which is distinct from intellection—is a delight in love and attachment [to God] attained by means of intellection. It is therefore self-evident that we ought to attribute to it [i.e. to the soul] both an active faculty and one that is acted upon. For the faculty of intellection is active and activates the delight in the substance of the soul, and the faculty for experiencing delight is thus the faculty that is acted upon. Once there have been identified in the soul an active faculty and one that is acted upon, it is not implausible that passing-away be necessitated for it. For the cause of the passing-away of things is precisely the failure of acted-upon faculties to yield to active faculties.[155] Therefore, when the active faculty in the soul, which is the faculty for intellection, is acquiesced to by the faculty that is acted upon, which is the faculty for experiencing delight, it [viz. the soul] is then left to its nature and continues on and does not pass away. But when the active faculty in the soul is not yielded to, the soul remains in a condition opposite to its nature, and suffering befalls it. The degrees of suffering, however, vary, and the suffering might intensify to the point of necessitating the soul's passing away. That which is under investigation, however, is: Does it pass away into something or into nothing? And if it passes into something, then into what? Even if the doors to investigation are locked in this matter, it would nevertheless appear that the final passing-away, after the suffering called Gehenna, is the passing-away of the disposition that the substance has by its nature, as if there could remain a spirit naked of all disposition. This is what the Rabbis call ash, which is the remnant of a burnt thing after it has been burned.[156] Even if it has not reached the final level of passing-away, it is not implausible that it undergo temporary purgation, in accordance with divine wisdom, and, with the passage of time, remain at this stage. This is in accordance with God's graciousness, may His name be forever exalted. Thus do all these difficulties appear to be resolved.

The fifth difficulty concerns the idea that a person is judged according to the majority of his deeds. This may indeed be resolved by saying that this concerns the corporeal promise alone. And if this idea is nevertheless confirmed with respect to the spiritual promise, we shall seek a mean between the two extremes. For there is a

---

[155] See II. vi. 1 n. 414 for how passing-away occurs in the body. Crescas here considers a structurally comparable process for the soul.

[156] The Vienna and Florence manuscripts have: "after its usefulness (תועלתו) has been burned."

mean between one who repents and one who is firm in his rebellion. This is someone who fails to repent either because he became lax in this regard on account of forgetfulness or because he was caught up in sin on account of not protecting himself from the snare of his inclination—but neither out of rebellion nor out of treachery. In cases such as this, "He who abounds in kindness tips [the scales] toward kindness."[157]

The sixth difficulty has to do with divine justice: how can God reward or punish anyone different in species from the one who is obedient or transgresses? It is fitting that we say by way of resolution that, since the soul is, as was established, a substance by definition, then, although it is the form of the body insofar as it bestows on the body its human perfection when it unites with it, it nevertheless does not change in its own essence but only separates from the body. Since it is the noble part of a person, and this part, before it separates, is unchanging in its essence and then only separates from the body, and since bodily good and bad are not true good and bad, it is therefore reasonable that true reward and punishment, true good and bad, are spiritual good and bad.

The seventh difficulty concerns the question: how could divine justice not choose for a man reward and punishment affecting his body and soul, since the agent, whether of obedience or of rebellion, is this man insofar as he is body-and-soul? This solution is very easy, in accordance with the tradition, since the intention behind the resurrection of the dead, as it appears, is this end itself, namely, that reward and punishment be appropriate and correct—as it is said: "And many of those who sleep in the dust of the earth shall awaken, some to everlasting life, and some to reproaches and everlasting abhorrence"[158]—as will be explained below, God willing.

Since "the measure of good is more abundant,"[159] we have found that some of the pious, according to the tradition, did not experience the taste of death. Among them is Elijah the prophet, peace be upon him, of whom it is said explicitly in Scripture: "Today the Lord will take your master from your head"[160]—to the point that he ascended with horses of fire and a chariot of fire, and he is still alive and will soon be revealed, as the prophet said: "Behold I will send you Elijah the prophet before the coming of the great and awesome day of the Lord."[161]

Thus are all difficulties resolved. Praise is to God alone, who is exalted above all blessing and praise.

Part IV

CONCERNING resurrection of the dead.

Since this root-principle is recognized in the nation as affirmed in the Torah, as the Mishnah explicitly reports,[162] there are four matters that need to be clarified: first, an account of this view itself; second, its end and benefit; third, the severe punishment that awaits one who denies this root-principle—to the point that the Sages, specifically with respect to this view, set as the punishment for one who says that it is not affirmed in the Torah that he has no portion in the world-to-come; and fourth, the

---

[157] BT *Rosh Hashanah* 17a. There is here a play on words between "abounds" (רב) and "majority" (רוב).
[158] Dan. 12: 2.   [159] BT *Sotah* 11a; BT *Sanhedrin* 100b.   [160] 2 Kgs. 2: 3.
[161] Joel 3: 4; Mal. 3: 23.   [162] BT *Sanhedrin* 10a.

resolution of some of the difficulties that attend it. We therefore assigned four chapters to this issue.

Chapter I

AN account of this view itself.

Four things must be determined in this connection. The first is whether resurrection is universal or partial; and, if partial, which part [is resurrected]. The second is the timing of the resurrection. The third, whether or not the dead will use their senses and will die after they come to life. The fourth, whether there will be at that time a day of judgment, as our Rabbis of blessed memory held.

There is no way to apply knowledge of the truth to such matters; one must rely on tradition, on what Scripture says about them, and on considered judgment and reasoned deliberation alone. I assert first[163] that, according to what is said explicitly, "And many of them that sleep in the dust of the earth shall awake, some to everlasting life, and some to reproaches and everlasting abhorrence,"[164] it would seem that resurrection is not universal. And the interpretation of our Rabbis of blessed memory concurs. They say: "'And many of those who sleep in the dust of the earth shall awaken, some to everlasting life': not all of those who sleep."[165] Since resurrection is thus partial, there remains a doubt as to which part [of mankind] will be resurrected, but reasoned consideration determines that it is the completely righteous alone who will be resurrected. Yet the opposite of this is explicitly stated: "and some to reproaches and everlasting abhorrence." This is what increases perplexity in knowing which part will be resurrected. It appears that the right way, which leads directly to knowledge of the truth in this matter, is for us to focus on the end for the sake of which this magnificent wonder is created. For if we focus on this end, perhaps we will easily discover the part [of mankind] in whom it will actually be realized. We have therefore deferred this investigation to Chapter IV, which has been designated for the resolution of some of the difficulties. For we shall focus on the end in our discussion in Chapter II, God willing. And this should now suffice for the first.

The second concerns the timing of the resurrection. Based on the dicta of our Rabbis of blessed memory, it would seem that there is a dispute in this matter. According to tractate *Yoma* it would appear that the resurrection will take place at the time of the building of the third Temple in the days of the Messiah.[166] For they asked there: "Of the miter and the tunic, which is to be donned first?" They were puzzled by the question, and said: "When the Temple is built, Moses and Aaron will be there, too."[167] They regarded it as evident that the resurrection will occur when the construction of the Temple begins. One may not simply say that they were speaking loosely and that all they intended was that there was no place for that question until the time of the coming of the Messiah. For, most of the order of *Kodashim* and the

---

[163] "First" is not found in the Ferrara edition.
[164] Dan. 12: 2.
[165] Implicit in BT *Rosh Hashanah* 16b–17a.
[166] BT *Yoma* 5b.
[167] BT *Yoma* 5a. The reason the Sages are puzzled by the question being raised concerning which priestly vestment will be donned first is that, on the assumption that the resurrection occurs at the same time as the building of the Third Temple, Moses and Aaron, having been resurrected, would be there to answer it.

disputes it contains concern "the laws of the messianic age."[168] Indeed, how could it be otherwise? Furthermore, many reforms were instituted in the days of R. Joḥanan ben Zakkai because of this doubt [regarding the timing of the resurrection], as they say in *Gemara Rosh Hashanah*: "The Temple will speedily be rebuilt, and they will say, 'Last year did we not eat [the new produce] from daybreak? Now, too, let us eat.'"[169] From the straightforward meaning of a statement by Samuel which is found in many places, it appears that the resurrection will not occur in the days of the Messiah. For Samuel said explicitly that, "the only difference between this world and the days of the Messiah is the freedom (of the Israelites) from servitude to foreign kingdoms."[170] If the resurrection were at this time, it would appear that there would be an enormous difference between the two epochs, for in those days all the nations will be of one accord[171] to worship God, and all the promises that appear in the Prophets will be fulfilled then, since they will observe God's statutes and instructions, and will recognize God, to the point that the sons and daughters will prophesy, as Joel has said,[172] along with many other such promises. Therefore, according to Samuel's statement, the time of the resurrection will not be at the start of the coming of the Messiah. He thus disagrees with the straightforward sense of the *Gemara* in *Yoma*. Samuel's statement is not, however, one upon which there is general agreement in the *Gemara*, for there are among the Sages those who disagree with him. Yet it is not implausible that he would agree with the statement in *Yoma*, for we might say that it was accepted by them that the building of the Temple will not occur immediately with the coming of the Messiah, and that Samuel's statement applies solely to the coming of the Messiah, but that the resurrection will occur at the time of the building of the Temple—just as the straightforward sense of *Gemara Yoma* appears to suggest. Be that as it may, we may not disregard the straightforward sense of that discussion, for they dealt with the question straightforwardly. Therefore, it appears that, regardless of what occurs at the start of the days of the Messiah, there will be resurrection when [the building of] the Temple begins, according to the true tradition. This is the second matter.[173]

The third concerns whether or not the resurrected will use their senses and will die after they come to life. In this connection we have not found in the discussions of our Rabbis of blessed memory a sufficiently clear statement. Later commentators of blessed memory treated this matter in accordance with their own considered judgment, and differed from one another on this question. The Rabbi of the *Guide*, in his

---

[168] The expression, הלכתא למשיחא, is found at BT *Zevaḥim* 45a.

[169] BT *Rosh Hashanah* 30a. The time for eating the new produce will change once there is a Temple; it will no longer be at daybreak, as it was before.

[170] BT *Berakhot* 34b; *Sanhedrin* 99a.   [171] The expression, שכם אחד, is found at Zeph. 3: 9.

[172] Joel 3: 1.

[173] According to *Gemara Yoma*, the two events that will occur nearly simultaneously are the building of the third Temple and the resurrection of the dead. Thus if, on the one hand, as Samuel has maintained, the only difference between the epoch known as "the days of the Messiah" and the current state of the world is that the former marks the end of Israelite servitude, and if, on the other, the resurrection heralds an epoch that is vastly different from the state of this world, the only way to reconcile Samuel's statement with the prophetic descriptions of the epoch of resurrection is to say that the days of the Messiah precede the building of the Temple and the concurrent resurrection.

great composition,[174] and especially in the epistle he composed on the question of resurrection,[175] held that the world-to-come, which is mentioned in the discussions of our Rabbis of blessed memory, is the world that comes to each and every person immediately following his death. And of that world they said that "there is in it neither eating nor drinking nor anointing nor sexual relations, but the righteous sit with their crowns on their heads, enjoying the radiance of the Divine Presence."[176] But at the time of the resurrection there is eating and drinking, and the righteous will experience wondrous enjoyment and will apprehend what they failed to apprehend at first. After that they will die, and their souls will remain in the world-to-come at a level even higher than that which they attained earlier. He regarded as highly implausible the view of those who held that this dictum applied to the time of resurrection. He strengthened his view by saying that God would not create anything in vain and would not make anything that was not for something. For, God forbid that God's works resemble those of idolaters ["who have eyes but do not see"[177]]. He put it this way: "Perhaps according to these people the children of the world-to-come have no limbs, but are only bodies; perhaps they are spheres, or cylinders, or even cube-shaped beams. The view of these fools is only an amusement for the nations. If only they would be silent, and have their silence be their wisdom."[178] This is his view. He along with many Spanish sages embraced this view regarding the explication of "world-to-come" as it appears in discussions by our Rabbis of blessed memory.

In this matter that is before us, some later philosophizers followed the Rabbi, but R. Meir Halevi,[179] along with the great ones, among whom was Ramban of blessed memory, took serious exception to this view, and understood the statement literally to refer to the time of resurrection. For with regard to the world that comes immediately after death there would have been no need to teach that there is in it neither eating nor drinking. There are indeed many rabbinic dicta that teach that this term [viz. "world-to-come"] refers to the resurrection. We find as well that they have explicit dicta which, when taken literally, indicate that those who are resurrected do not die. They say, for example: "The dead whom God will in the future resurrect do not return to the dust."[180] Ramban expanded on this in *Sha'ar Hagemul* ("The Gate of Reward"),[181] and responded to what was maintained by the Rabbi of the *Guide*, namely, that the body's organs exist in order that they be used. Ramban said that their creation was for the sake of use before the resurrection, and that afterwards God did not wish to annul their creation. He maintained, in addition, that the human form harbors deep secrets for which it was created initially, and for those reasons God wished to preserve it. As for a comprehensive preservation of body-and-soul,

---

[174] The reference is to the *Mishneh Torah*. See *Hilkhot Teshuvah* 9: 2, and *Hilkhot Melakhim* 11 and 12.
[175] *Iggeret Teḥiyat Hametim*. [176] BT *Berakhot* 17a.
[177] Jer. 5: 21. Fisher adds this bracketed phrase for clarification. It is not found in the Ferrara edition or in the manuscripts. The "gods" of the idolaters have mouths that do not speak, eyes that do not see, and ears that do not hear. If God were to make men with organs that are useless—as they would be if at the resurrection people would neither eat nor drink—He would, God forbid, be like the idolaters.
[178] This quote is from Maimonides' *Epistle on Resurrection*. The final sentence is in the spirit of Job 13: 5.
[179] The reference is to Rabbeinu Meir son of Rabbi Todros Halevi Aboulafia, in his *Yad Ramah* (*An Upraised Hand*), "Ramah" being a play on the acronym of his name, R. Meir Halevi, on BT *Sanhedrin* 90a.
[180] BT *Sanhedrin* 92b.
[181] This is the final chapter of his work, *Torat Haadam* (*Instruction for Humanity*), par. 124.

owing to its having united with the supreme intellect, this is not improbable by nature, as [we see] in the case of Moses and Elijah. This is the view of this Rabbi [viz. Ramban]. He alluded in it to secrets of the tradition. And there is no doubt that the dicta of our Rabbis of blessed memory in their literal sense support this view. Yet it appears that this term [viz. "world-to-come"] encompasses two senses, and they use it in each of them, as will be discussed in Chapter IV, God willing. I shall also say that, when we delve deeply into the end and benefits of the resurrection, we will discover that this view is correct and clear, and that it leaves no room for the objections of the Rabbi of the *Guide*, to the effect that the organs of the body would then be in vain. We will therefore defer the determination of this view to Chapter IV, where we will explain the difficulties that apply to it. This should suffice for the third matter.

The fourth is whether there will be at that time a day of judgment, as our Rabbis of blessed memory held. According to the literal sense of the prophecies it would appear that the day of the great and awesome Name will come at the start of the time of the resurrection, as it is said: "And many of those who sleep in the dust of the earth shall awaken, some to everlasting life, and some to reproach and everlasting abhorrence."[182] It would appear that this miracle will be performed through Elijah, may he speedily be revealed. As it is written: "Behold, I will send you Elijah the prophet before the coming of the great and awesome day of the Lord."[183] This is indeed fitting, since everything found in Scripture concerning the wonders of God was performed through a prophet, and not through anyone else. It was therefore fitting that this great miracle be performed though a prophet after he was made an angel in body and soul, as has been verified in the case of Elijah of blessed memory. This is what we intended with respect to the fourth matter.

Chapter II

CONCERNING the intended end of this wondrous miracle and its benefits.

Since the end common to all the miracles and wonders is the imparting of true faith to the deniers, and the affixing of it in the heart of those who already subscribe to it, it is established of this universal miracle, common to our nation and to other nations, that it is worthy to strengthen faith in the heart of those who subscribe to it to the utmost, and to impart it to the heart of those who waver and deny. For when they show and tell their children—and the children, their fathers—what they experienced when their souls separated from their bodies, those who subscribe to the true faith will affix it in their heart and in the heart of their children most firmly; and those who deny it will come to believe without any residual doubt, and will say: "Our fathers have inherited only lies," as the prophet predicted.[184] The following is my understanding of the verse, "And he shall turn the heart of the fathers to the children, and the heart of the children to their fathers":[185] the resurrection will occur both for the

---

[182] Dan. 12: 2.   [183] Mal. 3: 23.   [184] Jer. 16: 19.
[185] Mal. 3: 24. On the usual interpretation of this verse, its meaning is that the fathers and the children are reconciled to one another. Crescas, however, interpreting the preposition על (ʿal), which means literally "on," as "on account of" rather than as "to," takes the verse to be speaking of the turning of both fathers and children to the proper faith because of the account each received from the other.

children and for the fathers. If for the children, they will have died before their fathers. The prophet through whom this great miracle will occur will turn the heart of the fathers [to faith], on account of the children who will explain to them what they experienced in those days; and the heart of the children he will also turn on account of the fathers [who will report to their children]. Scripture selected those who are closest, for it is fitting that they trust one another.

Since this miracle will be the greatest of those that are recorded in the Torah—whether insofar as it is universal or whether because the end that is intended in miracles generally ensues from this one more perfectly than it does from all past miracles, as the prophets predicted—it is fitting that this miracle be distinguished by being performed by means of a prophet who achieves the rank of the angels.

I say further that this miracle is intended for an additional end on account of which it is fitting that it be performed by Elijah the prophet and by no other. For since it is fitting according to political justice that true reward and punishment befall, respectively, the obedient one himself and the transgressor and not another, how much more so is this true of divine justice; it is insufficient that reward and punishment befall a soul once it is separated from the body. This is so even though obedience and transgression are more appropriately attributed to the more eminent part of man [viz. the soul], and while it is in the body reward and punishment do not befall it, as was discussed earlier. Thus, were it not for this miracle, there would indeed be a flaw, God forbid, in divine justice. Therefore, divine wisdom decreed this great miracle, through which divine justice and righteousness will be perfected in every respect. Since what was intended by this miracle is reward and punishment for body-and-soul, it is indeed fitting that this miracle be performed by means of the first prophet who merited this rank in body-and-soul, and this is Elijah, may he be remembered for good. For even though the midrash states that Enoch was also privileged to receive this honor,[186] he preceded the Torah. In addition, there is Elijah's vigorous effort in securing this end [viz. that of strengthening faith] in the days of Ahab, as it is said: "How long do you waver between two opinions?"[187] Nor is that midrash [concerning Enoch] uncontested, for Onkelos the Proselyte disputed it in his translation: "and he is not, for God has killed him."[188] And even if our Rabbis of blessed memory have indeed told us of others among the pious who were privileged to attain this rank, nevertheless, the first prophet to be so privileged, and who exerted effort toward this end,[189] was Elijah, may he be remembered for good. It is therefore

---

[186] The primary source for this legend is the Book of Enoch, which was excluded from the Hebrew biblical canon. The classic *midrashim* are sharply divided on the question of Enoch's ascent to heaven. Some, such as *Gen. Rabbah* 25: 1, cite it as a view held by heretics and refuted by the Rabbis. Other sources (*Midrash Aggadah*—a work by Solomon Buber, published in Vienna in 1894—and *Targum Yonatan*, both commenting on Gen. 5: 22; also *Zohar* I, 56b), however, affirm the view. It seems likely that the affirmation of Enoch's ascent was popular in late medieval Spain due to the influence of the *Zohar*.

[187] 1 Kgs. 18: 21. Elijah tried to keep the Israelites true to God and away from idolatry; Enoch never expended any comparable effort.

[188] Gen. 5: 24. Onkelos renders the Hebrew, לקח, "has taken," as the Aramaic, אמית, "has killed." For Onkelos, then, Enoch was not privileged as Elijah was with being removed from this earth while still alive.

[189] See n. 187.

fitting and necessary in accordance with divine justice that this miracle be performed through him.

I say, furthermore, that with this act the end of the creation of[190] the human species is fulfilled, which is in itself identical with the end intended by the Torah, as we discussed earlier at the end of Book II. This is so—whether in respect of the Creator or in respect of man. This end is the complete uniting with and attachment to God. In respect of God, it is the utmost benefaction possible, as was established there. Since this is so, it is fitting that it be fulfilled by means of one who was privileged to experience this uniting constantly—and such a one is Elijah who is remembered for good.

Chapter III

CONCERNING the severe punishment that awaits one who denies this root-principle.

It has been established with respect to this root-principle that through it the end[191] of the human species is perfected to the greatest possible extent, both in respect of God and in respect of man, as was discussed earlier. It has been established in addition that it strengthens the truth in the heart of those who know it, and divine justice becomes widely known through it. It is therefore most necessary to believe it, and it is fitting that one who denies it be severely punished.

This promise [of resurrection] is unique to this divine Torah, inasmuch as the earlier divine teachings from Adam to Noah did not promise this end: it is something that is as contrary to nature as is possible, unlike the case of psychic reward, which was well known in the earlier divine teachings. The latter is a matter that is natural for souls, as was discussed in Part III of this Book. It is therefore fitting that this promise be contained in this Torah, as was discussed earlier in relation to the corporeal promise. It was not, however, stated explicitly, since corporeal promise is something perceived by the senses, both generally and by the truly obedient, and this [viz. resurrection] is something that is not perceived until the time that it comes to pass. Because of the preciousness and great value of this matter, divine wisdom ordained, as our Sages of blessed memory held, that he who denies that resurrection is promised in the Torah will not be privileged to experience it. The Sages in *Gemara Sanhedrin* put it this way: "He denied the resurrection; therefore, he will have no portion in the resurrection."[192] This dictum is one of those which indicate that they regard the world-to-come as the resurrection of the dead. And indeed this is indicated as well by the interpretation they offered in *Sifrei*: "'That your days be multiplied and so, too, the days of your children':[193] 'your days' refers to this world; 'the days of your children,' to the days of the Messiah; 'as the days of the heavens

---

[190] Both Fisher and the Ferrara edition have צורת, "the form of," which Smilevitch renders, "*la forme de.*" The Florence and Vienna manuscripts have יצירת, "the creation of." "Form" might be correct since the human form is the soul. It is creation, however, that has the same end as the Torah. In Chapter IV as well we have: "and to further the end of creation." And Crescas refers the reader to the end of Book II, whose concern is creation's end.

[191] Following the manuscripts. The Ferrara edition omits "end," תכלית.

[192] BT *Sanhedrin* 90a.

[193] Deut. 11: 21. The verse continues: "in the land which the Lord swore to your fathers to give them, as the days of heaven above the earth."

above the earth,' to the world-to-come." It indeed appears that the Rabbis listed these epochs in order.

Chapter IV

RESOLUTION of some of the difficulties that attend it.

There are indeed serious difficulties in the phenomenon in itself, as well as in the way it was posited. Let us begin with the possibility of the phenomenon in itself. For we indeed noted in Book II Part III that the term "power" does not apply to anything the possibility of whose existence is inconceivable[194] by the intellect. Therefore, the term "power" does not apply to those intelligibles that cannot be contradicted. And since this is so, when the composite individual passes away as his simple parts decompose into their elements, even if it is verified that the parts that were part of Reuben recombine [at the resurrection] by the will of God, it is unavoidable that a new creature would emerge and it would not be confirmed that this one is the very same one. Yet according to what was posited, namely, that one of the essential ends of this miracle is to make divine justice manifest by bestowing reward and punishment[195] on the obedient individual or the transgressor himself, if it is not verified of him that he is his very self, the reward and punishment will not affect that individual himself.

Second, if we concede that when the simple parts recombine divine justice will be made manifest, then, if some of these parts were in the convexity of fire and some in the center of the earth or in other composites, to the extent that some were part of the body of a lion and some the part of an ant, would the animals break apart and return to being parts of the individual who merits resurrection? This is beyond inconceivable.

Third, once it is posited that one of the essential ends [of resurrection] is that divine justice be made manifest, how can it be that this miracle will occur for some but not for others? For this is indeed what was posited in Chapter I of this Part. For divine justice will not be manifest to that part that will not be privileged to experience this miracle.

Fourth, it is doubtful that the resurrection[196] will affect our entire nation in the straightforward sense of the Mishnah's dictum, "All Israel has a portion in the world-to-come,"[197] if all will have to die before the time of the resurrection. For the proposition that they will arise and live after death even if they die after the resurrection is utter nonsense, for that would necessitate that the resurrection be drawn out steadily. And indeed Scripture cries out and says, "before the coming of the great and awesome day of the Lord,"[198] which indicates that this comprehensive miracle takes place at one instant and is not drawn out steadily.

Fifth, since the promises found in the Prophets that apply to our nation as a whole bypass the custom of nature—such as length of days, as it is said: "For the youngest

---

[194] The manuscripts add "and unintelligible," בלתי מושכל.

[195] From this point until the end of the paragraph I translate in accordance with what appears only in the manuscripts: לאיש העובד או העובר בעצמו, הנה (אם) לא יתאמת בו היות הוא הוא, הנה לא יהיה הגמול והעונש לאיש ההוא בעצמו.

[196] The manuscripts contain the term "general," כוללת, modifying "resurrection."

[197] *Sanhedrin* 10: 1.   [198] Joel 3: 4; Mal. 3: 23.

will die a hundred years old, and the sinner being a hundred years old will be accursed,"[199] and the promise of prophecy, as it is said: "Your sons and daughters will prophesy, your old will dream dreams, your young men will see visions"[200]—it is uncertain whether these promises pertain to the time of the resurrection or to the days of the Messiah. Either way, it is something puzzling. For if these promises pertain to the time of the resurrection, it would appear that the resurrected would be using their senses and will die—which is the opposite of what was assumed. And if it pertains to the days of the Messiah, the dictum of Samuel opposes it, for he says: "The only difference between this world and the days of the Messiah is the freedom (of the Israelites) from servitude to foreign kingdoms."[201]

These are the objections raised with respect to the issue of resurrection in accordance with what was posited. It is fitting that we respond in the following way in resolving them.

With respect to the first and second, which concern the very possibility of resurrection, it has been established that God's power is infinite, that His knowledge, too, encompasses an infinite number of matters, and that all things are within His purview. Even things that are improbable to the greatest extent from the point of view of nature are to the greatest extent within God's reach—to the same extent and with no difference among them. It is therefore not unlikely that at the time ordained by God's wisdom for the occurrence of this great miracle the parts of the composite would be arranged in such a way that they are disposed to recombining as at first, without the need for the separating of the parts of other animals.[202] But it would appear that there is no need, for the purposes of this miracle, that these parts be the original parts themselves. For it is evident that even if those parts were those themselves, it would not be true of them that they would constitute the very same individual. There is therefore no benefit in those parts' combining, especially if they have to be separated from other animals. Nevertheless, divine justice would indeed be made manifest in them. For if God were to create a creature possessed of, for example, the temperament and traits of Reuben such that not one hair of his head fall to the ground,[203] which is something that is possible in the case of God, and Reuben's soul, which is an independent substance that would unite with that creature, there is no doubt that this soul and its faculties would use this body, upon uniting with it, precisely as it had formerly used Reuben's body. Since among its faculties as a whole are memory and imagination, the soul in this body will remember how it was at first, as if it had united with the simple parts of the elements that composed its body initially. For an amount of the element water, for example, bears no imprint that would indicate whether it derives from the element's concavity or its convexity. This is self-evident. Since this soul will use this body, it is right that divine justice be proved true through it. Indeed, how could it be otherwise? By way of analogy let us consider Reuben, who was born short of stature in terms of his vegetative soul and subsequently grew taller. Just as the parts of his body came to be from the food that descended through his body's organs—and it is evident that each and every part of

---

[199] Is. 65: 20.   [200] Joel 3: 1.   [201] BT *Berakhot* 34b; BT *Sanhedrin* 99a.
[202] The Ferrara edition and Fisher contain an "or," או, so that the phrase reads: "of animals or of others."
[203] 1 Sam. 14: 45.

his body came to be from food that was outside his body—and nevertheless his body is one substance, so, too, in the case of this soul: when it unites with this body, that is, when this body's parts, which, even though they come from places outside nevertheless constitute a body equivalent to Reuben in terms of his traits, unite with the soul, they constitute one substance together with it.[204] And since the soul provides the essential form to its possessor, and imparts to him its essence, this soul is the body's form and imparts to it its essence. And since the soul's essence is unchanging, it is necessary that the body that unites with it become assimilated to it, just as the food becomes assimilated to the receiver of the food and becomes in turn his body.

This would appear to be so on the basis of what our Rabbis of blessed memory endorsed and said: "The righteous are destined to stand clad; this is an a fortiori inference from the case of wheat."[205] The intent of this dictum is that the exposure of one's private parts is shameful, so much so that God decreed for man, once he knew good and evil, [that he be clad:] "And He made for them garments of skin and clothed them"[206]—for it is not fitting that they remain naked. The Rabbis drew an a fortiori inference from wheat in order to indicate that God brings things into existence in the most praiseworthy way; and just as wheat comes out [of the ground] in its covering to protect it from injury, so, too, do the righteous stand clad to protect them from shame. But it is clear from this dictum that, just as there is no special attention paid to whether the garment is composed of the parts themselves in which he was buried—so long as the garment mimics his shape, as if he had slept in his clothing, for in this there is some indication of the person's individuality—so, too, with respect to the body there is no special attention paid to the parts of the elements' being precisely those that separated from it—so long as they are in the same relation, as was said above. If, however, we cannot avoid saying that these parts are the same as those that separated out of the first composite, there is no harm in it. This is what appears to be the solution to these objections.

The third concerns that which was posited with respect to this miracle, namely, that it occurs for some and not for others: how is this accommodated by divine justice? It is fitting that we add to this what we promised in Chapter I, namely, an account of the part [of mankind] in which the manifestation of divine justice is confirmed. I assert that, since the straightforward sense of Scripture, which indicates that there will not be a universal resurrection, is inescapable, and since it was indeed established that one of the essential ends of resurrection is that divine justice be made manifest, it would appear that resurrection should occur in the case of the consummate righteous and the consummate wicked. For this would suffice to make divine justice manifest, as it is said: "Some to everlasting life, and some to reproaches and everlasting abhorrence."[207] But for those who are intermediate, those who do not attain the standard that would merit that this great and astounding miracle occur for them, psychic reward suffices. And if they do not attain corporeal[208] reward in their lifetimes, this is attributable to their inferior level. For the Judge is faithful in weighing in the scales of His wisdom the

---

[204] Following the Florence manuscript which has עצם אחד עמה; Fisher has עצם אחד ממש, "one actual substance."
[205] BT *Ketubot* 11b; BT *Sanhedrin* 90b. [206] Gen. 3: 21. [207] Dan. 12: 2.
[208] Only the Florence manuscript has, correctly, הגשמי.

amount of corporeal recompense due, so that He compensates the person in psychic reward either twofold, or as His simple kindness ordains.

Divine justice is thus confirmed, that is, in the weight of these two kinds of reward. For it will be seen that this is what the Psalmist says: "The *mishpatim*[209] of the Lord are true; they are righteous altogether."[210] That is to say, even if the corporeal recompense with respect to some is not just, the combined corporeal and psychic recompense is just. We saw fit to interpret this [verse] as applying solely to the judgments with which God compensates man, and not to interpret it as applying to the issuing of the ordinances, for the terms true and false do not apply to these, but rather such terms as fine and inferior, correct and appropriate, or incorrect and inappropriate.[211] According to this, those who are privileged to experience resurrection are the consummate righteous, for divine justice determines[212] that the intermediates, who do not merit this great miracle, will not be privileged to experience it. Therefore, that it is said: "All Israel has a portion in the world-to-come,"[213] may be understood in one of three[214] senses.

One is that the majority of Israel is intended. For we have a root-principle: "Inferences ought not be drawn from general rules, not even where an exception is specified."[215]

A second is that what is meant by [the dictum] that all Israel has a portion in the world-to-come is that it is their inheritance and a promise of this Torah—even though in other earlier divine teachings it was never promised—so that *if* they were all righteous they would indeed be privileged to experience resurrection. The prooftext for this is: "The people shall all be righteous; they shall inherit the land forever"[216]— that is, the land of life. And this is not something that pertains to other peoples.

A third is that the world-to-come encompasses both the time of the resurrection and the psychic reward after death. This is seen in the Rabbis' dictum: "The righteous among the nations of the world have a portion in the world-to-come,"[217] yet it does not appear as if they will experience the pleasantness of resurrection. And it is seen too in the idiom of the Sabbath blessing of the celestial luminaries, in which four epochs are alluded to, as follows: "There is none comparable to You, O Lord our God, in this world; there is none other than You, our King, in the life of the world-to-come; there is none but You, our redeemer, in the days of the Messiah; and there is none like You, our deliverer, during the resurrection of the dead." Apparently, they were listed in order: first, "this world"; next, "the world-to-come," which follows immediately upon death; next, "the days of the Messiah," which precedes the resurrection; next, "the resurrection," which comprises the arising and the pleasantness that follows afterwards. Since the other dictum, as well as yet others besides, imply that "the world-to-come" denotes the time of the resurrection, it appears that this term

---

[209] Crescas will now go on to explain his preference for "judgments," as one of two possible meanings of the term *mishpatim* (משפטים), which can also mean "ordinances."

[210] Ps. 19: 10.

[211] Crescas is rejecting Maimonides' interpretation of the verse, as found in *Guide* III. 26. As Maimonides interprets it, it is affirming the utility of all God's commandments.

[212] The Ferrara edition has להם; the manuscripts, יתן בהם.   [213] *Sanhedrin* 10: 1.

[214] In both the manuscripts and the Ferrara edition the number of senses is listed as two, yet explicitly three senses are discussed.

[215] BT *'Eruvin* 27a.   [216] Isa. 16: 21.   [217] *Tosefta Sanhedrin* 13: 2.

includes both [viz. the time immediately following death and the resurrection]. If we should say, however, that it includes only the time of the resurrection, it would be necessary to interpret the idiom of the blessing otherwise, to imply that "this world" comprises this world both in life and in death, and that "the world to come" refers to the pleasantness of the time of the resurrection following the arising. The Sages would then have arranged first the two extremities of the time period, followed by the intermediate ones, namely, the days of the Messiah and the arising. This is what they intended by the resurrection of the dead.

Regardless of how this term is interpreted, once the intended end and the benefits of this miracle—to make divine justice manifest, insofar as reward and punishment are dispensed appropriately; to engender faith; and to further the end of creation—are established, it becomes evident that the correct view, which is that those who are privileged to experience resurrection will not die, and do not eat, but rather, as the dictum says literally, "the righteous sit with their crowns on their heads," that is, the crowns of their perfection will be on their heads, as they are "enjoying the radiance of the Divine Presence,"[218] leaves no room for the Rabbi's understanding of the matter.[219] It is indeed necessary that they be in their bodies, and have their limbs and organs, in order that divine justice be made manifest. Furthermore, even though they do not drink and do not make use of the sense of taste or their reproductive organs, they will nevertheless speak and hear and serve God and hold fast to the Torah, as was the case with Elijah. Moreover, along with this they will impart the correct faith to others, as we will yet establish in resolving the fourth objection.

The fourth concerns whether all will die in the time preceding the resurrection. For if we take the Mishnah literally, and say that "all Israel has a portion in the world-to-come" intends the resurrection of the dead, it will be thought necessary that all die prior to the resurrection. I assert, however, that even if we take the dictum literally with respect to the resurrection, and affirm a universal arising, it is still not necessary that all die before that. For the world-to-come includes the arising and the time following the arising. And[220] with respect to the generation of the time of the arising, even if they are not privileged to experience attachment and uniting [with God], even if they use their sense organs and die, they will still have a portion in the world-to-come. For it was established above that among the benefits of this miracle is that it engenders faith in the hearts of others, as a result of which they will be privileged to experience that which they would not have been privileged to experience were it not for this miracle.[221] It is thus verified that all Israel has a portion in the world-to-come. It is acceptable to interpret the dictum that affirms that the pious of the nations of the world have a portion in the world-to-come to refer to the generation that exists at the time of the resurrection and to the generations that follow it, without necessitating that they be privileged to experience arising.

---

[218] BT *Berakhot* 17a.
[219] Maimonides' view is that at the time of the resurrection there will be eating and drinking—and death.
[220] The *vav* of conjunction is omitted in the Ferrara edition and in Fisher.
[221] Following the manuscripts which read: זכו למה שלא היו זוכים בו אם לא היה הנס ההוא, as opposed to the Ferrara edition which reads: זכו למה שהיו זוכים בו עם הנס ההוא, "they would be privileged to experience what they are privileged to experience through this miracle."

Be that as it may, the resolution of the fifth objection is very easy. It is that the promises found in the words of the prophets will come to fruition in the generation that exists at the time of the arising and in subsequent generations. For they will be influenced by those who arise, by the spirit of knowledge and fear of the Lord.[222] Even if they use all their senses, and live long, and reproduce, no absurdity will result.

This is what appears to be correct with respect to the resolution of these objections in accordance with the propositions we have acquired from the tradition, and from what appears to result from considered judgment and reasoned deliberation. God, may His name be praised, is the one who knows; He is exalted above all blessing and praise.

Part V

CONCERNING the eternality of the Torah.

There are two chapters devoted to this matter. The first concerns the proper way for this to be understood in accordance with what the tradition has transmitted, and the way in which we have come to know it. The second concerns the resolution of one objection that may be raised against it.

Chapter I

According to what the tradition transmits, this divine Torah, which includes the written Torah and the oral Torah, is eternal, as our Rabbis of blessed memory have said: "This teaches that a prophet is not permitted to introduce anything new from now on."[223] Therefore, it is impossible in any respect that any one of the Torah's commandments be cancelled or changed, even by a prophet. Our root-principle, however, is that a prophet may, as a temporary measure, invent a new instruction or permit something forbidden, as Elijah did on Mt. Carmel, so long as it does not involve idolatry.[224] And so, too, a court may conditionally enjoin the uprooting of something in the Torah when it involves abstention from [a permitted] action, and this for the purpose of erecting a protective barrier for the commandment. This is not considered an abrogation, for it is integral to the Torah and the tradition. Indeed it is confirmed by the tradition itself, as all of this is recorded in *Gemara Sanhedrin*.[225]

The eternality of the Torah may be arrived at as well through considered judgment and reasoned deliberation. For it was established on the basis of our earlier discussion that this Torah is at the height of perfection in leading those who hold fast to it— whether they are perfected or deficient—to human happiness and to the yearned-for end, and also that it provides the most excellent guidance toward the perfection of the virtues of character and intellect, as well as the utmost rousing of service and attachment to God. Consequently,[226] it is impossible that it be nullified, in whole or in part, other than by being replaced by another. For the proposition that it will be nullified and not replaced by another is absurd, since the end desired by God, and which is characteristic of Him, namely, benefaction, cannot be nullified. Therefore, were this Torah to be nullified, it would of necessity be replaced in whole or in part.

---

[222] Isa. 11: 2.   [223] BT *Shabbat* 104a.   [224] See 1 Kgs. 18.   [225] BT *Sanhedrin* 90a.
[226] Reading, with the manuscripts, הנה א"כ, rather than, with the Ferrara edition, אחר כך, "subsequently."

Yet it is inevitable that this replacement-Torah be either of the same measure of perfection as the first or of an inferior measure. It cannot be of an inferior measure, for that would not accord with God's desired end. And it is absurd that it be of the same measure of perfection as the first, for then the act of replacement is futile and without benefit. It is therefore evident on the basis of considered judgment and reasoned deliberation that this Torah cannot be changed in any way.

One later author argued plausibly from another perspective. For since this act of the giving of the Torah ensued from an agent of infinite perfection, it is necessary that the act be the most perfect possible. According to the previous argument it is necessarily impossible that the Torah be nullified in whole or in part. Yet even though this argument is sound when considered in itself, it will not yield the truth concerning this question from every perspective unless something extra is added. For one might object that the act which God, may His name be blessed and praised, performed in giving this Torah, was the most perfect possible for those who received it; the necessity that engendered it will not extend any further. Therefore, were the recipients either more perfect or more deficient, the nullification of this Torah, in whole or in part, and its replacement with one more suitable to the recipients, would have been possible. This is what happened in the case of the directive issued to Adam forbidding meat to the people [of that generation], for meat was later permitted to the sons of Noah. It happened similarly in the case of the directive issued to the sons of Noah, from whom the Israelites were later distinguished by their Torah, that is, by the Torah that included some changes from the previous [Noaḥide] commandments, as well as additional commandments—as is obvious.

Once it is established, however, on account of what this Torah contains, that it is at the height of perfection, whether for the perfected ones, such as the thinkers and the elect, since it contains the perfection of wisdom, or for the deficient, since it contains the perfection of the virtues and the awakening of hearts to service, to attachment [to God], and to love, which is eternal happiness—all of which was discussed at the end of Book II—it follows necessarily that this Torah as a whole is eternal. This is what we wished to establish.

Chapter II

RESOLUTION of the objection that may be raised with respect to this root-principle.

This objection is as follows. It is not unreasonable to say, with respect to the part of the Torah received by way of tradition, that is, the oral Torah, that it gives rise to uncertainties and disputes; and even with respect to the written Torah, that it contains a thing or things that are subject to doubt. Indeed, how could it be otherwise? Disputes between factions have indeed occurred with respect to this divine Torah: its divinity is accepted, but there are disputes concerning its root-principles. Some believe that a part of it is eternal and a part of it not. Some disagree concerning the interpretation of a part of the written Torah and of the majority of the oral Torah. They hold fast to their error[227] by saying that they received their tradition

---

[227] Following the Florence manuscript which has מחזיקים בטעותם; the Ferrara edition has מתחזקים בטענותם: "they are strengthened in their argument."

from the sages of their nation and from their elders, as, for example, the Sadducees, who are called Karaites in the Orient and in the south. Is there anything in this on which a person of true faith might rely that would determine[228] his faith? For in the faith of each of the members of the various sects there is a dominant belief, perhaps barring the entry of any suspicion or wavering with respect to the truth of his view and the falsehood of the view of others. Apparently, however, this determination [of the true faith] is not given to each from the perspective of his apprehension. For if the gate were open for each person to choose a faith as seemed best to him, there would not be a single sect that preserved its faith, since people's apprehension is constantly changing. Since this is so, how can a person possessed of the true faith be secure in his faith? If only I knew.

The resolution of this objection is not difficult, in light of what the Torah says about this and what is well known in the tradition, which is that we have a root-principle to the effect that whenever there is a doubt or a dispute regarding one of the matters in the Torah, the determination is assigned to those who are seated before God in the place of His choosing. As it is said: "If there should arise a matter too hard for you in judgment...then you shall arise, and go up.... And you shall come unto the Levite priests, and unto the judge."[229] If there is no single agreement, we are obligated to follow the majority. This obligation is in accordance with the tradition: "Even if they tell you of the right that it is left and of the left that it is right."[230] They based this on what is said: "You shall not turn aside from that which they shall declare unto you, to the right or to the left."[231] This was accepted to the point that we have the following in *Gemara [Baba] metzia*[232] concerning the dispute between R. Eliezer and the Sages regarding the oven of ʿAkhnai, when a voice emerged [from heaven] and said: "Why do you dispute R. Eliezer?" R. Joshua then stood up and said: "It is not in the heavens."[233] The interpretation is then offered that God has already given us the Torah, and in the Torah it is written: "Follow the majority."[234] They established in this way that even though R. Eliezer had truth on his side regarding the intent of the Torah, once the majority of the Sages of Israel agreed to something else, then, even if this was not the intent of the Torah, they are the ones to be heeded. This is because the Torah's root-principle is to follow the majority even if they say of the right that it is left.

It is indeed fitting that it be so. For if this requirement were to follow the priests or the Sanhedrin of the time, but only so long as they all agreed on matters of practice, the door would be open to any stubborn dissenter to dispute with them and to disobey them, claiming that they do not agree on matters of practice. This would be,

---

[228] Fisher has יכריח, "necessitate," where the manuscripts have יכריע, "determine." The latter is surely correct, since just a few lines later the text refers to "this determination," הזאת ההכרעה.

[229] Deut. 17: 8–9.   [230] *Sifrei* on Deut. 17: 8.   [231] Deut. 17: 11.

[232] BT *Baba metzia* 59b. The case concerned whether an oven made out of separate clay coils one atop the other with sand between the coils is susceptible to defilement. R. Eliezer declared it not susceptible to defilement; the Sages declared it susceptible. As separate coils they would not be susceptible, but the question is whether an outer coating of mortar or cement renders them a single unit.

[233] R. Joshua is quoting the verse Deut. 30: 12 in support of the Sages. He insists that the law is determined by majority rule and not by a heavenly voice or even by what is "objectively" correct.

[234] Exod. 23: 2.

too, a cause of the proliferation of disputes in Israel, and the Torah would become as if a thousand Torahs. But with this requirement, it is impossible for a dispute or a doubt to remain with respect to anything in the Torah, unless it were doubtful to all or to most of them, which is very implausible. And even if this unlikely thing were to happen, there is still a certain way to behave with respect to it, according to the root-principles of the tradition. Since this is so, one who maintains his faith in accordance with the unanimous agreement of the judges, or with the agreement of most, can be secure and free as much as is possible from suspicion and doubt.

Should the sects who oppose us respond: how is one to know which sect adheres to the ruling of the judges or to the majority of them? we assert that it is known and recognized by all the sects that, when the dispute of one sect began,[235] all the Sages of Israel held fast to this Torah and its interpretations, as we do today. The sect that opposed us and was the founder of this dispute was the mass of the people, who had no share at all in wisdom or study. It is therefore evident that their dispute with us is not something that should be called a dispute and be regarded as something that gives rise to an objection.

What does seem to count as an objection against us is the sect of the Sadducees, who take pride in the tradition they have from their sages. Yet it is well known, too, according to what has been transmitted concerning the events of that time, that at the time of the Men of the Great Assembly, in accordance with whose dictates we conduct our lives, both the high priests and the Sanhedrin consisted of Pharisees. It is they who transmitted the tradition to the Sages of the Mishnah. And they were exceedingly careful and punctilious in gaining a precise understanding of the Torah and in applying reasoning to it, employing the thirteen interpretive techniques devised for the Torah's interpretation, until the later Sages came along and added more notions and matters in the Talmud. It is in the category of the impossible for one who delves into them [viz. the Pharisees] to regard them as delusional, while this is without doubt appropriate with regard to the Sadducees. The basis for their delusion is well known, for to take the Torah's words literally is an easy fiction and approach to adopt. This is the opposite of the tradition of our ancestors, which has roots and branches, and whose branches have branches, upon which there is utmost agreement, and which renders impossible the creation of fictions and the invention of new things, unless it stems from the true tradition. As the Rabbi said in his *Introduction to the Mishnah*:[236] "When R. Ashi completed this noble compilation, it served for us as a faithful witness to 'that the holy spirit of God resides in him.'"[237] Therefore, no suspicion or wavering about it remains at all on account of their disputes. Praise is to God alone, who is exalted above all blessing and praise.

---

[235] The text that follows, until "was the mass of the people," is found in the manuscripts, but it is omitted in the Ferrara edition no doubt because of fear of censure inasmuch as the sect in question is surely the Christians. היו כל חכמי ישראל מחזיקים בתורה הזאת ובפירושיה, כמו שאנו מחזיקים בה היום. ושהכת שכנגדנו אשר יסדו המחלוקת חזה, היו מהמון העם....

[236] Maimonides, *Introduction to the Commentary on the Mishnah*, also known as his *Introduction to the Talmud*, ch. 9.

[237] Dan. 4: 5.

Part VI

CONCERNING the difference between Moses our Teacher and the other prophets.

According to what the Torah reports, the difference is evident—both in respect of miracles and in respect of the essence of the prophecy. We therefore assign two chapters to this Part.

Chapter I

CONCERNING the difference between them in respect of miracles.

The difference in respect of miracles is explicit in the Torah, where it is said: "[And there has not arisen since a prophet in Israel like unto Moses] ... in all the signs and the wonders, which the Lord sent him to do in the land of Egypt ... and in all the mighty hand, and in all the great terror, which Moses wrought in the sight of all Israel."[238] Moses' miracles were distinguished in three domains: in their number—which is indicated by its saying: "in all the signs and the wonders"; in their having been performed publicly before the sect opposed to the Torah, which was renowned largely for their wisdom, as our Sages hinted in *Gemara Menaḥot*: "Joḥani and Mamre said to Moses our Teacher: 'Moses, you are bringing straw to ʿOfraim'"[239]—which is indicated by its saying: "to do in the land of Egypt before Pharaoh and before his servants and before all the land"; and for their duration—which is indicated by its saying: "and in all the mighty hand." For the duration of the miracles [is seen] in the manna's descending and the Israelites' being led by the clouds of glory for forty years, as it is said: "and in all the great terror," and as our Rabbis of blessed memory put it: "'and in all the great terror': this refers to the revelation of the Divine Presence." Along with this we might include the phenomenon of Moses' face sending forth beams of light, as it is said of him, "And they feared drawing near to him":[240] all this is "the mighty hand." It seems to me, too, that this is alluded to in its saying: "the work of the Lord that I am about to do with you, that it is tremendous."[241] This confirms for me the promise of great wonders, since we do not hear after the assembly at Sinai of the occurrence of new great wonders that had not been previously created. Therefore, its saying, "that it is tremendous" is related to its saying, "and they feared drawing near to him." So, too, its saying, "with you" indicates only for him, after it was said in that verse, "before all your people I will do marvels";[242] and so, too, "and all the people among which you are," necessitates that its saying, "that I am about to do with you," refers to Moses.

Because of their [viz. the miracles'] number and because they were performed publicly before Pharaoh and his servants, whereas their duration was in the sight of Israel alone, the verse was ordered so that "Pharaoh and all his servants" preceded its saying "and with all the mighty hand," and so that "in the sight of all Israel" appeared last, for this [refers to that which] was for their eyes only.

---

[238] Deut. 34: 10–11.
[239] BT *Menaḥot* 85a. Joḥani and Mamre were two Egyptian magicians who were unimpressed by Moses' first miracles. ʿOfraim is presumably a land renowned for its straw. The expression is like ours of carrying coal to Newcastle.
[240] Exod. 34: 30.   [241] Exod. 34: 10.   [242] Exod. 34: 10.

It indeed appears that the order in Scripture exhibits a perfect progression. Since the miracles engender perfect faith in the soul, it is their number, first, that strengthens faith; then, it is their public display that strengthens it further, for it confirms their validity and frees them from the suspicion of trickery; and then they are even further strengthened by something that is beyond doubt, namely, their duration, for this frees them from the suspicion of sorcery, magic, and the creating of illusions, for these have no steadfastness or permanence. And it ended with "the great terror," for this is the most marvelous miracle without bounds, since it is the attachment of the Divine Presence to Israel, especially to Moses, steadily over time. And this alone would establish Moses' superiority to the other prophets, even if we did not appeal to the tradition's setting us straight regarding the sun's standing still for Moses. For even if Joshua's miracle were greater than Moses' insofar as it occurred in something more eminent than that in which Moses' miracles occurred, nevertheless, the miracle of the attachment of the Divine Presence to Moses is much more significant, because its subject is immeasurably more eminent.

We have agreed with the following view of our Rabbis of blessed memory in tractate *Baba batra*: "Hillel the Elder had eighty students. Thirty of them were worthy of having the Divine Presence rest upon them as it did upon Moses our Teacher, and thirty of them were worthy of having the sun stand still for them as it did for Joshua son of Nun."[243] There is no doubt that in saying, "were worthy of having the Divine Presence rest upon them as it did upon Moses our Teacher," they intended the attachment to God. For if they intended prophecy, Joshua too had the Divine Presence rest upon him. We hinted at this in Book II Part IV, in the resolution of the difficulty we mentioned. This should suffice for our discussion of miracles, along with what was said there. It was indeed established in Part I[244] who the agent of the miracles is, so as to leave no doubt. There is no value in repeating what was said there.

Chapter II

CONCERNING the difference between them in respect of the essence of prophecy.

The difference in respect of the essence of prophecy is explicit in the Torah. It is said, "If there be a prophet among you, I the Lord do make myself known unto him in a vision, I do speak with him in a dream. My servant Moses is not so."[245] At the conclusion of the Torah it is said: "And there has not arisen since a prophet in Israel like unto Moses, whom the Lord knew face to face."[246] The Rabbi in his *Commentary on the Mishnah* established this difference on four counts.[247] First, the prophecy of the other prophets involved an intermediary; in Moses' prophecy there was no intermediary. Second, other prophets could prophesy only in a dream at night, or, during the day when sleep descended upon them, or in a condition in which their senses were rendered ineffective and only thought itself remained—this is called a "vision" (מראה; *mar'ah*) or an "apparition" (מחזה; *maḥazeh*) but Moses received prophecy in the daytime while fully awake, between the two cherubs. Third, when

---

[243] BT *Baba batra* 134a.   [244] Fisher has ההוא בכלל for הא בכלל. See especially Part I Chapter V.
[245] Num. 12: 6–7.   [246] Deut. 34: 10.
[247] Maimonides, Commentary on *Sanhedrin* 10: 1, seventh principle.

the other prophets prophesied through either a vision or an angel, the limbs of their bodies shuddered and they themselves were seized with fear to the point that they nearly expired; but Moses was not afraid, even though he spoke to God face to face. Fourth, the other prophets did not prophesy at will, and some required preparation, as in the case of Elisha, who said, "And now, bring me a minstrel";[248] but Moses could prophesy at any time as is indicated by its saying: "Stand, and I shall hear what He commands."[249] A dictum of our Rabbis of blessed memory concurs, for they said: "'Speak to your brother Aaron, that he come not at all times into the holy place'—Aaron is forbidden to come in but Moses is not forbidden."[250] These are the words of the Rabbi.

The core of all the differences is its saying: "whom the Lord knew face to face." For the superior rank of Moses consists in the permanence of his prophecy and his attachment to God, and in the great extent to which his senses and faculties obeyed his intellectual faculty, all of which is alluded to in the Torah's saying, "My servant Moses is not so; he is trusted in all My house."[251] For in the case of the most faithful servant in the house of his master, all his efforts are devoted to the service of his master, and because of this, because of his greater attachment [to God], his prophecy was without the mediation of an angel. Also, because of the greater obedience of his senses and faculties to his intellectual faculty, his prophecy occurred while he was awake and without his being afraid and not by way of parables and riddles. Furthermore, because of the tenacity of his attachment, prophecy occurred at all times. Indeed it occurred in a special place, namely, between the two cherubs, for this is a place disposed to perfecting to an even greater degree Moses' extraordinary attachment [to God].

The other prophets, who did not attain the level Moses attained in attachment, did not receive prophecy face to face. Since they did not attain his rank in the obedience of their faculties [to the intellect], their prophecy occurred through the mediation of the imaginative faculty, which was alluded to in its saying: "I the Lord make myself known unto him in a vision (מראה; *mar'ah*), I speak with him in a dream."[252] It was indeed established in the book, *Sense and Sensibilia*,[253] that a dream occurs through the intermediation of the imagination—just as in the case of a mirror (מראה; *mar'ah*), in which the forms of those who look at it are imitated in it and it seems as if they are engraved in it, yet all this is the work of the imagination.[254] I assert that, since the prophecy of all the other prophets occurs at times while they are dreaming, at times while they are awake, but they imagine the thing they are seeing, the prophetic emanation comes from there [i.e. from the imagination]. Such is the case with Abraham who saw angels in the form of men; even though they were not men, speech came to him through them. So, too, in the case of Joshua's speaking with the angel. He did not see the essence of the angel, but speech reached him: "I am captain of the host of the Lord; I am now come."[255] Since the ranks of the prophets differ with respect to the extent to which they subjugate their [other] faculties to the intellectual

---

[248] 2 Kgs. 3: 15.   [249] Num. 9: 8.   [250] *Sifra* on Lev. 16: 2.   [251] Num. 12: 7.
[252] Num. 12: 6.   [253] An Aristotelian work cited previously in II. iv. 1.
[254] Crescas is connecting the term *mar'ah*, vision, to *mar'ah*, mirror. In both cases the imagination is operative.
[255] Josh. 5: 14.

faculty and their [other] faculties obey it, there are those who, because of how limited the subjugation is, experience a shuddering of their limbs and sudden travails,[256] as in the case of Daniel.[257] This must therefore be experienced at the start of the process, which is the moment of the battle between the other faculties and the intellect. But when the intellect triumphs over the other faculties, and a state of spiritual contemplativeness is achieved, the prophet should not experience any conflict. This is why it is said there: "Let my lord speak; for you have strengthened me."[258]

It is thus fitting that the details of these differences be understood without a doubt. But to take literally the idea[259] that the prophets are seized by fear and great terror, to the point that they nearly expire—God forbid.

Thus the faithful prophet Samuel at the start of his prophecy,[260] and in his reply with respect to the donkeys,[261] and so, too, Elisha in his reply to Na'aman,[262] among other occasions, demonstrate that they were not seized with great fear, nor did a deep slumber descend on them. Samuel even imagined that Eli was calling him;[263] it would appear that he imagined the voice [of God] to be Eli's voice with which he was undoubtedly quite familiar, as our Rabbis of blessed memory said: "How is it that a woman is permitted to a blind man? Because he is accustomed to her voice."[264] Since that speech was precisely like Eli's speech, that experience is called a vision, for the voice was imagined. Yet in Abraham's case, a deep slumber descended on him, as well as great fear. This is attributable to several possible factors. Perhaps prophets who do not prophesy constantly differ in their dispositions on account of the loosening of their attachment to God and the undoing of their bond with Him—possibly because of an overpowering external factor. Perhaps after Abraham exerted himself in the battle of the kings, this exertion affected his prophecy and a deep slumber descended on him. Another possibility is that this is an allusion to and parable of exile. Perhaps it was two of these things together. But in any event this does not entail that a deep slumber was experienced by the other prophets.

At the eminent assembly [at Mt. Sinai], however, the Israelites apprehended that which they apprehended, and particularly, according to the tradition, as the straightforward sense of Scripture indicates and as was discussed at the beginning of this work, the first two utterances of the Decalogue, "I am" and "You shall not have." [Their fright] was undoubtedly due to the mighty miracle and marvel; moreover, not all the Israelites, no doubt, were worthy of or disposed to prophecy. For this reason we must conclude that they discerned the words in these two utterances, and not mere sound.[265]

It is not fitting to say in interpreting the dicta of our Rabbis of blessed memory that they intended these utterances [viz. the first two utterances of the Decalogue] to be demonstrable things, such that the prophet and the scholar are equal in their

---

[256] The expression ויהפכו ציריו recalls an expression found in 1 Sam. 4: 19, כי נהפכו עליה ציריה, which means: "her [labor] pains came suddenly upon her."
[257] See Dan. 10: 16.   [258] Dan. 10: 19.
[259] This idea is Maimonides', as seen at the beginning of this chapter.
[260] See 1 Sam. 3: 20.   [261] See 1 Sam. 10: 2.   [262] See 1 Kgs. 5.
[263] See 1 Sam. 3.   [264] BT *Gittin* 23a.
[265] Maimonides contends in *Guide* II. 33 that the Israelites heard only sound and could not discern words.

judgment of them. For the intention of the second utterance is not the cornerstone of divine unity, as some thought, but rather [the commandment of] distancing oneself from idolatry.[266] It is true that once we acknowledge God's unity, we would not worship another, for example, one of His servants, in order to honor Him;[267] but this is not a matter of demonstration. Moreover, although this is not a matter with regard to which one would be prone to error, nevertheless, we have seen among the commentators some who have written the opposite. Yet the truth bears witness to itself.

This is what we intended in this Part. Praise is to God alone, who is exalted above all blessing and praise.

Part VII

CONCERNING the *Urim* and *Tummim*.

This root-principle is one known to us from the Torah and the tradition. Our discussion of it concerns two aspects. The first, the matter itself; the second, the resolution of the objections that may be raised with respect to it.

Chapter I

CONCERNING this root-principle itself.

According to the tradition, when the priest, while engaged in priestly activity, employs this instrument, which is a garment unique to the high priest, he is enveloped in the holy spirit as he meditates on the question that was asked. He imagines that the letters that are engraved protrude and arrange themselves in the order of the word from which he will glean the answer to his question. This, according to the tradition, occurs only under three conditions—the first having to do with the inquirer; the second having to do with the question; the third having to do with the person consulted.

With respect to the inquirer, it must be a king, or a high court, or someone to whom the care of the community is entrusted. With respect to the question, it must be something that concerns all Israel. And with respect to the person consulted, it must be the high priest on whom the Divine Presence rests. All of this is established in the seventh chapter of tractate *Yoma*.[268]

There is not a description of this instrument presented in the Torah, and only Moses was given instructions as to how to construct it. This accords with what some Sages have said, namely, that it contained the written explicit name of God. When the high priest, who is unique in the performance of the divine service, would observe the engraving of the tribes with the words "tribes of God," and his thoughts would linger on them, and he would focus on the apprehension of the divine name written there

---

[266] Here, too, Crescas opposes Maimonides.
[267] The version in the Ferrara edition, כאלו אמר ממשרתיו לבד, is difficult to render. I follow the manuscripts which have: כאלו תאמר אחד ממשרתיו לכבודו. "His servants" are the celestial bodies: the sun, the moon, and the stars.
[268] BT *Yoma* 73b.

and would direct his thought to God's service, divine wisdom ordains that he be clad in the holy spirit and attain the correct answer to his question.

Even though this is a standing miracle, like other standing miracles in the Torah, speculation does not discredit it. For the prophet himself requires external preparations on occasion, as occurred in the case of Elisha who said: "'But now bring me a minstrel.' And it came to pass, when the minstrel played, that the hand of the Lord came upon him."[269] And so, the high priest, even if he is not at the rank of prophet, could, through certain preparations, and through general divine providence, be clad in the holy spirit, so long as he was worthy of it. This is what we wished to establish.

Chapter II

RESOLUTION of the objections that may be raised with respect to it.

The first of these is that, as we have already seen, the rank of prophecy is higher than that of the holy spirit, and it was one of the conditions of this practice that the priest be such that the holy spirit could rest on him, but it was not required that he be a prophet. How then could it be that Joshua, who received the Torah from Moses; who was, at God's command, the one upon whom Moses placed his hand; and who was known to be a prophet, so much so that his prophecy became part of the written Torah[270]—which is something that we find concerning no other prophet but Aaron; and who amazed by performing the greatest of miracles, namely, that the sun stood still in the midst of the firmament for him—how could it be that he required a practice [performed by the priest] for which the holy spirit sufficed? Yet Scripture says: "And he shall stand before Eleazar the priest, who shall inquire for him of the judgment of the *Urim*."[271]

Second, since, as we have seen, the rank of prophecy exceeds that of the holy spirit, and since prophecy contained predictions that could fail to materialize, as was established in Book II, how could that which our Rabbis received by way of the tradition be true, namely, their saying that even if the predictions of prophecy may fail to be realized, those of the *Urim* and *Tummim* cannot fail?[272]

Third, as we saw in Part VI, one of the differences between the prophecy of Moses and that of the other prophets is that Moses could prophesy whenever he wished, which was not the case with any other prophets. How, then, could it be possible for this practice, in which only the holy spirit is involved, to receive an answer whenever it was needed?

The solution to the first difficulty is simple. Even if the prophet needed this practice, this does not mean that the holy spirit is superior to prophecy. Rather, since prophecy was not accessible to the prophet whenever he wished—this is a privilege that only Moses enjoyed—divine wisdom devised this practice, so that the whole of the nation might use it at a time of need, when there might not be a prophet who is in a position to prophesy.

---

[269] 2 Kgs. 3: 15.
[270] This refers to the view of certain Sages that Joshua was the author of the end of the Torah, which, according to them, was written after Moses died, since it recounts Moses' death. See BT *Baba batra* 15a.
[271] Num. 27: 21.   [272] BT *Yoma* 73b.

The second, too, is easy. Since the benefit attained from this practice is the giving of an answer when a question is asked at a time of need for the whole of Israel, then, if the prediction were to fail to materialize, the benefit would be forfeited. For there is no benefit in asking for an answer if, after the answer is received, the uncertainty remains. Therefore it is fitting that, because of the providence of God for the whole nation,[273] the prediction contained in the answer hold and not be reversed. This is self-evident.

It appears that the solution to the third difficulty, which concerns [the supposition] that, through this practice, the answer comes whenever there is a time of need, consists either of two reasons taken together or of just one of them. One is that God is provident for the whole nation, as in the case of some of the commandments, such as the sabbatical year and the festivals, for which, because of God's providence for the whole nation, there was a general standing miracle.[274] [The second is that,] with respect to the inferiority of the rank of the holy spirit as compared with that of prophecy, it is not unreasonable that concentration and a certain preparation would suffice for attaining what prophecy could not attain. Therefore, employing this practice at a time of need does not entail the superiority of the holy spirit to prophecy.

This is what we wished to establish in this chapter. Praise is to God alone, who is exalted above all blessing and praise.

Part VIII

CONCERNING the Messiah.

This discussion concerns two matters: the first, a description of the Messiah and issues related to him; the second, the timing of his arrival. We therefore assigned two chapters to this Part. We also added a third chapter, to explain with regard to the root-principles comprised in this Book that, although these are true beliefs, and those who deny them are heretics, they are not among the cornerstones and foundations of this divine Torah without which its existence would be inconceivable.

Chapter I

A DESCRIPTION of the Messiah and issues related to him.

That which has been related in Scripture and established in the tradition and has occasioned no dispute is that from the line of Jesse and his son David a king and prophet will arise, who will rule over Israel and Judah and will gather the dispersed of Israel and Judah from the lands of their dispersion. And they will be united under him, and will no longer be divided into two kingdoms, and never will there cease to be a king of this lineage occupying this throne of the Lord. No one has ever contested this description.

---

[273] From this point on the passage is corrupt in the Ferrara edition and in Fisher; missing is the text from here until the expression "as is the case with some of the commandments" in the next paragraph. The following is the version found in the manuscripts and translated here. אמנם שיהיה היעוד בתשובה קיים ובלתי חוזר, זה מבואר בעצמו. הג' יראה שהתתשובה במעשה הזה בכל עת הצורך היתה לב' סבות יחד או לא' מהן. הא' להשגחת השם על כלל האומה....

[274] See II. vi. 2.

What *has* engendered disagreement is the matter of whether or not a new order will be instituted in the days of the Messiah, one that diverges from the natural order, as some of the predictions found in the Prophets suggest. Nothing definitive has been established concerning this matter. Nevertheless, there is the view of Samuel, which appears in several places in the Talmud, and which it seems that the Sages of that generation accepted, namely, that "the only difference between this world and the days of the Messiah is [the freedom of the Israelites from] servitude to foreign kingdoms."[275] Be that as it may, the prophecies predict the abundant perfection of the messianic age, and, according to the Midrash, the Messiah would be privileged to experience something that Moses himself was not privileged to experience, namely, individual eternality. For thus did they interpret the verse, "Behold, my servant shall prosper":[276] "'he shall be exalted'—above Abraham; 'and be extolled'—above Moses; 'and be very high'—above the ministering angels."[277] If he was privileged to experience psychic reward and to delight in the radiance of the Divine Presence while a body-and-soul, he would already have become an angel. It seems likely, however, that, insofar as he was still in a body, he was even more exalted than the angels.

As for the question of whether or not the resurrection of the dead and the building of the Temple will occur immediately upon the Messiah's arrival, this is something we discussed sufficiently in Part IV. Some midrashic texts, however, regard the arrival of the Messiah son of Joseph as preceding that of the Messiah son of David, and they apply to him most of the prophecies contained in the section [in Isaiah], "Behold, my servant shall prosper." And some of the Geonim spoke of this as well. Nevertheless, since the truth of this has not been established, we saw no reason to speak of it at length.

Chapter II

CONCERNING the timing of the Messiah's arrival.

To discuss the precise timing of the Messiah's arrival is enervating and involves futile exertion. If we consider the Writings, we find that, far from specifying the time, they attest to its inaccessibility, as it is said: "And I heard, but I understood not ... for the words are shut up and sealed till the time of the end."[278] If we consider what our Rabbis of blessed memory said, we find: "Blasted be the bones of those who calculate the end.[279] As for that his coming will be in the future and has not taken place as yet, surely speaking about this at length is superfluous. For it was known widely and for a long time that, through the entire span of time whose events have been transmitted to us, we have neither heard nor was it ever related to us that there was a king who ruled Israel, or gathered our dispersed from the four corners of the earth, or, a fortiori, reigned for an extended period of time; rather, our senses attest to our having been dispersed in this exile of the kingdom of Edom, of Ishmael, of Persia and Media, and of Togarmah.[280]

---

[275] BT *Berakhot* 34b; *Sanhedrin* 99a.   [276] Isa. 52: 13.
[277] *Tanḥuma Toldot* (Buber ed.) 20, on Isa. 52: 13.   [278] Dan. 12: 8–9.
[279] BT *Sanhedrin* 97b.
[280] Crescas seeks here to discredit as absurd the Christian view that the Messiah has already come, since none of the predicted events associated with the advent of the Messiah have occurred.

Therefore, the current discussion concerns the length of this exile and the delay in the Messiah's coming even now, which is the year 1337 following the destruction of the Temple.[281] For it seems that the exile in Egypt lasted no longer than two hundred ten years. And the Babylonian exile, whose cause was idolatry, sexual immorality, bloodshed, and public violation of the Sabbath, lasted only seventy years. With regard to the current exile, the Rabbis disagreed as to its cause. For at the time of the destruction of the [Second] Temple, the Israelites did not commit these sins but, according to the first chapter of *Yoma*, they were righteous, as our Rabbis said there: "Since they were all righteous, for what reason were they punished?"[282] Some said it was due to gratuitous hatred between them; others, that they did not respect the Sages. But even if this is likely to have been their sin, the length of this exile is alarming. For it would seem, according to the rule of justice and equity, that the duration of punishment ought to reflect how serious or how minor the offense is. And since the transgressions that were responsible for the Babylonian exile were far more serious than those that entailed this one, it would seem fitting that the duration of this exile be shorter in comparison to that of the Babylonian exile. Yet our common knowledge and perception suggest just the opposite, namely, that this exile is far longer than the Babylonian exile, and to this day it remains unknown when divine anger will cease and when there will be an end to these wonders.[283]

To be sure, God's thoughts are deeper than ours, and His ways exalted above ours,[284] and it is not for us to evaluate them or to compare His to ours, for God is the one who knows His end, intention, and will. In the same way we do not know God's end in the matter of the flourishing of the wicked and the suffering of the righteous, nor the proportionality between them. So, too, is it well known with respect to the nations generally that they lack religion and a divine law, yet they enjoy a great measure of happiness—in the size of their population, the extent of their territory, their wealth, assets, and prestige. It is not our responsibility to assess and to evaluate God's chastisements, or to weigh on the scales of our intellect the punishment of exile as against our transgressions. God is the one who knows the end of His will, and we trust in Him as our judge.

Since in our time, however, many among the multitude are emboldened to challenge this view, to measure the exiles in relation to one another, and to assess the transgressions that preceded them and caused them, it is fitting that we say a bit more by way of resolving this problem, especially since, upon serious consideration, it is not difficult to do so. For if the punishment mandated for transgressions were exile of a certain duration, there would be occasion for the objector to object, and to assess the relation between the amount of time in relation to these transgressions versus those. But the true punishment was the destruction itself, and the dispersion

---

[281] Fisher follows the Florence manuscript here, making the year in question 1405–1406 CE. At the end of the work the manuscripts set its date according to the Jewish calendar, at 5170 since creation, which corresponds to 1410 CE. The manuscript was apparently completed in 1405–6, and was then revised and completed for a second time in 1410 CE.
[282] BT *Yoma* 9b.   [283] Dan. 12: 6.
[284] Based on Isa. 55: 8–9: "For My thoughts are not your thoughts, neither are your ways My ways, says the Lord. For as the heavens are higher than the earth, so are My ways higher than your ways, and My thoughts than your thoughts."

into exile of those who sinned in their souls. The duration and length of the exile is natural for those in exile. It is their redemption and ingathering that is miraculous and is consequent upon the divine will and the merit of those who are obedient to Him. If in the Babylonian exile, when there were the craftsmen and the smiths,[285] the Men of the Great Assembly, and prophets, the people merited the miracle of their deliverance, this nevertheless entails nothing for us. For if no miracle is performed for us that would gather our dispersed from the four corners of the earth, it is because we do not deserve it in the way our predecessors did. In a related case it is said: "Do not say: 'How was it that the former days were better than these?' for it is not out of wisdom that you inquire concerning this."[286]

This certainly suffices for the resolution of this matter, even if we concede the legitimacy of comparing exiles to one another. Yet the absolute truth is that this comparison is not legitimate, for it is known that this exile in which we find ourselves today is an exile that was mandated for us by the destruction of the First Temple. Those who were in Babylonia were remembered[287] [by God] but only by leave of Cyrus, king of Persia, and they remained under his governance and were not delivered ever, but were always under the rule of the kings of Media. Indeed only forty thousand were delivered, as is stated explicitly in the Book of Ezra.[288] At times they would rebel against the Greeks, and God wondrously performed miracles for them of which they were worthy[289] on account of their perfection and piety. And so it continued for most of the Second Temple period. They had the Great Assembly then, which was authorized by the kings of the nations, as is seen in the work of Yosef ben Gurion[290] and in some midrashic texts. With respect to them, the prophet said: "The glory of this latter house shall be greater than that of the former."[291] The exact opposite of that which occurred in the case of the First Temple occurred in the case of the Second Temple. For after the death of Solomon, the majority of Israelites rebelled against his royal line and erected two calves, as is well known. But in the era of the Second Temple they brought an offering on behalf of the kings of the nations. But because they had gratuitous hatred for one another and their hearts were not united, they failed in their rebellion so that Titus came and conquered them. In the final analysis, in the Second Temple period it was as if the king of Egypt who now rules in the beautiful land[292] were to permit the Jews in some of the lands over which he is sovereign to go up and build the Chosen House on condition that they remain under his rule. It would hardly be surprising if, after a number of days, they would rebel

---

[285] 2 Kgs. 24: 14. According to the Rabbis in BT *Sanhedrin* 38a, these terms actually signify the greatest Sages of that generation.

[286] Eccles. 7: 10.

[287] The term is נפקדו (*nifqedu*), which I take in the biblical sense of divine remembering of a promise followed by divine action to fulfill it. What happened in Babylonia, Crescas tells us, is that this "remembering" was at the pleasure of Cyrus who retained his power over those exiles who returned to Zion with his permission. See the end of the paragraph for more on "remembering."

[288] Ezra 2: 9.

[289] Fisher, following the Ferrara edition, has: והפליג השם לעשות עמהם נס באשר היו ראויים לעשות עמהם נס. The current translation follows the manuscripts, which have: והפליא ה' לעשות עמהם נס באשר היו ראויים לעשות להם נס. The difference in sense is negligible.

[290] The reference is to Flavius Josephus, the renowned Jewish-Roman historian of the 1st Century CE.

[291] Hag. 2: 9.   [292] ארץ הצבי, an expression found in Dan. 11: 16.

against him, he would exile them, and he would enslave them. This is the equivalent of what happened in the Second Temple. Therefore, the full truth, as it would appear, is that the current exile is an exile continuing from the destruction of the First Temple, which was alluded to in the Torah by the expression, "and you shall have been long (ונושנתם; *venoshantem*)[293] in the land." But they were remembered in the days of Ezra, as it is said: "After seventy years are accomplished for Babylon, I will remember you."[294] Clearly, this was not a complete redemption; it was only a remembering (פקידה; *peqidah*).

As it appears, this agrees with what is contained in the Psalm known as the Great Hallel.[295] It is apparently so called because it is entirely devoted to the recounting of God's kindnesses, from the time of creation until the end of days. It begins first with the wonders in Egypt, through its saying, "an inheritance for His servant Israel."[296] Next it alludes to the Israelites' being remembered in Babylon, as it is said: "who remembered us at our low estate."[297] The text specifically uses the term, "remembered" (זכירה; *zekhirah*), which is one and the same as *peqidah* (פקידה), for it was not a redemption but a remembering. Next it hinted at the future redemption, as it is said: "And has delivered us from our adversaries,"[298] for this will be a complete redemption. He again hinted at the mending of the world in its entirety, since it is said that they will serve Him "with one consent,"[299] and all people will speak one language as a result of the influence of the radiance of God's glory, and they will be guests at His table, as it is hinted at the Psalm's conclusion: "Who gives bread to all flesh, for His steadfast love endures forever."[300] This is the nature of truth, which bears witness to itself and is in agreement with itself from all perspectives.

It is thus established that the length of our exile affords no grounds on which to challenge our view. This is especially so for it indeed appears that the fruit of this exile is most wondrous. From the perspective of the whole of our nation, the sufferings in this world are a great treasure and an advocate for us for the world-to-come. It is reasonable to say that, just as in the case of the exile in Egypt no known explicit warning of punishment preceded it but it was a means of bringing us to the worship of God—as is hinted in its saying: "I am the Lord your God who has taken you out of the land of Egypt from the house of bondage; you shall have no other gods before Me"[301]—so, too, in our current exile. Since what we experienced of God's kindnesses was insufficient to render us perfect in loving Him, His wisdom ordained that we undergo this extensive exile, in order that we surrender our hearts to the greatest extent possible, and that God increase His kindnesses to us, and that, by gathering us from among the nations after this prolonged exile, we desist from following the desires of our heart as at other times and gain courage through loving God and serving Him. This is the good that is extended to our nation as a whole.

And [this exile also benefits] other nations—both insofar as we will be disposed to draw them to the service of God in the end of days, and insofar as they will derive

---

[293] Deut. 4: 25. The *gematria* of ונושנתם is 852, suggesting that they would be exiled from the land after eight hundred fifty-two years.
[294] Jer. 29: 10. [295] The reference is to Ps. 136. [296] Ps. 136: 22. [297] Ps. 136: 23.
[298] Ps. 136: 24. [299] Zeph. 3: 9. [300] Ps. 136: 25. [301] Exod. 20: 2–3.

benefit, on account of the merit of this nation, as it is said: "The whole world is sustained for the sake of My son Ḥaninah, and Ḥaninah My son has to subsist on a *kab* of carobs from one weekend to the next."[302] This is the intent of the prophet in the section, "Behold, my servant shall prosper," for it would appear that he spoke there[303] of the whole of Israel during this exile. Yet he began to hint at our Messiah, in saying, "he shall be exalted, and extolled, and very high," as the Midrash explains. For the exaltedness of Israel's king will secure Israel's becoming exalted. This should suffice now to fulfill my intent.

Chapter III

AN exposition of the view that the root-principles comprised in this Book, although they are true beliefs and there is no doubt as to their truth, are nevertheless not among the cornerstones and foundations of this divine Torah without which its existence would be inconceivable.

This may be easily established by means of induction. For with respect to the first root-principle, which is creation, we have already established earlier that, even for those who believe in anterior eternity, the power of God, His knowledge, and His will are necessitated, and on the basis of these the existence of the Torah may be conceived. Similarly, the Torah is conceivable without immortality of the soul, and without reward and punishment. For it was already established that true worship is not for the sake of reward. That the Torah is conceivable without the resurrection of the dead is certainly true. And whether the Torah is eternal or temporary, its existence would certainly be conceivable. So, too, the distinction between Moses and the other prophets: for even if there were no distinction between them, and even if it were possible to conceive of a prophet greater than Moses, the existence of the eternal divine Torah would be conceivable, for it is impossible that a prophet, even one greater than Moses, would deny the pronouncement of any other prophet, even if the other be inferior to him. And even without the Messiah, the existence of the Torah is conceivable. Moreover, with respect to the root-principles tied to specific commandments, there is no doubt that, were those commandments to be nonexistent, the existence of the divine Torah would nevertheless be conceivable.

Therefore, we counted the root-principles that are included in this Book among the true root-principles, such that one who denied any one of them would be considered a heretic, but we did not count them among the cornerstones and foundations without which the existence of the Torah would be inconceivable.

We did not think it right to count the avoidance of idolatry in this Part, as another has done,[304] since it is not a belief but a commandment.

This is what we wished to establish. And with this Division A of this Book is completed. Praise is to God alone.

---

[302] BT *Berakhot* 17b.
[303] Reading דבר שם (*dibber sham*) with the manuscripts, rather than שם דבר (*shem davar*) with Fisher and the Ferrara edition.
[304] The reference is to Maimonides.

Book III: Division B
Concerning beliefs tied to specific commandments.

When we investigated this matter, we discovered that there are three. The first is prayer and the priestly blessing. The second is repentance. And the third, the Day of Atonement and the four periods of the year that are established as festivals for the Lord. We therefore assigned three Parts to them.

We did not, however, see fit to include the belief tied to the ritual of the woman suspected of adultery, for it is an individual case. So, too, the belief tied to the pilgrim festivals and to joyous occasions, for the promises attached to their observance are of bodily benefit and, even though they will be balanced with psychic good, what applies to the other commandments and their promises will apply to these as well.

Part I

Concerning prayer and the priestly blessing.

Although these are commandments, they entail beliefs, namely, the belief that God is responsive to the person who prays to Him and to the priests who bless Israel. And since these are of the same genus, we included both in this Part, though we have devoted two chapters to them.

Chapter I

Concerning prayer.

The belief tied to this commandment is that we believe that God responds to the person who prays and places his trust in God in his heart in the right way. As it is said: "The Lord is nigh unto all who call upon Him, unto all who call upon Him in truth."[305] The intent of this verse is that the calling [upon God] not be by the mouth alone, with no regard for what is in the person's imagination and the thought in his heart, such that he is of the sect of which it is said: "You are near their mouth, but far from their hearts."[306] The phrase, "unto all who call upon Him," indicates that even if the person, without prayer, would be unworthy and unfit to receive that which he seeks, nevertheless prayer renders likely his attaining it—in addition to the reward [he receives] for the fulfillment of a commandment—if he places his trust in God in the right way. This

---

[305] Ps. 145: 18. [306] Jer. 12: 2; literally, "far from their kidneys."

is the secret of trust in its entirety. For it includes some of the cornerstones of the Torah, such as divine knowledge and individual providence, as well as that God is an agent who emanates by will. These conditions are explicitly stated in the tradition.

This root-principle is alluded to in Solomon's prayer, in which he said, "Also concerning the stranger,"[307] which indicates that even if a person is not worthy in himself, nevertheless, by means of prayer, it is likely that he will attain what he seeks. And what the Psalmist said attests to this as well: "O You who hear prayer, unto You does all flesh come."[308] It would appear that he said this because it is established among the conditions of prayer that the praises [of God] are arranged first, as is recorded in the first chapter of *'Avodah zarah*: "One ought always arrange his praises of the Holy One Blessed Be He first and petition only afterwards."[309] Since it is indeed thought that the articulation of God's praises should be withheld from the masses and reserved for the elite few, the Psalmist began by saying this with respect to it: "To You is silence praise, O God in Zion, and unto You will the vow be performed."[310] His intent in saying, "in Zion," is that Zion is the city in which God chose to dwell and on which He chose to set His sanctuary, and it is in Zion where, from one point of view, silence is praise to God, because of the trepidation that eminent men experience [there] with respect to praising God, for the reason which we shall set forth in what follows, God willing. From another point of view, his intent in saying, "will the vow be performed," is that, when sacrifices are brought either to fulfill a vow or voluntarily, it is as if those who offer them are setting a table for God as they would for people. And this despite the fact that everything comes from God, and everyone needs Him and all place their trust in Him. Therefore, he continued by saying: "O You who hear prayer, unto You does all flesh come"—that is, those who are perfect and those who are not perfect. This resembles the conclusion of the Psalm, "Praise to God,"[311] which is constructed on the model of a eulogy to God: "My mouth shall speak the praise of the Lord; and let all flesh bless His holy name for ever and ever."[312] "My mouth shall speak" refers to the Psalmist himself, the measure of whose perfection is obvious; and the Psalmist continues: "and let all flesh bless His holy name for ever and ever"—to include those who are imperfect. For this reason those who arranged the prayers attached to this: "And we shall bless the Lord from now until forever,"[313] to indicate that once the wisdom of God determined this [viz. that we may all praise God], as the Psalm of David suggests, it becomes fitting that we bless God from now until forever.

It is appropriate to expand on this matter somewhat, since some scholars have inferred from the words of the Rabbi of the *Guide* that ascribing attributes to God is to be avoided, since all positive attributes are impossible with respect to God. They relied on the view and words of R. Hanina, for they said: "Someone who came into the presence of R. Hanina said [in his prayer]: 'God the great, the valiant, the terrible, the mighty, the strong, the tremendous, the powerful.' R. Hanina said to him: 'Have you finished all the praises of your Master?... To a flesh-and-blood king who has

---

[307] 1 Kgs. 8: 41. Solomon entreats God to answer everyone's prayer, and in this verse he specifies the prayer of the "stranger," by which he surely means the non-Israelite. But Crescas interprets him to mean the individual who is unworthy.
[308] Ps. 65: 3.   [309] BT *Avodah zarah* 7b.   [310] Ps. 65: 2.
[311] Ps. 145.   [312] Ps. 145: 21.
[313] Ps. 115: 18. The *ashrei* prayer reproduces Ps. 145 but begins and ends with verses borrowed from other Psalms.

thousands of gold dinars and is praised for having silver ones; is this not an insult to him?'"[314] They interpreted this text, therefore, to mean that the terms [of praise] were to be regarded as equivocal [as applied to God and to man], on analogy with the striking comparison to praising a king for possessing silver, which is not even of the same species as gold. Yet as we noted earlier in our discussion of this matter, the attributes apply to God and to us by way of priority and posteriority, which is a kind of analogy. For the attributes are predicated of God as infinite, and of us as finite. And they are predicated of God also insofar as He bestows their existence on us, and of us insofar as we acquire them from Him. And from this point of view alone they differ in species, which is hinted at in the analogy of the silver coins and gold coins. But positive attributes are not excluded with respect to God—God forbid. And so the straightforward sense of the passage indicates. "Have you finished all the praises of your Master?" indicates that completing the praises is impossible with respect to God, inasmuch as they are infinite. We spoke of this matter at length, however, at the end of Book I, and what was said there is the very truth.

Since the attributes of God uttered in the framework of prayer are in the form of allegory or poetry, it was fitting that the Rabbis formulate the Kaddish prayer so that it attests to this. It therefore says: "who is above all blessing and song and praise," in order to suggest that blessings are not received by God but rather bestowed by Him. They said "song and praise" to indicate with respect to the attributes that they are intended as poetry or praise.[315] And they said "[and above] regret,"[316] to indicate petitioning for things one needs, lest it be thought that God is affected by prayer and is then regretful, for it is not so. Rather, God's eternal will wishes to respond to prayer when it is worthy. We have departed somewhat from the intent of this chapter, but this matter is something about which many have been misguided, as they followed the literal sense of the language of the *Guide*.

Let us return then to where we were, and let us say that it has indeed been established as well—in the narratives in the Torah, in the prayer offered by Moses on behalf of the Israelites, in the prayer of Abraham on behalf of Sodom and Gomorrah, in the prayer of Isaac on behalf of his wife, and in accounts of events in the Talmud on this matter—that through the merit of the prayer of a righteous man it is likely that God will respond to him even if he prays for another. Our Rabbis went so far as to hold that God will respond to the prayer of a righteous person even on behalf of the dead after they have died, and even on behalf of the wicked, as they did in the case of David and Absalom.[317] Even though this is a matter of midrash and homiletics, nevertheless, the standing custom throughout Israel is to bless even the dead and to pray on their behalf. On this and on similar things the Rabbis said: "Let the Israelites be, for even if they are not prophets, they are the children of prophets."[318]

---

[314] BT *Berakhot* 33b. The omitted text is as follows: "Now, even the three [praises] that we do say we should not have said had not Moses our Teacher said them and had not the Men of the Great Assembly instituted them in the liturgy, yet you come and say [all these]! To what may this be compared?"

[315] As opposed to literal truths.

[316] In the Kaddish prayer, the term that follows "above all blessing and song and praise" is ונחמתא (*venehemata*), which may be translated either as "and comfort," or as "and regret."

[317] See BT *Sotah* 10b.   [318] JT *Pesahim* 67a; See 2 Sam. 19.

Chapter II

CONCERNING the priestly blessing.

The belief tied to this commandment is explicit in the Torah: "So shall they put My name upon the children of Israel, and I will bless them."[319] Even if the Sages disagreed in *Ḥullin* regarding its interpretation—there are those who think that "them" refers to the Israelites and those who think it refers to the priests—nevertheless, the Israelites were not excluded from the blessing. And since the blessing was not conditional upon the perfection of the priest or upon his righteousness generally, we believe that when we were worthy of the blessing, that is, when the obstacle was not on account of us, there was then no obstacle on account of the priests—unless there were some things standing in the way of the fulfillment of the commandment, as was explained there.[320] What proves this is that, according to the Torah, even a drunk priest may bless the people; this practice is forbidden only by the Scribes. Similarly, it is said there that one suspected of a transgression may perform the benediction. It is thus evident that the performance of this commandment is not conditional upon the priest's being wise or righteous. Rather, since the priests are intermediaries between Israel and their Father in heaven, then, when this benediction is at the congregation's behest—at which time the priests are obligated to perform this commandment, as the Rabbis interpreted its saying, "Say to them,"[321] to refer to the priests[322]—the Israelites had already placed their trust in God. Since our root-principle maintains that communal prayer is more acceptable [than private prayer], as is stated in *Gemara Berakhot*,[323] there is no requirement that the priests be perfect such that if they were not, the benefit would be entirely forfeited.

In addition, God vested the commandments with special properties, like those of drugs. Just as drugs work because of their quality and in themselves, so, too, do the commandments of the Torah. But just as one drug interferes with the efficacy of another, so, too, in the case of keeping commandments and transgressing. Sometimes the effect of a commandment is to lead to a certain bodily benefit, but that very same benefit will be prevented by a transgression. Or, the other way around: a certain transgression produces a certain bad thing for the body, but the fulfillment of a single commandment, because of its beneficial nature, will prevent that bad thing. According to what is established in the Torah, God imbued the priests with a certain distinction, that of serving as intermediaries to receive the blessing from God and

---

[319] Num. 6: 27.

[320] Possible impediments include faulty defective speech, physical defects, certain transgressions, excessive youth, wine-consumption, and impure hands. See Maimonides, *Mishneh Torah, Hilkhot Nesiat Kapayyim* 15: 1.

[321] Num. 6: 23.

[322] BT *Sotah* 38a. The clause, "Say to them," is normally taken to mean "Say to the Israelites": Moses is to instruct the priest Aaron and his sons to bless the Israelites by addressing them, by "saying to them"—that is, by using the prescribed formula that follows. The Rabbis, in parsing this clause, interpret it to be directing the prayer-leader in the synagogue to "say to them," i.e. to call upon the priests, to recite the blessing-formula. For Crescas, then, when the community calls upon the priests to bless them, the priests must comply.

[323] BT *Berakhot* 8a.

to bestow it on Israel. It is therefore as if, by raising their palms upward as they were commanded, they receive the blessing in their hands to transmit to Israel. And it is indeed well known that hands are disposed to receiving blessings, as it is said: "And to bless all the work of your hand."[324]

It has been established explicitly in the tradition that God's acceptance of prayer is reserved especially for those who are attached to Him and who serve Him, even if their rank in the wisdom of Torah[325] is not high, more than it is for those whose wisdom is greater but are not at the same rank in service. *Gemara Berakhot* recounts an incident that supports the truth of what we said: "When R. Joḥanan ben Zakkai's son became ill... his wife said to him, 'Is R. Ḥanina greater than you?' He replied, 'He is like a servant before a king, while I am like a prince before a king.'"[326] It is fitting to understand that his status as prince represents his superiority to R. Ḥanina in wisdom, but R. Ḥanina lived ascetically and served God constantly and, for that reason, his prayer was more acceptable to God.

This is what we wished to establish. Praise is to God alone, who is exalted above all blessing and praise.

Part II

CONCERNING repentance.

This Part contains two chapters. The first clarifies this root-principle and the way in which we arrived at our knowledge of it. The second concerns the solution of difficulties that might be raised with respect to it.

Chapter I

EXPOSITION of this root-principle and the way in which we arrived at our knowledge of it.

According to what the Torah says and what is made explicit in the tradition, one of God's kindnesses is to welcome the sinner who returns to Him. Our Rabbis of blessed memory magnified this point by saying: "In the place where penitents stand the consummately righteous may not stand."[327] And they said in another place that their transgressions are counted as merits.[328] The reason for this is obvious, for the force that works to subjugate the will to service to God must be much stronger in the case of someone who conquers himself and returns to the service of God than in that of someone who does not need to conquer himself and is simply inclined to service. The one in whom the force effecting the submission is stronger deserves to be more attached to God and more favored. For the attachment and love that exert the stronger force would have to be stronger [in the case of the penitent than in the case of the righteous].

---

[324] Deut. 28: 12.
[325] The manuscripts have: "in wisdom—that is, in the wisdom of Torah"; בחכמה ר"ל בחכמת התורה.
[326] BT *Berakhot* 34b. R. Joḥanan ben Zakkai had asked R. Ḥanina ben Dosa to pray for his son's recovery.
[327] BT *Berakhot* 34b.   [328] BT *Yoma* 86b.

Even though there is no doubt that this is a wondrous kindness on God's part, nevertheless speculation concurs. For it is established of God that He is the absolute good, and that the end He most favors is benefaction. Therefore, even when a person has rebelled and has grown distant from service to God, nevertheless, when he mends his ways and awakens from the slumber of his foolishness, it is fitting that God welcome him, to the point indeed that God helps us and activates in our hearts a love for Him. This is especially so considering what was established earlier in Book II Part V,[329] namely, that on account of this [i.e. on account of our freedom to choose and hence to repent] we permitted ourselves the prayer in which we ask that God return us to Him in full repentance and draw us near to His service,[330] for otherwise the end of creation and of the giving of the Torah would not be. This is what we wished to explain.

The procedures for repentance and its levels are set forth in the book concerning rectitude known as *Gates of Righteousness* (שערי צדק; *Sha'arei Tzedeq*), by the righteous Rabbi, R. Jonah son of R. Abraham.[331]

Chapter II

THE resolution of two objections that may be raised with respect to this.

The first is that, once it is seen as fitting for God that He welcome repentance as an expression of the abundance of His kindness and goodness, how is it conceivable that one who intends repentance be prevented by God from repenting and, in addition, be punished for having been thus prevented? The tradition says explicitly in the Mishnah: "He who says I will sin and then repent is not permitted to repent; and for the one who says I will sin and the Day of Atonement will atone, the Day of Atonement will not atone."[332] Our Sages said as well: "There are twenty-four things that hinder repentance."[333] And the Torah says: "And the Lord hardened Pharaoh's heart,"[334] and God himself says explicitly: "For I have hardened his heart."[335] The Rabbi of the *Guide* already took note of this difficulty in his great composition.[336]

The second is that it would seem that one of the paths of repentance—and this is something on which earlier thinkers concurred—is the sorrow and sighing occasioned by the transgressions committed in one's [past] treachery against God through which one rebelled against His holy spirit. Must these arise only at the start of one's awakening to repentance and during the motion toward it? For the proposition that he [viz. the penitent] will experience sorrow at the completion of the path of repentance seems implausible and nearly impossible once we accept that his transgressions are counted as merits. If we should say that it is a matter of different perspectives, such that from the perspective of the sin alone, he would

---

[329] II. v is dedicated to the issue of human free choice.

[330] These expressions are found in the weekday *'amidah* prayer.

[331] This book is better known as *Gates of Repentance* (שערי תשובה). R. Jonah Gerondi was for a time one of Maimonides' principal opponents.

[332] *Yoma* 8: 9.   [333] There is no precise Talmudic source for this statement.

[334] Exod. 9: 12.   [335] Exod. 10: 1.   [336] See *Mishneh Torah, Hilkhot Teshuvah* 6: 3.

necessarily feel sorrow over what has happened in the past, but from the perspective of his repentance, it is permitted that he be happy over what has passed, we would in turn reply that the sense of the proposition that there is sorrow from the perspective of the sin alone is the sense intended by one who says that sorrow is required of the sinner who does not repent; but now that the sinner has completed the path of repentance, is he permitted solely to rejoice with respect to his earlier sin? And even if it is not possible that he be without some sort of sadness, nevertheless, when we measure the sorrow and the joy, will not the joy outweigh the sorrow, for joy is necessitated by the act's end, and it has been established that the end is the most eminent of the four causes?[337]

The resolution of the first objection is not difficult. It is of the nature of the twenty-four things that hinder repentance that they delay it and induce in man a laziness with respect to being aroused to it. Some of these [do so] by trivializing the transgressions in the eyes of those who commit them; some by habituating them to sins and drawing them to transgression; some because the transgressors hate rebuke, as is easily established of them. Yet it does not say that they "prevent" repentance but only that they "hinder"[338] it, that is, that they delay and defer it. But the one who says, "I will sin and then repent," is not provided the wherewithal to repent. Although the nature of this trait necessitates this, it is also a matter of measure-for-measure. For since in his stubbornness he relied on repentance and used his trust in repentance as an instrument to further his sinning and his rebellion against his creator, it is fitting that this support be removed from him. Yet since in most cases the force of Talmudic principles resides in their generality, it would seem that if he awakens from the slumber of his foolishness, and feels that he sinned in relying on repentance, and sees himself as the fool [who] rages and is confident,[339] and his whole desire is to return to God and abandon that sin, he will be accepted in his repentance. Yet since for the most part one who is like this will not be aroused in this way, the Talmud said simply: "he is not provided the wherewithal to repent."[340]

Concerning what is said about Pharaoh's being prevented from repenting, this need not be included in this category. For because of God's kindness and His providence for those who are attached to Him, He increases His wonders as well as

---

[337] This objection concerns whether the penitent will continue to feel sorrow over his past transgressions or, since he has now repented, will feel only joy. It would seem that whatever sorrow he would have experienced at the start of his path to repentance would dissipate completely by the time he reached the end of his path, especially since his very transgressions increase the worthiness of his repentance. Yet should one who has transgressed against God feel only joy, or at least very great joy and only minimal sorrow?

[338] Not מונעים but מעכבין.

[339] Prov. 14: 16. This verse contrasts the wise man who is fearful and avoids evil with the fool who is incautious and confident. Crescas plays on the term "confident" (בוטח; *boteaḥ*), taking it to mean "reliant on repentance."

[340] There are psychological hindrances to repentance, but none of them is such that it cannot be overcome. Even one who repeatedly sins and repents, abusing his repentance as a way to keep on sinning, may repent. When the Talmud suggests that such a person will be prevented from repenting, its intention is only that in almost every case such a person will not repent sincerely. Here, too, the hindrance is psychological in that repeated sinning strengthens the disposition to sin and weakens the disposition to do right. Nevertheless, should even such a person repent sincerely, God would welcome his repentance.

the plagues He visits on the wicked. And the reason is explained as follows: "For I hardened his heart and the heart of his servants, in order that I might show these My signs in their midst."[341] This is the proximate end. The final end is: "and that you may tell in the ears of your son, and of your son's son ... that you may know that I am the Lord."[342] The Rabbi approached the solution to this objection differently, and held generally that there are transgressions whose punishment is the precluding of repentance. But even if this is so, we do not need it to explain the plagues in Egypt because the Torah indeed supplied the reason, as we have seen.[343]

With respect to the resolution of the second objection, it might be said that one who defies the word of God deserves, in accordance with justice and equity, a punishment without limit. If, then, it is out of God's kindnesses that he who repents is welcomed in repentance, it is not fitting that there be a fixed measure, at which, once he reaches it, it may be said of him that he has completed the path of repentance in truth. This may be said only figuratively or metaphorically. Yet even if we assume that there is a certain limit at which, once a person reaches it, it may be said that he has completed the path of repentance in truth—as some Rabbinic dicta suggest[344]—it is still not hard to resolve this difficulty. For it was already established earlier that the final end for which man yearns is attachment and service to God. And [man's] happiness and pleasure, since this is the final good, is the end desired by God. Therefore, if receiving good and reward were the final end for man, a great difficulty would be entailed.[345] For since his earlier transgressions increased for him the amount of good, it would surely be fitting that he be happy on their account. But since the yearned-for end is love, and since the servant is the true lover,[346] he will be pained that his past conduct was hateful to God. Therefore, it is fitting that his having been for even a single hour wicked before God, may He be blessed and exalted, would pain him terribly, despite the increase of good that that time may have yielded.[347]

In this way another difficulty, one that troubled earlier thinkers, may be resolved as well. It concerns Moses' plea in saying: "Let me go over, please, and see."[348] They said that, since it is self-evident that there is no relation or comparison whatsoever between psychic reward and corporeal reward, it would seem to be fitting and

---

[341] Exod. 10: 1. [342] Exod. 10: 2.

[343] God's purpose in hardening Pharaoh's heart was, proximately, to exhibit His power, via the plagues, before the Egyptians. His final end was to foster faith among the Israelites for generations to come. The hardening of Pharaoh's heart, then, has nothing to do with depriving him of the ability to repent or relent, and so does not constitute a proper objection to the notion that God welcomes the penitent.

[344] See BT *Yoma* 86b, where the Rabbis celebrate the greatness of repentance and of God's compassion in receiving penitents, no matter how grievous their transgression.

[345] The manuscripts have in place of מחיב, "would be entailed," the exclamation, בחיי, "by my life."

[346] The translation here follows the manuscripts: אבל להיות התכלית הנכסף האהבה, והעובד הנה האוהב האמתי, כבר ...קשה. The Ferrara edition, followed by Fisher, has: אבל להיות התכלית הנכסף האהבה והעבודה, הנה האוהב האמתי כבר ...קשה. The translation of this version would be as follows: "But since the yearned-for end is love and service, the true lover will be pained...."

[347] The penitent will inevitably experience sorrow because his penitence can never be complete. But even if it could be complete, nevertheless, he could not be completely joyful. For however rewarding his current repentance—especially if his past transgressions count as merits—he will surely be pained over his past wickedness, since the true lover wishes only to serve.

[348] Deut. 3: 25. Moses pleads with God to be permitted to enter the Promised Land.

necessary that Moses yearn to the utmost that the psychic reward come speedily, and, a fortiori, that he not seek to delay it for even an instant. Yet this objection is not a difficult one. For it is possible that, considering the way Moses conducted his life in steadfast service and attachment, he might have hoped to attain his psychic reward, namely, the future reward of the resurrection of the dead, as has been established, while he was still alive, as was indeed the reward that Elijah was privileged to experience in his lifetime. We may assume, however, that once death was ordained for him, Moses no longer hoped for that end. I assert, then, that, since the final end for which man yearns is service and love, and since attachment[349] is in respect of service and not in respect of the pleasure attained, it is fitting that Moses yearn to go over into the land so that he might increase his service, even if that delayed the pleasure attained via psychic reward. This is especially so since, by persevering in service he would increase the level of his psychic reward, which would be better than rushing to attain the measure of psychic reward he was worthy to attain at this point.[350] This is, to be sure, constructed on two premises, whose truth is indubitable. The first is that psychic reward is infinite in potentiality—that is, it can increase infinitely. Thus, had Moses our Teacher, for example, who was at a far higher rank than any mortal, lived for a thousand years and been steadfast in his service, his rank would have been far higher. Otherwise, the reward determined for one who serves God for one hundred years and for one who serves Him for one thousand years, both doing the same kind of service, would, God forbid, be equivalent. The second is that the effort expended for the attainment of psychic reward is confined solely to one's lifetime. This is something our Rabbis of blessed memory established in the Mishnah. They said: "One hour of bliss in the world-to-come surpasses all of life in this world; and one hour devoted to repentance and good deeds in this world surpasses all of life in the world-to-come."[351] With this they establish the second premise, in which it is also implied that the final end for which man yearns is service, which is attained by means of repentance and good deeds. This is something understood in itself, for if the end of service and love were the pleasure attained, the pleasure would be yearned for more than the love, and the love of God would not be the greatest thing possible. Yet it was indeed established that it is fitting and necessary that the love of God be the highest and greatest thing possible, as we discussed above in Book II.

This is what we wished to establish in this Part. Praise is to God alone, who is exalted above all blessing and praise.

---

[349] The Florence manuscript does not have "attachment," דבקות (*deveiqut*).

[350] One might have thought that Moses would prefer to die since he would then be with God: what could be better? But as Crescas has argued, even though from the perspective of God, the end of the Torah is for human beings to be attached to Him, from the perspective of man, the end is service. Moses therefore prefers to continue to serve God rather than to enjoy immediately the pleasure of basking in His presence. Moreover, the longer the service, the greater the eventual pleasure. Even so, the greatest reward from the perspective of man is the service itself; no amount of pleasure of being in God's presence can outweigh it.

[351] *Avot* 4: 17. Crescas reverses the order of the two clauses.

Part III

CONCERNING the Day of Atonement and the four periods of the year.[352]

It was established already in our previous discussion that God's divine benefaction sought to render us as perfect as possible, devising all sorts of clever means to bring us to this end and to select us, those who hold fast to His Torah, to receive His providence, by specifying certain services for certain periods of the year, in order that we be directed by His direction and not by the direction of another. These times were therefore designated for the judgment of people, in accordance with what His wisdom has ordained and what we noted in our previous discussion. This also provides for us a wonderful utility, for by there being a time or times singled out for various services, one is powerfully aroused to focus one's thoughts on service. Since acts and their sustained practice establish firm character traits and dispositions in the soul, a person will gain perfection as he focuses on that service, and it is likely that he will persist in it. Thus at this season of the year, as the turn for the service approaches,[353] he will be more aroused than he was previously at this same time, and he will gain strength in this continually, as our Rabbis of blessed memory say: "The reward for a commandment is the commandment."[354]

We have thus completed Book III Division B, with the help of God, may He be blessed and may His name be praised forever. Amen.

---

[352] There are four seasons of divine judgment. On Passover the world is judged with respect to produce; on Shavuot, with respect to fruit; on Rosh Hashanah, all creatures are judged; and on Sukkot, with respect to rain. See BT *Rosh Hashanah* 16a.

[353] The expression בהגיע תור, "when the turn approaches," is reminiscent of the expression, בהגיע תור אסתר, "when Esther's turn approached" (Esther 2: 15).

[354] *Avot* 4: 2: שכר מצוה מצוה. The idea is that the performance of a commandment is its own reward. It is also possible to interpret this adage to mean that the reward for the fulfillment of one commandment is the opportunity to fulfill another.

Book IV

CONCERNING the beliefs and views toward which the intellect inclines, in accordance with the tradition.

There are thirteen issues [to be investigated] here;[1] (1) whether the universe is posteriorly eternal; (2) whether another universe or many other universes might exist; (3) whether the spheres are living and rational; (4) whether the motions of the celestial bodies affect and direct the course of human affairs; (5) whether amulets and incantations affect the acts of people; (6) demons; (7) whether a human soul transmigrates, which is what one sect of Sages calls *gilgul* (גלגול); (8) whether the soul of a child who has not yet begun his education is immortal; (9) Paradise[2] and Gehenna; (10) whether "the account of creation" (מעשה בראשית; *ma'aseh bereishit*) refers to physics, and "the account of the Chariot" (מעשה מרכבה; *ma'aseh merkavah*) refers to metaphysics, as some of the sages of our nation have held; (11) whether or not the intellect, the intellecter, and the intellected are one thing; (12) the prime mover; (13) the impossibility of apprehending the truth of God's essence.

Since the correct determination regarding these issues has not been established explicitly in the Torah, whether positively or negatively, we shall observe the following method of investigation. We shall present plausible arguments in support of each of the two contradictory positions, so that one who investigates will easily distinguish the correct from the incorrect.

Issue I

WHETHER the universe is posteriorly eternal.

It seems that there are many plausible considerations that support an affirmative answer. One is all the proofs and arguments that some philosophers thought necessitated its anterior eternity. For all the plausible considerations in support of the impossibility of the universe's coming-to-be support as well the impossibility of its passing-away. This is most evident with respect to them.

Another is that, even if we assume the universe's creation and coming-to-be, nevertheless, since existence is in itself good, as was established elsewhere, it follows

---

[1] The term דרוש (*darush*), which I have translated "issue," is sometimes rendered "inquiry" or "investigation." Smilevitch renders it "*enquête*." In my view דרוש is best regarded as that which is being investigated.
[2] Or, Garden of Eden.

that the nonexistence of the universe is bad. Since it was established that bad does not ensue from God, as was agreed to in the dicta of our Rabbis of blessed memory, in their saying: "No bad thing descends from on high,"[3] it would seem that it therefore follows that its nonexistence is impossible. Eternality means nothing but this.

Another is that physics has established that natural passing-away is a function of matter and not of form, when the passive powers dominate the active powers.[4] But this applies only to that which has an opposite. Since it is evident that celestial bodies have no opposite, it is evident that they have no cause of passing-away. And since the celestial bodies, through their motions and their luminosity, act upon and influence what is in this realm, it is also evident that it is impossible for what is in this realm to pass away, for the bodies that act upon it are constant and eternal.

Another is that, once it is assumed that the comprehensive coming-to-be is a matter of [divine] will, it follows necessarily that if it were to pass away, its passing-away would similarly be a matter of will. Not only is it impossible to attribute to God a change of will, but it is inconceivable that the absolute Good would will a total passing-away.

From all these points of view it would seem that speculation mandates that the world is posteriorly eternal. Indeed, the straightforward sense of Scripture concurs. It is said: "You, O Lord, are enthroned forever, Your throne is from generation to generation."[5] "Your throne" hints, as it would seem, at the heavens, as it is said: "The heavens are My throne."[6] It is said, too: "The Lord sits as king forever."[7] And it is known that "king" is a correlative term; a king is necessarily a king over a kingdom. As it is said: "The Lord will reign forever."[8]

On the negative side there are also plausible considerations. One is that, since it is assumed that the world came to be, as was discussed earlier, and it is a widely held belief that everything that comes to be also passes away, it follows necessarily that the universe will pass away.

Another is that, since opposite motions are detected in the celestial bodies, such as that some move from east to west and others from west to east and some combine many motions,[9] it would seem that passing-away is possible for them. If it is possible, it will necessarily become actual at some point. For the proposition that something which is possible in itself will never be actualized is impossible.[10] Therefore, the passing-away of the universe is necessary. Indeed one dictum of our Rabbis of blessed memory concurs. They said: "The world will exist for six thousand years, and for one thousand years it will be destroyed."[11] Since there are plausible considerations supporting both the positive and the negative, it is fitting that we distinguish the correct from the incorrect.

The first argument for the affirmative view relies on proofs that were thought to support anterior eternity and is therefore illegitimate. It was already established

---

[3] *Gen. Rabbah* 51: 3.   [4] See II. vi. 1 n. 414.   [5] Lam. 5: 19.
[6] Isa. 66: 1.   [7] Ps. 29: 10.   [8] Exod. 15: 18.
[9] The reference is to the eccentric and the epicycle, mentioned above in IIIA. i. 2.
[10] See Aristotle, *Metaph.* IX. iv. The idea seems to be that to assert of something possible that it will never—not even in infinite time—become actual is in effect to negate its possibility.
[11] BT *Rosh Hashanah* 31a.

that these proofs fail to necessitate this conclusion. On the contrary, creation was established beyond a doubt.

The second relies on the proposition that states that bad does not ensue from God. But since this proposition is conditional, that is, bad does not ensue from God essentially though it can ensue from God accidentally through what the nature of matter necessitates, the nonexistence of the universe is not impossible through what the nature of matter necessitates. Thus, bad does not ensue from God essentially but it can ensue accidentally on account of that which is acted upon.

The third relies on the nature of the celestial bodies which [purportedly] have no cause of passing-away since they have no opposite. This argument does not yield the truth in this matter. For one thing, the celestial bodies do exhibit opposition in terms of the direction of their motions. And it is acceptable to say of them that this opposition derives from their essence, even if their nature escapes us because of their extreme distance. Therefore, the foundation on which they constructed this argument is shaky and false.

For another, even if we admit that the celestial bodies do not pass away by their nature, nevertheless, since their coming-to-be and their enduring are volitional, as was explained earlier, the possibility of their passing away is not precluded.

And for another, even if it is conceded that the passing-away of celestial bodies is impossible, it does not follow that the passing-away of what is in this [lower] realm is impossible. For insofar as the configurations of the celestial bodies are constantly changing, it follows that, just as it is possible for the inhabited part of the world to be destroyed, so destruction is possible for the whole [of this realm]. The discrediting[12] of this argument, however, does not compel the possibility that the [entire] universe will pass away into nothing.

The fourth relies on that the volitional nature [on God's part] of [the universe's] coming-to-be is directed toward the end of benefaction, in which case volitional total passing-away would be inconceivable for the absolute Good. This is true in itself. Nevertheless, it does not yield the absolute truth. The absolute truth is that the world would not pass away unless it gave rise to an even better world. In this way it would proceed along a path of perfection to another world—something that is possible for the world in which we exist, as was discussed earlier. What *is* confirmed by this argument is that it is impossible for the world to pass away into nothing.

The plain meaning of Scripture does not guarantee the universe's eternity. For the divine throne does not persist other than from generation to generation. So long as the generations persist, God's throne will not pass away. But when the generations cease, the passing-away of the throne becomes possible. Similarly, God's kingship will endure with the enduring of the world, as it is said: "You will sit as long as the world."[13] This is especially the case once [it is accepted that] the [current] world will not pass away into nothing, for that into which it will pass away will indeed also be a

---

[12] Following the manuscripts which have אלא שהבטול, as opposed to the Ferrara edition and Fisher which have הנה למה שהבטול, "thus, since the discrediting."

[13] Lam. 5: 19. The expression, לעולם תשב, is normally rendered, "You will sit forever," but לעולם is here interpreted hyperliterally by Crescas to mean "for [the duration of] the world."

throne of God, and therefore it will turn out in fact that the throne and the kingship will be posteriorly eternal [even if the current world is not].

The first argument on the negative side relies on the proposition that everything that comes to be passes away. The falsity of this is easily established. For it was already dealt a severe blow and its truth was not established. Moreover, even if we were to concede its truth, it would apply only to natural coming-to-be but not to the sort of coming-to-be that is volitional.

The second relies on the opposition found in the celestial bodies and maintains that, because of this, passing-away is possible for them. This does not supply the truth in any way. For the difference in their motions does not necessitate essential opposition in them. Rather, it has been established that their coming-to-be is volitional, and a matter of providence, for the sake of perfecting that which is in this realm. Furthermore, even if we concede that opposition is found in them, then, just as their coming-to-be was volitional for the end of benefaction, so it is possible and fitting that their enduring be volitional, for the very same end.

When we consider carefully the dictum of our Rabbis of blessed memory, which affirmed the world's destruction after a certain amount of time, we will see that it more strongly supports the enduring of the world. This support may be seen, first, from the perspective of their limiting the time of destruction: "for one thousand years it will be destroyed." For if it were destroyed permanently after six thousand years, there would be no point in limiting the destruction to one thousand years. This is self-evident. Second, from its saying "destroyed" (חרוב; *ḥaruv*): for the term "destruction" does not apply to nonexistence. For this reason it seems that they affirm its enduring, whether in terms of species or in terms of individuals, and accept its being in a state of destruction for a limited time.

Therefore, what emerges from all that has been said is the affirmation of the posterior eternity of the world in terms of its species. In other words, it will not pass away into nothing, but it may pass away into another world, one that would progress beyond this one on the path of perfection. It seems, however, that that to which our Rabbis of blessed memory attested through their dictum is a certain destruction of this realm for a limited time. With respect, however, to the celestial bodies, they affirmed nothing. It is therefore more fitting that we affirm their individual eternity in accordance with the Torah. And this is especially so considering what was established concerning the existence of individual eternality during the time of the resurrection of the dead, as we saw previously. This should suffice for the first issue.

Issue II

WHETHER another universe or many other universes might exist.

There are plausible considerations supporting both sides. On the affirmative side, there are the following plausible considerations.

One is that, regardless of whether the universe came to be by will or by necessity, what could prevent that will or necessity from bringing about another world or worlds besides this one?

Another is that, since it has been established that the coming-to-be of the world was indeed a matter of will, a matter of benefaction and grace, and since it is evident that there is no stinginess or niggardliness in God's benefaction, the more universes, the more benefaction. It is therefore reasonable that there would be many worlds here. From these perspectives, the affirmative answer would seem to be the correct one.

On the negative side, however, there are plausible considerations as well. One is that, if there were many worlds here simultaneously, the following disjunction in this matter[14] would be inescapable. Between the worlds there must be either empty space or a body. According to the ancients, empty space is impossible. Therefore, by necessity, there is between them a body. The body would have to be either transparent or not. If it were transparent, we would necessarily see occasionally more than one sun and moon, when both were above the horizon. If it were an opaque body, it would receive its light from another source, since it appears that the opaque celestial bodies receive their light from another source. For according to those who maintain this position, the moon receives light from the sun, as do some of the planets. In this case, then, the body between the worlds would receive its light from the suns, and one would expect that we would see many planets from the other world or worlds. It is necessarily the case, therefore, according to the testimony of the senses, that there is no more than one world here.

Another is that, since a plurality of individuals is found only in the case of individuals that are subject to coming-to-be and passing-away, such as animals and plants, it would seem that their plurality is for the sake of preservation of the species alone. Therefore, for individuals that are not subject to passing-away, there would be no plurality. It follows necessarily, therefore, that, once it has been established that the universe is not subject to passing-away, it would also not be plural.

Another is that, since the agent of the universe is one, to the highest degree of simplicity, it would seem to be fitting that that which exists be one—either because of the accepted principle that from a simple one nothing ensues other than a simple one, or because it would seem that the greatest perfection for an emanated existent is that it resemble the emanator as much as possible; and, since this emanator is one, the oneness of the emanated existent would necessarily count as a perfection for it. From these considerations it follows necessarily that a multiplicity of worlds is impossible.

Since, however, there are plausible considerations on both sides, it is fitting that we distinguish the correct from the incorrect. We assert that:

The first argument on the affirmative side, the one that relies on the possibility that either by will or by necessity there would be a world other than this, would, in the case of will, necessitate not the existence of another world but only its possibility. If, however, there is an impediment from the perspective of plurality itself, even its possibility would be eliminated. It indeed seems likely that there is an impediment from the perspective of plurality because of one of the plausible considerations in support of the negative conclusion—either the one that sees plurality as superfluous in the case of individuals that are eternal,[15] or the one that regards oneness as a perfection—as was mentioned above.

---

[14] The Ferrara edition, followed by Fisher, has העולם, "the world," rather than הענין, "the matter."

[15] The purpose of plurality is to preserve species whose individuals pass away.

The second argument is the one that relies on the world's coming-to-be being volitional for the sake of benefaction and grace. Even were this to necessitate plurality, this plurality would inescapably have to be either limited or unlimited. It could not be limited, for no matter how many worlds are assumed, they could always be increased in order to increase benefaction. But it is also not possible that it be unlimited, for then the number of simultaneously existing bodies would be unlimited. Yet since it is also impossible that benefaction entail a plurality that is neither limited nor unlimited, it is evident that it does not necessitate plurality at all. Since it is thought that coming-to-be from the perspective of grace entails increased benefaction through an increase in the number of worlds, it is inescapable that one of two possibilities obtain. One is that divine wisdom ordained that the coming-to-be be limited—and it is not fitting to attempt to understand why the increase stops where it does, for no matter at what point it stops, the same question would arise once the number is fixed. The other is that divine wisdom ordained that the emanated existent be one, inasmuch as it resembles the emanator.[16]

With respect to the first argument in support of the negative conclusion, the one that relies on the necessary disjunction concerning what is between the worlds, namely, that it must be either emptiness or fullness, I assert that either way no absurdity follows. For it has not yet been established that empty space is impossible, and perhaps it is even the case that its necessity was established, as we explained in Book I. Therefore, if between the worlds there is emptiness, no absurdity will ensue. If there is fullness between them, the absurdities [associated with fullness] will not result either. For because of the great distance between worlds, it is plausible that we would not see anything of those planets.

With respect to the second argument, which is based on induction, it does not determine the truth in this issue. For one cannot base a proof on an analogical syllogism.[17] Moreover, even if it is the case with respect to eternal individuals that their plurality within one world is not necessitated and perhaps is even detrimental, no inference may be drawn from this to the impossibility of their plurality in different worlds.

The third argument, which derives from the perfection of the agent and from the resemblance of the emanated existent to God in respect of the attribute of oneness, also fails to necessitate the impossibility of plurality. For with respect to its own perfection, each world is independent of the others. And since the oneness that this world exhibits is not in any way dependent on another world, the plurality in the number of worlds need not detract from the perfection of the oneness that this world exhibits. Even if [generally] the emanated must be one since the emanator [is one],

---

[16] If God's goodness were to necessitate many worlds, yet there could neither be limited worlds (because there is no limit to God's goodness) nor unlimited worlds (because there cannot be unlimited simultaneously existing bodies), we would have to conclude that God's goodness does not necessitate plurality. If nevertheless there is plurality (which has not been ruled out but only shown not to be necessitated), then there would seem to be an arbitrary plural number—one whose point is opaque to us. The only other alternative is that the number of worlds be one, so that what emanates would most clearly resemble the emanator.

[17] We do not know if what is true for the individual within the world, namely, that if it is eternal there would be no need for plurality, is true for the world as a whole.

nevertheless, since the end of His emanating is benefaction and grace, a plurality of recipients of His benefaction is not precluded. This is self-evident.

Since this is so, that is, since it is established that in all the arguments we have mentioned, whether in support of an affirmative or of a negative conclusion, there is nothing that determines the truth about this issue, and all they do establish is the possibility of plurality, it is fitting that we not depart from the interpretation offered by some of our Rabbis of blessed memory. They said in Chapter 1 of ʿAvodah zarah: "this teaches that God courses through eighteen thousand worlds."[18] Their intent here is that God's providence traverses all those worlds. And this is what they intended with respect to this issue.

We saw no reason to extend this discussion by discrediting some of the analogies the Philosopher presented to establish that there is but one world. According to him, if we concede the existence of many worlds, we eliminate natural places. For he said that if we accept them, it would follow necessarily that, for example, parts of the earth in one world would move to their natural place in another world. But these are seductive words that are baseless. For in positing many worlds, we accept that there are natural places in each one. That is, earth will find its center in its world, and fire will find its periphery[19] in its world. This is self-evident. This should suffice for this issue.

Issue III

WHETHER the celestial bodies are living and rational.

There are plausible considerations supporting both sides. On the positive side, there are the following plausible considerations. One is that, since it has been established that the motions of the celestial bodies are the most perfect of ways in which the lower realm is constantly perfected, it is evident therefore that their source is an intellectual conception. It would appear that they apprehend this conception. For if we posit them as not apprehending it, then it is inescapable that their extraordinary order is either in them—whether as a matter of nature, as is the case with the motions of the elements, or as a matter of a compeller compelling this order. For it is absurd that this order be by chance, insofar as it is magnificent, constant, and suited for perfecting that which is in the lower realm. It would seem to be absurd, however, for it to be a matter of nature, for all motions which are a matter of nature move from a distinct that-from-which to a distinct that-to-which, just as happens in the case of the elements and of composites that are devoid of souls. Similarly in the case of chance motion, which occurs when things are in a place not their own but come to rest in their natural place. Celestial bodies, however, have no that-from-which from which they move, and no that-to-which to which they move. For, that from which they move is that to which they move.[20] And they also do not rest at all for the duration of

---

[18] BT ʿAvodah zarah 3b. The Rabbis fancifully interpret the clause in Ps. 68: 18, רכב אלהים רבתים אלפי שנאן, to mean: "The chariots of God (or the lands He traverses) are 20,000, with 2,000 missing," reading אלפי שנאן ("thousands upon thousands") as אלפי שאינן ("thousands that are missing".)

[19] The Ferrara edition has "its center," מרכזו, here as well, but the manuscripts have, clearly more correctly, "its periphery," מקיפו.

[20] Since they revolve.

an extended time. It would therefore seem to be impossible for their motion to be a matter of nature. It is evident, however, that it is also not a matter of compulsion, for something that is moved by compulsion is not in constant motion, and such motion is rare. And this is the opposite of how it appears.

Moreover, we find in things that follow a course of nature, that nature endows each and every one of them with its own particular principle to manage their ordered activities. The more eminent a thing, the more sufficient is this principle. You will therefore find that the human being, insofar as the activities needed for the preservation of his body and species are ordered, is more self-sufficient than animals are, and animals more than plants, all of which was established in Aristotle's book *Parts of Animals*.[21] Once this is established, and once it is further evident that the celestial bodies are more eminent than other natural things, it is clearly fitting that nature endow the celestial bodies with a more sufficient principle than other natural things have for carrying out their activities. This is because of the eminence of their rank and their being the perfect ones within the realm of coming-to-be.[22]

In addition, even if their order were compelled, it would be necessary that the compeller be a body. For how could a celestial body be in any way subject to the motive intellect without the intermediation of a body? Since it has been established that a body will not move without being moved, it follows necessarily either[23] that the entity moves by choice insofar as it has a soul, or that it is moved by another body[24] that compels it. But since this process cannot go on without end, it necessarily culminates in a mover possessed of a soul. Since this is so, it is fitting that this be posited as the start of the speculation. For nature does nothing in vain. It is thus evident that the celestial bodies move by apprehension and choice in order to perfect that which is in the lower realm.

Another is that the straightforward sense of Scripture indicates that the celestial bodies are capable of apprehension. For it is said: "The heavens declare the glory of God."[25] These are the considerations that support an affirmative answer.

Yet there are plausible considerations on the negative side as well. One of these is that, since the celestial bodies are material—and we shall see that material perceptions are acquired via the senses—and since the celestial bodies have no senses, as they are devoid of qualities, as was discussed in the book, *On the Heavens*,[26] it follows that they cannot apprehend.

Another is that if they could apprehend, their motion would be a matter of a desire and choice to perfect the lower existents. If they were acting for the sake of a certain end, they would have to apprehend the particulars of the motions of the planets, and the changes in their angles, and their combinings, through which the end is achieved. Yet since the apprehension of particulars is unimaginable without the senses, it

---

[21] See Aristotle, *Parts of Animals* X.

[22] The celestial bodies are frequently said to perfect, להשלים, that which is in the lower realm. The term used here, however, שלמי ההויה (*shelemei hahavayah*), suggests not their role as perfecters but their own state of perfection within the realm of coming-to-be.

[23] The אם is missing from the Ferrara edition and from Fisher.

[24] I follow the manuscripts that have "body," גשם, rather than the Ferrara edition that has "soul," נפש.

[25] Ps. 19: 2.   [26] Aristotle, *On the Heavens* I. iii. 270ª22ff.

follows that it is impossible for their motion to be a matter of apprehension. These considerations render plausible a negative answer. Since, however, there are plausible considerations on both sides, it is fitting that we distinguish the correct from the incorrect among them.

We assert that the first argument on the affirmative side does not provide the truth on this issue. For we see that natural motions contain a certain opposition and a certain diversity. For the motion of some of the elements is toward the center, the motion of others away from the center. And since this is the case, what would prevent the natural motion of the celestial bodies from occurring around the center?

Furthermore, if it is true of the elements that their natural state of rest occurs when they are in their natural place, what would prevent the natural state of the celestial bodies from being motion, such that there would be two differences between them and the elements, just as the elements themselves differ both in their motion and in their rest?

In addition, what was said concerning the impossibility that their motion is compelled, namely, that since it is fitting that nature endow them, because of the eminence of their rank, with a principle more sufficient than that with which it endows other natural things—this begs the question. For if the celestial bodies are inert bodies,[27] then the rank of an ant would be higher than theirs, for the elements, despite being greater in size, do not measure up in importance to an animal, and, a fortiori, to a human being, even if the latter is much smaller in size as compared to them.[28]

Also, it indeed appears that the matter of the motion of the celestial bodies cannot escape the following disjunction.[29] Either motion is natural for them, or rest is, or neither rest nor motion is natural for them, or both rest and motion are natural for them. It is absurd for both rest and motion to be natural for them, for if that were the case, they would necessarily rest and move simultaneously. It is also absurd for rest to be natural for them, for if that were the case they could not move other than by a compeller, which is precisely the possibility which they [viz. those who argue in the affirmative] sought to avoid. It is also absurd for neither motion nor rest to be natural for them. For it is inescapable that nature endowed them with a principle of motion and rest, unless it did not endow them with this potentiality at all. Yet if it did not endow them with this potentiality, neither motion nor rest could be attributed to them, and it would be impossible for them to move—yet we see them constantly in motion. And if it endowed them with a principle of both motion and rest, and both motion and rest are natural for them, they would have to move and rest simultaneously.

---

[27] The term "inert," מתים, is missing in the Ferrara edition and in Fisher.

[28] The eminence of the celestial bodies is precisely what is at issue. Whether they are superior or inferior to animals—and to human beings—has not been established.

[29] The text of the Ferrara edition from this point until the end of the paragraph is defective. It lists only one of the disjuncts and follows it with garbled refutations. I reproduce here the correct text based on the Florence manuscript, which is the version translated: אם שתהיה להם התנועה טבעית או המנוחה, ואם שלא תהיה להם טבעית לא המנוחה ולא התנועה, ואם שתהיה להם טבעית המנוחה והתנועה. ושקר שתהיה להם טבעית המנוחה והתנועה, שאם היה כן יחויב בהם שינוחו ויתנועעו יחד. ושקר ג"כ שתהיה להם המנוחה טבעית שאם כן לא היה אפשר בהם שיתנועעו, אלא מפאת מכריח והוא מה שברחו. ושקר ג"כ שלא תהיה טבעית לא התנועה ולא המנוחה, חה שלא ימלט מהיות הטבע שם בהם התחלה שיתנועעו וינוחו, אם שלא שם בהם כח על זה. והנה אם לא שם בהם כח על זה, הנה לא יתוארו בתנועה ולא במנוחה, והיה נמנע בהם שיתנועעו ואנחנו נראה אותם מתנועעים תמיד. ואם שם בהם התחלה שיתנועעו ושינוחו והנה התנועה והמנוחה טבעית להם, והיה להם שיתנועעו וינוחו יחד. יחויב א"כ בהכרח שהתנועה להם טבעית, ולזה נראה אותם מתנועעים תמיד, מבלתי שנרגיש בהם מנוחה בכל הזמן הארוך שהתעתקו אלינו קורותיו.

It therefore follows necessarily that it is motion that is natural to them, and that is why we see them always in motion, without sensing their ever being at rest in the entire long span of time whose events have been transmitted to us.

If one should object that their motion is not natural but by choice—in order to perfect the inferior existents in this realm—just as is the motion of human beings and animals who move by choice—I would respond that we would not rule out their motion's being by choice, although I would acknowledge that there is no escaping that it is natural. For it is impossible that nature would not have endowed them with a general principle of motion—just as in the case of human beings and animals whose motion is in a certain way by choice, while motion in general is natural to them. Yet although it is confirmed that the motion of the celestial bodies is natural, it does not follow that their motion is by choice. Rather, nature endowed them with a principle of motion in order to perfect that which is in this realm.

It has thus been established that the affirmative argument in this issue, the one that the Philosopher constructed and which the commentators on his books as well as some of the sages of our nation followed, does not establish the truth of the affirmative position.

The second argument, which is founded on the straightforward meaning of Scripture, also fails to prove the affirmative, although there can be no doubt that the celestial bodies convey, poetically and metaphorically, a powerful lesson concerning the glory of God. As it is said, poetically: "Then shall the trees of the wood sing for joy,"[30] and others of this sort.[31]

The arguments in support of the negative may have shown that it is unimaginable that the celestial bodies have particular apprehensions, but they nevertheless failed to dispel the possibility of their having a general apprehension in respect of their mover, insofar as they move in order to perfect that which is in this realm.

It is therefore evident that the gates to the investigation of this issue are locked. It would therefore seem that it is improper to divest scriptural texts and the formulations of the Men of the Great Assembly of their plain meaning, especially if one interprets "*ofanim* and holy living beings" mentioned in the Chariot envisioned by Ezekiel and in the formulated benedictions[32] as spheres and planets.[33] Let this suffice for the third issue.

Issue IV

WHETHER the motions of the celestial bodies affect and direct the course of human affairs.

It has been established in physics that the celestial bodies move the elements and produce their compositions, and bestow on the compounds the potentiality

---

[30] 1 Chr. 16: 33.

[31] The verse Ps. 19: 2, "The heavens declare the glory of God," need no more be taken literally as implying that the celestial bodies are capable of apprehension than other similarly poetic biblical verses, such as 1 Chr. 16: 33.

[32] This phrase appears in the Sabbath morning liturgy in the introduction to the *Shemaʿ*.

[33] If the Men of the Great Assembly took the angels depicted in Ezekiel's vision to be the celestial bodies, then they very probably regarded the celestial bodies as being capable of some sort of apprehension.

and disposition to receive their natural forms. There is no doubt that, in accordance with the mixing of these compounds from the four qualities, various attributes and impressions derive. This influence can extend so far as to bestow on certain human beings the propensity to receive the divine prophetic emanation, in accordance with the disposition of their natural virtue. This kind of direction of the course of human affairs was never subject to doubt. But doubt has been raised as to whether the celestial bodies have an influence and effect on men with regard to things that are not necessitated by the mixture of the four qualities, such as, whether a man is poor or rich, prosperous in commerce and in the discovery of treasure or the opposite, a husband to many wives or to just one, and, a fortiori, righteous or wicked, and other matters of this kind.

The affirmative position is well known to those adept at astrology. It was confirmed for them, through many repeated experiences, that, according to the configurations of the planets in the Zodiac, and their mutual disposition, and their connection to one another, and other conditions they discuss, these things are necessitated, even if they do not influence the properties of things.

There are plausible considerations on the negative side as well. One is that, since it has been established that for everything—whether natural or a product of art—there are four causes: efficient, material, formal, and final, it is evident that, if the celestial bodies had power and influence over these things, they could only function as the efficient cause if the matter were so disposed and prepared. It would appear, therefore, that the existence of those things would not depend solely on the influence of the celestial bodies. For if that in itself could necessitate, matter would not have true potentiality.[34]

Another is that it is known that among the causes of things, some are natural, some are volitional, and some are by chance. But if things were determined and necessitated by the celestial bodies, chance would not be chance, and will would not be will.

Another is that it is known that immaterial substances are of higher standing than material substances. This is so to the extent that, in truth, the immaterial are the agents, and the material are that which is acted upon. Since the human soul emanates from the higher sort of thing, how could it be that material bodies would act on it?

Another is that if human affairs were necessitated, the prescriptions and proscriptions of the Torah would be in vain, and reward and punishment would be undeserved.

Another is that, if this part [of the account of how things happen] had some veracity, it would seem not to be fitting for it to be forbidden the way soothsaying or divination is forbidden. For apparently it is this latter part alone, namely, the part that is not dependent on the mixture and nature of the qualities, that the Torah has prohibited. Thus have the Rabbis interpreted soothsaying, ʿonenut (עוננות), as, for example, determining the favorable time to go, from the root, ʿonot (עונות), "times"; and divination, niḥush (ניחוש), as, for example, from a gazelle crossing one's path.[35]

---

[34] If the configuration of the celestial bodies could fully determine on their own the course of events in the world, then it would make no difference on what sort of matter they, in their capacity as efficient cause, were operating. But in fact, not every kind of matter has the potentiality to be any kind of thing. The kind of matter receiving the influence would thus also be a factor.

[35] What the Torah forbids are superstitious predictions of good and bad fortune having nothing to do with the natures and mixtures of natural qualities.

Yet since the affirmative position is established on the basis of sense-experience repeated many times, and is especially reinforced by talismans and astrological tables which those adept at astrology[36] maintain are things that cannot be derived from the four qualities, it would seem that the plausible arguments on the negative side raise difficulties for the positive. It is fitting that we seek to resolve them.

We assert that the first argument, based on there being possibility in things, does not discredit the influence of the celestial bodies. And this for two reasons. The first is that, even though the celestial bodies act on compounds that have possibility, they are possible [only] in respect of themselves, but in respect of their causes they are necessitated. For example, the matter silver has the possibility of becoming a goblet or a ring, and when the artisan fashions it in the form of a ring, it is necessary in respect of the artisan that it be a ring, but in respect of itself its possibility remains. The second is that, although the celestial bodies act on and dispose the matter, they do not operate by constraint, especially in the case of the human being who has intellect and choice. We explained this at length in Book II Part V. In the same way we eliminate as well the second objection, which concerns things that are by chance and volitional.

The third concerns the rank of the intellecting soul. We have already conceded that choice is of higher rank than the constellation, and it is possible for a human being's individual providence to trump the constellation, as was established beyond a doubt in Books II and III. We explained there how the prescriptions and proscriptions serve an extraordinary purpose. Thus is the fourth difficulty resolved as well.

The fifth concerns the Torah's forbidding this part [of the account of how things happen]. This is easy to resolve. For soothsaying and divination are things that cause the multitude of the people to divest themselves of trust in God and to dispense with effort.[37] This is because of their ignorance of the secrets of possibility and necessity; they think that all things are absolutely necessitated, and that investing concerted effort into things is absurd. Yet this is undoubtedly an absurdity.

Thus have the doubts concerning this issue been dispelled, and the affirmative side established. This is something on which our Sages of blessed memory have agreed in many places in the Talmud, even as they insisted that true providence is superior to the constellation, just as this is the very truth. This should suffice for the fourth issue.

Issue V

WHETHER amulets and incantations affect the acts of people.

Even though some of the sages of our people thought it highly improbable that things such as these have any influence, and saw those who believe in them as misguided and foolish, we will not deny our senses and contradict what was well known to our Rabbis of blessed memory in many places in the Talmud. Rather, it is necessary that we try to resolve the following serious objection, which plausibly supports the negative side: how can an action directed by an agent through amulets and incantations come

---

[36] I take בעלי המשפט as a shortened form of בעלי משפט הכוכבים.

[37] In this respect the belief that the celestial bodies exert influence on human beings is dangerous for the people in the way soothsaying and divination are.

to pass, when the action falls outside nature's course? It was established in the *Metaphysics* that, whenever something effects the transition of another thing from potentiality to actuality, that which exists potentially in the thing acted upon exists actually in the agent.[38] Since it is evident that amulets and incantations do not contain in actuality anything of that which they intend to effect, it would seem that amulets and incantations are not the agents of this act. From this perspective alone it is evident that the celestial bodies, too, are not the agents, for there is no relation between them and amulets and incantations.[39] It would indeed appear that God, may His name be blessed and exalted, is also not the agent, for the following reasons.

One reason is that, since it is evident that these practices are subject to the will of the practitioner, it would follow that God, may His name be blessed and exalted, yields to the practitioner's will as well. Yet this is most nonsensical.

Another is that since, of these intentional practices, some are for good and some are for evil, it would follow that God sanctions evil, God forbid.

Another is that, if God were the agent—when it is evident that at the same time the practices are products of human choice and will—it would follow either that God has a new will, which is impossible for Him, or that the practice at this time stems from God's anteriorly eternal will, which threatens the nature of the possible—since man's will is then necessitated and constrained, and not one that wills and chooses.[40]

It is thus evident that God is not the agent. But it is evident, too, that man is not the agent, for it is clear that he, insofar as he is a man, cannot act outside nature's course. And if he does act, he necessarily acts through the intermediation of amulets and incantations. What, then, is the relation between them and the action that ensues from them? If only I knew.

Even though this objection is serious, it is not difficult to resolve it. For as it appears, the agent proximate to the act that ensues from amulets and incantations is not always the same but rather it varies. Sometimes, the proximate agent is the celestial bodies. Sometimes the proximate agent is God. What these agents have in common is that the amulets and incantations serve them at the level of instrument. For sometimes a caveat or condition is attached, namely, that their agent be wise and fear sin, and that he perform these practices out of holiness and purity and the proper intention, so that this and other such things are a kind of prayer and worship, which, as was already established, benefit him and others. These practices are but imitations, and pillars upon which to lean his thoughts. Therefore, amulets and incantations are the sorts of thing that operate at the level of instrument, for they instill faith and right thought in the hearts of the practitioners who work through them. And sometimes they contain no condition or caveat requiring that the agent be someone who fears sin or satisfies any of the other conditions. It is not implausible that agents of this sort are the celestial bodies, and that these practices serve [them] at the level of instruments,

---

[38] Aristotle, *Metaph.* IX. viii.
[39] In the absence of a relation between the celestial bodies, on the one hand, and amulets and incantations, on the other, the celestial bodies cannot be the actuality that could effect their transitioning from potentiality to actuality.
[40] The manuscripts, but not the Ferrara edition, contain the word, ובוחר, "and chooses."

because of the connection and relation that obtain between the celestial bodies and the inferior existents. As for us, even if we are ignorant of this relation and resemblance, we cannot escape that there is some relation between them—even if the Philosopher imagined the celestial bodies to be devoid of qualities. Since the relation is either essential or accidental, and since—due to the difference in their essence and their distance from one another—it is evident that it is not essential, it follows that it is accidental. Insofar as the relation is accidental, it necessarily resembles those qualities found in the inferior existents.

Yet how is this to be established? As I shall now show. We see that the sun warms the air and the moon cools it. If it is established that these planets do not have these qualities, and if, at the same time, it is evident that whenever something effects the transition from potentiality to actuality in another thing in a certain respect, that which is present in potentiality in that which is acted upon must be present in the agent in actuality, I cannot fathom how the sun and moon can give rise to heat and cold. The only way to explain it is by saying that the rays of the sun are related to the nature of heat, and the rays of the moon are related to the nature of cold. It is possible that the difference in their natures has influence in this way. At any rate, since the rays are related to them, it follows necessarily that they are members of the same genre of quality, for it is evident that things that do not share the same genre are unrelated—as there is no relation between sweet and white, and, a fortiori, between sweetness and a surface. It is evident that, for us, even if we are ignorant of the quality or qualities characterizing the celestial bodies, they must in any event still relate to the qualities of the inferior existents. How indeed could they fail to do so? For the efficacy of the talismans and the astrological tables are confirmed through repeated experience. And if there were no relation or resemblance between the celestial bodies and the inferior existents, they would have no efficacy. Why, then, should we dismiss as implausible the efficacy of talismans and incantations? Rather, it is because of the relation between the celestial bodies and these that through their intermediation the emanation from the celestial bodies reaches us. They serve at the level of instruments for those actions. And it is likely that the apprehension of the practitioner is a great aid in this. For the Rabbis say the following, as well as other similar things: "One [instance of healing] is to prove the [legitimacy of the] person; one is to prove the [legitimacy of the] amulet."[41]

Relation and resemblance have already been established by what is seen of the circular motion of the elements. For it is agreed that the element fire is moved by the sun. And it is impossible that it would move it by way of pushing or cutting off a part[42]—for three reasons. One is the distance between them. Second, the sun is not characterized by hardness and softness. And third, the sun is set in its sphere,

---

[41] BT *Shabbat* 61b.

[42] By pushing the element of fire downward and cutting off a part of it, the sun would be enabling it to mingle with the other elements. Leonard Levin points out that, although the Ferrara edition as well as Fisher have והחתוך, here rendered "cutting off," and rendered by Smilevitch "*un sectionnement*" (1171), both the Florence and the Vienna manuscripts have והכחוך, which means rubbing or scratching. In that case Crescas would be saying that the sun cannot move fire by rubbing against it because the sun is distant from fire, has no texture, and does not move from its place.

not moving from its place. It is inescapable, then, that its rays warm the fire and move it. Relation and resemblance are, then, inescapable as well. This should suffice for this matter.

Issue VI

CONCERNING demons.

Since the existence of demons is explicit in the Torah and in the words of our Rabbis of blessed memory, is also well known and long-accepted among the nations, and is verified by the senses, the investigation into them will concern two matters: what their quiddity is, and what the end of their existence is. Since we have no access to the science of their causes, the way we shall conduct our inquiry into these matters is by beginning with what is later and working back to what is earlier. For what is later is that which is known longer and more widely.

Four things are known about them. One is that they have knowledge of present and future natural matters, for through their intermediation such knowledge passes to man. The second is that they seek honor and obeisance, for through rituals they are gratified and implored to fulfill the requests of their worshiper, as it is said, "They sacrificed unto demons, non-gods,"[43] and as it is recorded in the books dealing with this art. The third is their preference for evil, such as to incite to sin, as Satan did with Job, and lies are in their nature, as it is reported in tractate *Sanhedrin*.[44] The fourth is that they operate with exceeding ease, and take on suddenly a human guise, as is well-known from incidents recorded in the Talmud on this matter. There is no need to mention them here.

I therefore assert that, since demons have knowledge of things present and future, there is no escaping that they have an intellectual aspect. And since they seek honor and prefer evil, which are things that ensue in them from their appetitive faculty, there is no escaping that in them the light elements dominate, despite their being composed of the four elements. Perhaps they contain mainly elements of fire and air. This would fit well with their preference for evil. For it was established that the best character traits are those at the mean, so that if one contained a mixture of equal parts of the four elements, he would be disposed and suited to a preference for good. Those who contain earth in large measure would be angry and envious and would covet honor and prestige beyond what is proper, because they deviate from the mean. Therefore, demons whose elements are fire and air, which are at the farthest extreme, are disposed to exhibiting the highest degree of arrogance, anger, and envy, to the point of urging and propelling people to as much evil as possible.[45] This is how I assess the quiddity of demons. I am in agreement with what our Sages of blessed

---

[43] Deut. 32: 17.

[44] BT *Sanhedrin* 101a. The Rabbis regarded demons as dangerous. When R. Jose forbade consulting demons not only on the Sabbath but on weekdays, R. Huna maintained that he ruled thus only on account of the danger of this practice. It is told of R. Isaac son of Joseph that when he consulted a demon he was swallowed up in a cedar tree, but a miracle was wrought for him: the cedar split and cast him forth.

[45] The idea here may be that any deviation from the mean at which all elements are equal results in a disposition to vice, but an excess of fire and air disposes one to greater evil than does an excess of earth.

memory have said of them, namely, that they have some properties similar to those that people have, and some similar to those of the ministering angels.[46] Therefore, the end of their existence is the good, whether to test people and to perfect them by way of their trials, which is what happened to Job at the end of his experience; or to serve as a hammer applied to those who defy God's word, in accordance with what divine wisdom ordains.

One flourishing sect of the Mutakallimun has regarded the quiddity of demons as incorporeal intellects, which, as soon as they were created, were conscious of their superior rank and so were disposed to arrogance. They were either resentful of their subjugation to God, or they envied the status of the perfected human being, for they knew he was destined to be of their rank. Yet the way they were was a matter of choice, for they were created possessors of choice and will and they chose evil. Their punishment was therefore to exist and persist in their evil choices.

This, however, is a self-refuting proposition. For it is known that evil and deficiency arise from matter, and good and perfection from form. This is so all the more when the form is an intellectual form that is precluded from choosing evil and defect. Once the proposition that demons were created possessors of choice and will is understood to indicate the goodness of their will for perfection and joy, this becomes true beyond a doubt. But if we see the proposition as indicating that they are possessors of choice such that they can do good and bad, it [viz. the notion that they are incorporeal intellects] becomes something inconceivable considering the nature of intellect.

Furthermore, their sin must inescapably occur either at the time of their creation or after their creation. Yet it is impossible that it occur at the first instant of their creation, for what incites their sin is their sense of their own greatness. In general, since sin consists of a certain act on the part of an agent, the agent must from all perspectives precede the sin in time. Therefore, since it is necessary that the sin follow their creation, they must have remained in a state of perfection for a certain amount of time before their sin. It is evident that they have no opposite, thus it is inescapable that a new cause would be required to turn their will toward sin and evil choice. It is, however, impossible for a new cause to arise in a simple incorporeal intellect. It is evident, therefore, that sin is impossible for such an intellect. This is especially so in light of what is assumed by those who hold that the rest of the intellects have persisted [in this perfection],[47] and that God has ensured their choice of good immediately upon their creation. It was fitting that the demons, too, receive this assurance of their choice of good, insofar as they existed for a time free of sin.

Since these things escape us and the gates of speculation are nearly locked, it is improper for us to stray from the tradition of our Rabbis of blessed memory, according to which demons have some things in common with human beings and other things in common with the ministering angels. This should suffice for the sixth issue.

---

[46] BT *Ḥagigah* 16a.
[47] Reading נתקימו (past tense), with the manuscripts, rather than יתקימו (future).

Issue VII

WHETHER a human soul transmigrates, which is what one sect of Sages calls *gilgul* (גלגול).

Since it has been established in a preceding discussion that the soul of man is a substance disposed to intellection, it would appear that transmigration is impossible for it in anyone who has acquired some of the intelligibles in actuality. For otherwise, the second being will be born intellecting in actuality without having learned, which contradicts what sense-experience attests through the entire span of time past whose events have been transmitted to us—unless, by God, the intelligibles he acquired were rendered nonexistent in him by the will of God, for some end known to Him.

Yet since the sect that affirms transmigration has a foundation in the tradition, the doors of investigation are locked in this matter. If it is a received tradition, we shall receive it favorably. Let this suffice for the seventh issue.

Issue VIII

WHETHER the soul of a child who has not yet reached the age of obligation to fulfill the commandments is immortal.

Since it was established earlier that the soul is a substance disposed to intellection, it would seem that its immortality is necessitated, regardless of how small or large the person's body is. But according to what has been said of immortality, namely, that it is a reward for service [to God], if the soul does not succeed in serving, its being deprived of immortality seems appropriate. It is fitting that it return to its source, just as the atoms of matter return to their source, and that it not achieve immortality[48] in itself, as we have noted with regard to this matter in Book III Part II.

According to the tradition received by our Rabbis of blessed memory, however, immortality is in effect from the moment the eye of the child's intellect is opened. That is what they implied by saying: "From the time he knows how to answer amen."[49] This is tantamount to their saying: "the child who knows to whom benedictions are addressed," for this word [viz. amen] is generally the answer that follows a benediction. Therefore this is tantamount to the Rabbis' having said, "From the time he understands a blessing and can respond to it, he merits immortality." Immortality can also be attained by virtue of the merit of circumcision through which the child enters the covenant of Abraham our father. Let this suffice for the eighth issue.

Issue IX

CONCERNING Paradise and Gehenna.

There is no doubt about the existence of Paradise[50] and Gehenna, since the existence of Paradise is explicit in the Torah as well as in several places in the Talmud, and even

---

[48] The manuscripts contain in addition the term קיום, "sustained existence."
[49] BT *Sanhedrin* 110b.   [50] Or, Garden of Eden.

though the existence of Gehenna is not explicit in the Written Torah, nevertheless, the Talmud makes explicit in many places that its existence is well known to and accepted by the Rabbis. Where there is doubt is concerning whether these are places set aside for reward and punishment for souls alone, whether they are set aside for the Day of Judgment,[51] or whether they are common to souls upon their separation from the body and to human bodies on the Day of Judgment.

With respect to Paradise, it is located in the inhabited world, for Scripture states explicitly that it was the dwelling-place of Adam and Eve before they rebelled. It is therefore more appropriate and reasonable that it be the dwelling-place of the righteous as body-and-soul who merit resurrection and will be alive at the time of the resurrection. The following dicta of our Rabbis of blessed memory concur: "In the future the Holy One Blessed Be He will prepare a meal for the righteous in Paradise";[52] "In the future the Holy One Blessed Be He will arrange the righteous in a ring, and His glory in their midst, and all will point with their finger toward Him."[53] With this they indicated that the attachment of the righteous to the radiance of the Divine Presence will be of such a measure that, even though they use their senses, the connection will not be severed in any way.

That there will be a place designated for souls alone is a notion that requires the application of speculation, insofar as souls are spiritual and are thought not to be confined to a place. Therefore, the Paradise reserved for the righteous, which, according to the plain meaning of what appears repeatedly in the words of our Rabbis of blessed memory, occurs immediately after death, indicates a Paradise on high, which is attachment to the radiance of the Divine Presence.

Yet from what is said in the tradition regarding the limitations placed on the duration of punishment for the wicked,[54] it would seem to be beyond doubt that that punishment occurs immediately after death. Since there are many places where it is said to take place in this lower realm, which is termed in places in Scripture, *Avadon*, *Shaḥat*, and *Tofteh*,[55] it would appear that souls, despite their being spiritual, are confined to a place and experience intense pain. This pain, which we have discussed earlier, is something that speculation does not dispute. In general, since it is agreed by our opponents that the soul experiences pleasure and joy when it apprehends what it is in its nature to apprehend, it is fitting that it experience suffering and pain when it fails to apprehend this. It is not implausible for this pain to lead to destruction and annihilation in the end. Also, because of its having been tainted by materiality, it is not implausible that at the time of death some materiality and the barest trace of quality linger on with it, on account of which it would also suffer pain and be confined to a place. Therefore there is no reason to dispute the tradition of our Rabbis of blessed memory. And it is established as well that speculation does not dispute this. This should suffice for this issue.

---

[51] Following the Florence manuscript: אם הם מקומות מיוחדים לגמול ועונש לנפשות לבד, או הם מיוחדים ליום הדין.
[52] BT *Baba batra* 75a.   [53] BT *Taʿanit* 31a.   [54] *ʿEduyot* 2: 10.
[55] See, respectively, Ps. 88: 12, Ps. 7: 16, and Isa. 30: 33.

Issue X

WHAT is intended by "the account of creation" (מעשה בראשית; *maʿaeh bereishit*) and by "the account of the Chariot" (מעשה מרכבה; *maʿaseh merkavah*), and whether these refer, respectively, to physics and to metaphysics, as some of the sages of our nation have held.

It is self-evident to one who is well-acquainted with the rabbinic dicta on this subject that what these terms intend is not what has been thought—even though the Rabbis elevated these accounts to heights of greatness and sanctity. They said, for example: "'A small thing': this refers to the discussions of Abaye and Rava; 'a great thing': this refers to the account of the Chariot."[56] They said as well, that when R. Eleazar ben Arakh engaged in the interpretation of the account of the Chariot, R. Joḥanan ben Zakkai wrapped himself up and sat upon a stone beneath an olive tree, and fires encompassed all the trees.[57] The point of this is to highlight the sanctity of these matters and their stature. But none of this can be apprehended through metaphysics, for most of what is established there is extremely weak, as was shown earlier. To be sure our Rabbis of blessed memory were exceedingly secretive about these things, as the Mishnah says in the section [that begins],[58] "One may not teach the account of creation in the presence of two, nor the account of the Chariot even in the presence of one." They even recounted many stories about the punishment that befalls anyone who seeks to publicize these matters—to the point that they themselves refrained from studying them until their old age, as they said in that chapter: "Come, I will instruct you in the account of the Chariot. He replied: I am not old enough."[59] Nevertheless, there is in these things, that is, in physics and metaphysics, nothing that requires secrecy and concealment—unless, by God, one calls that which is in them that is heretical and destructive to the divine religion: "the secrets of the Torah." How could it be otherwise? This [purportedly] concealed material was indeed publicized to youth and to children, and also to others of the nations[60] in their houses of study whose students are twenty years of age or younger. They also spoke most expansively[61] before their assemblies and in large crowds about things opposed to the Torah.

One thing that proves that what they imagine is illusion and fiction is that it is known that the science of physics necessarily precedes metaphysics in order of study, as was established there. Yet in the *Gemara* there is the incident of the two Sages, the one who was well versed in the account of creation, the other in the account of the Chariot, who agreed that the one would teach the other what he knew on condition that the other would teach the one what he knew. After the one taught the other the account of creation, when he then asked the other to hold up his end of the

---

[56] BT *Sukkah* 28a.   [57] See BT *Ḥagigah* 14b.   [58] *Ḥagigah* 2: 1.   [59] BT *Ḥagigah* 13a.
[60] Reading, with the manuscripts, לזולתנו מהאומות, as opposed to with Fisher, לזולתנו, "to others."
[61] Reading with Fisher, הרחיבו תכלית ההרחבה, rather than with the manuscripts, הרחיקו ההרחקה, "they avoided to the utmost." (It appears that הרחיבו may have been changed to הרחיקו in the Florence manuscript.) The sense of the manuscripts would be that a certain care was exercised not to say anything publicly that opposed the Torah. Crescas may be returning, however, to his criticism in the Introduction of the "rebellious slaves" who defile the words of the Rabbi. The "also" (גם כן) suggests that these miscreants not only revealed matters that were to be kept secret but, *in addition*, brazenly publicized ideas at odds with the Torah.

agreement, the other replied: "You are not old enough."[62] This indicates explicitly that they do not, God forbid, intend by the account of creation and the account of the Chariot physics and metaphysics, respectively.[63] Even more than this they do not intend that these are at a higher level than the Talmud, which explains the commandments of the Torah and its divine laws, which confer on man true happiness.

It would seem, therefore, that what is intended by the account of creation is, literally, a description of the act of creation,[64] and this is the crux of what is discussed in *Sefer Yetzirah* (*Book of Creation*), which was known to Abraham our father. This is what is alluded to in the interpretation of our Rabbis of blessed memory: "With the letter *heh* the world was created, for it is said: 'when they were created',[65] בהבראם,[66] that is, ב' ה' בראם, 'with *heh* they were created'";[67] and they said: "The world-to-come was created with the letter *yod*, for it is said, 'For ביה, that is, with *yod-heh*, the Lord formed the worlds.'"[68, 69] And since this connection and successive procession, which our Rabbis of blessed memory received by the tradition, derives from the secret of the explicit name of God,[70] it follows that this matter is a secret that is closed and concealed, due to the greatness of His name and the fear He inspires. What is meant by the account of the Chariot is what it is possible to apprehend of the higher beings, and their interdependence one on another.

These matters which were known by tradition are of the utmost eminence and subtlety, and deviation from a correct understanding of them[71] [both] leads to destruction and distances a man from his happiness. The Rabbis therefore required the utmost secrecy and maturity, for which reason this science was kept from young people whose temperament is heated and who act too lightly. The Rabbis also forbade the expounding of these matters other than to the sage[72] with extreme secrecy and with only chapter headings. Yet this is to be understood as applying to the times in which one comes to discourse on scriptural texts that allude to these matters, when all this is done for the sake of instilling fear of God in the hearts of the auditors. It does

---

[62] BT *Hagigah* 13a.

[63] Crescas supposes that, were physics the appropriate preparation for metaphysics, and were the account of creation physics and the account of the Chariot metaphysics, then once one had mastered the account of creation one would be able to proceed directly to the account of the Chariot. Since, however, the Sage who was taught the account of creation could not proceed directly to the account of the Chariot, they are clearly not equivalent to physics and metaphysics, respectively. Even more tellingly, the Sage who mastered the account of the Chariot had not mastered the account of creation. Yet, presumably, one cannot successfully study metaphysics without first having mastered physics.

[64] The following text found in the Florence manuscript is missing in the editions: "and this is the successive procession (השתלשלות) of existents and the connection between the upper and the lower ones, the secret of which is not known via speculation."

[65] Gen. 2: 4.

[66] The letter ה appears elevated in the Torah scroll in accordance with the Masoretic tradition.

[67] See BT *Menahot* 29b.

[68] Isa. 26: 4. Note the plays on words: יה, usually translated "God," is taken here in the sense of: the letters *yod* and *heh*; צור, usually rendered "Rock," is taken as a verb meaning "formed."

[69] See BT *Menahot* 29b.

[70] The Ferrara edition and Fisher omit "the secret of," בסוד.

[71] The Ferrara edition and Fisher have והבנת העניינים בחלקי מה שהם, which suggests partial understanding; the manuscripts read: והבנת הדברים בחלוף מה שהם, which suggests mistaken understanding. I follow the manuscripts.

[72] The word, לחכם, "to the sage," is missing in the Ferrara edition and in Fisher.

not pertain, however, to the time of study. For it is unreasonable to think that these matters, in which deviation [from the correct understanding] entails serious rebellion, should be transmitted at the time of study only through chapter headings. And this is even more the case insofar as they are matters that are not knowable through investigation. Rather, to one who grasps these matters on his own, the Mishnah applies the name sage (*ḥakham*; חכם), as the Rabbis have said: "unless he is a sage and understands through his own intelligence."[73] It is when an occasion arises for one to speak with such a person about the interpretation of scriptural texts and to relate these matters to those texts, that it is appropriate to employ chapter headings. For he is a sage, and it will be easy for him to understand through his own intelligence how these matters accord with the texts.

Since the explicit name of God and its vocalization supply hints to these matters, the grandeur of the name of God and His sanctity was transmitted to the priests. The Rabbis forbade everyone but the priests to read it as it is written, and permitted it only in the Temple. This is because the name is unique in its indicating God's power to perform miracles, as is indicated by its saying: "And my name, 'Lord' [i.e. the Tetragrammaton], I did not communicate to them"[74]—that is to say, that despite God's having revealed himself to the Patriarchs with the name El Shaddai, which points to God's directing and ordering of existence generally, He did not make himself known to them, that is, He was not well known to them by things outside the natural course. This may be seen as well by the priest's having the woman suspected of adultery take an oath with this divine name and its being effaced by water, until this wondrous feat is accomplished.

It may indeed be seen that what this name teaches is in accordance with the sanctity of the holy tongue. For it teaches the constant creation of all existents, as was established in Book III. It is a sign of its status as a proof[75] that it teaches the necessity of the constancy of creation, which is the secret of God's power and unity. Therefore, the divine name is at the highest level of grandeur and sanctity. There is no doubt that its vocalization indicates the superiority of that name and its greatness and its wonders, on account of which this concealment is fitting and necessary. It is in this way that the words of the Rabbi of the *Guide* in his relevant chapters are to be understood, even if this is not what the straightforward sense of his language suggests. Concealment is not mandated for the notion of necessary existence of which he spoke; rather, this is something that ought to be publicized to the multitude of men and women.

Although we have deviated a bit from the intent of this chapter, we saw fit to mention this here, for this [divine] name, despite how little is apprehended of it, is the foundation for the account of creation and the account of the Chariot, as the words of our Rabbis of blessed memory intended. This is what we sought to establish.

---

[73] *Hagigah* 2: 1.
[74] Exod. 6: 3. Although "Lord" is the common English substitute for the Tetragrammaton, it is not, of course, the divine name. It is the Tetragrammaton that appears in the verse in the Hebrew.
[75] The Ferrara edition has אות האיתן, "a strong sign"; the manuscripts, אות ראייתו, "a sign of its proof." I follow the manuscripts.

Issue XI

WHETHER or not the intellect, the intellecter, and the intellected are one thing.

The affirmative answer is widely accepted by the philosophers. They believe this because, since the intellect is in actuality, it is not confined to a place,[76] and it is nothing other than intellection; and the intellected, when it is abstracted from the thing intellected,[77] is nothing but intellection. It has been established for them, therefore, that the intellecter, the intellect, and the intellected are one thing. This was necessitated for them with respect to the separate intellect, which is constantly in actuality. And it is evident that it would be necessitated as well with respect to human intellect when it is in actuality. The Rabbi indeed expanded on this in Part I of his book.

The negative answer is established as follows. If we posit that the intellect, the intellecter, and the intellected are one thing, it follows that the intellect is constituted by the things it intellects. Since it was established in our earlier discussion that this premise is false inasmuch as many absurdities follow from it, it follows therefore that when the human intellect intellects in actuality, it is impossible for the intellecter and the intellected to be one thing. For the intellecter is something other than intellection, though intellection is necessitated for the intellecter by an essential necessity. It is therefore evident that this premise is false with respect to human intellect, even if we posit it with respect to intellect in actuality. This is necessitated as well for the separate intellect, for intellection is an essential attribute and not an essence. Many philosophers have stumbled in this matter, having failed to distinguish between an essence and an essential attribute.

What is surprising about these philosophers is that this matter cannot escape the following disjunction. Either intellection of various different intelligibles is one thing or it is not. If it is one thing, it would be necessary for the intelligibles to be one thing, since intellection and the intellected are one thing. Yet the intelligibles were assumed to be different from one another. It would be necessitated as well that when a man knew one intelligible he would know them all, since they are one thing. But if their intellection is not one thing, it is necessitated that the intellect be composed of various intelligibles. If they are substances, it would be composed of many substances. All of this, however, is absurd in the extreme. This should suffice for this issue.

Issue XII

CONCERNING the prime mover.

Is the prime mover an effect of the First Cause, or is the prime mover God? The great philosophers disagreed on this issue. Avicenna and Alfarabi, as well as R. Moses Halevi who sided with them, held that the prime mover was an effect of God. Averroes, however, held that God *is* the prime mover. It is fitting to explain their views briefly and what troubled them in this controversy. It will become evident from this that the grounds of the controversy are shaky.

---

[76] Following the manuscripts I remove the *vav* of ואינו, which is found in Fisher and the Ferrara edition.

[77] Beginning the new clause with "and the intellected," והמושבל, and then reading באשר with the manuscripts, as opposed to ואשר with the Ferrara edition.

They [all] accepted two propositions. One is that the First Cause is at the height of simplicity. The second is that from one simple cause nothing but one simple effect can ensue. Therefore some have said that, since the first intellect is the cause of the sphere that activates the diurnal motion, and the sphere is some sort of composite, it follows necessarily that its mover be composed as well of some sort of composition. Since, according to what was established in the second proposition, namely, that from a simple, nothing but a simple ensues, and since that which has necessary existence is at the height of simplicity, as was established in the first proposition, it follows that the prime mover is not the necessary existent. Since everything that does not have necessary existence is an effect of it, the prime mover must be an effect of the necessary existent. This is the view of Avicenna and Alfarabi, and R. Moses Halevi joined them.

But Averroes, even though he conceded these propositions, held that the prime mover is the necessary existent. He said that the second proposition is true only of the efficient cause but is not true of the formal cause. Since the necessary existent is the formal cause of the existents, the simplicity of the first effect is not necessitated. He established that God is not an efficient cause, for the act of an efficient cause involves the act's transition from nonexistence to existence. Once it makes the transition to existence the act no longer depends on the efficient cause. Since the act of bringing something into existence is a change that is finite, and an act that is finite cannot be attributed to the infinite—for the infinite always exists at the final perfection and is therefore not one who is active at one time and not at another—it follows for him, then, that the necessary existent is not an efficient cause. It is therefore not necessary that the mover of the final sphere be one of its effects.

The sage, R. Moses Halevi of blessed memory, however, maintained that this is true only of quiddity and not of the agent [acting] absolutely. Yet this [agent] is that on which the existence of everything depends, no matter what sort of existence it is, whether eternal or not eternal. He therefore determined that the prime mover is an effect of the First Cause.[78]

These are the conclusions of their approaches in brief. And it is evident that their foundation is shaky. The second proposition is true from the perspective of [the universe's] necessity. But once it is established beyond doubt that the agent acts through will and benefaction, it is not necessitated that the effect be simple. It is evident to one who delves into this book that, indeed, since it is a tradition of our Rabbis of blessed memory that the angels were created on the first day, there is no reason to depart from their tradition. Even more is this the case inasmuch as it concurs with speculation. This should suffice for this issue.

---

[78] Since for Averroes, God is not an efficient cause—operating at one time and not at another and, via His acts of bringing things into existence, producing finite change—but rather a formal cause, He can be the mover of the sphere, i.e. the prime mover, and remain a simple necessary existent. R. Moses Halevi salvages God's efficient causation by distinguishing between being the cause of quiddity, which would indeed involve the agent in temporal and finite change, and being the cause of existence itself. According to R. Moses Halevi, God's causal agency brings into being existence itself of whatever sort—eternal or not—but not the quiddity of that which exists. God for him is therefore not the prime mover (which causes changes in quiddity) but rather the efficient cause of all existence. The existence of all existents depends on God as First Efficient Cause.

Issue XIII

THE impossibility of apprehending the truth of God's essence: does this derive from the Torah alone, or does speculation concur? And if speculation concurs, does this impossibility have a permanent nature, such that possibility [of apprehension] is inconceivable?

I assert that, since it is agreed by the majority of the horde of philosophers that the intellect, the intellecter, and the intellected are one thing, it would seem that speculation agrees with them about this impossibility, and that the impossibility of this is such that possibility [of apprehension] is inconceivable. For if God's quiddity were intellected by another, then the other, namely, the intellecter, along with that which is intellected, would, God forbid, be one thing. But this proposition is evidently false, as we saw earlier in several places in this book. Therefore, even though this impossibility is required by the Torah, as it is said: "For man shall not see Me and live,"[79] and even though speculation concurs as well with the notion that there is no possibility for another to grasp the truth of God's quiddity, nevertheless the impossibility is not such that it is inconceivable for God's power to override it by way of a miracle. Onkelos may be in agreement with this inasmuch as he renders "and live" as "and endure,"[80] which is in accord with what is said in another place: "We shall surely die because we have seen God."[81] It is therefore not unthinkable that Moses asked to apprehend God's quiddity by way of a miracle. According to the Rabbi of the *Guide*, however, this possibility is inconceivable in every way, since he concedes the proposition that the intellect, the intellecter, and the intellected are one. According to his words, the request to know God's quiddity is far removed from Moses' rank. But be that as it may, Onkelos's translation does not compel the conclusion that the apprehension of the truth of God's quiddity is possible for the separate intellects. As we have already established, the request to see God's face alludes to the essential attributes, for the proof of the impossibility of apprehending them is not decisive. Therefore Onkelos rendered "and live" as "and endure."

This is what we saw as sufficient for these issues. With this Book IV of this first part called "Light of the Lord" is complete. This completion occurred in the month of Ziv,[82] in the year one hundred seventy of the sixth millennium since creation, in Saragossa in the kingdom of Aragon.

Praise is to God alone, who is exalted above all blessing and praise. Amen, amen, amen.

Blessed is God who aided me to this point. He in His mercy will afford us the privilege of understanding and apprehending the truth. Amen, amen.

---

[79] Exod. 33: 20.

[80] Crescas is suggesting that Onkelos did not think immediate death was the inevitable result of seeing God—that is, of apprehending the divine essence.

[81] Judg. 13: 22. Manoaḥ and his wife did not die.

[82] See 1 Kgs. 6: 1, where the month of Ziv is identified as the second month, viz. the month of Iyyar. The year is 5170, corresponding to 1410 CE.

Bibliography

Primary Sources

Editions of Light of the Lord (Or Hashem)

Hasdai Crescas. *Or Hashem*. Ferrara 1555.
Hasdai Crescas. *Or Hashem*. Florence MS. Institute of Microfilms of Hebrew Manuscripts, Jewish National and University Library, Jerusalem, no. 17997 (ed. and annotated by Crescas's students).
Hasdai Crescas. *Or Hashem*. Vienna MS. Oesterreichische Nationalbibliothek Cod hebr. 46, Catalogue Schwarz Wien NB Vienna Austria 150, Institute of Microfilms of Hebrew Manuscripts, Jewish National and University Library, Jerusalem, no. 1323 F.
Hasdai Crescas. *Or Hashem*. Introduction, Preface, and Book I Part I. Vilna 1905. With Commentary *"Otzar Hayim"* by H. Y. Plensberg.
Hasdai Crescas. *Or Hashem*. Ed. Rabbi Shlomo Fisher. Jerusalem: Itri Edn., 1990 (Heb.).
Hasdai Crescas. *La Lumière de l'Éternel*. Fr. trans. Éric Smilevitch. Paris: Hermann (Ruben Éditions), 2010.

Other Works by Hasdai Crescas

Hasdai Crescas. *Refutation of the Christian Principles* (*Sefer Bittul Iqqarei Ha-Nozrim*), Heb. trans. Josef Ben Shem Tov, ed. Daniel J. Lasker. Ramat-Gan: Bar-Ilan University Press, 2002.
Hasdai Crescas. *Refutation of the Christian Principles*. Trans. with introd. Daniel J. Lasker. Albany: SUNY Series in Jewish Philosophy, 1992.
Hasdai Crescas. *Sermon on the Passover* (*Derashat ha-Pesah le-Rab Hasdai Crescas u-Mehqarim be-Mishnato ha-Pilosofit*), ed. Aviezer Ravitzky. Jerusalem, 1988 (Heb.).
Hasdai Crescas. *Epistle to the Jewish Communities of Avignon*. In Weiner edn. of Judah ibn Verga, *Shevet Yehudah*, Hanover, 1855. Eng. trans. F. Kobler, *Letters of Jews through the Ages*, vol. i. London, 1952.

Works by Other Medieval–Renaissance Jewish Philosophers

Abarbanel, Isaac. *Commentary on the Bible*. Jerusalem, 1964.
Abarbanel, Isaac. *Mif'alot Elohim*. Lemberg, 1863.
Abarbanel, Isaac. *Nahalat Avot; Commentary of Rabbeinu Don Yitzhak Abarbanel on Masekhet Avot*, ed. Oren Golan. Ashkelon, 2013.
Gersonides. *Wars of the Lord*. Trans. Seymour Feldman (3 vols.). Philadelphia, New York, and Jerusalem: Jewish Publication Society, 1984–99.
Maimonides. *Guide of the Perplexed*. Trans. Shlomo Pines (2 vols.). Chicago: University of Chicago Press, 1963.
Maimonides. *Guide for the Perplexed*. Trans. Saul Friedländer. London: Routledge & Kegan Paul, 1904.
Maimonides. *Le Guide des égarés*. Trans. Salomon Munk (2 vols.) Paris: A. Franck, 1856.
Sefer Habahir (*Book of Brightness*). Ed. Reuven Margaliot. Jerusalem, 1951.

Secondary Sources

Ackerman, Ari. 1994. "The Composition of the Section on Divine Providence in Hasdai Crescas' *Or Ha-Shem*," *Daat* 32/33: 37–45.

Ackerman, Ari. 2012. "Ḥasdai Crescas and his Circle on the Infinite and Expanding Torah," *Jewish Studies Internet Journal* 11: 217–33.
Ackerman, Ari. 2013a. "Ḥasdai Crescas on the Philosophic Foundation of Codification," *AJS Review* 37: 315–31.
Ackerman, Ari. 2013b. "The Attribution of 'Sod Ha-Kaddish' to Ḥasdai Crescas," *Kabbalah* 30: 65–73.
Ackerman, Ari. 2017. "Ḥasdai Crescas and Scholastic Philosophers on the Possible Existence of Multiple Simultaneous Worlds," *Aleph* 17: 139–54.
Assis, Y. T. 1989. "R. Ḥasdai Crescas's Plans for the Rehabilitation of Spanish Jewry after the 1391 Massacres," *Proceedings of the World Congress of Jewish Studies* 10: 145–48 (Heb.).
Aviezer, Rivka. 1982. "The Development of R. Ḥasdai Crescas's Views on the Question of Freedom of the Will," *Tarbiẓ* 51: 445–69 (Heb.).
Baer, Yitzḥak. 1940. "Abner of Burgos' *Minḥat Qenaot* and Its Influence on Ḥasdai Crescas," *Tarbiẓ* 11: 188–206 (Heb.).
Baer, Yitzḥak. 1966. *A History of the Jews in Christian Spain*. Trans. from the Hebrew by Louis Schoffman. Philadelphia: Jewish Publication Society.
Ben Porat, Eliezer. 2001. "Notes on Crescas's View Regarding Determinism and Freedom of Will," *Daat* 46: 29–44 (Heb.).
Ben Porat, Eliezer. 2008. "Notes on Crescas's Discussion of Beliefs Related to Special Mitzvot," *Daat* 63: 75–86 (Heb.).
Ben Porat, Eliezer. 2011. "Notes on Crescas's Discussion of the Divine Attributes," *Daat* 70: 35–47 (Heb.).
Ben Porat, Eliezer, Eliezer ben Moshe Hacohen, and Eliezer Portman. 2001. "The Cornerstone of Free Will—Notes on the Method of Rabbi Ḥasdai Crescas," *Shemaʿtin* 145: 91–7 (Heb.).
Ben-Shalom, R. 2012. "Hasdai Crescas: Portrait of a Leader at a Time of Crisis," in Jonathan Ray (ed.), *The Jew in Medieval Iberia,*. Boston: Academic Studies, 309–51.
Bleich, J. David. 1983. *With Perfect Faith*. New York: KTAV. (Contains translations by Warren Zev Harvey and Seymour Feldman of selections from *Light of the Lord*.)
Bleich, J. David. 1997. "Providence in the Philosophy of Hasdai Crescas and Josef Albo," in Yaakov Elman and Jeffrey S. Gurok (eds.), *Hazon Nahum: Studies in Jewish Law, Thought, and History*. New York: Michael Sharf Publication Trust of the Yeshiva University Press, 311–58.
Bloch, Philipp. 1879. *Die Willensfreiheit von Chasdai Kreskas*. Munich: T. Ackermann.
Bondi, Dror. 2002. "Fundamentals of Crescas's Doctrine of Cognition," *Maʿaliyot* 23: 194–219 (Heb.).
Davidson, Herbert A. 1987. *Proofs for Eternity, Creation, and the Existence of God in Medieval Islamic and Jewish Philosophy*. New York: Oxford University Press.
Davies, Daniel. 2010. "Creation and the Context of Theology and Science in Maimonides and Crescas," in David Burrell et al. (eds.), *Creation and the God of Abraham*. New York Cambridge University Press, 65–76.
Ehrlich, Dror. 2010. "The Status of Divine Retribution in Ḥasdai Crescas' Dogmatic System," *Daat* 68/9: 3–13 (Hebrew).
Eisenmann, Esti, and Shalom Sadik. 2015. "Criticism of Aristotelian Science in Fourteenth-Century Jewish Thought," *Journal of Jewish Studies* 66: 116–37 (Heb.). DOI: 18647/3214/JJS-2015.
Epstein, Isidore. 1931. "Das Problem des göttlichen Willens in der Schöpfung nach Maimonides, Gersonides und Crescas," *Monatsschrift für Geschichte und Wissenschaft des Judenthums* 75: 335–47.
Eran, Amira. 2016. "Love Sets One Free: The Influence of Raavad's Understanding of Love and Will on Crescas's Understanding of Love and Will," in Shmuel Wygoda, Esti Eisenmann,

Ari Ackerman, Aviram Ravitsky (eds.), *Adam le-Adam (Homo Homini)*, Jerusalem: Magnes, 340–65.
Feldman, Seymour. 1980. "The Theory of Eternal Creation in Hasdai Crescas and Some of his Predecessors," *Viator* 11: 289–321.
Feldman, Seymour. 1982. "Crescas' Theological Determinism," *Daat* 9: 3–28.
Feldman, Seymour. 1984. "A Debate Concerning Determinism in Late Medieval Jewish Philosophy," *PAAJR* 51: 15–54.
Feldman, Seymour. 2012. "On Plural Universes: A Debate in Medieval Jewish Philosophy and the Duhem-Pines Thesis," *Aleph* 12: 329–66.
Fraenkel, Carlos. 2008. "From the Pythagorean Void to Crescas' God as the Place of the World," *Zutot* 5: 87–94.
Fraenkel, Carlos. 2009. "Hasdai Crescas on God as the Place of the World and Spinoza's Notion of God as 'res extensa,'" *Aleph* 9: 77–111.
Fraenkel, Carlos. 2013. "Philo of Alexandria, Hasdai Crescas, and Spinoza on God's Body," in *Envisioning Judaism*, Raánan S. Boustan et al. (eds.), with the collaboration of Alex Ramos. Tübingen: Mohr Siebeck, 809–19.
Frank, Daniel, Oliver Leaman, and Charles Manekin (eds.). 2000. *The Jewish Philosophy Reader*. London: Routledge. (Contains translations of some passages in *Light of the Lord* by Warren Zev Harvey.)
Guttmann, Julius. 1933/1964. *Die Philosophie des Judentums*. Munich: Ernst Reinhardt, 1933. Eng. version: *Philosophies of Judaism*, David Wolf Silverman (trans.). 1st edn., New York: Holt, Rinehart & Winston, 1964; 2nd edn., Northvale, NJ: Jason Aronson, 1988.
Guttmann, Julius. 1955. "The Free Will Problem in the Thought of Ḥasdai Crescas and the Muslim Aristotelians," in Julius Guttmann, *Dat u-Madda*. Jerusalem: Magnes, 149–68 (Heb.).
Harari, David. 1998. "Who Was the Learned Jew that Made Known Ḥasdai Crescas' *The Light of the Lord* to Gianfrancesco Pico Della Mirandola?" *Jerusalem Studies in Jewish Thought* 14: 257–69.
Harvey, Warren Zev. 1973a. 'Ḥasdai Crescas's Critique of the Theory of the Acquired Intellect,' doctoral dissertation, Columbia University. (Microfilms, Ann Arbor, no. 74-1488.) (Contains extensive translations of passages in *Light of the Lord*.)
Harvey, Warren Zev. 1973b. Ḥasdai Crescas and His Critique of Philosophical Happiness," *Proceedings of the World Congress of Jewish Studies* 6: 143–9.
Harvey, Warren Zev. 1980a. "The Term '*hitdabbekut*' in Crescas' Definition of Time," *Jewish Quarterly Review* 71: 44–7.
Harvey, Warren Zev. 1980b. "The Authorship of the Reservations concerning Determinism in Crescas's *Or Adonai*," *Kiryat Sefer* 55: 210–38 (Heb.).
Harvey, Warren Zev. 1982–3. "Kabbalistic Elements in Crescas's *Light of the Lord*," *Jerusalem Studies in Jewish Thought* 2: 75–109 (Heb.).
Harvey, Warren Zev. 1984. "Comments on the Expression 'Feeling of Compulsion' in Rabbi Ḥasdai Crescas," *Jerusalem Studies in Jewish Thought* 4: 275–80 (Heb.).
Harvey, Warren Zev. 1986. "R. Ḥasdai Crescas and Bernat Metge on the Soul," *Jerusalem Studies in Jewish Thought* 5: 141–54.
Harvey, Warren Zev. 1988a. "Crescas versus Maimonides on Knowledge and Pleasure," in *A Straight Path: Studies in Medieval Philosophy and Culture*, ed. Ruth Link-Salinger. Washington, DC: Catholic University of America, 113–23.
Harvey, Warren Zev. 1988b. "The First Commandment and the God of History: Halevi and Crescas vs. Ibn Ezra and Maimonides," *Tarbiẓ* 57: 203–16 (Heb.).
Harvey, Warren Zev. 1989. "Review of Ravitzky, *Crescas's Sermon on the Passover*," *Tarbiẓ* 58: 531–5 (Heb.).

Harvey, Warren Zev. 1990. "The Philosopher and Politics: Gersonides and Crescas," in L. Landman (ed.), *Scholars and Scholarship: The Interaction Between Judaism and Other Cultures*. New York: Michael Scharf Publication Trust of the Yeshiva University Press, 53-65.
Harvey, Warren Zev. 1991. "R. Ḥasdai Crescas on the Uniqueness of the Land of Israel," in Moshe Ḥalamish and Aviezer Ravitzky (eds.), *The Land of Israel in Medieval Jewish Thought*. Jerusalem: Yad Yizḥak ben Zvi, 151-6.
Harvey, Warren Zev. 1992. "Nissim of Gerona and William of Ockham on Prime Matter," in Barry Walfish (ed.), *The Frank Talmage Memorial*. Haifa: Haifa University Press, ii. 87-98.
Harvey, Warren Zev. 1997. "Bewilderments in Crescas's Theory of Attributes," *Proceedings of the Israel Academy of Sciences and Humanities* 8: 133-44 (Heb.).
Harvey, Warren Zev. 1998a. "Knowledge of God in Aquinas, Judah Romano, and Crescas," *Jerusalem Studies in Jewish Thought* 14: 223-38 (Heb.).
Harvey, Warren Zev. 1998b. "*L'Univers infini de Hasday Crescas*," *Revue de Métaphysique et de Morale* 4: 551-7.
Harvey, Warren Zev. 1998c. *Physics and Metaphysics in Hasdai Crescas*. Amsterdam: J. C. Gieben. (Contains short extracts from *Light of the Lord* translated into English.)
Harvey, Warren Zev. 2010. *Rabbi Ḥasdai Crescas*. Jerusalem: Zalman Shazar (Heb.).
Harvey, Warren Zev. 2013. "Arabic and Latin Elements in Ḥasdai Crescas' Philosophy," in Haggai Ben-Shammai, Shaul Shaked, and Sarah Stroumsa (eds.), *Exchange and Transmission across Cultural Boundaries*. Jerusalem: Israel Academy of Sciences and Humanities, 106-15.
Joël, Manuel. 1866. *Don Chasdai Crezkas' religionsphilosophische Lehren*. Breslau: Schletter H. Skutsch; Heb. trans. Tel-Aviv: ha-Shaár, 1928.
Kellner, Menachem. 1979. "Maimonides, Crescas and Abravanel on Exod. 20:2," *Jewish Quarterly Review* 69: 129-57.
Kellner, Menachem. 1983. "Inadvertent Heresy in Medieval Jewish Thought: Maimonides and Abrabanel vs. Crescas and Duran?" *Jerusalem Studies in Jewish Thought* 3: 393-403 (Heb.).
Kellner, Menachem. 1986. *Dogma in Medieval Jewish Thought: From Maimonides to Abravanel*. Oxford: Oxford University Press.
Klein-Braslavy, Sara. 1980a. "Gan eden et Gehinnom dans le système de Hasdaï Crescas," in G. Nahon and C. Touati (eds.), *Hommage à Georges Vajda*. Louvain: Peeters, 262-78.
Klein-Braslavy, Sara. 1980b. "The Influence of R. Nissim Gerondi on Crescas's and Albo's 'Principles of Faith,'" in *Eshel Beer-Sheva* (Jerusalem), 2: 177-97 (Heb.).
Kreisel, Howard. 2001. *Prophecy: The History of an Idea in Medieval Jewish Philosophy*. Dordrecht: Kluwer.
Krygier, Rivon. 1998. *À la limite de Dieu: L'énigme de l'omniscience divine et du libre arbitre humain dans la pensée juive*. Paris: Publisud.
Langermann, Y. Tzvi. 2012. "No Reagent, No Reaction: The Barren Transmission of Avicennan Dynamics to Ḥasdai Crescas," *Aleph* 12: 161-88.
Lasker, Daniel J. 1997. "Chasdai Crescas," in *History of Jewish Philosophy*. Routledge History of World Philosophies 2, ed. Daniel H. Frank and Oliver Leaman. London: Routledge, 399-414.
Lasker, Daniel J. 1988. "Original Sin and its Atonement According to Ḥasdai Crescas," *Daat* 20: 127-35 (Heb.).
Lemler, David. 2011. "À propos de *Lumière de l'Éternel*, de Ḥasdaï Crescas," *Labyrinthe* 37: 157-61. (Review of Smilevitch's French translation of *Light of the Lord*.)
Leone, Alexandre. 2015. "Considerações sobre a prova da Existência de Deus Elaborada por Hasdai Crescas (1340-1411)," *Kriterion* 56: 191-212.

Levy, T., 1992. "*L'Infini selon Rabbi Hasdaï Crescas* (1340–1412)," in D. Banon (ed.), *Inquisition et pérennité*. Paris: Éditions du Cerf, 161–6.

Maccoby, Hyam. 2003. "Crescas's Concept of Time," in Gerhard Jaritz and Gerson Moreno-Riano (eds.), *Time and Eternity: The Medieval Discourse*. Turnhout: Brepols, 163–70.

Manekin, Charles (ed.) 2008. *Medieval Jewish Philosophical Writings*. Cambridge: Cambridge University Press. (Contains translations of some passages of *Light of the Lord* by Manekin.)

Melamed, Yitzhak. 2014. "Ḥasdai Crescas and Spinoza on Actual Infinity and the Infinity of God's Attributes," in Steven Nadler (ed.), *Spinoza and Medieval Jewish Philosophy*. Cambridge: Cambridge University Press, 204–15.

Musall, Frederek. 2008. *Herausgeforderte Identität Kontextwandel am Beispiel von Moses Maimonides und Hasdai Crescas*. Heidelberg: Schriften der Hochschule für jüdische Studien, Universitätsverlag Winter.

Nehorai, Michael. 1997. "Determinism and Ethics in the Teachings of Rav Hasdai Crescas and Rav Abraham Isaac Hacohen Kook," in Charles Manekin (ed.), *Freedom and Moral Responsibility*. Bethesda, Md.: Capital Decisions, 205–15. (Trans. from Heb.)

Netanyahu, Ben Zion. 1995. *The Origins of the Inquisition in Fifteenth-Century Spain*. New York: Random House.

Neumark, David. 1929. "Crescas and Spinoza," in *Essays in Jewish Philosophy*. Cincinnati: Central Conference of American Rabbis, 308–16.

Oḥayon, Avraham ben Avner. 2008. "Resurrection of the Dead in the Thought of R. Hasdai Crescas," *Mikhlol* 25: 167–77 (Heb.).

Ophir, Natan. 1993a. 'Rabbi Ḥasdai Crescas as a Philosophical Commentator on the Words of Chazal,' doctoral dissertation, Jerusalem: The Hebrew University (Heb.).

Ophir, Natan. 1993b. "A New Reading of R. Ḥasdai Crescas's *Or ha-Shem*: The 'Conversos' Perspective," *Proceedings of the World Congress of Jewish Studies* 11: 41–7 (Heb.).

Ophir, Natan. 1999. "Love in the Philosophical and Educational Teachings of R. Ḥasdai Crescas," *Hagut be-Ḥinukh ha-Yehudi* 1: 81–95 (Heb.).

Ophir, Natan. 2001. "The Secret of the Kaddish: A Kabbalistic Text Attributed to R. Ḥasdai Crescas," *Daat* 46: 13–28 (Heb.).

Pines, Shlomo. 1967. "Scholasticism after Thomas Aquinas and the Teachings of Hasdai Crescas and His Predecessors," *Proceedings of the Israel Academy of Sciences and Humanities* 1: 1–101.

Rabinovitch, Nachum L. 1970. "Rabbi Hasdai Crescas (1340–1410) on Numerical Infinities," *Isis* 61: 224–30.

Ravitzky, Aviezer. 1976. "A Forgotten Work by R. Ḥasdai Crescas," *Kiryat Sefer* 51: 705–11 (Heb.).

Ravitzky, Aviezer. 1982. "Crescas's Theory of Human Will: Development and Sources," *Tarbiẓ* 51: 445–70 (Heb.).

Robinson, James T. 2003. "Ḥasdai Crescas and Anti-Aristotelianism," in Daniel H. Frank and Oliver Leaman (eds.), *Cambridge Companion to Medieval Jewish Philosophy*. Cambridge: Cambridge University Press, 391–413.

Rosàs Tosas, Mar. 2015. "Performativitat i aporia derridianes en la creació del món segons Hasday Cresques," *Enrahonar* 54: 77–92 (Catalan).

Rudavsky, Tamar. 1990. "The Theory of Time in Maimonides and Crescas," *Maimonidean Studies* 1: 143–62.

Sadik, Shalom. 2008. "Crescas's Critique of Aristotle and the Lost Book by Abner of Burgos," *Tarbiẓ* 77: 133–55 (Heb.).

Sadik, Shalom. 2010. "Human Choice and Animal Will in Jewish Philosophy at the End of the Middle Ages," *Jewish Studies Internet Journal* 9: 181–203 (Heb.).

Sadik, Shalom. 2011. "The Definition of Place in the Thought of Abner of Burgos and Rabbi Hasdai," *Jerusalem Studies in Jewish Thought* 22: 233–46 (Heb.).
Sadik, Shalom. 2016. "Hasdai Crescas," Edward N. Zalta (ed.), *The Stanford Encyclopedia of Philosophy* (Winter 2016). URL = <https://plato.stanford.edu/archives/win2016/entries/crescas/>, accessed 1 June 2018.
Schweid, Eliezer. 1970. *The Religious Philosophy of Rabbi Hasdai Crescas*. Jerusalem: Mekor (Heb.).
Schweid, Eliezer. 2008. *The Classic Jewish Philosophers: From Saadia through the Renaissance*, trans. Leonard Levin. Leiden: Brill.
Sirat, Colette. 1985. *A History of Jewish Philosophy in the Middle Ages*. Cambridge: Cambridge University Press.
Tartakoff, Paola. 2012. "Apostasy as Scourge: Jews and the Repudiation of Apostates," *Between Christian and Jew: Conversion and Inquisition in the Crown of Aragon, 1250–1391*. Philadelphia: University of Pennsylvania Press, ch. 5, 106–16.
Tobiass, Marc, and Maurice Ifergan. 1995. *Crescas: un philosophie juif dans l'Espagne medieval*. Paris: Éditions du Cerf.
Touati, Charles. 1971. "*La Providence divine chez Hasday Crescas*," *Daat* 10: 15–31.
Touati, Charles. 1974. "*Hasday Crescas et ses paradoxes sur la liberté*," in *Mélange d'histoire de religions offerts à Henri-Charles Puech*. Paris: Presses universitaires de France, 573–8.
Touati, Charles. 1983. "Hasday Crescas et le problême de la science divine," *Revue des études juives* 142: 73–89.
Urbach, Symcha Bunem. 1961. *The Philosophical Teachings of Rabbi Hasdai Crescas: Pillars of Jewish Thought*, vol. iii. Jerusalem: World Zionist Organization (Heb.).
Urbach, Symcha Bunem. 1965. "Halakhic and Aggadic Innovations in the Teaching of R. Hasdai Crescas," *Bar-Ilan* 3: 186–212 (Heb.).
Waxman, Meyer. 1920. *The Philosophy of Don Hasdai Crescas*. New York: Columbia University Press. (Repr. 1966, AMS.)
Wolfsohn, Julius. 1905. *Der Einfluss Gazâli's auf Chisdai Crescas*. Frankfurt am Main: J. Kauffmann.
Wolfson, Harry A. 1916. "Crescas on the Problem of Divine Attributes," *Jewish Quarterly Review* 7: 1–44, 75–121.
Wolfson, Harry A. 1919. "Note on Crescas' Definition of Time," *Jewish Quarterly Review* 10: 1–17.
Wolfson, Harry A. 1929. *Crescas' Critique of Aristotle*. Cambridge, Mass.: Harvard University Press. (Contains Heb. text and facing Eng. trans. of *Light of the Lord*, I. i. 1–25; I. ii. 1–14.)
Wolfson, Harry A. 1934. *The Philosophy of Spinoza*. New York: Schocken.
Wolfson, Harry A. 1953. "Emanation and Creation *ex nihilo* in Crescas," in *Sefer Assaf*. Jerusalem: Magnes, 230–6 (Heb.).
Wolfson, Harry A. 1977a. "Studies in Crescas," *Studies in the History of Philosophy and Religion*. Cambridge, Mass.: Harvard University Press, ii. 247–337.
Wolfson, Harry A. 1977b. "Emanation and Creation *ex nihilo* in Crescas," *Studies in the History of Philosophy and Religion*. Cambridge, Mass.: Harvard University Press, ii. 623–9 (Heb.). (Repr. 1953.)
Zonta, M., 2001. "The Influence of Hasdai Crescas's Philosophy on Some Aspects of Sixteenth-Century Philosophy and Science," in J. Helm and A. Winkelmann (eds.), *Studies in European Judaism, Religious Confessions and the Sciences in the Sixteenth Century*. Leiden: Brill, 71–8.

Citations Index

BIBLE

Genesis
1 229
1-2 23
1: 1 277
1: 16 17
1: 26 16
1: 31 158, 239
2: 4 16, 350
2: 16 291
3: 21 302
5: 22 298
5: 24 279, 298
6: 6 116
9: 27 23
12: 5 144
14: 19 277
15: 6 184
15: 8 184
17: 4 2, 161
18: 20 11
18: 21 122
18: 26 179
21: 12 161, 291
22: 8 162
22: 12 122, 157
22: 13 163
22: 14 162
25: 7 17
26: 5 17
28: 15 172
28: 17 163nn158, 159
32 12
32: 7 179
32: 27 143
32: 30 143
32: 31 143
48: 15-16 143

Exodus
1: 22 284
3: 13 115
3: 14 115nn239, 240
3: 19 126
4: 22 284
6: 3 351
7: 9 143
9: 12 326
10: 1 326, 328
10: 2 328
11: 4 168
12: 2 277
12: 12 144
12: 23 144
12: 29 168nn191, 192
14: 21 143
15: 18 332
15: 26 283
18: 11 284
19: 5 161, 227
19: 5-6 209
19: 17 13, 204
20: 2 27
20: 2-3 319
20: 3-5 224
21: 26-7 208
23: 2 307
23: 7 208
23: 20 144
24: 1 144
25: 8 163, 235
25: 22 163
32: 10 173nn214, 215
33: 11 98, 144
33: 12 129
33: 18 98
33: 19 109
33: 20 109, 354
33: 23 109
34: 6-7 107
34: 10 309nn240-1
34: 24 152, 227, 284
34: 30 309

Leviticus
7: 23-5 153
7: 26-7 153
16 230
19: 17 209
19: 17-18 209
19: 18 209
23: 9-14 231
23: 40 165
23: 43 234
25: 1-7 208
25: 8-17 208
25: 20-2 152
25: 21 284
25: 46 207

Leviticus (*cont.*)
 26: 3   177
 26: 8   152
 26: 15 177

Numbers
 5: 11–21   152
 5: 11–31   285
 5: 19–20   227
 6: 23   324
 6: 27   324
 9: 8   311
 10: 9   230
 12: 6   180, 311
 12: 6–7   310
 12: 7   311
 12: 8   98, 144
 14: 20   179
 16: 29   177
 22: 28   168
 22: 30   185
 23: 10   279
 23: 19   181
 27: 21   314

Deuteronomy
 1: 17   208
 2: 5   148
 3: 25   225, 328
 4: 19–20   145
 4: 25   319
 5: 7–9   224
 5: 16   284
 5: 26   199
 6: 4   114, 215
 6: 5   215, 224, 228, 235
 6: 7   19
 7: 10   285
 8: 5   14, 193, 283
 9: 4–5   290
 10: 12   215
 10: 15   118, 219
 11: 12   163
 11: 13   215, 233
 11: 21   299
 11: 22   17
 13: 4   156, 235
 15: 1–11   208
 15: 4   152
 17: 8–9   307
 17: 11   229, 307
 17: 20   208
 18: 21   177
 18: 22   171, 174, 176
 19: 19   229
 22: 7   284
 22: 8   198
 23: 16   208
 26: 18–19   209
 28: 12   325
 28: 28   132
 30: 12   307
 30: 15   279
 30: 16   215
 30: 20   17, 215
 31: 6   208
 31: 18   146, 149
 31: 29   130
 32: 7   229
 32: 9   161, 229
 32: 17   345
 32: 20   146, 149
 33: 4   27, 29
 33: 10   144
 33: 26   162
 34: 10   129, 180, 310
 34: 10–11   309
 39: 29   209

Joshua
 1: 8   19
 5: 14   311
 5: 15   144
 10: 13   185
 22: 5   17

Judges
 13: 22   354

1 Samuel
 3   312
 3: 3   17
 3: 19–20   171, 175
 3: 20   312
 4: 19   312
 10: 2   130, 178, 312
 10: 9   130
 14: 45   301
 25: 10   23
 25: 29   279

2 Samuel
 19   323
 23: 2   170

1 Kings
 1: 39   163
 5   312
 6: 1   354
 8: 2   164
 8: 41   322
 8: 48   163
 9: 3   163
 18   305
 18: 21   298

2 Kings
 1: 10   177
 2: 3   279, 293

CITATIONS INDEX

3: 15 188, 311, 314
13: 21 274
17: 9 121
20 179
24: 14 318

Isaiah

2: 5 17, 26
2: 6 23
3: 24 23
5: 21 17
6: 1 16
6: 3 77
11: 2 305
12: 1 150
16: 21 303
26. 2 220
26: 4 350
28: 16 17
29: 8 182
29: 14 23
30: 33 348
32: 16 16
40: 18 102, 106
40: 25 102, 106
41: 8 219
41: 18 2, 118
50: 6 179
50: 20 23
51: 1 2, 17, 160
52: 13 316
55: 6 164
55: 8–9 317
63: 7 17
63: 10 116
65: 20 301
66: 1 332
66: 5 24

Jeremiah

5: 21 296
10: 6 102
12: 2 321
16: 19 297
18: 6 27, 243
18: 7–10 172
20: 7 23
20: 9 180
20: 10 23
21: 8 17, 204
23: 29 235
28: 8 176nn226, 227
28: 9 175nn221, 224, 176
28: 15 172
29: 10 319
30: 15 214
45: 5 188
49: 35 183

Ezekiel

1 229
1: 4–26 23, 229
3: 12 77
18: 32 279
26: 12 214
28: 12 16

Hosea

4: 14 149
12: 5 143

Joel

3: 1 295, 301
3: 4 293, 300

Amos

3: 7 126
8: 11 231

Jonah

3: 4 172
3: 10 172

Zephaniah

3: 9 295, 319
9: 3 186

Haggai

2: 6 23
2: 9 318

Malachi

3: 23 293, 297, 300
3: 24 297

Psalms

1: 2 19
4: 4 103
7: 16 348
12: 1 233
12: 4 16
16: 11 16
17: 15 182
19: 2 185, 277, 338, 340
19: 10 303
29: 10 332
30: 6 158
31: 17 16
31: 22 16
33: 14 17
36: 8 164
37: 23 230
49: 16 279
51: 7 234
62: 13 285
64: 4 177
65: 2 103, 322
65: 3 322

Psalms (*cont.*)
   68: 18 337
   73: 17 279
   80: 13 214
   82: 5 17
   83: 41 214
   84: 2 163
   85: 10 17
   85: 13 275
   86: 11 16
   87: 2 163
   88: 12 348
   91: 15 116
   104: 31 116, 117
   113: 2 16
   113: 5 16
   115: 17 279
   115: 18 279, 322n313
   118: 23 25
   119: 105 16
   119: 126 20
   136 319
   136: 1 239
   136: 22 319
   136: 23 319
   136: 24 319
   136: 25 319
   136: 26 239
   139 12, 229
   139: 1 121
   139: 2–3 121
   139: 3 107
   139: 4 123
   139: 15–16 123
   139: 16 108
   139: 17 123
   139: 17–18 107
   139: 19 229nn467, 468
   139: 23 124, 229
   139: 24 124
   145 322
   145: 18 321
   145: 21 107, 322

Proverbs
   3: 27 188
   6: 23 16, 23, 24, 204
   8: 34 19
   9: 5 231
   14: 16 327
   20: 27 17, 25, 282
   28: 22 187

Job
   1: 21 16
   13: 5 296
   16: 9 87

Lamentations
   5: 19 332, 333

Ecclesiastes
   1: 14 82, 154
   5: 6 23
   5: 7 198
   6: 6 239
   6: 11 72, 82, 214
   7: 10 318
   7: 20 225
   7: 24 17
   12: 7 279, 281
   12: 13 224

Esther
   1: 20 23
   2: 15 330
   9: 27 13, 204

Daniel
   2: 22 282
   4: 5 308
   6: 11 163
   10: 16 312
   10: 19 312
   11: 14 23, 126
   11: 16 318
   12: 2 293, 294, 297, 302
   12: 6 317
   12: 8–9 316
   12: 9 23

Ezra
   2: 9 318

Nehemiah
   8: 10 164nn178, 180
   9: 5 16
   9: 6 16

1 Chronicles
   16: 33 340nn30, 31
   28: 9 121, 230

MIDRASHIM
Midrash Rabbah
Genesis Rabbah
   3: 7 90, 276nn69, 70
   8: 2 238
   9: 5 158, 239
   14: 8 164
   25: 1 298
   30: 8 17
   39: 1 119
   51: 3 149, 288, 332
   68 77

Leviticus Rabbah
  7: 40 203
Numbers Rabbah
  12: 4 17
Song of Songs Rabbah
  2: 32 118

Midrash Tanḥuma
Tanḥuma Toldot
  9 118
Tanḥuma Toldot (Buber edition)
  20 316
Tanḥuma Vayishlach (Buber edition)
  6 179
Tanḥuma Pekudei
  3 17

Midrash Halakhah
Sifra on Leviticus
  Introduction 18
  16: 2 311
Sifrei on *Parashat Berakhah*
  16 181, 183
Sifrei on Deuteronomy
  16: 19–20 208
  17: 8 307
  17: 11 229

Mekhilta
Mekhilta, Ki Tissa
  1 77

MISHNAH
Berakhot
  5: 1 157
  9: 5 224
  17: 1 118
  31: 2 119
Peah
  1: 1 18
Shekalim
  4: 1 162
Yoma
  8: 9 326
Sukkah
  1: 4 234
Ḥagigah
  2 171
  2: 1 116, 349, 351
Sanhedrin
  10: 1 300, 303
Ketubot
  8: 1 116

Sotah
  7: 6 105
Gittin
  4: 6 163
Kiddushin
  1: 10 211
Makkot
  3: 16 18
Avot
  1: 3 224, 225
  1: 14 199
  2: 5 187
  2: 17 224
  3: 11 129, 185
  3: 15 197, 198n315, 212, 287
  3: 21 231
  4: 1 187
  4: 2 330
  4: 4 208
  4: 17 329
  4: 22 225, 289
  6: 11 18
'Eduyot
  2: 10 288, 348
Tamid
  6: 1 230

TOSEFTA
Ḥagigah
  2: 2 197
Sanhedrin
  7: 6 28
  13: 2 303
  13: 4–5 154

TALMUD
Babylonian Talmud
Berakhot
  3b–4a 168
  4a 172
  7a 173
  8a 324
  17a 165, 280, 282, 296, 304
  17b 24, 320
  19b 24, 110
  30a 163
  31b 122
  32a 107, 228
  33b 103, 323
  34b 295, 301, 316, 325nn324, 325
  54a 166

Babylonian Talmud (*cont.*)
Shabbat
  6b 20
  23b 207
  30b 188
  31a 209
  32a 198
  61b 344
  88a 204
  92a 187
  96b 20
  104a 305
  119b 220
  137b 160nn139, 141, 161
  146a 160
  152a 157, 280
  152b 221, 223
  156a 288, 290
'Eruvin
  6a 24, 110
  13b 24nn92, 93, 225
  27a 290, 303
Pesaḥim
  50a 211
  68b 239
  112a 129
Rosh Hashanah
  16a 162, 164, 165, 330
  16b 164
  16b–17a 294
  17a 154, 200, 212, 286nn125, 127, 287, 288, 293
  18a 164
  30a 295
  31a 332
Yoma
  5a 294
  5b 294
  9b 317
  11a 233
  29a 203
  39b 105
  73b 313, 314
  86b 325, 328
Sukkah
  28a 349
  29a 199
Beitzah
  21a 235
Ta'anit
  20a 181
  31a 348
Mo'ed katan
  25a 164
  28a 288, 290
Ḥagigah
  5b 116
  11b 82

  12a 286
  13a 349, 350
  14b 349
  16a 346
Yevamot
  47b 186
  64a 118
Ketubot
  11b 302
  49b 207
  110a 163
Nedarim
  25a 77
  27a 203
  32a 17
Sotah
  8b 285
  10b 323
  11a 293
  14a 225
  38a 324
  [38b] 144
Gittin
  23a 312
  45a 208
  60b 18, 19
Kiddushin
  20a 207
  22a 207
  24b–25a 208
  30b 235
  39b 211, 288, 291
  40b 18, 157, 198, 212, 286
  71a 105
Baba kamma
  92b 290
Baba metzia
  59b 307
  92a 20
Baba batra
  10b 211
  13b 171
  15a 314
  75a 280, 348
  134a 310
  160b 137
  161a 137
Sanhedrin
  10a 293
  17a 24
  32b 208
  38a 318
  38b 144
  76b 207
  88b 20
  89a 180, 183
  90a 200, 296, 299, 305
  90b 302

92b 296
97b 316
99a 295, 301, 316
100b 293
101a 345
105b 185
110b 220, 347
Makkot
5b 229
11b 199
23b 186
23b–24a 27
Shevuot
7b 77
29a 77
30b 208
31a 208
39a 77
'*Avodah zarah*
3b 337
4b–5a 198
5a 199
7b 322
25a 181
40b 77
Horayot
11b 77
Zevaḥim
45a 295
Menaḥot
29b 350nn66, 68
43b 233
85a 309
109b 105
Ḥullin
7b 198, 230
60b 118
142a 284
Temurah
14b 18, 19

Jerusalem Talmud
Pesaḥim
50a 211
67a 323

CLASSICAL JEWISH SOURCES
Maimonides

Guide of the Perplexed
Guide I
38 109
54 103, 109
61 104

62 105nn204, 206
72 237
74 279
Guide II
Intro. 32, 50
32 188nn289, 290
33 312
Guide III
13 240n518, 240n519, 241nn520, 521, 243
26 303
Introduction to Tractate *Avot*
4 224
Commentary on the Mishnah (Introduction to the Talmud)
9 308
Commentary on Mishnah *Sanhedrin*
10 242n2
10: 1 310
Mishneh Torah
Hilkhot Teshuvah
6: 3 326
9: 2 296
Hilkhot Tefilah
14: 10 105
Hilkhot Nesiat Kapayyim
15: 1 324
Hilkhot Melakhim
11, 12 296

Gersonides (Levi ben Gershon)
Wars of the Lord
I. viii 280
VI. i. 23 259

Judah Halevi
Kuzari
I. 67 278

Naḥmanides
Sha'ar Hagemul (Gate of Reward)
par. 123 223
par. 124 296

Kabbalistic Works
Zohar
I. 56b 298
Sefer Yetzirah (Book of Creation)
2: 3 77
1: 6 112
Sefer Habahir (Book of Brightness)
fr. 107 105

CLASSICAL GREEK SOURCES
Aristotle
Posterior Analytics
II. iv. 91^{a}16 49
On the Soul
II. iii. 414^{b}27ff. 223
II. v–III.viii 138
III. vii–viii 219
III. x 191
III. xii–xiii 223
On the Heavens
I. iii. 270^{a}22ff. 338
I. iii. 270^{b}1–4 88
I. v–vii 31
I. xii 246
On Generation and Corruption
I. iv. 319^{b}31ff. 47
Meteorology
IV. I 219

On Parts of Animals
X 149, 338
Physics
II. iii 189
II. iv–vi 189
III. iv–viii 31
VI. iv. 234^{b}10ff. 51
VIII. v. 256^{b}9–10 53
Metaphysics
I. iii. 983^{a}32 236
III. ii 987^{a-b} 24
VII. xv. 1039^{b}23ff. 211
VIII. i. 1042^{b}3–5 48
VIII. v 211
IX. iv 332
IX. v–ix 190
IX. viii 343
IX. ix. 1051^{a}15ff. 149, 211
XI. x 31
XII. vii 206

Subjects and Names Index

Aaron 147, 235, 294, 294n167, 311, 314, 324n320
Abarbanel 11
Abaye 349
Abigail 279
Abner of Burgos 15
Abraham (patriarch) 1-2, 17-18, 250, 311-12, 350
  attachment to/covenant with God 10, 17, 118-19, 184, 219n411, 347
  courage and generosity of 208
  God-fearingness of 122, 122n11, 130, 130n37, 157n129
  God's promises to 291, 291n153
  prophecy and 119, 122, 312
  trial (Binding of Isaac) and 5, 122, 157, 161-2, 289
  see also circumcision
R. Abraham Ibn Daud 30, 279n92
Absalom 323
Abu Bakr al-Tsayigh, see Avempace
Abu Ḥamed, see al-Ghazali
Abu Nazzr, see Alfarabi
accident(s) 33n14, 61-2, 83, 83nn142-4, 250-1, 266
  bodies and 54-5, 62, 86-7
  essential/nonessential 54n65
  existence and 99-101, 137
  God and 110
  motion and 49-50, 52-3, 85, 94
  quantity, shape, and position of 54n65, 62
  time and 58-60, 89-90, 105
  see also force(s)
actual/actuality/actualization/actualizers 60-1, 95, 246-7, 247n17; see also motion/movers/moving things: potentiality to actuality; potential/potentiality
Adam/Adam and Eve 2, 160-1, 278, 299, 306, 348
agents 61, 95
  amulets and incantations and 343-4
  God and 143-5, 248-9, 273-4, 273n61
  indispensability of 64-5
  miracles and 273-4
  providence and 143-5
  see also intermediaries; motion/movers/moving things
Ahab 298
Ahitofel 124
R. Akiva 197n312, 287
Alexander (of Aphrodisias) 30, 52

Alfarabi 112, 114, 352-3
Amalek 184, 208
Amoraim (s. Amora) 20
amulets and incantations 342-5
angels 143-5, 211, 298, 340n33, 353
  as communicators 132
  created on first day 313
  of death/the destroyer 144, 283
  demons and 346
  human beings at rank of 279, 297-8, 316
  as intellectual substances 281
  as intermediaries 144
  not subject to passing away 236
  prophecy, agents of 311
  realm of, highest of three 236
  referred to as *elohim* or Tetragrammaton 143-4
  as separate intellects 145
anterior eternity 3, 69-70, 240, 262-71, 275-8, 320, 331-2
  arguments for 244-9
  creation and 268-72
  Gersonides' view of 249-62
  infinite potentialities and 246-7, 246n14, 247n18
  Maimonides' view of 249-50
  motion/time and 244-5, 254n32, 255
Apollonius of Perga 202n333
apprehension/apprehenders 196-7, 221-2
  celestial bodies, capable of 251, 266, 337-40
  divine 13, 197n310; see also God: knowledge of particulars
  human (of God) 102-4, 111-14, 118, 151, 211, 307, 354
  intelligibles and 214
  Moses' (of God) 108-9, 109n221, 115
  pleasurable 116-18, 211, 221-2, 286-7, 348
  will and 272
Aristotelianism/Aristotle 1, 3, 3n1, 24, 70-91, 252nn24-5
  assumptions and propositions 6, 70n103
  on bodies: composite nature of 62
  on change/motion 47-53, 57-8, 60-1, 64-5, 88
  on coming-to-be/passing-away 246, 248
  on empty space 31, 34-7
  on existence of God 30-1, 67
  on existence/nonexistence 61-4, 247n17
  on first principle 167
  on forces in a body 53-8, 62
  on heaviness and lightness 38, 38n29, 50

Aristotelianism/Aristotle (cont.)
  on imagination/intellect 55, 169
  on infinity 37–47
  on matter and form 64
  on number 59–60
  on place/time 58–9, 65, 75–6, 247, 253
  on substratum 64
  on the universe 9, 337
  works, see *Metaphysics*; *On Generation and Corruption*; *On the Heavens*; *On the Soul*; *Parts of Animals*; *Physics*; *Sense and Sensibilia*
arousing/awakening 164, 226–8, 232–4, 306, 326–7, 330
R. Ashi 308
attachment/connection/service to God, see God
attributes of God, see God
ʿAtzeret (Shavuot) 231, 231n478
Avempace 52, 72, 82, 84, 91, 98, 112
Averroes 32n9, 36, 36n23, 72, 278, 280n98
  on change 52
  Commentary on the Physics 82
  on corporeal form of celestial bodies 86–7
  on existence/quiddity 98, 99n187
  on God 99
  on infinity 47, 82
  on the intellect 132–3
  on prime mover 352–3, 353n77
  On [Aristotle's] Sense and Sensibilia 132
  on unity/quiddity 101
Avicenna 280n98
  on corporeal form of celestial bodies 86
  on existence/quiddity 98
  on infinity 47, 82
  on prime mover 352–3
  on unity/quiddity 101

Baal 183
Babylonian exile 317–19
Babylonian Talmud 20; see also Oral Torah
Balaam 168, 180–1, 183–5, 279
Balak 134
Baruch son of Neriah 188, 188nn289–90
belief/beliefs 2, 30
  choice/will and 200–4, 201n331
  commandments and 242–3, 242n1, 321
  in creation 243–4
  effort and joy in 203–4
  in existence of God, see God: belief in existence of
  involuntary 13, 27, 202
  required, not necessary for Torah's existence 6, 242, 321
  required, not tied to commandments, see creation; immortality; Messiah/messianic age; Moses: prophecy/other prophets and; reward and punishment; resurrection of the dead; Torah, eternality of; under individual beliefs; *Urim* and *Tummim*
  required, tied to specific commandments, see festivals; prayer(s); priestly blessing; repentance; Rosh Hashanah; Yom Kippur
  required, for Torah's existence, see cornerstones
  reward and punishment for 201–5
  undetermined by Torah 331–54
  see also faith; religious beliefs; root-principles
benefits/harms 14, 151n104, 284–5, 315, 324
Binding of Isaac 2, 122, 157, 161–3, 180, 230, 291
bodies 54n66, 72–3, 258
  accidents and 54–5, 62, 86–7
  anteriorly eternal 268–71, 270n59
  composite/composition of 42n40, 53–4, 62, 68, 93–6, 93–4n171
  dimensions 72–3
  division of 55
  finite/infinite 37–45, 37n27, 39nn32–3, 73, 87
  forces and 56, 56n79, 87–92, 94n172
  motion and 43, 51
  natural form and 86
  numbers and 59–60
  separation from 219, 219n414
  simple 42n40
  tangible 37, 37n27
  see also celestial bodies/spheres
Boethius 197n310
Book of Fruit (*Liber Fructus*; *Sefer Haperi*) (Ptolemy) 162, 162n148, 186
borders/boundaries 45, 81; see also shape

Carmel (Mount) 305
causation/causal necessity 10; see also necessitation/necessity
causes/effects 46–7, 269
  choice and 193nn301–2, 194n304; see also choice (free will)
  efficient 34n18
  existence and 61–2
  final 34, 34n18
  finitude/infinitude and 46, 82–4, 83n138, 84n145
  first 83–4, 113–14, 191; see also F(f)irst C(c)ause
  formal 34n18
  intellection and 113
  material 34n18
  motion and 53n62
celestial bodies/spheres 9, 246–54, 246n12, 252nn24–5, 254n32, 337–44
  creation of 251–2, 260n46
  diurnal 18n39

eminence of 9, 339n27
influence on human affairs of 340-2, 341n34
as intermediaries 145
living and rational 145, 337-40
motion and 250, 337-40
Chaldeans 188
change 249
  categories of 47
  continuous 88, 88n157
  division and 51, 84, 84n147
  external/internal 48n48
  motion and 48, 48nn48-9, 57, 260
  potential to actual 249, 262n52; *see also* potential/potentiality
  time and 48n49, 51-2
Chariot, account of 23, 23n78, 349-51, 350n63
children 207, 220, 223, 347
choice (free will) 27, 188-205, 193n303
  belief/beliefs and 200-4
  causal necessity vs. constraint 10, 12-13, 193-204
  as cornerstone 10-13
  divine foreknowledge and 12, 196-8
  effort and 10, 12-13, 195-203
  joy and 12-14, 188, 203-5
  reward and punishment and 203
  see also commandments; cornerstones; freedom; will
Christians and Christianity 4-5, 308n234, 316n279
circumcision 17, 160-1, 184, 232-3, 292, 347
combiner, need for 69, 95-6, 95n177
coming-to-be/passing-away 54, 54n66, 245n10, 246, 248, 331-5
commanded/commander 26, 120, 226; *see also* God
commandments 10, 14, 17-29, 21n69, 205-10
  belief/beliefs and 242-3, 242n1, 321
  children and 207
  knowledge and performance of 18n42, 21-3, 212
  love and 209
  memory aids for preservation of 17-22
  negative 28n15
  number of 27-8
  positive 26, 28n15, 207n345
  reward and punishment and 291, 330n352; *see also* reward and punishment
  slaves and 207-8
  will/choice and 27
  women and 206-7
  see also circumcision
commentaries:
  on Aristotle 30, 82, 132
  on Maimonides 32, 62
  on the Mishnah 308, 310
  on the Talmud 20-1

Commentary on Maimonides' Twenty-Five Propositions (al-Tabrizi) 32n9
Commentary on the Mishnah (Maimonides) 308, 310
Commentary on the Physics (Averroes) 82
communication 133-4, 133n44, 150-2
composites/composition 62, 237-8; *see also* bodies
compulsion/constraint 122-3, 124n19, 188, 190, 196-7
Conics (Apollonius of Perga) 202n333
cornerstones 6-7
  choice (free will) 188-205
  end (purpose) of Torah 205-41
  God's knowledge of existents 120-42
  God's power 166-8
  God's providence 142-65
  prophecy 169-88
covenant 17, 160-1, 168, 181, 184, 232, 347; *see also* Abraham (patriarch)
creation 16, 90, 229, 243-78
  account of 23, 23n78, 349-51, 350n63
  belief in 141-2
  constant 276-7
  as emanation from God 271-2
  end (purpose) of 239-40
  from nothing 155, 167, 213, 248, 252, 255-6, 265-6, 271-6, 281
  God's power and 167, 167n188
  see also Gersonides; Maimonides, R. Moses
Crescas, Ḥasdai 1-6, 32n9

Daniel 170
David (king) 12-13, 123-4, 170, 279
Day of Atonement, *see* Yom Kippur
death 177, 211-12, 278-9, 348
  goodness and 158, 239
  intellect and 90-1, 221-3
  seeing God and 354
  see also resurrection of the dead; soul: immortality of
deeds:
  commandments and 200
  reward and punishment for 292-3
  sinful, *see* sins
  see also majority, judgment according to
demons 345-6
deplorable condition 125, 127, 139, 148-59
Diaspora 163
distance/distanced:
  between worlds 336
  of celestial bodies 251, 333, 344
  divisible 35-6
  from God 14, 158-9, 227
  heaviness/motion/time and 35, 40-1, 45
  lines/radii and 43-4, 79-80
  sensation and 197

divination 341-2
divine attributes, see God
divine governance 161-5; see also God: providence
divine-human bond 2, 10, 16-17, 105-6
divine judgment 162, 294, 297, 330n350
divine justice 195, 197
  compatible with causal necessity 141, 200-1
  compatible with judgment according to majority 158
  David (king) and 124
  deprivation of celestially ordained good and 157
  for good end and perfection/good in itself 158, 201
  political 14, 195-6, 289
  resurrection and 300-4
  wicked intellectuals and 151
  see also reward and punishment
Divine Presence (shekhinah) 17n32, 310
divine providence 10; see also God: providence
division 32, 66, 125
  bodies and 54-5
  change and 51, 84, 84n147
  motion and 51
  time and 244
Doeg the Edomite 229
dreams and magic 169-70, 175, 180, 182, 310-11
duality, see God: oneness/unity of

Eber, see Shem and Eber
effort:
  belief and 203-4
  causal necessity and 193-4, 194n304, 199, 199nn324, 326
  choice and 178, 190
Egypt/Egyptians:
  exile in 317, 319
  exodus from 227-8
  gods of 291
  magicians 309
  plague of the first-born 144, 168, 284
  suffering of 283-4, 328
Eleazar (son of Aaron; priest) 314
R. Eleazar ben Arakh 349
R. Eleazar Hakalir 234
elements 9, 37, 37n27, 51n55, 71, 82, 300-2, 345-6n45
  four 40, 50-1, 345
  infinite 74-7
  motion and 92, 339, 344
Elements (Euclid) 35, 202
Eli (priest) 312
R. Eliezer 307
Elijah (prophet) 279, 293, 297-9, 304-5, 329

Elisha (prophet) 179, 188n291, 274, 274n66, 311, 312, 314
emanation:
  from celestial sphere 161, 164-5, 344
  constant 252
  of divine overflow 235
  of effect from cause 83
  God's glory as 77
  necessary/volitional 271-2, 275
  prophetic 311, 341
  of spheres 252
empty space 3n1, 9
  creation and 274-5
  Gersonides' view on 256n35
  homogeneity of 71n104
  impossibility of 33-71, 248, 335
  locomotion/motion and 34, 34n19, 71-2
  metaphor for God's glory 77
  as place for body 256-7, 274
  possibility of 71-7
end (ultimate purpose/final cause of Torah/existence) 205-41, 224n436
  divine/human perspective on 225, 225n446
  as God's will 241
  as love of/service to God 215, 225, 234, 241, 328-9
  perfection and 206, 210, 215
  Torah and 214-15, 224-5
Enoch 279, 298, 298nn186-8
Epicurus 65
Epistle on Resurrection (Iggeret Tehiyat Hametim) (Maimonides) 296
equivocation vs. priority/posteriority 99n186, 108, 323
  Averroes on 99
  "exists" as applied to God/other existents 100, 100n190
  Gersonides' view on 135
  Maimonides' view on 99, 136-7, 137-8n54
  Tetragrammaton and 104
error 182-3
Esau 12, 172, 178-9
essence 63; see also God
eternality and eternal/non-eternal 69n101; see also anterior eternity; posterior eternity
Euclid 35, 202
Eve, see Adam/Adam and Eve
evil 148-53, 151n104; see also the wicked/wickedness
excision 153-4, 284
exile 150, 186, 188, 312, 316-20
existence/existents/nonexistence 100n190, 136-7, 246-7, 247nn16, 18
  accident and 99-101, 137
  end (purpose) of 236-40
  finitude/infinitude of 247n19

SUBJECTS AND NAMES INDEX 373

God and 3, 140, 197, 272
quiddity and 98-9, 99n187
see also creation; God: belief in existence of
Ezekiel (prophet) 23n78, 171, 229n460, 279, 340

faith 307-8
 foundations of 2
 imparting of 297-8
 see also belief/beliefs
festivals (pilgrim) 165, 227, 231-2, 234, 284n108; *see also* ʿAtzeret (Shavuot); Passover; Sukkot
finitude/infinitude 31-3, 32-3nn10-12, 55-6
 acting and being acted upon and 42-3, 78
 bodies and, *see* bodies
 cause and effect and 46, 82-4, 83n138, 84n145
 lightness/heaviness and 40-1, 77-8, 78n127
 motion and 36n23, 78n128, 267-8; *see also* motion/movers/moving things: circular; motion/movers/moving things: rectilinear
 size and 267
 time/place and 9
F(f)irst C(c)ause 6, 69, 83-4, 100-1, 113-14, 191, 259, 352-3
force(s) 30n6, 33n14, 60, 167
 bodies and 53-7, 56n79, 59, 87-92, 94n172
 motion/mover and 35-6, 65-71
form 45, 64-6
 matter and 54, 258-9, 258n40, 261
 see also natural form
four species on Sukkot 165n183
freedom 12-14, 197; *see also* choice (free will)
fringes 233

Garden of Eden, *see* Paradise
Gates of Righteousness/Repentance (Shaʿarei Tzedeq/Teshuvah) (R. Jonah Gerondi) 326n329
Gehenna 222, 288, 347-8; *see also* world-to-come
Gemara, see Talmud
gematria 17n37, 27, 27n9, 29n21, 319n292
Geonim (s. Gaon) 20-2
Gersonides 126n25, 157, 281
 on creation 243, 250-62, 264-71, 274-5
 on God's knowledge of particulars 133-5, 133n42, 133n44
 on Maimonides 135-7, 137-8n54
 on potentiality 259-61, 259n43, 261n47, 268
 on prophecy 173-5, 173n212
 on time 252-5, 259
 Wars of the Lord (Milḥamot Hashem) 135
al-Ghazali:
 on corporeal form/celestial bodies 86
 on existence/quiddity 98

 on infinity 47, 82
 on prime mover 352-3
 on unity/quiddity 101
Gideon 144
God:
 attachment/connection/service to 187-8, 201-2, 220, 225-6, 235, 241, 329, 329n348
 attributes of 2, 102-12, 102n197, 107n214, 322-3; *see also* equivocation vs. priority/posteriority
 attributes of (essential) 102, 104, 107-15, 107n216, 108-9n219, 115n237, 354
 attributes of (negative) 100n190, 102n197, 115, 137, 137-8n54
 belief in existence of 6, 8n5, 26-9, 91-3, 97-101
 belief in, not a commandment 26-9
 concealment of 97, 115
 connection to people Israel 2
 creation and, *see* creation
 essence/glory of 2, 77, 98, 104, 108-12, 115, 126, 126n23, 354; *see also* God: omniscience of
 fear of 199n323; *see also* Abraham (patriarch)
 as First Cause 100-1
 foreknowledge 121-37, 126nn23-24, 136n51, 140-1, 141n61, 197
 human beings and, *see* divine-human bond
 incorporeality of 115-19
 joy and 116-18
 kindness of 17-19, 107n214, 147, 162, 186, 195, 226-8, 232-3, 239, 241, 293, 303, 319, 325-8
 knowledge of particulars 128n30, 129-37, 136n51, 153
 love for/God's love 1-3, 11, 117-18, 156-7, 159, 180, 187-8, 201-2, 215, 218-20, 224, 225-6, 228, 281, 325-6, 329
 names of 104-5, 105n206, 109, 351; *see also* Tetragrammaton
 omniscience of 12-13, 110-11, 121, 138-42, 153, 197n310
 oneness/unity of 68-70, 91-3, 101-15
 power and transcendence of 27, 110-11, 166-8, 226-8, 243
 praising/worship of 106-7, 107n213, 179-80, 182, 186; *see also* R. Ḥanina
 proofs for existence of 31-70
 providence of 10, 142-65; *see also* providence
 punctiliousness of 229-32
 see also divine governance; Divine Presence (*shekhinah*)
 the good 226-7, 236, 238, 241, 272-3; *see also* reward and punishment; the righteous
Greeks 20, 188, 279, 318
Guide of the Perplexed (Dalalat al haʿirin; Moreh Nevukhim) (Maimonides) 1, 21, 23

374 SUBJECTS AND NAMES INDEX

R. Hananiah son of ʿAqashia 18, 186
hakhamim (s. hakham), see Sages; sages
Hananiah son of Azur (prophet) 175–6, 182, 183n265
R. Hanina (Sage) 103, 103n201, 106–7, 322, 325
happiness 209–11, 226, 232; see also joy; pleasure; reward and punishment
Harvey, Warren (Zev):
　on innovations in physics in Light of the Lord 3n1
　on metaphysical proof of God 8n5
heaviness/lightness, see lightness/heaviness
Hebrew language 15, 19n45; see also gematria
Hezekiah (king) 172
high priest 199, 199n326, 235, 308, 313–14
Hillel 209, 310
R. Hiyya 20
R. Hisda 290
holy name 110; see also Tetragrammaton
Horeb 134
human–divine bond, see divine–human bond
hylē (matter) 36n22, 54–5, 278
hylic faculty 124, 124n20, 127, 129, 139, 192, 192n300
hylic intellect 210, 210n374, 213

ibn Bajja, see Avempace
ibn Nazzr, see Alfarabi
ibn Rushd, see Averroes
ibn Sina, see Avicenna
ignorance 117–18, 148, 149n94
　absence/negation of 110–11, 135–6, 141
　as defect 12, 131–2, 141
immortality 132
　apprehension of intelligibles and 219, 223
　children and 223, 347
　of the soul 219, 223, 278–82
impurity 206, 232–4
incantations, see amulets and incantations
the infinite/infinity 74–5; see also finitude/infinitude
the intellect 2, 17n19, 55, 55n74, 210–18, 217–18nn408–10
　acquired 55n71, 212–16, 213n386, 280
　active 91n163, 150, 152, 212, 280–1
　constitution of 112–13, 112n230, 138–40, 213–14, 216, 280
　hylic, see hylic intellect
　as one with intellecter and intellected 351–2
　post-death 212
　as receiver of spiritual overflow (prophecy) 169–70
intellection 113, 213–14, 219, 292, 352
intelligibles 117n251, 150, 154, 210–18, 280
　apprehension of 214
　souls and 202
intermediaries 143–5, 144nn84–5; see also agents

Isaac (patriarch) 5, 161–2, 291, 291n153, 323
Isaiah (book) 316
Isaiah (prophet) 171–2, 179
Israel (land) 163–4
Israel (people):
　acceptance of Torah 204
　connection to God 2
　election of 17, 161–3

Jacob (patriarch) 12–13, 132, 143, 163, 172–4, 175n219, 178–9
Jeremiah (book) 172, 175, 178
Jeremiah (prophet) 170, 175–6, 179, 183n265
Jerusalem Talmud 20
Jethro 284
Joan I of Aragon (king) 4
R. Johanan ben Zakkai 295, 325, 349
R. Jonah Gerondi 326, 326n329
Jonah (prophet) 172
Joseph 143
Josephus 318n289
Joshua 144, 179, 181, 280, 310–11, 314
R. Joshua 307
joy 12–14, 89
　in attachment to/in presence of Divine Presence 118, 164, 221, 280, 286, 296, 304
　in apprehension 116–17, 348
　at beginning of year 165
　in belief 203–5
　of demons 346
　experienced by God 116–19
　festivals and 230
　of giving 118
　in performing commandments 12, 201, 215
　in repentance 327, 327n335
　and will 117, 201
R. Judah Halevi 278, 278nn78–9
R. Judah Hanasi 20–1
R. Judah son of R. Simon (Sage) 90
judgment/justice 124, 125n21, 202, 208, 233, 286, 317, 328
　political 14, 195–6, 198, 200, 200n327, 298
　see also divine judgment; divine justice

Kaddish prayer 323
Kuzari 278, 278nn78–9

lamp imagery 25
Lamp of God 17, 25n100
Lamp of the Commandment 13, 16, 17n29, 23, 26
Lamp of the Lord 5, 16, 17n29, 25–6, 25n100, 282
law, see Talmud
R. Levi son of Gershon, see Gersonides
light imagery 25

SUBJECTS AND NAMES INDEX   375

lightness/heaviness:
  finiteness/infiniteness and 40–1, 77–8, 78n127
  of the four elements 50–1
  traversing distances and 41
Light of the Lord 5, 17, 23n76, 25–6, 25n100, 26n3
lines 41, 52, 55, 58, 62, 70, 70n103, 140
  infinite 37, 44, 73–4, 79–81, 80–1nn133–4
  intersecting 44n44, 80, 80–1nn133–4
  parallel 44, 79
  see also radii
location, *see* motion/movers/moving things; place(s)
locomotion 47–50, 65, 78n128, 89
  continuousness of 57–8, 88
  empty space and 34–6, 34nn18–19, 71
  precedence of, among types of change 58, 58n82
  precedence of, among types of motion 89, 89n159, 245, 260
  rectilinear 39–40, 43, 45, 50, 57, 57n80, 72, 76–9, 78n126, 79n130, 88, 92
  see also motion/movers/moving things
love 1–4, 6, 10, 17, 19, 24, 117–18, 209, 219, 233–5, 286
  afflictions of 157, 285
  distinct from intellection 215, 220, 287, 292
  intensity of 118, 218–19, 224, 325
  as ultimate end 220, 226
  see also God

maʿaseh bereishit (account of creation), *see* creation
maʿaseh merkavah (account of the Chariot), *see* Chariot
magic, *see* dreams and magic
magnets/magnetic attraction 53, 86
magnitudes/substances:
  infinite corporeal 37–45, 74–5; *see also* finitude/infinitude
  infinite incorporeal 32–7, 70–3
  infinite in number 46
Maimonides, R. Moses 1–3, 21–4, 26, 32n9, 47–8
  on the 13 principles of Jewish faith 242–3
  on accidental motion 85
  on causes/effects 83
  on change 47–52
  Commentary on the Mishnah 308, 310
  on creation 243, 243n6, 249–50, 262–4, 263nn53–4
  on divine attributes 102–4, 322–3
  on the end (purpose) of existence 205, 240–1
  Epistle on Resurrection (Iggeret Teḥiyat Hametim) 296
  on eternity 243, 249

  on God 6, 9, 65–70, 91–7, 105, 134–7, 137–8n54
  Guide of the Perplexed 1, 5, 21, 23
  on incorporeal entities 91
  on the intellect 55
  Mishneh Torah (Code of Jewish Law) 5, 21, 22, 23n75, 26n2
  on potentiality 262–3
  proofs of root-principles 30–8
  on prophecy/prophets 171–2, 174–5, 310–11
  refutations of 29n21, 135–6, 262, 262n52
  on resurrection and the world-to-come 295–7, 304n218
  on the soul 55n74
  on time/motion 52, 65, 105
majority, judgment according to 157–8, 198, 286–90, 288–9nn137–8, 292, 293n157
majority rule 306–8, 307n232
matter 9, 36n22, 64–5
  coming-to-be/passing-away 54, 54n66, 248, 248n20
  form and 54, 87n155, 258–9, 261
  possibility and 64, 91
  prime 195, 248, 248n20, 261–2
  privation and 63–5
  see also hylē (matter); hylic faculty; hylic intellect
measure-for-measure 284–7
measure(s) 70–4, 89–90, 306
  finite/infinite 33, 41, 46, 253
  limits of 38, 267, 275–6
R. Meir 220
R. Meir Halevi Aboulafia 296
Men of the Great Assembly 20, 106–7, 308
Messiah/messianic age 294–5, 301, 303–4, 315–20
metaphysics, *see* physics
Metaphysics (Aristotle) 48, 149, 190, 244
  on the intellect 210
  on potentiality to actuality 343
  on ultimate good 206
Metatron 144
mezuzah 232–3
miracles 152, 168, 227–8, 274, 297–304, 318;
  see also Balaam; Moses; prophecy/prophets; signs and wonders
Mishnah 20, 308
Mishneh Torah (Code of Jewish Law) (Maimonides) 5, 21–2, 23n75, 26n2
monotheism 2, 6; *see also* God: oneness/unity of; religious beliefs
Moses 27, 98
  level of perfection of 183, 183n266
  miracles performed by 181, 185–6, 309–10
  prophecy/other prophets and 169, 171, 173n215, 177, 177n237, 180–1, 309–13
  providence and 144
  requests made to God by 98, 104, 108–9n219, 115, 328–9

R. Moses Halevi 112n228, 113, 352-3, 353n77
motion/movers/moving things 9, 34-5, 50, 60, 64-71, 245n11
  accidental 49-50, 53, 85
  anterior eternity and 245-6
  bodies and 53, 86, 94
  categories of 89, 89n159
  causation and 49n51, 49n53
  change and 48-9, 48nn48-9, 260
  circular 40, 43-5, 79, 81
  continuous 57; *see also* locomotion
  division and 51
  empty space and 71-2
  essential 49-50, 85
  finitude/infinitude and 36n23, 77-8, 81, 96-7
  forces and/forcible/natural 35-6, 35n20, 49-50
  place(s) and 75-6, 76n115
  from potentiality to actuality 49, 49n51, 60
  prime, *see* prime mover
  rectilinear 39-40, 45, 77-9, 78n126
  time and 35-6, 35n21, 41, 44-5, 58-9, 71-2, 89-90, 139, 252-4
  unmoved and indivisible mover 66-7, 67n98
  the up and the down 40, 50-1
  see also agents; locomotion; receptacles and movers

Naʿaman 312
Naḥalat Avot (Ancestral Inheritance) (Abarbanel) 11
Naḥmanides, R. Moses:
  on resurrection of the dead 296-7
  on reward and punishment 222-3
  Shaʿar Hagemul ("Gate of Reward") 223, 223n425, 296, 296n181
Narboni, R. Moses 63
  on accidental motion 85
  on causes/effects 83
  on Maimonides 63-4n89
natural form 53-4
natural order, *see* order
necessitation/necessity 10-13, 188-204
  divine justice and 200
  effort and 193-4, 194n304, 199, 199nn324-6
  in respect of causes/itself 10-12, 193-204
  see also causes/effects; choice (free will); the possible/possibility (category); reward and punishment
negation and affirmation 109-11, 113-15, 166-7
Nineveh 172
R. Nissim of Gerona 4, 184, 277
Noah 153, 184, 299
Noaḥide commandments 291, 306
numbering/numbers 59-60, 82; *see also* under other entries

ʿOfraim 309
omniscience/foreknowledge:
  change/the possible and 140-1, 140n60
  God and, *see* God
oneness/unity, *see* God
On Generation and Corruption (Aristotle) 47, 134
On the Heavens (Aristotle) 31, 246, 338
Onkelos 354
On the Soul (Aristotle) 138, 191, 194, 219, 223
Oral Torah 18-19, 19n48, 20, 20n57
order 47, 89n159
R. Oshaʿiya 20

Paradise 222, 347-8; *see also* world-to-come
parts, *see* bodies; elements
Parts of Animals (Aristotle) 149, 338
passing-away, *see* coming-to-be/passing-away
Passover 231
Patriarchs 145
  God and 219
  spiritual promise to 291
  see also Abraham; Isaac; Jacob
peace in the home 207
penitents 325-7, 327n335, 327n338, 328n345
perfection:
  reward and punishment, to foster 283
  of the soul 219-20
  in views 210-15, 226
  in virtues 206-9, 226
  see also end (ultimate/final cause of Torah/existence)
Pharaoh 126, 192, 228, 284n114, 309, 326-7, 328n341
philosophers:
  on God 2, 112-13
  on the intellect/soul 117, 214, 219-23
  on pleasure 116, 220-2
  see also Alfarabi; Aristotelianism/Aristotle; Averroes; Avicenna
phylacteries 233, 233n485
physics 3, 349
  celestial bodies and 246, 340-1
  metaphysics and 349-50, 350n63
  on motion 245
  theology and 7-9
  things subject to coming-to-be/passing-away 190, 332
Physics (Aristotle) 37, 71, 189, 244
  Book I 216
  Book VI 51
  Book VIII 53, 56
Pico della Mirandola, Giovanni 6
place(s) 38-40, 72-7, 72n107
  God and 77
  infinite/set 40n34, 41-2

motion and 75-6, 76n115
providence and 163-4
pleasure 13, 116-19, 221-3, 329n348; *see also* happiness; joy
pogrom of 1391 (Spain) 4
the possible/possibility (category) 21n68, 187-97
  alternatives and 141n61, 192-3, 203; *see also* God: foreknowledge
  causation and 188-204
  matter and 64
  nature of 142, 192n300, 196n308
  see also cornerstones
Posterior Analytics (Aristotle) 49
posterior eternity 69n101, 74, 94n173, 271, 331-4
potential/potentiality 61, 63, 63-4n89, 246-7
  potentiality to actuality 48, 150, 260
  unactualized 247n17; *see also* actual/actuality/actualizers; motion/movers/moving things
power 300
  finite/infinite/unlimited 166, 168, 272
  of God, *see* God
  Torah and 166
prayer(s) 228, 241-2, 321-3
  God and 7, 117-18
  of praise 103, 106-7
prescriptions (positive commandments), *see* commandments: positive
priestly blessing 324-5
priests 235, 324-5; *see also* high priest
prime matter, *see* matter
prime mover 64, 95, 95n175, 352-3, 353n77
priority and posteriority, *see* equivocation vs. priority/posteriority
privation, state of 63, 63-4n89, 90
prophecy/prophets 169-88
  definition/essential properties of 169-72
  errors and 182, 182n262
  the intellect and 169-70
  as intermediaries 143-5
  miracles/signs/wonders and 179, 181
  root-principles and 8
  superiority of Moses' 309-13
  testing of 172-8, 175n219, 175nn222-4, 176nn230-1, 177n237
  veracity of predictions of 171-3, 172nn206-7
  worship of God and 179-80, 182-3, 186
proscriptions (negative commandments), *see* commandments: negative
proselytes 182, 186
providence 142-65
  agents and 143-5
  deplorable condition and 125, 127, 139, 148-59

end (purpose) of 143
God's love and 159
Sages on 144
people/places/times selected for 163-4
Torah and 10-12, 142-52, 158
Psalmist, *see* David (king)
psychic happiness 209-11
Ptolemy 162, 162n148, 186
punishment, *see* reward and punishment
purification/purity, *see* impurity

quality 47, 52, 62, 88-9
quantity:
  as an accident 54n65, 62
  as a category of change 47-8
  continuous 125, 128, 139
  finiteness/infiniteness of 253, 266-7
  incorporeal 32-3, 33n16
  time and 252-3
quiddity 59n83
  existence and 98-101
  of God 97-9, 112-15
  see also God: oneness/unity of

Rabbah 290
the Rabbi, *see* Maimonides, R. Moses
the Rabbis, *see* Sages
radii 43-4, 79-80, 81n134
Ralbag, *see* Gersonides
Rambam, *see* Maimonides, R. Moses
Ramban, *see* Naḥmanides, R. Moses
Rashi 277, 285n120
Rava 204, 349
receptacles and movers 35-6, 71-2
recompense 284-5, 287; *see also* reward and punishment
Refutation of the Principles of the Christians (Ḥasdai Crescas) 5
repentance 325-9, 327n335, 327n338; *see also* reward and punishment; the wicked/wickedness
resurrection of the dead 293-305
  denial of 299
  manifestation of divine justice and 300-3
reward and punishment 14, 147-52, 154-6, 155n120, 213, 282-93
  belief/beliefs and 201-5
  body-soul compound and 289n140, 289n142
  choice (free will)/will and 203-4
  commandments and, *see* commandments
  corporeal 157-8, 283-4, 287-90
  degrees/types of 222, 287-90
  divine justice and 213, 289, 293, 298, 303-4; *see also* divine judgment; divine justice
  necessity/compulsion and 190, 194-7, 200-2
  primary intent of 283

reward and punishment (*cont.*)
  psychic/spiritual 155–6, 158, 286–9, 291–3, 302–3, 329
  Torah and 158
  see also resurrection of the dead
the righteous 148–57, 221 *see also* reward and punishment; the wicked/wickedness
root-principles 2, 26–31, 97–101, 114–16, 119–21, 287–93
  of monotheism 6–8
  Torah and 119, 320
  see also belief/beliefs
Rosh Hashanah 162, 164–5, 330n350

Sabbath 232
sacrificial offerings 162, 230–1, 233
Sadducees 307–8
Sages (*ḥakhamim*) (Rabbis of the Mishnah and Talmud) 20, 20n61, 24n95, 116
  investigation, forbidden by 82, 116
  on Israel's acceptance of Torah 204
  on providence 144–5
  rank of 145
  on world-to-come 220, 222–3
sages (*ḥakhamim*) (post-Talmudic Jewish thinkers) 20n61
  on amulets and incantations 342
  on the Chariot/creation 349
  on final end as perfecting intellect 210
  on freedom to choose 197
  on God's creating wonders 187
  on God's knowledge of particulars 126–7
  influence of philosophers on 23, 120–1, 142, 214
  on Moses' sun miracle 186
  of other nations 19
  on prophecy 170, 183
  on providence 148–9
  on reward 202
  see also Gersonides; Maimonides, R. Moses; R. Moses Halevi
Samuel (prophet) 171, 175–6
  prophecy and 312
  on the resurrection of the dead 295
  Saul and 130–1
Saul 124, 130–1, 229
Savoraim (s. Savora) 20
Sefer Habahir (*Book of Brightness*) 105n207
Sefer Yetzirah (*Book of Creation*) 112, 350
Sense and Sensibilia (Aristotle) 169, 311
Sermon on the Passover (Ḥasdai Crescas) 5
service to God, *see* God: attachment/connection/service to
sexual relations 206, 231–2
Shaʿar Hagemul ("Gate of Reward") (Naḥmanides) 223, 223n425, 296, 296n181

shape 62, 81
  definition of 44–5
  preservation of 256–7, 269–71, 270n59
Shavuot, *see* ʿAtzeret (Shavuot)
shekhinah, *see* Divine Presence (*shekhinah*)
Shem and Eber 277, 291
Shemaʿ 11, 118, 226, 228, 232, 284, 340n32
shofar 162–4, 238
Sifra 20
Sifrei 20
signs and wonders 130, 166, 171, 179, 243, 273–4, 309, 328, *see also* dreams and magic; miracles; prophecy/prophets
simple one 237, 250, 264, 269, 272, 335
Sinai 13, 27, 160, 199n323, 204n340, 227, 309, 312
sins 153, 198, 198n321, 203, 288; *see also* the wicked/wickedness
slowness and swiftness, *see* motion/movers/moving things
Smilevitch, Éric 14
Sodom/Sodom and Gomorrah 122, 124, 323
Solomon (king) 170, 224n435, 318
  on the commandments/Torah 24
  on immortality of soul 279, 281
  prayer of 163, 322
soothsaying 341–2
soul 55, 90–1
  children and 347
  happiness of 209–10
  immortality of 278–81
  passing-away of 292
  perfection of 219–20, 223
  quiddity of 282
  reward and punishment and 154, 154n115, 154n118
  spiritual aspects of 215–16, 219, 219n414, 286–7
  suffering of 212
  transmigration of 347
space, *see* place(s)
space, empty, *see* empty space
Spain, Jews of 4–5
spheres, celestial, *see* celestial bodies/spheres
Spinoza, Baruch 6
spiral 58
study:
  the Chariot and 349–51
  performance and 18n42, 212
  of Torah 18–19
substance(s), *see* magnitudes/substances
substratum 33n13, 54n66, 59
sukkah 234
Sukkot 165, 234

al-Tabrizi 37, 43–4, 63, 73–4, 74n110
  on causes/effects 83

on entities subject to change 84
on locomotion 48
on Maimonides 32n9, 62, 63-4n89
Talmud 20-3, 154n118, 290, 327; *see also* Oral Torah
Tannaim (s. Tanna) 20
tefillin, see phylacteries
Temple 228, 235, 294-5; *see also* priests; sacrificial offerings
Ten Utterances (Ten Commandments; Decalogue) 28-9, 28n14, 29nn20-1, 312-13
testing and trials 156-7; *see also* Abraham (patriarch)
Tetragrammaton 25n100, 104-5, 105nn205-6, 208, 144n75, 162, 351, 351n73
theodicy, *see* providence
Themistius 52
Theriac 134n45
time 59, 65, 74n110, 89, 252
    anterior eternity and 244-5, 259
    division and 244
    finiteness of 41-3, 252-5, 253n27, 253n29, 261n48, 267-8
    motion and 35-6, 35n21, 41, 44-5, 58-9, 71-2, 89-90, 139, 252-4
    place and 9, 276n68; *see also* place(s)
    providence and 164
Torah:
    beliefs and 6-7, 331-54
    commandments and 17-18, 24-5, 205-11, 226-35; *see also* commandments
    eternality of 305-8
    final cause/ultimate end 205-25, 236, 238-9
    four human perfections and 206-9
    God's knowledge/power and 134-5, 166
    legitimacy of 276-7, 277n77
    providence and 10-12, 142-52, 158
    reward and punishment and 158
    root-principles and 119, 320
    seven notions taught by 226-35
    study of 18-19
    see also Oral Torah; Written Torah
Tosefta 20n56
transgressions, *see* reward and punishment; sins
transmigration 347
truth 8, 24, 26, 30n1, 228; *see also* root-principles
tzitzit, see fringes

unity, *see* God
universe 238-9, 248n21, 249n22
    coming-to-be/passing-away of 245n10, 250-1, 335
    creation of 257nn36-8; *see also* creation; Gersonides; Maimonides, R. Moses
    eternality and 333-4
    possibility of others 334-7
    views on 9, 250
the up and the down 38, 40, 78n126
Urim and *Tummim* 235, 242, 313-15
Usha 207

the vegetative 93, 93n170
views, perfecting of 210-15, 226
virtues, perfecting of 206-9, 226
vocalization (spare and full) 19, 19n45, 171, 171n199

Wars of the Lord (*Milḥamot Hashem*) (Gersonides) 135
whatness, *see* quiddity
the wicked/wickedness 148-59, 222, 285n120; *see also* sins
will 193-4, 196-7, 219, 273
    apprehension/apprehenders and 272
    belief/beliefs and 200-4, 201n331
    commandments and 27, 197
    reward and punishment and 203-4
    see also choice (free will)
Wolfson, Harry A. 3n1, 14
world(s) 4n2, 82; *see also* universe
world-to-come:
    allusion to in Scripture 279
    children in 220, 223
    as eternal happiness 209
    goodness of life in 225, 329
    incorporeal substance in 155
    portion in 200, 212, 293, 303-4
    reward and punishment in 220
    timing of/relation to resurrection 296-7, 299-300, 303-4
    see also Gehenna; Paradise
worship of God 179-80, 182-3, 186; *see also* God; prayer(s)
Written Torah 18-20, 19n48

R. Yitzḥaq 277
Yom Kippur 164-5, 230, 326, 330